THE ULTIMATE FILM FESTIVAL SURVIVAL GUIDE

SECOND EDITION

CHRIS GORE

ifilm publishing

THE ULTIMATE FILM FESTIVAL SURVIVAL GUIDE
The Essential Companion for Filmmakers and Festival-Goers

LONE EAGLE PUBLISHING COMPANY, LLC™
1024 N. Orange Dr.
Hollywood, CA 90038
Phone 323.308.3400 or 800.815.0503
A division of IFILM® Corporation, www.ifilmpro.com

Printed in the United States of America

Cover design by Lindsay Albert
Book design by Carla Green
Edited by Lauren Rossini
Maps created by Marion Gore

Library of Congress Cataloging-in-Publication Data

Gore, Chris.
    The ultimate film festival survival guide / by Chris Gore.--2nd ed.
        p. cm.
    Includes index.
    ISBN 1-58065-032-5
    1. Film festivals--Directories. 2. Film festivals. I. Title.
PN1993.4.G67   2001
791.43'079--dc21   00-052034

Books may be purchased in bulk at special discounts for promotional or educational purposes. Special editions can be created to specifications. Inquiries for sales and distribution, textbook adoption, foreign language translation, editorial, and rights and permissions inquiries should be addressed to: Jeff Black, IFILM Publishing, 1024 N. Orange Dr., Hollywood, CA 90038 or send e-mail to: info@ifilm.com

Distributed to the trade by National Book Network, 800-462-6420

IFILM and Lone Eagle Publishing Company are registered trademarks.

This book is dedicated to filmmakers who strive
to make breakthrough independent movies.
Be realistic about your dreams and remember—never quit.

CONTENTS

SECTION 2—BUILD BUZZ: EVERYTHING ABOUT INDIE MOVIE MARKETING

SECTION 3—THE ARTISAN OF THE DEAL

SECTION 4—FILMMAKER WAR STORIES

SECTION 5—FILM FESTIVAL LISTINGS

APPENDICES

SPECiAL THANKS

There are so many people to thank, here is a list, in no particular order, of the people and organizations without whom this book would not have been possible: the unbelievably cool Jeff Black; my amazing editor, Lauren Rossini, who still laughs at all my jokes; the ever-amazing Carla Green, who makes this book look so damn good; Jeff "The Dude" Dowd, Arthur Borman, Lance Mungia, Stephen Gates, Mark A. Altman, David E. Williams, Anthony Miele, Dan Mirvish, Margot Gerber, Linda Brown, Rich Raddon, Joal Ryan, Ron Wells, R.J. Millard, Sarah Jacobson, Geoff Gilmore, Joe Carnahan, Roger Nygard, Heidi Van Lier, Mark Osborne, Taz Goldstein, Richard Schenkman, Dan Myrick, Eduardo Sanchez, Babette Perry, Mark Cronin, Gary Auerbach, Haxan Films, Merle Bertrand, Stephanie Donnelly, Adam Hauck, Mike Monello, James Rowley, Ken Crosby, Joe Zeoli, Tara Georgenes, Jennifer Matthews, Gary Whitta, *Total Movie Magazine*, the readers of *FilmThreat.com* and especially my wife, Marion. A special thanks to all of my interview subjects for their cooperation and candor. I'd also like to thank all the various members of the film festival staffs for their assistance in this project—you really made this book possible. I thank you all sincerely. The biggest thanks goes out to all the filmmakers themselves—without their daily battle to make uncompromising films, there wouldn't be any film festivals. Thank you.

RE-INTRODUCTION

Into the Next Decade—sex, lies and the Blair Witch

So much has happened since the first edition of this book that I think it helps to go back to the roots of the current independent film scene to put things into perspective. In 1989, Steven Soderbergh's feature directing debut *sex, lies and videotape* surprised everyone when it took top honors at both the Sundance Film Festival and the Cannes Film Festival. This low-budget movie was somber, thoughtful and slow-paced. It offered moviegoers something they had been craving for some time—an engaging, intelligent story that explored the problems of real people. The movie was made for about a million bucks and went on to gross almost $25 million. If we look at box office as the barometer that measures a film's popularity to the moviegoing public, then the world was forever changed after the theatrical release of *sex, lies and videotape*. Face it, the late eighties gave us a lot of bad movies in genres that became increasingly tiresome and lame. Audiences were no longer satisfied by a diet of formulaic comedies, clichéd action films, cheesy drama, sci-fi and horror flicks—they wanted something more fulfilling. The overwhelming success of *sex, lies and videotape* was evidence that independent films had finally arrived and indies quickly became a staple in the regular diet of moviegoers everywhere. *sex, lies and videotape* was followed by the unexpected success of other independent movies—films like *Slacker*, *Clerks*, *The Brothers McMullen* and many others. In the '90s, two cable networks emerged to showcase these bold new movies: the Independent Film Channel and The Sundance Channel. Film festivals flourished and grew as the pursuit of the next independent film "discovery" became like a maddening gold rush. *sex, lies and*

> .....
> *"The Blair Witch Project* is as significant to independent film in 1999, as *sex, lies and videotape* was in 1989."
> .....

videotape had set the tone for the next decade of independent film-making.

Ten years later, another independent film would change the rules in a revolutionary way. This film was primarily shot on video, featured reality-based storytelling set in the horror genre, had no stars or structured script and was chiefly promoted through a website. It would go on to become the highest grossing independent film of all time. In 1999, *The Blair Witch Project*, made for only $22,000, would go on to make over $140 million dollars at the box office. This movie proved that stars are no longer an absolute necessity, and that digital filmmaking really has the opportunity to be the future. *The Blair Witch Project* is as significant to independent film in 1999, as *sex, lies and videotape* was in 1989. The triumph of *Blair Witch* and what it represents will reverberate long into the next decade. A new generation of filmmakers will be inspired by *Blair Witch*, just as others were inspired by *sex, lies and videotape*.

I'll see you at the next festival; I'll be waiting in line to see those movies.

—Chris Gore

A BRiEF HiSTORY OF FiLM FESTiVALS

Film, being only about 100 years old, is a young medium. The film festival, a medium for exhibiting and celebrating film, is likewise still in its youth.

While the date of the very first film festival may be lost to antiquity, the oldest still in business is the Venice Film Festival, founded in the 1930s by Italian Dictator Benito Mussolini. It was originally an adjunct to a larger, pre-existing arts festival but proved so popular that within a few years it had become a free-standing festival of its own. Unfortunately, in the days leading up to World War II, the Venice festival leaned heavily toward films from the Axis powers and Americans ultimately boycotted the gathering, which was subsequently suspended for the remainder of the war. While Il Duce did not survive the global conflict, the Venice Film Festival was revived in the late forties and remains an important international exposition today.

The Cannes Film Festival was also conceived in the 1930s and materially affected by the war. Set to debut on September 1, 1939, such Hollywood luminaries as Mae West, Gary Cooper and Tyrone Power traveled to the French seaside community for the festivities. Establishing a Cannes tradition of excess, a replica of the Notre Dame cathedral was built on the beach to promote the release of the *Hunchback of Notre Dame*. As it happened, *Hunchback* was the only film presented at the fledgling festival because that same day Adolph Hitler invaded Poland and began his own festival of destruction: the Second World War. The first Cannes Film Festival was cancelled and Hitler went on to invade France. Thankfully, the good guys ultimately won, Hitler was defeated and the Cannes festival made its real debut in 1946.

The third of the old-line European festivals, the Berlin Film Festival, was established in 1951 as an outpost of post-war culture sanctioned by the occupying Allied forces in West Berlin. Initially slighted by the commission that tried to oversee and coordinate the

European festivals, Berlin eventually rose to its current position as one of the top ranking European film festivals.

And so it went during the early years. Organizations like the Society for Cinephiles established festivals that were quietly run by aficionados and favored older films. Film festivals were not a rarity, but you didn't find them everywhere you turned. Ironically, rather than one of the big international festivals, it was the Society for Cinephiles' Cinecon, which traveled to different cities each Labor Day to view rare silents, that was the forerunner of the festival that ushered in the modern era.

Like Cinecon, The Telluride Film Festival was created as a film buff's festival. It even involved some of the same fans, such as the late William K. Everson. But unlike the humble Cinecon, Telluride was a pricey and exclusive affair held (also during the Labor Day holiday) in the privacy of a remote area of Colorado. When the Sundance Film Festival was founded, it used Telluride as a model.

The Sundance Film Festival, devoted to independent films, was founded in 1978 as the United States Film Festival. The first two sessions were in Salt Lake City; in January 1981, the festival moved to its current home in Park City, Utah. Robert Redford's Sundance Institute (founded in 1983) took over festival operations in 1984. The name was formally changed to the Sundance Film Festival in 1989, the year *sex, lies and videotape* put the festival on the map as the place where iconoclastic young directors could achieve a commercial breakthrough. Bloated and weighted by success, Sundance eventually became its own kind of establishment film festival and a concurrent festival of Sundance rejects, the Slamdance festival, debuted in 1995, also in Park City. The Sundance organizers reportedly admired their pluck.

With the success of Sundance and the upstart Slamdance, the floodgates were well and truly opened. Aspiring filmmakers who couldn't make the cut at Sundance might instead opt for Cleveland, Ohio's film festival. In the realm of tourist-bait, there was the late Sonny Bono's Palm Springs Film Festival. Over the years, significant film festivals have established themselves in Chicago, Denver, Portland (Oregon), Edinburgh, Krakow and Hong Kong.

Today, if you are a professional or a lover of film, you can go to Santa Barbara. If you want to see naked starlets, you can go to Cannes. If you're into animation, you can go to Annecy or Ottawa.

If you like edgy and inexpensive, there is the New York Underground Film Festival. There are also the film buyers markets, such as those held in Milan and Los Angeles.

Film festivals have both proliferated and changed. Once upon a time, festivals were predominately creatures of the arts, and powerfully connected to politics. In 1968, the Cannes festival was shut down as a result of French student riots. Similarly, in 1970, the Berlin festival was cancelled as a result of controversy over a German film titled O.K., about an American rape and murder in Vietnam. This kind of excitement is lacking at the more modern film festivals, which seem built around the entertainment/business model rather than the traditional art/politics combination. But the current era features a different kind of excitement. As entertainment has become the central element of our culture, film festivals have become veritable markets of celluloid, wherein dreams are bought and sold; lives are made and destroyed. On that very human level, they are exciting as hell.

D.i.C.—DO iT CHEAP

In all things related to your film—whether it be casting, production, post-production, marketing, promotion, anything—you will face one seemingly impossible barrier to getting what you want: money. Money is an obstacle filmmakers face at every level, whether producing a $100 million dollar big budget Hollywood extravaganza or a $900 digital indie feature. Those filmmakers who are able to master the art of Taming the Triangle will get what they want without compromising their vision. The Triangle represents the way a filmmaker wants everything done all the time: Fast, Good, Cheap. In any task related to a film, you almost always have the luxury of choosing only two in order to achieve your goal. It's a depressing reality, but only two of the three are possible for any given task. As an example, let's say you need an explosion for your film. The big budget Hollywood movie producer may choose to do a giant special effects-laden explosion and they can do it fast and good, but it will *not* be cheap. The no-budget digital movie producer may choose to do an explosion as well, but selects the path of fast and cheap, but it will *not* be good. Or the no-budget may choose good and cheap, but it will *not* be fast. That producer will encounter time as an enemy. In the making of your film, you will come up against the Triangle and the Fast, Good, Cheap decision many times. For most indies, the logical choice will be good and cheap as time is usually the one thing you have available. Many filmmakers make the mistake of rushing their film to meet a festival deadline. While this may seem wise at the time, if meeting that deadline in any way may compromise the quality of the film, you will only hurt your chances. Take a look at the choices on the Triangle and choose the path that best supports your final vision. You don't think filmmakers at all levels face the same dilemma? Even George Lucas, one of the most successful independent filmmakers of all time, waited over fifteen years to revisit the *Star Wars* universe while he waited for the quality of digital filmmaking effects and technology to improve while becoming cost-effective. Live by the Triangle, and as a filmmaker, evaluate every decision toward making the best finished film possible.

iN FiLM, POLiTiCS iS NOT A DiRTY WORD

In the film industry, politics means meeting the right people, rallying them to your cause (your film) and enlisting them in your mission to get your movie made and seen by as many people as possible.

Unfortunately, the question is not always, "Who is the best filmmaker?" More often, it comes down to the question, "Who excels at the political game of the film industry?" You must learn to become astute in politics if you intend to be a successful (i.e., working and solvent) filmmaker. Let me let you in on a little secret—you already know how to do this. You may not be aware of it, and you might not have done it on purpose, but you have used politics to your advantage every moment you have been working on your film.

- You raised the money you needed for your film from somewhere.
- You secured the perfect location—for free!
- You begged the lab to go the extra mile—and they did.
- You fought to have that scene kept and shot your way.
- You convinced the rental house to give you a break on your equipment.
- You kept spirits up when disaster struck and rain ruined a day of shooting.
- You inspired the cinematographer to come up with a solution for that troublesome set-up—and it turned out beautifully.
- You talked the entire crew into working through the night.
- Your sense of humor saved the first A.D.'s life when the entire crew wanted to kill him.
- You even persuaded your actor to do that embarrassing nude scene. (Full frontal. You rock!)
- You assembled a group of people to create a film and see your vision through to completion and you smiled through it all (even though you know you could have made a better film under more ideal circumstances).

So you see, you are a political animal, you just never thought of it that way before. Now, you must take these Svengali-like abilities and translate them into selling your movie. (Pay attention and commit the next sentence to memory. It's a run-on and completely grammatically incorrect. I already know that, and I've beaten my editor over the head to keep it just the way it is; basically, it is the crux of the entire book.) All you have to do is use these very same skills to apply to festivals, lobby the festival staff, convince them your film must be seen, get into the festival, hire a publicist, a lawyer, a producer's rep, an agent, travel to the festival; don't forget to make a killer poster, an EPK, a trailer and a website; get some press, create great buzz for your movie, pack the screening with press, friends, celebrities and acquisitions executives; be humble, engaging and funny at the post-screening Q&A session, get some good reviews, create more good buzz, get "the call," make the distribution deal, negotiate tough to get the best deal, read the trades to look for your name and the announcement, travel the world showing your film at other festivals, support the release of the film by doing interview after interview—and during this whole process get into as many parties and have as much fun as possible while exhibiting your ability to remain witty after far too many drinks. That's it. That's all you have to do.

The rest of this book explains how the above can be achieved. I would like to point out that no two filmmakers realize success by following the same path. Each one "makes it" differently and your experience will be completely different and completely your own.

WHAT MAKES A GREAT FESTiVAL

I have been attending film festivals for over ten years now and had my share of good and bad experiences. I rate a film festival as "great" based on a very specific set of criteria. I try not to judge a festival by a few technical mistakes because those can plague even the largest and most respected festivals. As a festival-goer, there are three key elements that make a festival enjoyable for me and they are great films, good organization and fun parties. These are three very simple things, but too many festivals get bogged down in other details—seminars, panels, charging exorbitant amounts—and neglect the these three things that matter most.

I want to see great films. I look for a festival, first and foremost, showing films that I am interested in seeing. This may sound pretty obvious, but you'd be surprised at the hype that can be generated for certain films no one would ever go to a theater to see if they were at home, much less watch on television or rent on video. Quality films are key to the success of a great festival and a memorable festival experience. I attend a festival to discover films I'd never have the chance to see anywhere else and to see uncommercial movies that seem available only on the independent circuit.

If a film festival is well organized, you probably won't even notice it because things are running so smoothly. Badly organized festivals call attention to their shortcomings and can be miserable for everyone involved. But, even the best festivals can have organizational difficulties—that is the price of success and high attendance. However, there are no excuses for keeping audiences waiting, creating nonsense rules or projectors that chew up prints. Good organization is key. You only seem to notice when things go wrong, but when things run smoothly, it's pure joy.

And fun parties are always crucial. Duh. Having a good time at a party is due in large part to the guest list and this varies greatly from festival to festival. For me, a pretension-free party devoid of snobs is generally the first ingredient of a successful party. Great conversation and partygoers interested in doing something totally ridiculous (like, for example, jumping into a swimming pool fully clothed—not that I've ever done anything like that) is the second. Add an open bar that doesn't close, and you've got a really good party.

For filmmakers, the criteria for a great festival are slightly different, since it is all about how the festival can advance their film or career. But a festival with these three elements will always be a good one.

STAYiNG ALiVE: TiPS FOR THE FiLM FESTiVAL TRAVELER

Simple Suggestions for Survival

While a tour book about your festival destination will contain the best regional information, I've learned some tried and true tips along the way that will enhance your travel experience. Sometimes, I've learned the hard way.

- **Make reservations.** For hotel, car, plane, the works. You cannot overdo it when it comes to reservations—and that includes dinner reservations. Be sure to check the restrictions on any reservation (cover your butt and make sure to find out if there are penalties for late cancellations). Remember, the further in advance you make the reservations for flights, the more money you will save. Flights fill up fast, so reserve your ticket early. Do not wait until the last minute. Making advance dinner reservations is key as well; you don't want to wait more than an hour for a table. Robert Redford's restaurant, Zoom, is always booked up months before Sundance. Also, sign up for every frequent flyer plan in existence. You'll be surprised how quickly those points and free trips add up. And also be sure to check on restrictions for flying standby. Some airlines will tell you over the phone that you must pay $50 or more to change your return flight. If you just show up to the airport and wait on standby, you can often bypass this flight change fee altogether. It depends on the type of ticket you purchase, so be sure to check.
- **Planning.** Get the festival schedule in advance—either by mail or from the festival website—and make a plan. Don't be afraid to modify the plan as you go; you can always pawn off a few tickets to a movie you discover you want to avoid. I type up a schedule before I leave so I know what films I'm seeing when, what parties I'm going to (or crashing) and who I'm meeting with and when. I never follow my plan exactly, but it helps me

to start with some kind of structure before I begin to deviate from it by crashing parties.

- **Address book.** On my schedule, I also print a mini-address book. Essentially, this is just a collection of local phone numbers and the cell phone numbers of pals I plan to meet. This is all printed in very tiny type and I make multiple copies so I never lose it. The info is printed small enough so it fits right in my wallet. (Is it just me, or am I sounding like a compulsive geek?)

- **Backpack.** You have to have one. It's the guy's version of a purse and totally essential to navigating a festival. I'm prepared for anything with my pack in tow. Mine always contains: the all-important address book, festival schedule, lip balm, water bottle, cell phone, pens, flyers, a folder of party invitations, something to read, energy bar (emergency meal), camera, map, tape recorder, notepad, batteries, gum, business cards, matches, headache pills, eyedrops, eyeglass cleaner, Kleenex, comb, sunglasses, mini flashlight and a hat. (The hat is used for early morning screenings. When bedhead is at its worst, a hat can be a lifesaver.)

- **Vitamins and water.** Film festivals can get exhausting very quickly. Plan on sleeping less, drinking probably more alcohol than normal and know that you'll be surrounded by cigarette smoke at every party. During Sundance, I get about four hours of sleep a night. I make it a point to drink lots of water and take extra vitamins. (I'm partial to vitamins in the B category myself.) I also keep a bottle of pills with a mix of capsules that includes Tylenol, aspirin, Pepto-Bismol pills, sinus headache medicine, migraine headache medicine, Tums and plenty of other remedies all crammed into one bottle. Sometimes my friends think I'm nuts—until I whip out this pill bottle and cure them of what ails them.

- **Clothes.** Obviously you should be prepared to bring clothes that match the climate for the festival. Wear mainly casual clothes, but it's also important to bring at least one dressy outfit so you're ready for a meet and greet event at which you have to impress. Also keep in mind, clothes make the filmmaker. Be unique. If you want to stand out from all the other filmmakers wearing the artist's favorite uniform—you know, black—

choose something really outrageous to wear. A bright hat, a loud jacket or a bold pair of shoes is not a bad idea. When members of the audience run into you during the festival, your unique "look" will be remembered. Clothes are about image building, so have fun with it.

- **Learn a foreign language fast.** When travelling to a foreign country, it's extremely helpful to get one of those quickie learn-a-language courses on tape. While learning the language is crucial, be sure to pay as close attention to local customs, which can be even more important than words. Reciting phrases over and over again is great for getting pronunciations correct, but you might want to try my own personal favorite way to learn another language—by watching movies. Many movie geeks like myself have the dialog for certain films memorized from beginning to end. Purchase a DVD with foreign language tracks, a foreign language version of your favorite video, or a videotape with closed captioning, or even watch television with the SAP channel turned on. By watching your favorite flick in another language over and over, you'll know that "Que la Fuerza te acompane" means, "May the Force be with you" in Spanish. You'll be quoting popular movie lines to all your new international pals in no time! And after all, movies are the international language.

- **See the world**. While you're travelling, don't forget to take at least a day away from the festival to see the local sights. You may never be back to this part of the country or the world. It's also refreshing to take a break from the fest and get away from people constantly talking about movies. But only for one day!

Use basic common sense when travelling. Don't hesitate to ask a festival staffer or a local for advice or help when lost. You'll almost always find them ready to give you the information you need.

SECTION 1
CONQUERING FILM FESTIVALS

"Like the lottery, you can't win if you
don't play. Sundance is the mother of
all film festivals—you MUST apply."

—Joal Ryan, filmmaker, *Former Child Star*

APPLY YOURSELF

Getting into the Best Festivals for You

So, you've worked hard, had the wrap party, you're close to finishing your film and it's now time to begin to send in that festival application and travel the world showing your masterpiece. Having finished a film you certainly have the right to be on a creative high, but don't let that sway you from reality; it's time to get serious.

Aimlessly filling out applications and writing checks is generally how most filmmakers go about submitting to festivals. That method usually results in paying a cool $40 bucks for each rejection letter—a total waste of cash. You can do better than that. You need a submission plan.

First, you need to get to know the festivals. (Which is why we included the handy festival appendix in the back of this book.) Choose a group of festivals that best fit the profile of your film. There are many factors to consider when choosing festivals that are right for you.

10 Important Factors to Consider When Applying to Festivals

As the filmmaker (writer, director, producer, or combination of the three), your job is to act as the ambassador of your film. When you travel to a festival, you represent everyone who worked on the movie and the movie itself. Make no mistake, selecting the festivals to submit your film to is an important decision. You will be throwing away vast amounts of time and money if you do not consider these ten important factors before submitting to any festival. In approximate order of importance, they are:

1. **Prestige.** Submitting your film to a prestige festival will give your movie its best chance to be sold to a distributor, receive loads of press coverage, get your next film deal and (cross your fingers) launch your brilliant career as a filmmaker. Also, even

something as simple as being *accepted* into a prestige festival can make a great quote on a video box—something as simple as "Official Selection Sundance Film Festival." I'll bet you've noticed that on more than a few video sleeves. Prestige counts for a lot. To just be accepted into one of the top ten festivals is an honor, so keep that in mind.

2. **Distributors.** Is this one considered a "discovery" film festival that distributors attend? If the ultimate goal is to sell the film, this must be of paramount concern to you. Make sure to ask the festival staff which acquisitions executives will be attending.

3. **Reviews and press coverage.** Getting coverage in publications like the *Los Angeles Times,* the *New York Times, Entertainment Weekly, Total Movie, Filmmaker, Premiere* and the trades is another important factor to consider. Your chances of being reviewed by these publications, and others, increase when they send representatives. But it's also your job to be sure that they attend a screening of your film. Ask the festival office to provide a list of the journalists attending the festival. If the festival has only attracted local press, it may not be worth your time. Unless, of course, that local press is in one of the top ten markets in the U.S.

4. **Prizes and awards.** From sizable cash awards to film equipment to lab deals, prizes should play a role in your decision to submit. The winner of the Grand Jury Prize at the AFI Los Angeles International Film Festival receives $10,000 in cash—that's a damn good prize! Cash awards are always a nice dividend. Be sure to research the prizes awarded and consider this when submitting. Inquire about audience awards, judges awards, etc. . . . Any type of award that your film receives only serves to increase its overall value.

5. **Location.** Could this film festival be a well-earned holiday as well as a chance to schmooze with the bigshots of the movie world? If it's a choice between the Hawaii Film Festival and a festival in Ohio, the choice is clear. Surf's up! Hawaii!

6. **Perks.** How does the festival treat you? Is the flight paid for? Are you put up for free? For example, The Florida Film Festival treats filmmakers like royalty, even offering passes to Disneyland and Universal Studios Theme Park while the film-

makers are in town. Be sure to inquire about paid expenses and other perks.

7. **Application fee.** Festival application fees can be really steep. Upwards of $50 for some. At that price, enter twenty fests and you've spent a $1,000 bucks. With over 1,000 festivals worldwide and new ones being announced on a weekly basis (or so it seems) those application fees can add up. You could end up spending enough in application fees to finance your next film!

Be sure to ask if a festival is willing to waive the fee. Some of them will actually be willing to. If your film has no chance of being accepted anyway, why bother writing the check and submitting the film? Do your homework. Don't submit your ultra-violent *Pulp Fiction* wanna-be to the Transgender Documentary Film Festival, since you obviously don't have a chance.

8. **Recommendations.** There are recommendations contained in the appendix at the end of this book, but you should consider contacting others who have either attended or had their films shown at that particular festival, if at all possible.

9. **Contacts.** It's vitally important to make contacts for investors in future films, distributors, acquisitions executives, agents, lawyers and especially other filmmakers who often turn out to be very helpful. Or simply to make friends in the industry. You never know how these contacts can pay off later. For many, a festival can be an opportunity to meet their heroes in a social setting. I know a filmmaker who attended a small film festival for one reason only—the Coen brothers were going to be there and he wanted to meet them. Nothing is more fun than slugging down beers and talking film until all hours of the night with a longtime film hero. You'd be shocked at what John Waters will tell you when he's feelin' loose at a party. (God, I love that guy.)

If you decide to go the route of self-distribution, making contacts will be a major factor in your submission plan. You'll need to find others in the industry willing to champion your film.

10. **Fun.** Yes, fun. If it's going to be miserable, why bother? Working the festival circuit, plugging a film day in and day out can be grueling after the fiftieth post-screening question and answer session. Select festivals in places you'd like to visit so if the fes-

tival is a bore, at least you'll have the opportunity to explore the nightlife in a new city. Ohio may not have the beach, but there are some great bars and even better people.

Basically, you need to think of your film as an investment. The value of your film (and yourself as a filmmaker) increases as you receive good press, awards of any kind and acceptance into prestige film festivals.

FORMiNG A FESTiVAL STRATEGY

In order to successfully break your film into the festival circuit, you must have a strategy. First, this involves getting to know your film. Be aware of festivals that may be more friendly to a film that fits a particular genre—whether it be gay, lesbian, documentary, digital, student, underground, animated, ethnic—there are festivals specializing in these types and your film may best fit into one of these. It's better to be the toast of a smaller festival than be overlooked at a larger festival.

When it comes to entering festivals, there are three that you absolutely must enter: Sundance, Berlin and Toronto. These are the "A" festivals and are also markets for indie films, heavily attended by acquisitions executives.

Next, you must plan a fallback strategy in case you do not get into any of the top three. This is the category most filmmakers will fall into. There are just not enough slots, no matter how many American Spectrums or Midnight Shows Sundance schedules. Compile a list of "B" festivals and these are the ones you will submit to simultaneously. These include festivals like the Hamptons International Film Festival, Austin, Montreal, Venice, Atlanta and the Los Angeles Independent Film Festival among others. (See the listings for other good "B" festivals.) These are all great festivals, don't get me wrong, but when it comes to getting a distribution deal, statistically speaking, the top three have had more films walk away with distribution than all the "B" festivals combined. These second tier fests are great for creating buzz, getting the word out and even getting a deal. Apply to ten or twenty of these festivals and lobby just as hard for admittance as you do for the top three.

Then, and this is optional, take some chances; apply to some wild card festivals. The weird ones and the strange sounding ones located overseas. Foreign festivals can be a blast. You may end up with a free trip to Spain for your film's European debut, all because you took a chance on a smaller festival.

All told, you should apply to close to twenty or forty festivals. Sure, you could apply to hundreds, but why bother? Once your film gets circulated, it will make it to other festivals because directors of festivals talk to each other. And while one fest may view your film and conclude that it is not right for them, they may call their buddy in Austin and pass along a recommendation to the Austin Film Festival. Once your film is in the pipeline, it is in the pipeline. It's better to focus on lobbying these film festivals first than to use a scattershot strategy and apply to the more than 600 festivals in this book. Remember, lobbying festival staff (politely, correctly, in a way that gets their attention and does not annoy) is time better spent than applying randomly. Work smarter, not harder.

Once your film plays one festival, other festivals will extend invites. Some invites will be very direct and others will simply imply that *if* you send in your tape, it will most likely make it in, and oh, by the way, you don't have to send in the application fee. Anything to get around paying another forty or fifty bucks.

SEEKiNG ACCEPTANCE

Avoiding Mistakes on the
All-important Festival Application

All you have to do is fill out the application, write a check, enclose a video, mail it off and you're in, right? *Wrong!* Filmmakers who follow this path are only fooling themselves. There are some very simple things you can do to make the lives of the people running the festival a little easier and increase your chances of acceptance. Follow this advice and avoid the mistakes that turn many festival entries into recycled videotapes.

1. **Follow instructions.** The first thing that can leave a film teetering on the fence of rejection is not following the directions on the application. This only serves to upset busy festival workers. If you have any questions or extenuating circumstances regarding your film, be sure to call the festival.

2. **Label correctly.** A package sent to a festival generally includes the check, application, the film on video, the sleeve and press kit, press materials, photos, etc. Be sure to label every single one of these things and include your contact information. If you send a video, the contact info should be on the video sleeve *and* the video itself.

3. **Inquire about a festival's pre-screening process.** Most festivals won't admit this, but many submissions are viewed on video, generally by subordinates, and only the first five to ten minutes are actually viewed. This is an unfortunate reality. However, when you consider that some festivals receive over 800 films, resulting in close to 1,500 hours of viewing time (that's about two straight months with no sleep in front of a VCR—hey, you try that!), you can't blame them for rushing through the screening process. If you pay the application fee, make sure someone is going to watch the entire film.

4. **Research the number of submissions accepted.** Your chances may be better at a smaller festival with fewer submissions.

5. **Write a competent synopsis that truly describes the film.** If you must, get a publicist or friend to write the synopsis for you. Remember, the synopsis is made to *sell* the film. Let the sales material do its job.

   If the synopsis is poorly written, it will reflect on the film itself. Also, avoid being esoteric. Here are a couple of examples of what to avoid, courtesy of the Atlanta Film & Video Festival. If you are making an experimental film, don't write something like, "This film is a cinematic meditation . . . this film transforms the viewers sense of possibility for inner and world peace." That film quickly transformed into a reject.

   Avoid being pretentious like this synopsis from a rejected submission: "Put simply, this film is a romantic fable. However, as a film, it is a composition of auditory and visual components. Please keep in mind, the same person both photographed and scored this film thereby creating a structure of audio-visual counterpoint. Using an original, yet light archetypal story, the filmmaker has sought to compose a film that 'works' not only as an intensive audio-visual approach, but also as a carefree ride right into a big fat smile!" Uh, yeah.

6. *Do not* **include a long apologetic letter pointing out your film's faults.** "The sound is a pre-mix . . . this is our first rough cut . . . we plan to take out another 20 minutes . . . we're still doing some reshoots . . . " Dailies are for *you* to examine, not the film festival. Send as close to a finished film as possible.

   Your cover letter should include all the basic details and should be no more than one page. If the film is an answer print, certainly point that out, but don't dwell on it or go into exhausting detail.

7. **Make a personal connection.** Any kind of connection you can make in your cover letter or follow-up phone call to the festival is helpful. Attaching a voice to a name makes you human and not just another applicant.

8. *Do not* **include promotional junk.** T-shirts, stickers, pens and other promotional give-aways will often make their way into the garbage. You'll need this stuff later to promote your film—*after* it has been accepted.

9. **Have a story.** I mean your own personal story. There is a reason that you made your film and your struggle to get it on screen can be as compelling as the film itself. It makes a great story in a festival program and will set you apart from the pack. Is the film auto-biographical? Why is your film so important that people would pay to see it? What hardships were endured to tell your tale? The viewers of your film will look differently at it if they know you had to sell blood to get it made.

   If you really have no story, be creative. The Slamdance Film Festival program book includes information about each film-maker including a short bio. I still remember reading: "Eric Kripke is a millionaire playboy director who solves baffling crimes in his spare time." His short film, *Truly Committed,* was hilarious and went on to win the audience award at Slamdance.

10. **Submit on time.** Submitting late will only give the festival staff an easy excuse to reject your film. It also means that most screening slots have already been filled and that your film will most likely not be viewed in its entirety. By now, the bloodshot eyes of the screening committee in the festival are highly trained to spot films they don't like. If they are not hooked in the first five to ten minutes, your film becomes a reject.

GETTiNG A "THUMBS UP" FROM THE GATEKEEPER

Behind the Scenes with Geoff Gilmore, Director of the Sundance Film Festival

Sundance gatekeeper Geoff Gilmore
PHOTO BY FRED HAYES

The Sundance Film Festival is the leading festival in the United States, if not the world. It is where indie films are picked up for distribution, where new talent is discovered and where people from all over the world travel to make deals. All festivals have gatekeepers, screening committees that often make group decisions about what films to accept. For Sundance there is only one. Geoff Gilmore: gatekeeper for Sundance. While the festival has a trusted group of screeners, he alone is responsible for the final decision to accept or reject a film for Sundance. This makes Gilmore one of the most powerful people in the independent film industry today.

Gilmore came to Sundance in 1989 when it was still called the United States Film Festival. He has been instrumental in the festival's emergence as the number one market for independent films in the United States. He teaches film classes at UCLA and has an unbridled passion for cinema that I have not seen in any other festival director. Gilmore truly cares about supporting independent films and has used Sundance to forward this admirable agenda.

In order to get into Sundance, you've got to get into the mind of Geoff Gilmore. He alone must embrace your film. In this extended interview, Gilmore reveals how he selects films and his philosophies about what makes a successful independent film.

As Director of the Sundance Film Festival, what does your job entail?
Generally speaking, I am where the buck stops in terms of what gets into the Festival. I help shape the vision of Sundance—what it is

and what it will become in the long term. I also manage many of the day-to-day things that we have to deal with as an institution.

Sundance sets the tone for a lot of the smaller film festivals. Many of those festival directors attend Sundance to see what's hot and then try their best to program those films at their festivals.

That's partially true, although in the past few years, we've really gone out of our way to offer another thirty or forty films to those festival directors to say, "Hey, guys, you didn't see this at Sundance but look! This wasn't ready for us when we had to make our decision, or, we just couldn't include this one. Why don't you take a look at this?"

You are essentially choosing forty features out of eight hundred—an impossible task. Both my staff and I will really try to offer up some options; we go out of our way not to just say, "Hey, program the stuff that's come out of Sundance." So, for a number of different festivals (SXSW, Los Angeles International Festival and others), we make recommendations about work that we think they might be interested in.

This also gives the filmmaker another chance. There's a real need to support a range of different independent filmmakers. Theatrical distribution is very hard to get right now, and many independent filmmakers tend to see Sundance as an all or nothing goal. If they attain it, they've achieved victory and if they don't, then they've lost. I very strongly want to make the point that this is not true and that good films do surface. Good films will find a way out and they'll find a way out through a number of different paths.

Playing at Sundance goes a long way toward helping a filmmaker secure distribution.

I am not going to argue that Sundance has a place in putting work into the marketplace or helping get work viewed, and not just for acquisition but for a lot of things. I don't think Sundance should be seen as only a market; that's too narrow. There are films at Sundance that people *don't* get to see, that *don't* become the buzz films and therefore people don't understand that those are also very much part of the independent world. But one of the things we're really interested in trying to do is continue to expand the sense of what the aesthetic possibilities are. Ten years ago, festivals were aesthetic enterprises for critics who went and talked about the movies and talked about the nature of the film and they talked about whether it was exciting or not. It was amazing, you could go to the Berlin Festival and not hear any talk about business whatsoever. Business was just not a big part of the film festival culture.

Now you go to these festivals and the topic of conversation is acquisition deals, or whether or not new films could have been found. That's unfortunate, because it really overloads and categorizes only one aspect of a festival's function. I think there are a range of functions. That said, I never apologize for the fact that Sundance has become a market. I think probably the nicest thing you can do for young filmmakers is to get them out of debt and get their films sold.

It's actually refreshing to hear another person in the film industry say that they are tired of hearing about the business side of film being talked about and written about more often than the art of film. Who cares whether a film was successful at the box office—I want to know whether it was successful creatively speaking.

It becomes a horse race; number one is the only position that matters. They report whether or not something is the number one grosser of the weekend; that's ridiculous because independent release distribution patterns are now similar to studio patterns. It's so much harder to keep a film in a marketplace and watch it actually find an audience.

It's amazingly difficult, the way that sets up what films the acquisitions executives are looking for— because they don't know anymore. They're finding it difficult to try to figure out what can stay out there and what can't. You can argue that it's a hit driven marketplace. But what does that mean? Was *The Full Monty* something that someone tried to hit as a home run? You bet it wasn't! It was given away by the people who produced it because they already had a working-class drama. So it becomes a question of what one thinks is the overall function of a festival. Clearly, you want to try to broaden those possibilities. I am not so naïve that I

> .....
> **"I never apologize for the fact that Sundance has become a market. I think probably the nicest thing you can do for young filmmakers is to get them out of debt and get their films sold."**
> .....

think people should come there and debate Fellini; yet I would hope that at least some of the discussions would be aesthetic and ideological discussions.

The generation of filmmakers currently very much involved in producing independent films strikes me as being similar to the '90s professional athlete—very interested in what's in it for them, in making money, having their own position and their own status, but not necessarily winning championships. A lot of guys have huge contracts without ever winning a playoff game. And in some ways that seems to be what's going on with independent filmmakers. They don't really care about making films that will be memorable, films people will talk about ten years from now. They care desperately about making a film that can get them into the industry so they can recoup some of the investment they've put into the film. More than that, they want to go onto a career that's lucrative and glamorous. I meet more and more filmmakers who are extremely knowledgeable about the business side of the industry and don't really know anything about film. They have a better understanding of who's who and who is influential in the business of film than they do an appreciation for the craft.

I don't hear anyone justifying their festival by saying, "The films we showed at our festival were great." They justify themselves by saying, "We had as many films picked up as they did!" Or, "We have as many acquisitions coming out of it as they do." That should not be the justification for a festival. You have to look at your program and say, "I like this program. This is a strong program. This is what we should be showing. These are the choices we made because these are the films that have value on a number of different levels."

Even so far as Sundance goes, I am not sure that we are in an era of great filmmaking at all. In fact, there are very few American independent films that we are going to be talking about as being memorable in the coming decades. But maybe the great independent films have yet to be made. Maybe a few of them have been and maybe a few in the past, yet not enough that we can really argue about it. When people talk about the twenty-somethings taking over the business the way the '70s generation did in Hollywood twenty-five years ago, I say, "Well it may appear that there's a lot of interest in that, but look at the films. Tell me, which are the key works that we are going to compare to, say, *Nashville* or *Raging Bull?*" Where are those films that signify aesthetic achievement?

The younger filmmakers are clearly savvier about the industry than they are about cinematic achievement.

I think the Rick Linklaters and the Kevin Smiths have made more interesting films as they've gotten older, which is part of the maturation process. It's a hell of a burden to place on a twenty-something filmmaker and say, "Not only do you have to produce films that are successful in the marketplace, but you have to produce great films."

Too often the critique made is "Oh, there were no wonderful things at Sundance this year." When the critique should really be, "They're flawed, but probably no more flawed than a number of the Hollywood films being made, and they indicate talent." Those are the filmmakers to be embraced, instead of those whose films were sold to the highest bidder.

Hasn't Sundance become a part of this emphasis on the business side of the film industry?

One of the odd complaints of Sundance is that the agenda we've set for everyone is the business agenda, yet I don't think that's the crisis. You really have to have a degree of balance. I would hope that to some degree that balance comes from the filmmaker: that they have not chosen filmmaking as a career because they like the accoutrements that go with being a movie director, but because they actually have some passion and a kind of creative vision and a voice they need to express. I don't know if I see that as much. You can ask a lot of filmmakers questions about any of those filmmakers in their fifties, or about guys who are dead—and they don't know them; they haven't seen them. When they do, it really shows. It comes out in their work, which doesn't always make it the most commercial, but makes it interesting. And this fails to be lauded enough by critics and by journalists, who used to be part of that mechanism that helped support the aesthetic dimensions of independent film.

Too often, that's dismissed; we are almost moving to a kind of dismissal of independent work by older critics. They just say, "This doesn't have power, it's not great." I sometimes think that they are throwing out the baby with the bath water. There is a lot of talent there, but it's not yet something that deserves to be spoken in the same voice as the guys who changed Hollywood.

How does Sundance actually select the films?

When you look at about eight hundred independent fictional features and another couple of hundred documentaries and another three or four hundred films in other categories, you really just don't have time to go through them all yourself. So the primary staff is responsible for viewing that work. We have a support staff, and we make sure that no film is seen by fewer than at least a couple of people. I screen a lot of films cold, off the shelf. Recently, that percentage has dropped a bit. Instead of picking up fifty percent of those old films and taking them home, maybe the number is down to twenty-five percent or so. That means that there are a number of other major staff members that see material cold. We have screeners as well, and they are there to make sure the films get dealt with in a very professional way.

People think that we just throw in a tape for two minutes and that's it, and that's not what happens at all. My wife yells at me, "Haven't you seen enough of this? This is terrible," and I've watched thirty-five minutes of it; I try to give it a chance. I think that all the staff members here do the same.

The one thing I have always given my staff credit for is that they are very thoughtful. They really take a lot of time to consider work. They argue it passionately and persuasively—often fighting over different films. You are not looking for five of six people to sit there and agree. You are looking for people to support the work and you are trying to think about what they are saying. You are trying to be a professional programmer who is able to pick a film out and say, "This film should be shown. It's not necessarily my taste or a film I would buy if I were an acquisitions person, but it is a film that should be shown." You make that decision as a professional because you have reasons for this film to be shown as part of what's out there in the independent world. That's the goal for your staff and for yourself. That's what you strive for.

Unfortunately, too many people take for granted the kind of pressures that are put on you. They figure, "Well, there is a lot of political pressure coming from individuals or companies, therefore they have to respond that way." We are not about that pressure. We are certainly in a situation where some of the films we show will be distributed, but if we show six or seven films from Miramax one year, people will say, "God, Harvey [Weinstein] put in whatever he wanted this year." What people don't realize is that we looked at twenty films from Miramax and we didn't take fourteen others. The films we choose are those we think make up the best festival and represent what the independent universe is all about.

The competition is fierce now, and it continues to grow.

Promotion and advertising (P&A) costs have tripled in the last two years. Any film you buy has to gross theatrically at a certain level to make it profitable. You can't release a film with less than $2 million of P&A. You are going to be in that situation regardless of what the film cost to make in the first place. So, you have these acquisitions executives looking around and asking themselves, which are the films worth investing the huge amount of P&A required to make them profitable? Those are the questions that I don't think people think through clearly enough.

You need to know who your audience is. Think through what the film is about. Thinking for an audience doesn't mean that you've somehow gone commercial, or that you have to put elements in the film to make it commercial or to sell it to your audience. No, it's the opposite. It's actually thinking through what you, as a voice, are trying to say, and knowing who is listening. I don't think that anybody who isn't a wonderful filmmaker doesn't think about the audience. I have talked to a lot of the major filmmakers, who talk very much about how they have the audience in mind when they are writing. I think it's kind of a myth that the true artist doesn't pay any attention to that.

Are there common mistakes that you see filmmakers make over and over again?

Rushing. I keep saying don't rush. Don't create a situation where everything is dependent on a schedule only to get into X or Y festival. You know, you spend an awful lot of time putting this project together. Make it good; take the extra time to not only shoot that extra take, but to really think about quality. Try to take a step back. Have naysayers around you. Don't just let people say, "Great, great, great!" Have someone who really gives you a critical eye. You don't want a whole bunch of people arguing with you; what you really want is someone you can trust to help support your vision and not rush it.

We look for a lot of different things, but I've always said our strength is that we respond to a lot of different things. We have a very diverse and eclectic level of response that allows us to look at a work from one kind of experimental point of view to something much more casually mainstream. People really need to look at the range. You are not trying to do something as narrowly defined as "a Sundance film."

For many years, we have attacked the industry as making formulaic work and pushed the independent film as the realm in which creative vision flourished. Yet, we have now moved into an era in which the independent world has become a derivative mess. Some of the initial perspective that motivated the independent world has been lost: the capital "Q" quirky comedy that reflects only a series of quirky comedies that have come before; the generic "Tarantino-wanna-be" work; the coming-of-age angst story that really isn't fresh or doesn't have the depth to make it profound, but is simply another version of the same tale.

Without being too harsh, you want to say those films aren't going to make it anymore. You really need to find something or think about something that runs with freshness and originality. People hear these words and then go and do something straight out of a primetime network sitcom.

When it comes to films that are rejected, do they make many of the same mistakes?

Casting and story are the simple answers to that. Story is the most obvious one; casting is the second. People realize they can't get major actors, so they make poor decisions. Even films that have a lot to offer lose any dramatic impact because you can't squeeze a performance out of an actor who just isn't able to give it. This is something that really takes more experience and it's certainly something that filmmakers should pay more attention to. Filmmakers have to understand that they have to make a *great* film, not a good film. I think that means a lot of different things, but it really means bringing quality to the film. And it's not just the standard required to get into Sundance. It's the standard required to get

> .....
> "Filmmakers have to understand that they have to make a *great* film, not a good film."
> .....

your money back. It's the standard required to be able to find any kind of distribution deal whatsoever.

My belief is that most films fail at the stage of the script—it always goes back to the script. The script is often underdeveloped. The thing that irks me even more is when I hear a filmmaker brag that they wrote the film in a week.

Isn't it amazing that they do that? They say things like, "This film was done on first draft." You want to tell them—*it shows.*

What is the future—the unexplored territories in independent film?

I think digital is going to open up a lot of different possibilities when it becomes cost-effective for independent film, and it's getting there very quickly. So far, almost everyone has left the realm of special effects to the industry and they haven't realized that computers have brought those costs down dramatically. You can now do special effects on a computer that could never have been done optically. So the question is, are you going to be able to create a digital on-screen persona? That's a little bit different and would cost a fair amount of money but it's definitely interesting. It's very much part of a new world.

Many times filmmakers get so wrapped up in everything film that they tend to lose a sense of real life experience; I think that some of the better films come from filmmakers with actual life experience.

I think you need life experience outside of the film world because you aren't going to find creative inspiration just by watching movies. You can learn a lot, you can find a great deal to think about in terms of your craft and you can find creative inspiration, but in terms of your stories, you really need to find those elsewhere.

What makes a good professional in this field is a real eclecticism. Being narrow or critical in your taste is a real deficit. We have tried to support a lot of different things and have managed to avoid a narrow agenda. We understand mainstream filmmaking and filmmakers and traditional aesthetics; we are supportive of those but we see try to see the world more inclusively. Filmmakers of color, gay and lesbian filmmakers, different points of view and different voices, all became part of the definition of the Sundance festival.

We try to be responsive to the perspectives and the voices of both the U.S. and other continents, but we don't try to be inclusive of it in a broad way. That isn't what the festival is about. What Sundance helped do was to expand the field. When those films became not only successful at Sundance but then achieved a certain success in the marketplace, people began to say things like, "There was no gay or lesbian film up to that point." Or that there were very few African-American films that people were embracing and had a certain kind of commercial definition. So what we were doing was breaking through some of those old generalizations and saying, "Hey, look at this work."

Diversity has always been a key definition of what Sundance is about. Though to me that diversity isn't simply a position of the color of the skin. It's a diversity of aesthetics, a diversity of points of view and that sometimes has to do with the creator's experience but it also comes from a creative mind.

If you could sit down with some of these independent filmmakers before they started writing their screenplays and give them some advice, what would you tell them?

Don't just go out and make a film, make a great film. It's so hard to make films and I have so much respect for people that do it. A lot of people are very often angry at us for having to make choices, for being in a position where we have to say: these are the films we have chosen and these we have decided not to take. So often, we have people filled with righteous indignation at being rejected. We have people who think, because it is so hard to make films, that just having made a film is a significant enough accomplishment in itself. It's just not enough to spend a couple of years of your life making a movie, finally finish it, think, "Oh my goodness, I've made a movie!" and pat yourself on the back. You really have to look at what you made and say, "Is this successful? Does this convey the kind of energy and inspiration and storytelling and excitement? Does it work the way I want it to work?"

They read these stories in the paper about this guy making a film or that girl making a film. They feel they have to get their film made and they go out and make it—and too often it is just not good enough. That's a phrase we use around here all the time. "It's not good enough." That doesn't mean that it's bad and it's not that it doesn't have certain elements. It means it isn't cast well or it doesn't have any visual style, or it doesn't necessarily have the kind of creativity to it that really makes it stand apart. So you have to say to yourself—if you are a filmmaker and you have to spend all these resources and all this time—why not shoot for the top? Not enough people do.

Filmmakers need to be encouraged to really take their time. Sometimes that means you won't make it this year and that you need to work on your script. People don't like hearing that their third draft wasn't good enough, that they need to go into a fourth draft. They don't want to do that; they want to say, "Let's make it!" That sort of thinking will ultimately create something without any kind of effect and people won't care about it.

> "It's just not enough to spend a couple of years of your life making a movie, finally finish it, think, "Oh my goodness, I've made a movie!" and pat yourself on the back."

I don't believe that this generation doesn't work hard. I feel that the twenty-something generation right now is almost Protestant in its work ethic. Film students feel they should have no other life outside of their film schools. They don't even see movies because they're working so hard in school. When I was in film school, we used to say, "Are you going to go to the Nuart and watch this film?" Because it was presumed that was what you were going to do. Now, though, people are saying, "No, I've got to finish my project or I've got to work on my script or do my essay." The goal should be to go see those films. My advice is, seek that inspiration, seek that knowledge, broaden yourself, and take the time for your project to really get it right. Or else I fear we are not going to have a generation of filmmakers that will be considered memorable.

What so many of these young filmmakers forget is that you find a lot of major filmmakers doing great work in their late thirties, their forties and their fifties rather than in their twenties. You need life experience and you just don't get it when you are twenty.

It's interesting how many of the filmmakers who have made really low-budget films have become the filmmakers of note for this generation. Maybe the creative ingenuity you need when you are working with a low budget really marks them. I wonder if there isn't something to be said for that sort of initiation. I wonder if really struggling and making those really small $100,000 budget films forces them to overcome obstacles and marks them as filmmakers with ingenuity and promise for the future.

Gilmore and Gore: The Conversation Continues

For this second edition of the *Ultimate Film Festival Survival Guide*, I thought it would be important to check in with Geoff Gilmore for an update. As always, he has honest opinions and real thoughts about what's happening in film today.

I've heard this many times, primarily from filmmakers who have been rejected from your festival, that getting into Sundance is very "political." Some say it's "who you know." How do you respond to that kind of criticism?

That's a "I hear you've stopped beating your wife" remark. If you tell anyone what the reality of the situation is, no one believes you. I've heard a lot of people try to take credit for getting films in Sundance. They want to claim credit for getting films in based on the calls they make. I still have to smile and say, "Guys, it just isn't true." It's very hard to get inside these doors.

The ability to program comes from an ability to look at a lot of different kinds of things—even though some of them may not be your cup of tea—and say, "this one is terrific." And this is a skill that recognizes a genre film, like *Blair Witch*, and gives it credit for what it has. *Blair Witch* knows horror. It knows documentary. It understands independent work. It understands how to mix and play with genres. It has self-reflexivity in it. It brought digital filmmaking into another world, and that hadn't been done before. These guys are playing with various different elements. For all of the lambasting the film has taken, it doesn't get credit for what it did and what made it interesting in the first place.

It was revolutionary.

It was not just a marketing win or just a victory of website marketing. It actually had interesting things in it.

Has the web changed Internet marketing for independents?

Quality and talent are what really make things work; nothing can substitute for either one of those.

Tell me about the Sundance Online Film Festival, what exactly are you going to be looking for in films venturing into this new frontier?

The first thing it's *not* is taking the work from the Sundance Film Festival and putting it online; they're separate programs. A lot of the short films have populated the Internet, a lot of them are wonderful and a lot of them are there right now because of a certain accident of technology. Because a certain attention span, the ability to provoke, make people laugh and titillate the viewer are things that people are embracing right now. It's a "you can't do that on television" type of filmmaking that the Internet embraces. I'm actually trying to ask another question, which is "What is it about the aesthetic of the web that is going to be developed in the next couple of years?" That aesthetic is something that hasn't been discovered yet. It's really a new realm of storytelling that will actually go into something else. And that's what I'm looking to create an opening for.

Since the first edition of this book came out, there are now over 100 new film festivals. I've heard some say that there are too many festivals. I disagree. What do you think?

The functions of film festivals are now so numerous that you have festivals being created for regional tourist bureaus only to raise the media profile of a small resort, rather than to fill any function on the national scheme of things.

But is that necessarily a bad thing? The way I see it, these festivals bring independent film and filmmakers to audiences that might not otherwise see them. In a way, they're providing alternative distribution outlets for indies. The irony is that these, in some cases very non-commercial independent films, will play thirty, forty, fifty festivals and more people will see them on the festival circuit than after they get picked up by a distributor. It's as if the "festival tour" itself is really the thing filmmakers should focus on and rather than trying to get distribution. These films are, in a sense, already being distributed to an audience passionate about indie film.

Well, I agree with you. I think that those who say that there are too many film festivals are those who come from a perspective that flows from the industry, a kind of media nexus in which their sense of what the function of film festivals are is a specific and rather limited one. Festivals are for discovery of work for later distribution. Or they're meant to be launch places to get into specific national markets. I think the film festival circuit is a little bit like the cinematheque circuit in the '60s. Except the cinematheque circuit failed because they didn't have the marketing dollars. I do think that there are audiences for this. There's very much a pay-off for filmmakers and audiences that are able to see work that is not simply what the major multiplex world and major mainstream sources would have us see. So, in some ways, it is a substitute for some kinds of theatrical distribution.

I believe that after a film has had its debut, if it's invited to another festival, the filmmaker should be paid. I think they should get a percentage of that box office take.

Unfortunately, most festivals are not in a position to do that. And most of the smaller film festivals are in an even slighter position than the big festivals. There is a *quid pro quo* in this business that says, "I'm supplying the theater, I'm bringing in your audience, I'm providing an exhibition platform for you—and then you want me to pay you for it?"

True. The reality is that most festivals don't make money. That's the bottom line. But most of these indie films will never get significant distribution beyond a video release. If it weren't for the filmmakers and their movies, there wouldn't be film festivals.

It might be worth exploring, but there are myriad complexities associated with a plan like that. In the meantime, film festivals continue to broaden the possibilities and the opportunities for filmmakers as well as audiences, for which I am grateful.

THE DUDE, DUDE-ARiNO, THE DUDE-iNATOR, HiS ROYAL DUDE-NESS

A conversation with Jeff Dowd, indie film's most notorious Producer's Rep

Jeff Dowd is The Dude. Jeff's last name, Dowd, kind of sounds like "dude," so it's not unusual that he was given this nickname in elementary school. He's been known as Dude ever since. He has enjoyed a lifelong love affair with movies, having fallen in love in the theater when he saw *Some Like it Hot* at age nine. The Dude will also tell you that he has a passion for life. This guy knows how to party. And Jeff's very often the life of the party. There is always that one guy who gets everyone fired up—he's the one who cranks the music, taps the keg or starts the conga line. Jeff Dowd is that guy.

Producer's rep Jeff Dowd

The Dude has been at the center of the indie scene at its very beginnings having helped an astonishing number of films and filmmakers including *Blood Simple, The Black Stallion, Chariots of Fire, Gandhi, Hoosiers, The Stunt Man, Desperately Seeking Susan* and too many more to name. One of his more recent finds is *Smiling Fish and Goat on Fire*, a coming of age story that debuted to great notices at the Toronto Film Festival. It opened to positive reviews at the festival due, in no small part, to the Dude's relationships in the industry. When the Dude talks, people listen. He knows how to get a film into the hands of the right people and form the necessary strategy to put that movie into the best possible position to get noticed and sell. It's hard to say exactly what a producer's rep like The Dude actually does, but it is a rare talent. His job involves everything from script evaluation to marketing to publicity to just plain sweet-talking. And he's damn good at all of it, especially the sweet-talking. Jeff's recent accomplishments include selling films such as Raymond DeFelitta's *Two Family House* (Sundance Audience Award Winner) to Lions Gate Films, Kevin Jordan's *Smiling Fish and Goat on Fire* to Stratosphere Entertainment, Finn Taylor's *Dream with the Fishes* to Sony Pictures Classics and Michael Davis' *Eight Days a Week* to Warner Bros. The Dude also finds time to sit on the boards of the Independent Feature Project, the International Documentary Association, the Sundance Film Festival and the Sundance Institute. Jeff is such a well-known and strangely unique person that filmmakers Joel and Ethan Coen paid tribute to The Dude by basing a character in their film *The Big Lebowski* on him. Anyone who has spent more than five minutes with The Dude will notice that Jeff Bridges' mannerisms in that film are strikingly similar.

I met The Dude at the SXSW Film Festival where we ended up on a panel together. This resulted in a night I only half remember, bar-hopping through the streets of Austin, Texas. I don't recall everything that happened, I only know that I had an amazing time. Jeff is the cowboy I want leading the wagon train through a flurry of parties. He's also the perfect guy to have on your side when making and selling a movie.

What can a really good producer's rep do for a filmmaker?

What you do is prepare the filmmakers for what lies ahead in the marketplace. What their strategic choices are. What that means is that you help them creatively get as much feedback as they can on the movie—have screenings so they can make creative adjustments. And believe me, the best movies that we have all seen have made creative adjustments in post-production. Whether that means extra shooting, whether it means music addition. At the same time, it's strategic planning. How are we going to show this movie the first time? Are we going to show it at the festival? Are we going to show it to all the distributors at once? Or are we going to show it to only one distributor? What are we going to do in terms of domestic versus foreign? What's the filmmakers' agenda? There are going to be different people involved in the filmmaking team, and each one will have a slightly different agenda. Is this a stepping stone to their next movie? Do they want to get the investors' money back? Both? It's helping creative discussion so the people can focus in on the very important decisions they have to make. There are no right or wrong answers, but most of the time, people don't understand the alternatives. So, I try to get them all the information they can use to make good decisions. Also, we discuss all the things they have to do . . . whatever it takes to put your best foot forward. I essentially join the team in every aspect of it.

> .....
> "There are no right or wrong answers, but most of the time, people don't understand the alternatives. So, I try to get them all the information they can use to make good decisions."
> .....

I've noticed a disheartening trend in indie movies these days, and that is an alarming number of movies about making movies . . .

It's funny, I was in this meeting today and they were talking about a movie to look at and it was yet another movie about making movies. Which leads to the whole thing of "get a life." Doesn't anyone have any life experience outside of making movies? Although some of these movies are actually kind of good.

But are they going to have an appeal to anyone outside of people like you and me?

They might, but it's the sociological phenomenon—that so many people are making movies about the process of making movies at a time when there's a real world out there with other interesting things to do.

Can a filmmaker sell a film themselves without a producer's rep or an agent or lawyer?

Of course you can, if you are very lucky. But even Michael Jordan tended to like to go on the court with four other guys. The answer is that you are absolutely insane if you try to do it alone. What I'm all about is trying to build a team. I'll work with all the agents and lawyers to put together the best possible team. Anybody who goes out into today's extremely competitive, expensive, harsh world without a good team—well, they might as well take a gun and just start shooting off body parts of all the people who helped them make the movie. It's the most irresponsible thing to do, but it happens all the time. The problem with independents is that they're independent. It's important in today's world to make strategic alliances. I would recommend that independents also make strategic teamwork alliances. In the worst case, it's going to get them more information.

And by the way, any smart investor really wants the best team to protect their investment. A lot of producers have underbudgeted the production and a lot of directors have underpaid themselves and so they start to think, "Why should I let someone else get involved with this and take another piece?" And that's a legitimate feeling, but they're not seeing the big picture. The big picture is getting your film into the marketplace in a proper way. It's great to have a whole team of passionate, smart players.

> .....
> **"The problem with independents is that they're independent. It's important in today's world to make strategic alliances."**
> .....

Before the filmmaker even begins shooting, what do they need to know?
When you are making a movie for $100,000, that's a lot of money. You can save people's lives for that much. Think of what you could've done with that money other than making a movie that no one is ever going to see. You have to ask yourself some questions first. Just because anyone *can* make a movie, doesn't mean everyone *should* make a movie. I can't believe someone thinks people would actually go see these movies on an opening Friday night as opposed to all the other choices in the world! If your movie isn't enough for people who go see over every other choice, then it's never going to go theatrical. Is it so special that it's going to get on some cable show? And there's really no direct-to-video anymore, so what makes it so special? Hopefully television and the Internet will become a place.

1. Ask yourself, "Who is my intended audience?"

2. People really don't do enough dramaturgical work on their scripts. They should do readings and more readings and not just get the advice of a couple friends. Actually pay for some advice. If you're going to spend $100,000 on a film, you can use $5,000 on dramaturgical feedback. It could make the difference between the film getting released and not getting released. That's why we started the Sundance Institute. We try to say to people, "Do not make your film yet, stop. Reassess it. Put it on its best feet. Try filming some scenes here to get some feedback."

Paper is ultimately cheaper than film.

Right. The problem is, a lot of filmmakers are filmmakers first and storytellers second. Hitchcock, Sayles, Tarantino—these filmmakers were all writers first, directors second. Audiences go to stories, not to films. Form may be equally exciting as content sometimes, like in either *Trainspotting* or *X-Men*, but it's still the way the story affects the audience emotionally and viscerally. Most of the people who end up being successful in the independent market are phenomenally well versed in the history of cinema and they bring that to the table—Tarantino and Spielberg—these people could be working at the film library as archivists. The things that people don't pay enough attention to is stopping to get all the dramaturgical feedback that you can, studying films and talking to people about the marketplace. I guarantee I personally can increase peoples' chances 1000 percent if they talk to me earlier rather than later in terms of whether a film will get to distribution.

> .....
> "Hitchcock, Sayles, Tarantino— these filmmakers were all writers first, directors second. Audiences go to stories, not to films."
> .....

How does a filmmaker best go about showing their film to a distributor for the first time?

You have to think whom you are trying to sell it to in the first place. We're talking about domestic distributors here for the most part, and there are only a small number of them out there. There are really fewer than twenty or so American distributors.

And Miramax isn't really buying these days are they?

Regardless of that, the question is really, what is a distributor looking for?

So, what is a distributor looking for?

Several things: Distributors are looking to see how it plays for an audience. They are assessing how it plays for critics. That's why distributors often like film festivals. They are able to get a sense of how a movie plays for audiences and how critics are likely to respond. The other thing that's important at the end of the day, is how the distributors emotionally respond to the film, how they feel about the filmmakers. They're not going to do it just for economic reasons, believe me. And, of course, there are critical and economic evaluations. So, how you assess your first showing is: maybe there's one distributor who is perfect for your film and maybe they don't like film festivals and they like to see things in their own screening room and maybe that's the way to do it. Maybe a film festival is. But, you often want to screen a film in front of the target audience. It depends on the kind of film it is and what kind of experience you want to have. Sometimes a particular actor or director is going to be the key to selling the film. That's one thing that distributors assess. Who is going to represent this film in the media for us? They often need to see that person in action at a film festival or something. You need to come up with a way to screen the film that helps convey what it's going to do in the marketplace.

> .....
> "Distributors are looking to see how it plays for an audience. They are assessing how it plays for critics. That's why distributors often like film festivals."
> .....

Then perhaps the distributor screening, basically a few people sitting in the room, is not the best way to go?

Maybe not, but there are certain films that have been very successful, and that's how they were sold. It really is case by case. It's also what you do before you screen the film. How do you position it to the distributor? How do you describe it? They are very busy people and you have to do some of the homework for them. That might mean press, artwork, trailers—coming up with a way for them to get a feel for why or how the film might interest the public. That's all part of the process. The key thing is for the studios to understand how the continuum goes all the way through to the public.

So in a way, it's about demonstrating to the distributor that the public has an appetite for this type of movie.

Two key words are marketability and playability.

Are there other ways to get to distributors?

You can screen it at a festival, but the critical thing is what you do before, how you position it. You can do a one-two punch and screen it at a festival and then screen it right afterwards in New York and Los Angeles with audiences. No one is going to buy a film until the president of marketing makes a decision. That's how a big film is acquired. So, when you go to a film festival, there are times when only half of those people are there. You are rarely going to sell a film on the basis of its first screening. There will be tremendous interest and heat and then they're going to catch it at its second film festival screening. Or they're going to want to screen the print so other people in their company can see it. The other route is having a distributor screenings in New York and Los Angeles and there are lots of variations on that. The other alternative is to pick one or two distributors and just screen it for them. The advantages of that are quite obvious. The disadvantages . . . well, you've only kissed one girl, so to speak, and you'll never know what everyone else might think.

What are the best ways to create buzz to build interest from distributors?
One way is to have certain people in the media doing it. (e.g., *Variety, Hollywood Reporter*). Try to position the movie for them. You can also sometimes show a film to select members of the press.

Obviously, everyone sends out postcards and faxes and things like that. A website. You can have other people, who may not be interested parties but who have some credibility with distributors, call on your behalf. You could also have a couple of screenings that don't include distributors, but include people who have relationships with distributors.

If you're in a film festival, hiring a publicist is 100 percent recommended. If you're not in a film festival, there isn't really much for a publicist to do, to be honest. If you have one magazine article or something to generate some advance interest, that's okay, but you really don't need much more than one piece. You only need one or two examples of the buzz the film might generate. And, between the producers, the producers' rep and the publicists, that information will get to the distributors. Film festivals are a one-time opportunity to have people look at your film.

What is the number one thing that gets you to see a film, in any scenario; whether at a film festival or if someone hands you a videotape—what gets you to sit down and watch it?
If I get a really strong recommendation from somebody I trust— that would be the number one thing.

What's the next thing?

Subject matter is quite important. It's very hard to judge a film on subject matter. Sometimes it's the level of talent in the movie, a certain actor or director.

What are some of the important things for a filmmaker to be aware of in any distributor negotiation?

Meet the people who are going to be marketing your film—the ones at the company who are going to be marketing your film! The people who are involved acquiring your film are going to have a lot of contact with you ahead of time, but when your movie is coming out, they may be off in Cannes. The people who are marketing your film, those are the people you're going to be married to. The person you're going to be working with everyday is the head of marketing.

So meet those people in the company, and have them sell you on the plan of how they are going to market your movie. Brainstorm a little, even have some disagreements. The success of the film isn't about the price of the film, it's about how it is handled in the marketplace.

> **"The success of the film isn't about the price of the film, it's about how it is handled in the marketplace."**

The real test is in the extra marketing things that the distributor is going to do. How much are they really going to put into screenings programs for word of mouth? How much are they going to put in at a local level?

I'm sure there are other questions—like what about publicity? How are they going to publicize it? Do they have their own in-house publicity?

Right, but how much extra support are they going to need? Are they willing to pay to put the filmmakers on the road? It can make all the difference in the world in Boston if you show up there for a few days or not. Each film is a new business. There are few films that you market the same way you did your last three films. The audiences are quite distinct.

Ultimately, you're really looking for an individual in the company, an actual person, who is involved in the marketing who is going to give you a personal commitment as to how much they're going to do and how much they're capable of doing. You're looking for a strategy for your film. And someone with the ability to be flexible. Can these people be focused in the season your film is coming out? How many other films are coming out then? This is a human business. The biggest part of the deal you're looking for is who are the human beings you're going to be dealing with and then pray that they're going to be there when your film comes out and that the company doesn't change hands.

There are a lot of filmmakers who get their movies sold, but a certain breed of filmmaker can actually build a career. What are the things they need to do for that?

One of the things you want most is to have some idea of what your next movie is. Either have your own script ready or go buy one. There never seems to be enough time in the day, but make time. There isn't much an agent can do for you, except maybe get you work for hire, unless you have another product they can help get made.

A second project is definitely helpful, but what other things?

You want to build your team. You want to have your agents and your lawyer and your producers. I think some of the people who build a career have a team of people to work with and that team keeps them going. Quentin Tarantino has Lawrence Bender. That's often tough because first films often have odd couples together, mismatched and not necessarily partners for life.

Even if you have all the money in the world and have your own studio, you need to have a script. A lot of the time, what people are doing, is they're barely making post-production. They're racing every second. I've showed up at Sundance with dripping wet prints. But you have to find an hour a day to start writing things or reading things. Or, you put the word out that you're looking for something. You have to be ready for the next effort.

A lot of films get made these days by attaching talent, getting a bankable name attached to some independent film. What is the best way to get someone attached?

To start with, I highly recommend that you do get some names attached to your film. You've taken your odds and made them dramatically tougher without names. On the other hand, David Arquette in the *Dream Life of Fishes*, is not a superstar, but he is enough of a name that the foreign markets recognize that they can do something with that name. The domestic people know they can get him on television and radio shows and they can do something on radio and cable.

At the end of the day, an actor will be attracted to a great script. So, doesn't it all come back to the screenplay itself?

The absolute best way is to write parts, because actors will be your best friends. If you write a really good script, with really good parts, you can get really good actors to do it. Agents can become great allies if you have a good script. There are enough smart people who are producers, actors, agents, etc. . . . that if you can build a good enough team, you can get your film to the critical mass, for example, *Boys Don't Cry*. It's almost a litmus test. If your script is good, you will be able to get a name actor.

LEARN FROM THE DUDE

- Get feedback. Paper is cheaper than film. Write. Rewrite. Get more feedback. Rewrite and repeat. Shoot some test scenes on video. Get more feedback and keep rewriting until the script is perfect. Ask yourself, "Why am I making this film?"
- Study films. Become a student of film history.
- Build a team. A combination of publicist, manager, producer's rep, agent, lawyer, etc. . . . They should be as passionate about your film as you are.
- Talk to people about the marketplace. What kind of films sell? What doesn't sell? What are the realistic expectations for my movie?
- Prepare for your film festival debut by thinking carefully about a strategy.
- Be willing to take helpful advice from others.
- Demonstrate to others how your film might best be sold to a paying audience in theaters. Your own early marketing materials (poster, trailer, website) along with the hype those generate in the form of publicity (articles in magazines and newspapers, on television and the web) will show a distributor that there is a market for your movie.
- Get to know the players in distribution that are interested in your film. Especially the marketing people. They are the ones who will be selling your film to the public, make sure they "get it." You only have to make *one* distribution deal—make the right one. Deals are made with people, so get to know and trust them.
- Have your next movie, a "go-to" project, ready. Either a script or idea you're working on, another piece of material you'd like to adapt, or option another script. It doesn't matter, just have *something*.Get some life experience, so you don't end up making a movie about making movies. Or at least save that idea for your eighth or ninth film.
- If your movie sucks, at least put on a great party. The Dude and I will be there.

SECTION 2
BUiLD BUZZ: EVERYTHING ABOUT iNDiE MOViE MARKETiNG

"The success of such films as *The Blair Witch Project,* in which millions of people knew about the film from the internet almost a year before its release, make it clear just how important the internet can be in getting the word out about your film. The pre-awareness of that project through the internet is directly responsible for the success of that film. Period."

—Linda Brown, Publicist

iNTRODUCTiON TO GUERRiLLA MARKETiNG

What do I mean by guerrilla marketing? Basically, it means "Be different." (I would also add that it means you intend to market inexpensively.) You must think beyond simply slapping the logo for your movie onto a T-shirt. You have to think, "out of the box." Get creative when it comes to getting your film the attention it deserves from festival attendees, press and especially distributors.

Take Sarah Jacobson, whose film *Mary Jane's Not A Virgin Anymore* played the 1997 Sundance Film Festival. She made cheap stickers that said "Not A Virgin." Jacobson, her mom and a posse of pals stuck them onto the festival badges of Sundance attendees. Within a few days, everyone was wearing them. One well-attended Sundance party found Geoffrey Gilmore himself wearing the "Virgin" sticker. It was hip because it was mysterious—and because it wasn't a T-shirt.

Jacobson took the concept further as she began passing out cigars with the logo of her film emblazoned on the wrapper. She printed these up quickly at Kinko's and put them onto some cheap, no-brand cigars.

Sarah Jacobson's film had great buzz because she was able to think "out of the box." She didn't spend a lot of money and yet she produced unexpected attention-getters and presented her film in a creative and unexpected way. And she did this all with almost no marketing budget! This doesn't mean that you should be passing out cigars yourself, but it certainly means you should consider something other than T-shirts, which are very typical, and often boring and uncreative. (Uh, that doesn't mean you shouldn't give me a T-shirt if you see me at a festival; I always keep the cool ones.)

Following is a list of ideas that should get your creative juices flowing so you can come up with your own ideas. The ideas below are really clever, and I think they're great—but they've been done, so use them to inspire your own wacky concepts.

"Out of the Box" Quick Marketing Ideas

Get your film known with these simple and cheap ideas.

- Create a flyer for your film and make it look like a parking ticket. Put it on all the cars at the festival and in the festival parking lots.
- Make a flyer that looks like a $20 bill. On the other side is info about your screening. Spread them all over town. NOTE: Feds don't like this one. So be careful. Counterfeiting is illegal, so make sure to replace Abraham Lincoln's photo on the five-dollar bill with your own, or do something else to make it obvious that the money is fake. Many copy stores will not make copies of money, as they already know these laws.
- T-shirts are easy, but depending on the local environment, you can come up with better items of clothing like ear muffs (cold weather), sweatshirts, ski caps, boxer shorts or G-strings. (Hey, that'll get attention!)
- A cereal box (the single-serving, tiny kind) with the poster of your film on the front and back. Screening info is printed on the sides where the ingredients should be.
- Give Viewmaster viewers to the press with still images of your film printed on the still frames in the viewer. The frames on a Viewmaster are made from 16mm film and custom Viewmaster sleeves could be made cheaply. This one would be really cool, but likely expensive.
- A comic book. This worked well for the film *Six String Samurai,* which premiered at the Slamdance Film Festival in 1998.

There are plenty of ideas to come up with on your own; the point is to do something unique so people talk will about it and ultimately attend your screening.

A POWERFUL PRESS KiT

All good marketing begins with a press kit. It contains all the information a media person will require to do a story about your film. A large festival will be attended by hundreds, sometimes thousands of members of the media from newspapers, magazines, television, radio, the Internet, the wire service, all types of local media and international media—you name it, they're here. They're all going to need a press kit. Many times the press kit will act as your only sales tool to convince journalists to write a story about your movie. The writing should be smart and witty, as well as completely accurate. A little humor is okay, exaggeration is fine, but outright lying will end up in the loss of all your credibility—it's always best to stick to the facts. I often find that the stories behind many indie movies are better than the movies themselves. Tell me that story and get me excited by it. An interesting story about how your film got made can prove just as helpful toward getting press as the movie itself.

Most festivals require that you provide them with a certain number of kits to give out to the media. Be prepared with a master press kit and enough extra materials so that you can turn around several hundred kits on a moment's notice. Get your film's logo professionally printed on some slick stickers. (You can also print really nice stickers using your home computer and laser printer; it depends on how high you want the quality to be.) The stickers can be placed on the front of a folder that will hold all your materials. **QUICK TIP:** If you get some really nice stickers printed, they can also be placed on anything, turning that item instantly into an inexpensive promotional piece of merchandise. A baseball bat, a candy bar, a pen, a lunchbox, a backpack, a shoe horn, a bag of microwave popcorn, a jar of olives, a lampshade—anything can be instantly transformed into a cool promo give-away simply by slapping on an "official" sticker.

The Seven Items That Must Be in a Press Kit

1. **Cover Sheet.** The cover sheet to your press kit should include the logo for the film, the contact info for your publicist, your own contact info—or both. Be sure to include a local contact number for the particular festival, perhaps on business cards with your name, contact number and description of the basic plot of your film. Having a cell phone number (with voice mail) printed on this page is essential because you need to be available at every moment.

2. **Synopsis.** You need to have three versions of your synopsis:

   The One-Liner. A sentence, but not a run-on sentence. This one-liner version is much like the logline that you use to describe the story of your film to others. Basically this sentence is how others will talk about your movie, so take the time to craft it and try it out on people. It will be used to sell your film as much as it will be to describe it. Think about this one carefully—it must be a grabber.

   The Short Synopsis. About 100-250 words, this should share a page with the one-liner. This gives an overall description of the movie in a longer form and might give away some details from the first and second act of your film while offering just a hint of what might happen in the climax. If well written, it will only encourage readers to dig into other parts of your kit.

   The Long Synopsis. From 500-1000 words. This one describes the entire film and teases at what happens at the end, but it should not give away the ending. This detailed synopsis is for really lazy journalists who either skip your screening and pretend they saw your film, or who fell asleep at your screening. Try not to blame them; sitting on your ass watching movies all day can be really hard work. Really.

   These three synopses work to the benefit of one another offering deeper levels of information about your film depending on how far the reader wishes to delve. Most will only read the one-liner and the short synopsis, but having all three is crucial.

3. **About the Production.** A behind-the-scenes story detailing the making of the film that includes interviews with the cast, anecdotes about the shoot and the true tale of what inspired the filmmakers to make *this* movie. The best way to go about writ-

ing this is to interview the cast and crew during production and include their quotes. Journalists like numbers, so include details like how long it took to shoot, how many years you worked on the script, etc. . . . This document can be 500-1,000 words or more.

4. **Bios**. Include the bios of the key players in the production—the director, writer, producer, and actors along with other key crew like the cinematographer. Bios can run anywhere from 100-500 words generally speaking, but there is no rule here. If any of the crew or actors have their own bios, start there. The best way to write a bio is to tape record interviews and just say, "Tell me about yourself; how did you get into film? What is your background and experience?" Include details about schooling and other films they may have worked on. Highlight experiences with name actors or name filmmakers who journalists might recognize. If the director started as a production assistant working with Kevin Smith, that must be mentioned and will be a great starting point for any journalist to ask questions. Personal details are always important. If the film is about working at a fast food drive-thru and the writer worked at one for five years, include that. As they relate to the film, personal details make the bio that much more interesting to read.

5. **Credits**. Include a list of *all* the credits that appear in your film. It's important that this is completely accurate, as anyone who writes about your film will use this document to find the correct spellings of names of the actors, characters and anyone else associated with the picture.

6. **Other press clips**. Any positive press, no matter how small, should be included. If you have done your homework, you should at least have a mention of the movie in the local newspaper where shooting took place. Any mention may help. Online press counts, so include those printouts. Also, include other reviews *only* if they are positive and *especially* if they are written by name critics or for well-known outlets. You don't want someone to decide that they should not write about your film because someone else has already reviewed it. Be careful about this, particularly before your debut. After your premiere, include as many positive reviews as will fit in the folder.

7. **Photos.** You should have at least one good photo that best represents the film. Include caption information identifying the actors, their characters, what is depicted in the photo and any other pertinent info. Captions should say something like: Jack Jones as Dick Starkiller, a video store clerk in *Revenge of the Clerks*, an independent feature film written and directed by Keith Jones. Don't forget to include a photo credit and copyright information. You should have three different formats for photos: black and white stills, color slides and digital stills on floppy discs or a CD-ROM. Different outlets have different needs—generally newspapers want black and white stills, magazines want color (they'll also probably ask for some kind of exclusive picture, so be ready for that) and websites will want their photos in a digital format (on a floppy disk, a CD-ROM or they may download them from your site—more on that later). If you're sending out press kits in advance, ask the contact what kind of photos they require rather than wasting pictures on an outlet that may not use them.

POSTER THE TOWN

Most film festival movie posters just plain suck. But don't worry, plenty of successful films have had bad posters as well. Weak tag lines are commonplace even in mainstream movies. Consider Orson Welles' *Citizen Kane,* whose memorable tag line was: "It's Terrific!" Wow. Or George Lucas' *Star Wars,* whose original tag line read: "It's about a boy, a girl and a galaxy." Yikes. That sounds like *crap*!

Most posters seen at film festivals have an amateur look that, well, represents the film in a bad light. The festival is like a job interview and here you are in jeans and a grubby T-shirt. You need a poster that feels like a smooth Armani suit, not a stinky T-shirt. The first piece of advice for any filmmaker wishing to create an eye-catching poster is to acknowledge that you are a filmmaker—not a poster designer. Filmmakers, especially on small productions, have a tendency to want to make the poster themselves. You made the film, now back off and allow others to do their jobs. If you tell a designer exactly what you want them to do, they will do exactly as you tell them. If you allow your designer some creative freedom, you are more likely to get some new and cool ideas. However, if your budget does not allow for a poster designer and you are forced to create your own poster, there are some basic things you should know.

Wildposting is key to getting attention for your film. Michael Moore's The Big One *got it with some cheap posters and an overworked staple gun.*

PHOTO BY RANDALL MICHELSON

Jon C. Allen designs movie posters for a living. Allen began collecting one-sheets when he was young and knew he wanted to create them for a living. He has a degree in Visual Design and has worked at various Hollywood advertising agencies. These days, Allen freelances and has designed movie posters for Sony, Castle Rock, Miramax, New Line, HBO and many others. Allen's poster credits include films like *American History X, Spice World, Three to Tango, Go, The Fall* and *Palmetto,* along with countless video box designs for films like *The Brothers McMullen.* Now, don't blame him for some of these bad movies, the posters are all cool. However, a designer's job is also about pleasing the client and Allen is ultimately a gun for hire.

Allen suggests asking the right questions before embarking on a design. "Is the poster positioning this film in the best possible way? Does it invoke a good reaction? Can you tell what it is as you drive by it at forty miles an hour, looking at it in a bus shelter? Really, a designer has to be aware of the issues beyond the obvious aesthetics and layout. For me, a great poster is one that manages to straddle all of the fences just mentioned: sell the film, offer the slightest hint of something new, be well balanced in layout and design—and look really cool."

In order for an indie to create a poster that stands out at a film festival, it's important to know your market. "There are a lot of factors—film markets, for example. Some foreign markets lean towards more action oriented posters (and movies)." says Allen. "As far as the U.S. film market goes, I would take advantage of the fact that you aren't in the studio system and avoid some of the clichés that tend to creep into those type of projects. You don't have to do the over-used and -abused "Two-Big-Heads-Floating-in-the-Sky" look that so many studios rely on. The best piece of advice I can give you for your poster look (whether on your own, or hiring a designer to do it for you) is to *keep it simple.*

"Whenever we work on a smaller film, we always make it simple to make the movie feel *bigger.* Less really is more, in this case." Allen recommends a simple approach. "So often smaller indie projects with low advertising budgets fall into the kitchen sink design trap—let's show everything this movie offers so they know how hard we worked on it. Granted, in some cases, a distributor wants you to show all kinds of action, explosions, sex, etc., in your poster.

But sometimes, it might be better to show less. Especially if you have no stars, no photography—often in those cases, we go with a simple icon, or a concept idea that captures the viewers attention."

Allen offers a few final thoughts: "People ask me, 'Why do the majority of movie posters suck?' Well, it's all subjective, but those same people should ask, 'Why do the majority of movies suck?' Film advertising mirrors many of the same traits (good and bad) as the rest of the film industry. Whenever you have to please a significant number of people, compromises will be made. Sometimes this will improve something—often it will not. 'Design by committee' just like 'Filmmaking by committee' doesn't always work. I encourage someone working on their own one-sheet to make the film poster their own vision. Please yourself first, everyone else second. Hopefully, those same rules applied when you made your movie."

Poster designer Jon C. Allen can be reached via his website: http://onesheetdesign.com

10 Elements of Great Movie Poster Design
Follow these simple rules and you are on your way to a memorable one-sheet.

1. **Invoke feelings**. Create some sort of emotion. This can be done through color, image, etc. A great poster sparks interest, makes people stop on the street or in a theater lobby. For example, a poster for a comedy should make you laugh.
2. **Well thought out typography**. Type should compliment the image, yet not attract undue attention to itself, and it should work with the imagery as a unit.
3. **Second read**. In other words, something you don't notice the first time you look at it. For example, take a look at the FEDEX logo. Have you ever noticed the hidden arrow inside the type?
4. **Good photography**. Head strips of stars' heads on doubles' bodies sometimes work, but it's always nice to have an idea for a photo shoot, have that star shot the way you envisioned, and use the resulting photography to make your design work.
5. **Great copy**. Always important, especially for comedies. "Four Score and Seven Beers Ago . . ." made my *Senior Trip* poster work.

6. **Logo**. A logo that stands on its own. A great logo compliments the poster and works well in its own context, because it will often be used on its own in other mediums, such as trailers. The logo should actually compliment the poster, instead of "floating" out in front of the poster, and not acting as part of the artwork.

7. **Translatable**. Translates well to other formats. Some things may look great at 27" x 41" on a one-sheet, but how will it look on billboards, bus sides, websites, or in black and white in a newspaper?

8. **Relevant to the film's story/plot**. Sometimes a poster has nothing to do with anything that happens in a film—for example, an idea that services the marketing, but is completely removed from the film itself.

9. **Show something new**. This is always a tricky issue. Movie posters mirror the movies themselves—it's rare that something new is tried as opposed to giving them what they've seen before.

10. **Hit the target**. It should please the intended audience. Know your demographic and be sure the poster appeals to this group. Studios not only hold focus groups for movies, but for the poster ideas themselves.

10 Most Common Mistakes of Poster Design

These mistakes result in amateurish posters and poor design.

1. "Kitchen sink" design.
2. Not thinking conceptually.
3. "It looks cool" being a design's only redeeming quality.
4. Thinking of it as art, instead of *commercial* art . . . it's about marketing, not just what looks good.
5. Not positioning the film well.
6. Not designing everything to work together. Say, typography not working with the imagery.
7. Unwillingness to compromise for the best overall design. Sure, there are compromises left and right, some of which will drive the designer crazy. Every movie poster designer has had the client change/alter their "vision" and felt it was a fatal mistake. But that's the nature of the business; you're trying to market a movie. Being able to play within those limits and boundaries and produce something worthwhile is part of the challenge.

8. Not using all the available elements to produce good work. Typography, layout, color, imagery, concept.
9. Bad finishing skills. Sure, you have a brilliant idea that will make you the next Saul Bass, but the fact that it looks like crap because you aren't comfortable in Adobe PhotoShop will hinder your idea.
10. Again, not pleasing the client. Sure, it's easy to dismiss them if you don't agree with their views/opinions, but since they are *paying you* to market *their movie*, you should work with them, not against them.

TEASE YOUR AUDiENCE

Posters are fine; good buzz and press always help, but nothing gets an audience more hyped to see a film than a great trailer. I love movie trailers—they're just plain cool. They're my favorite part of going to the theater and I never miss them. The truth of the matter is that you really don't need a trailer to take a film to a festival. Creating a trailer can be a costly distraction when the real order of business should be to make the best film possible. Consider very seriously how setting time aside to make a trailer may impact on everything else you have to do to prepare for your festival debut. My advice is to put making a trailer at the very bottom of your "to-do" list.

However, if you have the luxury of time and some extra money to invest in a trailer, it becomes yet another helpful tool to aid in selling your movie. Trailers can be digitized and posted on the web. This exposes a bit of your film to tens of thousands of people, whetting their appetite before your festival premiere. In addition, the trailer can be used to get distributors in seats. While it is not recommended that you send your entire film on video to a distributor, an effective trailer on tape is yet another way to get a distributor or a producer's rep interested in attending a screening. It's hard to get them to sit still for 90 minutes, but two minutes of their time is not a lot to ask. In addition, a powerful teaser assists in spelling out your movie's selling points and explaining how exactly a distributor may market the film to a wider audience.

To learn about trailers, I spoke with one of the best in the business. Dave Parker is an award-winning, veteran trailer editor and has been toiling in the industry for the last fifteen years. Currently employed at Seismic Productions, he has worked on countless campaigns for everything from big Hollywood movies to independent film projects including *Saving Grace, Casino, The Mask, Philadelphia, Mortal Kombat, Tomorrow Never Dies; Me, Myself and*

Irene and *Dungeons and Dragons*. I met with Dave, who broke down for me exactly what makes an effective movie trailer.

10 Elements of an Explosively Effective Trailer

1. **Quick Cuts**. If you've got some cool shots and a really simple-minded story, cut each shot down to about a 1/3 of a second and slap on some pumping driving music. The unfortunate reality is that often style wins over substance.

2. **Use Graphics That Grab You**. Decent graphics are a plus. Be creative and make an impressive title treatment that is different from your main title.

3. **Original Music is Important**. Be careful with the music you use. There are plenty of affordable tracks from companies that supply music specifically for trailers. Be sure to use music that is legally cleared. Of course, there *is* another way. For the purposes of the *trailer only*, if you want music that *sounds* similar to a certain movie soundtrack to capture a particular mood, have an original song or piece of music composed. The secret is this: if you want to blatantly rip off a tune, remember to *change every seventh note*. By changing the tune slightly, you can avoid being sued.

4. **Tell the Story (but don't ruin it)**. If you've got a great story, don't be afraid to spell it out. It doesn't hurt to do a little hand-holding. A narrator can go a long way toward dramatizing the story in broad strokes. Also, don't tell the *whole* story. Leave them wanting more.

5. **Use Positive Reviews**. If the film has gotten early positive reviews from notable critics or credible press outlets, use them. Big, bold quotes in a white typeface against a black background look impressive when cut quickly into the trailer. Generally, these are most effectively used near the end just before the title screen. Be sure to clear the use of these quotes from the outlets that provided them.

6. **Great Sound is Critical**. Spend time on the sound mix. If you have a slight problem understanding what your actor said, then you can bet your ass that the guy looking at your trailer doesn't have a clue. Also, don't be afraid to record dialog for the trailer only to clarify the story. In *The Negotiator* trailer, Kevin Spacey says, "They're gonna have to deal with both of us!" Spacey

looped that line for the trailer only and never said anything like that in the finished feature. Imagine that! Lying in advertising! Hard to believe, huh?

7. **Star Power**. If your film has a recognizable star, make sure to feature your star very prominently. Even if you've got only one celebrity in a cameo, make sure those shots are used extensively in the trailer.

8. **Keep it Short**. The shorter the better, about a minute or two, but absolutely make sure it is under two and a half minutes. Why? Because that is the time limit imposed by the MPAA for all theatrical trailers. The audience watching your little masterpiece has been trained like a pack of Pavlov's dogs. Anything over two and a half minutes and they're looking at their watches.

9. **Start with a Bang!** Open with an attention grabber. The opening of the trailer for David Lynch's *Lost Highway* features Robert Blake and Bill Pullman engaged in a creepy conversation. Man, that was cool. Opening with an explosive image or a memorable line of dialog will keep them watching.

10. **End with a Bang!** Close with the best shot and/or best line. What sold *The Perfect Storm*? Was it the brooding presence of surly George Clooney? How about the clichéd dialog mouthed by Marky Mark? C'mon, we all know it was that awesome wave!

10 Mistakes to Avoid in Making a Trailer

1. **Do Not Use a Feature Editor**. Use a trailer editor only and don't even consider hiring your feature editor to cut the trailer. A feature editor is used to letting things play out and is not as good at the short sell. A trailer is an advertisement, plain and simple. It's essentially a commercial or a music video and is a completely different animal than a feature, so get a good editor with experience cutting trailers.

2. **Don't Fear Outtakes**. Don't be afraid to use some original scenes or outtakes that didn't make the final cut. Remember in *Twister* when that tractor came crashing down in front of that car? Nope, me neither . . . it existed only in the trailer. It's also fine to shoot footage specifically for the trailer.

3. **No Nudity**. Keep the trailer PG-13 at least. Even if your film has a lot of sex, there's no reason to flaunt it. Violence, of course, is

never frowned upon. But you never know who may see it or download it. Make sure the trailer is acceptable to air on network television.

4. **No Expanded Scenes.** Use sound bites only. Don't use really long expository dialog. Make every shot concise.

5. **Boring is Bad.** Get to the point. What is your movie about? Define it in the first ten seconds.

6. **Do Not Use Uncleared Music.** A distributor may assume you have the rights and you'll be shooting yourself in the foot if you use music for which you don't have the rights.

7. **Bad Transfer.** Make sure not to skimp on the transfer. The picture should look as good, or even better than your feature. Footage from your dailies or rough cut is not suitable for use. Transfer clean for the trailer.

8. **Never Use Stolen Shots.** Eventually, they'll see the finished film, so don't try to cut in expensive shots that are gratuitously lifted from another movie—like, say, a giant explosion or a train wreck.

9. **Do Not Give Away the Ending.** Never ever give away the ending. Yeah, I know that trailers for big studio movies do it all the time. The trailer for *Double Jeopardy* gave away the entire movie and still every housewife on the planet went to see it. Look at the acquisitions people as the big fish and your trailer as the little, convulsing worm. You want them to bite, but not feel full.

10. **Too Long.** The most common crime committed by an amateur trailer editor is cutting one that is too long. Shorter is better.

WHY AN EPK iS ESSENTiAL

An EPK or "electronic press kit" is an invaluable tool when it comes to getting press on television. While creating an EPK sounds like yet another costly distraction with all the work you already have to do to make the film, it is worth doing for several reasons.

- An EPK is incredibly helpful for television producers and makes getting press on TV much easier.
- Content from the EPK (trailer, behind-the-scenes footage, interviews) can also be used for promotion on the web and later on as extras for the DVD release.
- The material on the EPK is an asset that will have value when it comes to negotiating a distribution deal.

Television journalists are perhaps the laziest members of the media, trust me. They often need stories spoon-fed to them. Why not make their jobs a snap by suggesting they do a little story on your movie? In addition to your press kit, it's to your advantage to produce an electronic press kit that will, in a way, do a little hand-holding to help deadline-crazed television producers fill some airtime. The more material you provide, the chances increase that your story will go from a five second mention in a festival round-up on local television to a full blown review taking up a minute or more of time on the air. In addition, television producers will archive your EPK for use later in case the need for a follow up story presents itself. Either they'll archive it or throw it in a pile to be turned into a blank tape, you can never tell. With this in mind, it is helpful to label the tape: *Please Return After Use.* But tapes like this are rarely returned, so you shouldn't expect it. Just be grateful to get any press at all on TV.

Producing the EPK Begins with the Movie

Work on the EPK should begin along with start of production. When you are shooting, you know that you should have a photographer shooting stills of key scenes such as the production at work and slick pictures of your cast. It doesn't hurt to shoot some Hi-8 or digital video footage of behind-the-scenes for use on the EPK. Members of the cast are often waiting around for the next set up. Don't waste this downtime, get the actors to sit in front of the camera for twenty minutes for an interview. Be sure that the actors are coached to speak in soundbites—no more than thirty seconds on any one question and preferably much shorter, like ten or fifteen seconds. The person off-camera will not be heard asking the question, so make sure the actor repeats the basic question within their answer so their comments are put into context. Ask the actor about their character in the film, and the actor should respond, "Well my character Max Power is a blah, blah, blah." (Except, you know, make sure they say something more clever than, "blah, blah, blah.") Prepare ten to fifteen questions, and give the actors time to formulate some clever responses. Trust me, your actors will leap at the chance to offer their own witty comments.

What's On the EPK Tape?

The EPK must include a legal disclaimer at the beginning of the tape itself. Issues such as a specific time frame that the outlet may use the material can vary, so consult your lawyer. The legal disclaimer should include the following language:

This film/video/digital footage is for publicity and promotional use only. Any use, re-use or unauthorized assemblage of this film/video/digital footage is strictly prohibited without the prior written consent of [PRODUCTION COMPANY NAME]. All rights reserved. Property of [PRODUCTION COMPANY NAME], promotional use only. Sale, duplication or transfer of this material is strictly prohibited. Use of material is granted for a six month [TIME PERIOD MAY VARY] window.

The legal disclaimer is followed by the title card or logo. Then, a menu screen in which text scrolls outlining the content contained on the tape. Indicate how long the tape is within the text with a TRT (total running time) in parenthesis [e.g. (31:30)] and then scroll the menu and indicate the TRT for each individual section. The sections include the following elements and should appear in the order outlined below:

1. **Two trailers**. There should be two versions of the trailer, one that includes the complete trailer and a second version of the same trailer with the sound split into two tracks—one for dialog and effects and another track for music. In addition, if your trailer has a narrator, the second version of the trailer should either delete or isolate onto the second track with the narrator. This is so that a television commentator can add their own commentary over clips from the film. This second version is very important. Be sure to indicate the second version has NO NARRATION and has dialog and effects on one track and music on a separate track. Many television producers are wary of airing anything they even suspect might be uncleared music, so even if you have done your homework and cleared your music, be sure to leave them the option of omitting the music entirely when running clips.

2. **Selected scenes**. This is your opportunity to highlight the best scenes from your film. You may choose from just a few or as many as ten scenes, there is no rule, but offer a variety of scenes that accentuate your film's greatest strengths. Every scene should be under a minute, in fact, the shorter the better. Spend some serious time thinking about what clips represent the best of your movie. TV time is very precious and a gripping fifteen-second scene is going to deliver more of an impression than a drawn-out one-minute scene. Be sure to introduce each clip with the title of the movie and a title, in quotes, for the scene along with a TRT for the clip. Example: JOE INVADES PARK CITY "Joe and Bob Lose Their Car Keys" (TRT :20 sec.).

3. **A "making of" featurette**. (Optional) This is totally optional and it's not likely to be used on television, but it will come in handy when talking to a distributor who will use it for promotion and for use later as an extra on the DVD. Featurettes can run anywhere from just a few minutes to up to thirty minutes. This behind-the-scenes look at your film offers another opportunity for coverage of your movie if it has already been covered

in another way. It's not necessary to have behind-the-scenes footage on the EPK, but it doesn't hurt. If your featurette has a narrator, it's also wise to put two versions on the tape with the soundtracks split so that a TV commentator can add their own spin to the footage.

4. **B-roll footage with key scenes.** (Optional) This is yet another optional element and often just contains raw footage of the production of certain scenes.

5. **Interviews with the cast, director, writer, producer, etc. . . .** (Optional) This should be presented in the same way that scenes are shown—with a title for the clip keeping the comments from the cast in clever soundbites under thirty seconds or less. A few comments from each crucial cast and production member are acceptable. Be sure to title each clip, for example: JOE INVADES PARK CITY, Director Joe Jones "Joe on making a movie on a lunch-size budget." (TRT :15 sec.).

6. **Still frame of the title.** A still frame of the title logo is crucial because this will be used as a computer graphic and appear in the background when the TV commentator mentions your film. Don't forget to include the logo—or even the poster—as a still running for thirty seconds or so on the tape, so it can be turned into a graphic.

It's not important that your EPK contain every one of the above-mentioned elements, however the two things you must have are the *trailer* and some *selected scenes*. The EPK can become a huge distraction, an animal as large to deal with as the movie itself. Do not go about producing an EPK if it will take time that is better spent on the film itself. Have an EPK with a trailer and scenes; that's really all you'll need.

Get Press Online with a CD-ROM Press Kit/EPK

When most people refer to an EPK, they think in terms of television press only, but this amazing PR tool can also help toward getting press on the Internet as well. When it comes to online press, your EPK material can be digitized and used on your film's official website. In addition, you can also take the digitized content and burn it on a CD-ROM to give to major online press outlets. The CD-ROM version of your EPK should be readable by a Mac and a PC and it must also include a decent selection of digital stills in the form of JPEGs. Stills are the most important addition to the CD-ROM press kit. It also is wise to include text from the press notes like cast and crew bios, the synopsis and production notes.

HYPE iT ON THE WEB

The Internet is the most important promotional tool for the independent filmmaker. The website you create for your movie has the potential to reach more people than any other mass medium—more than radio, magazines, or television. And the best part about it—you have total control over the content. In other sections I've discussed how to make various promotional materials like a press kit, a trailer, an EPK, a poster. They are all valuable, but if you can choose only one of these marketing tools to put your time, money and energy into, I would tell you to build a website. When you consider the impact that *The Blair Witch Project* website had on that movie, you cannot ignore the importance of the Internet for building awareness of your own movie. A website is a vital tool to build buzz in advance of your festival debut and is necessary to communicate with your greatest supporters—the moviegoing audience. In fact, promoting a movie today without a website is wasting a fantastic opportunity to increase the value of your film. Consider it this way, an effective website can help double the value of your movie. You must have a site. **QUICK TIP:** Be sure that you use your "dotcom" name, your www.thenameofyourfilm.com on everything. Your website URL should be on your poster, stickers, press kit, and on your business cards.

Create a Supreme Website

The basic steps for creating a site don't necessarily need to be done in the order listed below; in fact, it makes sense to work on many parts simultaneously. I don't have the space for all the details necessary and there are whole books on how to build a site, I'm just going to give you the fundamentals. Here's how to do it:

1. **Register the name**. It costs about $70 bucks to reserve a URL name for two years and takes about ten minutes—if you type really slowly. There are many places to register a name on the web and they even offer other services like site hosting, e-mail,

etc. . . . Start by checking out www.register.com and take the time to research other places to register your name. When you have settled on a name for your film, do it as soon as possible, even if you don't plan to launch the site until much later. If the name of your film is taken, you can always do what Hollywood does and add the word "movie" to the end. I suggest registering the name of your production company as well and letting this be the home for all of your films.

2. **Create Content**. Here is where the word "re-purpose" comes into play. By creating the materials for the press kit, you have already done the hard work of putting together a synopsis, bios, credits, production details, trailer, photos and a logo for your movie. These will be elements used to launch your site. You may want to write other material exclusive to the site by keeping a production diary, but the basics from a press kit will be the early building blocks to release the initial version of the site. More elements will be added later, but starting with these key elements is essential. Don't forget this key element—your contact info. Have this visible at the bottom of every page of the site.

3. **Flow Chart**. Here is where the site really begins to take shape. The site itself is like a collection of pages from a magazine or a book, the difference is that instead of either of those, a web surfer can bounce from page to page. The flow chart identifies all the pages of your site and shows how they connect. On paper or on a computer, build a flow chart that demonstrates how a reader will use the site and how every single page is linked. The easiest way to begin is to start with the home page and then spell out the most important aspect of the site, which is the menu bar. Make it simple, logical and easy to navigate. The key word to keep in mind is "intuitive." Ask yourself—Does it make sense that this page connects to that page? Can the reader get back to the home page or any other page on the site efficiently? The easiest way to go about this is to design a menu bar that contains all the sections for your site. Name those sections Home, Movie Synopsis, Bios, News, About the Production, Trailer, Photos, etc. and so on. The best thing to do is to look at other sites and see how they did it. Spend considerable time poking around to see what works and what doesn't. Ultimately, an intuitive site will have your readers focusing on the content

instead of the flow (or the lack thereof). Visit as many other sites as you can to get a feel for what works best for you.

4. **Design the Site**. When I say design, I am talking about the way it looks. This is where you can get creative and have a blast. In a way, it's like decorating your room or apartment. Your site should, in some way, reflect the theme or mood of your film. Choose graphic elements that say something about the movie. It's like painting the outside of the house and deciding exactly how you want it to look. Almost all of the filmmakers interviewed in these pages have their own sites. Check them out and see what they did to create a mood. The subject matter of your movie will dictate much of the design. When designing a look for the site it makes a difference to make it fun, have it express other levels of your movie and (for some this may be the hard part), be original. Make sure it does not look like any other movie site.

5. **Build It**. There are so many ways to build a site, it would be like me telling you exactly what kind of film you should make. Here are just some of the options you may consider

Off the shelf software. There are plenty of programs made for building sites. They vary in levels of complexity, but for under $100 bucks, you can find numerous programs made to build a site from scratch.

Build it on the web. Some websites offer space on their sites to build your own. There are thousands, like Yahoo and Homestead.com, but research them closely before building the site. These sites have software built into the browser that walks you through building your own simple site. The advantage here is that you won't be paying for space. The disadvantage is that you may outgrow it quickly. Be sure you have the option to move the site to another server, should that happen. All of these sites require that you click on "Terms" or "Agreement" when using their sites. Check any restrictions that apply before you put in the energy. Explore all of these options fully and choose the best path for you.

Hire a web design company. This is a smart choice if you have the money to do it. You'll provide them with the content and design and they build it. Most charge upwards of $100 or more per page of the site, so if you plan on a large site that you'll want to grow, then this may not be cost-effective.

Get a friend. Most students in high school now know HTML and web design better than they can spell. Get a student or a friend to do it. If you are technically inclined, you may just want to do it yourself. If not, or if you are busy making the movie, delegating this responsibility is a wise choice. The only option you don't want to exercise is putting it off. It's helpful for the site to go live during pre-production. Even if it is not perfect, you can always alter it or add to it later. And don't forget to test the site for bugs. This involves looking at every page of the site using different computers and different browsers with different types of Internet access (T1, DSL) or modems. Ask some friends to look at it for you and report any problems so they can be fixed.

Ingredients of an Awesome Movie Website

Here are the do's and don'ts you must know to make a movie website that readers will not only revisit, but also tell their friends about.

1. **Don't get too flashy**. Bells and whistles like Flash and Shockwave look really cool. That intro movie to your site is great to watch—but it only works once. Web design sometimes gets too caught up in trends. (Remember "frames"? Does anyone use frames for their site anymore?) There is one mistake that novice web designers make time and again and that is over-designing a site. Just because you *can* add some cool new effect, doesn't mean you should. To reach the maximum number of people with your site, avoid adding flashy extras. For example, the Film Threat website (which I designed, by the way), is tested and able to work at a reasonable speed using a 28.8 modem and AOL's own web browser. The design does not have to be compromised, but avoid jumping headlong into new technologies without weighing how that might limit the potential audience for your site.
2. **Interact with your audience**. Adding production diaries, interviews, exclusive video footage and such adds a personal touch to the site. Speak directly to your audience and have a message

board so readers can offer feedback. Make it a priority to answer that feedback and make yourself accessible.

3. **Keep it simple**. This one should be self-explanatory. An overly complex site will only turn off readers and they'll surf elsewhere.

4. **Update the site yourself**. If you design the site yourself, this should not be a problem. Make sure that you are trained to add simple updates to the site as often as you need. Don't be a slave to some web design firm that must be paid each time you add a minor update or news story. Don't be slave to the friend or student who built your site. Learn how to update the site yourself. Then, be sure to follow my next suggestion . . .

5. **Update often**. I can't stress this one enough. Weekly updates are preferred and even more often if that is at all possible. The latest news about your film should be right on the front page. Attach a date to each new news item so readers know when the site was last updated. If new features are added, be sure to let others know about it as well. You are taking the readers on your journey. Tell them about all the ups and downs—the sometimes personal and real-life drama you encounter making the film can make the best stories. It will also endear the audience to your cause, which is making your movie. And when you experience triumphs, like your debut festival screening, they will share in those successes.

Do-It-Yourself Internet Publicity

Now that you've spent all this time building the coolest movie site on the web—I'm sorry to have to break this to you, but I've been completely honest up to now so I have no problem telling you this—your website is worthless. Like farting in a car with the window rolled down, no one is going to notice it *unless* you promote the site. The best way to do that is to start by sending out e-mail and promoting it virally. I don't mean literally sending out a virus to all your friends; I mean a piece of e-mail that spreads virally on the net to everywhere it needs to go. Start with an announcement that the site is live and contains information about your movie. Send the e-mail announcement to your address book of friends and family and encourage them to tell others. Be sure to have an area on your site where readers can sign up for an e-mail newsletter about your film.

Send out updates when new things are added to the site, but not too often. There's enough junk e-mail on the net already, so when you send out news about your site or film be sure you really have something to say. There are no rules, but sending out an e-mail once a month or so is usually considered plenty.

One of the best places to announce the launch of your new site is at FilmThreat.com, which is my website. On the site, we announce new indie movie sites every week and filmmakers tell me they get a tremendous number of hits. (One filmmaker complained that he got 500,000 hits within two weeks and his site was nearly shut down!) Drop me an e-mail and send it to input@filmthreat.com and I'll write something about your site. You'll also want to send a more formal announcement to members of the online media. Cruise those sites and build a list of general e-mail addresses to send out a mass e-mail. All entertainment and movie sites on the web have a general e-mail address for news, so gather those addresses and send out your announcement. Build your list starting from production and add everyone you meet to the list. A quick note about communicating via e-mail: Be understanding when it comes to dealing with members of the media online. I get hundreds of e-mails daily and I do my best to answer all of them. Make sure that all of your e-mail communications include the very basic details about your film so I have all the information I need to write up a story. Guys like myself are constantly bombarded, so don't assume that I, or any other member of the media, will remember all the details about your film off the bat. At the end of the day, I want to support indie filmmakers, so help me to help you.

> All entertainment and movie sites on the web have a general e-mail address for news, so gather those addresses and send out your announcement. Build your list starting from production and add everyone you meet to the list.

HiRiNG A PUBLiCiST: WHAT YOU NEED TO KNOW

Filmmakers entering the festival game for the first time quickly learn the value of good PR. Great public relations can take an average movie and increase its value by creating hype. An average film with heat behind it is much more likely to be sold to a distributor than a great film with no heat: this is an unfortunate reality at film festivals. Really good films can get lost in the shuffle. However, with a great press kit, an amazing website, some well-timed articles in the trades, a few positive reviews and some friends in the media, you'll much better positioned to achieve a sale and begin your filmmaking career.

On the Publicity Trail with PR Pro LINDA BROWN

Linda Brown began her career at PMK Public Relations where she worked for five years on publicity campaigns with actors such as Winona Ryder, Andie MacDowell and Gregory Hines; films such as Luc Besson's *La Femme Nikita* and *My Left Foot* and television shows such as Fox's *The Simpsons*. After leaving PMK in search of some kind of life, she stopped briefly at Bragman Nyman Cafarelli, then went on as Director of Motion Pictures Los Angeles for Rogers & Cowan, where she headed up campaigns and promotions for a countless number of films including *The Mask* with Jim Carrey. Currently Brown heads one of the premiere public relations firms for independent filmmakers, the Los Angeles-based Indie PR. Getting press is not just a job for Brown; she passionately believes in her clients and

Indie PR partners Linda Brown and Jim Dobson at Sundance.

their films. Indie PR has been in existence since 1996 and has been successful in providing promotion, marketing campaigns, parties, festival debuts and more for indie filmmakers.

How can a publicist help a film?

A publicist does different things at different stages of a campaign for a film. For a festival, a publicist prepares the press to receive your film (in the intellectual and emotional sense). Presentation means a lot; a publicist advises you on the look of your poster, chooses the stills you will use in representing your film, your clips for electronic interviews and will prepare that all-important press kit—which serves as a bible to the press when they write about your film.

Equally important, a publicist comes up with a strategy for presenting your film to the public. A filmmaker's idea of how a film should be presented may be entirely different from what is going to sell. That doesn't mean the filmmaker is wrong, it just means that it's only one opinion and it sometimes helps to go at it from other angles as well.

I worked on a film at the Santa Barbara Film Festival called *Confessions of a Sexist Pig* by director Sandy Tung. Sandy came to me and said he thought the film was essentially about the love story between his two leads. Now, with a title like *Confessions of a Sexist Pig,* I figured the love story might play a part in the campaign . . . but was it the part that would bring someone into the theater? Would the love story make a distributor, given a choice among four films playing at the same time at a festival, choose ours? The title was just too brilliant to not play up.

So I made a suggestion. In our target audience for the film, who makes the decision as to what movie a couple would see? Women. Okay, what is it about this film that women would want to see? I just knew that what women want more than anything else is to get *inside of a man's head* and find out what they are really thinking. I knew that men would be okay with seeing this film simply because of the title. It was *women* we needed to attract. And we did with that very campaign . . . we put it in our press kit, on our poster, on our promo cards . . . it commanded attention. We were on every radio station, newspaper and magazine that covered the festival.

Why does a filmmaker need a publicist?

The smartest filmmaker takes on a publicist at the very onset of a project and keeps one throughout the entire process. (That can get costly, but deals can sometimes be made.)

There is so much for the press to cover during a festival, from reviewing films to covering parties to eavesdropping during breakfast for items. Unless you have someone out there vying for ink and creating a buzz about you or your movie, you run the risk of getting lost in the noise pollution. My campaigns start a month prior to the festival when I start making calls to the magazines and columnists who can put a little "pre-festival buzz" on my movie. I get the press excited about your film by letting them in on it early and in a personal way. At this point, a lot of the members of the press are friends of mine, so it is very much like my calling a friend to let them in on something they just shouldn't miss.

What do filmmakers need to know when it comes to publicity?

Publicity is less effective when it is a "one-shot-deal." It is so much better to have continuity and a steady flow of information going out to the press throughout all of the stages of your film. That way, when it comes time to do the festival thing, it's a matter of instant recognition for both the press and distributors. It is also essential in getting all of the materials you will need to help sell the film— whether it be a press kit complete with clippings (to show a studio that your film can get press), or photos and an electronic press kit complete with interviews and behind-the-scenes footage.

Can filmmakers do their own publicity? Is that method recommended? What are the advantages and disadvantages of a filmmaker going about their own publicity?

Filmmakers can do their own publicity as easily as publicists can make their own films and do it well . . . it just isn't smart. First of all, it takes up a lot of the filmmaker's time that should be spent other ways, but mostly because it's smarter to have those who do what they do best—actually *do* what they do best. The only advantage a filmmaker has in doing his/her own publicity is that it will save a few thousand dollars. That's it. Without the advice and careful planning of someone who lives this kind of work, an uninformed filmmaker could miss the opportunity to present his film with the perfect spin to catapult his campaign and film into the arms of a dream distributor. Without the forethought and careful planning that went into the PR campaign for *The Full Monty,* most ticket buyers would have passed it up for another film. Think of the distributor as an audience member with a checkbook. You still have to stand out and grab their attention.

What is a publicity campaign that you were not involved in that you admired?

The most recent and perhaps most obvious is *The Full Monty;* you just can't deny the brilliance of the Fox Searchlight team on that one! I think that campaign worked so well because it was not at all about the "hype" and "glitz" which the public is so aware of at this point. There was no "slick spin" put on that film. Instead, they played on the humanity and the "realness" of their cast; they presented this almost voyeuristic look into the down-and-out lives of people just like you and me, but they made it fun. How many of us can relate to the unemployment line scene? It was such a real moment and these were such real people with which everyone could identify. *And* it was strong enough to carry the weight of a good portion of their campaign.

> .....
> **"Filmmakers can do their own publicity as easily as publicists can make their own films and do it well . . . it just isn't smart."**
> .....

What kind of advantages do filmmakers who have publicists have, over ones that don't?

For all of the reasons I mentioned before and because, ultimately, the more people you have talking about your film at a festival, the better your position. And who has bigger mouths and talks to more press, distributors and festival-goers than publicists? We're with the press at breakfast, between screenings, *at* the screenings, in the bathroom, in their rooms . . . we never stop! We get 'em while they're drunk and make them commit . . . we're relentless and you need that kind of energy on your side when your film is at a festival.

What sort of questions should a filmmaker ask when hiring a publicist?

When hiring a publicist, the most important question to ask is: "How many other films are you working on at the festival?" I see it all the time: Bigger agencies pile on the clients telling them that they are at an advantage in being "in the company" of other big films. This is simply not true unless you are working with a publicist who can't get Sheila Benson on the phone *without* a bunch of big films.

There is no way you can effectively work with an exorbitant number of films—*effectively* being the key word. I don't like to work with more than four films per festival. Part of a campaign is spending time with the filmmaker at the social function (it's where most of the interviews are set up) and if you're chained to a desk in a hotel room working on fifteen films, you just can't do that. Film festival PR is not like publicity at time of release, where you *can* chain yourself to a desk and pump out the calls. The press is out and about . . . they're at the parties, they're at the panels. You've got to have the freedom to pound the pavement and hunt them down.

What can a filmmaker expect to pay for a publicist?

Most agencies charge anywhere between $3,000-$5,000 for a film at a festival. You should allow for expense monies as well, which should cost you another couple of hundred (depending upon the festival).

What was the best deal you were involved with and why?

One of my most successful festival campaigns (and certainly the most fun campaign) was with the indie film *20 Dates,* by director Myles Berkowitz at the Slamdance Film Festival in 1998. Myles came to me late in the game; we were two weeks away from opening night of Slamdance. Myles had no photos, no poster and no press kit . . . but what Myles did have a lot of was enthusiasm to do whatever it took to make *20 Dates* "the" talked-about film of the festival.

By the end of festival, *20 Dates* had won the audience award at Slamdance and was picked up for distribution by Fox Searchlight. It was all about getting the decision-makers in the room—and that was all me, baby!

How important is it to get good online press these days?

The success of such films as *The Blair Witch Project,* in which millions of people knew about the film from the Internet almost a year before its release, make it clear just how important the Internet can be in getting the word out about your film. The pre-awareness of that project through the Internet is *directly* responsible for the success of that film. Period

Early on, it seemed that online activity was most effective with genre or cult films, but in the past year or so, the Internet has taken over as a primary way to reach worldwide audiences with current information. The key word here being "current."

As publicists and promotions people, we used to rely on magazines or shows like *Entertainment Tonight* to get the word out. Most magazines require a three to four month leadtime, and entertainment shows give you three to four minute spots and that's that. With the Internet, it's happening right now. And the cyber-sky is the limit as to the amount of content you can have, so online press is becoming more important than any other form. The fact that studios now have entire departments of publicists and promoters who deal specifically with the online community is evidence to the fact.

How do you approach getting press on the web differently?

The web is a visual tool and its audience is more visual than, say, the *Los Angeles Times* reader, who is going to sit down and read a feature, then maybe glance at a photo. When we approach a web outlet, our job is to incorporate more interactive participation and make it more interesting for the site's audience. With print, it's a bit more cut and dry and somewhat more controlled.

Does a filmmaker need to hire a publicist to do online press?

I think that anyone can do online promotions themselves. But a publicist is able to come to the table with more of a strategic campaign, which will compliment any promotions a filmmaker has already done online. But a filmmaker doesn't necessarily have the relationships with outlets like AOL, who would do the larger entertainment features on their film, and as with traditional publicity . . . you need to have someone open the door for you.

What are the important things for a filmmaker to remember when working with a publicist?

A publicist is not a miracle worker. The ultimate sale of your film depends upon how good it is. But a publicist can be an essential part of your team in creating awareness and the infamous "buzz" that everyone listens for at a festival.

> .....
> "A publicist is not a miracle worker. The ultimate sale of your film depends upon how good it is."
> .....

QUESTIONS AND ANSWERS

After the screening of your film, you'll want to offer a few quick thank-yous, introduce members of your cast and crew in attendance and are expected answer some questions from the audience. It helps to be prepared. This is your opportunity to show some personality and potentially win some points. Believe it or not, it is beneficial to wear something outrageous—a bright orange jacket, a wild hat or a loud shirt. You may even consider dying your hair a bright purple. The reason is so that you stand out. When members of the audience run into you during the festival, your unique "look" will be remembered. Besides being an opportunity for a fashion statement, the Q&A is also, much like an important speech delivered by a politician, a way to win people over to your cause. The best advice is to be genuine, be honest, tell some funny stories and anecdotes and keep your ego in check. Be gracious. Have a little humility. You may be the "filmmaker" up front doing the Q&A, but the reality is that there are at least a hundred or more people behind you that helped make the movie possible. Giving them some type of acknowledgment on stage goes a long way toward earning the respect of the audience.

As for any feelings about being nervous when speaking in front of a group, that old trick about picturing the audience naked really works, just don't let it distract you. There are some typical questions you can expect to hear at almost every Q&A, so be prepared to answer any of these:

- How much was the budget?
- How long did it take to shoot?
- Is the film autobiographical?
- Where did you find that actor?
- How did you get the money?
- Where did you get the idea for your film?
- What does the title mean?
- What kind of film did you use?
- How did you shoot that one scene?
- Who are your influences?
- Where did you shoot your film?
- What's the film about?
- What's the film *really* about?
- Do you have another film in mind?

The answers to these questions should be easy; you have struggled to make your film and you know all of this. Keep the answers short, don't meander and don't play politics—answer the question asked.

Don't fret about money questions, most audiences just don't know any better. The last thing you want to do is reveal the actual budget for your picture. Even if you do give a specific number, people will think you are either naïve or lying—so either way, they won't believe you. Just be vague and say, "Just below $10 million."

JOURNALIST DAVID E. WILLIAMS ON GETTING PRESS

How can a filmmaker without a publicist compete to get your attention?

Blindly pitching stories is not the way to go.

If you want press, first you have to know the press and understand what each particular magazine wants. When I worked for *Film Threat,* I specifically looked for films that were in some way rebellious—either through the story, filmmaking style, or simply the maker's guts for doing what they did. For *American Cinematographer,* I look for visual accomplishment, whether the picture was shot on Super 8, 16mm, 35mm or video.

So the filmmaker has to research the target publication and devise a pitch based on that magazine or newspaper's field of interest. If someone asked if I wanted to interview the star of their picture, I'd immediately know that they had not done their research. If they had, they'd know that I'd only need to talk to the director, cinematographer, gaffer and other key production people.

David E. Williams is now the Executive Editor of Special Issues at the *Hollywood Reporter.*

THE PARTiES

Get Invited, Make an Impression, Crash, Avoid Spilling Something

The single most important event at a festival (other than your own screening) is the party. You may be as talented as Orson Welles when it comes to filmmaking, but your talent is truly judged by how comfortable you are with idle cocktail chit-chat. Yes, yet another unfortunate entertainment industry reality.

At the parties you'll be schmoozing with agents, entertainment lawyers, acquisitions executives, distributors, development executives, producers, actors, festival staff and other filmmakers—basically, the masses of the movie industry. It's important that you make a good impression.

So get social. Grab a drink, grab a table, grab some food and scan the room. (Hey, you'll probably be too busy to grab dinner, so you'll save a little money on meals by eating party appetizers for days, keeping the cost of your trip very low. Living on chicken fingers and wing dings for a week won't kill you. At least, not right away.)

Now, you've got that person in your sights. The one you need to talk to. The actor for your next film. The agent you want to rep you. The festival director you want to

Leonard Maltin and James Coburn hit the festival parties.

accept your film. The executive you want to pitch for your next film. The bartender you want to pour your next drink. (Okay, I'm getting carried away, but it can be just as hard to get the bartender's attention as is to spark an agent's interest at these overcrowded events.) There are a few important things to remember at a party when you are there for business. Here is my version of the inevitable list of "Do's and Don'ts."

The Party Do's

- *Do* introduce yourself to people. Most will have festival badges with their names and companies on them. At any given party you'll find at least a few people you should meet to further your personal agenda. As annoying as it sounds, remember that you are attending these parties to further your personal goals. If you think otherwise, you are only lying to yourself.
- *Do* try to find some common ground to begin a conversation. For example, films you each enjoy, a common city, a favorite drink, a popular actor, a filmmaker—anything at all to establish the conversation on a positive note.
- *Do* make friends with other filmmakers and get invited to their screenings.
- *Do* tell inoffensive and clever jokes.
- *Do* talk passionately (yet unpretentiously) about your love of film and how your life was changed by the defining moment of one important film. People at film festivals get all mushy when this subject comes up.
- *Do* talk business—that's what these parties are really about anyway.
- *Do* be bold and walk up to Harvey Weinstein of Miramax and invite him to your screening.
- *Do* take every person you speak with seriously, even if they do not initially seem important to your immediate agenda. The assistant of today is the festival director, agent or studio head of tomorrow. They'll remember that you showed them respect when no one else would. That's important.
- *Do* hand out business cards.
- *Do* make it a point to follow up and send letters to people you have met when appropriate. Again, you never know how those relationships will pay off.

The Party Don'ts

A party can be a great opportunity to make new friends, make an impression and, most importantly, to make deals. If some studio executive likes to hang out and party with you, certainly, he may also want to work with you. That's the secret of the business—people hire other people they like. It's very simple. So keep some things in mind.

- *Do not,* as I have done, make inappropriate jokes in mixed company.
- *Do not,* as I have done, charge room service to your pals at 3 a.m.
- *Do not,* as I have done, put drinks on the tab of "the table in the corner."
- *Do not,* as I have done, drink way too much alcohol.
- *Do not,* as I have done, try to dance after drinking that alcohol.
- *Do not,* as I have done, schedule 5 a.m. wake up calls for your colleagues.
- *Do not,* as I have done, mercilessly criticize the award-winning festival film as a total piece of crap when the director can hear you.
- *Do not,* as I have done, stand on a chair and thank everyone in the room for coming and for their support for your film, when you haven't made the film that the party is for.
- *Do not,* as I have done, avoid the festival party scene to see local bands, find the strip clubs and visit the after-hours bars.
- *Do not,* as I have done, yell "Fire!" at a crowded party.

I really mean it. Don't do any of these things. I've made every possible mistake anyone could possibly make at a party. Sometimes I just can't resist putting some pretentious moron in his place, or making a point through humor. Sure, I have a great time, but generally I'm attending a festival to have fun; I like to leave the business at the office. If your goal is to have fun, a few "don'ts" are fine. But more likely, you have a goal in mind—you're trying to sell a film or get another one made. Leave the hard partying for the final festival party.

CRASHiNG FiLM FESTiVAL PARTiES

In order to get the opportunity to do some schmoozing, you have to *get into* the party. Do whatever it takes to get into the party legitimately first, but when all else fails, it's time to crash!

It's always best to get on the list before arriving at a party but that's not always possible. Because if you're like me, you're probably not invited. But I've never let that little piece of reality stop me, and neither should you. I am the party crashing king and I'll crown you a prince (or princess) if you simply follow my lead.

The first piece of advice I can offer is to put on your poker face. Security is generally loose at film festival parties and it's up to you to take advantage of that. Remember: you were invited to this shindig and there must have been some mix-up. Make sure to deliver lines like an actor.

Also, never get upset. The publicists or people at the door are constantly bombarded with Hollywood egos, why add to their grief? Act understanding. Do something different—be nice. Be cool. Don't be a jackass. Knowingly shake your head as the jerk in front of you mouths off to the publicist. They'll appreciate it. They'll especially appreciate your patience as they frantically flip through the list, then just give up and wave you in.

You can always use someone else's business card. In fact, some fancy computer work with a handy laser printer can now produce pretty convincing business cards with the click of the print button. In fact, I'm amazed how many times my own business card has been used as my golden ticket into a party.

One tried and true trick is to execute the bum's rush. Just walk in with a large group as if you know exactly what you are doing. If caught, just simply point way up into the crowd, too far to see and declare, "I'm with them." Wave and act convincing. Never fails.

And heck, if all else fails, there's always, the back door. Yes, the back door—this is not a movie cliché, I have actually used it to gain entry. Sure, you'll be stumbling through the kitchen, but you're *in* baby! Sometimes restrooms will have windows and those can be easily accessed from the outside. If you know of a great party that you must attend, it's best to do a little reconnaissance and check out the place first. Heck, you may even make a few new friends in the kitchen.

10 ALL NEW Lines to Use When Crashing a Party!

No invite? Not on the list? No problem! These lines, if delivered correctly, will guarantee you entry into any party. However, it is getting even more difficult to crash parties now than it used to be just a few years ago. In fact, a recent party I attended required me to show a picture I.D. to get in. Stop the madness! It's not as easy to crash as it used to be, so you've got to be inventive. Try these sure-fire lines.

1. **"I did RSVP, but I understand if I can't be let in. Can I just try to find my friend? He's in there? Somewhere?"**
2. **"Excuse me, coming through! Watch it!"** Carry a large box filled with something. Could be a case of beer, equipment, posters, flyers—the important thing is that it must be so large and heavy that people have to make way for you to get by or you may drop the damn thing and hurt yourself or somebody else. Be polite and walk right in like you know what you're doing. If stopped, say that you have to get these in there or you'll be in a heap of trouble. If you really want to go for realism, have a walkie-talkie on your belt, tons of laminated credentials around your neck and carry a flashlight.
3. **"I think I'm going to be sick, can you tell me where the bathroom is?"** Women are much more convincing for this line. A man would never stand in the way of a sick woman. This works even better if you spit out a mouthful of corn chowder.
4. **"I'm here to drop off my roommate's keys."** Pretend to know one of the waiters, waitresses, or someone working the bar. Just in case, have an old set of keys you don't mind losing in case they decide to pass them along for you.
5. Weasel your way to the front of the line and walk in like you're supposed to be there. When stopped (and you will be), look shocked and say, **"Hey, I'm *in* the movie."** Enter party. A variation on this is to wear a baseball cap and say, **"Hey, I'm the director!"** Don't even bother to try "writer" since it won't work.

6. **"Is this the party for the *best* film at this festival?"** Now this is going to take a little pre-planning and might get you in trouble, but give it a shot. Business cards can easily be printed now from laser printers and they look perfect. Make some phony cards from a really big press outlet. You can even go on the web and get a logo to make it ultra-realistic. When your name doesn't show up on the list, just be apologetic and pass along your card. Once the impressive card hits the hands of the person holding the list, you'll be let in.

7. **"Hi, I was here earlier and I lost my wallet, do you have a lost and found?"** This one's called "Lost and Found." Now, here's the trick, you are *not* asking to get into the party like everyone else standing in line. No siree. Why? Because you were *already there*, why would you want to go into that awesome party? You're asking about the *lost and found,* so you have deflected the door person's attention from your true intentions. Act distraught. When your *"wallet"* (or purse, or keys, or jacket, or scarf, whatever) does not turn up in the lost and found box, ask very nicely, "May I go in and take a look around? Maybe I can find it myself." Be sure to nicely wave your wallet to the person on your way out. "Found it!" Everyone loves a happy ending, you found your missing item and you got in. Piece of cake.

8. Wave like a you're insane and say **"Heeeeey!!!"** I call this one the "Wave and Hug." Wave hysterically to someone that is *way* beyond the eyesight of the people guarding the door. This could be someone you barely know or no one at all but wave and act like you're seeing an old friend you haven't seen in ten years. You're so caught up in seeing them after all this time that you merely "forget" to check in. Be sure to really close the deal with a convincing hug. (Hopefully, you'll know the person you're hugging, if not, hopefully you'll find someone overly friendly.) This one only works at a really packed party.

9. This one is still effective and works even better if you learn to read upside down. Casually lean over, without letting the person see you, glance at the list and pick out a name. Try to select one that is not checked off. Then say: **"I'm the plus one with _____. I have to meet him/her here."**

10. **"Hi, I'm Jack Affleck. Ben Affleck's brother? I'm supposed to meet him here."** The famous always get into parties, but you're

not famous. So, who's to say that Ben Affleck doesn't have some less attractive brother named Jack? He might, maybe they're step-brothers, who knows. This line has actually worked for me. Celebrities are like royalty and publicists never want to offend a celebrity. Just be sure the celebrity you intend to impersonate as a distant relative is not actually going to attend. If they were there, it would be bad. To say the least. You may find yourself escorted to the VIP lounge being introduced to other celebrity folk. So go ahead, pose as Kate Hudson's cousin or William H. Macy's step-brother, why not? This is also only recommended as a last ditch effort to get into a really exclusive party since there could very well be repercussions involving the cops when using this method. Remember, I warned you about this one.

Okay, so the last two are from the first edition of the book, but they still work. And I can't give away all my secrets. Now remember, I'm a master, so for me it's easy—but practice makes perfect. In fact, very soon, these lines will be useless because lots of people will be using them, so be creative and come up with your own. The best advice I can give novice party crashers is this—any plausible excuse delivered with a straight face, in a polite manner, should get you in.

PUTTiNG ON A SUCCESSFUL PARTY

Create Buzz and Leave Them Talking

Nothing helps create buzz for a film better than a party. (Nothing except, well, maybe a really good film.) The most successful parties are the ones that are impossible to get into. Even as you hand your party passes to friends or associates, make sure to let them know, "This is my last pass, it's going to be really tough to get in so show up early. I can't guarantee you'll make it in, but you can try."

Of course, this statement is repeated to every single person you hand the pass to which will guarantee that your party becomes a "must attend" event. It's as if you are giving each person a challenge and they will rise to the occasion. The harder it is to get in, the more they will want to go.

There are certainly different opinions about what makes a great party. If you really want them to leave happy, your party must live up to the following:

1. **Make everyone RSVP.** This gives you an idea of how many will attend. The harsh reality is that 50 percent or more of those who do RSVP will *not* show up. However, those people who choose to skip your party will be offset by the party crashers, friends and members of the press who decide to just "show up."
2. **Hold the party at a venue that you know is too small for the number of people showing up.** If you leave at least some people at the door, it's considered a party worth getting into. If it doesn't present some challenge—if it's not at least somewhat overbooked—then it's not considered a hot party.
3. **Open bar, free food.** Another unfortunate reality is that if you charge for drinks and food or use some annoying "ticket" system, you'll only piss people off. The two most feared words among journalists are "cash bar." Believe it or not, making people pay for drinks can result in bad buzz. Keep the free drinks flowing and let people know when it's last call.

4. **Avoid loud music or bands.** It's hard to have conversations with any type or distraction; music set to the max is the worst.

5. **Keep any speeches really short and funny.** Most "speeches" or "announcements" given at party gatherings only serve to stop the party cold. In most cases, this is when the walk-outs begin. Start any speech about a half-hour before the scheduled end of the party and keep it to less than three minutes. Say your thank-yous, tell a joke and then encourage people to attend your screening. That's it. Otherwise, you can kill your own party.

6. **Send 'em home with something for free.** A goodie bag is always a good idea. The bag should contain some type of useful freebie that advertises your film. A T-shirt, soundtrack CD, poster or some useful item (like lip balm in cold climates or suntan lotion in warm climates) works wonders.

7. **Invite celebrities.** Yeah, they can be a distraction, but the fact that they showed up means something. I know, I think it's lame too, but that's reality. A good publicist will "book" a celeb to stop by and people at the party will talk about it. I am definitely *not* a celebrity, but invite me anyway. Please?! (See Appendix for a list of people you *must* invite to your party.)

8. **Do something different.** The party for the film *20 Dates* required that each male and female wear a badge with a number. The number corresponded with a male or female partner that partygoers were "required" to meet up with and ask a series of questions. The questions were typical of what one might ask on a date. It might sound stupid, but it was a load of fun and people talked about this party afterwards. I have always wanted to go to a film festival party with a carnival dunking booth. You know, one of those ones that people throw baseballs at so the person is "dunked" in a vat of cold water. It would be cool to see world-famous critics or movie actors in that dunk tank. Well, that's just my idea, but anything you do that is unique will get attention. Having your friend's band play will not help and is really not recommended.

THE MOST iMPORTANT GOAL AT A FESTiVAL

To prepare for your film festival debut, the list of things you need to accomplish can seem insurmountable. The "to do" list below is just to help you get started. You will think of many more things to add to this list, based on your individual needs. Aside from all the distractions and small tasks that come with preparing for a festival, the most important goal you have is to complete the greatest film possible with the resources at your disposal. Do not even consider compromising the integrity of your movie to make a festival deadline—making the best movie is the top priority.

THE ULTIMATE FILM FESTIVAL "TO DO" LIST

→ **Submit to Film Festivals**
   ❑ Do not allow deadlines to affect the quality of your film.
   ❑ Research festivals.
   ❑ Submit to 10 "A" Film Festivals.
   ❑ Submit to another 10-30 "B" Film Festivals.
   ❑ Follow up with festivals.
   ❑ Promote movie online with website.
   ❑ Get local media to do some press.
   ❑ Set aside funds for festival debut.
   ❑ Build buzz.

→ **Build the Team**—Get the best team members possible with a combination of the following:
   ❑ Publicist
   ❑ Lawyer
   ❑ Agent
   ❑ Producer's Rep
   ❑ Manager
   ❑ Friends (for support and for assisting with tasks)

→ **Create Marketing Materials**
  - ❏ Stickers with movie logo
  - ❏ Press Kit (with B&W, color and digital photos)
  - ❏ Poster
  - ❏ Flyers
  - ❏ Postcards
  - ❏ Website (with e-mail newsletter to promote site)
  - ❏ EPK (electronic press kit)
  - ❏ CD-ROM Press Kit
  - ❏ Promo Item (clever and original)
  - ❏ Trailer (post it online)
  - ❏ Invitations/Postcards to screening
  - ❏ Plan a party

→ **Don't Forget**
  - ❏ Book travel.
  - ❏ Restaurant reservations.
  - ❏ Make a schedule.

→ **During the Festival**
  - ❏ Invite reviewers, distributors and VIPs.
  - ❏ Distribute flyers.
  - ❏ Contact local media.
  - ❏ Give out promo items.
  - ❏ Promote screening.
  - ❏ Wear something that stands out at your premiere.
  - ❏ Throw party.
  - ❏ Go to parties.

→ **Remember**
  - ❏ Send thank you letters.
  - ❏ Make contacts with distributors.
  - ❏ Set up post-festival screenings.
  - ❏ Collect all press and reviews.
  - ❏ Explore attending other festivals.
  - ❏ Have a next project.
  - ❏ Get distribution.

THE ARTISAN OF THE DEAL

"All of a sudden, you're talking about years of work, years of dedication and you have your whole heart in this film. And suddenly that film has been turned into a monetary figure."

—Daniel Myrick, co-writer/co-director
of *The Blair Witch Project*

BEHIND THE *BLAIR WITCH* DEAL

How two unknown filmmakers made the most financially successful independent movie of all time: The shocking story behind the deal of *The Blair Witch Project*. (Okay, it's not that shocking.)

The filmmakers behind *The Blair Witch Project*, co-writers and co-directors Daniel Myrick and Eduardo Sanchez, were as unprepared for their success as was the entire industry. The two met as college students attending the University of Central Florida in 1990. Their mutual passion for movies sparked a friendship that began a ten-year journey, culminating in the astounding and

Dan Myrick,
co-writer/co-director of
The Blair Witch Project
PHOTO BY JULIE ANN MONELLO

unpredictable box office accomplishment of their very first feature. I've talked to countless filmmakers in my career and I have never spoken to anyone who made more of the right choices than Ed and Dan did. Their accomplishment was no accident—these guys really know what they're doing. They made all the right decisions when it came to virtually every choice facing them in the production, marketing and selling of *The Blair Witch Project*. Perhaps the best decisions involved getting the

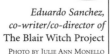

Eduardo Sanchez,
co-writer/co-director of
The Blair Witch Project
PHOTO BY JULIE ANN MONELLO

right people on board as part of the team that would bring them to the 1999 Sundance Film Festival with more hype than any other movie.

So, exactly how do two unknown filmmakers spend years making an indie film for about $22,000 that goes on to make $140 million at the box office? What follows in this next section is an interview with Ed and Dan, along with some lessons worth noting. Keeping these lessons in mind when making a film will not guarantee your success, but it may increase your chance of standing out in what is now a very crowded marketplace of indie films. Along with the interview, I spoke to Haxan Films co-producer of *Blair Witch*, Mike Monello, who helped fill in all the details for a chronology documenting the decade-long journey to bring the film into reality. In addition, I had a conversation with producer's rep Jeff Dowd, who adds his insight into what it takes to effectively tackle the seemingly impossible task of making a good movie and then selling it.

Ed and Dan could very well have made all of the same decisions and still not sold their movie. They could have sold the film and the box office might not have been so spectacular. Certainly, the unprecedented box office achievement of *The Blair Witch Project* has as much to do with luck and timing as anything else. But clearly, making the right choices absolutely gave them a head start.

You both went to film festivals before taking The Blair Witch Project *to Sundance. What festivals did you attend and what was your film festival experience like?*

Daniel Myrick: The Florida Film Festival, which I have been to twice, has really become the hub of the indie film community here in Orlando. It's really valuable, I think, in that it gives the locals the opportunity to work with people in the industry from Los Angeles and New York. You don't usually get exposure like that in areas like Orlando. For me, the Florida Film Festival has been a good place for that in the early days.

Eduardo Sanchez: Sundance is actually the first one we got into. I entered some stuff in a local festival called the Rosebud, and I won a couple of prizes there, but that was still a local festival. Other than Florida, we hadn't really entered. *Blair Witch* was the first film we took out to festivals and Sundance was the first one we got into.

You met John Pierson at the Florida Film Festival, so your experience at Florida really led to helping your film get made. Can you talk about how you met John and how you convinced him to get involved?

Dan: Pierson specifically tries to hire local filmmakers to help him shoot segments for *Split Screen*. Mike Monello, who was our co-producer on *Blair Witch*, was working at the Florida Film Festival and recommended that I be his shooter on one of the segments. John was going to do some segments when he came to the Florida Film Festival, so basically I was shooting the project with him for the four or five days he was in Orlando, and I got to know him. At the same time, we were in the process of developing *Blair Witch* and we had produced a little eight minute investor trailer to help solicit funds for the movie. And after I shot with John for a few days, I asked if it would be okay if I just sent him the trailer and he said, "Sure." So when he went back to New York, I packaged it up and sent it to him. He thought it was all true. I told him it was a fictional premise for a movie we wanted to do called *Blair Witch*. He loved it and asked if he could put it on *Split Screen*. He gave us money and that helped out. It definitely heightened the awareness for the film, which ultimately helped get the website going. With the money John gave us, combined with credit cards and money from friends and family, we were able to shoot the first phase of the movie.

LESSONS LEARNED: Attend film festivals for two reasons: 1) To get to know what a festival is like, especially one that you are planning to enter. 2) You never know who you might meet and how they might help you down the road. So be cool.

The website was a critical part of creating the hype behind the movie. When did the idea behind the website launch, which was critical in the success, I think, of getting the film sold?

Ed: We had always planned on doing a website. We had been using the Internet for a while because it seemed like the best way to get the information out there pretty cheaply. Sometime after the second *Split Screen* segment aired (which was six or seven months after we actually shot the film), the discussion board on John Pierson's website—www.grainypictures.com—exploded with questions about *Blair Witch* and the controversy and this and that. So we were like, "Well, I guess it's time to put up a website." So our strategy was to make the site be just another part of the whole myth. We based it on the actual events about the myth in the film and not the film itself. And we just started building the site and slowly putting it out. We started in May of 1998 and by the time we got to Sundance we had a lot of fans already. The site made the film one of the buzz movies at Sundance for that year.

LESSONS LEARNED: You must have a website. Build the website throughout pre-production, right up until the film's release.

When you entered The Blair Witch Project *at Sundance, did you do anything other than mail in a check and a video?*

Dan: Yeah, we screened a rough-cut of the film at the Enzian Theater prior to the whole Sundance thing. That's when we met Kevin Foxe, our executive producer, who ultimately helped us raise the rest of the money. When he saw the rough cut—we caught this on camera—he said, "This movie is going to Sundance." We were just kind of laughing, but that hyped us up because he was the first real industry guy of any kind who had seen the movie even in rough form and had given us such great praise. Also, he had contacts. He hooked us up with publicist Jeremy Walker. And he also handed the tape off to some people at the Endeavor agency, who saw the movie and came down and signed us up. We also did a screening in New York. There was a lot of industry buzz around the movie, and I think this helped to lobby the Sundance admissions committee to really look at it; it was really generating a groundswell of buzz. So Kevin was really instrumental in helping us put a team together to get it into Sundance. The movie had to be judged on its own merit, but it certainly helped to have these individuals attached to us before Sundance to help the Sundance committee take us seriously.

"The (web)site made the film one of the buzz movies at Sundance for that year."

Well certainly it speaks to the power and the quality of the film that all of these people were attracted and wanted to work on it.

Dan: Stuart Rosenthal, our attorney, was also on board prior to Sundance. And it was just that, they really liked the movie. It was something they hadn't seen before. So some agents from Endeavor flew into Orlando, went out and played pool, had a few beers with us and said they wanted to be involved. The same with Stuart, and with Jeremy Walker. They really believed in the movie, and that gave us a lot of hope that even if we didn't get into Sundance, we might still have a chance at selling it.

LESSONS LEARNED: Build a team prior to your festival debut. The team includes someone with connections, a lawyer, a publicist and an agent. You might also consider a producer's rep. Line up your team members as soon as you can and make the success of your movie in their best interests, even if it means giving away a percentage.

Did you have a "Plan B" should you not get into Sundance?

Ed: We did definitely target Sundance, but we also had some other plans. Other festivals were talking to us and we were hoping that if we didn't get into Sundance we would possibly go to LAIFF. We also had a lot of ideas about self-distributing the film. And even taking it up to New York and making a deal with HBO. We were so desperate and so in debt. We couldn't count on Sundance being our only option. So, we did have a Plan B, but luckily we didn't have to put it into effect.

"We were so desperate and so in debt. We couldn't count on Sundance being our only option."

LESSONS LEARNED: Always have a "Plan B." (It also helps to have a Plan C, D, E, F, and so on.)

You did have a publicist working for you, but in a way your web page acted as the best publicist for the film.

Dan: Yeah, the website was huge. The site was a destination that wasn't like any web page before, it wasn't just a promo for the movie. It really let people dive into the mythology and they ended up walking away with a tremendous number of questions that needed to be answered. And the movie was being portrayed as having those answers. These three students got lost and we found their film, so come see our movie, which is their film. Also, the industry people were interested because this film had so many marketing angles.

LESSONS LEARNED: Having a website is not enough—offer more information beyond the story of your film in order to generate more interest. Interact with the readers of your site and speak directly to them to form a relationship. You will begin to build a fan base and more importantly, your indie movie will become their cause.

Is that something you intended—to make a movie that would be easily marketed? Was that something you had in your thought process?

> *Ed:* Not really. As we came up with the idea, we just added more and more details. We realized there are a lot of things that made it very unique. Like the fact that the weaknesses that are common in independent film were our strengths, really. We couldn't use name actors and we had to shoot on video or cheap film. As we came up with the mythology and the ideas for the website we started to realize . . . I mean, we knew it was a cool little idea. But, no, we didn't sit down and say, "Alright we're going to make a film that has this and this and that." It just kind of came naturally and I think that's why it was so effective.

LESSONS LEARNED: Even an independent film without name actors has a chance, especially when the movie has a clever hook. Look for ways to capitalize on your film's marketability.

And Sundance is the perfect venue since Park City is surrounded by woods. The movie actually made me consider sleeping with the light on. So, what things did you do in terms of planning to get ready for that very first debut screening at Sundance?

> *Ed:* Luckily, we had already started planning. You find out you're at Sundance at the end of November and you have to have a print by early January. Our film was on video. So, we already had a plan that if we did get to Sundance, we'd have to transfer the film to 35mm. And we had designed a poster before that and were designing little pins and our hats. Mike Monello, our associate producer, had been to Sundance a few times and he knew a lot of the films were smart and had little things to hand out to people—like hats and stuff. So we made these cool knit caps with the Blair Witch guy on the front, and they were a hit. Everyone was asking for them (unfortunately, we only made fifty of them). It was something we could hand out. We also had to raise the money. Fortunately, Kevin Foxe (executive producer) came through for us again and had somebody waiting to write the check as soon as we got the news from Sundance. As soon as we got the news, everything was mobilized; we got the money, we got the film transferred from video and we were ready with the marketing things.

Dan: We had two phases of the budget—and I think this is a really important part of thinking ahead—one version of the budget to get the movie done, and then a broader version with a line item for film festival expenses. So, when we got that last chunk of money through Kevin, there was enough money to pay our way to Sundance and pay for some of this marketing material that Ed is talking about. A lot of filmmakers forget to do that, they you get into a festival and then you realize that you have no money to do posters or any promotional stuff. Fortunately, we were able to think a little bit ahead and kind of account for that. Also our thinking was, what do you hand out to people that they are going to use right then? You know, you go to film festivals and you get stuff handed to you all the time and unless it's something useable, you just end up tossing it in the garbage. Like Ed mentioned, we had these cool knit caps made that were really warm and comfortable, and they looked cool so people wore them instead of the baseball caps that they ended up putting in their duffel bags. If you're going to go to the extent of making marketing materials for your film, make it something that people will use at the festival.

> **"If you're going to go to the extent of making marketing materials for your film, make it something that people will use at the festival."**

Yeah, lip balm is always a good promo item and is especially useful in Park City during the winter . . .

Dan: Lip balm . . . note pads to write things down, all that stuff. You can get really creative with it. Hats are always great and the pins were a big hit for us.

LESSONS LEARNED: Have a poster along with other unique promo items ready to go. Be prepared to deliver a print in time for the film festival. And most importantly, plan to have funds available in order to pay for expenses at the festival. Budget for all of these costs and be ready when you get "the call."

So, now you're at Sundance, you've got your print, you've mobilized your crew, you're handing out hats and pins, what methods did you use to get distributors in the room?

Dan: We had a real advantage with the web campaign and one thing lead to another. You start with a little website that generates a little interest and then all of a sudden we had this promo reel about the

movie that ran on *Split Screen*. That generates interest in the immediate film community. So now you have agents sniffing around and
publicity people sniffing around, and once you get them on board
and get to Sundance, you have a really highly-anticipated movie. So
it wasn't real difficult for us to fill the theater with distributors and
have it play in a real favorable environment. I think that one of the
biggest challenges for filmmakers is generating that anticipation. It's
one thing to get in, but to try to figure out what kind of angle your
film has and how can you generate anticipation for your movie is
another thing altogether. What is it about your film that's so unique
that people will want to go to the screening? *Blair Witch* definitely
had a hook, and we explored that as much as we could prior to
Sundance, so there were lines outside the door when we got there.

Had you screened it for an audience before?
Dan: We had a couple test screenings here in Orlando to get feedback from an audience—as objective an audience as we could get,
to find out what was working and wasn't working. That was helpful
to us when it came down to making a final cut for Sundance. Once
Artisan bought it, we did a recut on it.

*Was it important that the distributors see it with an audience? Was that
something you insisted on?*
Ed: We weren't going to send any copies of the film out beforehand
because we wanted the distributors to be in with an audience as they
watched it for the first time. So, for us it was crucial to keep it under
wraps. We knew that we were going to have a good showing so we
just tried to keep our heads together and waited for the show to start.

LESSONS LEARNED: Do whatever it takes to build anticipation and have
your first industry screening with a real audience. Test screenings and
feedback from a real audience also help toward making the best film possible. However, I would add, that you should take any advice from test
audiences with a grain of salt.

Did you target any specific distributors?
Dan: We did a little research on distributors and had read up on
Artisan because we liked what they did with *Pi*. But I think our
agents were doing more targeting than we were. We were just hoping people would show up and like the movie. I think in a lot of

ways that was helpful for us. We were just glad that people were showing up and that screening went pretty well. But when it's all over and everybody leaves, you're not sure what's going to happen. We were happy that two or three distributors came up to our agents and said they wanted to meet the next day. We didn't know if that was just status quo or if meant that a deal was imminent. We didn't know what kind of deal it might be, but it seemed that the screening went so well that some distributor was going to be interested in something.

LESSONS LEARNED: Do your research on distributors or have the best people possible doing research on your behalf. Look at distributors and find out which ones have been successful with films that may fit your mold. Your representation should know who's buying and what they're looking for. They'll all tell you that they're looking for "good films" but that definition varies greatly depending on the person. Bottom line: Having a great screening really helps.

Now, I want to talk about that negotiating the actual distribution deal.
> *Ed:* We weren't there.

Seriously?
> *Ed:* We deliberately made that part of our strategy so no distributor could back us up against a wall and force us to do something we might not want to do. Essentially, we made sure that our producers had an escape route which was, "Well, we have to go confer with these other guys." That way, they could at least go into the next room and call us.

So, your absence was a strategy in and of itself?
> *Ed:* Yeah, exactly. But, it was just me and Dan in our hotel room trying to get to sleep because we were so nervous. Gregg Hale, our producer, would call us every half hour or so and say, "Well, we talked about this and that and this is the advance, and this is the deal." Finally around 6 or 7 a.m. they said, "This is the offer and I think we should take it." Dan and I agreed.

What kinds of things did you ask for?
> *Ed:* We went in asking for the world. We were very naïve. We talked to our agents and lawyers and asked for merchandising rights and

sequel rights. They laughed at us and said, "Well, we'll mention it." But you go into Sundance as an unknown filmmaker, and unfortunately, you have to give everything away. The only thing we wanted to carve out (and we did), was the interactive rights, so we have rights to do video games.

> .....
> "We went in asking for the world. We were very naïve . . . But you go into Sundance as an unknown filmmaker, and unfortunately, you have to give everything away."
> .....

So, Artisan took all the other merchandising rights?
   Ed: What we did with *Blair Witch 2*, we gave them the sequel rights, so they can do whatever they want with it.

Well, certainly, you must see some benefit to that.
   Ed: Yeah, it goes both ways. There are some benefits and there are some bad things about it. You know, imagine if 20th Century Fox had gotten the sequel rights to *Star Wars*. I mean, it'd be gone now.

It's funny because George Lucas basically said "I don't want to get paid a lot for Star Wars, *I just want the merchandising and the sequel rights." And 20th Century Fox gave Lucas a pay cut and thought they were getting a deal. Lucas got the kind of deal that no other filmmaker in the future will ever get.*
   Ed: Nobody knew what those things were worth. He was smart. We tried to be smart, but we just had absolutely no power.

Then how do you, with no power, go through that process and get the best deal?
   Ed: I don't know if Dan would agree with me, but I would say that you have to get proper representation.
   Dan: Yeah, you have to get a good team.
   Ed: And we had a great team around us. There are a lot of great people who do just that every year at Sundance. Artisan had just done *Pi*, which did about three or four million dollars at the box office. So we were operating within that state of mind. You know, here's *The Blair Witch Project*, maybe a bit more commercial, but it's shot on video. Issues like merchandising were just kind of a throwaway topic at the time. We were thinking advance. Fortunately, our agents negotiated performance bumps based on the box office according to *Variety*. So if the movie made over 10 million dollars,

we'd get a performance bump. Artisan threw that in. They didn't think this movie would make anything near 10 million dollars.

LESSONS LEARNED: Filmmakers make movies. Producer's reps, agents and lawyers negotiate deals. Assemble a negotiating team comprised of the best people possible. You can ask for the world, but be realistic—it's about getting the maximum amount of money possible up front. And, more importantly, it's about exposure to launch your career as a filmmaker.

The Blair Witch Project *is the most financially successful independent film in history and no one expected it. I'm sure underestimating the film's potential worked to your advantage?*

Ed: Artisan kind of gave in (on the performance bumps) because they thought they weren't going to have to pay out. And they did pay out an enormous amount of money because of the things we put in our contract. But, the most important thing, you have the proper representation when you go into the room with the distributors. Because the thing about it is that the distributors know all the tricks, so you need someone who knows them too. Jeff Dowd is a good example; he's done this a bunch of times before and knows what to do. One of the big mistakes we made, we signed a two-picture, first look deal with Artisan. Months later. we realized that having a first look deal could mean giving the distributor the option to keep your film hostage—keeping the idea of the film that you really want to make. When Robert Rodriguez made the three-picture deal with Universal, I thought, that's what I want to do. Now we realize that's not the best thing really. It just gives them a little power, and that's not really something you want to do. Artisan really wanted a three picture, first look deal with us—we compromised on two.

Is that what the "first-time filmmaker" is up against? First-time filmmakers are unproven commodities in the marketplace, so they are always negotiating from weakness . . . ?

Dan: You have to realize that we weren't there as George Lucases or Spielbergs. We were basically two dudes off the street who made this movie. I think it has a lot to do with coming to terms with the reality of what's going on around you. You're in there with this movie. You've made the movie, you have a distributor that wants to distribute and buy your movie. You have to assess—what is this distributor, who are they about, what are they about, do they seem like they're going to work well with you? You have to assess all these things from a gut instinct. You also have to come to terms with the fact that you're probably not going to get rich off this film; the odds are stacked way against you. Look at this as a calling card project, or as something that's going to get you to your next film. That's usually what happens; you don't get rich or wealthy off your first sell. Even with the advance, we didn't see that money for six months, almost a year. Our approach at the time was, "Let's just use this to get to the next level." *Blair Witch* was a fluke with regard to commercial success. But, in most cases, if *Blair* had made three or four million at the box office, I'd be making another modest independent film right now, which, in a sense, we are. But, our plans weren't really to get rich off of *Blair Witch,* we just wanted to pay off our credit cards, get enough money to pay everybody back and move on to the next project. Then let the merits of the film help our reputation as filmmakers to move up the ladder. In one sense, you have to be realistic about who and what you are. You're a nobody filmmaker trying to get a sale. But at the same time, be careful and remember, "What if this film really does make $50 million or $100 million. Do I want merchandising rights? How much do I want to fight for a performance bump?" That's where a good representative can help you out lot. They'll angle for the unforeseen things, little bits and points that you don't think about as a filmmaker, and then if something really big happens with your film, those things will kick in for you.

.....
You're a nobody filmmaker trying to get a sale. But at the same time, be careful and remember, "What if this film really does make $50 million or $100 million. Do I want merchandising rights? How much do I want to fight for a performance bump?"
.....

Ed: We were lucky in some places in the deal and unlucky in others. Nobody thought this film would make more than $10 million, so we lucked out that it did. But in other places in the contract, we put caps on certain things and they were kind of blown out of proportion. You can basically cap the expenses that a distributor can write off for actually marketing a film or whatever. If we were negotiating a big film, I'm sure all this stuff would be built into the contract. With us, nobody expected this film to have to address those problems. But, you live and learn and we have nothing to complain about. We made a lot of money with *Blair Witch* and we got our careers started, which is all we really hoped to do. Now we're making *Heart of Love* and we learned from the mistakes we made on *Blair Witch* and we've tried to implement that knowledge into the new contract for *Heart of Love*. Chances are, we're going to learn from our new mistakes on that. The whole point is trying to keep artistic control on our films, at least for Dan and me. We want to just make our own film, have a final cut. And something else people should keep in mind is that just because a distributor buys your film doesn't mean they're actually going to distribute it.

Certainly you can ask that it open on a certain number of screens?
Ed: If the advance they're offering you is half a million or a million dollars they say they can't give you that guarantee. But they can give you that guarantee for $200,000 less. It's a negotiation, but it's worth it. Everybody's heard the horror story of the vault at Miramax and I'm pretty sure most distributors have vaults like that. Sometimes your film doesn't work out; it doesn't fit into their schedule. There are a lot of films out there that people have put their entire lives into that haven't ever been released.

LESSONS LEARNED: Have realistic expectations. You're not likely to get rich and your lifestyle is not likely to change. Look ahead to your next film project.

Did you celebrate when the movie sold? Tell me about that moment . . .
Dan: Well, we woke up to get the call and tried to go to sleep. We had been up all night. It was more a sense of relief. For me, what was surprising was the sense of loss.

Was it kind of like handing your baby over to a stranger?
Dan: It really was like that. All of a sudden, you're talking about years of work, years of dedication and you have your whole heart in this film. And suddenly that film has been turned into a monetary figure. "For all this work and sacrifice, we'll give you this." Not that the money was bad, but suddenly it's like, "Whoa, now you own it and now you can decide what happens with it?"

Ed: Also, in a sense, it's a strange transition. Before, you're an unknown struggling filmmaker and there's a kind of comfort in your own group of friends and the anonymity that comes with that. Then all of a sudden you're doing interviews and you're considered a "real" filmmaker now. You've got to put up or shut up. Going from a student to doing commercial work. You can't use that excuse anymore. So, now that you're considered the real deal. There's that insecurity inside of you that maybe you just got lucky. It's a scary thing to be ushered into that world so quickly. These are all great problems to have, but it's still a strange transition to make.

Dan: I think a lot of the success of *Blair Witch* was timing. Not only did we have this no budget, nobody movie, but we were this rags-to-riches story and we did this improv shooting style along with the Internet marketing angle. There were a lot of hooks about the movie to get people actually into the theater to see what all the hype was about. We had a lot going for us. But it definitely woke up Hollywood and the indie community to the possibility. Don't count anybody out. Just because you spend thirty grand or sixty grand or whatever on the film, doesn't mean you can't compete if you have a solid concept and good execution. But I think Hollywood is Hollywood. It's a huge machine. When you look at the odds of big budget success driven movies on what they make and what they lose, I think there's a reason why they're still getting made. They make money. There's a reason why people go to see those films. I'm as big a sucker for those films as anybody. I loved *Star Wars* and *T2* and *Titanic.* Those are great films to go see. At the same time, I love heartfelt movies that really move you on an emotional level. And fortunately *Blair* did that for a lot of people. You don't need a lot of money to do that, you just need a good story.

LESSON LEARNED: The sale of the film is not the prize. Making the film itself was probably the best part, you just didn't know it then.

THE BLAiR WiTCH PROJECT CHRONOLOGY

From concept to wrap, from sale to release, the complete story.

1990
College students Daniel Myrick and Eduardo Sanchez meet in 1990 at the University of Central Florida (UCF) in the very first class of the new film program there. They also meet Mike Monello, another film student. They work on each other's films and go through the usual bonding experiences that college is so good at providing. Ed and Dan, in particular, often found themselves on the same wavelength when it came to movies and spent a great deal of time spitballing ideas for features.

1992
Dan and Ed come up with the basic idea for a "scary woods movie" while continuing their film studies at UCF in Orlando, Florida. Originally the story takes place in the 1970s and the found footage ends up as reels of Super 8 film.

July 1994
Dan and Ed go to Maryland to work on a project called *Gunther and Telis* and discuss more ideas for the "scary woods movie."

March and April 1995
Ed and Dan compile notes for an outline for a film whose working title at the time was *The Black Hills Tapes*. It later became known as *The Blair Witch Incident*.

Summer 1996
Over the course of the summer, Ed and Dan, now teamed with producer Gregg Hale, shoot footage to create the "investor trailer." The footage includes a rundown of the Blair Witch mythology leading up to the disappearance of three students and the release of the tapes to Haxan Films for investigation. The trailer runs about 11 minutes.

August 1996
Gregg, Dan and Ed form Haxan Films inspired by the Benjamin Christensen witchcraft documentary, *Häxan*, made in 1922. College buddy Mike Monello assists in putting together the investor package.

September 7, 1996
The first formal presentation to investors is made and they are told that the mythology and story of the missing kids is real—the footage had not been shot yet. Some potential investors are left shaken, but nobody writes a check.

September 11, 1996
A second investor meeting takes place, but Haxan is unable to raise any money.

October 1996
Haxan originally plans to shoot the film in October, however, unable to get the necessary funding in place, the filmmakers disband temporarily to get "real" jobs.

June 1997
At the Florida Film Festival, Dan does some extra work shooting footage for John Pierson's television show *Split Screen*. Dan gives a copy of the investor tape to Pierson, hoping that he may help them.

Late June 1997
Disturbed by the tape, Pierson calls up Dan. He totally buys the reality of the film. Dan eventually lets Pierson in on the truth. Pierson purchases the rights to air the segment on *Split Screen*. The segment will run as the cliffhanger for the first season's final episode.

June–July 1997
Casting sessions take place in New York, Los Angeles and Orlando, Florida. The casting starts as open cattle calls with small ads in *Back Stage*. During these sessions, actors are thrust into improvisational situations. The sign outside the door of the office describes a simple scenario such as *"You've murdered your child and have been serving a twenty-year sentence in prison. You are now sitting in front of the parole board."* The moment the actor walks in, he or she has to be in character. Ed and Dan immediately ask questions as if the fictional situations are real. Candidates are judged on their ability to improvise and think on their feet. If anyone walks in who is not immediately in character, they are checked off the list.

During these casting sessions the filmmakers meet actors Heather Donahue, Mike Williams and Joshua Leonard.

August 1, 1997

The filmmakers have just enough money in place from their savings, credit cards and the airing on *Split Screen* to shoot. The money in place is just enough to shoot the footage in the woods.

Mid-August 1997

The 11 minute trailer airs on *Split Screen* without any mention as to where the footage comes from, or whether or not it is real.

Ed and Dan choose the cast and decide on Heather Donahue, Mike Williams and Joshua Leonard. They will use their real names as their character names in the movie.

August –October 1997

Rob Cowie signs on as producer with Gregg Hale and writes a check to kick-start pre-production. Local legal counsel Bill Whitacre is brought in and the investment package is rewritten to reflect a significantly lower budget.

October 23–30, 1997

Production begins. The filmmakers go into the woods to begin the grueling shoot. Over the next eight days, shooting is done in Gaithersburg, Maryland. Filming in the woods also takes place in Seneca Creek State Park, Maryland, and in Western Montgomery and Frederick counties. A global positioning system (GPS) is used to identify their locations so the filmmakers do not actually get lost.

The three principal actors shot nearly all of the movie using a CP-16mm camera for the black and white footage and a Hi-8mm camera for the video footage. This is the first time in motion picture history that actors have ever shot an entire movie.

Locations are programmed into the GPS to guide the actors through the woods and lead them to specific points, either to where something unusual happens (stickmen in the trees), or to a stopping point where they find a basket with food and three little 35mm still film cans marked "H," "J" and "M." Each can has notes from Ed and Dan with secret instructions— the actors are not to show or tell each other what the notes say. They (the actors) would also leave tapes, film and batteries and collect fresh supplies. Ed and Dan would get the tapes and look at them to make sure they were getting what they wanted. Examples of the kind of notes the actors received:

Heather—Your film project is getting away from you. You should take control and lead this project.

Josh—Heather has no idea what she is doing. You should try to lead more often.

Heather, Mike and Josh were requested to interview the townspeople, who were often, unbeknownst to them, planted by Ed and Dan. As a result, the expressions on the actors' faces were unrehearsed.

Mike and Josh received no information on the Blair Witch mythology. Heather received a two-page explanation of the legend.

All lines are improvised and nearly all the events in the film are unknown to them beforehand, and are often on-camera surprises. The cast live off PowerBars for the entire shoot.

October 31, 1997 (Halloween)
The final day of shooting. Only two scenes were shot more than once—the "running from the tent scene" and the end sequence in the house, which is shot the night of Halloween. After the shoot, Heather and Mike are brought to Denny's and told to feast—all the "Moons over My Hammy" they can eat, and not a PowerBar in sight. It is quite a surreal experience for them, as the whole wait-staff are dressed as ghosts, goblins, vampires and witches.

November–December 1997
The film is in the can, but money has run out completely. The arduous task of logging all the film and tapes begins. Scenes that stand out are pulled out and highlighted. From 22 hours of footage a rough cut is assembled to get a feel for the movie as a whole.

January–February 1998
Dan gets some commercial work cutting videos for Planet Hollywood. An office is set up with AVID editing equipment. Every spare minute is spent working on cutting together footage. During this time, the second *Split Screen* segment is cut. Mike Monello is brought in to co-produce *The Blair Witch Project*.

February 13, 1998
Haxan registers www.haxan.com and www.blairwitch.com. Work begins on the website.

April 1998
The second *Blair Witch* segment airs on *Split Screen*. Pierson directs viewers to the *Split Screen* website where the message boards explode with response to the footage.

May 1998
The Blair Witch Project website goes live. Readers from *Split Screen's* website are directed to continue their discussions at www.haxan.com to get more information about the mysterious footage.

The site contains a small timeline, a shot of the actual tapes, a brief history of the Blair Witch and a discussion board. The discussion board is the key element that brings readers back to the site as they add their own theories about the Blair Witch. Around this time, Haxan collects e-mail addresses and offers an e-mail newsletter called "Haxan News" which is also archived on the site.

June 15, 1998

Haxan News, an e-mail newsletter written by Ed in a casual, first-person voice, lets readers in on the secrets of *The Blair Witch Project* and the film-making process. It is e-mailed to subscribers sporadically whenever there was important news.

June 1998

Haxan leases two Media 100s—one to continue to cut *Blair Witch* and one to cut videos for Planet Hollywood. They move out of their tiny offices and rent a duplex.

Once the lease is signed, the Planet Hollywood work stops dead. Other commercial work is sought out to support the lease. At this point, the Haxan payroll stops. All food is bought from discount stores like Costco. Fast food is a luxury and the Haxan team lives on packaged ramen noodles (four for a buck!). Wives and girlfriends are now supporting the staff. All money is spent on the basics—like keeping the phones turned on.

Dan and Ed complete the edit of phase one of *The Blair Witch Project.*

June 27, 1998

The Blair Witch Project is screened at the Enzian Theater in Orlando, Florida, on a Saturday morning at 10 a.m. Two hundred and fifty friends and associates pack the theater for the first test screening. The audience witnesses a two and a half hour cut of the film. Forms ask questions of the audience such as "What moments stand out? What did you like? What did you not like?"

Christian Gueverra invites Kevin Foxe to the screening. Immediately afterwards, Kevin walks into the lobby and says, "Who is responsible for this movie?!" He introduces himself to Ed, Dan and the Haxan team. Kevin proclaims, "You guys are going to Sundance with this and I want to help you get there."

Shortly thereafter, Kevin signs on as executive producer whose job it is to raise money to get a print, complete the film and get it sold. Kevin has already been to Sundance with another film, so along with his experience, he is a welcome addition to the Haxan team.

July 1998

Feedback from the screening leads to a shorter, one hour and 45 minute cut of the film, which is then shown to a film history class at the University of Central Florida. Forms are passed out to get more feedback.

After both test screenings, one thing is absolutely clear to Ed and Dan—the audience wants to know more about the legend of the Blair Witch. The decision is made to shoot footage for phase two, which will elaborate on the myth.

July–August 1998

Using the footage they already have, money is quickly raised.

July 23, 1998

Shooting of phase two commences. Several fake newscasts, an interview with Heather's mom (not really Heather's mom), and footage from the initial search for the students is shot entirely in Orlando, Florida. "The Old Jail," a tourist trap in St. Augustine, Florida, is used to shoot a 16mm black-and-white newsreel from the '40s of Rustin Parr in jail. (Rustin is played by Frank Pastor, who first met the Haxan guys in June, when he knocked on the door of the duplex they were moving into and offered to cut the grass for 20 bucks.)

September 1998

In an effort to make the film more commercial, attempts are made to integrate the phase two footage into the movie. These additional scenes explain the myth of the Blair Witch. It is not working; every attempt to weave in the new footage does not work. During the last week of September, Haxan looks at all the cuts in an effort to find a solution. Ed and Dan believe the film is better without the footage explaining the myth. All of this footage is cut. In its place, a title card is used explaining the origin of the footage. (All of this footage is used to explain the backstory and winds up becoming the documentary, *The Curse of the Blair Witch*, which later airs on the Sci-Fi Channel as a special. This documentary also appeared as an extra feature on the DVD.)

Late September 1998

The final cut of the movie now runs 87 minutes. There are now 125 people on the "Haxan News" e-mail list. The Sundance deadline looms.

October 1, 1998

An application and a videotape of *The Blair Witch Project* are sent by Fed-Ex standard overnight to the Sundance Film Festival, just making the deadline.

Early October 1998

Haxan submits *The Blair Witch Project* to other festivals, like the Los Angeles Independent Film Festival, Slamdance, San Diego, Taos Talking Pictures, SXSW, San Francisco International, Berlin and Rotterdam, among others.

Soon after, bootleg copies of the film penetrate the pirate market. Haxan regrets not having put the names of the festivals or dates in chyron on each individual video copy. By labeling each video with a name or date, the source of the bootlegs could have been tracked. In hindsight, the bootlegging only helped fuel interest in the movie.

Work continues on cutting and tweaking the finished film along with necessary sound work. Preparations move forward to get it as ready as soon as possible for a festival debut somewhere.

October 1998
Kevin shows the film to attorney Stuart Rosenthal, who agrees to sign on and to rep the movie. He will be the deal lawyer. Rosenthal is a highly respected attorney whose client list includes independent filmmakers like George Lucas.

October 19, 1998
Kevin Foxe arranges a screening for the Anthology Film Archives at the Maya Deren theater in New York with one goal in mind—to get publicist Jeremy Walker to sign on as the film's publicist. It is at this screening that Heather and Mike see the film for the first time. A night vision video camera captures the reactions of the audience watching the film—including the horrified looks on the faces of Heather and Mike. The screening is heavily policed so absolutely no acquisition people are in attendance. However, lower level people in the business are invited to help build buzz, including guys who work in the Miramax mailroom. The screening ends with complete silence followed by immediate applause. Blair Witch symbols are hung up in the lobby to creep out the audience. Jeremy Walker approaches the Haxan team and says, "This is an incredibly commercial movie." Walker immediately signs on to do publicity for a piece of the film.

October 31, 1998
Halloween—The Mark and Brian radio show in Los Angeles has a discussion about scary websites. Jeff Johnsen, one of the earliest Blair Witch fans, calls up the radio station and Mark and Brian discuss this creepy site and the legend on the air. The increased traffic to the site shuts it down temporarily.

November 9, 1998
The *Haxan News* e-mail list reaches 200 subscribers, and over 7000 visitors have checked out the Blair Witch webpage.

November 1998
The Haxan office situation becomes desperate as money begins to run out. Every time the phone rings, everyone jokes, " . . . it must be Sundance calling."

November 23, the Tuesday before Thanksgiving 1998
The phone rings and Ed picks up. Ed's face contorts into a look of disbelief as he calmly repeats, "Yes. Yes." John Cooper, Sundance Programmer, tells Ed that they are officially inviting *The Blair Witch Project* to the Sundance Film Festival. Everyone cheers! There is some concern about being invited to be a part of the Midnight Screenings—that not being in competition and showing at midnight could marginalize the film. All

thoughts are set aside as Haxan definitely chooses to go to Sundance. They call back and accept the invitation.

The entire Haxan staff celebrates by getting drunk and forming a drum circle.

Late November 1998
Money continues to be raised to take the film to Sundance.

Early December 1998
Once word spreads that *The Blair Witch Project* is going to Sundance, the Haxan Five, as they begin to call themselves, are heavily pursued by big agencies. After seeing the film, the Endeavor Agency flies several of their agents to Orlando. At a chain restaurant, Steve Rabineau, Tom Strickler and Phil Raskind from Endeavor talk with Ed, Dan and the Haxan team. After several rounds of cheap margaritas and bad Mexican food, the meeting goes well. As the only agency who flew out to meet with Haxan in person, Endeavor ends up repping the film and the Haxan Five.

December 1998
Haxan chooses not to hire a producer's rep with percentages already being divided between a lawyer, agent and publicist. The team is in place—Stuart Rosenthal (lawyer), Jeremy Walker (publicist) and Endeavor (agent). This group of all-stars prepares to go to Sundance with one goal in mind—to sell the movie and get the best deal possible.

Major preparations take place all throughout the month of December to mobilize for the Sundance Film Festival debut of *The Blair Witch Project*:

- Only fifty hats and fifty stickman pins, made from real silver, are produced. These promotional items are very selectively handed out.
- Postcards and posters are also produced. Backbone Design (now Vibranium) in Orlando does the poster and logo for the movie. The decision is made to design the marketing materials around the signature shot of Heather. Extra money is spent on the poster with a five color run that includes a clear glossy ink so it looks as if there are hand prints all over the poster. Haxan produces a huge run of posters without dates or specifics about the movie.
- Haxan chooses not to screen the film before Sundance for critics or acquisitions executives.
- The *Haxan News* list grows to over 900 e-mail addresses who are the most vocal fans of the film and help spread the word on the Internet.
- Rebecca Yeldham writes a description of the movie for the Sundance catalog that helps generate interest. This description is used in all the press materials.
- Travel arrangements are made for Park City.
- Sundance provides a limited number of tickets, so Haxan begins buying up extra tickets for screenings.

Late December 1998
The Haxan Five (Ed, Dan, Gregg, Rob and Mike) have a congratulatory dinner on the corporate credit card. During a toast Gregg says, "If this is as far as it goes, it was great."

January 7, 1999
4MC finishes the four 35mm prints—one goes directly to Sundance, one to Orlando, one to New York and one stays in Los Angeles. The strategy is to keep a print in New York and Los Angeles just in case quick screenings are required for a sale while the film screens at Sundance in Park City.

Early January, 1999
Dan and Ed are interviewed by *Filmmaker* magazine, to appear in the Sundance issue.

Much of this time is spent strategizing for Sundance—investigating the distributors while they investigate the Haxan Five. Haxan decides not to hold any pre-Sundance screenings for distributors, despite the immense pressure to do so.

Thursday, January 21, 1999
Arrival at Park City, Utah. The Sundance Film Festival begins.

Friday, January 22, 1999, 12 Noon
Endeavor sets up "meet and greets" with representatives from all the major distributors—Fox Searchlight, Miramax, October, Fine Line, and Artisan. Artisan tells Haxan about their success with *Pi* and wins them over with their "filmmaker friendly" pitch. Ultimately, however, it all hinges on the screening and who (if any) of this group is interested in the film.

Saturday, January 23rd 1999, PREMIERE Midnight Screening
The Blair Witch Project is just about to debut at Sundance and play its very first screening. All the distributors are in attendance including representatives from Fine Line, New Line, Fox Searchlight, Artisan, October Films and Miramax, among others.

The Haxan team takes their seats in the very back row of theater and some admit to being so nervous, they feel as if they are about to vomit. 180 people are turned away, most of them non-industry locals from Salt Lake City who trekked up the mountain to see the film.

Sunday, January 24th 1999, 12:20 AM
Ed and Dan introduce the film and give a quick thirty-second introduction. After thank-yous, the two sit down, the lights dim and the film unspools.

Five minutes into the film, Ed takes out a camera to take a picture of the screening in progress when his flash goes off.

A few walkouts occur during the screening, however, everyone survives. In the theater anyway. Audience response is fantastic. Everyone laughs in the right places and for the last twenty minutes no one even moves in their seats.

1:48 AM
The screening ends with dead silence and then enthusiastic applause. Dan and Ed introduce the cast and everyone involved. The question and answer session is lively and exciting.

2:05 AM
Haxan's Endeavor agents take cards from interested distributors. The reaction is swift. October is not interested. Fox Searchlight is not interested. Miramax is mildly interested. New Line/Fine Line is interested. Artisan is interested. The agents set up meetings with everyone for the next day. Some of the smaller distributors say they'll wait to see how negotiations proceed.

2:15 AM
The anticipation of the meetings set up for the next day is too much and no one can sleep. Thinking ahead (and knowing Utah's liquor laws well), Bob Eick and Kevin Foxe make sure that beer is waiting at the condo. An impromptu party begins.

2:50 AM
The party comes to an abrupt halt when a call comes through from Endeavor—Artisan wants to talk right now. Gregg Hale, Stuart Rosenthal, Rob Cowie (Haxan) and Bill Whittaker, Haxan's local attorney from Orlando, leave the party to go to the meeting. Ed, Dan and Mike do not attend the meeting so that the lawyers and agents could not make a decision in the room—they had to check with the Haxan boys.

Just after 3:00 AM
Gregg calls Ed, Dan, and Mike—"They're serious about buying the film." Gregg calls every half-hour or so with an update on the negotiations to get a consensus.

3:30 AM-ish
During negotiations, the representatives state that Haxan wishes to hold onto all sequel and merchandising rights. The Artisan crew stands up, thanks everyone for coming out and heads for the door. Those rights are immediately given up.

4:00 AM
Negotiations continued into the morning. Progress reports continue to be made about every twenty minutes.

6:05 AM

Gregg Hale makes the final call: "We just sold the film." Everyone goes to sleep and tries to rest before meeting in the lobby of the Yarrow Hotel later that morning.

6:15 AM

Ed, Dan and Mike do their best to try to sleep.

Sunday, January 24th 1999, Noon

Ed and Dan are rushed to publicist Jeremy Walker's suite for a press day. *The Blair Witch Project* is the first film to sell at Sundance 1999 and quickly becomes the must-see movie at the festival. The Haxan Five do an interview with *Entertainment Weekly*, and Ed, Dan, Heather, Mike and Josh also do a photo shoot for *Premiere Magazine*.

January 25-29, 1999

The rest of the week, Haxan does press, watches movies and plays foosball at Burgies on Main Street. At one point in the week, Haxan makes a bet with an Artisan exec—if *The Blair Witch Project* makes over 10 million at the box office, the executive will buy Haxan a competition grade foosball table.

Saturday, January 30, 1999, 9:00 PM

Sundance adds another screening at the Eccles Theater, a 1,300 seat theater and the largest venue in Park City—230 standby people are turned away. The screening is phenomenal—during the Q&A afterwards, one guy just stands up, screams, "Wow!" and sits down again. Roger Ebert is at this screening and word comes through the pipeline that he enjoyed the film.

Saturday, January 30, 1999, 11:10 PM

The Haxan Five, Kevin Foxe, and Heather, Mike, and Josh race out of the Q&A to race down the mountain to Salt Lake City for the screening there.

Sunday, January 31, 1999, Midnight Screening in Salt Lake City

The Sundance screening of the film in Salt Lake City is completely sold out and filled with fans, mainly kids. It is the very first Sundance film to sell out in Salt Lake City. The Haxan gang, along with Heather, Mike and Josh arrive after the movie has already started. After the screening ends, the audience erupts in applause, which grows after seeing the cast is there. The cast and crew and hand out posters to the audience. Heather, Josh and Mike sign autographs and are instantly famous. The reaction from the audience is incredible, and most importantly, it's a real screening—no agents, journalists, critics, or lawyers, just regular moviegoers.

February 1, 1999
After unsuccessfully trying to send e-mail from Sundance, Ed sends out a "Haxan News" report just hours after returning to Orlando. The report includes the great news about the sale of the film to Artisan. Haxan is inundated with fans sending congratulatory e-mails.

February 1999
Artisan holds a test screening in New Jersey. Initial reaction is tepid, and the twenty or so people they keep behind to interview can't seem to describe what *The Blair Witch Project* is like—no one mentions *COPS* or *The Real World* or any reality-based TV. The focus interviewer is stymied by the inability of the audience to give any kind of reasonable feedback until Gregg Hale yells from the back "Were you scared?" and everyone nods their heads. Artisan realizes they are going to have to educate people as to what this movie is like.

Artisan sends Haxan a cut of the first teaser trailer. The Haxan Five are pleased to see that the trailer is frightening, mysterious and totally nails it.

Artisan requests different endings under condition that Haxan has final say on the finished cut. Artisan also agrees to maintain the integrity of the Blair Witch website.

March–April 1999
The reshoots provide much needed money for living expenses for all involved. Ed, Dan and the Haxan group live on the money made from the reshoots. Some of the additional shots include:

- Mike hanging in the corner.
- Mike floating in the corner.
- Mike hanging and bloody in the corner.
- Mike floating and bloody in the corner.
- Mike standing in the corner covered in blood.
- Mike hanging and bloody right at the entrance to the room, where Heather's camera bumps into the body before falling.

Virtually none of the extra footage shot is used in the completed film. The only shot Haxan considered changing was the final shot with Mike in the corner. Haxan is not enthusiastic about altering the ending and despite protests, tells Artisan to use the original. Thankfully, Artisan stays true to their word and releases the film with the original ending.

April 1999
All materials delivered. Final deal points are negotiated.

Late April 1999
The first check from Artisan finally arrives.

May 1999

The Haxan Five go to the Cannes Film Festival, where *The Blair Witch Project* screens as part of Director's Fortnight. Dan and Ed sit on a panel moderated by Roger Ebert, with John Sayles, Ron Howard and Spike Lee. Gregg tears up at the sight of Ed and Dan sitting next to these giants and takes a lot of pictures. *Blair Witch* wins the "Prix de Jeunesse" (Award of the Youth). This award is given by a select group of European teens who screen all the films in the festival.

July 16, 1999

Artisan releases the film, which premieres on twenty-seven screens in limited release. *The Blair Witch Project* grosses $1.5 million. There are lines around the block for the first showing and all the screenings are packed to capacity.

July 30, 1999

The Blair Witch Project release is expanded to a total of 1,101 screens in North America. It becomes the second highest grossing at the box office that weekend bringing in a total of $28.5 million. (Second only to Julia Roberts in *Runaway Bride*, which makes $35 million the same weekend. *Runaway Bride* is also playing on more than twice the number of screens, 3,158 in total.) Hollywood and the entire industry is stunned that a film made for $22,000 could outperform other movies opening that week such as Warner Bros.' *Deep Blue Sea* with Sam Jackson. The top ten box office for the weekend broke down as follows:

1.	Runaway Bride	$34.5 million
2.	**THE BLAIR WITCH PROJECT**	**$28.5**
3.	Deep Blue Sea	$18.6
4.	The Haunting	$15.1
5.	Inspector Gadget	$14.0
6.	American Pie	$6.7
7.	Eyes Wide Shut	$4.4
8.	Big Daddy	$3.5
9.	Star Wars Episode I	$3.4
10.	Tarzan	$3.0

July 31, 1999

Some moviegoers experience nausea from the handheld camera movements and actually had to leave to vomit. In some Toronto theaters, ushers ask that patrons prone to motion sickness sit in aisle seats and "try not to throw up on other people."

August 1999

A competition grade foosball table is delivered to the Haxan offices in Orlando, Florida.

Late Summer 1999

The Blair Witch Project appears on the covers of both *Time* and *Newsweek*. The success of the film spawns hundreds of articles and press about what this means to the Hollywood moviemaking machine.

September 1999–July 2000

After the insanity and all the attention, Haxan decides to stay in Orlando and make *Heart of Love*, a comedy that Dan and Ed wanted to make before *The Blair Witch Project*.

In September, Mike marries his long-suffering fiancée, Julie, which kicks off marriage mania at Haxan. Ed marries his longtime squeeze Stefanie the following May. Dan outdoes them all by marrying his fiancée Julia on the island of Kauai in July 2000.

Most of the year is spent promoting *The Blair Witch Project* in the rest of the world territories, sharpening their foosball skills and negotiating the *Heart of Love* deal with Artisan. In January, 2000, Haxan returns to Sundance to watch movies, hang with the crowds and launch their second film, *Heart of Love*.

December 1999

The final box office take of *The Blair Witch Project* stands at $140.5 million. It joins *Star Wars: Episode I: The Phantom Menace* as one of the top ten highest grossing films of 1999 and remains the most profitable independent film ever.

March 26, 2000

The Blair Witch Project wins an Independent Spirit Award as the best film made for under $500,000.

SECTION 4
FILMMAKER WAR STORIES

"First things first, you have to really want this. No one who's on the fence about being a filmmaker ever succeeds."

—Heidi Van Lier, writer/director of *Chi Girl*

FROM THE FRONT LiNES OF FiLMMAKiNG

I've interviewed countless filmmakers at festivals and most of the interviews turn out badly—they're just incredibly lame and boring to read. In fact, I don't think I've ever gotten a good interview at a film festival. I suspect it's because the subject is painfully aware that they are being interviewed for a magazine, newspaper, television or whatever, so they immediately launch into "spin mode." They talk nice about the producer, nice about the director, nice about the actors, nice about the festival, *everyone* is nice. You'd think that these interview subjects had just consumed some type of happy drug! (In some cases, they actually have.) The truth is that they are merely doing the right thing and being political. They don't want to say anything that might offend or piss someone off and hurt their chances of getting a deal, winning the prize or launching their career.

The subjects that I've gathered for this section were *not* interviewed at film festivals. They each take a truthful, and sometimes painful, look at their experience. What you are about to read are less interviews and more like confessionals—each person offering a detailed account of their triumphs and their failures.

I have carefully selected interview subjects who would avoid politics and offer useful information to filmmakers and festivalgoers. These interviewees comprise the best and the brightest in independent film. Each person delivers the real deal—hard information, free of polite spin.

The filmmakers interviewed for this second edition of this book have created a strangely diverse range of films; from an earnest indie about the search for a long lost friend, to a bloody flick about fast-talking used car salesmen, to a documentary about the UFO-obsessed, to a short film about a dancing cow, to a narrative feature about a washed-up child star, to a movie that is best described as "*Swingers* with *Star Trek* geeks," to an Oscar®-nominated short filmmaker making his feature debut with a comedy about suicide.

The movies are clearly diverse and the experiences of each film-maker are even more so. Each of these filmmakers represents the numerous paths a filmmaker can take when seeking success through a film festival. These myriad paths include:

- Submit to Sundance, make it into Sundance, screen at Sundance, sell film for theatrical distribution.
- Submit to Sundance, make it into Sundance, screen at Sundance, film *does not* sell to distributor, filmmaker chooses to self-distribute movie.
- Rejected from Sundance, make it into Slamdance, sell film for theatrical distribution.
- Rejected from Sundance, rejected from Slamdance, enter other festivals where the movie is then discovered.
- Rejected from Sundance, rejected from Slamdance, become a hit on the international film festival circuit.
- Rejected from Sundance, rejected from Slamdance, rejected from almost every festival, go home empty, but filled with hard lessons.
- Rejected from nearly every film festival on the planet, pursue self-distribution as the final option.

There are certainly more roads than those I've mentioned and new ones that filmmakers will invent for themselves out of necessity. And you can easily replace "Sundance" and "Slamdance" for other great festivals like Toronto, Telluride, Cannes, Florida, SXSW, Berlin, Chicago and many others. Read these interviews for inspiration, entertainment and enlightenment, but most of all, learn from their experiences.

MARK A. ALTMAN, Writer/Producer

Before starting independent production company Mindfire Entertainment, Mark A. Altman was an entertainment journalist and magazine editor. As editor of *Sci-Fi Universe* magazine (a magazine he and I created together), Mark received an inside glimpse at the real world of science fiction fandom. He has already produced two independent films, including *Free Enterprise* which he also co-wrote with Director Robert Meyer Burnett. *Free Enterprise* chronicles the misadventures of two devoted science fiction fans who meet their idol, William Shatner, and learn he's more screwed up than they are. It's best described as *Swingers* with *Star Trek* geeks. Mark wrote the script around William Shatner before the Canadian over-actor had even committed to being in the film. While this indie comedy never played Park City, *Free Enterprise* successfully played many smaller festivals and was picked up for distribution by Lions Gate Films.

Writer/producer Mark A. Altman
PHOTO BY AL ORTEGA

Where did the idea for Free Enterprise *come from?*

My co-writer and I were deeply involved in scripting another project, a supernatural thriller involving Jewish mysticism, but we were having some problems licking it and I started writing *Free Enterprise*, then known as *Trekkers*, as a lark. The high concept was *Swingers* meets Woody Allen's *Play It Again, Sam*. We were able to interest a producer we were working with, Dan Bates, and he raised the money to make the film.

How did you get William Shatner for your film?

It was a difficult road. Shatner's representatives rejected our over-
tures several times. Eventually, our persistence sort of wore him
down and he called us to say that he wasn't doing our movie. This
was in response to a letter that he now refers to as "the tear stained
letter." We made all sorts of claims—that this movie would do for
him what *Boogie Nights* did for Burt Reynolds and *L.A. Confidential*
did for Kim Basinger—by changing his image. The irony is that it
sort of has. The Priceline.com commercials that he sings in were
inspired by *Free Enterprise.* The Priceline people were actually at the
premiere and called for copies of the film the next day for their
advertising agency. And now Shatner has a whole second career as a
pitchman and as a comedian, with roles in *Miss Congeniality* and
Third Rock from the Sun. It's funny because when he first called, he
said, "You've written a very funny movie, but I'm not doing your
film." He was written like Humphrey Bogart in *Play It Again, Sam,*
as an imaginary muse who keeps appearing to give the guys life
advice. But he didn't want to be a god-like figure. He told us, "I'm a
screwed up guy, I can't play a guru." As a result, we retooled the
script to make the character of "Bill" a real character with foibles
and feet of clay. He responded to this version of the script and we
were off to the races.

What did you do to increase your chances for acceptance into festivals?

We tried to generate as much press as possible. And we made sure
to send all the press we had to the festivals with the applications. We
also made sure we had good black and white and color art to send,
along with cast availability. For many festivals, having the cast come
and discuss the film is a major plus. Especially if you have William
Shatner. Also, since the film was somewhat semi-autobiographical,
Rob and I were good guests and that helped create a lot of goodwill
among audiences.

Free Enterprise *played a lot of small festivals, which eventually led to even
more festival showings.*

Well, we did a lot of the B+/A- film festivals. We had our world premiere at the Sitges Festival of Fantastic Film in Spain, which was
both professionally and personally one of the greatest experiences
I've ever had. Given our sci-fi backgrounds, we had a delightful time

going to see many of the genre movies they showed. The culture was just so wonderful and seeing the film shown with Spanish and Catalan subtitles was a kick. I can't say enough good things about this film festival. There is a real respect for film and no condescension to the genre of sci-fi films. I was concerned about the language barrier, but the film was very warmly received. After Sitges, we literally hit the road like door-to-door salesman. A week later we were back in Los Angeles and the film had its U.S. premiere at the AFI International Film Festival where we won Best Film and Best Screenplay. But we weren't able to accept in person because we were already off to Atlanta where we won Best Independent Film at the Peachtree International Film Festival . . . and we weren't able to accept that award in person because we were in Hawaii at the Hawaii International Film Festival! (Hawaii is another terrific festival and celebrates a lot of Pacific Rim cinema.) We couldn't ask for more, but unfortunately—despite the through-the-roof response— the acquisition exec who flew in for this screening couldn't sell his people on the film back in Los Angeles. Quentin Tarantino was at that screening and we actually spent some time with him at a tree-house party in the hills above Waikiki, which was fairly surreal. Just watching Quentin do his Shatner impersonation was worth the flight over.

Any other memorable festivals?

We also were accepted into the Newport Beach Film Festival where the film screened several times. We won the Audience Award—in no small part thanks to the efforts of Captain Blood, the proprietor of the theater where the film played. He became a huge advocate for the movie and wanted to release the film himself if no one else picked it up.

Subsequent to Hawaii and Newport we went to a small but well-run little festival in Tahoe, were closing night at the USA Film Festival in Dallas and then went to Edmonton, Canada, for the Local Heroes festival. This was another pleasant surprise, where the warmth of the organizers was very tangible and there was a terrific love of film. They made us feel very welcome and the film was a tremendous success. We shared a marquee with the closing night film, Arthur Hiller's *The Americanization of Emily.* Ironically, by now, we were taking a lot of crap from people for spending too much time at what some people called "second rate festivals," which they said wouldn't do anything to get distribution for our film. However, we were meeting people, networking on panels and we ended up being offered the Opening Night slot at the inaugural Winnipeg Local Heroes Film Festival. They wanted Rob and I to come up and introduce the film since the screening in Edmonton had been such a huge success. A lot of people thought it was ridiculous for us to go to Winnipeg. The irony is that this is where we sold the film. We met up with Paul Colichman from Regent Entertainment on the last night of the festival; he was there for a *Gods & Monsters* fund-raiser. I told him about how a deal we had with another distributor looked like it was going to fall through and he came to the rescue. Paul came to the table and acquired the film and released it in theaters several months later.

> .....
> "A lot of people thought it was ridiculous for us to go to Winnipeg. The irony is that this is where we sold the film."
> .....

What was your best festival experience?

We went to the Cannes Film Festival with Shatner, and that was an experience I will always cherish. We did three days of non-stop publicity with the worldwide press, screened the film, actually invited fans to come in costume and watched Shatner wax poetic to E! Channel about the virtues of topless women on the beach. Nothing had ever prepared me for that experience. We actually missed our plane because Rob and I were buying French movie posters and ended up staying in Nice for an extra day. Shatner actually gave one of his costumes from *Free Enterprise* to the Cannes Planet Hollywood in a big ceremony in which he made up a long, elaborate and completely untrue story about the history of the outfit and it was a huge hit with the paparazzi. I came up with the idea as a lark and it was one of our most successful press functions.

How were you accepted into so many small festivals at once?

In many cases, we were accepted into festivals we didn't apply to because of word-of-mouth from other festivals. Many of the later festivals came to us because we had won awards and had either seen it or heard people really responded to the film. At the very least, they'd waive their application fees. If you're strapped for money, you should always ask.

When Free Enterprise *did not get into festivals known for acquisitions like Sundance, what kind of strategy did you take to get the film seen by distributors?*

Obviously, not getting into Sundance or Toronto, the ten ton gorillas of the festival scene, was a disappointment. We hoped to use the AFI fest as a springboard in Los Angeles for getting execs to see our film, but when the attendance there wasn't what we hoped, we used our award as a way to get people to check the film out at acquisitions screenings we set up in town. We had some great screenings, but we just couldn't seem to get anyone to come to the table because they felt the film was a "tweener"—too big for a small indie, but too small for a mainstream romantic comedy.

> .....
> "We had some great screenings, but they felt the film was a tweener, too big for a small indie, but too small for a mainstream romantic comedy."
> .....

What has been great for me as a filmmaker is that I'm a film lover first, and the opportunity to travel to these festivals around the world has just been a great bonus. Sure, we're there to sell and promote the film, but we're also there to revel in much of the great unseen cinema that exists throughout the world and to me that's the ideal kind of experience to have combining business in pleasure.

How did you promote for your first festival screening?

We made sure to have posters up and that the print had arrived and checked the projection booth. We spoke to the projectionist to ensure the right aspect ratio was being screened and the sound was up, but other than that, we sat back and enjoyed the film with the audience. I can't emphasize enough how important it is to work in concert with the projectionist. In one case, they were showing a short in 1:33 and our film was in 1:85 and they were just going to show everything in 1:33. If they did, you would have seen boom mikes and c-stands and it would have looked like *Santa Claus Conquers the Martians*. We had to scream at the festival organizers (which we very rarely do), to make sure to show the film in 1:85. It usually doesn't pay to be difficult and we always tried to be low-maintenance when it comes to accommodations, travel and the like, but when it comes to the actual screening of the film, it pays to be a huge pain in the ass. This is the one area you have to have zero-tolerance for screw-ups.

Free Enterprise *received a lot of great press, due in large part to William Shatner's role in the film, but did you hire a publicist?*

Because of my background as a journalist, I have a pretty respectable contact list. I worked very closely with the press to ensure coverage of the film. In addition, I made sure that we had extensive art from the set available as well as the participation of the cast in interviews and publicity. This may be the least interesting and glamorous thing to a first-time filmmaker, but as a former magazine editor, I knew what editors needs would be and tried to appeal to that. It worked fairly well, and we got quite extensive coverage of the movie prior and during the release for being a small indie film. We also had a good press kit that I put together and lot of B-roll we shot on set which ended up making it onto the electronic press kit (EPK).

I had some friends shoot digital video on the set to cover some of the behind-the-scenes. We got *Entertainment Tonight* to agree to do a story on the film, but then when Shatner wasn't available they were going to kill the story—so we offered them an interview we had shot with Shatner on set. They took it and ran a great piece. So it really pays to make sure you have your publicity bases covered. We ended up using all the cast interviews and behind-the-scenes footage for a documentary on the DVD. Thanks to the special edition features, the DVD has become one of the best selling non-studio DVDs of last year for Pioneer, and it was nominated for several VSDA awards. The extensive material helped us get a video deal for our second film, based on the success of the first film.

> .....
> **"Hype is like a seduction. Before you jump into bed, you have to tease a little."**
> .....

What did you do to build buzz to get acquisitions executives excited?

Hype is like a seduction. Before you jump into bed, you have to tease a little. And the way to tease a film is to keep as much under wraps as you can, so people are begging you to see it. We made the mistake of letting some acquisitions people see it early. I probably would have really kept the movie under wraps until its premiere and made sure no footage, screeners, nothing got shown before its first premiere at a film festival. Once an acquisitions exec has seen it, you're finished unless they love it. Even then, without a bidding war, it gives them a chance to hem and haw and find reasons not to buy it. This is what happened to us with a major studio. When they thought another studio was interested, they were all over us, but once they had some time to think about it and pass it onto their superiors, the heat subsided and in the cold light of day they reassessed their feelings about the film. Don't give them a chance to say no. Put your film in front of as many acquisitions people as possible. Also, it helps with an audience if the talent—namely you, the filmmaker—are at the screening. They're much more inclined to like a film if you come out and are avuncular and enthusiastic and they can see the film is the culmination of a lifelong dream. If the film just unspools without the filmmaker there, it's easier to be dispassionate and walk out if the film doesn't appeal to you in the first ten minutes.

It's funny, when we were at an *Empire Magazine* party in Cannes, Rob got on top of a statue of a naked woman, stripped down to his boxers and yelled, "I'm the director of the film *Free Enterprise* and I'm doing this to promote my movie!" The next day a reporter from the U.K. asked Shatner what he thought of this stunt, and he asked the reporter, "Well, what did you think?" They said, "It was brilliant," and he said, "Well then, you know, I gave him the idea."

Any things you would have done differently in pursuing the deal?

If a studio guy wants to see your movie, make them watch a print in their screening room. Tell them you don't have a tape. Lie. Make them watch it on film. Otherwise it's easy to think of the film as a cable or video premiere and not a feature film. Did I mention don't show them a tape? You'd much rather them see the film in a public venue with a crowd than on tape. You want to avoid people screening your film on tape at all costs. They can get up, take phone calls, go to the bathroom, whatever. And, if it's a comedy, a screening on tape can really kill you.

You've been a journalist yourself, can you offer any unique insights on how to handle critics?

Always get the business card of anyone you talk to in the press and keep a list. Keep a data base so you can approach them when you need to. Also, if you get a good review, send a thank you. Critics get a lot of negative mail, but they very rarely get positive mail and they appreciate the vote of confidence. They like to know they're nurturing a career and supporting an underdog if it's something they believe in. If they don't like your movie, don't hold it against them. Maybe they'll like the next one. (This is easier said than done, of course.)

Did you do anything different to support the release?

We did everything we had to do. In Hawaii, for instance, we literally gave out fliers at every comic book store and campus to make sure the theater was full when we knew we had an acquisition exec coming to see it. You do what you need to; we hand carried posters, we called sci-fi clubs in advance of the screenings and later the release. We spoke to college film programs and screened the film and, of course, did radio and TV promotion and interviews. Nothing was too small for us. We were literally giving out posters and promotional material to people waiting on line to buy *Star Wars: Episode I* toys at midnight at Toys 'R' Us, and going to midnight shows of *Star Trek II* to promote the film. With our second film, *The Specials*, it's been much of the same. Grassroots publicity supported by print and media buys in support of the film. Of course now, the Internet is becoming more and more important, so we're scheduling chats, doing more and more ambitious websites, earlier and earlier in the course of production.

Your film toured a lot of festivals, did the Q&As ever become routine? And what was it like to work with Shatner?

Oh yeah. We used to joke before the Q&A all the time. By the end of the festival circuit, we had our routine down to a science. We had a snappy response to everything.

"What was it like working with Shatner?" "God, you mean?"

> .....
> "How much did the film cost? More than *El Mariachi* and less than *Desperado*."
> .....

"Did you put my life on screen, man?" "It was our life first, dude."

"How much did the film cost?" "More than *El Mariachi* and less than *Desperado.*"

There were a lot of great anecdotes, so it was real easy to talk about the film and everyone was interested in what it was like to work with Shatner, and later, Eric McCormack (who went onto great success with *Will & Grace)*. And, for the record, working with Shatner was *great.* He was a real trooper and loved the spirit of indie film and our enthusiasm. On the last day of filming, he turned to Rob and me and said, "You know guys, I'm really glad I did this movie." In a way, that was the most satisfying thing of all.

....

After the success of *Free Enterprise*, Mark produced a second film called *The Specials*, which is an indie comedy about dysfunctional superheroes and their life when they're *not* fighting crime. In addition to serving as producer on several upcoming Mindfire films including *The House of the Dead*, based on the Sega video game, Mark is also developing a television series based on *Free Enterprise*. You can read more about Mark and his upcoming films at www.mindfireentertainment.com.

JOE CARNAHAN, Writer/Director

Joe Carnahan's debut feature film, *Blood, Guts, Bullets & Octane (BGB&O)*, tells a gruesome tale of fast-talking used car salesmen who stumble upon a car wanted by every hit man in the country. Carnahan cast himself as one of the motor-mouthed car salesmen, and upon meeting him you have to agree with his decision. He's more than "high-energy," this guy spits words out like bullets from a machine gun. *BGB&O* played the midnight slot at the 1998 Sundance Film Festival and later sealed a distribution deal with Lions Gate. *BGB&O* was recently released in a special edition DVD from Universal Home Video.

Writer/director Joe Carnahan (left) and actor/producer Dan Leis at the IFFM where they made a remarkable impression, which helped get them into Sundance.

Carnahan was working at a tiny local television station, struggling at a nowhere job, shooting his film on weekends. The movie was shot for less than $8,000. He did all of that while balancing the responsibilities of family life with a wife and two kids! The gutsy filmmaker just woke up and decided to do it and the result is a fast-paced debut oozing with creativity.

How does a filmmaker successfully apply to Sundance and gain acceptance?

Network like a sonofabitch. Anybody who believes that simply mailing in a VHS tape and a check for forty bucks will guarantee democratic privilege in the judging process is completely deluded. Don't be afraid to approach people like Geoff Gilmore or John Cooper or any of the programming staff if you see them at a festival or some other indie gathering. We have a tendency to deify these people and put them on a pedestal. Keep in mind a very basic precept—without the films to make the festivals, these people would be out of work. So strap on the same set of balls you used when you broke your ass for months on end to make your film in the first place; walk up to them and introduce yourself. If you fancy yourself the shy, inhibited, introspective type, let me tell you, that will get you about as far as the front door.

> .....
> "So strap on the same set of balls you used when you broke your ass for months on end to make your film in the first place; walk up to them and introduce yourself."
> .....

If you want to GETYOURFILMINFESTIVALS, get proactive about it. Now. Case in point, Sarah Jacobson—she's a one-woman marketing machine. Her film (*Mary Jane's Not a Virgin Anymore*) might not have been picked up, but you'd be hard-pressed to find somebody on the festival circuit who doesn't know who she is. And that's it right there, kids; that's what it's all about. Sarah, through her own force of will and undaunted hustle, is in a position to go out and make more films and find people to make those films with her. It all boils down to bare bones determination.

How did you find out you were in Sundance?

I was in the trenches, pulling an all night edit since we were still doing our AVID cut for the lab. My wife called in a frenzy, saying John Cooper had just called. I called, and Cooper confirmed that *BGB&O* was in.

It sounds flippant as all hell, but I had a pretty good idea we were already in. Don't get me wrong; there was a tremendous sense of relief, because after month upon month of aimless speculation and second guessing, our wish came true. Even though almost nine months earlier, our producer's rep—the dazzling, debonair, Patrick Lynn—had a fleeting confab with Geoff Gilmore in Toronto, and Geoff basically told Patrick that he intended to program the film. Even knowing that, we couldn't relax until we got "real" confirmation. Usually the festival programmers, particularly in Sundance, are notoriously tight-lipped about their line-up. Nothing short of the rack and razor blades around the ear can pry that priceless inside skinny from the staff.

What other festivals did you apply to?

Toronto tossed us very early on, and that was tough to swallow, but after Sundance, we were carpet-bombed with fest invites. My favorite was Berlin, hands down. It is the most structurally sound festival on the face of the planet. You could drop D-Day on that festival and it will still run as smooth as a tuned engine. Next Wave films, run by the esteemed prince of indie print, Peter Broderick, was our partner in crime since they kicked in, along with IFC/BRAVO, the necessary monies to finish the film in 35mm. They were really instrumental in landing a lot of festival attention.

Were you concerned about applying to other festivals before you got word from Sundance?

No. Primarily because I believe that it is fundamentally inane to put that much into a single film festival, even the great and almighty Sundance. Everybody says how Sundance frowns on playing other festivals before you play theirs. While there is no arguing a preference for North American premieres and debuts in the festival, there were plenty of films that had played previously in Toronto and other big festivals prior to their Sundance dates. If your film is good enough, it's not going to be ignored.

How did you prepare for your first Sundance screening?

I didn't have a lot of time considering that the sound mix was still being done five days prior to our screening. I just sat around contemplating the disaster that would ensue if the print didn't arrive on time. When it did, I thought it was only about seventy percent of what the film was in my original straight-to-video cut. Basically, I just stuck with my family and played it very low key in Park City. The showing didn't end up starting until almost one in the morning, which I felt hurt us even more than the poor print quality. In the end, I just bit the bullet and trusted in the fact that key people (Lions Gate and more importantly, Mark Urman) had viewed my original version of the film and were already big fans.

What did you do to hype your film at Sundance?

The same way we hyped it everywhere else. We gathered en masse and marched through the streets of Park City like a parade of thugs—wearing parkas emblazoned with the film's logo, shoving it in everybody's face, creating a maelstrom of hype—getting that critical "buzz" going early and all the rest of that requisite catchphrase stuff. I openly despise and deplore ham-handed marketing techniques, the notion of jamming something down peoples' throats ad nauseum. Unfortunately, the film business doesn't give you the option of subtlety. Sometimes you have to forsake your better judgment and basic common decency and just get it done . . . hawking your wares come hell or high water. Now, I'm not saying run up, jump on Harvey Weinstein's back and blast your film's synopsis in his ear with a bullhorn; I *am* saying stop just short of that.

Did you hire a publicist?

The PR firm of Dennis Davidson & Associates, and the wonderful Nancy Willen and Melinda Hovee, cut us an incredible rate after repping the film gratis for almost five months. The fee they ended up collecting from us was a pretty pitiful per diem considering the tremendous effort they put into publicizing it.

We publicized it until we were pretty sure everyone was so sick and tired of us that they'd watch the film, even if it was just to have a reason to ridicule us. Fortunately, it worked out for the best and people really dug the flick. In the end, when your film hits the street it had better deliver; particularly if you've been bragging that it cost less than eight grand to put in the can. When the lights go down, it's gutcheck time. I can't stress that enough: you can come down on people with the trumpet of God, if the film can't back your claim, scuttle the ship, the ride's over.

What would you have done differently in preparing for your film's debut?

I would've gotten a much earlier jump on the extensive post-production work that had to be done. This is the kind of thing you don't want to delay. Unfortunately, my lawyer and other lawyers were off doing their "lawyering." A process requiring you to sit on your hands for weeks at a time, waiting for contractual crap to clear and a bunch of other fascinating bits of tedium that have miraculously little to do with filmmaking. I really can't say I would have changed a thing, because the PR machine we were able to put together at that point, as well as Amy Taubin's glowing review in *The Village Voice,* really put everything on track.

How can other filmmakers create the much-needed hype for their own films?

Number one, get your film into a forum where it can be shown on a screen. This means a place like the Independent Feature Film Market (IFFM), held annually in New York. This is the single best place to develop a platform for your film. They have a marvelous staff of people who will really go the distance for you if they believe in your work. I missed the deadline for the '97 IFFM by more than a month, but because they really believed in the film, they found me a slot. This was primarily the work of two fabulous souls, Milton Tabbot and Sharon Sklar. Once you get there, adopt a style that suits your personal preference and acts in the movie's best interest. You can be obnoxious, overbearing and pushy in a very subtle and effective way if you tailor your marketing plan to your strengths as well as your shortcomings. If you don't do well speaking to other people, or you stumble or stutter or stammer or whatever, find someone in your group who DOESNOTDOTHESETHINGS. Make them the point person for public relations. Understand that this is a temporary arrangement since at some point you will be required—nay, *obligated*—to speak on behalf of your work because you are the filmmaker. So beat back the bashfuls and get verbal.

Get as many press people on board as possible. If you have some outside connection or some way of getting a tape to a local critic or movie reviewer or features editor, get it to them. For me, two people were absolutely instrumental early on: Mark Ebner, formally of *Spy* Magazine and Lisa Derrick from *New Times LA*. I met them both online and they agreed to view the tape; both were jazzed about the film's prospects. They provided gutsy praise and some stellar copy for the one-sheet. I owe them both a tremendous debt since it was their initial reviews that paved the way for Amy Taubin's and others. So far, I have yet to meet Lisa in person, and it just goes to show you, you don't have to live next door to these people to get them your film.

Understand that there are tremendously creative people out there with a lot riding on a movie. This is not a normally cheap endeavor and I know people who have gone several hundred thousand dollars in debt and seen bupkes on their return. These are the relentless, competitive types you will encounter and are forced to compete against. At IFFM in '97, I put my most menacing actor,

Hugh McChord, in the lobby of the Angelika and taped a huge poster-sized standee for our film to the table. This was something that was frowned upon by the theater's management, but since Hugh stands about 6'3" and is upwards of 240 lbs., nobody was willing to say anything (and with good reason; this guy never smiled once and when you walked in, your eye immediately went to him). It worked, and two days after our screening, we were the talk of the market. I'm not condoning antisocial behavior or implied physical violence as viable marketing tools, but if you've got the bulk, use it. I had six guys, averaging six feet in height, walking around New York with matching T-shirts and hats promoting the film. We may have looked like idiot tourists, but the message got across. Since no one wanted to risk a public beating by what appeared to be a goon squad, snide comments were minimal.

Just don't be afraid. Don't shy away from contact and do what you need to do to make your point. There are thousands of filmmakers out there willing to do the necessary things to sell their film. Set yourself apart as much as possible, do the unusual and the extreme and ignore the whispers.

Were you nervous at the first screening?

I was more agitated than nervous because I knew the audience was not going to be seeing the film the way I intended. I sat out in the hall outside the Park City library looking at my six-month-old son and hoping the freaking roof wouldn't fall in on me and my career. I dealt with it by staying as loose as I could and joking with my brother Matt who, like the best of the bomb squad, can always take the tension off and clip the right wires. Bob Hawk, my hero, introduced the film and that helped, too. Bob was a huge fan and his high praise for the film went miles toward calming me down and helping me focus.

What did you learn from that first screening?

That I had homicidal impulses where sound designers are concerned. That a library is just that, a library, and therefore not acoustically kind. And that what I did in two months I should have stretched over six months. And finally, that films should never start after midnight unless they have "Rocky," "Horror" or "Picture Show" in the title.

What did you do to get acquisition executives into your screenings?
That was more Patrick Lynn's doing. He, in concert with my wonderful agent Neil Friedman, drummed up early support for the film,
months before the festival. We already had an idea that Lions Gate
was going to come on strong—which was great since most in the
business believe that Lions Gate will soon surpass October Films as
the heir of the Miramax throne. Lions Gate also has a history of
brilliantly handling small films like *The Daytrippers* and *The Pillow
Book,* so this was a thrilling proposition for me.

Who negotiated the deal?
Neil Friedman primarily, who is truly a brilliant man. He and
Patrick worked the seams to get me the best possible deal. Lions
Gate put the offer on the table one week after Sundance.

What did you look for in the deal?
A company that I knew could put the film in play, which Lions
Gate can so clearly do. Also, I wanted to work with guys like Mark
Urman and Tom Ortenberg at a young company that is clearly
going places. This was as exciting as anything else since we knew
how much Mark loved the film and how doggedly he would push
it. They gave us a great backend deal and a pretty substantial
advance, so I was ecstatic.
    The deal went for a modest six figure sum with great ancillary
perks. Like $50,000 bumps as the film surpassed certain gross rev-
enues. Remember, when a company, particularly one as upstart as
Lions Gate, takes a flyer on a $7,300 film, there ain't much they can
do wrong as it pertains to a relationship with their filmmakers.
They even assumed the costly "Errors & Omissions" insurance and
agreed to pay for the MPAA rating because they knew how little
money we had. Those expenses alone more than doubled the film's
original budget.

Any advice on getting the distribution deal?
Yeah—don't show the film to *anybody* who has *anything* to do with
acquisitions. If distributors are going to see your film, it's best that
they all see it at the same time. It's what is known as an "Acquisitions
Screening" and it's done all the time in Los Angeles. Press is one
thing—you need that. That's a risk you have to assume, try to pref-

ace all conversations with potential reviewers with the request that they not show the tape around. They're going to do it anyway, but you still want to try to contain it. When you send your film in to an agency, they will almost immediately make copies of the film if they like it. They do this almost as a reflex, so at some point it's really out of your hands as to who is seeing your film. But, do your best to contain it early. In my own experience, it came to light that a rather powerful, prominent indie agent, one who reps some pretty big names, got a hold of my tape, liked it, and without my permission, passed it on to some distribution companies. He may have thought he was doing me a favor, but he wasn't and he should have known better. Guard your film. I sent mine out to only three people at the outset. One of them, Patrick Lynn, went on to rep my film. I sent my fourth out to DDA, which gave the copy to Neil Friedman, and he instantly became my agent. From that standpoint, I was fortunate.

Any advice on handling press?

Yeah, watch your ass . . . and keep that switchblade taped to your ankle. Understand that the people interviewing you can put whatever spin on whatever word of yours they choose. I got interviewed by this punk kid from *Variety* and thought I was coming off humble, gregarious and generally happy to be there. What he wrote down and more importantly, put in print, made me look like a colossal ass and consequently blew my whole notion of "objective" journalism sky high. Press people want three things: funny shit or semi-scandalous shit or shit that makes you look like you were eating Top Ramen noodles and living in a shoebox prior to making your debut film. That's it. Look at most print media about festivals and its participants and you'll find those tenets are absolutely true. You can be all bright-eyed and bushy-tailed, just so long as your answers aren't.

How were you, as the filmmaker, expected to handle supporting the release of the film?

I think, with the incredible proliferation of independent films, anything you can do to support your film is going to help. I will do print interviews, TV, radio, everything. In the last four months, a slew of Sundance films have opened theatrically and thoroughly tanked. Movies like *Hurricane Streets* and *TwentyFourSeven* and fell right off the radar . . . why? I think a certain amount of the blame falls on the companies releasing them—they don't aggressively go after the indie filmgoer.

....

Joe Carnahan Today

Joe has done a lot of writing since the debut of his film, the Sundance favorite *Blood, Guts, Bullets and Octane.* He is currently writing and rewriting a few scripts for Warner Brothers and penning a project called *Pride and Glory* for New Line. Joe is juggling a couple more scripts including *The Surrender of Washington Hansen* (which Harrison Ford has expressed interest in) and *Narc* (which Ray Liotta may star in). Joe is also in pre-production on a digital feature called *Excursion* that he plans to shoot himself.

TAZ GOLDSTEIN, Short Filmmaker

Taz Goldstein's career has taken about as many twists and turns as a complex Hollywood thriller. His first job in Hollywood was as a tape screener for *America's Funniest Home Videos.* Taz's college degree came in handy as he watched endless hours of people falling into pools, dogs peeing, babies vomit-

Short filmmaker Taz Goldstein

ing and dads getting hit in the groin. Shortly after, he became an associate director on several television shows, like Fox's *Studs.* On the brighter side, he did earn an Emmy nomination for music composition, which didn't help his pursuit of a career as a director at all. After working in the industrial and commercial world, and after several attempts to sell a feature script, Taz chose to make a short. I saw his hilarious twenty minute film at the USA Film Festival in Dallas where I gave it a special award. His short, *The Dancing Cow,* has played over fifteen festivals and has already won three awards as best short film.

How did you come up with the idea for The Dancing Cow?
My partner, Rob Moniot, came up with the idea while we were sitting in some creative executive's office on the Universal lot. The executive split in the middle of the meeting to take a twenty-minute phone call. Rob turned to me and asked, "What would you do if Harvey Weinstein called to praise your film, but he was talking about the wrong film?" We spent the twenty minutes the exec was gone coming up with a twenty-minute movie. If he had been gone

longer, we would've written a feature. Sure, he was a rude little shit . . . but now we have a movie. We'd like to thank him—but we don't remember who it was. So if you happen to know any rude creative executives, let us know.

We were planning on shooting on 16mm or DV. Once the script was finished, it was read by John A. Alonzo (cinematographer for *Chinatown, Scarface*, etc.); he loved the script and called to offer his services for free. John's involvement changed everything. Now we were shooting on 35mm (and HD) with donated film, equipment and locations. The same sort of thing happened with the music. We sent a rough cut to Mark Snow (composer for *X-Files, Disturbing Behavior*, etc.) because a friend thought he might be able to suggest a young, hungry composer. He watched the cut, loved it and offered to score it himself. The entire experience has seemed charmed . . . we know that this will never happen again.

I directed the film, and Rob produced. We only made the movie to show what we could do. It was just going to be an example for our reel. Much to our surprise and delight, it became a lot more then that, and has been playing the festival circuit all year. We planned our festival strategy with the first edition of this book; and I'm not just saying that to suck up. Oh wait. Yes, I am.

How did you raise the money?

Mom and Dad . . . who I still haven't paid back. Perhaps seeing their names in this book will delight them to the point where they forget about the loan. What do you think, Seth and Judy?

Did you do anything in particular to increase your chances for acceptance into a festival?

For the most part, we just sent in the entry and kept our fingers crossed. However, in one case, after sending in the tape, we had all our friends call the main festival office and excitedly inquire if the rumors were true . . . that *The Dancing Cow* was accepted into their festival. Of course, there really was no rumor, but the festival staff didn't know that. I think the hype helped us in. Couldn't hurt, right? Waiting to hear back from a festival is

> **"Waiting to hear back from a festival is always tough. The general rule to keeping your sanity is to hope for everything, but expect nothing."**

always tough. The general rule to keeping your sanity is to hope for everything, but expect nothing.

How did you find out you were in the U.S. Comedy Arts Festival?

We were finishing up a major project, and hadn't slept for several days, when we got the call from the director of the U.S. Comedy Arts Festival telling us that we had been accepted. He said, "You guys rock!" We jumped around. Called our moms. Fell asleep.

What other festivals did you apply to?

The only festivals we applied to, and were rejected by, were Sundance, Slamdance and Telluride. But we're not at all bitter. The bastards.

What was your goal in making a short?

I directed *The Dancing Cow* solely to demonstrate my abilities. We expected only production companies and studio executives to view *Cow*, but it took on a life of its own.

Were those goals achieved by exposure from film festivals?

For us, the initial exposure came from tapes being passed around town, from office assistants to executives, from mailroom clerks to producers. And as soon as the film started playing at festivals, those executives and producers started taking the film, and us, more seriously.

What did you do to hype your film?

Hype creates Hype. The more you make, the less you need to make yourself. For example, after returning from the U.S. Comedy Arts Festival, we wanted to hype the fact that we got a development deal while we were there. So I designed a postcard featuring a doll (the film's iconic logo character) wearing a T-shirt that reads "My Parents went to Florida and all I got was this lousy T-shirt." I altered the T-shirt with a marker to read "My movie went to Aspen, and all I got was this lousy Development Deal." We sent out the cards and got great response. Next thing you know, we get a call from the director of the Comedy Arts Festival. They want to use our T-shirt concept in their full page, color, "Call for entries" ads in the

FILMMAKER WAR STORIES: TAZ GOLDSTEIN

Hollywood Reporter and *Variety*. However, instead of a doll wearing the shirt, they want us wearing the shirt! So right now, there are trade publications with big-ass photos of me and Rob. More hype! It's contagious. People love passing along hype.

Something else to remember is that everyone loves a good story. I'm not talking about the story in your film. I'm talking about the story of how you lost your actor halfway through shooting. I'm talking about the story of how you made your film in your basement for $75. Have an amazing story to tell. It will be remembered, and passed along at parties.

Hyping the film was just like making the film. Pulling off miracles with no money.

We knew we wanted to send out some unusual stuff, but we didn't want it to get tossed aside like much of the swag that flies around. So, we decided *not* to send stuff to people at production companies or studios, and instead focused on people who *talk* for a living—publicists, managers, magazines, etc.

> .....
> **"Hyping the film was just like making the film. Pulling off miracles with no money."**
> .....

First, we sent out 300 naked baby dolls with tags stuck in their ears displaying the name of the movie. They were accompanied by tall index cards with quotes about us from the biggest people we could find who were willing to go on record.

A week later, we sent each of those same people a bottle of "Dancing Cow" Steak sauce and an information card about the movie. We found the sauce on the Internet, and asked the owner if he would be interested in helping us out. He sent 300 bottles to us the next day. We love him . . . and his steak sauce kicks ass (www.dancingcow.com). In fact, one bottle found its way to the executive dining room at the Culver Studios. It was a big hit. Now, their menu has "The Dancing Cow Burger" which comes with fries, a drink, and the movie's website address (www.thedancingcow.com). Again, hype creates hype.

A week later, those 300 people received a soundtrack CD, featuring Mark Snow's score. We got the CD's for free as well. There are a lot of film fans out there who are willing to help if you just ask nicely. Rob asks very nicely.

The day the tapes went out, we took out full page ads in the trades. We bartered our editorial services in exchange for the space. We owe a lot of people favors, but it was worth every karmic cent.

What would you have done differently in preparing for your film's debut?
Had a feature script ready to go. We were not expecting the huge response we got, and were therefore unequipped to completely capitalize on it. Production companies and studios wanted to see our next project. We were planning on writing a feature after we finished the short. In hindsight, we should have done it the other way around.

Were you nervous at the first screening and if so, how did you deal with it?
"Nervous" is not the right world. "Paralyzed with fear" is probably a bit more accurate. I had finally directed a film. This was something I'd wanted to do my entire life, but was never really sure if I could do successfully. And now, for the first time, a crowd of strangers was prepared to give me my answer. I intended to stand in the back and pace, but my path was blocked, and the lights were dimming. So I grabbed a seat next to my partner and sweat into the seats. I don't remember much. Lots of laughs, groans and applause.

> .....
> **"We owe a lot of people favors, but it was worth every karmic cent."**
> .....

How did you go about getting a distribution deal for your film?
As soon as the film hit the festival circuit, we were approached by *lots* of online distribution companies and several traditional distributors as well. We were getting fairly impressive offers, and some promises of wide distribution. However, getting distribution was not our primary goal. First and foremost, we wanted exposure. We initially went with Pop.com because we figured Steven Spielberg + Jeffrey Katzenberg + David Geffen + Brian Grazer + Ron Howard = Exposure, right? Our choice paid off right away. We were the topic of a feature article in the *Hollywood Reporter* the day after Pop.com acquired our film. Rob has been quoted twice in the trades since then. Since then Pop went under, so we're shopping the film around.

Your received a fair amount of attention for a short film, any advice on handling the press?

Stories of imminent doom and funny quotes—pick one and go with it. The best place to get quoted is at the after screening parties. We've also had luck sneaking into festival press rooms and asking, "Who wants some big news?" Be bold, but don't be an ass.

....

The Dancing Cow was released as part of a DVD compilation packed with *Total Movie* magazine. Taz Goldstein co-founded a production company Built-D Pictures (which stands for "But Ultimately, I'd Like to Direct," www.built-d.com) with his partner, Robert Moniot. Together they've produced and directed industrials, commercials, music videos, film trailers and radio spots. Their client list includes Universal Studios, Columbia/TriStar Motion Pictures, Paramount Pictures, Fuji Film, Miramax and New Line Cinema. Information about Taz's short *The Dancing Cow* is available at www.thedancingcow.com.

ROGER NYGARD, Documentary Filmmaker

Documentary filmmaker Roger Nygard

Roger Nygard's first film was a horror-comedy short called *Warped*. The film went on to capture the top award at the 1990 Houston International Film Festival. Roger followed up with a feature comedy, *High Strung*, starring and written by comedian Steve Oedekerk. This independent film was shot in two-and-a-half weeks on a $300,000 budget and premiered at the San Jose Film Festival. His second feature, an action/comedy called *Back to Back*, starred Michael Rooker and Bobcat Goldthwait and premiered at film festivals in Dallas and Seattle. Roger moved away from narrative features but could not leave his comic sensibilities behind him. He next directed and edited *Trekkies*, a documentary that took a humorous look at the world of *Star Trek* fandom. *Trekkies* was acquired by Paramount Classics after screenings at the Hamptons and AFI Los Angeles festivals. Jumping back to narratives, Roger co-wrote, directed, and edited, *Suckers*, a dramatic-comedy about new car salesman, which premiered at the U.S. Comedy Arts festival in Aspen, and the Minneapolis/St. Paul Film Festival. Roger's success in the independent film world is directly related to his success at film festivals. His latest documentary, *Six Days in Roswell*, offers an inside look at the cult of fanatics fascinated with the prospect of an alien spacecraft that supposedly crashed in Roswell, New Mexico, in the 1940s.

How do you go about raising money for a documentary film?
I have directed and/or produced five independent features so far. Ideas come from everywhere. But the best are ideas with which you have personal experience. Don't try writing a car salesmen movie if you have never sold cars, shadowed some car salesmen or at least ridden somewhere in a car.

I've had good luck talking investors out of their money. It helps if you wash up and put on a nice shirt first. And don't make a lot of sideways, darting glances. Nobody invests in nervous people. Usually, forty-nine of fifty "committed" investors will back out prior to writing a check. It's a numbers game, so be prepared to talk to a lot of rich windbags. Be bold; don't be afraid to ask them for their money, they've got plenty and there's no reason they can't wager some on such an exciting investment as your movie.

Virtually all of your films have broken at festivals, how do you account for your success at getting accepted into major festivals?
Film festivals are another numbers game. I use the shotgun approach and hit as many festivals as I can. Programmers' tastes vary greatly—some are going to love you and some are going to hate you. Film festivals have personalities, and some will mesh with you and with your film's tone better than others. Don't wait for Sundance, the Starbucks of film festivals, investigate the more exotic festivals as well. The smaller festivals can be cozier and more fun. Have contingency plans and be realistic and realize that the odds are that you will be one of the 95 percent who don't get into Sundance.

Conventional festival strategy says wait to see if you get into one of the top festivals. I agree that you should choose your premiere festival with care, because you can only premiere once. After that, attend every festival that invites you. That way you can build up a press kit of glowing reviews. If you don't have a top star, or if you don't win a top prize (and don't count on that, unless you are counting on winning the lottery, too), the reviews are what the

> .....
> **"Don't wait only for Sundance, the Starbucks of film festivals, investigate the more exotic festivals as well. The smaller festivals can be cozier and more fun."**
> .....

distributors will care about. That's how they sell small films; indie releases are review driven.

My films generally have gotten accepted at the same groups of festivals each time around. The programmers at those festivals apparently have the same twisted sensibility as I do. The "important" festivals sometimes get a bit pompous and overblown, which means the more "serious" films have a better shot there. The smaller festivals tend more toward the quirky.

What can you do to improve your chances?

First of all, submit early. Many films are never even viewed in their entirety because they come in at the deadline with the crush of hundreds of other tapes. Always follow up to make sure your tape was received. Fed-Ex tracking numbers are a blessing on that count. Submit only a finished version of the film. When programmers see timecode, they see a film that won't be ready in time. As with screenwriting, your film's story has to grab people in the first ten minutes, or it probably won't be viewed past the first act. Also, an eye-grabbing photo or artwork on the tape's cover won't hurt.

You're something of a film festival veteran by now, so what elements make up a good festival for you?

The thing to keep in mind is that this industry is all about entertainment. If you are an interesting, entertaining person, you and your audience will enjoy the experience that much more and the festivals will look forward to having you back again. If you're a boring, depressed whiner, you'll drive them away in droves. If you don't give the audience what they want, you'll be back to making home movies. The best festival experiences are the ones where they have all the logistics worked out and you don't have to worry about a thing. At the top of my list are the festival people in Dallas and San Jose. They are the nicest people you will ever meet. The worst festivals are the ones that charge you $150 to reject you. Festivals that charge more than a $70 entry fee are likely making a profit off of you. What can you do about that? Absolutely nothing. Except start your own festival.

.....
"If you don't give the audience what they want, you'll be back to making home movies."
.....

Festival screenings provide a receptive audience who made the effort to be there; they bought a ticket and are motivated to have a good time. Distributor screenings are only slightly more painful than back surgery. You generally have a small audience of jaded highbrows who couldn't make a film to save their lives but think they know it all. Don't expect much. Their reactions and feedback will be minimal. Try to screen for distributors with an audience. Invite all your friends in the industry, who will help you pack the house and spread the good word to other people in the industry.

When your film did not get into festivals like Sundance or Toronto, how did you get the film seen by distributors?

Everybody gets to have one hyped screening. If you don't premiere at a big festival, you can hype your own screening in Los Angeles or New York, where the acquisition scouts are. The acquisition scouts will have to attend your screening just in case. Don't let them make you feel guilty about that. It's their job, the lazy bastards.

> **"Anybody can be your publicist as long as it's not you."**

What did you do to hype your film to acquisition executives?

If you've got a track record, use it. If you're related to Bob Dylan, use that. If you've got a lot of money, spend it. If you've got a dead horse, beat it. If you have none of the above, rely on your own creativity and your own cheap, clever PR ideas. Your reach is increasing with the spread of the Internet. You are no longer limited to buttons, posters, flyers, mailings, bear costumes, bribes or strippers.

Everyone has access to the same lists. Make sure you do too. Get the distribution directories and blanket the town with your clever, colorful, irresistible invitations. If you've got great review quotes already, use them.

Did you recommend hiring a publicist?

Your film is fantastic, you say? Nobody's going to believe you. You're hardly in a position to be objective. That's why publicists exist. Anybody can be your "publicist" as long as it's not you. Publicists are expensive and you will never feel that their results are sufficient, but sometimes you can't afford not to hire them. You spent all that money making the film, so why not burn some more cash with a PR machine? Of course, talk them down in price first, just like you did with your vendors when making the film. Get people talking about your film any way you can, short of committing really serious crimes.

Be sure to canvass the local media outlets in the city hosting the festival. They are faced with covering dozens or hundreds of films and you want yours to be one of those chosen. Your timely letter or phone call may be what brings your film to the top of the pile. Contact them on the pretext of alerting them to you or your stars' availability for interviews. Journalists are often grateful for your call. You aren't bothering them. It's their job to write about this event and you are there to help.

How important was your website in promoting your film?

Every film needs a website. This *is* the 21st century, in case you haven't noticed. The sooner you get your site up, the sooner the search-engine spiders will list it. Once you build it, the site virtually maintains itself, aside from general updates. It should be the one-stop shop for everything anybody could possibly want to know about your film. Post all your press kit information, including high-resolution color photos that a reviewer can download in a pinch. Make the site lively and entertaining, make it stand out from the competition.

Does having an unusual doc at a film festival give you an advantage over filmmakers making narrative movies?

Documentaries are addicting. I had never planned to make documentaries, but I was presented with an opportunity and I'm glad I took it because it was a blast. Unlike a scripted feature that never quite lives up to the extent of your imagination, a documentary takes you on a journey where the story continually evolves. You may not know your ending until you get there. The process is exhilarating—but not necessarily lucrative. If you set out to make a doc, you're embarking on an endeavor that historically has not lead to large box office grosses.

Distributors are scared of the "D" word because audiences are scared. Audiences just don't show up in the same numbers, the idiots. But thanks to reality-based programming, they seem to be learning how superior documentary entertainment can be. Lazy idiots are more willing to click a button to see your documentary than they are to drag a date miles and miles to a theater to see it. The good news is that domestic and foreign television markets have a huge appetite for documentary programming.

Did you have to employ different strategies when selling your doc?

Consider the strengths of your project when selling it. Is the subject matter going to be interesting to a wide audience? If you don't pick a subject with some kind of commercial appeal, you're not going to get paid for the next year of work, and you better understand that you may be making a glorified home-movie—which is fine, if that's your goal.

Your strongest selling point (if your documentary is not about a star like Madonna or Muhammad Ali) will be the story. A documentary needs a story just as much as a narrative film does. *Hoop Dreams* is terrific because the story is so engrossing. You need a set-up, rising action, and an ending. Many have built in endings like: the verdict (*Brother's Keeper*); will the protagonist find who he's searching for (*Roger and Me*); who will win the big game (*Hoop Dreams*). Your film's subjects and their engrossing story will be your strongest selling point.

Making a documentary is so much work, you must choose a subject you really like. One that will amuse, inspire, and engage you. Your film won't inspire anybody else if it doesn't inspire you first. Keep the length manageable and keep it moving. Don't lose sight of the fact that a successful documentary entertains. A documentary that is all "message" is propaganda. Not even your mom is going to sit through that garbage.

How do you find a distributor supportive of documentary films?

Know your market. Who are you planning to sell this film to? Have they purchased similar product in the past? Were they successful? Classy? Did they pay the filmmakers? Get references and call them. Certain companies handle documentaries, and only a few do it well. A big studio simply can't think in terms of anything less than 800 screens—and *that's* low budget. Discover the right companies first.

What is the most important thing for a documentary filmmaker to keep in mind when negotiating a deal?

Dealmaking for documentaries is the same as it is for narratives, except for one primary difference: distributors want to pay you much less.

Keep in mind that that your goal is to get as much money up front as possible, and any product is only worth as much as two people are willing to pay for it. Try to get simultaneous, multiple interest. Always counter-offer; nobody offers the best price first. In fact, they'll feel badly if you don't counter-offer. They'll assume they paid too much and be pissed about it. They'll actually be happier if you don't make it too easy.

Have an exhaustive list of deal points that you need to cover. You can't remember everything. Don't forget to hit the foreign sales companies; that cash flow can save you.

> **.....**
> **"Dealmaking for documentaries is the same as it is for narratives, except for one primary difference: distributors want to pay you much less."**
> **.....**

If you are fortunate to have a film rep interested in your documentary, keep in mind that, to be effective, a salesman has to believe in his product. Don't sign with just anybody. Talk to a few people. If someone is blown away by your film, they will push harder and persevere longer than someone who is lukewarm. You will be able to sense the enthusiasm.

Try for the advance, but be aware that it's the rare documentary that gets one. Many distributors will want you to give them your film for free, in exchange for a share of the back-end profits. You can kiss your back-end good-bye at this stage and hope the attention you get from the film's release will make up for the lack of financial return. If this is all you can get, it's better than nothing. You made your film to be seen, right?

....

Roger Nygard's *Six Days in Roswell*, has toured over fifteen film festivals including Hawaii, Ft. Lauderdale and São Paulo, and was recently released on DVD. Roger maintains a site with information about all of his movies at www.rogernygard.com.

MARK OSBORNE,
Short Filmmaker with
a Feature Debut

Mark Osborne attended Pratt
Institute where he studied film. He
quickly discovered a passion for animation and transferred to CalArts
where he was enrolled in the experimental Animation program from 1990-
92. After graduating, he finished his first
animated film, *Greener,* and went on to work
for five years in TV graphics, winning several
awards. His career took off when he co-directed an

*Filmmaker
Mark Osborne*

animated *Jurassic Park* spoof for "Weird Al" Yankovic, which
earned him a Grammy nomination for Best Music Video. Mark's
second animated effort, *More,* garnered him an Academy Award®
nomination for Best Animated Short Film in 1998 and Best Short at
the Sundance Film Festival in 1999, as well as a dozen other prizes.
From the success of his short, Mark sought to make his mark as a
feature director. His feature debut, *Dropping Out,* is a live action
dark comedy penned by and starring his brother, Kent Osborne.
The story involves a man so bored with life, he decides to commit
suicide. A group of underground filmmakers decide to document
his journey into the abyss of death when a studio actually gives
them funding to make a big-budget version of the story. The result
is a brilliant, satiric look at the worlds of independent filmmaking
and Hollywood. Since *Dropping Out*'s premiere at Sundance 2000,
Mark and Kent have toured the festival circuit seeking distribution.

*How does a filmmaker make the transition from a successful short to a fea-
ture film?*

When I made *More* it was a very stressful and difficult process. What
began as a 35mm short became a 70mm/15perf (IMAX format)

film due to an opportunity presented to me by a couple of friends that I couldn't pass up. We all decided the film would be appropriate for the screen and it was exciting because no one had really done a complete stop-motion film in the large format. Production was on a shoestring budget and riddled with technical problems as we were flying by the seat of our collective pants. We were using borrowed equipment from some amazingly generous large format companies, such as Graphic Films and Imagica USA. The idea came from the New Order song *Elegia*. It became the score of the film mainly because I had derived the structure and all of the visuals from listening to it over and over. We shot *More* using one camera for fifteen weeks to create enough footage for a six minute film. I was pretty happy a year later to make close to a two hour film in only four weeks of shooting.

Dropping Out has been a long and hard road and it feels like we have been trying to make it forever. Kent wrote the script five years before production began, and it seemed like we would never get funding. It wasn't until my Academy Award® nomination, and Kent's considerable popularity as a television host of TBS's *The Movie Lounge*, that we had enough momentum to get the financing. As far as production goes, I guess we did a very unorthodox thing. We made a small independent film on the scale of a small studio film. We wanted as high production value as possible and our producers had amazing connections to get us stuff that we never dreamed we would have access to. This allowed for some very un-independent film type things, like clearing actual TV clips that were much needed for the saturated media theme.

Your short and your feature both made it into Sundance. Most filmmakers have difficulty getting one movie into Sundance, much less two. How did you go about getting accepted by Sundance twice?

When it came to getting the attention of Sundance, I got really lucky with *More*. Our premiere was in the Los Angeles IMAX theater and we got a great half page article with a picture in the *Los Angeles Times* about the short. I couldn't help but think that this helped us get noticed by Sundance. I think my acceptance call came a few days after that. I had sent a few cool invites to the premiere of *More* to the Sundance office, but I don't think they got farther than the receptionist's circular file.

Getting *Dropping Out* some visibility was a little trickier because we were one of several hundred entries without any major stars or studio backing to help the Sundance officials decide. Since I had won best short with *More,* I guess that made me a little more noticeable in the pile, but we felt we needed an edge. I realized too late that I had missed the grand opportunity to kiss a lot of ass after winning the prize the year before. I just got too busy making *Dropping Out* and figured the Sundance folks would rather I make a movie instead of hang around the offices. I did write a letter at one point describing in detail all of the effects and fixes that would be in the final print. (I was submitting updates of my Avid cut to them weekly).

How did you find out you were in?

For *More,* my wife got a call from Trevor Groth, the short film coordinator at Sundance, asking if I had a 35mm print. She then called me and I spent a few minutes wondering what that meant before realizing that this was pretty serious, they wouldn't ask this question to a rejected film.

For *Dropping Out,* I actually was waiting and waiting and after Thanksgiving I gave up hope. My *More* call came early, so I figured that no call yet was a bad sign. On Friday I got a casual congratulatory message from Trevor, who said, "Congrats. See you in Park City." I flipped out and waited until Sunday and tried calling the office. I finally got through and someone official in programming got on the phone and said "Oh . . . congratulations!" It turned out they had gotten so behind and bogged down that some calls hadn't gone out. I was excited and terrified at the same time. A lot of work needed to be done to get ready and in the case of *Dropping Out,* we had to finish the final film print. Both times I didn't know what to expect, so I spent a few weeks giving myself ulcers and generally freaking out.

Were you concerned about applying to other festivals before you got word from Sundance?

I really didn't apply anywhere else since Sundance was a major target from the outset for both projects. Sundance was the first application for both films and luckily, I got in each time. You always want to save your premiere for a significant festival, if you can. Most fests want to discover someone and they love to premiere films on some level even if it's a regional premiere. Sundance was the first I applied to for both films. Next was SXSW, the USA Film Festival, Cannes, Berlin, Gen Art and of course Aspen Shortsfest for *More*. Almost all of my decisions were based on your first film festival book, which my wife bought me. There are so many festivals and it's such a crapshoot—you really have to do your research.

How did you prepare for your first Sundance screening?

For *More* I actually missed the first two screenings since I didn't go for the whole ten days. I didn't know what to expect so I didn't plan too much hype for my screenings at all. I discovered while at Sundance what it was all about and found that you really have to rise above all of the hundreds of films to get any attention at all. We did make flyers and hats and that seemed to help us get associated with our film once people saw it.

> .....
> "i discovered while at Sundance what it was all about and found that you really have to rise above all of the hundreds of films to get any attention at all."
> .....

For *Dropping Out*, our first screening was scheduled on day seven of the festival and it was way down in Salt Lake City. This was hardly ideal and seemed to be the least desirable slot in the whole fest. We planned to hype all week leading up to our screening, but no one really cared about our film until the premiere was close at hand. Our publicist had a hard time getting anyone to give a crap about a film that wasn't the news of the moment. It stunk because by the time we premiered some papers were already printing their "wrap-up" articles . . . and we hadn't even shown yet! We got great reviews but by the time they were printed, it was a little late to get noticed.

What did you do to hype your film at Sundance?

For *Dropping Out*, we had the typical hats, posters, flyers and throngs of people walking the streets to create some visibility. I knew early on that I wanted to capitalize on the fact that I had won best short film the year before with *More*. So I premiered *More* on the web at IFILM.com and tried to get some attention in Park City that way. It worked for the most part, as it seemed that most people knew that *Dropping Out* was by the guy who made *More*. IFILM® was cool enough to make postcards for me and they were all over town too. On day five I handed someone a postcard and they said, "Oh, I heard this was great," and since we hadn't screened yet, I figured we had some buzz somewhere, somehow.

The web is a great tool for hype, but you really have to be smart and unique in what you do there. Don't assume that posters will get the word out because they get torn down or covered in minutes. Plan something clever that refers in some way to your film and then be relentless with it. Kent wanted to ski nude and since no one had done that yet, it seemed like a good idea. We then realized that it didn't relate to our film too much, so he kept his clothes on.

Did you hire a publicist?

We had a publicist for *More*, because we felt that was important, but boy were we wrong. They got a big, fat, free trip—and we got a smattering of mentions, but no real press. I think for shorts, it's pretty silly to have one. In retrospect, I wouldn't have had one at that point. This was in 1999 before the whole dot-com frenzy, so no one cared too much about shorts. In 2000, it was much different and shorts were all the rage.

We did hire a publicist for *Dropping Out,* but it was an uphill battle to get any buzz since our premiere was so late in the fest. Our publicist had lots of other films to tend to also, which wasn't the best situation. He was busy elsewhere until it was time for our moment. Then, it really felt as though it was too late to get noticed. It was a very strange situation.

What would you have done differently in preparing for your film's debut?

I think I would have organized a stunt or some sort of really flashy move early in the week. We toyed with so many ideas that weren't very feasible given the fact that we were broke and really overwhelmed by the whole thing. I guess I would have tried to have more fun. I spent a lot of energy trying to get noticed and it was quite fruitless because my film was so far off from opening weekend, Sundance is all about what's hot and right at that moment.

> .....
> **"I guess I would have tried to have more fun."**
> .....

Were you nervous at the screening and if so, how did you deal with it?

I was terrified. At the first *More* screening I attended, my publicist told me to talk for two minutes or so. I prepared a horribly detailed speech about my film's original IMAX format and blah, blah, blah . . . . After I spoke and before announcing the feature, Sundance's John Cooper said, "Thanks, Professor," and the audience erupted with laughter. It was pretty funny, but I later learned that most feature directors got up there and said stuff like, "Thanks for coming," and sit down. My advice, keep it simple.

For our *Dropping Out* premiere, we had as many people there as possible. I think about twenty-five crew and friends were there and that made it really feel special and relaxed. We had done some local radio in Salt Lake that morning and that seemed to help the turnout. We were blown away that we had the longest wait list lines of any film that was in Salt Lake, about 300 people showed up without tickets, and everyone got in. It was amazing.

What did you learn from that first screening?

Well, for *Dropping Out* we learned a lot about our film since it was our first audience screening ever. We were thrilled at the stuff that worked, we were freaked out at the stuff that somehow didn't work and we were relieved that some of the bolder, riskier stuff we had done was appreciated. One thing we learned, always bring goodies, especially to your premiere. Throwing out buttons or T-shirts or anything is a big hit, no matter how cool the festival-goers are.

How did that first Q&A go at Sundance?

It was really great, we had two theaters full of people all crammed into one for the questions. They were really thrilled because we had made it clear that they were the first audience ever to see the film. They were very happy and eager to get some inside scoop and see our reactions to their reactions. They asked things like, "How did you get the clip of *CHiPS* and *Punky Brewster*?" Audiences love practical info. "What did the squirrel and the mayonnaise mean?" We had some bizarre imagery that threw some people off, but it was always fun to answer. And my favorite question of all time, "How did you find your lead actor? He was perfect for the part." He's my brother! I found him in my parent's house when we were little.

The worst thing that can happen in Q&As is the audience can pick apart holes in the plot or something like that. We didn't have any of that. Sometimes, audiences can be pretty harsh so, be prepared for that.

The Gen Art film festival in NYC was undoubtedly the worst of all. Right before the screening they announced that the first 100 people to leave the theater would get a free bus ride with beer to the after film party. Well, needless to say, only about thirty people stayed for the Q&A. Even my Mom tried to get on that bus. It was pretty depressing.

What did you do to get acquisition executives into your screenings?
For *Dropping Out* we sent a bunch of execs T-shirts and invites that we'd stuffed into mayonnaise jars (sounds weird, but it does tie in with the film). We had our agents calling the distribution folks to make sure they knew where and when we were playing.

It was pretty tough to get through to them so we really were praying for reviews to get printed or for any kind of press. Word of mouth was useless because we were so late in the week.

More *has appeared in short film compilations on DVD and is downloadable on IFILM.com. How did you negotiate those deals?*
My *More* deals were—sadly—all negotiated by myself. I now have a lawyer to do it, and I highly recommend one. The deals can be tricky and will hardly ever be in your favor. Remember, everything is negotiable. The first offer is never a good one, they will always lowball you. *More* deals were actually few and far between. Even after the Academy Award® nomination, it was hard to squeeze some cash out of that film. DVD compilations are popular and Internet money is scarce, but you'll find it if you are careful and persistent. My advice is hold on to as many of your rights as possible. Don't give anyone an exclusive deal unless they really pay for it. Split up the rights carefully and maximize on all platforms.

Be careful of the Internet and be wary of promises from anyone. Some companies try to act like friends when they are trying to steal your babies. You have to value your work and make sure that you

> .....
> **"The deals can be tricky and will hardly ever be in your favor. Remember, everything is negotiable."**
> .....

are doing the best thing for it. Don't expect too much money and never give your rights away for free. *More* was courted by several websites, which accidentally started an awkward bidding war. Try to find a site you really like and then pursue the best deal you can. And you don't have to go to the web right away. Actually, having your film on the web sours some potential TV deals and makes some festivals feel like second fiddle.

Some short filmmakers feel as if their films are being exploited. Where do you stand on this?

The Yahoo Internet Life Festival for shorts was the worst. Yahoo used all of the filmmakers' movies for online audience voting and we basically created the content for their site for a couple of months. When all was said and done they gave a few prizes—but oddly, no Internet voting prizes. They actually promised far more prizes than they actually gave away, then they acted like they did the filmmakers a favor by exploiting us. The festival turned into a giant dot-com boasting contest with a huge market of website companies, half of which weren't even launched yet.

Can you describe your whirlwind film festival tour?

If your film turns out good and you start getting into festivals, drop everything and make yourself as available as possible. Some fests will pay your way, and some will treat you pretty well. Try to make yourself as visible as possible throughout your tour, because that will help your career in the long run. You will find a lot of the same filmmakers on the circuit too, so, make friends, be nice and don't get too drunk. The hardest thing, I think, is seeing some of the same films over and over, but you have to do it, even for the ones you don't like so much. It's a crazy time. Write down numbers and take notes about the people you meet. You never know who's going be what in the years to come.

What were some of your best festival experiences?

Aspen Shorts Fest and American Short Shorts in Japan are neck and neck in my book for first place for short film festival. They both really treat filmmakers. ASS Fest (as we all called it) was great at helping us all have a good time in Tokyo. They organized fun tour outings and they really took care of us, giving us native tour guides and translators to help.

For features, so far, the best time would have to be SXSW. Austin is a great town. It was a blast and everyone was so nice. It's a smaller festival, but we really felt like an important part of the whole thing. We did a couple of panels, including a case study on how we made *Dropping Out* and that was really cool. The trade show and the panels were all really cool and they managed to get a really impressive group of people to come out and support the fest.

What is the most important thing you've learned having screened your films at so many festivals?

Film festivals are a total crapshoot. Don't get too excited about the prizes you win and don't get too devastated if you don't get into a target festival. It is random at times and you never really know what is going on behind the scenes. I have won top prizes at some and not even gotten past the first round of screeners at others. Send your film off and don't even think about it again. If it's the day that they said they would notify the filmmakers about acceptance and you are rushing to the mailbox, forget it. Most festivals call, fax or email you ahead of time to make sure you want to participate. Don't put too much emphasis on getting into any of these festivals because you never really know what goes on, and the film is most important thing after all.

Mark Osborne's short film *More* has played over sixty festivals and won twenty major awards. Mark's follow-up feature *Dropping Out* has played more than ten major festivals including Sundance and SXSW. Despite very positive feedback from audiences, the feature remains undistributed. Mark is hopeful that a recent re-edit of *Dropping Out* will attract distributor interest. Mark maintains a website about his film: www.droppingout.com.

JOAL RYAN,
Writer/Director

For each success story of film-makers like Darren Kronofsky, Richard Linklater and Robert Rodriguez, there are hundreds, perhaps thousands of failures. Unfortunately, while the press heaps attention on the chosen ones, the losers, the filmmakers who didn't quite make it, are left with nothing but hard lessons—learned most often in the form of a mountain of credit card debt, an unsold film and worse, an unfulfilled dream. Regrettably, these lessons are rarely passed on to those who could really use the information—first-time filmmakers ready to make their movie and enter the festival meat grinder. One such tale of woe is that of Joal Ryan.

Joal Ryan is a journalist-turned-filmmaker. Her debut indie feature, *Former Child Star,* failed to get into Sundance, Slamdance or Slumdance or Slamdunk, failed to get much good press, failed to launch her film career or get her the elusive three-picture deal; the movie itself failed to sell.

Showing tremendous vulnerability, Ryan documents every single mistake she made along the way. She details, with refreshing honesty and a rare flair for the truth, the trials and tribulations of making her first indie feature.

How did you begin the process of making your film?
I put an ad in *Drama-Logue,* the Los Angeles casting magazine. *Former Child Star* was, more or less, official. I was going to make a movie—a real one, with film and everything.

I was twenty-eight. A journalist. A film buff with no "official" film background. A magazine subscriber with one too many clipped-out articles about Kevin Smith. Inspired by the do-your-own-movie movement, I'd shot a 67-minute flick on Hi-8 video the year before called *How to Make a Generation X Movie*. And that project was how I came to be making a real movie.

Some quick back story on *How to Make a Generation X Movie*—the video thing. I wrote, I directed, I cast my friends. Amateur hour? Maybe. But we approached it professionally. A month of rehearsals. I even scribbled out a couple of storyboards before I (a) got bored and (b) realized I had little talent for storyboards.

In the end, Filmmakers United, a screening series in Los Angeles, invited us to show the flick in Hollywood. A very nice gesture that turned out pretty badly. The screening was a disaster. The audience just kind of looked at it—as opposed to, you know, laughing. (It was a comedy. Or, it was supposed to be.)

And then there was the review. The bad one. The very best the old *L.A. Village View* could say was that it was "coherent." That was it. "Coherent."

How did you handle the bad press?

That word—"coherent"—became my albatross. I could do better than "coherent," couldn't I? Why, sure I could! I could make a *great* "coherent" movie. Write a better script. Extend my casting net. Get more input. Shoot on film. And, yes, spend more money. *Much* more money.

So, that was how I got to *Former Child Star*.

The story for that thing was something I'd kicked around for a while: What would happen if someone you grew up watching on TV suddenly burst into your life—became a living, breathing character in your own personal drama? Sounds kind of deep. And it probably could have been. Except when I was writing, I was studying Woody Allen's *Bananas*. I thought my video movie had been too slow, too boring. I wanted peppy, fast, funny. So, I dissected *Bananas* scene by scene and wrote a farce. Except I didn't write farcical characters. Or farcical situations. (This, I would learn later. About two years later, while squirming in my seat and watching the final product with a silent, mummified audience.)

So, fine, we had a script. The actors—a strong bunch, I still think—came mostly through *Drama-Logue* (and our subsequent auditions). The locations? My apartment and a bunch of other friends' apartments. (Yes, terribly imaginative. And, as it turned out, terribly uncinematic.) The camera? Hired a camera guy who owned his own CP-16. (Thought about renting a camera and trying to shoot the thing myself, but insurance costs made that idea impossible.) The sound? Hired a sound guy who owned his own Nagra. If it sounds like I hired a lot of people, I did. Too many. There were four paid crew members, in all, I think. Ultra-cheapo, to be sure. But still too many.

Former Child Star taught me the great lesson of self-financed independent filmmaking: Don't.

Rant all you want about what a great learning experience making an ultra-indie movie is. Sooner rather than later, that deluded line leaves you with a wallet full of maxed-out credit cards. The artistic reality of moviemaking is that if your idea, script, cast and commitment is strong enough, you'll find funding. Maybe not as much as you want, but you'll find something. The economic reality of moviemaking is that it's an expensive hobby. And a hobby is exactly what it remains until you get someone to offer you so much as a nickel for the reels.

This was your first mistake?

Moviemaking is not novel writing. You can tap away in your attic for a year on the "Next Great Event in Fiction," produce an unreadable mass of pages and not endanger your future ability to, say, buy a can of tuna fish.

But moviemaking? The second you start rolling is the second you start losing money. The only way to stay ahead of the game is to *spend as little as possible.*

Before hindsight set in, I was seduced. I was convinced I could shoot a feature-length 16mm movie in color, with sound, for about $5,000-7,000. (I'd spent $5,000 on the video project. Also way too much but I considered it to be an "acceptable" loss.)

I probably could have pulled it off, if I'd slowed down and done my homework. Ingratiated myself to techies. (I didn't know any.) Enrolled in a class on how to operate a camera. Enrolled in a class on how to edit the old-fashioned way—by hand, with film. And, hey, genius, how about this one? Decided to shoot in *black and white.*

Where did you end up getting the money?

I talked up my movie idea to my father and—bingo!—that's where our money came from. He enthusiastically bankrolled *Former Child Star.*

Bad, *bad* idea.

Not on his part. (Hey, he's my father; he thinks he's investing in genius.) On my part.

Beg, borrow, steal, but do not—Do Not—let your parents subsidize your artistic whims. It'll save you the trouble of developing a taste for Pepto-Bismol and a springing a guilty head of gray hair.

Anyway, I told my father we could shoot and do a video edit for about $10,000. He ended up being in for $19,000. Not counting the $3,000-plus I spent on processing, food and assorted sundries. That's $22,000-plus on a film—without even getting to the print stage. What can I say? Shameful. Embarrassing. Stupid.

Surely an ultra low budget film will have flaws an audience will look past?

The thing you learn quick enough—even on the festival circuit—is that a $22,000 movie gets no extra credit for being a $22,000 movie. Maybe it did once, but certainly not today. You compete against the big boys and the semi-big boys. If you're not good enough, you're not good enough and your film ain't going nowhere—and you, loser, are out $22,000.

Did you apply to Sundance?

Okay, so I'm either a defeatist or a realist, but I knew *Former Child Star* wasn't getting into Sundance. Not a chance. Three reasons:

(1) In the mistaken belief that the Independent Feature Film Market (IFFM) was the place to take a brand-spanking new movie, we screened at the event in September 1996. (To give you an idea about how naïve I was—I remember nervously awaiting word on whether we'd been "accepted" to the IFFM. And then to compound naïveté with stupidity, I remember thinking that we'd "achieved" something by being "accepted." Then I got to New York and realized that quality control amounted to conferring with the bank to see if the check cleared. The IFFM is a must-*see* for an aspiring indie filmmaker; it's not necessarily a must-*screen*.)

Anyway, back to our IFFM screening. People from Sundance attended. From Slamdance, too. And the Chicago Underground.

And probably a half-dozen other festivals. Nobody from these out-fits contacted me after the screening. In this case, silence meant a big, fat, loud "No."

(2) I didn't do my homework. Again. Going into the IFFM, I did little to aid my cause. Sure, I hyped our screening time to as many studio and festival types as I could. But a press release and a phone call is not enough. I showed up in New York with a fresh-from-the-lab print. Nobody *really* knew me. Nobody knew my film. Nobody cared. Sure, it would have helped if the fresh-from-the-lab print featured something akin to *Citizen Kane: 1996*, but it also would have helped if I'd worked the festival circuit like Sarah Jacobson, whom I met at IFFM that year.

Jacobson had made a short, *I Was a Teen-age Serial Killer,* in the early 1990s. She screened it everywhere, she pushed it relentlessly. She made people care about her passion for film. When she showed up at IFFM with her first feature, *Mary Jane's Not a Virgin Anymore,* she was ready to make people care about that project, too. And they did. A couple months later, Sarah got accepted into Sundance. That was not luck; that was hard work.

(3) My film wasn't very good. Just another waste of celluloid and money in the post-*Clerks* world of wannabe filmmakers. At least that was my review.

So why did you bother applying to Sundance?

Again, three reasons:

(1) Like I said before, filmmaking is expensive. You've got to do everything you can to protect and preserve your investment, includ-ing lying. ("It's a comedy. Really funny!") The results can be embar-rassing when someone actually screens the thing and tells you, "It's a mess. Really sucky!," but consider that part of your penance.

(2) Art is subjective. Who knows? Maybe the Sundance guy will actually like the thing. It's not your job to tell him he won't like it. (See the bit about lying in the item above.)

(3) Like the lottery, you can't win if you don't play. Sundance is the mother of all film festivals—you *must* apply. Especially if your father, who paid for the movie, tells you to.

So, anyway, in the fall of 1996, I did what 800 other filmmakers did and mailed off our movie, our press kit and a fifty dollar check. (Why Sundance needs fifty dollars to reject a film its advance team already essentially rejected at the IFFM, I don't know. "To make money," would be my first guess.)

What other festivals did you apply to?

That fall and subsequent winter I also applied to: Toronto, SXSW, Film Fest New Haven, San Francisco, New York Underground, Los Angeles Indie, Portland, Taos Talking Picture, New York's Gen Art, Hudson Valley, Laguna Beach and Florida.

Most required entry fees—from twenty five to forty dollars, usually. All of which I wrote. Stupidly so.

Not having yet learned my lesson from IFFM, I failed to realize that unless a festival scout contacts you first, the chance of your unsolicited tape working its way out of the slush pile and into the acceptance pile is minimal. That's not an indictment of festivals; that's reality.

How do you get a festival's attention?

Think about how the screenplay business works. Do you send your hot, new script directly to Warner Bros.? Or do you send it first to an agent, who, if he likes, can get the ear of Warner Bros. on your behalf? You send it to an agent, of course. He's your "in." That's what you're looking for at film festivals.

Before you get to the check-writing, application stage, what you want to do is get your movie before the eyes of festival types. Maybe you do it at IFFM. Maybe you do it at a local fest that takes all comers. Maybe you do it at a private screening on your Moviola. Whatever. Just get them to watch. If they like, they'll let you know. They won't tell you you're a lock. But they'll suggest you apply. That's something; that's one person on your side. You might even get your entry-fee waived.

What festivals accepted your film?

Of all the festivals I listed above, only Los Angeles Indie contacted me first. The program director called. Somebody had listed *Former Child Star* on a list of should-sees. I didn't get in, but at least I knew I had a chance. (I also ended up getting invited—and accepted—to the USA Film Festival in Dallas and the Chattanooga Film Festival in, yes, Chattanooga.)

Anyway, the rejection from Sundance came via the post office. Sundance was classy enough to send a "Dear Filmmaker" letter. It arrived a couple days *after* the lineup was released in the trades, but still . . . the other festivals I entered didn't bother to call, write or e-mail. About the best their organizations did was send a sales brochure hyping their events, i.e., the slates of movies that got picked instead of mine. (Not that it's a bad idea to go to a festival where you're just an observer. In fact, it's a great idea. I need to do it more—to see what my peers are up to, to gauge the market, and above all, to learn—maybe even steal a couple tricks.)

How did you handle all the rejections?

Since Sundance never even seemed as real as a pipe dream, I wasn't exactly crushed when the rejection letter arrived. It was more like, "Next." I didn't wait for Sundance. I didn't expect Sundance. I didn't get Sundance. Fine. Next. Time to move on.

Actually, I'd begun to move on even before that. In early November 1996, I sent a video copy of *Former Child Star* to this little thing in Cleveland that promised to show *anything*. No fee, no standards, no problem. The Off-Hollywood Flick Fest. My kind of crowd.

Was I worried about blowing my Sundance virginity by hosting my world premiere in Cleveland—two months *before* Park City? No. Remember: (a) there wasn't a chance I was getting in; and, (b) if by divine act of God or mislabeling I *did* get in—what was Robert Redford going to do? Shoot me? Yell at me? *"You screened at the Off-Hollywood Flick Fest?!?! Infidel!!"* The way I figured, Sundance wouldn't boot me from its shindig. Maybe it would move me out of the competition wing, but it probably would still screen me. And that's all you want. To play Park City in January . . . needless to say, it was a potential problem that I spent a nanosecond worrying about.

Where did you go at this point?

After Cleveland, after the no-go with Sundance, I pursued the one solid lead I got out of the IFFM: the USA Film Fest. The program director, Alonso Duralde, saw *Former Child Star* in New York and suggested I submit. The festival didn't actually solicit features—its entry form is for short subjects—but Duralde was willing to consider *Former Child Star*. Sounded good to me. I submitted, he considered; a couple months later, he said okay. We were going to our first "real" film festival.

What did you do to build hype for your film?

It was early 1997. Pauly Shore was in a new sitcom and the reviews weren't great. But instead of cracking a joke, turning the page and looking for somebody else to make fun of (like usual), I stopped and considered the case of Pauly Shore.

The guy's never been a critical darling or a mass-audience favorite. And yet . . . he keeps working. The world tells him he's not funny; he says he is—and keeps working. He does what he does, figuring that someone, somewhere, will, and does, like his work.

An empowering notion.

If Pauly Shore got rejected by Sundance, I thought, would he fold and file *Bio-Dome* away on a shelf? Ha! My man Pauly would keep sellin' it. Keep sellin' himself. And why not? No one has the right to tell you you're lousy. Except yourself.

So, with my new Power of Positive Pauly Shore Thinking in place, I decided to hype the one sure-fire angle of *Former Child Star*—the former child star angle.

If you grew up watching TV, you care about former child stars. You can't help but wonder what happened to Willis on *Diff'rent Strokes* or Natalie on *The Facts of Life*. These actors are our virtual peers. We wonder about their post-TV lives, like we wonder about the post-high school lives of old classmates.

That was my audience. That was my cause.

This was my platform: Former Child Star-Palooza. An e-zine. An e-mail newsletter designed to shamelessly hype the movie. And designed to provide real information on real former child stars—career updates, tabloid news, first-person sightings.

In February 1997, I sent out my first issue. I compiled a list of seventy-five e-mail addresses—mostly film companies, friends and film festivals. By the second issue, readership doubled. (It's now steadied at about 2,000 a month.)

The e-zine helped you get mainstream press?

Sure. Pretty soon, I was being interviewed by the *Boston Phoenix*. Getting invites to film festivals (Wine Country, Northampton,

Cinequest and Las Vegas, none of which I ended up getting into—but, hey, at least they were waiving the entrance fees now).

By summer, the e-zine and subsequent website had been blurbed in *Newsweek, Wired* and *Entertainment Weekly.* The e-zine took on a life of its own. It immediately found greater acclaim and acceptance than the film. In turn, it kept the film alive. It gave the film mystery. ("So, what's this *Former Child Star* we keep reading about?") It gave the film relevancy.

It *didn't* help the film get any press at our big-time film festival screening, but nothing's perfect.

How did you handle that first festival screening?

When we got into the USA Film Festival, some extra hype—beyond the e-zine—was required. Unfortunately, all I had was me. I know you're supposed to call in favors to get stuff like this done right, but I was lousy at asking for freebies. Really, you should be required to take a personality test before making an indie film. (Flunking out in the chutzpah department would have saved me thousands of dollars.)

So, anyway, I sat down, typed up a press release, attached it to our press kit and mailed the whole batch off to Dallas media, newspapers, weeklies, even a couple radio and TV stations. I followed up with regular faxes and phone calls. Even got a couple people on the phone. All very nice. All very noncommittal. No one asked for a screener. (Bad sign.) And, in the end, no one reviewed or mentioned *Former Child Star.* I mean *no one.* A couple months after the festival (we were there in April 1997), the program director sent me a round-up of clippings on the festival. Maybe twenty to thirty articles. I went through every single one. Not one word—bad or good—about *Former Child Star* in any of them. A complete swing and miss.

.....
"The festival paid for my airline ticket (cool!), paid for my hotel room (double cool!) and inexplicably treated me like a real filmmaker . . . I even got asked to sign an autograph."
.....

That said, the experience in Dallas was the highlight (so far) of the *Former Child Star* grind. The festival paid for my airline ticket (cool!), paid for my hotel room (double cool!) and inexplicably treated me like a real filmmaker. I got invited to a reception honoring me . . . and Liza Minnelli. (I showed; she didn't.) I even got asked to sign an autograph.

Nothing like a little adulation to keep you going. And that's all I was looking for, really. Again, I had no illusions about the USA Fest. It's not Sundance, Slamdance or SXSW. Agents and studio execs don't roam the theaters with cell phones and checkbooks. It's a local festival hosted and enjoyed by the locals. The focus in the press is not "$20,000 movies by out-of-town nobodies," but rather Hollywood movies *(Volcano, Traveller)* by Hollywood types. It's Dallas' chance to rub elbows with Tommy Lee Jones, Bill Paxton and Molly Ringwald (a few of the names there that year).

> .....
> "And then I thanked people profusely for not throwing stuff. At me. Or the screen. All in all, a pretty good night. To date, it's the best festival night I've had. Also, the only one."
> .....

Dallas didn't make me a media darling, but it gave me something more important: The belief that there's an audience for every movie.

Somewhere, somebody is testifying to what a fabulous character drama *Lost in Space* is. And, yes, somewhere, somebody is attesting to what a brilliant comedy *Former Child Star* is. I don't necessarily want to meet these somebodies, but it is nice to know they exist.

Dallas was where I learned this. As much as I paced and ducked out of the theater in anticipation of the "bad" parts, the movie did okay. Aesthetically, the print never looked or sounded better. (Much better than the tin-eared closet we screened in at the IFFM.) And artistically, the film was genuinely liked. They laughed, they applauded, they stayed for the Q&A.

How did the Q&A go?

The Q&A was a breeze. In my case, again, the stakes were low. I didn't have Mike Ovitz to win over. I merely had to be nice to an auditorium of nice people who liked my movie.

I told the requisite "funny-things-that-happened-while-we-made-the-movie stories" (#1: How we caused a police incident during the filming of a robbery scene because—rim shot, please!—bystanders thought a real hold-up was in progress; #2: How I unsuccessfully sought out real former child stars to appear in cameos; #3: How I successfully recruited real former child star Rodney Allen Rippy, who starred in TV commercials for Jack in the Box in the 1970s, to do a cameo.)

I stammered when a person asked the inevitable "So, how much did it cost?" (FYI: No one is shy about pumping you for info on that one, so don't get offended.) Anyway, I mumbled an answer—afraid if anybody heard me correctly, they'd charge right back: "You spent *how much*?!? . . . and it looks like *that*!?!"

And then I thanked people profusely for not throwing stuff. At me. Or the screen. All in all, a pretty good night. To date, it's the best festival night I've had. Also, the only one.

.....

"Film people want to see good films. They want to hear good stories. You got that, you're in."

.....

We've had theatrical screenings in New York, Las Vegas, San Francisco and Los Angeles (as the midnight show for a couple weekends at a local theater), but as far as festivals go, Dallas was the ballgame to date.

Sure, there were Cleveland and Chattanooga, but they didn't pay for my trip and I couldn't afford to go on my own. (Also, I lacked that chutzpah thing necessary to finagle myself free airfare, á la a scene from a Jennifer Aniston film.)

The organizers of those two fests weren't mad about my planned absences; they said they weren't anyway. I can't say for sure now. They never took any of my follow-up phone calls.

What did you feel you've learned from the experience?

Look, I was nobody—nobody—and people at film festivals and studios still took the time to watch my flick, to take my calls. Did everybody like what they saw? No. But I learned the access *is* there. Film people want to see good films. They want to hear good stories. You got that; you're in.

Naïve? I don't care. That's my one plucky attitudinal vice and me and Pauly Shore are sticking to it.

....

Joal Ryan Today

Since her unheralded debut as a filmmaker, Joal has poured her considerable thoughts on the subject of TV former child stars into a book on real TV former child stars, *Former Child Stars: The Story of America's Least Wanted* (ECW Press, 2000), a groundbreaking treatise on pop culture, celebrity and, yes, Gary Coleman. Her website, *Former Child Star Central* (www.formerchildstar.net), has been featured on CNN and reviewed in *Movieline, Newsweek* and *Entertainment Weekly*. She is self-distributing her movie *Former Child Star* through her site where a VHS copy can be purchased for only $13.

Ryan is also the author of the biographical tribute *Katharine Hepburn: A Stylish Life* (St. Martin's Press, 1999), and the upcoming *TV Poetry: A Collection of Television Verse* (TV Books, 2001), which is exactly what it sounds like—haiku, limericks and free verse about *Dawson's Creek, Gilligan's Island* and the lot.

Joal currently works as an editor at IFILM® (www.IFILM.com). She is also working on a screenplay which will only be committed to film, "if somebody actually buys the stupid thing."

JOAL RYAN'S ADVICE ON HOW TO WIN THE FILM FESTIVAL GAME (OR AT LEAST NOT BE REDUCED TO TEARS WHILE PLAYING):

1. Attend a film festival. (Preferably the one you'd really like to get into. And, yes, that means planning a year in advance—at least. Don't sweat the lag time. Trust me. I've tried the slap-dash method; I don't recommend it.)
2. Don't submit blind. (Until you know at least somebody at a festival is pulling for you, it's pointless. Take the time to do the proper leg work. Unofficially show your film to as many people as you can. Solicit advice. Make contacts. If all goes well, you'll save yourself a bundle on entry fees.)
3. Keep moving. (Satchel Paige's baseball wisdom works for movies, too. Don't wait for word from Sundance or Slamdance. Keep working other festivals. Keep writing scripts. Keep moving.)
4. If you get in, take your mother with you. (I took mine to Dallas. Parents make great conversation pieces at the nightly cocktail parties.)
5. Make a really, really good movie. (Go figure. Quality has a way of cutting down on the number of scams you need to run to get people to notice your movie.) The funny thing about *Former Child Star* is that even though I didn't enjoy, or deserve, being one of those Sundance Success Stories, the experience left me hopeful, not despairing.

RICHARD SCHENKMAN, Feature Filmmaker

New York native Richard Schenkman is a veteran indie film-maker. He started his professional career creating award-winning promos, network ID's, and documentary programs for MTV. Richard soon started his own production company, RSVP, producing and directing music videos and commercials for clients such as Swatch Watch, Honda Scooters, Pepsi Cola, and most notably his Clio-winning commercials for the children's cable network, Nickelodeon.

Director/screenwriter Richard Schenckman (left) with co-screenwriter Jon Cryer (right)
PHOTO BY TOM LEGOFF

Taking a break from the commercial world, he made a short film called *Overnight Success* in 1989, which premiered in the prestigious American Film Institute LA Film Festival and went on to win several festival awards. It was the success of this short that fueled Richard's festival fever. Over the next three years, he worked for Playboy in Los Angeles, creating original programming for their cable channel. It was here that Richard saw a lot of naked women which must have inspired his first feature, *The Pompatus of Love* which premiered at the Hamptons Film Festival in 1995, and was released theatrically the next year. His most recent film, *Went to Coney Island on a Mission from God . . . Be Back by Five*, has won seven major film festival awards and was released theatrically by Phaedra Cinema. This touching coming of age story is his second feature film collaboration with writing/producing partner Jon Cryer.

How did you and Jon Cryer meet and end up making two indie features together?

Jon and I had been friends for some years, and, as friends do, we'd spent plenty of time bitching about our respective careers. Jon was disappointed with the features he was making (or not making, as the case may be) and the perception of him as a "TV guy." I was disappointed that I had not been able to break into features, other than a B-movie I had directed "pseudonymously." So we said, "Why don't we write our own?" That's how *Pompatus of Love* came to be. There was a third writer/producer on that film, Adam Oliensis—a buddy of mine from New York who was a deeply talented playwright who had never written a screenplay and was curious about the process. Through the four years it took to write, produce, edit and eventually distribute *Pompatus*, Adam grew completely sick of show business and has since become an incomparably wealthy day-trader.

Jon and I, however, loved the process of making our own movie, and loved working together, so we vowed to do it again. In fact, we were staying in a shoebox in Cannes, trying to help sell *Pompatus* internationally, when he showed me the first pages on for a new script.

We spent a year or so on the first draft of *Coney Island*, then both got busy with different projects. One of the projects Jon got busy with was a doomed TV series that he had spent months turning down. He knew it would never work, but when they finally drove the money truck up to his front yard, he had to say, "Yes."

Well, as predicted, the series never got past the pilot stage, but he did get a rather large check, which he immediately committed to fund 50 percent of *Coney Island*.

We spent months (what feels, in retrospect, like years) working with various producers, trying to raise the other 50 percent, and finally, it seemed, we had, so we began production.

Well, several days into photography (and I shall never forget which day it was, because I was in my foolish "Freak Show Guy" wardrobe) there I was, standing in the cold, at an outdoor pay-phone, speaking to our investor in Germany. He was explaining to me that he couldn't release his half of the money (now weeks late) because *our* half of the money was no longer in escrow. Of course it wasn't in escrow any longer—it was being spent on the movie!

And that was that. We never lined up another investor. We just cut back on expenses as much as we could and we carried on, putting off post-production expenses as long as possible, delaying the payment of bills as long as possible.

While we were still editing, we showed the film to several indie and international distributors, in the hopes of getting finishing funds and a distribution commitment. But despite some strong interest and prolonged negotiations, nothing came to fruition.

Jon funded the entire film out of his pocket, and I sincerely hope that not only does it stop costing him money at some point, but that he actually gets some of it back some day.

Coney Island *played quite a few film festivals. What is the best strategy for getting accepted?*

I send in my tape like a schmuck and hope for the best. The one thing you can do is to get a high-powered producer's rep or agent on board, just as you are completing your film, and then let them use their juice and connections to get you into the "important" festivals.

> **"First let me be clear about one thing: we did not hire a producer's rep, and it was a huge mistake."**

Did we do that? No. Why? I'm not sure. Like many filmmakers, we believed in our movie. We saw what else was out there, and we said, "We have something special here."

I knew I could get Geoff Gilmore on the phone, since he had actually attended a screening of *The Pompatus of Love* in Los Angeles several years before. (While he told me at one point that he had "mixed feelings" about that film, and over the objections of several programmers did not accept it for Sundance, he did remember me.) He cordially agreed to look at an early cut of *Coney Island*. We gave him the early cut because even at that point it would have been a race to the deadline to get it finished in time, and the lure of a possible Sundance premiere was too strong to resist. Sadly, the film was rejected.

Our next thought was to try for Cannes or Toronto, but Cannes seemed impossible (I applied anyway and literally never heard anything back at all) and Toronto was too far away, time-wise. A high-ranking exec promised us a slot at the Hamptons (where *Pompatus* had its American premiere) but that promise was later rescinded by the chief programmer (who was, of course, well within his rights to do so, but it still hurt). So, I called my friend Robert Faust, and offered the film to the Los Angeles Independent Film Festival, which at that time had a rapidly growing reputation as a place where movies premiered and were acquired.

When your film did not get into Sundance, how did you get distributors to see it?

First let me be clear about one thing: we did not hire a producer's rep, and it was a huge mistake. A very classy guy even offered us his services, but we were so high on the film, and so confident in the assurances we were getting from various people that the LAIFF screening would be attended by every acquisitions person, that we did not take him up on his offer.

Later, in Germany, I met a director who had hired a producer's rep who did the following for her film: He got it into Toronto after the deadline had passed! Now that's a good producer's rep. I even hired the same rep later, but because we had already premiered, and been seen by most acquisitions execs, in the end there was very little he could do for us.

Having said that, I did have a clear understanding that our film was being "tracked" and that the acquisitions community was aware of it and planning to see it. One mini-major even took me to dinner the night before the first screening. I thought we were set.

This is an important lesson: There is *nothing* more important than your first screening. It is so important to *not show* your picture to the acquisitions exces until all of them are in a room, chomping at the bit to see it. You hear this all the time, but it really is true. Spend as much time as possible getting them interested in the film; if necessary whet their appetite with a trailer, and confirm that somebody from the company will come to that all-important first screening.

Sometimes this process feels like that old Steve Martin bit—how to be a millionaire and fix all the world's problems: "First, get a million dollars. . . " In this case, it's, "First, get a movie star to be in your movie, then get into

> .....
> "Spend as much time as possible getting them interested in the film; if necessary whet their appetite with a trailer, and confirm that somebody from the company will come to that all-important first screening."
> .....

Sundance." There is so much that's out of your control, it's important to maximize the opportunities that are within your control.

But the fact is, once you know you're not going to play Sundance, Toronto, Cannes, Berlin or New York or, in the second tier, Telluride, Hamptons, LAIFF or AFI, it doesn't matter much. At that point, you're not going to the festivals to sell your movie. Not directly, anyhow. You're going to the festivals for fun, for ego, for the thrill of showing it to an audience. And in the hopes that if you win a pile of awards. Because then you can say, "We won a pile of awards." And hope that people don't ask you if you won those awards at Sundance.

I love the give and take with an audience who just paid to see your movie. I love the meals and the panels and the parties that allow me to meet and bond with other filmmakers. I love traveling and seeing other cities, and I especially love when someone else is paying. My wife always says, "Don't get between indie filmmakers and a buffet." And boy, is it true.

Was the LAIFF premiere screening a success?
LAIFF did, in fact, accept the movie, and we geared up for our big premiere. We badgered them for a good slot and eventually got early Saturday afternoon, on the big screen at the Director's Guild of America. Thomas Ethan Harris, the programmer, assured me constantly that *Coney Island* was one of his favorite films of the festival; that he felt it was one of three or four most likely to be acquired. That in fact he was telling all the acquisitions people that the Saturday afternoon/evening lineup was made up of the big five titles—the ones they needed to see.

So, we concentrated on showing everyone a good time. I found a firm in Los Angeles that could provide hot dog stands to place in the DGA lobby and quickly feed 400 people "Coney Island Dogs" (with sauerkraut and mustard, 'natch). We got our old buddies from YooHoo® and Dr. Brown's Soda (who had given us product for the movie) to supply beverages for 600. The food turned out to be an enormous hit, and we ended up feeding everybody who was hanging around the festival that day, whether they'd seen our film or not.

What did you do to hype your film?

These questions give me a stomachache, because they keep reminding me of the mistakes we made. Which were especially stupid mistakes when you consider that we made almost the same exact ones on *Pompatus*.

We didn't hire a publicist for the same reason we didn't hire a rep. We thought we didn't need one. Everyone in the business seemed to know about the film, and the folks at LAIFF assured us that all acquisitions people would be there—that is, until about a week or so before the screening, when they said, "What do you mean you don't have a producer's rep? How do you know the execs are coming?" And I said, "I thought you were getting them to come!"

> .....
> **"The movie will not sell itself. No matter how good it is, or how good you think it is, unless Tom Cruise is in it."**
> .....

You are on your own. You must make the world aware of your movie, and you must get the acquisitions people to come down, or you must hire the people who will do this. There's virtually no way around this. The movie will not sell itself. No matter how good it is, or how good you think it is, unless Tom Cruise is in it.

What we did to hype our film was create a website, and we put Jon out there as much as we could. Jon did some radio, even some local TV appearances, promoting the LAIFF and our film's appearance in it. He even did an episode of NBC's *Later* (with Angie Everhardt, of all people), and they played clips from the movie. So in the end, we got a fair amount of publicity, and in fact our screening was a huge hit, selling out nearly every one of the 585 seats in the DGA.

How do filmmakers build good hype?

Good hype, I believe, grows intrinsically from the movie. If, for example, your movie is a fictional documentary about young filmmakers lost in the woods, spread the rumor that it's a real documentary, and the filmmakers really were lost in the woods.

If your movie is about male hustlers on the streets of Los Angeles, let people believe that you spent months with these hustlers, learning their true stories. People love dirty behind-the-scenes stories. Look at the success of the young filmmaker who supposedly lived in the subway tunnels with the subjects of his documentary.

If your movie features the theatrical debut of a huge TV star, get that TV star out into the world talking to the press about what a thrill it is to be in his or her first indie movie.

If the movie is autobiographical, sell your story to the tabloid. In other words, be as creative as possible with what you have.

How and when did you build the website for Coney Island?

I'm very lucky. Jon is a computer nerd from way back, and he started building the site as soon as we were done with the movie. It's been a useful tool to promote festival screenings, and to let the press have instant access to stills, our press kit materials and other information. It's gotten better and better as the years have gone by, and now it's as good as any non-studio film has. Jon's got the trailer up there for streaming or downloading, a free MP3 download of a track from the film, and links to buy our first movie at the lowest price. Soon we'll have links for the soundtrack CD, and eventually, the *Coney Island* DVD and poster.

How important was the site in promoting your film?

This is a tough question to answer, but to date, our site has gotten over 25,000 hits, so somebody's looking at it. Jon has been diligent about linking our site to zillions of other sites, and making sure that we're tied in to all the search engines, so that if, for example, someone does a search on *Coney Island*, we turn up.

Were you nervous at the screening?

When screening this film, I only get nervous about technical matters; will it be out of focus, will the projector break, will the film break, will the audience notice the bad splices in reel one? I have no qualms about the movie itself, because I love it, I think it's really, really good, and if someone doesn't like it, I usually think there's something wrong with them.

That might sound arrogant, even egomaniacal, but I don't think it is. After all, I don't think I'm so great, but I am damn proud of the movie—which a hell of a lot of people worked on.

> .....
> "i think it's really, really good, and if someone doesn't like it, i usually think there's something wrong with them."
> .....

A great way to deal with nervousness at film festival screenings is to flee the theater immediately after introducing the film, and go get a cocktail. I did this, for example, in Austin, Texas, and was able to be entirely absent when the film jammed in the projector at a bad splice and burned spectacularly. When I returned for the Q&A and the film was running oddly behind, someone explained the trouble to me, and asked, "Why weren't you here!!!???"

To which I replied, "And what could I have done if I were, besides freak out?" I've already got enough stress, thanks.

By the same token, however, Jon and I had the pleasure of screening the film opening night at the 1999 Rhode Island Int'l Film Festival, and we had planned to run away for cocktails as soon as it started. But the audience reaction was so strong, and so loud, right from the start, that we said, "Well, we'll just stay until the schoolyard scene . . . well, we'll just stay until the subway scene. . . . " Until we had stayed for the whole screening.

Were you prepared for the questions from the audience?

I had already been on the festival circuit with *Pompatus*, so I knew that especially at an indie film festival, people would ask about how the film was made, about the budget, technical matters, etc. . . . Frankly, I prefer European festivals for just that reason—people tend to ask about the theme, about acting, about the filmmaker's process and intention—not about how the picture got made. I'm continually amazed that people in other countries understand English so well that without subtitles they still completely "get" the movie.

The last festival we went to was the Local Heroes festival in Edmonton, Canada, and Jon was there alone. But the audience reaction was so crazy that he called me on his cell phone, while onstage doing the Q&A to let the audience shout their approval into my answering machine. That was great. In fact, the festival videotaped that and put it up on their website. And, of course, it's now up on ours.

When the film didn't sell at a festival, how did you go about pursuing distribution?

Well, as I said, when our festival debut came and went without a distribution deal, we went back on the festival circuit and tried to build buzz. We had some strong interest at Miramax, and went pretty far up the ladder there, but in the end, there wasn't enough interest and the lead died.

When I met Alison Swan and heard about her success with her rep, I hired him, and he tried to get some excitement going for the film. However, in the end, the best he could do was a pretty lowball offer from Showtime for the Sundance Channel.

I'd heard that Blockbuster was starting to buy indie movies for their exclusive program, and I asked him to send them the film. For some reason, he didn't. However, in the meantime, Blockbuster purchased a different film I had directed . . . a "director-for-hire" job I had done for Nu Image. I called the acquisitions exec at Blockbuster and said, "I'm the director of *October 22*. If you like that film, I have an even better one." He said, "Sure, send it down." And not a video, mind you—he asked for the 35mm print, which impressed me greatly. And, to make a long, long story short, we ended up making a deal with them.

What were the details of that video deal?
It was important to us that the film get a theatrical release. Of course we wanted audiences to have a chance to see it on film, on a big screen, and of course we wanted the higher profile within the industry that a theatrical release would give us.

But additionally, we knew that a theatrical release would positively impact the picture's value in the ancillary markets, especially foreign. One lesson that we had learned with *Pompatus* was that if you have a non-genre, non-star-driven title, you'd better have some sort of domestic theatrical release in place before you try to sell the international rights.

Initially, our Blockbuster deal was a simple, six-month video exclusive. Meaning, the title would debut on VHS tape—for rental only—exclusively at Blockbuster stores. We would get a tiny advance, and then a healthy share of the rental revenue. We would retain the right to release the film theatrically, if we could get a distributor. And of course we would retain cable, pay-per-view, international and video sell-through—even the secondary rental market. They just wanted those first six months of rental.

However, in the months it took to negotiate the deal, their needs changed, and they eventually came back and asked for all TV and Internet rights for three years. They improved the advance, and the deal finally made sense. We retained theatrical, foreign and DVD rights. In fact, I negotiated a facet of the agreement that allows the DVD to be released shortly after the rental video street date. My theory is that, at this point in time, most people who want to buy a movie like this for their collection will buy the DVD. We'll see if I'm right.

For the most part, I've negotiated our deals, but depending on the deal, we've had the help of an attorney. For example, while I negotiated all the initial, major deal points of our Blockbuster deal, our lawyer has—for months, now—been ironing out the details. And it's a good thing, too, because he caught some nasty gaffes that would have been very costly to us if not spotted.

How did you support the release of the film?

I've made myself available on every level to promote the movie. I even wrote the production notes myself. I've done interviews at film festivals, for TV, print and radio. I made sure that we had someone on set taking stills, and someone shooting 8mm footage for "behind-the-scenes" segments. However, as I said, for the theatrical release of the movie there has been very little interest from the press in talking to me. It makes it harder on Jon; he has to be everywhere, on two coasts, at the same time. Whatever it takes to sell the movie.

What do you love most about touring at film festivals?

I do love the relationships one forms with other filmmakers, from seeing them around the world on the "festival circuit." You find yourself in a strange town, and suddenly, there are these familiar faces, who are going through the exact same thing you are.

It is certainly much more pleasant when the festival really takes care of you. When they fly you in, have you picked up at the airport and brought to a nice hotel, all at their expense. When they cover most of your meals, either via a festival tent (Ft. Lauderdale fest, for example), a series of catered events (Austin, Oldenburg) or actual restaurant vouchers (Figueira Da Foz, Portugal). When they provide some outside-the-festival diversions (we had a great tour of the city of Ghent courtesy of the Flanders festival). It can get very, very exhausting when you're on your own, plus, frankly, you feel a little ripped off. After all, most indie filmmakers have worked for free for years to make their movie; the festival is charging admission for the tickets—it's only right that they pass some of it back to you, at least in living expenses.

I was invited to a small festival in Sacramento, and I made it very clear to the festival director that I was not working at that time, and that I could not attend the festival if it was going to cost me any money. He assured me that all expenses would be covered, and when I returned home, I sent him my receipts. To date, I have not received reimbursement.

Were the years of struggle worth it?

Since Jon and I started to make this movie, we've dealt with one aspect of it or another nearly every single day since, and that's over four years. Four years for one little movie! We finished the film in February 1998, and made our festival debut in April of that year at the LAIFF. I can't believe it's taken more than two years to get this movie out, and despite the long delay, it's still getting an extremely small release.

You look around, and you think, "How did this piece of crap get distributed, and not my film?" Sometimes there's an easy answer— the piece of crap has a big star, or lots of nudity, or extreme violence, or something else undeniably marketable—but more often there's no answer at all. Who can say?

The first time I read utterly conflicting reviews of *Pompatus*, something changed in me irrevocably. "How can this be?" I wondered. "How can two different, intelligent people completely disagree like this?" It remains a mystery to me, but a fact of life. Some people will love your movie, and some will hate it. And that would be fine, if those people were the audience. Unfortunately, there are many gates to pass through and miles to cross before you can ever reach a paying audience.

> .....
> "And that's why there are film festivals. People who love independent and foreign films, going out of their way to come see movies they've never heard of, simply out of desire. They're the best audiences in the world . . . it's worth attending festivals if only for the chance to show your films to this audience."
> .....

And that's why there are film festivals. People who love independent and foreign films, going out of their way to come see movies they've never heard of, simply out of desire. They're the best audiences in the world, and despite the difficulties and hardships and expenses, it's worth attending festivals if only for the chance to show your films to this audience.

....

Richard Schenkman and Jon Cryer have completed two new screenplays: *Brooklyn Down*, a drama, and *Reasons to be Cheerful*, a comedy. The two recently sold a TV pilot script, *Us & Them*, to 20th Century Fox Television. Jon Cryer personally built the website for *Coney Island* and you can check it out at www.evenmore.com.

HEiDi VAN LiER, First-Time Feature Filmmaker

Filmmaker Heidi Van Lier

Heidi Van Lier is a real character. Besides being a talented writer and filmmaker, she's damn funny. I would describe her as kind of a female Woody Allen with a nasal, whiny voice. In 1994 she wrote and directed a cute little short film called *Small Town Recollection*. The very next year she attended the Sundance Screenwriters Lab to develop her skills. Heidi is one of those people who is hilarious when she's doing absolutely nothing, so it's no surprise that she cast herself as the lead in her feature directing debut *Chi Girl*. In 1999, *Chi Girl* went on to win Slamdance's coveted Grand Jury Prize for Best Feature. I met Heidi at the USA Film Festival in Dallas, Texas where we sat on the jury for the short film program. In addition to offering sound advice, her unique experiences making films and travelling to festival could also provide plenty of material for a television sitcom.

Tell me about the making of Chi Girl?

I was in Los Angeles, attempting to be a screenwriter for years. Everyone kept telling me I needed something produced before I'd start getting work. So I knew at some point I was going to have to make my own little movie, whether I liked it or not. But I had no idea how soon I was actually going to be doing that.

When I broke up with my boyfriend I went to Chicago to get as far away from my old life as I could. In Chicago I would go see this band every Tuesday night at a little Capone speakeasy, and I met the band's manager. Out of nowhere I found myself telling him I wanted to use his band on the soundtrack for my movie. I wasn't even making a movie, but I didn't mention that part. I scrambled and came up with the idea for *Chi Girl* within a week. I spent two hours pitching it to the manager and at the end he said they'd do the film. Now I was screwed. I was going to have to make this movie.

One thing led to another, with some good name-dropping, since my father is somewhat of a hometown hero in Chicago (having played for the Bulls in the '70s), and now I had this band. And step by step I was putting a movie together.

One phone call to my mother and she started sending me the cash to get insurance and all the paperwork you need for pre-production. I found my only crewmember, my amazing DP, Anders Uhl. And I figured that's all I needed. Everyone I ran into told me, "Oh, no. You can't do it like that." But they were a little late, I was already about to shoot a feature, with one crew member, each scene done in only one take, on 35mm film.

Did you do research on film festivals before applying?

I'd been going to Park City and other festivals for years. The biggest mistake someone can make when applying is not knowing what they're really getting into. I'd met the people at Sundance and Slamdance over the years. Sundance didn't pay much attention to my film, Slamdance did. I'd made a movie that I thought was original enough to get some attention, even though I'd ripped off all my heroes at the same time. And once I applied to Slamdance I started giving them old computers and things, not so much to bribe them (wink, wink), just so they'd remember me. It all worked. Later I found out many people try to bribe them, and with some serious cash, but most of them don't get in. After Slamdance I just started going to any festival that invited me. Most of the film festival organizers go to Park City in January to program their own festivals. They watch out for films that have "buzz" and then invite them to their festivals.

How did you find out you were in?

A friend of mine was programming, and he wasn't allowed to vote for my film as a result. He came over and first told me I had not gotten in. Then confessed he was joking. It was a big let down to get in, for a couple reasons. 1) I went through the emotional breakdown of not getting in, which was painful, and 2) now I had to actually finish my film, and I didn't have the $30,000 to do so. Thus began six weeks of sobbing in my car on the Ventura Freeway. After that, I didn't really apply to any others, just went to festivals that invited me.

When your film did not get into Sundance or Toronto, what kind of strategy did you employ to get the film seen by distributors?

When I got into Slamdance, this sweet guy at William Morris, Shaun Redick, saw the film before the festival and started telling distributors about it. Somehow he motivated ten of the big distributors to show up at my first screening at Slamdance. We had sent out postcards and faxes for weeks as well, but I don't think they did nearly as much as Shaun did.

What did you do to promote your film at Slamdance and in Park City?

We talked to some publicists. But no one seemed that interested in our little $50,000 movie that I starred in myself. Fliers on the street. We were nice to everyone we met. We were willing to talk about the movie to everyone, including tourists who weren't even in Park City for the festivals. I still go to meetings now where the producer will say they met me on Main Street in Park City and I spent some time talking to them. Posters. Faxing. Calling people. We put together a street team to come up and meet the public while we were there. We made little notebooks with the *Chi Girl* logo on them. People still have those notebooks two years later. And we made tootsie pops with *Chi Girl* stickers on them so the audience would have a giggly sugar high in the middle of the screening. My mother spent days faxing people and we sent out thousands of postcards over the weeks before the screenings. Everyone knew our movie was at Slamdance.

How did the first screening go?

I was having some kind of strange panic attack in the lobby at the Treasure Mountain Inn. The line for our first screening was huge. My best friend was with me and watching my face go through odd contortions. The only way to get through it was to do it. I had a little silly thing I had to read before the film. I read it, people laughed, I was shaking, the lights dimmed.

I learned that it is impossible to die from nervousness. I'd seen enough Q&As to know what the deal was. I think I was a huge brat though, because I was still shaking, but for some reason people just thought I was being funny.

Also, everyone tends to think I *am* the character in the film. It usually takes them a minute to realize that I'm not an obsessive stalker with a mentally ill guy with a camera following me every-where . . . although I did marry the guy who played the mentally ill guy with the camera.

What were some of the questions you were asked at the Q&A?

"Are you seeing anyone?" When I said I was dating the other lead in the film, now my husband, the guy said, "No, I mean, like a thera-pist."

"Is that a prosthetic ass?" I had put on some Chicago winter weight while shooting the movie, and my ass was enormous.

"Did you ever think about cutting the film down?" I said, "Yes. I thought about cutting it down to three minutes, but that just wouldn't have been a feature film, now would it?"

Almost the entire audience stayed, and as I walked up to do the Q&A they were all leaning forward with these big smiles on their faces. I got great agents. Got a lot of distributor interest. Got a lot of press. Got a lot of buzz. It could not have been better.

When the film did not sell immediately at Slamdance, how did you con-tinue to pursue a distribution deal?

I just made myself as available as possible. I spent two months after the festival Fed-Exing my print back and forth from New York to Los Angeles so people could decide if they wanted to buy it. That was a full time job by itself. We have some distributor offers again, but there are some legal issues we'll need to clear up first, so we're doing that now. It's still up in the air, but at some point it'll see the light of day, even if it's part of some 1999 film retrospective in 2020. Other than that, my movie had a great little life. I got some jobs I love as a result. My career finally took the turn I'd been working toward, for many, many years.

> .....
> **"If the press like you, they'll help the distributors to pay attention to you. They can help you get an agent, and your agency can use your press as a way to get other producers to hire you."**
> .....

Any advice on handling the press?

Be nice to everyone! And talk to as many people as humanly possible. The press will sell your film for you and get you other jobs as well. If the press like you, they'll help the distributors to pay attention to you. They can help you get an agent, and your agency can use your press as a way to get other producers to hire you.

What were some of the other festival screenings like?

The first screening at Slamdance was by far the best. But the second best had to be the Cleveland Film Festival. That is an amazing little festival! The entire population of Cleveland has a deep understanding of how film works. I was very impressed. Three screenings of 600 people were sold out, and I didn't do any promo stuff at all. The worst was a screening at the Director's Guild of America in Los Angeles, where the "large ass" was discussed again, and people seemed to be a little irritated with the shaky-cam thing. I think they'd all just seen *Blair Witch* and were already tired of the mockumentary.

.....
"Bring plenty of nutrition bars, not every festival will feed you. And try not to drink, you'll end up in bed with someone who made a film you despise."
.....

Can you describe Chi Girl's *whirlwind film festival tour?*

Sex, drugs and rock and roll in every country in the world. Very fun if you're single. I wasn't. But you have to go where you're invited, especially with your first film. It's an experience you'll never forget, and you'll get to go places you'd never go on your own.

It does get really exhausting after a while, even if you're having fun. And it can be expensive, it costs money to stay in free hotels and eat out all day, even if the festival does provide a sandwich for you on occasion. They always ask for a credit card when you check in, which I didn't have the entire year, so I'd have to leave fifty bucks there, which was generally all the money I had for food.

At the end I'd just plan on going for three days only, and on the weekend, so that I didn't have to miss any meetings in town really. And I'd spend less cash that way. Three days is the perfect amount to be at any of the smaller festivals. Bring plenty of nutrition bars, not every festival will feed you. And try not to drink, you'll end up in bed with someone who made a film you despise. I've seen it happen a thousand times.

Did the screening of the film lead to other opportunities?

Greg McKnight from William Morris was at my first Slamdance screening and he was totally enthusiastic. I moved to William Morris a week after I came back to Los Angeles, and they had me going out on so many meetings I couldn't keep track. The really weird thing is, I love my agents! How many people can say that? Sara Bottfeld and Greg McKnight totally turned my career around. I started working in November on a film for MTV that I have finished writing and if all goes well, I'll be directing soon. And there are a few other cool projects I've been working on as well, thanks to Greg and Sara and the Slamdance experience.

You've also been involved with Slamdance as a programmer, what mistakes do filmmakers make when they apply?

I have so much frustration about how people "do" festivals. Most people who apply to festivals have no idea what they're doing, and they miss out on all the opportunities when they do, and even more when they get in. First things first, you have to really want this. No one who's on the fence about being a filmmaker ever succeeds. So as a result, you should be learning everything you can about everything. Don't slack; go to these festivals and start from scratch before you think about applying. I'd say before you even think about making a film. I don't think there's much "luck" involved in a film festival. You can make the best possible scenario for yourself by doing *everything* you can to be nice, to be available, to be prepared and to be aware of what else you could be doing. There are four things people try to get out of a festival: An award, a sale, press, other work and/or an agent. Granted, not everyone is going to win a big festival, but it doesn't mean you can't get one of the other three.

If you get even one, you've done well at your festival.

> .....
> "There are four things people try to get out of a festival: An award, a sale, press, other work/agents. Granted, not everyone is going to win a big festival, but it doesn't mean you can't get one of the other three."
> .....

Heidi Van Lier's *Chi Girl* never sold. Her film joins thousands of "cine-orphans," movies without a distributor. However, the buzz that *Chi Girl* received got Heidi a lot of meetings in Hollywood and she recently wrote *Tales from the Prom* for MTV Films. She is also a programmer for the 2001 Slamdance International Film Festival.

HEIDI VAN LIER'S 12 STEPS TO A SUCCESSFUL FILM FESTIVAL

1. Be nice to EVERYONE, especially people who are bugging the hell out of you. Be nice to the other filmmakers, sometimes they'll tell people to go see your film. Better that than they're all telling the press how much they hate your arrogant ass. And always be nice to volunteers. Give the volunteers gifts; they're the ones who do all the work for you that you can't do. They'll tell everyone whether you're nice or not, and if they like you they will play a huge role in selling your film or getting you more work that year.

2. Have another project ready to go that you can pitch while you're there. If you don't, you won't get another deal or an agent and then you're a big loser. And it better be totally original or forget it.

3. Know the lay of the land by going to the big festivals before you enter.

4. Maybe make a good film, this can occasionally help. Preferably not a mockumentary. I didn't listen to this, but my film still hasn't sold. You do the math. And don't make a "you and your twenty-something friends sitting around being clever" film. Only you think your friends are clever.

5. Abstain from your drinking and drug habits while you're there. You need to be alert when Bill Bloch's people approach you. If only to make a fool out of yourself in the end anyway.

6. Promote. Let the entire planet know your screening times weeks before you go. And keep telling them until that day. Faxing. E-mailing. Posters. Postcards.

7. Billboard on Sunset with a picture of yourself naked, if you can afford it.

8. Keep your introduction short and funny. No one wants to see a bad twenty minute stand-up routine.

9. Just because you've had your first screening doesn't mean you can sleep yet. You still have the rest of the week to get press and sell your film. Sometimes people buy a film a year after it ran at one of the big festivals. This will help you start your drug habit again when the festival is over because it's even more stressful than the festival was.

10. Be careful who you bring with you on your team. Don't bring your parents or kids unless they're media savvy; they'll say the wrong thing to the press and harass celebrities while you're there and it'll only embarrass you. Don't bring friends who don't like to work hard. They'll drive you nuts when they're getting up to go skiing every day and you've been up all night stuffing press kits.

11. Don't get jealous when other filmmakers sell their movies the first day you're there. They sold their movie before they even got up there and lied about it to get into the festival. They probably didn't make any money on the deal, and it'll probably only be in theaters for five minutes. And you could still sell your movie for nothing so it can be in theaters for only five minutes.

12. Gain some weight before you go. You will lose ten pounds at every festival.

LiFE AFTER THE FESTiVAL DEBUT

Pursuing a career in film is an ongoing series of battles that never seem to end. One moment you're basking in the glow of the premiere, and the next, you're scrambling to get your next project produced. For some, the realities of paying the rent become all too real, and the pursuit must often be set aside in order to "get a real job." However, that so-called "real" job is generally only a minor pit stop on the path to getting back in the race. None of the filmmakers interviewed for the last edition of this book have been taking it easy. They've all been working hard on new projects both film and non-film related. I checked in with all of them to see what they are up to.

Arthur Borman

The writer/director of *The Making of . . . And God Spoke* and *Shooting Lily* is in post-production on his most recent project, a documentary tentatively titled *Karaoke Fever*. He plans to have the doc ready to play the festival circuit in 2001. He's also in pre-production on a Bar Mitzvah comedy entitled *Bloom*. *Bloom* is being produced by his brother Mark and director Brett Ratner. Arthur maintains a site about his films at www.directorscut.com.

Mark Edgington

Mark Edgington's previous short film, *The Death of Mr. Frick & Other Hardships*, won numerous prizes and was seen at over thirty international film festivals. It was selected for the Channel Four (UK) Young Filmmaker of the Year Competition and is distributed by Jane Balfour Films of London. His acclaimed short, *Anna in the Sky*, has won more than ten major festival awards and played at seventy-five film festivals worldwide. *Sunburn*, a feature script that Mark co-wrote with Director Nelson Hume was produced by Jean

Doumanian (*Sweet and Lowdown, Spanish Prisoner*). *Sunburn* premiered at the Toronto Film Festival and is currently in negotiations for domestic distribution. Mark's feature screenplay, *Satellites*, won the $25,000 Minnesota Independent Film Fund Award. He still hopes someday to direct a feature. Mark maintains a site for his movies at http://home.att.net/~markedg/anna/

Brian Flemming

Brian is still infamous as the head organizer of the Slumdance Film Festival. The one-time event will remain a permanent part of Park City lore as having the best parties. The Slumdance website lay dormant except for a brief period in which Brian ran an online film festival, which he readily admits was essentially a get-rich-quick scheme. Apart from Slumdance, he has worked as a segment producer for John Pierson's *Split Screen* television show. Brian recently co-wrote a stageplay with Keythe Farley called *Bat Boy: The Musical,* which will open Off-Broadway sometime in 2001. His feature debut, *Hang Your Dog in the Wind,* remains undistributed. News about Brian's latest activities can be found at www.slumdance.com.

Sarah Jacobson

Sarah's movie *Mary Jane's Not a Virgin Anymore* debuted at Sundance and was later picked for video distribution by Turbulent Arts. She spent seven months as a segment producer for the Oxygen cable network, covering "edge-y" issues for the teen girl show *Trackers*. She also collaborated with Sam Green for a segment on the Independent Film Channel's *Split Screen*, about the lost girl punk classic film, *Ladies and Gentlemen, The Fabulous Stains* starring Diane Lane. Sarah is now developing her own show, *Underground Floor*, for Pseudo Programs (www.pseudo.com) which will cover underground film, music, politics, art and writing. "Now I can cover several different topics a week instead of spend five years on one film!" Sarah Jacobson maintains a website with information about all of her films at www.sirius.com/~lenny/maryj2.html

Dan Mirvish

Dan wears more hats than any one in the indie film scene working as a director, writer, festival organizer and family man. After successfully completing years of litigation (time well spent for any director), Dan is still trying to make his second film, the modern-day-postal-western, *Stamp & Deliver*. In the meantime, he works diligently as one of the chief organizers of the Slamdance Film Festival, which has now become a year-round operation. His most recent project includes the completion of a beautiful new baby girl. To get more Dan than you can handle, check out www.slamdance.com/mirvish.

Lance Mungia

After the successful Slamdance debut and theatrical release of *Six String Samurai*, Lance pitched several projects around Hollywood including a remake of the kitsch sci-fi classic *Tron*. Currently he is developing an action script with John Woo and Terrance Chang's company, Lion Rock Entertainment, as well as negotiating a *Six String Samurai* television series. Lance is also putting the finishing touches on a script he plans to shoot soon. He does not plan to rush into his sophomore film because he says, " . . . if you're not careful, you'll do mediocre work because you're rushed into something and you're just cocky enough to think it doesn't matter."

SECTION 5
FiLM FESTiVAL LiSTiNGS

"And that's why there are film festivals.
People who love independent and foreign
films, going out of their way to come see
movies they've never heard of, simply out
of desire. They're the best audiences in the
world . . . it's worth attending festivals if
only for the chance to show your films to
this audience."

—Richard Schenkman, filmmaker

THE TOP TEN FiLM FESTiVALS

This section contains the complete list of over 600 film festivals worldwide. I have identified the most important festivals and included detailed information to aid you in your decision to visit a festival or enter your film. In addition to the Top Ten festivals, I have compiled lists of festivals that excel in certain areas. Throughout the directory section you'll find lists of what I consider to be the "Best Film Festivals" in categories ranging from Best New, Best Touring, Best Awards, Best Video, Best Digital, Best Kept Secret, Best Underground, Best Documentary, Best Weird, Best International, Best Gay and Best Party to Best Vacation.

The Top Ten film festivals have been selected based on a number of factors, one of the most important being that they qualify as "discovery" festivals—wherein new talent emerges to take center stage on the independent film scene. Each brings a significant amount of prestige along with better opportunities for filmmakers to gain exposure in the form of national media attention. Receiving an award from any of the Top Ten results in much-needed publicity and the attention of the industry, which can go a long way toward launching a career. The Top Ten also act as launching pads for some of Hollywood's best work—studios view these particular film festivals as a chance to premiere their most distinguished films and even their Oscar® contenders. And, of paramount importance for independent filmmakers, these fests also act as backdoor film markets—movies that are shown at these festivals have a greater chance of getting picked up for distribution. And finally, this select group of Top Ten film festivals also make great vacation destinations, have the best parties and are just damn good places to see new movies.

1. Sundance Film Festival

The mother of all independent film festivals in the United States, Sundance sets the tone for the industry, which is why you will find as many festival directors from other film fests as you will agents and acquisitions executives. Sundance is the place to be in January; whether you're a film lover, filmmaker or film student, no festival comes close to matching the experience. There is an air of excitement and electricity about the films at Sundance. Hearing about the struggles of indie film directors at post-screening Q&A sessions only serves to motivate the next generation of filmmakers to pick up their cameras. Sundance has everything: whether you're looking for distribution, a script, an actor for your next movie, to crash some cool parties or you just want to see some quality films. And in an effort to address the unprecedented growth of film on the web, Sundance recently created the Sundance Online Film Festival as a way to showcase new work on the Internet.

The only negative thing one might say is that the Sundance Film Festival is a victim of its own success—there are just too many people trying to see films in too few venues. There can be a certain amount of frustration at the festival, with the insanely cold weather, sold out screenings and packed parties, but like a strained family gathering at Thanksgiving, you know you'll always come back— and love every minute of it. I never miss Sundance.

P.O. Box 3630
Salt Lake City, UT 84110-3630
California Headquarters:
8857 W. Olympic Blvd., Beverly Hills, CA 90211
Tel: 310-360-1981 (California); 801-328-3456 (Utah)
Fax: 310-360-1969 (California); 801-575-5175 (Utah)
Email: programming@sundance.org
la@sundance.org (California Office)
institute@sundance.org (Utah Office)
Web Site: www.sundance.org
Festival Date: January 18-28, 2001
2002 DATES: January 10-20, 2002 (Earlier because of the Olympics.)

Entry Deadline: September: Short subject entries and October: Feature entries.

For 2002 Festival:

Early Submissions for 2002: Friday, July 20, 2001

Shorts Submissions for 2002: Friday, Sept. 21, 2001

Features Submissions for 2002: Friday, Sept. 28, 2001

Contact: RJ Millard, Press Coordinator

Director: Geoffrey Gilmore, Programming Director (California office)

Other Staff: Elisabeth Nebeker, Press Coordinator

Category: Independent, International

Profile: The Sundance Institute is governed by a 26-member Board of Trustees, currently chaired by Walter Weisman. In 1981 Robert Redford gathered a group of colleagues and friends at Sundance, Utah to discuss new ways to enhance the artistic vitality of the American film. The result was the establishment of the Sundance Institute, dedicated to the support and development of emerging screenwriters and directors of vision, and to the national and international exhibition of new, independent dramatic and documentary films. A nonprofit corporation, Sundance's $8.5 million budget is met by 40 percent earned and 60 percent contributed income. Over 300 filmmakers benefit annually from Sundance's programs; over 20,000 people attend the Sundance Film Festival; millions more attend films originally developed by Sundance. The artists and films supported by the Sundance Institute are the recipients of numerous Oscar®, Emmy and International Film Festival awards. Sundance, Utah, is home to the artistic activities of the Sundance Institute, creating summer and winter artists' communities. Sundance's administrative and program offices are located in Salt Lake City, Utah, and in Los Angeles, California.

Awards: Jury Awards: Competition films compete for the Grand Jury Prizes, Directing Awards, Cinematography Awards, Waldo Salt Screenwriting Award (Dramatic Competition only), and Freedom of Expression Award (Documentary Competition only). Jury Prizes are also awarded to a Latin American film and to an American short film under 30 minutes in length. All jury awards are determined by a group of distinguished filmmakers, technicians and critics.

Audience Awards: Competition and American Spectrum films compete for the Dramatic Audience Award and the Documentary Audience Award. World Cinema films compete for the World Audience Award.

Application Tips and Fee:

Deadline: All films must be received at the Sundance Film Festival office no later than 5:00 p.m. on their respective deadlines.

Format: All films must be submitted on 1/2" VHS videotape format. All entries, as well as accompanying materials, will not be returned and will become property of the Sundance Institute.

Accompanying Materials: The following must be included with the videotape. Incomplete entries will not be considered.

- Official Entry Form
- Film Still: preferably a black and white print that best represents the film, clearly labeled. Production shots with director are not acceptable.
- Synopsis: a short, typed description of the film's content.
- Credits: a complete principal cast and production credits list.
- Entry Fee: Features, $50 or $35 for early submission (American Features only); Shorts, $20. Make checks payable in U.S. dollars to Sundance Institute. US$ money orders acceptable.

Eligibility Requirements: Language: All films must be in English or subtitled in English.

Financing: All Competition and American Spectrum entries must have at least 50 percent U.S. financing.

Completion Date: Films must have been completed no earlier than October 1999.

Running Time: Dramatic features, no less than 70 minutes; documentary features, no less than 50 minutes; dramatic shorts, less than 70 minutes; documentary shorts, less than 50 minutes. Running time is calculated from the head frame to the last frame of the end credits.

Prior Screenings: Entries for the Competition must be U.S. premieres and may not have played in more than two international festivals. Entries for other categories may have screened at two U.S. or international festivals prior to the Sundance Film Festival. Entries may not open theatrically or be broadcast in any format anywhere in the U.S. before February 1, 2001.

Independent Production: Films produced, financed or initiated by a major motion picture studio are not eligible for the Competition or American Spectrum. However, a film that conforms to the above guidelines and is produced, financed, or acquired by an independent division of a studio is eligible.

Festival Presentation: If selected, films must be made available as a 16mm or 35mm "composite" print with soundtrack and titles included. Films may also be presented as a completed Sony HDCam Digital Videotape program. Films requiring dual projection (interlock) or super 16mm projection cannot be screened at the Festival. (Please refer to the Technical Information section on Entry Form.)

Explanation of Categories: Premiere: World and U.S. premieres of high profile films by established American and international directors (by invitation only).

Independent Feature Film Competition: A Competition of independent American dramatic and documentary feature films.

American Spectrum: A showcase of independent American narrative and documentary feature films.

World Cinema: A program of foreign feature films.

Frontier: A program of American and international experimental and avant-garde films.

Park City at Midnight: An "after-hours" showcase of American and international feature films

Shorts: A competition of American short films and a non-competitive selection of international short films.

Native Forum: A program of feature and short films from Native American filmmakers.

Tourist Information: Hey, there's always time for snowboarding lessons.

Travel Tips: The Sundance Film Festival features a thoroughly integrated transit system effectively linking the Festival Transit with Park City Transit. Both systems are complimentary. Festival Transit stops at Festival Headquarters and at all official Festival venues. Express Festival Transit provides quick links with key areas. Maps designating Festival Transit routes and Park City Transit routes will be available in the upcoming Film Guide, at the Festival Headquarters Information Desk, the Main Box Office, each theatre location, and at local hotels.

Travel to the Festival:

Travel Desk—(800) 933-5025; (801) 355-2300

Email address: traveldesk1@juno.com

Contact Travel Desk, the official air travel agency of the Sundance Film Festival, for special Festival rates.

Delta Air Lines—(800) 241-6760

Delta Air Lines, Inc., in cooperation with the Sundance Institute and Travel Desk, offers special discounted rates on flights to Salt Lake City for Festival participants. To take advantage of these special discounted fares, call Travel Desk and refer to Sundance Institute File Number 122060A.

Express Shuttle—(800) 397-0773; (801) 596-1600 Fax: (801) 531-7882

Express Shuttle (formerly Rocky Mountain Super Express) provides round-trip shuttle service between the Salt Lake International Airport and the Festival in Park City. Service is also available between Park City and Opening Night events in Salt Lake City by reservation only. Vans depart the airport approximately every 30 minutes. To make a reservation, please have a major credit card and flight information ready when you call.

Lodging at the Festival:

• Festival Headquarters and Hospitality Suite Shadow Ridge Resort Hotel and Conference Center, 50 Shadow Ridge—(435) 645-7509 or (801) 328-3456, 8AM - 8PM daily

• The Yarrow Resort Hotel & Conference Center— (800) 927-7694 or (435) 649-7000

The Yarrow Resort Hotel and Conference Center is proud to be the Official Press Headquarters for the 1999 Sundance Film Festival. As a major Festival venue, the Yarrow Hotel features public and press screenings, with additional public screenings held at the Holiday Village Cinemas, located directly behind the Hotel. The Yarrow Hotel is conveniently located in the heart of Park City and is on the free Park City and Festival Transit routes for easy access to other Festival venues and Historic Main Street. As a full-service hotel, The Yarrow Hotel features and on-site restaurant and bar, outdoor year-round heated pool and hot tube and fitness facility. In addition, guests of the Hotel will enjoy a refrigerator, coffee maker, full-size ironing board, wall hair dryer, voice mail and data port telephones in every room!

• David Holland's Resort Lodging & Conference Services—(800) SKI-2002 or (435) 655-3315

David Holland's Resort Lodging offers a wide range of rental properties throughout Park City in locations convenient to Festival events and great skiing. If your needs include a condominium, an elegant hotel, an apartment or private home, call on us. For group sales, contact Shawn Lym: 435-649-0800.

• Gables Hotel—(800) 443-1045 or (435) 655-3315

• Park Station Condominium Hotel— (800) 367-1056 or (435) 649-7717

• The Lodge at Resort Center—(800) 824-5331 or (435) 649-0800

• Shadow Ridge Resort Hotel & Conference Center—(800) 451-3031 or (435) 649-4300

• Deer Valley Lodging—(800) 453-3833 or (435) 649-4040 or Fax (435) 645-8419

Deer Valley Lodging offers distinctive accommodations throughout Deer Valley and Park City. Relax in the luxury of unique one to four bedroom condominiums featuring spacious living areas, daily housekeeping and private spa options. New this year are The Lodges at Deer Valley offering hotel rooms, one bedroom suites and assorted condominiums. Call for Festival rates.

• The Lodging Company—The Inn at Prospector Square and The New Claim Condo Suites— (800) 453-3812 or (435) 649-7100 or Fax (435) 649-8377

Films shown daily in our Prospector Square Theatre, full service athletic club and spa (available at a discounted fee), outdoor 20 person jacuzzi, and Grub Steak restaurant.

• Park City Resort Lodging—(800) 545-7669 or (435) 649-8200 or Fax (435) 645-8419

Park City Resort Lodging features superior to deluxe accommodations throughout Park City. Select from conveniently located Main Street properties to delightful units near the Park City Mountain Resort. All properties feature comfortable living areas and easy access to the free city-wide shuttle. Call for assistance with Festival lodging.

• Radisson Inn Park City—(800) 333-3333 or (435) 649-5000

The award-winning Radisson Inn is minutes away from Park City's Historic Main Street and located on the free shuttle. Enjoy Radigan's restaurant and Cooter's Private Club. Relax in our indoor/outdoor heated swimming pool, hydro spas and dry sauna.

• Sundance—(800) 892-1600 or (801) 225-4107 or Fax (801) 226-1937

Sundance Film Festival

1 Egyptian Theater   **4** Holiday Village Cinema

2 Park City Library Center   **5** Prospectors Square Theater

3 Yarrow Theater   **6** Eccles Theater

◄HQ► FESTIVAL HEADQUARTERS   ◁1▷ **FESTIVAL RELATED**   **3 THEATER**

Ⓐ HOTEL

THE SECRETS OF SUNDANCE

Rent a car only if you must and be sure to share it with a group. Parking is sparse in Park City, though if you're from out of town, the first parking ticket you get is a warning. After that you have to pay, so watch the parking signs. The mass transit system works well enough that a car is not a necessity (and it can even be a nuisance).

The real trouble with Sundance is that there is no central meeting place other than the press office. Main Street is the closest thing to ground zero and you'll find lots to do there when you're not seeing movies. Parties take place in the great bars and restaurants on Main Street which include: Harrry O's (two floors of fun), The River Horse Saloon (home to many private functions), Mediterraneo (used for private luncheons), Cisero's (lots of schmoozing done here), Wasatch Brewing Pub (great microbrew at the top of Main), Lakota (home to many upscale parties), Grappa and 350 Main Seafood & Oyster Company. Just walk down Main Street and wherever you see a crowd forming, something's happening.

If you need a quick bite in an unpretentious setting, the Main Street Pizza and Noodle Restaurant is your best bet. It's located near the middle of Main, it's cheap and you don't need to make reservations. Their pizza is incredible and I find myself eating there just about every other day.

At the bottom of Main Street is Zoom, Robert Redford's restaurant. You won't get into Zoom without a reservation and it's often booked up months before Sundance. If you're willing to wait, Zoom may seat you based on a cancelled reservation, but don't schedule around it. (It's worth it though just to taste their mouth-watering garlic mashed potatoes.)

If you're having trouble getting tickets to Sundance screenings, or your idea of a good time isn't standing in a "wait line" for two hours on the slim chance you might actually get into the Egyptian Theater, you have the check out the alternative "dance" festivals happening in Park City. Main Street is host to the insanity caused by the presence of festivals like Slamdance (a personal fave located at the Treasure Mountain Inn at the top of Main), No dance, Lapdance, Digidance, Slamdunk and new favorite, TromaDance. The locations of these fests change regularly, so check their websites for updates; they are all worth a visit.

The Silver Mine is a location used for parties and events including the infamous Lapdance. It's a huge venue with nothing but a mountain view, so when you get there, plan on staying the whole night.

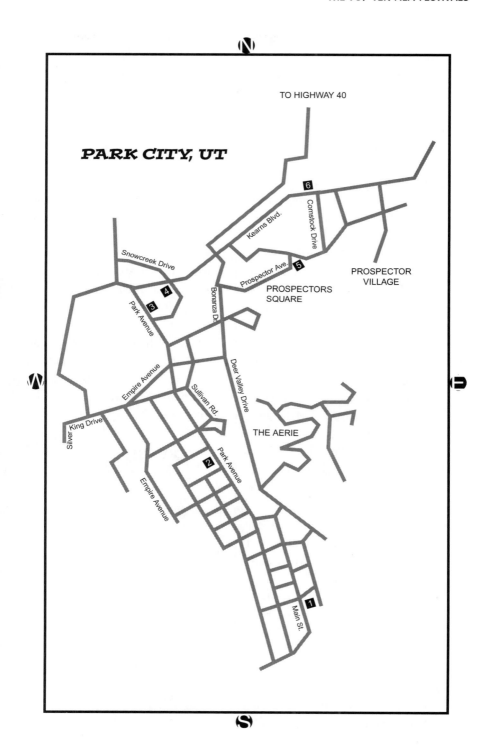

PARK CITY, UT

2. Toronto International Film Festival

The cosmopolitan city of Toronto in the great white north of Canada is host to one of the most respected festivals in the industry. Toronto breaks new talent and has premiered the first films of people like indie fave Tom DiCillo and wise-ass documentarian Michael Moore. Recently Toronto has become the festival of choice for debuting Hollywood's Oscar® hopefuls like the Academy Award®-winning *American Beauty* and the critically acclaimed *Almost Famous* and *The Contender*.

I first attended the Toronto Film Festival in 1988. Toronto, Ontario, was just a quick train ride from Detroit, Michigan, where I lived at the time. While I had gone to smaller film festivals before (having attended my first fest at the age of twelve), nothing could have prepared me for Toronto. I was initially overwhelmed at the sheer number and variety of films. From foreign film retrospectives, to independent film premieres, to Hollywood debuts, to Canadian work, there was almost too much to choose from. There is still an awesome amount to see and it just keeps getting better. Toronto's midnight movie program proves that the festival directors are not too full of themselves. (Nothing beats midnight showings of Japanese monster movies featuring my favorite giant turtle, Gamera.) The atmosphere is exhilarating as the whole city seems joined in a celebration of cinema.

Toronto is one of the best organized festivals in the world, and the amazing staff works diligently with filmmakers to help promote their films to the more than 1,000 members of the press that attend. Toronto is also a key festival for acquisitions executives looking for hot new films. The parties are a blast and the city of Toronto itself provides incredible opportunities for fun. If the bars were open later, it would be the prefect fest. As it is, it's just really, really close.

TORONTO INTERNATIONAL FILM FESTIVAL

2 Carlton Street, Suite 1600
Toronto, Ontario M5B 1J3
Tel: 416-967-7371
Fax: 416-967-9477
Email: tiffg@torfilmfest.ca
Web Site: www.e.bell.ca/filmfest
Festival Date: September
Entry Deadline: May (Canadian Shorts).
May (Canada). June (International Features).
Year Festival Began: 1976
Contact: Sarah Brooks, Manager, Programme Administration
Director: Piers Handling;
Managing Director: Michèle Maheux
Programmer: Kay Armatage, Noah Cowan, Liz Czach, Colin Geddes, June Givanni, Steve Gravestock, Piers Handling, Michèle Maheux, Ramiro Puerta

Other Staff: Director of Administration, Peter Roberts; Communications Director, Nuria Bronfman; Director of Development, Ana White; Director of Finance, Penny Weeks; Director of Public Affairs, Allison Bain; Film Reference Library Director, Sylvia Frank; Film Circuit Director, Cam Haynes; Sales Office, Kelley Alexandy

Category: International

Profile: To actively cultivate excellence and involvement in film as art and industry. The Toronto International Film Festival Group operates the Toronto International Film Festival; Cinematheque Ontario (a year-round screening programme, specializing in Canadian and international cinema, featuring both classic and contemporary films); The Film Reference Library; SPROCKETS Toronto International Film Festival for Children; and The Film Circuit (coordinates screenings for Canadian and international films for volunteer film groups in over 30 centres throughout Ontario).

The Toronto International Film Festival is a ten-day event held every September featuring nearly 300 films from over fifty countries. The Festival hosts over 700 accredited international media, in excess of 900 invited guests including directors, producers and actors, and more than 2,500 industry participants. The Toronto International Film Festival is one of the biggest in North America, is considered a *must attend* by industry professionals, and is ranked amount the top four film festivals in the world.

FESTIVAL HISTORY:

Starting out in 1976 as a collection of films from other festivals—a "festival of festivals," the Toronto International Film Festival has become one of the most successful cinematic events in the world, universally regarded as an ideal platform to premiere films. Boasting a public eager for the best in contemporary film, as well as international attention from media, distributors, producers, and buyers along with a galaxy of stars, the Toronto International Film Festival is considered the premiere film festival in North America. In 1998, *Variety* acknowledged that "the Festival is second only to Cannes in terms of high-profile pics, stars and market activity."

Seminars: The Rogers Industry Centre is *the* place to do business. The Centre provides a Canadian perspective on the international business of film and television. In 1997, it included: the Ultra Indie Experience, a series of daily up-close and personal discussions with five of the hottest new directors and their production teams; the Screenplay Café, where industry players peruse scripts from festival films; Micro-Meetings, sessions featuring key industry executives in informal one-hour meetings; Symposium, includes keynote addresses, main sessions, various workshops and panels; and, the Sales Office, representing films programmed in the current Festival, attracts the elite of the international film buying and selling community and has helped nurture the reputation of many young filmmakers.

Famous Speakers: Past speakers have included: Tom Schulman, Mike Newell, Sydney Levine, James Schamus, Roger Ebert, Michael Moore, Errol Morris, Chris Hegedus, David Thompson, Simon Perry

Awards: Yes

Competitions: No

Major Awards: The Toronto International Film Festival does not have a market, nor is it competitive but it does have the following awards:

Metro Media Award: *Boogie Nights* (d. Paul Thomas Anderson), *L.A. Confidential* (d. Curtis Hanson)

International Critics Award for film from Festival's Discovery Programme: *Under the Skin* (d. Carine Adler)

People's Choice Award: *The Hanging Garden* (d. Thom Fitzgerald)

Canadian Awards:

CITYTV Award for Best Canadian First Feature (cash prize of $15,000): *Cube* (d. Vincenzo Natali)

Toronto-City Award for Best Canadian Feature Film (cash prize of $25,000): *The Hanging Garden* (d. Thom Fitzgerald) and *The Sweet Hereafter* (d. Atom Egoyan)

NFB-John Spotton Award for Best Canadian Short Film (cash $2500 + $2500 benefits to be applied to costs of a future production): *Cotton Candy* (d. Roshell Bissett)

Application Fee: No entry fee.

Average Films Entered: 300+

Odds of Acceptance: 281 films from 58 countries; 233 features, 49 shorts; 1163 International Submissions; 47 first features; 130 international features making their world or North American premieres

Attendance: 250,000

Travel Tips: Special rates on Air Canada

Air Canada, the official airline of the Toronto International Film Festival, offers special rates to the Festival from Air Canada gates in North America and around the world (some conditions apply). Call your travel agent or Air Canada at 1-800-361-7585 or (514) 393-9494. Please ask that the Festival Event Number CV500910 be entered in the Tour Code box of your ticket regardless of the fare purchased.

Random Tidbits: Special hotel rates are available through the Festival's Guest Relations Office. If you require information or reservations, please call Festival Guest Relations at (416) 934-3210 or fax us at (416) 966-1329, and ask for PYO Hotel rates. Due to the volume of inquiries, please allow at least two weeks to process your requests. All hotel requests are subject to availability. Thank you for your patience.

Toronto International Film Festival

1 **Roy Thomson Hall**
60 Simcoe St

2 **Visa Screening Room (Elgin Theatre)**
189 Yonge St

3 **Famous Players Uptown Cinemas**
764 Yonge St

4 **Cineplex Odeon Varsity Cinemas**
Manulife Centre
55 Bloor St West, 2nd Floor

5 **Alliance Atlantis Cumberland Cinemas**
159 Cumberland St

6 **Royal Ontario Museum Theatre**
100 Queen's Park

7 **Massey Hall**
178 Victoria St

8 **Jackman Hall**
Art Gallery of Ontario
317 Dundas St (at McCaul St)

HQ **Park Hyatt Toronto (HQ)**
4 Avenue Road

2 **Executive Festival Offices**
Four Seasons Hotel Toronto
21 Avenue Road

3 **Public Box Office**
College Park
777 Bay Street, Lower Level

4 **Hazelton Lanes**
55 Avenue Road, Lower Level

5 **The Film Reference Library**
2 Carlton Street

6 **The Japan Foundation**
131 Bloor Street West

A **Park Hyatt Toronto**
4 Avenue road

B **Four Seasons Hotel Toronto**
21 Avenue Road

C **Bay Bloor Executive Suites**
1101 Bay St

D **Cambridge Suites Hotel**
15 Richmond St East

E **Comfort Suites City Centre**
200 Dundas St East

F **Courtyard by Marriott**
475 Yonge St

G **Days Inn Toronto Downtown**
30 Carlton St

H **The Grand Hotel and Suites**
25 Jarvis Street

I **Holiday Inn on King**
370 King St West

J **Hotel Inter-Continental**
220 Bloor St West

K **Metropolitan Hotel**
108 Chestnut St

L **Quality Hotel Midtown**
280 Bloor St West

M **Renaissance Toronto Hotel at SkyDome**
1 Blue Jays Way

N **Royal York Hotel**
100 Front St West

O **Sheraton Centre Toronto Hotel**
123 Queen st West

P **The Sutton Place Hotel**
955 Bay St

Q **Toronto Colony Hotel**
89 Chestnut St

R **Toronto Marriott Bloor Yorkville**
90 Bloor St East

S **Toronto Marriott Eaton Centre**
525 Bay St

T **Town Inn Suites**
620 Church St

U **The Westin Harbour Castle**
1 Harbour Square

V **Windsor Arms**
18 St. Thomas St

 FESTIVAL HEADQUARTERS   FESTIVAL RELATED   **3** THEATER

A HOTEL

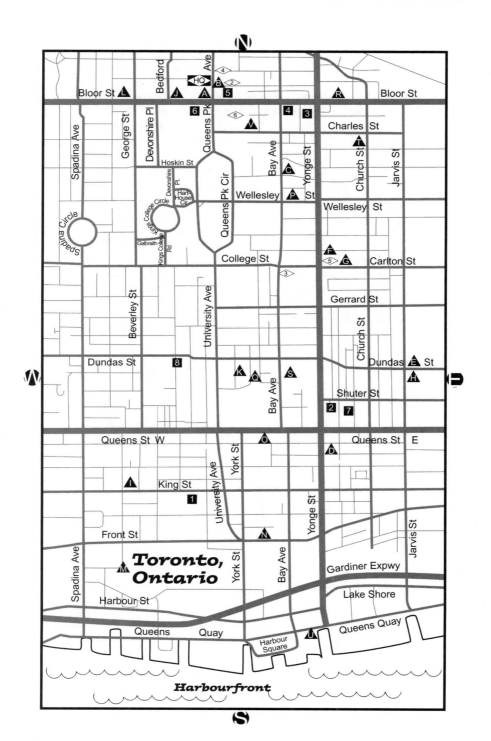

Toronto, Ontario

Harbourfront

THE SECRETS OF TORONTO

When visiting the Toronto Film Festival, don't even think about renting a car. Once you've mastered the subway system, perhaps the cleanest in the world, you'll miss it when you leave. When I used to go in the old days, the bars closed at 1 a.m., now the festival has become so important, the city has eased up on its drinking laws. During the fest many bars are open well until the wee hours. Hurray!

Ground zero for drinking and the official bar of the festival is Bistro 990 at 990 Bay Street. This is where you are most likely to see celebrities, and the bar is open to anyone. The Windsor Arms, a European-style hotel located at 18 St. Thomas Street, has become a hotspot for activity and has two bars, both of which are formal and a lot of fun. (It's also the place where John and Yoko did their bed-in in the early seventies.)

Across from the Cumberland Theater is an Italian restaurant called Toni Bulloni's (156 Cumberland Street). This is a great place for a fast meal and they make incredible pressed Italian sandwiches that you can eat while standing in line.

Unfortunately, the party scene at the Toronto Film Festival leaves a lot to be desired. There's a feeling that the Hollywood celebrity handlers want to separate the VIPs from the mucky-muck like you and I, so prepare for the two-tiered party system. If you really feel like visiting a gala so you may witness the "celebrity petting zoo" behind the ropes, go right ahead, but you're better off hitting the scene in the city than getting treated like cattle at a festival party.

3. Cannes Film Festival

Cannes is home to the most prestigious film festival in the world. (And remember, Cannes is pronounced CAN as in "trash can," not KHAN as in *Star Trek: The Wrath of Khan.*) Held in the sprawling city on the French Riviera, this May event, known as the Festival International du Film du Cannes (Cannes Film Festival), attracts top industry players worldwide—from studio executives to moguls, to the biggest celebrities, to press and filmmakers all the way down to the struggling indies.

There are five sections of the festival: Compètition (Competitive Section), Un Certain Regard (Showcase Section), La Semaine de la Critique (Critic's Week), La Quinzaine des Rèalisateurs (Director's Fortnight) and The Marchè (the Market).

While many film festivals shy away from their obvious market appeal, Cannes embraces this business reality by offering filmmakers a chance to sell their movies to overseas buyers. Any film is welcome to be a part of the market (for a price), which makes the whole event feel more democratic. And I mean everyone is welcome—both Troma and representatives from Slamdance attend every year to sell their films at the market.

Learn a little French, save up some cash (*everything* is expensive) and realize that no amount of preparation is sufficient for the largest and most prestigious film festival in the world. (But seeing topless women on the beach in thong bikinis doesn't require that much preparation, trust me.)

"The Festival is a non-political no man's land, a microcosm of what the world would be like if people could contact each other directly and speak the same language"

—Jean Cocteau

Association Francaise du Festival International du Film
99 Boulevard Malesherbes
75008 Paris
Tel: 33-1-4561-6600
Fax: 33-1-4561-9760
Email: festival@festival-cannes.fr
Web Site: www.festival-cannes.fr
Festival Date: May 9-20, 2001
Entry Deadline: March
Year Festival Began: 1946
Contact: Gilles Jacob
Category: Independent, International, Markets
Profile: The spirit of the Festival International du Film is one of friendship and universal cooperation. Its aim is to reveal and focus attention on works of quality in order to contribute to the progress of the motion picture arts and to encourage the development of the film industry throughout the world.
DETAILED HISTORY:
   In 1939, the French government decides to create the "Festival International du Film", and chooses Cannes because of its "sunny and enchanting location." The first Festival is postponed due to the war. In 1945 the "Association Française d'Action Artistique" is asked once again, to organize for the following year, a Festival that would be held under the aegis of the Ministry of Foreign Affairs, the Ministry of Education and from 1946 onwards, of the newly founded National Center for Cinematography (CNC). Despite the hardships of the time, the Cannes Film Festival, the first important cultural event after the war, starts on September 20, 1946. It is more a film forum than a competition as almost all the films presented are to receive a prize. Apart from 1948 and 1950(1), the

Festival has been held every year since 1946. In its early years it took place in September, but since 1951 it is held in May for approximately two weeks.
   At first the Festival was mainly a tourist and social event for the few hundred participants attending the many parties organized in the palace hotels of the Croisette and the luxurious villas of Cannes. Owing to the great increase of participants and the new economic stakes involved, the Festival then becomes the annual gathering of the film industry. In Cannes, the professionals can find a unique opportunity to meet, to build up future projects and to do business with partners from an increasing number of countries.
   The films were originally chosen by their countries of production, but in 1972 the General Delegate Maurice Bessy asks the President Robert Favre le Bret and the board of Directors to change the rules. The Festival will from then on select the films among the recent productions in each country, a decision that marked a turning point and has since been taken up by many other festivals.
   Thanks to a balance between the artistic quality of the films and their commercial impact, the Festival gains its fame and becomes the meeting place for the international film scene. Not only does the presentation of a film in Cannes guarantee international publicity thanks to the high concentration of the media, but the Festival reveals as much as it reflects the evolution and trends in the world cinema while defending the notion of "cinéma d'auteur for a large audience."
   Many film schools and foreign cinema owe their reputation to Cannes and the Festival has discovered, established and honored directors who, by their presence in Cannes, also contribute immensely to the prestige of the event.
   Besides the screenings, many cultural and artistic activities—debates, tributes, retrospectives, productions and filmed documents—have enriched the palette of the Festival thus helping both the art and the industry of cinema.
Market: The Cannes Film Festival is one of the most important media events in the world. About 4000 journalists, more than half of them belonging to the foreign press, contribute to the fame of the Festival and reinforce its role of a meeting place for the international film scene. Over 1500 media—print press, radio stations, televisions, press agencies, photo agencies and press online—representing about 80 countries, generate a huge international mediatic impact on the selected films, the attending personalities and the many cultural and artistic activities of the event.
Awards: Yes
Competitions: Yes
Major Awards: Palme d'Or, Grand Prix, Best Actress/Actor, Best Director, Best Screenplay, Special Jury Prize, Technical Grand Prix, Camera d'Or

Past Judges: The 53rd Cannes Festival will have two official juries:
- the Feature Films Jury which awards the winning feature films in the competitive section of the official selection.
- the Short Film and Cinefondation Jury (created in 1998) which chooses the award-winners in these two categories of the official selection.
The Camera d'Or is awarded to the best first-time film and is chosen by an independent jury.

Application Process Tips: Submission of Films—
The films must meet the following conditions, unless a special waiver is granted:
- films must have been produced during the 12 months preceding the festival
- films cannot have been presented in any other competition or exhibited in any motion picture event.
- short films that do not exceed 15 minutes in length
(Note: There is no documentary or video section at the Festival.)
Submission of a Film to the Selection Committee—
The Film registrar (Régie des Films) at the Festival's office delivers the rules & regulations and gives information on the deadlines for application and the dates of the Festival. The selection committees view films in Paris: 35 mm print or video-tape (VHS in PAL, Secam or NTSC).
The prints should be sent to France by the Festival shipping agent. Videotapes must be sent to the Festival's office by mail or by an express courrier service.
For any further information please contact the Régie des Films or consult the official web site of the Festival at: www.festival-cannes.org
Unless a special waiver is granted, films must comply with certain conditions :
- Films must have been made during the 18 months preceding the Festival,
- Films must not have been presented in major international festivals,
- Films must not exceed 60 minutes in length.
Note: Documentaries are not accepted.
For any further information (rules & regulations, application forms) please contact the Régie des Films.

Attendance: The Festival is only open to film professionals. An accreditation is necessary to have access to the "Palais des Festivals." Registration forms are delivered by the Festival's office in Paris, by film related organizations and by Unifrance Film.

Journalist Attendance: 4000. Press accreditation is only delivered to the representatives of the media accredited by the Festival's press office. Every year, numerous arrangements are made to facilitate the journalists' work.

4. Berlin Film Festival

While people are recovering from Sundance and the madness of Park City, the Berlin Film Festival is just getting started. Taking place at the beginning of February each year in Berlin, Germany, this fest is one of Europe's longest running (over fifty years) and most prestigious events. Filmmakers arriving at Berlin are given the best of treatment. Traveling overseas can be stressful for some and the incredibly helpful staff make navigating Berlin a breeze. The festival assigns a liaison to every attending filmmaker, who will answer questions and attend immediately to every need—whether it be a ride to a film, help exchanging currency, taking care of problems with your flight or where to get a cheeseburger—these liaisons are on the case. (This special attention comes in handy, especially as the theaters are spread all over town.) To say that the festival is well organized is an understatement—Berlin is perhaps the most well organized festival in the world. For example, each person attending the festival receives a badge that is swiped for each screening. Filmmakers are given a copy of the names, as well as the audience member's designation as a filmmaker, journalist, distributor or a viewer. In addition, there are no such things as "wait lines." The badges allow the ticketsellers to deduce precisely how many tickets are available for each screening, making attending screenings less of a hassle. For filmmakers there is also the European Film Market, which takes place during the festival and affords producers the opportunity to sell their films for theatrical, video or television to European territories. Being so far from Hollywood, there is no sense of pretentiousness about the festival. This is not a Hollywood schmooze-fest, Berlin is about an appreciation of film.

BERLiN iNTERNATiONAL FiLM FESTiVAL

Internationale Filmfestspiele Berlin
Abteilung Programm
Potsdamer Straße 5
Berlin, D-10785
Tel: 49-30-259-20-444
Fax: 49-30-25-920-499
Email: program@berlinale.de
Web Site: www.berlinale.de/
Festival Date: February 7-18
Entry Deadline: Late November
Contact: Moritz de Hadeln, Dieter Kosslick (2002)
Other Staff: Beki Probst, head of European Film Market
Category: Independent, International
Profile: The Berlin International Film Festival was founded in 1951 from an American cultural-political initiative; in a wider sense an initiative of the three Western Allies. Six years after the end of the war,

Berlin was a "showcase" for the free world, and only ten year later the Film Festival was an established and important part of the cultural life in Berlin. Ingmar Bergman, Satyajit Ray, Michelangelo Antonioni, Roman Polanski and the directors of the French Nouvelle Vague Jean-Luc Godard, François Truffaut and Claude Chabrol have all had great international success with their films at the Berlin Festival.

In the mid-sixties began a period of obvious stagnation. In 1970, there was a public outcry, not coincidentally over a film about Vietnam. In 1971, the International Forum of New Cinema was established besides the traditional competition. In 1974, the first Soviet film was seen at the International Film Festival, and a year later, the GDR was also represented. The political climate had changed; treaties with the GDR had been signed. Since then, the Festival has re-established itself as a mirror of international film production, and re-unification has given the Festival a stronger cultural and political role as meeting point and mediator between the West and East.

With an infrastructure integrated into the Berlin International Film Festival, the European Film Market seeks to complement the activities of the film business during the Festival by providing the means to further work and foster an atmosphere favourable to commercial transactions.

The European Film Market is open only to producers, distributors, exhibitors, exporters and importers of films as well as professionals active in the areas of video and television sales and acquisitions. Without being exclusive, the European Film Market is particularly interested in the exchange of productions of European origin or destination. It gives priority to films intended for theatrical distribution.

Awards: Yes

Competitions: Yes

Major Awards: The Golden Berlin Bear for the best feature-length film

The Silver Berlin Bear as the special Jury prize

The prize for the best director (Silver Berlin Bear)

The prize for the best actress (Silver Berlin Bear)

The prize for the best actor (Silver Berlin Bear)

The prize for an outstanding single achievement (Silver Berlin Bear)

A Silver Berlin Bear for an outstanding contribution, to be defined each year

The "Blue Angel," the prize of the European Academy for Film & Television (Brussels) to a European film.

The Alfred Bauer Prize to a long feature film which opens new horizons in the art of film

The Golden Berlin Bear for the best short film

A Special Award (Silver Berlin Bear)

Application Fee: About $100 U.S.

NOTE: Short films submitted for the Competition should not exceed 10 minutes in length.

Attendance: 50,000+

Berlin Film Festival

1	Cinestar	**◄HQ►**	Potsdamer Straße 5 (HQ)
2	CinemaxX	‹2›	Voxstraße 3
		‹3›	Weinhaus Huth
A	Grand Hyatt Hotel	‹4›	Arkaden
		‹5›	Berlinale-Palaste
		‹6›	debis Atrium
		‹7›	Galerie Berliner Volksbank

◄HQ► FESTIVAL HEADQUARTERS	‹1› FESTIVAL RELATED	**3** THEATER	
A HOTEL			

Random Tidbits: For a selection screening, films must be submitted in their original language. Films in German, French and English may be submitted without subtitles, but films in another language should either be subtitled or accompanied by a complete dialogue list in one of the three accepted languages.

In exceptional circumstances, work prints and doubleheaded prints may be accepted. For video-cassettes, the systems VHS or Beta SP are preferable. The PAL, SECAM, or NTSC (not on Beta SP) systems are acceptable.

5. SXSW: South By Southwest Film Festival

Austin is a party town and there is no better bash than SXSW. And they also show some cool films. I like to think that I go to Austin for the movies, but for me, Sixth Street is as much of a draw as the chance to see new indie work. The bars, clubs and restaurants lining Sixth Street during SXSW are not quite as wild as Mardi Gras in New Orleans (less nudity), but they come damn close. Austin's down-to-earth folks make the non-stop partying the main attraction along side the films. The informative panels, the prominent guests, the useful convention and the down-home openness of the people provide a whirlwind education in filmmaking. Spend a weekend at SXSW and you'll get almost the same amount of inspiration you'd get from four years in film school. It's really that cool.

The fest began as an extension of the SXSW Music and Media Conference and has quickly established itself as a formidable force in the indie film world. This slightly mesquite-flavored independent festival has attracted the likes of Quentin Tarantino, Richard Linklater (who lives in Austin) and Kevin Smith, among others, who attend annually to sit on panels and simply enjoy the

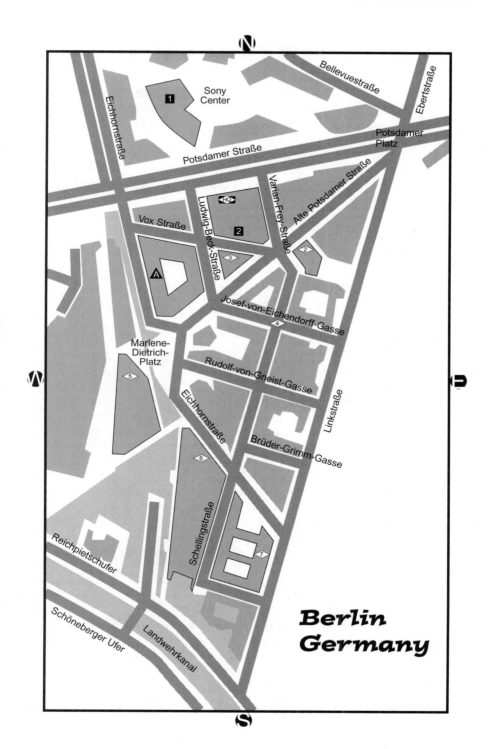

Berlin
Germany

SXSW Film Festival

1 D. Montgomery Theatre Austin Convention Center	◄HQ► **Omni Downtown** 700 San Jacinto	☀ **Scottish Rite Theatre** 207 W. 18th
2 Alamo Drafthouse & Cinema 409 Colorado	**A** **Driskill Hotel** 604 Brazos	☀ **Polly Esther's** 404 Colorado
3 Paramount Theatre 713 Congress	**C** **Four Seasons** 98 San Jacinto	☀ **Stubbs BBQ** 801 Red River
4 State Theatre 719 Congress	**D** **La Quinta Capitol** 300 E. 11th	☀ **Waterloo Brewing Co** 401 Guadalupe
5 Dobie Theatre 21st & Guadalupe	**E** **Radisson Hotel & Suites** 111 Cesar Chavez	☀ **Antone's** 213 W. 5th
	F **Wellesley Inn & Suites** 1001 S. IH-35	

◄HQ► FESTIVAL HEADQUARTERS	◄1► FESTIVAL RELATED	**3** THEATER	
A HOTEL	☀ HOT SPOT		

THE SECRETS OF SXSW

Austin, Texas, is already a party town as it is the home of the University of Texas. But if you're in town for the SXSW Film Festival and want to avoid the college kids and the frat party scene, there are still plenty of great places to visit. Sixth Street is really where it all happens and the entire street is closed off on Friday and Saturday (and some parts on Thursday.) Sixth Street highlights include Joe's Generic, Emo's Club DeVille (a lot of unofficial SXSW parties take place at Club DeVille, which is just off Sixth and Red River) and The Library—which is fun with if you're in the mood for pool and air hockey. The coolest hangout on Sixth Street is Casino El Camino. If you want to hang with the college crowd, Fat Tuesdays has live music and serves every alcoholic fruit drink known to man, and Logan's is a sports bar with enough televisions to find your home team. A real Austin favorite is The Black Cat, which began as an anti-Sixth Street venue—they have live music with no cover charge, and the original owner Paul Sessums (recently deceased), is a local hero. No matter where you are on Sixth Street, you'll find a place that suits your taste and by the end of the evening you might even remember where you were.

For authentic Tex Mex food head to Guerros on Congress. You'll also want to check out Ego's on the corner of Congress and Riverside, which is a cool, hidden away place with live music in a very intimate setting.

And you absolutely have to visit the world-famous Alamo Draft House, a venue that has perhaps the greatest movie theater innovation since widescreen or surround sound—they serve beer along with their other concessions. There are tables in the theater so you can enjoy food and a cold one during the movie. It's heaven! After a night at the Alamo, you can pop right across the street into a dance club called Polyester for retro dance tunes.

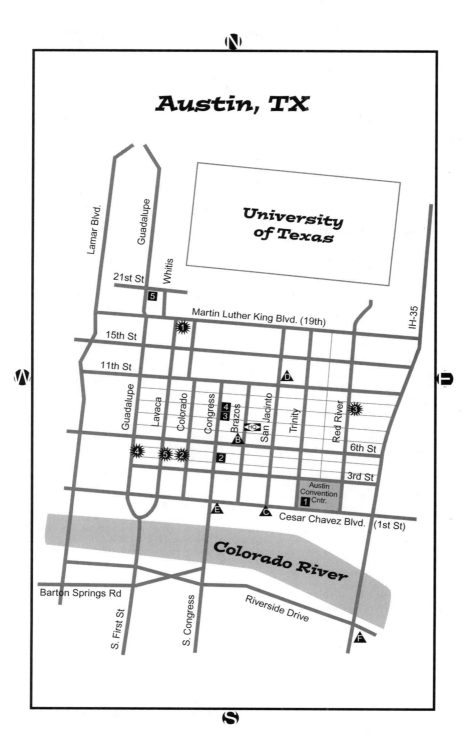

fest. Texas filmmakers are given their due with screenings, and this attention to regional artists gives out-of-towners a taste of something new to chew on other than the usual indie fare. The atmosphere is incredibly laid back, which accounts for a lot of their tremendous growth. People come back to Austin for this event.

1000 East 40th Street
Austin, TX 78751
Tel: 512-467-7979
Fax: 512-451-0754
Email: sxsw@sxsw.com
Web Site: www.sxsw.com
Festival Date: March 9-14
Entry Deadline: Early: Mid-November; Late: Early December
Year Festival Began: 1994
Contact: Louis Black
Category: Independent
Profile: SXSW Film is a four-day film conference and nine day film festival providing a unique place to listen to and learn from the best voices in all phases of independent filmmaking, as well as showcasing the best new independent films.

Festival categorization: Independent films from America and all over the world. Panels, workshops, mini-meetings, mentor sessions, demo reel sessions. SXSW Film is the conference for the working filmmaker. The SXSW Film conference is aimed at making movies and getting them seen. Panels, workshops, mentor sessions, and work-in-progress screenings at SXSW are geared towards new information, innovation, hands on work sessions, and the latest technology. Each March, working filmmakers from all aspects of the industry and around the world gather in Austin to talk about film. The conference concentrates on the million details that are involved in filmmaking. The talk and the Film festival are about the energy and future of film. The best professionals in the business come to share their expertise at SXSW because this is an audience of passionate intelligent filmmakers who love the unique dialogue opportunity that SXSW provides.

SXSW Film Festival attendees packed the houses for new films by a cross section of international filmmakers, who premiered a rich selection of over 200 of the best in U.S. and international features and shorts. Legendary cinema innovators D.A. Pennebaker and Monte Hellman were on hand to meet and encourage the next generation of filmmakers at retrospectives of their work. Other SXSW 2000 filmmakers included Michael Almereyda, Carlos Avila, Craig Baldwin, Barry Blaustein, Stephen Frears, Peter Greenaway, the Hughes Brothers, Barry Levinson, Ron Mann, Gregory Nava, Todd Phillips, Roger Spottiswoode, and Julien Temple.

In addition to the SXSWeek events, North by Northwest Music and New Media Conference and Festival (NXNW), held each Fall in Portland, Oregon, is a production of SXSW as well. In association with NOW, an alternative newsweekly in Toronto, SXSW is also involved in North by Northeast (NXNE), held in Toronto, Canada in late Spring.

Famous Speakers: Past speakers include: Robert Rodriguez, Quentin Tarantino, Kevin Smith, Ruby Lerner, Judith Helfand, Richard Linklater, Steven Soderbergh, Anne Walker-McBay, Caroline Kaplan, Rana Joy Glickman, John Sloss, John Pierson, Emanuel Levy, Susan Bodine.
Awards: Yes
Competitions: Yes
Major Awards: Best Narrative Film, Best Documentary Film.
Value of Awards: Feature and short film winners receive plaques commemorating the Silver Armadillo Award and feature length film winners receive lab, film stock and other services.
Application Tips: Yes, make a good film. And don't submit until you are ready. It doesn't do you any good to submit a cut that is so rough that it does not give you a good shot at getting in. Most festivals are amenable to accepting films for submission after the deadline, you just have to call and ask for an extension.
Application Fee: Early: $20 for shorts, $30 for features. Late: $25 for shorts, $35 for features.
Insider Advice: The wheel that squeaks the loudest does not get the oil. We would suggest not sending photos until your film is accepted into the Festival, it saves you money and photos do not influence our decision.
Odds of Acceptance: 1 in 7
Tourist Information: Austin is beautiful in the springtime, and there is much to do, although most fest-goers don't have time to see and do all Austin has to offer.
Travel Tips: It is hard to get to Austin on a direct flight, at least until the new airport opens in 2000. Also, Austin is a place where it is possible to get around without renting a car, but it makes life a lot easier if you have one.
Best Restaurants: Fonda San Miguel.
Best Bars: Dog & Duck Pub
Best Hangout for Filmmakers: Dog & Duck Pub
Best Place for Breakfast: Las Manitas

6. Telluride Film Festival

Telluride is the best vacation festival on the planet, period. Sundance may be the place where the industry does business, but in Telluride you'll make lifelong friends at the movies. Set in a former mining town in the Rocky Mountains at a breathtaking (literally) 9,000 foot elevation, the September event in Telluride, Colorado, transforms the whole tiny city into a celebration of cinema. (The town itself is very small and everything is within convenient walking distance—no need to rent a car.) The charming venues will remind you of the movie theaters of yesteryear—without the modern (and sometimes annoying) sound systems of theaters today that can leave your ears ringing.

There's something special about being at Telluride. Conversation in movie lines revolves around the "art" and appreciation of movies rather than "grosses," current box office or the latest "deal," all of which is incredibly refreshing. Leave your cell phone at home, you won't need it and you'll be booed at if it goes off—this festival is all about an appreciation and love of film; save the deal-making for another festival. This festival is also short, a four-day event that seems to end too soon, leaving you wanting more. There's just something in the air at Telluride that unites everyone in a cinema love-fest.

Telluride Film Festival

"I had a great time in Telluride, a sort of heterosexual Provincetown with mountains instead of beaches. Good parties, wonderful selection of films—a summer camp for lunatics. Only problem: it's difficult to smoke cigarettes and breathe properly in that altitude."
—John Waters, Director

379 State St. #3
Portsmouth, NH 03801
Tel: 603-433-9202
Fax: 603-433-9206
Email: Tellufilm@aol.com
Web Site: www.telluridefilmfestival.com
Festival Date: August 31 - September 3, 2001
Entry Deadline: July 15, annually.
Year Festival Began: 1974
Director: Stella Pence, General Manager
Category: Independent, Student
Profile: Snowcapped peaks that hover over a glacial-cut valley provide a visually spectacular backdrop for the Telluride Film Festival. Tucked in this valley is the idyllic turn-of-the-century mining town of Telluride whose Western appeal and small-town charm is still as genuine as its Victorian homes and storefronts. The Telluride Film Festival, held each Labor Day Weekend since 1974 in a Colorado mountain town, is an international educational event celebrating the art of film. It is a sympathetic gathering of film aficionados (both lovers and creators of cinema) who come together from all over the world and from all walks of life to see and discuss and celebrate the most interesting work of the past, present and future. Telluride is not a series of screenings for the press, nor is it a film market. It is a small, friendly festival, regarded by many as one of the most unique events in the world of film.

The Telluride Film Festival traditionally does not release information about the content of its programming until opening day. Despite this idiosyncrasy, the Festival sells out every year. Over 5,000 people make the trek to Telluride each Labor Day Weekend on the strength of the Festival's reputation for innovative and exciting programming, and many return year after year.

The program consists of a minimum of 27 major film events, which include three tributes to individual artists. These events are supplemented by for-

Telluride Film Festival

1	Mason's Hall Cinema	◄HQ►	Hospitality
2	Nugget Theatre	◇2◇	Monday Seminars
3	Sheridan Opera House	◇3◇	Conversations
4	Abel Gance Outdoor Cinema	◇4◇	Yahoo! Interactive
5	Chuck Jones Cinema	◇5◇	Food
6	The Max/Minnie	◇6◇	Picnic Area
		◇7◇	Festival Club

◄HQ► FESTIVAL HEADQUARTERS	◇1◇ FESTIVAL RELATED	**3** THEATER

THE SECRETS OF TELLURiDE

The first thing to remember when attending the Telluride Film Festival is to be very aware of the 9,000 foot elevation. Drink plenty of water and avoid alcohol, as its effects are enhanced at this high altitude. Being so high in the clouds also seems to have a slowing down effect among the locals as everything seems move at a much more leisurely pace—service is notoriously slow so make the time for it. You can expect a great sit down breakfast at Sofio's, which is located one block before the Mason's Hall Cinema—just don't expect it fast. Plan for an hour and a half (at least) for a sit down breakfast, or grab some quick take out at Baked In Telluride (located beyond the Nugget at Fir) any time of the day. Another place for some quick eats is the Downstairs Deli right next to the Nugget. The finest Italian restaurant in town is Rustico Ristorante (on Colorado near Mason's), and be sure to visit its sister establishment in Mountain Village called La Piazza.

For a powerful meal to die for, The Powder House is an amazing steak house and is located in the basement of the Sheridan Opera House. Near Pacific Street, you'll find Pacific Street Market, which is great for take out. Pacific Street is also home to Josie's Kitchen for great Mexican food on and Leimgruber's, a delectable German restaurant.

Take the gondola up to Mountain Village where the Chuck Jones Cinema is located for 15-20 minutes of relaxation and an awe-inspiring view of Telluride above the clouds. There you can visit a fantastic restaurant called 9545, which is also the actual altitude.

I cannot stress enough to drink lots of water, use sunscreen and wear your clothing in layers as the weather changes from one minute to the next. Most important, remember to breathe.

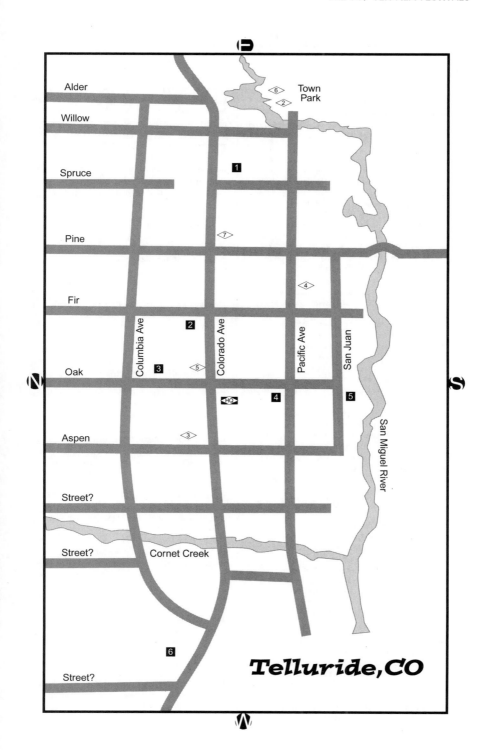

Telluride, CO

mal and informal conversations and seminars with the filmmakers and artists in attendance, as well as parties, picnics and, of course, popcorn!

FILMS

New films from around the world, classics of the first hundred years of cinema, documentaries, short subjects, animation, and works by student and emerging filmmakers are all presented at screenings in seven theatres. Each program is accompanied and introduced by at least one person key to its creation.

Telluride created and marked much in film history: it was the first to play Louis Malle's *My Dinner with Andre*, David Lynch's *Blue Velvet* and Billy Bob Thornton's *Sling Blade*. It hosted the World or North American premieres of such films as *Central Station, The Dreamlife of Angels, Happiness, Jesus' Son, The Straight Story, Ma Vie En Rose, Secrets and Lies, Cinema Paradiso, The Piano, The Sweet Hereafter, Au Revoir Les Enfants, Breaking the Waves, To Die For, Farewell, My Concubine* and *My Left Foot*. Telluride audiences were also the first to learn the secret of *The Crying Game!*

Seminars: Each year, three noon seminars are held, free to all, in a town park. The seminars are led by noted film scholar/educator Annette Insdorf and involve the filmmakers as panelists. The discussions revolve around such topics as "What are the challenges to portraying social and cultural issues in the movies?" and "To what extent can—or should—the actor be the 'author' of his screen character?" Panelists have included nearly every prominent film artist attending the Festival, from Robert Altman to Zhang Yimou.

Panels: People at the Telluride Film Festival are always talking about movies. Here the focus is on the creative talents behind the films and providing access to them for all passholders through a series of seminars, panel discussions and post-screening question and answer sessions. The intimate environment of the town, the various social events and even standing in theatre lines provide opportunities for connections between passholders and filmmakers.

Famous Speakers: Telluride has orchestrated ributes to the following: Shirley MacLaine, Mike Leigh, Alain Cavalier, John Schlesinger, Zhang Yimou, Judy Davis, Ken Burns, Harriet Andersson, Ken Loach, John Alton, Jennifer Jason Leigh, Elmer Bernstein, Cy Endfield, Harvey Keitel, Jodie Foster, Sven Nykvist, Clint Eastwood, Gerard Depardieu, John Berry and many more.

Awards: No

Competitions: No

Application Tips: Entry in the Telluride Film Festival is open to professional and non-professional filmmakers working in all aesthetic disciplines: documentary, narrative, animation, experimental, etc. Features and shorts of all styles and lengths are eligible for consideration provided that they are new works and will remain unseen by the public until the current Labor Day weekend.

Selected short films will play either with a feature or as part of three specially selected programs of "Filmmakers of Tomorrow," "Great Expectations," and "Celluloid Resumes" featuring works by emerging artists.

For students, the most important qualities we seek are: passion for film, an ability to interact with other students and Symposium guests, and a willingness to follow a rigorous, albeit free-form program of screenings and discussions. With only 50 slots available, each student's full commitment to the program is critical.

Application Fee: Entry fee based on length of film.

Odds of Acceptance: Over 400 films entered.

Travel Tips: The festival takes place in Telluride, Colorado which is at a 9,000 foot elevation. (Keep in mind that pilots in the Air Force are given oxygen at 10,000 foot elevations.) Steer clear from alcoholic beverages as their effect in the mountain air is greatly enhanced. Give yourself at least a day to get used to the thin air.

It is recommended that all attendees arrange lodging as well in advance as possible. For assistance, call the Film Festival travel desk of Telluride & Mountain Village Visitor Services, the Festival's travel partner, at 888-871-3646 in the U.S. or at 970-728-4431 to make a reservation request.

Best Parties: Telluride Festival goers value the opportunity to mix and mingle. Patron passholders enjoy the first event of the Festival on Friday morning—a brunch at a mountaintop ranch. The Opening Night Feed on Friday evening closes off several blocks of Telluride's main street to gather all passholders together for a buffet supper and spirits. On Labor Day the entire Festival convenes in Town Park for a relaxing picnic.

Random Tidbits: Non-competitive, premier event.

Special Programs: The Telluride Film Festival is also renowned for its unique once-in-a-lifetime special presentations. These have included such memorable programs as Tod Browning's 1931 *Dracula* with new score by Philip Glass and live accompaniment by Glass and the Kronos Quartet, *The Unknown Chaplin, Writing for Hitch, 100 Years Ago: Films by Lumiere, Walt Disney's Unseen Treasures, The Silver Age: The American Film 1967-1974* and 3D in the Movies.

Tributes: At the heart of the Telluride Film Festival are three tributes given each year to distinguished and at times overlooked talents in the art of film. The Telluride Film Festival was the first in the world to significantly recognize the careers of Michael Powell, Joel McCrea, John Alton, Andrei Tarkovsky and Clint Eastwood. Others who have come to Telluride to receive this honor include Gloria Swanson, Francis Ford Coppola, Abel Gance, Gerard Depardieu, Werner Herzog, Peter Greenaway, Sven Nykvist, Jack Nicholson, Chuck Jones, King Vidor, Harvey Keitel, Shohei Imamura, Jodie Foster, Janet Leigh, Andrej Wajda, Neil Jordan, Susumu Hani, Meryl Streep, David Lynch, Philip Glass and Catherine Deneuve.

7. Chicago International Film Festival

Even without a film festival, Chicago would still be a fantastic city to visit. Growing up in Detroit, Michigan, where we had no real film festival to speak of, Chicago was a favorite destination for me and my pals. (And less than a five-hour drive, which counts for a lot when you have to talk your folks into lending you the car.) Chicago was and still is a savior.

Recently celebrating its 36th year, the Chicago International Film Festival maintains an international flavor by showing amazing new work from all over the world—Argentina, England, Brazil, Mexico, Turkey, Russia, Belgium, Japan, France, Iceland, Germany, Poland, Taiwan, Australia, Spain, Thailand and Iran among others—all while avoiding an air of pomposity. Heck, besides an always incredible line-up of world cinema, their most recent fest paid tribute to Director Joe Dante and screened Gremlins 2: The New Batch, and the original Howling with Dee Wallace. Now that is cool.

In addition, their relentless support of issue-raising documentaries is to be applauded. The programmers at Chicago are not following anyone else's lead—they're taking their own lead and running with it. With over 100 films, a truly international line-up, an impressive variety of documentaries, Hollywood galas and guests like Laurence Fishburne, Robert Altman and Harold Ramis, the Chicago International Film Festival is—bar none—the best fest in the Midwest.

Chicago International Film Festival

"Martin Scorsese, probably America's greatest director, premiered his first film here. So did Bertrand Tavernier of France and Alan Parker of England. The German New Wave—Fassbinder and Herzog and others washed ashore in Chicago while others were scorning them. The Chicago International Film Festival has grown into an event which more than a million movie lovers have attended.
—*Roger Ebert, Chicago Sun-Times*

32 West Randolph St., Suite 600
Chicago, IL 60601-9803
Tel: 312-425-9400
Fax: 312-425-0944
Email: info@chicagofilmfestival.com
Web Site: www.chicagofilmfestival.com
Festival Date: October
Entry Deadline: Early August
Year Festival Began: 1965
Contact: Michael Kutza
Director: Michael Kutza, Founder and Artistic Director
Programmer: Helen Gramates
Jim Healy
Other Staff: Naomi Walker, Outreach Coordinator
Category: American Films, Animation, Documentary, Ethnic African, Ethnic Asian, Ethnic Black, Ethnic Jewish, Ethnic Latin, Ethnic Spanish, Experimental, First Time Independent Filmmakers, Gay Lesbian, Independent, International, Short, Student, Woman
Profile: Cinema/Chicago organizes the Chicago International Film Festival. Films from around the world have graced its screens for thirty-six years, making it the oldest competitive festival in North America. Always fresh, new and exciting, the Festival brings the world's most contemporary films to Chicago, along with their producers, directors and stars.

Chicago International Film Festival

**Chicago
(North Side)**

1 Leows Cineplex 600 N. Michigan Ave	**HQ** Festival Office 32 W. Randolph St	**C** The Claridge Hotel 1244 N. Dearborn Pkwy
2 Music Box Theatres 3733 N. Southport	**◇** Hilton Garden Inn (HQ) 10 E. Grand Ave	**D** Hotel Allegro 171 W. Randolph St
3 Max Palevsky Cinema 1212 E. 59th St	**A** Chicago Hilton & Towers 720 S. Michigan Ave	**E** Omni Ambassador E 1301 N. State St
4 The Chicago Theatre 175 N. State St	**B** Hyatt Regency Hotel 151 E. Wacker Dr.	**F** Regal Knickerbocker 163 E. Walton Place

HQ FESTIVAL HEADQUARTERS	**◇** FESTIVAL RELATED	**3** THEATER
A HOTEL		

**Chicago
(South Side)**

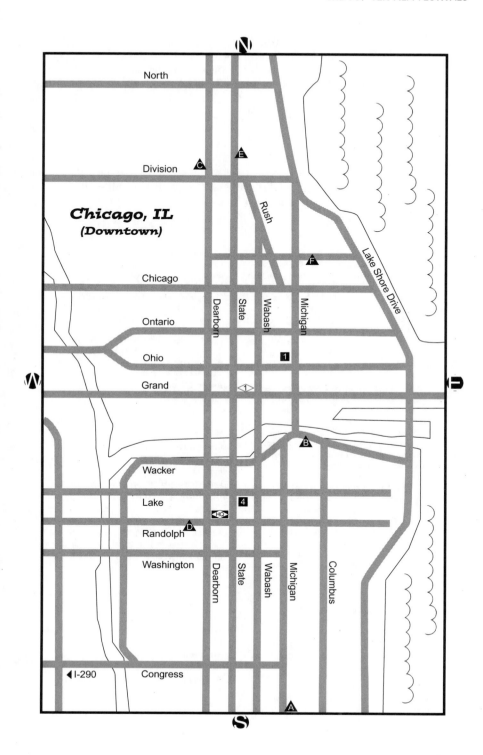

THE SECRETS OF CHICAGO

Whether you're in town for the Chicago International Film Festival or just in for a weekend getaway, Rush Street is always big for bar-hopping and restaurants. On the North side, Clark has a lot of cool bars, including Sluggers, a sports bar with actual batting cages and midget boxing. Plus, there's Raven's, which is open until 5 a.m. on Fridays and Saturdays. (The Lincoln Park area is also a hotspot at night.) I recommend sticking to screenings at the Music Box—the South side venues are not in the best neighborhoods. Just a few doors down from the Music Box is Cullen's, a fantastic Irish pub. Also look for O'Callaghan's and the Tiny Lounge, which is a very small, retro-type bar with great art deco design. Other great spots are John Barleycorn (the one on Belden, near the Biograph is where Dillinger was shot), Martyr, which is a cool punk bar and Goose Island Wrigleyville is one of the top microbrews in the Midwest. The best pizza in the city is at My π.

Through the Chicago International Film Festival we can explore our curiosity about different cultures, places and thoughts through the diverse films offered this year. For those of us who have strong ties to countries outside the U.S., these films can be poignant reminders of distant homelands. The Festival creates an opportunity for each of us to learn something about one another.

Cinema/Chicago is the parent organization of the annual Chicago International Film Festival, North America's oldest competitive international film festival.

Founded in 1964 by award winning filmmaker and graphic designer Michael Kutza, the Festival's goals were to provide an alternative to the commercial Hollywood movies that dominated the city's theaters, to discover and present new filmmakers to Chicago, and to award these filmmakers for their artistry. The first Festival opened in 1965 at the Carnegie Theater, where directors King Vidor, Stanley Kramer, and actress Bette Davis were honored for their contributions to American cinema. Since then, the Festival has continued to grow to become a world-renowned annual event. In 1998 more than 70,000 local and international audience members viewed over 110 feature film premieres and 60 short film productions from 36 countries on six downtown screens. Seeking out the best in cinema, the Festival discovered new talents and opened windows to a world of film previously unavailable in Chicago.

The festival introduced innovative directors such as Martin Scorsese, John Carpenter, Susan Seidelman, Victor Nunez, Gregory Nava (United States); Wim Wenders, Rainer Werner Fassbinder (Germany); Bertrand Tavernier (France); Peter Weir (Australia), Mike Leigh, Alan Parker, Michael Apted, Peter Greenaway (England); Vincent Ward (New Zealand), Krzysztof Kieslowski, Krzysztof Zanussi (Poland); Dusan Makavejev (Yugoslavia), Victor Erice (Spain); Jan Troell (Sweden) and Maria Louisa Bemberg (Argentina), plus many other internationally renowned directors.

The Chicago International Television Competition is also about quality television. As a division of the annual Chicago International Film Festival, one of the world's premiere cinematic events, we have made it our goal to celebrate the best in television. We do this by bestowing our highest honor, The Gold Hugo, upon work that compels, entertains, educates and informs a television audience. Most importantly, the television productions and commercials annually recognized in our competition propel the medium to higher levels of quality and distinction.

Panels: Different themes annually.

Famous Speakers: John Boorman, Monte Hellman, Spike Lee, Morgan Freeman, Lauren Bacall, John Frankenheimer, Ray Harryhausen, Jodie Foster

Market: No

Competitions: Yes

Major Awards: The Gold Hugo is awarded to Best International Feature Film.

Last Winning Films: *La Maladie de Sachs*

Last Winning Directors: Michel Deville (France)

Past Judges: Michael Wilmington, Jerry Schatzberg, Christopher Lee, Hill Harper, Michelle Reis

Application Fee: $30-$100 depending on which category the film is entered in. ($100 feature films)

Insider Advice: Submit early and adhere to all Festival regulations.

Average Films Entered: 1,000

Films Screened: 100 Feature Films, 80 Shorts and Documentaries

Odds of Acceptance: 1 in 10

Filmmaker Perks: Free travel and lodging; some meals.

Attendance: 70,000

Journalist Attendance: 75

Tourist Information: The Art Institute, The Museum of Contemporary Arts, The Shedd Aquarium, The Sears Tower, The John Hancock Building, The Field Museum of Natural History,

Wrigley Field, Komiskey Park, The Adler Planetarium, The Magnificent Mile.

Best Cheap Hotels: Motel Six—312-787-3580

Best Luxury Hotels: Hilton Chicago and Towers—312-922-4400

Best Restaurants: Low End: Hi Ricky's—773-388-0000

High End: Tsunami—312-642-9911

Best Bars: The Alcohol Abuse Center (Tuman's), on the corner of Leavitt and Chicago

Best Hangout for Filmmakers: Butcher Shop Gallery

Best Place for Breakfast: Leo's Luncheonette

Lodging at the Festival:
Headquarters Hotel:
• Hilton Garden Inn
10 East Grand Avenue, (312) 595-0000

Host Hotels:
• Hyatt Chicago
151 East Wacker Drive, (312) 565-1234
• Hilton Chicago & Towers
720 South Michigan Avenue, (312) 922-4400

Participating Hotels:
• The Claridge Hotel
1244 North Dearborn Parkway, (312) 787-4980
• Regal Knickerbocker Hotel
163 East Walton Place, (312) 751-8100
• Omni Ambassador East
1301 North State Street, (312) 787-7200
• Hotel Allegro
171 West Randolph Street, (312) 236-0123

8. Florida Film Festival

Located in the gorgeous city of Orlando, the Florida Film Festival has been called the best regional film festival and with good reason. This festival is an intimate affair offering the opportunity for attendees and filmmakers alike to interact in an atmosphere of unpretentious revelry. I attended the Florida fest as a judge for their shorts program in 1997 where I sat on the jury with John Pierson. (This is the same year Pierson met the Blair Witch boys and, well, the rest is history.) I have never been treated as well by any festival I have attended as I was by the Florida fest. Filmmakers are treated like royalty as the fest rolls out the red carpet for arriving artists. Now in its tenth year, films screen at the spectacularly beautiful Enzian Theater. (The Enzian is a classic movie house that hosts other fests, such as the Central Florida Jewish Film Festival, the South Asian Film Festival and a variety of festivals of films for kids.) The festival takes place in June, but the Enzian brings independent film to Orlando year round.

The festival ends with a gloriously star-studded awards ceremony attended by hundreds of filmmakers, members of the media and local luminaries. This elegant event is held on a sound stage at Universal Studios and is a gala on par with the Academy Awards®. Not to be missed for filmmakers and the lucky residents of Orlando.

1300 South Orlando Ave.
Maitland, FL 32751
Tel: 407-629-8587; 407-629-1088
Fax: 407-629-6870
Email: filmfest@gate.net
Web Site: www.floridafilmfest.com
Festival Date: June 8-17

Entry Deadline: Early Deadline: February 23 Late Deadline: March 23

Contact: Matthew Curtis

Director: James Green, General Manager

Programmer: Matthew Curtis

Other Staff: Kat Quast, Assistant Manager, William Gridley, Director of Marketing & Development, Jane Bohn, Volunteer Coordinator

Category: Independent

Profile: Celebrating its tenth provocative year, the Florida Film Festival (June 8 to 17, 2001) showcases the best in American independent and foreign films. Past year's guests include Oliver Stone, Christopher Walken, Dennis Hopper, Gena Rowlands, Steve Buscemi, and William H. Macy. Festival seminars have included such film industry notables as Bingham Ray, Cliff Robertson, and Victor Nunez; cinematographers Haskell Wexler and Bill Butler; animator Bill Plympton; and producers Gale Anne Hurd and Roger Corman. The Enzian Theater also hosts other festival events. Co-produced with the Asian Cultural Association, the South Asian Film Festival (February 3-5, 2001) takes place every February at Enzian Theater. The three-day celebration of Indian culture, heritage, and film artistry comprises weekend matinees and evening shows of four cinematic programs. In 2000, the films included Deepa Mehta's *Earth,* Sturla Gunnarsson's *Such A Long Journey,* and Santosh Sivan's brilliant *The Terrorist.* Every October, Enzian Theater hosts the Central Florida Jewish Film Festival in cooperation with the Jewish Community Center of Greater Orlando. The 2001 festival (October 29-30, 2000) featured four films: *Pick a Card, Train of Life, The Plot Against Harry* (with the animated short *Village of Idiots*), and *Kadosh.* Brouhaha (November 11-12, 2000) is an annual two-day festival, sponsored by Enzian Theater, that showcases the work of independent, Florida-based filmmakers and film students. Each year the showcase takes place over two November afternoons, with each afternoon featuring two programs of totally different shorts, trailers, and features. The 2000 Brouhaha featured dozens of works representing filmmakers and film students from around the state and half-a-dozen schools, including FSU, VCC, DBCC, UCF, Ringling, and U Miami.

Seminars: Topics change every year, usually five or six scattered throughout the ten days. Some of last year's subjects included "The Role of Digital Media in Film," "Successful Indie Film Development Strategies," "Shoot Today So It Will Play Tomorrow" (the Cinematographers seminar), and the always popular closing day "Filmmaker Forum."

Panels: Most of our seminars are panel driven.

Famous Speakers: Haskell Wexler, Oliver Stone, Joel Schumacher, Michael Apted, Brian Dennehy, Bob Hawk, Gale Anne Hurd, Diane Ladd, Rod Steiger, Roger Corman, Dennis Hopper

Awards: Yes

Competitions: Yes

Major Awards: Grand Jury Prizes for: Best Narrative Feature Best Documentary Feature, Best Documentary Short, Best Short Film plus one other award at each jury's discretion, plus Audience Awards for: Best Narrative Feature, Best Documentary, Best Short Film

Value of Awards: No $ value but a very nice trophy presented to the winning filmmakers at the Closing Night Awards Gala.

Last Winning Films: *The Headhunter's Sister, 35 miles from normal, Hang Your Dog in the Wind, Before I Sleep, Andre the Giant Has a Posse, Hands on a Hardbody, Blue City, Anna in the Sky, The Journey, Nobody's Business, The Spirit of Christmas, Only Child*

Last Winning Directors: Scott Saunders, Mark Schwahn, Brian Flemming, Kristen Schultz, Helen Stickler, S.R. Bindler, David Birdsell, Mark Edgington, Harish Saluja, Alan Berliner, Trey Parker, Christopher Landon & David Ogden

Past Judges: Peter Broderick, Jason Kliot, Robert Hawk, Bingham Ray, Stuart Strutin, Bruce Sinofsky, Chris Gore (!), John Pierson, Gale Anne Hurd, Jeff Lipsky, Seymour Cassel, Frederick Marx, Bruce Sinofsky, Paul Cohen, Karol Martesko

Application Tips: Do something original, spend more money on your film than your video jacket, send as finished a work as possible up to the entry deadline, edit!

Application Fee: $30 for features (50 minutes or more), $15 for shorts (less than 50 mins.), $15 late fee for entries postmarked after early entry deadline.

THE SECRETS OF FLORIDA

The Enzian Theater is the center of all the action at the Florida Film Festival. On the corner of Lake near the theater is The Copper Rocket, a very relaxing pub. If you're looking for wonderful Italian food, just across the street from the Enzian is the kitschy Buca di Beppo. South of the theater is Winter Park Village which has tons of shops, restaurants and bars. The real nightlife is downtown (just take Orange all the way). Downtown Orlando is host to amazing dance clubs like The Kit Kat Club, Icon and Cairo, all of which are located in an area called Wall Street Plaza. Take a cab because you won't want to be driving home.

Florida Film Festival

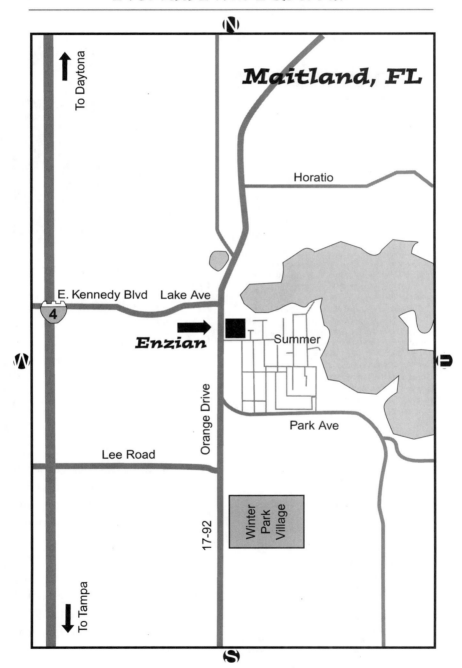

Maitland, FL

Insider Advice: Comedy is hard; work on your script; get your sound mix as good as possible; be original; longer is not necessarily better; get your film in early and be patient; pick your spots—it's hard to get excited over a film that has already played at numerous other in-state festivals; if you're not going to have a 16 or 35 print by late May you probably want to look for another festival.

Average Films Entered: Well-scripted, well-conceived, original visions competently brought to celluloid life...good ones!

Films Screened: 40-50 student works are screened during the ten days of the festival.

Odds of Acceptance: Approximately 150-200 features, 200-300 shorts, and 75-100 docs are submitted. About ten narrative features, ten doc features, and enough shorts to fill four live action and one animated shorts program (perhaps 30-40) are accepted. Then of course, we also program a dozen or so "Spotlight" films a national sidebar of five films, half a dozen Midnight Movies and a few tribute films. All-in-all, approximately 90-100 films

Filmmaker Perks: Due to the limitations of our sponsorships, we are able to fly in some but not all, of the narrative and documentary feature directors, and put them up for four days or so. Any filmmaker whose film is in the festival and makes their own way to Orlando we guarantee will be put up for at least two nights, regardless whether their film is a short or feature.

Filmmakers will also make contacts with the Orlando Film Commission, Universal Studios, other local and national industry professionals such as film distributors and entertainment lawyers, and many others that could be helpful in their future cinematic endeavors.

Travel Tips: It's hot! Pack light clothes, a bathing suit, and one decent outfit for the Closing Night Awards Gala at Universal Studios

Best Restaurants: Depending on your budget, the following are recommended by members of the festival staff: Enzo's, Chez Vincent, Cafe Tu Tu Tango, West End Grill, Tacqueria Quetzalcoatl, The Melting Pot, Bubbalou's Bodacious Bar- B-Q

Best Bars: Sapphire Supper Club, Kit Kat Klub, Go Lounge, Copper Rocket

Best Hangout for Filmmakers: All of the above plus Harold & Maude's and the Nicole St. Pierre lounge

Best Place for Breakfast: The Coffee Shoppe on Lee Road, First Watch

Festival Tale: A couple of years ago a very well known character actor with a history in Indie film going back to the '60s was being driven down the main drag in downtown Winter Park. As he passed the Victoria's Secret store, an absolutely spectacular woman in a very small dress walked out the front door and he leaned out the window of the car yelling, "Hey Babe! Love that Wonderbra!" The woman waved, the actor told the flabbergasted volunteer driver to pull the car over, and he ended up

asking the woman out. She agreed, and he still has a smile on his face to this day.

2) How about having your final closing night program, after ten days and nearly 100 films, be a subtitled French-Canadian film that unfortunately for your 98 percent English-speaking-only audience turns out to have no subtitles at all!? Lesson learned—make sure all "subtitled" prints really are subtitled during the inspection process.

9. Slamdance International Film Festival

Park City, Utah is not just about Sundance anymore as alternative festivals (sometimes referred to as "parasites") continue to invade. Each year is marked by the creation of a new -dance festival, with names like Slumdance, Souldance, Tromadance, Vandance, Lapdance and No Dance, with no end in sight. Each of these rebel film fests infiltrate the home of Sundance for one reason—to get massive media exposure for their own films and event. The streets are now so crowded with alternative events, I choose to call the entire anarchistic scene "Park City Madness." Only one alternative festival has endured the hardships and gained the respect of the industry. Primarily because the staff couldn't find "real" jobs, but also because they have stayed true to their core beliefs. Slamdance remains the true rebel film festival "by filmmakers for filmmakers." Besides the garage band-like atmosphere, what I admire most about Slamdance is their never-ending refusal to grow up and "become a 'real' festival." The filmmaker-friendly atmosphere is everywhere as festival founder and host of the event, the Mad-Hatter Dan Mirvish, keeps a low-key cool to the screenings. Slamdance screens about a dozen features by first-time directors in an environment devoid of industry snobbery or elitism. The spirit of DIY filmmaking is present in the halls, in the lines and at the parties in an incredibly supportive environment that at times feels more like a college dorm room than a festival. Coinciding with Sundance, screenings take place in January at the Silver Mine in Park City. (The timing is by design and attracts acquisitions executives willing to find their way to the top of Main Street to discover new talent.)

Slamdance has become the festival to watch for the next big thing. Several Slamdance premiere films have graduated to theatrical distribution, making acceptance to the event an achievement in itself. And festival directors in Park City attend the event to discover new films to invite to their own festivals. One word of advice, when you enter Slamdance, leave the industry air kisses at the door. This festival kicks serious ass.

"Slamdance has truly come into its own."
—Lauren Sydney, CNN

5526 Hollywood Blvd.
Los Angeles, CA 90028
Tel: 323-466-1786
Fax: 323-466-1784
Email: mail@slamdance.com
Web Site: www.slamdance.com
Festival Date: January 20-27
Entry Deadline: Early submission deadline: October 11; Late submission deadline: November 8
Year Festival Began: 1995
Contact: Peter Baxter, Dan Mirvish
Director: Peter Baxter
Category: Independent, International, Short
Profile: Slamdance is a film festival that was started in 1995 by a group of filmmakers. We've since expanded into other support mechanisms for filmmakers (including our Screenplay Competition), but the following pages will mainly talk about the Festival itself - which takes place every January in Park City, Utah, simultaneous with the Sundance Film Festival.

In 2000, Slamdance got over 2050 total submissions (slightly more shorts than features). We programmed about 80 films altogether, with 12 features and 16 shorts screening in the main competition. We had 21 shorts screening in the kick-off edition of the Anarchy online section last year, and the rest of the films screened as Special Screenings, or in the Lounge—competing for the Spirit of Slamdance award. Statistically this does make Slamdance harder to get into than Sundance, but that doesn't mean you shouldn't try.
Awards: Yes

Competitions: Yes

Major Awards: The Sparky and the Audience Award.

Value of Awards: Last year, the festival gave away over $35,000 worth of cash and prizes at its awards ceremony.

Last Winning Films: *Six String Samurai, The Bible and Gun Club, Ayn Rand: A Sense of Life*

Past Judges: Chris Gore, Steve Montal, Gabe Wardell.

Application Tips: Slamdance's main feature competition is devoted to first-time directors who have made films on a low budget and do not yet have U.S. distribution. "However, we usually show several films that fall outside of these criteria—including many shorts," says Peter Baxter. "We do not have any strict 'premiere' requirements and we welcome films in any subject matter, length, format (including video), finished or not."

If a film is accepted, entrants will be solely responsible for delivering their exhibition print/video materials to and from the festival venue. Complete press kits will be needed as soon after notification as possible. Slamdance can not be held liable for your exhibition print/video materials which are lost or damaged. If your film wins either a Grand Jury or Audience award, you are required to mention that fact in posters and other promotional material if and when the film gets distribution. Please note festival dates are subject to change. Unfortunately Slamdance does not provide room, board or travel for filmmakers, but we do suggest bringing a cushion.

Application Fee: The early deadline fee is $25.00 for all films under 40 minutes, and $40.00 for all films 40 minutes and over. The final deadline fee is $35.00 for all films under 40 minutes, and $55.00 for all films 40 minutes and over.

Average Films Entered: 1200 films.

Films Screened: About 14 features, 20 shorts.

Odds of Acceptance: 1200 films apply and only 14 features are shown, so your odds of getting into Sundance are actually better than Slamdance.

Filmmaker Perks: Free entry to all screenings. Filmmakers lounge provides breakfast and complimentary food and drinks.

Attendance: 2,000+

Best Parties: The parties at Slamdance are all free and generally easy to sneak into.

10. Cinequest:
The San José Film Festival

Celebrating a decade of bringing film to San José, California, and the surrounding areas, you can't find a film festival more ambitious than Cinequest. Growing at a tremendous rate, this festival screens over 100 independent films. Besides showing indie features, documentaries and several series of short films, Cinequest continues to champion digital filmmaking in a way unparalleled by any non-digital fest. Which is no surprise, since the festival is right in Silicon Valley's backyard. Awards are not only bestowed upon filmmakers, but also upon innovators of new filmmaking technologies. Cinequest's support of cutting edge filmmaking tools make it a must visit for the true filmmaker.

Over the ten-day event, the fest holds a series of useful seminars and panels and has even hosted events with filmmakers like Dario Argento.

With luck, the spirit of Cinequest will catch on and other festivals will include a more comprehensive approach to new film technologies. You can find the future of film at Cinequest.

"Cinequest is one of my two favorite festivals along with the Havana Film Festival. "Havana for its cigars and Cinequest for what it does for filmmakers."

—Christopher Coppola

"(Cinequest Film Festival) has consistently managed to pull in heavyweight guests."

—Dennis Harvey, Variety

The San Jose Film Festival
476 Park Ave Room 204
San Jose, CA 95110
Tel: 408-995-5033
Fax: 408-995-5713
Email: sjfilmfest@aol.com
Web Site: www.cinequest.org
Festival Date: February-March
Entry Deadline: October
Year Festival Began: 1990
Contact: Mike Rabehl
Director: Halfdan Hussey - Executive Director
Programmer: Mike Rabehl - Associate Director, Head of Programming
Other Staff: Kathleen J. Powell - President
Stuart English - Marketing Director
Wendi Hodgen - Operations Mangaer
Jens Michael Hussey - Publicity Director
Juliana Isaac - Special Projects Manager
Vikki Wolfsmith - Operations Manager
Profile: It was in the spirit of the maverick that filmmakers and Silicon Valley engineers founded Cinequest. Through a personable world-class showcase of maverick films, filmmakers and the technology that is reshaping the industry, Cinequest inspires and enables mavericks in their creative quests. Cinequest Film Festival is located in the heart of the Silicon Valley.

Sections of the festival include: A Maverick Competition of features, documentaries, shorts, and digital films. All styles and genres, i.e. African American, Latino, Asian, gay & lesbian, and midnight movies. The 11th Cinequest will be a spectacular festival of special events, VIP guests, Maverick tributes, seminars, technical presentations, digital screenings, catered celebrations and entertainment adding to the fun of this warm and extraordinary festival. Cinequest accepts all formats including 35mm, 16mm and video. A special student short film competition is available.

During the 10th festival (2000), Cinequest had 203 visiting filmmakers representing 24 countries and over 40,000 film fans indulged in 143 maverick films presented at 212 screenings. Cinequest's 11th anniversary is sure to be an incredible event for filmmakers and film lovers alike.

Seminars: Cutting edge seminars on the latest digital technologies that are created in Silicon Valley.
Panels: Panels that include world-renowned filmmakers and industry experts. Past panels include Produced and Abandoned, Women in Film, Sex in the Cinema, A Look at the Relationship of John Ford and John Wayne in the Western.
Famous Speakers: Alec Baldwin, Kevin Spacey, Jackie Chan, Peter Fonda, Wes Craven, Gabriel Byrne, Jennifer Jason Leigh, Rod Steiger, Barry Sonnenfeld, John Schlesinger, Vilmos Zsigmond, Jennifer Beals, John Waters, Bryan Singer, Sheila Benson, Peta Wilson, Cassian Elwes, Grace Zabriskie, Barbara Turner, Werner Herzog, Michael

Radford, Gus Van Sant, Russ Meyer, Robert Wise, Walter Murch, Walter Hill, Ron Shelton, Philip Kaufman, Elmer Bernstein.
Market: No
Competitions: Yes
Major Awards: Maverick Spirit Award
Value of Awards: (no cash prize)
Last Winning Films: The award most representative of the vision of Cinequest, The Maverick Spirit Trophy, went to *Janice Beard: 45 WPM*. Directed by Clare Kilner. United Kingdom.
Best Dramatic Feature went to *Under the Sun*. Directed by Colin Nutley. Sweden.
Best First Feature went to *Janice Beard: 45 WPM*. Directed by Clare Kilner. United Kingdom.
Best Documentary went to *Beyond the Mat*. Directed by Barry W. Blaustein. United States.
Best Short Narrative went to *Elimination Dance*. Directed by Bruce McDonald & Don McKellar. Canada.
Best Short Animation was a tie and went to *Humdrum*. Directed by Peter Peake. United Kingdom, and *Little Dark Poet*. Directed by Mike Booth. United Kingdom.
Audience Choice Award for Best Narrative Feature was a tie between: *Green Desert*. Directed by Anno Saul. Germany. *Mexico*. Directed by Lorena Parlee. United States. *Seven Girlfriends*. Directed by Paul Lazarus. United States. *Under the Sun*. Directed by Colin Nutley. Sweden.
Audience Choice Award for Best Documentary Feature went to *Life Afterlife*. Directed by Lisa F. Jackson. United States.
Special Jury Award, aka The Guilty Pleasure Award went to *Suckers*. Directed by Roger Nygard for which the jury felt deserved special recognition for the viewing pleasure they received for its political incorrectness.
Past Judges: Barbara Turner, Paul Bartel, Pam Walton, Sheila Benson, Jim Harrington, Gideon Bachmann, Lissa Gibbs, Dorothy Fadiman, Glenn Lovell, Zaki Lisha, Jack Nyblom, Karen Davison, Jan Kravitz, Susan Tavernetti, Kim Roberts, Katie Cadigan
Application Fee: Before October 1, 2000—$25; After October 1, 2000—$30
Common Mistakes: 1) Read *all* of the materials the festival sends you, and let them know immediately if there are concerns or questions.

2) Filmmakers often forget that to have a film is one thing. To get people to see it, you need to market it. Always consider your marketing for when the film is accepted. Too many filmmakers do not think about the media exposing their film. If you want reviews and/or exposure, spend enough on marketing—especially black and white photos for printing in newspapers (these are priceless items to have for all purposes).

3) If you do not have a full press kit, include as much as you can. The most important items that

Cinequest Film Festival

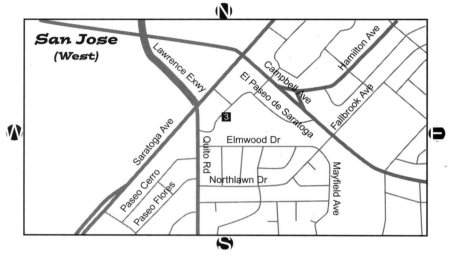

1	Camera 3 S. Second St & San Carlos		**4**	Morris Dailey Auditorium San Jose State University 4th St & San Fernando
2	Towne 3 1443 The Alameda		**5**	The Tech Museum 201 S. Market
3	AMC Saratoga 14 700 El Paso de Saratoga		**6**	The Fairmont 170 S. Market St

FESTIVAL HEADQUARTERS	◁▷ FESTIVAL RELATED	**3**	THEATER
A HOTEL			

THE SECRETS OF CINEQUEST

San Jose Airport is the hub for American Airlines, so you can fly right into San Jose for Cinequest. They completely revamped the downtown and now it is has lots of very cool cafés, bars and restaurants in an area called Market Street. It's also worth noting that Santa Clara Street has the best Vietnamese and Thai food in the entire Bay area. The festival takes place during hockey season, so you can catch a San Jose Sharks game or visit a museum downtown to get a break from the fest.

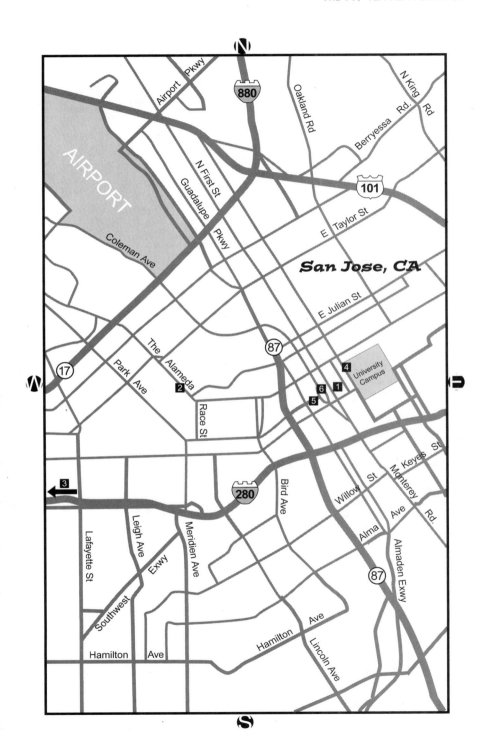

should always be included are: synopsis and cast and crew bios.

Insider Advice: 1) Submit early. 75 percent of the film submissions arrive in the last two weeks of the deadline. It's always better to have someone review your film who has not spent the last nine hours watching films. Works in progress are fine, as long as you let the festival know. The review committee is comprised of mostly filmmakers and understands the process.

2) Check for discounts on the entry fee.

Average Films Entered: Our focus is maverick films, which is open to all genres and styles. The more creative and/or challenging the film is, the better the chances are it will make it into the program

Films Screened: 143

Odds of Acceptance: 1 in 6

Filmmaker Perks: Travel and lodging are on a case-by-case situation. The earlier we can invite a film, the higher the chances our budget will allow for each.

Attendance: Over 40,000.

Journalist Attendance: Over 200 journalists do coverage on Cinequest.

Tourist Information: San Francisco, Santa Cruz, Monterey, Carmel, The Tech Museum of Innovation, local vineyards.

Travel Tips: Book your hotel and flight early! Silicon Valley is a bustling area.

Best Cheap Hotels: Ask Cinequest about how to get a special rate at local hotels.

Best Luxury Hotels: Why, The Fairmont of course!

Best Restaurants: The Grill at the Fairmont, Blakes, A.P. Stump's, Il Fornaio, Scott's Seafood.

Best Bars: The Grill, A.P. Stump's, South First Billiards.

Best Hangout for Filmmakers: Cinequest Hospitality Tent

Best Place for Breakfast: Il Fornaio

Festival Tale: Jackie Chan and his entourage left a film set with no sleep after shooting all night, drove through seven hours of torrential rains on the highway from Los Angeles, and said Cinequest was such a great experience he wanted to come back again another year. He was one class act. The fans went nuts.

Italian horror master and tribute guest Dario Argento told a packed house at the screening of his masterpiece *Suspiria* that "Working with animals is much better than working with actors. A rat, or a swarm of bees is more natural than Marlon Brando or Tom Cruise could ever be."

While introducing his *Tenebrae* screening the next day, Argento said he had already bared his soul the night before, and had nothing more to say. He then proceeded to disrobe to his boxer shorts, jokingly claiming that was all he had left to share. "Good vision to you all!" he said. Argento was a favorite among festival patrons for his witty and warm personality.

Random Tidbits: We treat people well. Filmmakers tell us all the time how they love Cinequest because it's friendly, we care about our guests, and they have access to meet powerful people. They have a good time. We are very casual and laid back, but work hard to provide a great experience for our filmmaker and patrons.

NORTH AMERiCAN FiLM FESTiVALS
United States and Canada

AFi DVCAM FEST Sponsored by Sony

2021 N. Western Ave.
Los Angeles, CA 90027
Tel: 866-234-7668
Fax: 323-462-4049
Web Site: www.dvcamfest.com
Festival Date: April
Entry Deadline: February
Year Festival Began: 2001
Contact: Jennifer O'Neal
Director: Christian Gaines
Programmer: Nancy Collet
Category: Digital, Documentary, Experimental, Independent, Fiction, Creative Events & Performance Coverage, Student, Video
Profile: The AFI DVCAM Fest, sponsored by Sony, is a competitive festival intended to identify, recognize and reward digital video professionals, including fiction and documentary filmmakers, event videographers, news gatherers and others professionally applying digital video technology.

The AFI DVCAM Fest will feature awards in five categories: fiction, documentary, experimental, creative events coverage and performance coverage. The competition will be adjudicated by a panel of professional celebrity judges, who will determine winners in each category, as well as an overall Grand Prize winner.

AFRiCAN FiLM FESTiVAL

154 West 18th Street., Suite 3B
New York, NY 10011
Tel: 212-352-1720
Fax: 212-807-9752
Email: nyaff@erols.com
Web Site: www.africanfilmny.org

Festival Date: April/May
Director: Mahen Bonetti
Category: Touring
Profile: The African Film Festival, a non-profit arts organization, explores ways to introduce African film to non-African audiences, not only to develop a much needed market for this growing body of work but to open a dialogue between artists and media professionals on the two continents. Through panel discussions and post-screening events where audiences and filmmakers meet, AFF offers opportunities for increased awareness of and interest in African culture and the development of new channels of distribution for African film throughout the U.S.
Competitions: No

AMERiCAN FiLM iNSTiTUTE (AFi)— LOS ANGELES iNTERNATiONAL FiLM FESTiVAL

"AFI Fest has established itself as a terrific platform for new talent. I am thrilled to be supportive of the Festival."
Billy Bob Thornton,
director/writer/actor

"A great festival for film professionals and the Los Angeles community to discover new talent from around the world."
Kevin Thomas, Los Angeles Times

American Film Institute
2021 N. Western Ave.
Los Angeles, CA 90027
Tel: 323-856-7707
Fax: 323-462-4049
Email: afifest@afionline.org

Web Site: www.afifest.com
Festival Date: Late October
Entry Deadline: Early: June 5; Final: July 17
Year Festival Began: 1986
Contact: Julianna Brannum
Director: Christian Gaines
Programmer: Nancy Collet
Category: American Films, Digital, Documentary, Ethnic Asian, Ethnic Latin, First-Time Independent Filmmakers, Independent, International, Short
Profile: AFI Fest combines its film programming with special events, capturing the cultural diversity of Los Angeles while providing new filmmakers with an avenue of exposure to the film industry. The American Film Institute is the preeminent national organization dedicated to advancing and preserving the art of film, television and other forms of the moving image.

Gore Score · · · · · · · · · · · · · · ·
AFI puts together an ambitious program. It's strange that big acquisition deals are not bursting from this fest since the line-up of American indies here certainly deserves more attention from the industry than it has been getting. Luminaries from Los Angeles always attend (including the mayor) and I hear the parties are great, though for some reason, I'm never invited.

Seminars: Digital Cinema Symposium
Panels: Financing, Screenwriting, Distribution
Famous Speakers: Spike Jonze, Oliver Stone, Steve Martin
Competitions: Yes
Major Awards: Grand Jury Prize
Value of Awards: $10,000

Jennifer Jason Leigh and Jennifer Beals at the AFI Fest in Los Angeles.
PHOTO BY KEVIN PARRY

Last Winning Films: *Not of This World* (Italy)

Last Winning Directors: Giuseppe Piccioni

Past Judges: Alison Anders, Victor Nunez, Emilio Estevez

Application Fee: Early: $30 shorts, $40 features; Final: $40 shorts, $50 features

Common Mistakes: Fill out every detail of the submission form and if you have questions, call the Festival. Don't go overboard with promotional materials or press kit. Keep it simple. And never send your tape in a fiber filled envelope...when we open them, the fibers get all over the tape and can damage it.

Insider Advice: Shoot on the highest format you can afford and pay special attention both content and quality. Finally, be prepared for rejection.

Sometimes great films are rejected due to the highly competitive nature of the festival. Don't let it be a reflection of your capabilities as a filmmaker.

Average Films Entered: Short and Feature length Documentaries and Narratives; Experimental and Animation are not as common, but are accepted.

Films Screened: 60-75

Odds of Acceptance: 1 in 23

Filmmaker Perks: Free travel, goodie bags, filmmaker pass, parties and possibly lodging, depending on hotel sponsors.

Attendance: 50,000 +

Journalist Attendance: 300

Travel Tips: Rent a car!

Best Cheap Hotels: The Standard

Best Luxury Hotels: Beverly Hills Hotel

Best Restaurants: Asia de Cuba or Spago in Beverly Hills

Best Bars: Skybar or 360

Best Hangout for Filmmakers: Sunset Marquis Bar

Best Place for Breakfast: Mirabelle

Festival Tale: Celebrity sightings at the Fest...Jack Nicholson, Shirley MacLaine, Tim Roth, Jennifer Jason Leigh, Tobey Maguire

Random Tidbits: We have been told by filmmakers and attendees that we are the most organized Fest with the friendliest staff and the best goodie bags!

AMERICAN SHORT SHORTS

"I am delighted to offer my support to the Committee of American Short Shorts...It is a pleasure to participate in a festival that showcases the work of young filmmakers from the United States."
—Martin Scorsese

1007 Montana Ave., #534 Santa Monica, CA 90403

Fax: 310-899-3758

Email: katyoc124@aol.com

Web Site: www.americanshortshorts.com

Festival Date: June

Entry Deadline: September

Year Festival Began: 1999

Contact: Doug Williams

Director: Doug Williams, Tetsuya Bessho

Category: American Films, Animation, Digital, Digital Animation, Documentary, DVD, Experimental, First-Time Independent Filmmakers, Independent, International, Multimedia, Online Festival, Short, Student, Super 8/8mm, Touring (Tokyo, Naha, Nagoya, Sapporo and Osaka), Underground, Video, Weird, Woman

Profile: American Short Shorts was founded in 1999 to bring American short films to Japanese audiences, who previously had rarely been exposed to the format. The festival was co-founded by Douglas Williams, an American who lived and worked in Japan for eight years as a reporter/anchor for American and Japanese news, and by Tetsuya Bessho, a well-known actor in Japanese film, television and stage. Doug and Tetsuya realized that the pure, boundless creativity of short film makes it an exciting, entertaining and ideal form of cultural exchange. Each year the festival also highlights the early short films of prominent filmmakers, who have so far included George Lucas and Martin Scorsese, to show how short films can launch a career in filmmaking. In 2000 we featured five vintage shorts to give audiences some perspective on the last 100 years of short filmmaking.

Gore Score · · · · · · · · · · · · · · ·
Simply one of the greatest showcases for short films and not to be missed.

Panels: Yes

Famous Speakers: Academy Award-winning documentary filmmaker Keiko Ibi (2000).

Market: No

Competitions: Yes

Major Awards: The American Short Shorts Award

Value of Awards: 3,000 feet of Kodak 16 mm film

Last Winning Directors: Ron Krauss; Mike Cargile

Past Judges: Committee for American Short Shorts

Application Tips: Make sure you submit all of your materials on time and that the information requested is complete. Remember that films in this festival will be subtitled.

Application Fee: None

Average Films Entered: Shorts.

Films Screened: 45

Odds of Acceptance: 1 in 5

Filmmaker Perks: We offer select filmmakers free business class travel to Tokyo, reduced rates on lodging, and student volunteers to act as translators and tour guides.

Attendance: 25,000

Journalist Attendance: 100; American press at 2000 festival included CNN, CBS Evening News, E! Entertainment Television (which will include coverage of the festival on "FYE", "Wild On", and an upcoming show about film festivals around the world), *Variety*, and *The Hollywood Reporter*.

Tourist Information: Sony, Asakusa Shrine and Market, Meiji Jingu Shrine, day trip to Kyoto...Tokyo has endless opportunities for sight-seeing, eating, shopping.

Festival Tale: The filmmakers celebrated a Shinto religious festival in Asakusa, where they happened upon a party thrown by the head of one of the Yakuza (yep, the Japanese mafia). Half-naked men with missing fingers and full-body tattoos insisted that Marliese Schneider, producer/actor in the hilariously profound *Turkey Cake*, go on stage to drink a giant bowl of sake to the gods!

Random Tidbits: Filmmakers are provided with detailed information about where to go and what to do in Tokyo. The festival also organizes special dinners, parties, and tours for all filmmakers who attend.

ANGELCiTi LOS ANGELES FiLM FESTiVAL & MARKET

"These guys really know how to put on a radical show."
—*Passions Magazine*

"This young film festival promises an annual helping of independent cinema that challenges our perception of what movies are, can and should be."
—*Cinematheque*

1680 N. Vine St., Suite 904
Hollywood, CA 90028
Tel: 323-461-4256
Fax: 323-466-7588
Email: Info@AngelCiti.com
Web Site: www.AngelCiti.com
Festival Date: February 8-18, 2001
Entry Deadline: December
Year Festival Began: 2000
Contact: Adam Zoblotsky
Director: Adam Zoblotsky
Programmer: Melanie Minella
Other Staff: Larry Hartman, Katherine Katz, James Hill, DeWayne Barron
Category: Animation, Documentary, Ethnic African, Ethnic Asian, Ethnic Black, Ethnic Jewish, Ethnic Latin, Ethnic Spanish, Experimental, First-Time Independent Filmmakers, Gay Lesbian, Independent, International, Markets, Multimedia, Short, Underground, Video, Woman
Profile: AngelCiti is dedicated to promoting talented independent filmmakers to the film industry community in Los Angeles and helping the dreamers of today to become the heroes of tomorrow.

Gore Score · · · · · · · · · · · · · · ·

If a film market is what you are after, this is adequate—though films playing in an alley in Park City, Utah, during Sundance are likely to get more press.

Seminars: Yes

Panels: Under consideration for 2001

Famous Speakers: Speakers from last year included acclaimed director George Hickenlooper, Lamar Card (CEO of

Directors.net), Santa Fe New Mexico Mayor Larry Delgado and Adam Merins.

Market: Yes

Competitions: Yes

Major Awards: Rita Anne Hartman Diamond Halo Audience Selection Award

Value of Awards: It is a statuette

Last Winning Films: *Cement* starring Chris Penn and Sherilyn Fenn

Last Winning Directors: DJ Paul

Past Judges: The audience

Application Fee: $275, includes market and is fully refunded if submission not accepted

Common Mistakes: Completing a film is a tremendous task. It is such a relief to complete a project that filmmakers sometimes don't pay as much attention to detail when submitting their project.

Insider Advice: First and foremost, follow your heart and your instincts; they will serve you well. Secondly, please realize that a film festival is a partnership between the filmmaker and the film festival. The film festival provides a wonderful opportunity for promotion, but filmmakers need to continue to strongly promote their individual project in order to get the most out of the festival.

Average Films Entered: We review and consider all genres and types; films are accepted (or rejected) based upon quality.

Films Screened: 105

Odds of Acceptance: 1 in 2

Filmmaker Perks: We arrange for discounted travel arrangements with local travel agents.

Attendance: 8,000

Journalist Attendance: 6

Best Luxury Hotels: Hollywood Roosevelt Hotel is the best buy for the money

Best Restaurants: Spago in Beverly Hills

Best Bars: The Standard

Best Place for Breakfast: Swingers on Beverly Blvd.

Never send your tape in a fiber filled envelope... when we open them, the fibers get all over the tape and can damage it (AFI Fest).

ANGELUS AWARDS STUDENT FiLM FESTiVAL

7201 Sunset Blvd.

Los Angeles, CA 90046

Tel: 800-874-0999; 323-874-6633

Fax: 323-874-1168

Email: info@angelus.org

Web Site: www.angelus.org

Festival Date: November

Entry Deadline: July

Contact: Monika Moreno

Director: Monika Moreno

Other Staff: Emily Patton, Submissions; Dennis Roverato, Technical Director

Category: Animation, Documentary, Independent, International, Short, Video, Woman

Profile: The Angelus Awards recognize and showcase student films of uncommon artistic caliber which explore the complexity of the human condition with creativity, compassion and respect.

Market: No

Awards: Yes

Competitions: Yes

Major Awards: Patrick Peyton Excellence in Filmmaking Award ($2500), Mole Richardson Production Design Award ($1500), Audience Impact ($1500), Documentary ($1500), Animation ($1500), plus industry prizes for all.

Value of Awards: $1500–$2500

Last Winning Films: My Mother Dreams Satans Disciples in New York

Last Winning Directors: Barbara Schock

Past Judges: Executives from 20th Century Fox, Dreamworks Animation, Disney, Universal Studios.

Application Tips: Be sure your film fits the theme and deals with hope, tolerance, respect, dignity and spirituality (over nihilism and despair).

Application Fee: $25

Common Mistakes: Sending us films rife with violence or gratuitous sex.

Average Films Entered: 200+

Films Screened: 10-12

Filmmaker Perks: We offer the winning filmmaker a stipend for travel expenses (if out of the Los Angeles area) and contacts. All ten finalists receive a screening at the Directors Guild in Hollywood, and all ten finalists receive prizes.

Attendance: 600

Journalist Attendance: 5-10

ANN ARBOR FiLM FESTiVAL

P.O. Box 8232

207 East Ann Arbor (Fedex/UPS)

Ann Arbor, MI 48104

Tel: 734-995-5356

Fax: 734-995-5396

Email: vicki@honeyman.org

Web Site: www.aafilmfest.org or www.citi.umich.edu/u/honey/aaff

Festival Date: March

Entry Deadline: December

Contact: Vicki Honeyman

Director: Vicki Honeyman

Programmer: Vicki Honeyman

Other Staff: Volunteer/Student Staff

Category: Independent, The festival accepts all genres: experimental, animation, documentary, personal documentary, narrative and encourages the works of mutli-cultural artists. It is all about the films and the filmmakers, providing an excellent screening facility for the works. A filmmaker's reception is held at the end of fest-week.

Profile: Started in 1963, the Ann Arbor Film Festival has a long-standing tradition of showcasing 16mm independent and experimental film. The festival is open to all films of all genres that demonstrate a high regard for film as an art form. Festival goals are to encourage the work of the independent filmmaker, to promote the concept of film as art, and to present a traveling tour of about 25 films in the Ann Arbor Film Festival Tour, which travels to over 20 locations around the U.S. late March through early August.

The festival is held in a huge renovated 1700-seat movie theater and has a very relaxed atmosphere with comfy seats

and good popcorn. The projectionists are perfectionists about sound and image. Filmmakers always remark on how great their films look on the Michigan Theater screen and are impressed with the professionalism of the projection staff.

Performance artists open each night's show. The theater lobby is taken over by local artists who create installation pieces, including film-loop installations.

The festival begins every year on a Tuesday night with an opening night reception that features a Mariachi band, free drinks and hors d'oeuvres.

Gore Score · · · · · · · · · · · · · · ·

This quaint little fest brings a bit of culture to the hippies in Ann Arbor (where getting caught with pot will land you what amounts to a parking ticket.) A bold fest that is a must attend if you live in Michigan.

Seminars: The three Awards Jurors, independent & experimental filmmakers/instructors/academics, present programs of their own work each afternoon during fest week.

Competitions: Yes

Major Awards: Best of Festival Award

Value of Awards: $2,000 ($13,000 total in cash awards)

Last Winning Films: Hauling Toto Big

Last Winning Directors: Robert Nelson

Application Tips: Read the entry materials, enter strong work.

Application Fee: $32 US / $37 overseas

Insider Advice: Don't enter until your work has gone beyond the "amateur" level.

Average Films Entered: 16mm films of any length, any genre, optical soundtrack or silent.

Odds of Acceptance: About 350 films entered; about 100 programmed into the festival-week screenings. In 1998, 371 films were entered; 113 were programmed.

Filmmaker Perks: We house filmmakers with people in the community. We provide fest-week passes to all screenings.

We throw a reception for all attending filmmakers.

Travel Tips: Call Ann Arbor Visitors Bureau: 800-888-8487 for housing, maps, etc

Best Restaurants: The Earle, Zanzibar, Kerrytown Bistro, Del Rio

Best Bars: Del Rio Bar

Best Hangout for Filmmakers: Angelos, Del Rio, Old Town, coffee shops are all over town.

Best Place for Breakfast: Angelo's Restaurant is where all the out-of-town filmmakers go.

ANNUAL AMERICAN INDIAN FILM AND VIDEO COMPETITION

2100 NE 52nd St.
Oklahoma City, OK 73111
Tel: 405-427-5228
Fax: 405-427-8079
Email: caroline@redearth.org
Web Site: www.redearth.org
Festival Date: June

Entry Deadline: TBA
Contact: Caroline Hogan
Director: TBA
Programmer: New chairperson every year—call for details
Category: Ethnic Other,

ANNUAL KIDFILM FESTIVAL

6116 N. Central Expressway, Suite #105
Dallas, TX 72506
Tel: 214-821-6300
Fax: 214-821-6364
Email: usafilmfestival@aol.com
Web Site: www.usafilmfestival.com
Festival Date: January
Entry Deadline: November
Contact: Ann Alexander
Director: Ann Alexander
Category: Kid
Competitions: Yes
Average Films Entered: 300
Attendance: 15,000

ANTIMATTER FESTIVAL OF UNDERGROUND SHORT FILM & VIDEO

F-1322 Broad St.
Victoria, BC V8W 2A9 Canada
Tel: 250-385-3327
Fax: 250-385-3327
Email: rogueart@islandnet.com
Web Site: www.islandnet.com/shortcircuit
Festival Date: September 21-30, 2001
Entry Deadline: Early: May 11, 2001; Final: June 8, 2001
Year Festival Began: 1998
Contact: Todd Eacrett
Director: Todd Eacrett
Programmer: Deborah de Boer
Other Staff: Kyath Battie, Erin Gawne, Charo Neville
Category: Animation, Digital, Digital Animation, Documentary, DVD, Ethnic African, Ethnic Asian, Ethnic Black, Ethnic Jewish, Ethnic Latin, Ethnic Other, Ethnic Spanish, Experimental, Fantasy/Science Fiction, Gay

Lesbian, Independent, International, Super 8/8mm, Touring, Underground, Video, Weird, Woman

Profile: Antimatter exists to provide a public platform for underground productions of short film and video—imaginative, volatile, entertaining and critical works that exist outside of the mainstream. It is a forum for innovative and radical ideas overlooked or marginalized by contemporary culture.

Antimatter is a noncompetitive series of screenings chosen by jury/curatorial committee.

Antimatter is dedicated to film and video as art. It is anti-Hollywood and anti-censorship.

Gore Score · · · · · · · · · · · · · · ·
One of the only underground fests in Canada, so run to see the movies before they get shut down.

Market: No

Competitions: No

Application Fee: Early: $10; Final: $15

Common Mistakes: Incomplete forms, missing info, missing entry fees, unlabelled cassettes.

Insider Advice: We need you more than you need us.

Films Screened: 110–140

Odds of Acceptance: 1 in 5

Filmmaker Perks: Billeting (lodging), exposure, contacts, free drinks (usually).

Attendance: 4,000

Tourist Information: Victoria is a world renowned tourist destination. Its Olde English charm wears thin for us, but they keep coming anyway. There are other options: Ross Bay Cemetery, cold water surfing up-island, Rogue Art.

Travel Tips: Victoria is on an island. There is no bridge. You must fly, take a ferry or be a damn good swimmer.

Best Cheap Hotels: Crystal Court Motel

Best Luxury Hotels: The Empress

Best Restaurants: Ferris' Oyster Bar & Grill

Best Bars: Thursdays

Best Hangout for Filmmakers: Mexico City

Best Place for Breakfast: The Butter Dell

Random Tidbits: Antimatter is not a "celebrity" festival. Don't expect to schmooze with Hollywood stars or industry snits.

ARIZONA INTERNATIONAL FILM FESTIVAL

P. O. Box 431
Tucson, AZ 85702
Tel: 520-628-1737
Fax: 520-628-1737
Email: azmac@azstarnet.com
Web Site: www.azstarnet.com
Festival Date: April
Entry Deadline: February
Contact: Giuilo Scalinger
Director: Giuilo Scalinger
Programmer: Giuilo Scalinger

ARIZONA STATE UNIVERSITY SHORT FILM AND VIDEO FESTIVAL

ASU Art Museum
Tenth St. and Mill Ave.
Tempe, AZ 85287-2911
Tel: 480-965-2787
Fax: 480-965-5254
Email: Spiak@asu.edu
Web Site: www.asuam.fa.asu.edu/filmfest/main.htm
Festival Date: Late April 2001
Entry Deadline: February 16, 2001
Year Festival Began: 1997
Contact: John D. Spiak
Director: John D. Spiak
Programmer: Bob Pece
Category: American Films, Animation, Digital Animation, Documentary, Ethnic African, Ethnic Asian, Ethnic Black, Ethnic Jewish, Ethnic Latin, Ethnic Other, Ethnic Spanish, Experimental, Fantasy/Science Fiction, First-Time Independent Filmmakers, Gay Lesbian, Independent, International, Multimedia, Short, Student, Super 8/8mm, Touring (Santa Ana and Santa Barbara), Underground, Video, Weird, Woman

Profile: An annual one night outdoor festival to celebrate the

artistic and creative endeavours of individuals with different visions and levels of experience.

Gore Score · · · · · · · · · · · · · · ·
More than a festival, it's like a giant party. Plus, entry is free!

Competitions: Yes

Major Awards: Juror Choice Awards; LeBlanc Audience Choice Award; AZ Award—Given to an outstanding Arizona film/video artist

Application Fee: None

Common Mistakes: People forget to include contact information or don't cue up their tapes.

Insider Advice: Send your work. We're free to enter and we have no messy paperwork. What do you have to lose?

Average Films Entered: A mix of everything.

Films Screened: 22

Odds of Acceptance: 1 in 6

Filmmaker Perks: Our one night festival was attended by 1,183 individuals last year. We have an outstanding contact and press mailing list who receive our press release and invite. All entrants receive a copy of the entire festival on VHS once the festival has been completed. Our website receives of 1,000 user sessions per month and all past festival information remains on the site as a recorded history of our event.

Attendance: 1,183

Journalist Attendance: 10

Tourist Information: Arizona State University Art Museum, Desert Botanical Gardens, Tempe Town Lake, Mill Avenue, Phoenix Art Museum, Scottsdale Museum of Contemporary Art, AZ Diamondbacks Baseball

Travel Tips: We are ten minutes from Phoenix Sky Harbor airport. A quick one-hour flight from Southern California or a short 5.5 hour drive.

Best Cheap Hotels: Holiday Inn

Best Luxury Hotels: Mission Palms

Best Restaurants: Sahara's Middle East, House of Trix's

Best Bars: Arizona Roadhouse

Best Hangout for Filmmakers: Valley Arts Theater

Best Place for Breakfast: Harlow's

Festival Tale: Tons of celebrities on our mailing list who all happen to live in the Phoenix area.

Random Tidbits: Not only is it free to submit your work, it is also free for everyone to attend. The only thing that is required is for you to bring your chair to this outdoor event. The festival is presented in VHS format.

ASIAN AMERICAN INTERNATIONAL FILM FESTIVAL

c/o Asian Cine Vision
133 W. 19th. St., 3rd Floor
New York, NY 10011
Tel: 212-989-1442
Fax: 212-727-3584
Email: acvinfo@yahoo.com
Web Site: www.asian cinevision.org
Festival Date: July
Entry Deadline: March
Director: Vivian Huang
Category: Ethnic Other
Application Fee: None

ASPEN FiLMFEST

110 E. Hallam, Suite 102
Aspen, CO 81611
Tel: 970-925-6882
Fax: 970-925-1967
Email: filmfest@aspenfilm.org
Web Site: www.aspenfilm.org
Festival Date: September-October
Entry Deadline: July
Contact: George Eldred
Director: Laura Thielan
Category: Documentary, Independent, International
Profile: This is a six day festival celebrating American independent films, documentaries, and foreign films. Over 6,000 attend.

Gore Score · · · · · · · · · · · · · · · ·
Any excuse to go to Aspen is okay with me.

Awards: Yes
Competitions: Yes
Application Fee: $20
Films Screened: 25 screened
Odds of Acceptance: 1 in 15

ASPEN SHORTSFEST

110 E Hallam, Suite 102
Aspen, CO 81611
Tel: 970-925-6882
Fax: 970-925-1967
Web Site: www.aspenshorts fests.org
Festival Date: April
Entry Deadline: Early Deadline November; Late Deadline January
Contact: Jennifer Swanson
Director: Laura Thielen
Category: Documentary, Experimental, Fantasy/Science Fiction, Gay Lesbian, Independent, Commercials, Music Video, Short, Student
Market: No
Competitions: Yes
Value of Awards: over $22,000 in cash and prizes
Application Fee: Early Fee $35 Short Late Fee $45
Average Films Entered: Shorts (30 minute maximim)

ATHENS INTERNATIONAL FiLM AND VIDEO FESTIVAL

Box 388
75 W. Union St., Rm. 407
Columbus, OH 45701
Tel: 740-593-1330
Fax: 740-597-2560
Email: bradley@ohiou.edu
Web Site: www.athensfest.org
Festival Date: April/May
Entry Deadline: February
Director: Ruth Bradley
Category: International

ATLANTA FiLM AND VIDEO FESTIVAL

"Other people within the film industry and the entertainment industry and other important festivals are aware of the Atlanta festival, and it's growing to the extent that filmmakers feel like it's important to come down here and meet the audiences and talk about their films, futher their careers... They feel like this is a good place to do that"
—Anne Hubbell

IMAGE Film/Video Center
75 Bennett St. NW, Suite N-1
Atlanta, GA 30309
Tel: 404-352-4225;
404-352-4254 (Festival Hotline)
Fax: 404-352-0173
Email: afvf@imagefv.org
Web Site: www.imagefv.org/afuf
Festival Date: June
Entry Deadline: February
Year Festival Began: 1976
Contact: Gabriel Wardell
Director: Genevieve McGillicuddy
Programmer: Gabriel Wardell
Other Staff: Brian Newman, Executive Director, Kelly Williams
Category: Animation, Documentary, Experimental, Independent, Student
Profile: The Atlanta Film & Video Festival celebrates filmmaking from around the world. The festival focuses on the appreciation of independent, experimental and student films. Since 1976, the festival has introduced audiences to some of the most exciting

BEST VACATION FILM FESTIVALS

Acapulco Black Film Festival
Aspen FilmFest
Bermuda International Film Festival
CineVegas Film Festival
Florida Film Festival
Hawaii International Film Festival
Miami Film Festival
San Diego International Film Festival
Sydney Film Festival
Telluride Film Festival

new film and video work being created. Ranging from the hilarious to the visually arresting, from the provocative and highly controversial to the boldly experimental, the AFVF has become one of the country's premiere showcases for work by independent media artists in the U.S. and abroad.

Gore Score ···············

This fest is put together by a group of passionate people determined to expose Atlanta to exciting new indie work. The atmosphere and parties are unpretentious. The screenings offer an up close and intimate look at new filmmakers. This fest has also been known to take risks when seeking new films to screen, which is admirable as so often festival directors only book films they have heard about from other fests. The staff at AFVF have minds of their own. You will have a blast!

Panels: Yes

Awards: Yes

Competitions: Yes

Major Awards: Jury Prize

Value of Awards: $500

Last Winning Films: *Kitchen Party*

Last Winning Directors: Gary Burns

Past Judges: Chris Gore, Adolfas Mekas, Lise Raven, Harry Knowles, Liliana Oliveres (Rosebud), Eugene Haynes (October Films), Marlon T. Riggs, Barbara Hammer, Les Blank.

Application Tips: Follow directions. Make short films short (and good). Snappy Synopses.

Application Fee: $65 for early admission

Insider Advice: Get work in on time. Neat and easy to understand; clearly labeled.

Average Films Entered: Funny—wide variety—indie.

Films Screened: 100-150 screened

Odds of Acceptance: 1 in 5

Travel Tips: It is hot, but it is bound to rain. Pack accordingly.

Best Restaurants: Pasta Puccinello, Raging Burrito, Heaping Bowl & Brew.

Best Bars: Righteous Room

Best Hangout for Filmmakers: Manuel's Tavern

Best Place for Breakfast: Waffle House, Krispy Kreme or Majestic Diner.

ATLANTA GAY AND LESBIAN FILM FESTIVAL— OUT ON FILM

75 Bennett St., NW, Suite N-1
Atlanta, GA 30309
Tel: 404-352-4225
Fax: 404-352-0173
Email: afvf@imagefv.org
Web Site: www.imagefv.org
Contact: Genevieve McGillicudy
Director: Genevieve McGillicudy
Category: Gay Lesbian

ATLANTIC FILM FESTIVAL

5600 Sackville St., Suite 220
Halifax, Nova Scotia B3J 1L2
Canada
Tel: 902-422-3456
Fax: 902-422-4006
Email: festival@atlanticfilm.com
Web Site: www.atlanticfilm.com
Festival Date: September
Entry Deadline: June
Contact: Gordon Whitteker
Director: Gordon Whitteker
Category: Independent

AURORA ASIAN FILM FESTIVAL

1430 Larimer Square, Suite 320
Denver, CO 80202
Tel: 303-595-3456
Fax: 303-595-0956
Email: dfs@denverfilm.org
Web Site: www.denverfilm.org
Festival Date: June
Director: Ron Henderson

AUSTIN FILM FESTIVAL & HEART OF FILM SCREENWRITERS CONFERENCE

"Clearly, this is the coolest of film festivals. It celebrates the screenplay and the screenwriter as the heart of film."
—Dan Petrie, Jr.

1604 Nueces St.
Austin, TX 78701
Tel: 512-478-4795; 800-310-FEST
Fax: 512-478-6205
Email: austinfilm@aol.com
Web Site: www.austinfilm festival.com
Festival Date: October
Entry Deadline: Screenplay Competition Deadline: May; Film Competition Deadline: September
Year Festival Began: 1994
Director: Barbara Morgan
Programmer: Conference Director: Allen Odom
Film Programmer: Phil Scanlon
Film Competition Director: Courtney Davis
Other Staff: Screenplay Competition Director: BJ Burrow
Category: Independent, Short, Student
Profile: The Austin Film Festival & Heart of Film Screenwriters Conference is a non-profit organization committed to furthering the art, craft and business of screenwriters and recognizing their contribution to the filmmaking industry. The Austin Film Festival is the first event dedicated to celebrating the writer's contribution to the entertainment industry and to supporting the aspiring writer by providing education, monetary assistance, career opportunities, industry exposure and public recognition.

The four-day Screenwriters Conference presents over sixty informative panels, roundtables and workshops. The panels address various aspects of screenwriting and filmmaking and are conducted by established writers, directors, agents and producers. Additionally, the Austin Film Festival presents an eight-night film program, dedicated to providing an environment of recognition, opportunity and reward for those individuals who have realized their vision from script to screen. The film program consists of evening screenings and premieres dedicated to raising awareness of the writer's contribution to the entertain-

Robert Altman and Buck Henry at the Austin Film Festival.

PHOTO BY ANDREA TURNER/ JACK PLUNKETT

ment industry. The Festival also takes great pride in our retrospective series, honoring those who have achieved notoriety and success as a result of their prolific and breakthrough works.

Gore Score · · · · · · · · · · · · · · ·

If you are a screenwriter thinking about attending a film festival, this is the place to be. No other festival is as dedicated to the craft of screenwriting as AFFHFS. For film fans aspiring to write the great American screenplay or for screenwriting professionals alike—make the trip to Austin and thank me later.

Seminars: The Austin Film Festival's Screenwriters Conference presents over 60 panels, roundtables, and workshops, addressing various aspects of screenwriting and filmmaking. The Screenwriters Conference also features staged screenplay readings and numerous networking opportunities.

Famous Speakers: Robert Altman, Shane Black, James L. Brooks, Bill Broyles, Joel & Ethan Coen, Wes Craven, Scott Frank, Buck Henry, Dennis Hopper, Mike Judge, Larry Karaszewski, John Landis, Frank Pierson, Gary Ross, Eric Roth, David O. Russell, Paul Schrader, Whit Stillman, Oliver Stone, Ted Tally, Andrew Kevin Walker.

Competitions: Yes

Major Awards: Film Competition Best Feature Film
Best Short Film
Best Student Short Film
Audience Award for Feature Film
Screenplay Competition
Best Feature-Length Screenplay (Adult Category)
Best Feature-Length Screenplay (Family Category)
Best Feature-Length Screenplay (Comedy Category)

Value of Awards: Winners receive cash prizes, airfare, accommodations, an all-access pass to attend the Austin Film Festival & Heart of Film Screenwriters Conference, and the AFF Bronze Typewriter Award.

Past Judges: Miramax, Sloss Law Office, Comedy Central, Ocean Pictures, 20th Century Fox, Rhino Productions, MTV Films, Nu Image

Application Fee: $40

Common Mistakes: They don't include enough promotional/marketing material.

Insider Advice: Consider your market before you make your film.

Films Screened: Approximately 80

Filmmaker Perks: Film competition winners receive free airfare and accommodations courtesy of the Austin Film Festival. Our

Festival is considered one of the most accessible festivals and there are numerous networking opportunities.

Attendance: 15,000

Journalist Attendance: 500+

Tourist Information: Barton Springs, Zilker Park, the bats under Congress Avenue bridge

Travel Tips: Austin is very casual and very hot!

Best Cheap Hotels: The Austin Motel

Best Luxury Hotels: The Driskill Hotel, The Four Seasons

Best Restaurants: Ranch 616, The County Line, Chuy's

Best Bars: Lucky Lounge, Antone's, The Continental Club

Best Hangout for Filmmakers: The Carousel Lounge

Best Place for Breakfast: Star's, Kerbey Lane Cafe, IHOP on I-35, Katz's Deli

Festival Tale: Celebrity sightings: Willie Nelson, Anne Richards, Lyle Lovett, Sandra Bullock, Matthew McConaughey

Random Tidbits: Austin is the premiere town for networking, because when industry people are here, they are relaxed and friendly. And writers are the coolest people in the film business!

AUSTIN'S GAY AND LESBIAN FILM FESTIVAL

P.O. Box L
Austin, TX 78713
Tel: 512-302-9889
Fax: 512-302-1088
Email: kino@agliff.org
Web Site: www.agliff.org
Festival Date: August 24-September 6, 2001
Entry Deadline: June 30, 2001
Year Festival Began: 1988
Director: Sandra Martinez
Programmer: Scott Dinger
Other Staff: Bobette Mathis, Peter Dean, Bruce Weatherford
Category: Gay Lesbian

B-MOVIE FILM FESTIVAL

5858 E. Malloy Rd., Suite 163A
Syracuse, NY 13211
Tel: 315-428-9602
Fax: 315-478-1410
Email: webmaster@b-movie.com
Web Site: www.b-movie.com or www.bmovie.net
Festival Date: September
Entry Deadline: July
Year Festival Began: 1999
Contact: Ron Bonk
Director: Ron Bonk
Programmer: Ron Bonk
Category: Documentary, Short, Video
Profile: A celebration of lower-budget productions. Filmmakers seeking to carry on the rich tradition of B-Movies. The festival defines a "B-Movie" as a low-budget film which provides a level of entertainment and/or artistic value which rivals or surpasses big-budget mainstream pictures.

Gore Score · · · · · · · · · · · · · · ·
As a fan, I couldn't be more pleased to discover a festival that has the balls to acknowledge the contribution of B-Movies to cinema. A festival that celebrates the genius of filmmakers like Ed Wood, Russ Meyer and Troma is at the top of my list.

Application Fee: Received by July 14: $35 per feature and $25 per short; Received from July 14-August 4 $45 per feature and $35 per short.

BACA FILM AND VIDEO FESTIVAL

BACA/Brooklyn Arts Council
195 Cadman Plaza West
Brooklyn, NY 11201
Tel: 718-625-0080
Fax: 718-625-3294
Festival Date: March
Entry Deadline: December
Contact: Rob Orlinick, Chuck Reichenthal, Mark Dannat
Category: Video

BANFF FESTIVAL OF MOUNTAIN FILMS

Banff Centre
Box 1020, Stn. 38
Banff, Alberta T0L 0C0 Canada
Tel: 403-762-6125
Fax: 403-762-6277
Festival Date: November
Entry Deadline: September
Director: Bernadette McDonald
Category: Independent

BARE BONES INTERNATIONAL FILM FESTIVAL

Muskogee, OK
Tel: 1-888-560-6683 x 1014
Fax: 1-888-560-6683 x 1014
Email: barebonesmoviemakers@juno.com
Web Site: http://barebonesfilmfestival.bizland.com
Festival Date: March

BARGAIN BASEMENT INDEPENDENT FILM/VIDEOFESTIVAL

Colombia, MO
Tel: ; 573-449-7046
Email: pter@usa.net
Web Site: www.accidentalmedia.com/fest/
Other Staff: Peter Gerard, Co-founder
Category: Independent, Student

BERKELEY VIDEO AND FILM FESTIVAL

1939 Addison St.
Berkeley, CA 94704
Tel: 510-843-3699
Fax: 510-843-3379
Email: maketv@aol.com
Web Site: www.eastbaymedia.citysearch.com
Festival Date: November
Entry Deadline: June
Contact: East Bay Media Center
Director: Mel Vapour
Category: Video

BEVERLY HILLS FILM FESTIVAL

1680 N. Vine St., Suite 904
Hollywood, CA 90028
Tel: 323-978-0033
Fax: 323-461-4007
Email: Info@BeverlyHillsFilmFestival.com
Web Site: www.BeverlyHillsFilmFestival.com
Festival Date: April
Entry Deadline: February
Year Festival Began: 2001
Contact: Adam Zoblotsky
Director: Adam Zoblotsky
Programmer: Melanie Minella
Other Staff: Larry Hartman, Katherine Katz, James Hill, DeWayne Barron
Category: Animation, Ethnic African, Ethnic Asian, Ethnic Black, Ethnic Jewish, Ethnic Latin, Ethnic Spanish, First-Time Independent Filmmakers, Gay Lesbian, Independent, International, Short, Woman
Profile: The Beverly Hills Film Festival will showcase 25 premiere independent films (features and shorts) with the focus of selecting films with a significant likelihood of (i) being picked up for industry distribution (feature films) or (ii) receiving additional funds for completion funds (shorts).
Seminars: No
Panels: Yes
Market: No
Competitions: Yes
Major Awards: The Golden Palm Award

Application Fee: $50

Average Films Entered: We will be screening promising shorts and features with commercial appeal.

Films Screened: 25-30

Odds of Acceptance: 1 in 10

Filmmaker Perks: We arrange for discounted travel arrangements with local travel agents.

Tourist Information: The shops and restaurants on Rodeo Drive and Wilshire Boulevard

Best Luxury Hotels: Regent Beverly Hills Hotel

Best Restaurants: Crustacean

Best Bars: The Four Seasons

Best Place for Breakfast: Peninsula Hotel

Random Tidbits: A focus of the event will be charity functions and parties particularly targeted at the Beverly Hills community.

BIG MUDDY FILM FESTIVAL

Dept of Cinema and Photography
Mailcode 6610
Southern Illinois University
Carbondale, IL 62901-6610
Tel: 618-453-1482
Fax: 618-453-2264
Web Site:
www.bigmuddyfilm.com
Festival Date: February-March
Entry Deadline: January
Year Festival Began: 1978
Director: Eva Honegger
Category: Independent
Profile: The Big Muddy Film Festival is committed to supporting and generating interest in innovative, independent films and videos, encouraging artists who challenge the traditional boundaries of visual media. We seek to provide an artistic and cultural alternative to mainstream cinema in a region where access to this kind of work is extremely limited. Since 1978, the Big Muddy has annually featured an international film and video competition, presentations by guest film and video makers, community outreach programs, and screenings of quality feature films.

Famous Speakers: Past festival judges/guest artists have included Jim Jarmusch, Haskell Wexler and Reginald Hudlin

Competitions: Yes

Major Awards: Best of the Fest

Value of Awards: We give the judging panel $3000 to divide up however they seek fit.

Application Fee: $30-$40, depends on length of film.

Average Films Entered: A wide range of quality work: animated, documentary, experimental, narrative, cross-genre, all lengths, 16mm or video (1/2 inch or 3/4 inch)

Films Screened: Approximately 70

Odds of Acceptance: 1 in 3

Travel Tips: The closest major airport is in St. Louis (2 hours); Amtrak passes through town.

Best Restaurants: Tokyo Restaurant

Best Bars: Tres Hombres

Best Hangout for Filmmakers: Long Branch Coffee House

Best Place for Breakfast: Melange Cafe

BIRMINGHAM INTERNATIONAL EDUCATIONAL FILM FESTIVAL

P. O. Box 2641
Birmingham, AL 35291-2711
Fax: 205-933-9080
Festival Date: Awards ceremony in May
Entry Deadline: January
Contact: Victoria Baxter
Category: Education

BLACK FILMWORKS FESTIVAL OF FILM AND VIDEO

1322 Webster, Suite 400
Oakland, CA 94612
Tel: 510-465-0804
Fax: 510-839-9858
Email: bfhfinc@aol.com
Web Site: www.blackfilmmakers hall.org
Festival Date: September—October
Entry Deadline: June

Contact: Dorothy Karvi
Director: Felix Curtis
Category: Ethnic Black
Profile: Its focus is to encourage black filmmakers and to explore black culture. Entrants in this festival are to be black directors, producers and film writers. Over 5,000 attend annually.
Awards: Yes
Competitions: Yes
Major Awards: There are over 10 categories with 3 prizes awarded in each.
Value of Awards: First Place: $1,500; Second Place: $750; Third Place: $500
Application Fee: $25-32
Odds of Acceptance: 33-50 films entered

BLACK HARVEST INTERNATIONAL FILM FESTIVAL

Film Center at the School of the Art Institute of Chicago
Columbus Dr. and Jackson Blvd.
Chicago, IL 60603
Tel: 312-443-3733
Fax: 312-332-5859
Email: bschar@artic.edu
Web Site: www.siskelfilm center.org
Festival Date: August
Entry Deadline: May
Director: Barbara Scharres
Category: Student
Application Fee: None

BLACK MARIA FILM AND VIDEO FESTIVAL

c/o Fries Hall Room MA 112
New Jersey City University
2039 Kennedy Blvd.
Jersey City, NJ 07305
Tel: 201-200-2043
Fax: 201-200-3490
Email: BlackMariaFest@aol.com
Web Site: http://elserver1.njcu. edu/TAEBMFF/
Festival Date: January
Entry Deadline: November
Contact: John Columbus
Director: John Columbus
Category: Touring (Alabama, Smithsonian, California, Alaska,

Rhode Island, Virginia, Atlanta, Vermont, Korea, New Jersey, New York, Boston, Chicago, Ohio, Pennsylvania)

Profile: We're the biggest small film/video festival going; we are anti-establishment; we are semi-underground; we are not bogus radical; we show really experimental, explorational, intelligent and inventive work.

Value of Awards: $17,000 in cash prizes

BLACK TALKiES ON PARADE FiLM FESTiVAL

3617 Montclair St.
Los Angeles, CA 90018
Tel: 323-737-3292
Fax: 323-737-2842
Web Site: www.wsbrec.org
Festival Date: August
Contact: Dr. Mayme A. Clayton
Director: Dr. Mayme A. Clayton
Category: Ethnic Black

BLUE SKY INTERNATIONAL FiLM FESTiVAL

4185 Paradise Rd. #2009
Las Vegas, NV 89109
Tel: 702-737-3313
Fax: Office will be moving, please call for new number
Email: info@bsiff.com
Web Site: www.bsiff.com
Festival Date: September
Entry Deadline: Ongoing—please call for accurate date
Year Festival Began: 1998
Contact: Gottfried Hill, Frank Montgomery
Director: Jeffrey Matthews Hill
Programmer: Jeffrey Matthews Hill
Category: Animation, Documentary, Independent, International, Short
Profile: An artisans forum dedicated to the discovery of new talent within the filmmaking community. We offer opportunity for all filmmakers, no matter how large or small their audience may be.
Awards: Yes
Competitions: Yes

Value of Awards: BSIFF Directors Award: $1000, BSIFF Best Screenplay: $1000, Plus a staged reading by the Blue Sky Players.
Application Fee: $15-$30
Films Screened: 100
Odds of Acceptance: 100 films submitted, 100 films screened.
Tourist Information: The Las Vegas Strip, Hoover Dam and Freemont Street.
Best Bars: Sunset Station

BOSTON FiLM FESTiVAL

P.O. Box 516
Hull, MA 02045
Tel: 781-925-1373
Fax: 781-925-3132
Email: gemsad@aol.com
Web Site: www.bostonfilm festival.org
Festival Date: September
Entry Deadline: July
Contact: Susan Fraine
Director: Susan Fraine
Programmer: Mark Diamond
Competitions: No
Application Fee: $60—Features; $45—Featurettes; $30—Shorts
Average Films Entered: 50+
Attendance: 25,000

BOSTON GAY & LESBiAN FiLM & ViDEO FESTiVAL

Museum of Fine Arts
465 Huntington Ave.
Boston, MA 02115-5523
Tel: 617-369-3454
Fax: 617-437-0293
Email: TBA
Web Site: None at this time
Festival Date: May
Entry Deadline: January
Director: Bo Smith
Programmer: Bo Smith
Application Fee: None

BRAiNWASH MOViE FESTiVAL

"This event trains culty, poly-glot focus on odd and obscure shorts, performance videos, works made for TV and out-of-genre efforts"
—Dennis Harvey, Variety.

P.O. Box 23302
Oakland, CA 94623-0302
Tel: 415 273-1545
Email: shelby@brainwashm.com
Web Site: www.BrainwashM.com
Festival Date: July/August
Entry Deadline: May
Year Festival Began: 1994
Contact: Dave Krzysik
Director: Dave Krzysik
Programmer: Vikki Vaden, Dave Krzysik, varies w/jury selection
Other Staff: Andy Wills, Vikki Vaden, Neel N. Kizmiaz, Scott Moffit.
Category: American Films, Animation, Experimental, First-Time Independent Filmmakers, Independent, Markets, Microcinema, Short, Underground, Video, Weird
Profile: The Brainwash Movie Festival is dedicated to presenting new, original, exciting movies at theatrical events and on television. Starting with shorts (less than 13 minutes) for the first six years, we are now expanding into feature movies.

Gore Score · · · · · · · · · · · · · · ·
If weird is what you like, or weird is what you've got, this is the place.

Market: Yes
Competitions: Yes
Major Awards: The 2nd Grand Prize
Value of Awards: $150.00—$500.00
Last Winning Films: *The Sex Life of the Chair, Madame DJ*
Last Winning Directors: Bernard Roddy, Johanna Hibbard, respectively
Past Judges: Les Blank, Annie Coulter, Barbara Traub, Scott Arford, Michelle Barnett
Application Fee: $20.00 early (by May 1st) for shorts (under 13 min.), $30.00 until May 10th.

$50.00 for features (under 130 min.), by May 1st, $75.00 until May 10th.

Films Screened: 30-60

Odds of Acceptance: 60%-75%

Attendance: 100-300 per screening

Journalist Attendance: At least 20-30 from major local press

Best Restaurants: The Mission Villa on 20th and Mission—oldest Mexican restaurant in town.

Best Hangout for Filmmakers: The Werepad

Festival Tale: It was the time of our second Festival and the featured guest to present the awards didn't show. So Matt Mitler, who did *Cracking Up* dressed up as Jesus and did it. We have video to prove it.

Random Tidbits: Robin Williams lives in Sea Cliff. Showtime acquisitions attended our Festival.

BRECKENRiDGE FESTiVAL OF FiLM

P. O. Box 718

Riverwalk Centre, 150 W. Adams

Breckenridge, CO 80424

Tel: 970-453-6200

Fax: 970-453-2692

Email: filmfest@brecknet.com

Web Site:
www.breckfilmfest.com

Festival Date: September

Entry Deadline: June

Year Festival Began: 1981

Contact: Tamara K. Johnston/ Julie Bullock

Director: Terese Keil

Category: Independent

Profile: This is a four day program of films, receptions, premieres, tributes, writers' seminars and film education activites providing unique and varied filmfare shown at venues throughout the community. Approximately 50 independent U.S. and international films presented from over 300 entries. Since 1981, Breckenridge Festival of Film has emphasized a relaxed atmosphere in which guests are readily accessible to filmgoers. Writers, directors, producers and performing artists attend to discuss their work with audiences in

informal sessions following screenings, at seminars, receptions and at the outdoor film forums.

Competitions: No

Major Awards: Best of the Fest

Application Tips: For initial selection, film entries must be in VHS format. Final screening accepted in 35mm, 16mm, 3/4". Scripts should meet US Motion Picture Industry standards and be 90-130 pages.

Application Fee: $35 US

Odds of Acceptance: 300 films entered, 50 presented.

Filmmaker Perks: Lodging accomodations and discounts on ground transportation provided for filmmakers during the festival.

Attendance: 1,500

BURBANK iNTERNATiONAL CHiLDRENS FiLM FESTiVAL

201 E. Magnolia Blvd., #151

Burbank, CA 91501

Tel: 818-841-3901

Fax: 818-841-3666

Email: pattedee@cs.com

Web Site: www.burbankfilm.org

Festival Date: October

Entry Deadline: September

Contact: Patte Dee

Director: Chris Shoemaker

Programmer: Patte Dee

Category: Short, Student

Application Fee: $100 Features; $50 Shorts; $80 Screenplay; $40 Student Filmmaker and For Children by Children

BWAC FiLM & ViDEO FESTiVAL

PO Box 020072

Brooklyn, NY 11202

Tel: 718-633-5490

Festival Date: May

Entry Deadline: March

Contact: Liz Longo

Application Fee: None

CANADiAN iNTERNATiONAL ANNUAL FiLM FESTiVAL

25 Eugenia St.

Barrie, Ontario L4M 1P6 Canada

Tel: 705-733-8232

Fax: 705-733-8232

Email: ciaff@canada.com or ciaff@iname.com

Web Site: www.ciaff.org

Festival Date: Varies

Entry Deadline: June

Contact: Ben V. W. Andrews

Director: Ben V. W. Andrews

Programmer: Kevin Harrison

CANYONLANDS FiLM & ViDEO FESTiVAL

59 South Main, Suite 214

Moab, UT 84532

Tel: 435-259-3385

Fax: 435-259-9868

Email: canyonfilm@hotmail.com

Festival Date: November

Entry Deadline: August

Contact: Howard Trenholme

Application Fee: $25

CAROLiNA FiLM AND ViDEO FESTiVAL

Broadcasting/Cinema Dept.

100 Carmichael Bldg.

UNC-Greensboro

P.O. Box 26170

Greensboro, NC 27402

Tel: 336-334-4197

Fax: 336-334-5039

Email: cifvf@uncg.edu

Web Site: http://cfvf.cjb.net

Festival Date: March

Entry Deadline: February

Contact: Sarah Westmoreland

Category: Independent, Student

Profile: This festival screens films by students and independents. Over 600 attend.

Awards: Yes

Competitions: Yes

Major Awards: Categories and amount awarded are determined by the festival's jury.

Value of Awards: At least $2500 awarded.

Application Fee: $30 U.S. (Independents) / $20 U.S. (Students)

Films Screened: 45 screened

Odds of Acceptance: 1 in 6

CHARGED 60-SECOND FiLM FESTiVAL

1700 Broadway, 9th Floor
New York, NY 10016

Tel: 212-765-5239

Fax: 212-765-5933

Email: dfalcone@charged.com

Web Site: www.charged.com

Contact: Daneil Falcone

Category: Animation, Short, Weird

Profile: The Charged 60-Second Film Festival is a competitive festival dedicated to films and videos one minute or less.

CHARLOTTE FiLM AND ViDEO FESTiVAL

c/o The Light Factory
809 West Hill St.
P.O. Box 32815
Charlotte, NC 28232

Tel: 704-333-9755

Fax: 704-333-5910

Email: wfishman@lightfactory.org

Web Site: www.lightfactory.org

Festival Date: April

Entry Deadline: February

Year Festival Began: 1989

Contact: Wendy Fishman

Director: Wendy Fishman

Category: Independent, Video

Profile: The Charlotte Film and Video Festival seeks to foster and encourage the art of independent film and video makers, especially those with a unique point of view. Affirming this commitment, the festival also seeks to increase public awareness and accessibility to this art form.

Awards: Yes

Competitions: Yes

Major Awards: Jurors Choice Award, Directors Choice Award

Value of Awards: $1000—$500

Application Tips: Films that are truly independent typically do better than standard documentaries or narratives. Creative and experimental films are encouraged. Films that are art, but not necessarily about art, do well. Don't send toys, T-shirts or props. Past screenings or awards are helpful.

Application Fee: $40 Feature $30 Short

Insider Advice: Make sure preview tapes are in good shape. No works in progress.

Average Films Entered: 600

Films Screened: 25 Features, 20 Shorts

Filmmaker Perks: All accepted films in the festival receive cash. Range is from $50 to $1000.

Festival Tale: In 1997, we screened *It's Elementary*. Two county commissioners came to the screening and alerted the local news. After the screening, the commissioners said the film should never have been screened and was about recruiting homosexuals. (It's about tolerance in public schools for all, including gays and lesbians.) All local news stations led with the story. Later that month the same commissioners voted to eliminate

$300,000 of taxpayer funding from the museum.

CHARLOTTE GAY & LESBiAN FiLM SERiES presented by OutCharlotte

PO Box 32062
Charlotte, NC 28232-2062

Tel: 704-563-2699

Fax: 704-569-8190

Email: director@outcharlotte.org

Web Site: www.outcharlotte.org

Festival Date: January-May (4th Thursday of each month)

Entry Deadline: We accept VHS tapes from June 1-November 1 each year.

Year Festival Began: 1991

Contact: Dan Kirsch

Director: Dan Kirsch

Category: American Films, Documentary, Ethnic African, Ethnic Asian, Ethnic Black, Ethnic Jewish, Ethnic Latin, Ethnic Spanish, Experimental, First-Time Independent Filmmakers, Gay Lesbian, Independent, International, Video, Woman

Profile: OutCharlotte is a regional organization that proactively celebrates the diversity and creative culture of the lesbian/gay/bisexual/transgender (LGBT) community through education, the arts, training and commitment to personal and community growth and development while striving for acceptance, respect and inclusivity for all.

OutCharlotte produces an annual cultural festival in October, presents the Charlotte Gay & Lesbian Film Series, and conducts various leadership development workshops for the community.

The Film Series and an annual Cultural Festival held every October celebrate the diverse contributions of the LGBT community. Our purpose is to foster awareness and appreciation of LGBT culture through arts-related, educational and historical programs.

Famous Speakers: Ruth Ellis visited Charlotte when we showed

BEST VIDEO FILM FESTIVALS

Arizona State University Short Film and Video Festival
Atlanta Film and Video Festival
Central Florida Film and Video Festival
Charlotte Film and Video Festival
Golden Shower Video Festival
New York International Video Festival
Northwest Film & Video Festival
Savannah Film and Video Festival
Victoria Independent Film and Video Festival
PXL THIS

her film in April 2000. We will look for opportunites to bring in filmmakers and/or subjects of documentaries to expand our communities awareness of LGBT people.

Market: No

Competitions: No

Films Screened: 20

Attendance: Average audience is 150 per film showing on the series.

Journalist Attendance: None

CHiCAGO ALT. FiLM FEST

"An event for filmgoers whose tastes fit somewhere between the foreign-centered International and the edgy Underground.... Programmed with emerging American directors in mind and indie-loving audiences at heart."
—Erik Piepenberg, MSNBC

3430 N. Lake Shore Drive, Suite 19N

Chicago, IL 60657

Tel: 773-525-4559

Fax: 773-327-8669

Email: chialtfilm@aol.com

Web Site: members.aol.com/ChiAltFilm/Fest

Festival Date: June

Entry Deadline: April

Year Festival Began: 1998

Contact: Dennis Neal Vaughn

Director: Dennis Neal Vaughn

Programmer: Dennis Neal Vaughn and Sandra Kay Zielinski

Other Staff: Leticia G. Esquivel, Pamela J. Stephens

Category: Independent

Profile: Chicago's premiere film festival of American Independent filmmakers–quality over quantity.

Seminars: Scripts—writing, buying, selling; Working with the Guilds, Film technology

Awards: Yes

Competitions: Yes

Major Awards: Founder's Award to most promising filmmaker.

Value of Awards: $1000

Application Tips: Be professional

Application Fee: $50

Insider Advice: Learn to write a good twenty-five word synopsis

of the film that details the protagonist, antagonist and their basic conflict. Get decent press photos.

Average Films Entered: narrative features and shorts

Films Screened: Total 35 features, shorts, and docs

Odds of Acceptance: 1 in 13

Filmmaker Perks: VIP/Filmmaker networking lounge and private dinner party

Tourist Information: Wrigley Field, the lake front, State Street, Michigan Avenue, Michael Jordan's restuarant

Travel Tips: Be prepared for anything—the weather can change in five minutes here.

Best Bars: The Rainbo Club

Best Hangout for Filmmakers: The Rainbo Club

Best Place for Breakfast: The Rainbo—Just ask any cab driver

CHiCAGO iNTERNATiONAL CHiLDREN'S FiLM FESTiVAL (CiCFF)

c/o Facets Multimedia, Inc.

1517 West Fullerton Ave.

Chicago, IL 60614

Tel: 773-281-9075

Fax: 773-929-0266

Email: kidsfest@facets.org

Web Site: www.cicff.org

Festival Date: October

Entry Deadline: May/April

Director: Nicole Dreiske, CICFF Founder and Executive Director

Category: Animation, Live Action Television, Short, Video

Profile: The Chicago International Children's Film Festival (CICFF) is the largest and most prestegious competitive festival of films for children in North America. Screening over 150 films and videos from over 40 countries in a marathon eleven days in October, the Festival has a local, national, and global impact, as is considered by many the point of entry for international children's films into the United States.

Competitions: Yes

Major Awards: Special Awards:

Best of the Fest Prize (selected by audience vote, cash prize $2500)

The Kenneth F. and Harle G. Montgomery Award (cash prize, $2500)

Whole Foods Market's Green Screen prize (cash prize, $1000)

Liv Ullmann Peace Prize

Rights of the Child Prize

Application Fee: Shorts are 59 min. or less ($35.00 USD entry fee); Features are 60 min. or more ($75.00 USD entry fee)

CHiCAGO iNTERNATiONAL FiLM FESTiVAL

See "The Top Ten Film Festivals" beginning on page 214.

CHiCAGO LATiNO FiLM FESTiVAL

"...One of the city's premier film events..."
—Chicago Tribune

Chicago Latino Cinema

600 S. Michigan Ave.

Chicago, IL 60605-1996

Tel: 312-431-1330

Fax: 312-344-8030

Email: clc@popmail.colum.edu

Web Site: www.latinocultural center.com

Festival Date: April-May

Entry Deadline: January

Contact: Pepe Vargas

Director: Pepe Vargas

Programmer: Jesse Rodriguez (Feature Film Programmer)
Carolina Posse (Short Film & Video Programmer)

Category: Animation, Digital, Digital Animation, Documentary, Ethnic Asian, Ethnic Black, Ethnic Jewish, Ethnic Latin, Ethnic Other, Ethnic Spanish, Experimental, First-Time Independent Filmmakers, Gay Lesbian, Independent, International, Multimedia, Short, Video, Weird, Woman

Profile: The Chicago Latino Film Festival promotes Latino culture and supports Latino films and directors by presenting the best and most recent films and videos

Learn to write a good twenty-five word synopsis of the film that details the protagonist, antagonist and their basic conflict (Chicago Alt Film Fest).

from Spain, Portugal, Latin America and the United States. The Festival stresses the artistic and educational value of film. Works from other countries are considered if the director is of Iberoamerican descent, or the subject matter is directly related to Latino culture. Preference is given to premiers, although works of strong historical or artistic value are often show-cased.

Market: No

Awards: Yes

Competitions: No

Major Awards: Audience Choice Award

Value of Awards: $5000

Last Winning Directors: Cristián Galaz Garcia

Past Judges: Audience

Application Tips: Submit complete promotional package: A VHS videotape (NTSC preferred), completed entry form with entry fee, synopsis, photos or slides, reviews if applicable, contact information, print source information.

Application Fee: $20

Average Films Entered: 300

Films Screened: 60 Features, 40 shorts

Best Cheap Hotels: Days Inn-Gold Coast, Motel 8—downtown

Best Luxury Hotels: Four Seasons

Best Restaurants: Tru, Nacional 27, Cite, Lalos

CHICAGO LESBIAN AND GAY INTERNATIONAL FILM FESTIVAL

c/o Chicago Filmmakers

Attn: Reeling

5243 N. Clark St.

Chicago, IL 60640

Tel: 773-293-1447

Fax: 773-293-0575

Email: reeling@chicagofilm makers.org

Web Site: www/chicagofilm makers.org/reeling

Contact: Brenda Webb

Director: Branda Webb

Category: Gay Lesbian

Application Fee: $15—First entry $10—each additional entry by same entrant

CHICAGO UNDERGROUND FILM FESTIVAL

3109 North Western Ave.

Chicago, IL 60618

Tel: 113-866-8660

Fax: 773-327-3464

Email: info@cuff.org

Web Site: www.cuff.org

Festival Date: August

Entry Deadline: May

Contact: Bryan Wendorf

Director: Jay Bliznick

Programmer: Bryan Wendorf

Other Staff: Donna Jagela, Wendy Solomon, Sonja Pachmeyer, Chris Tillman, Mike Miller, Michael Kopp

Category: Independent, Underground, Weird

Profile: Our festival is designed to showcase the truly independent filmmaker. We don't promote any sort of political agenda other than the free expression of views outside of the entertainment mainstream...we're just about the films. We won't discriminate on content but we are firm about intent. We also don't discriminate between first-time and established filmmakers. If you suspect your film is underground, it probably is.

Gore Score · · · · · · · · · · · · · · ·

My personal favorite underground film festival. The most recent fest honored Alejandro Jodorowsky. From John Waters to Nick Zedd, there is no better place to get a taste of the real underground scene. As an added bonus, the parties rock.

Seminars: Yes

Famous Speakers: John Waters, Beth B, Jack Sargeant

Awards: Yes

Competitions: Yes

Major Awards: Golden Sewer Cap

Value of Awards: $500

Last Winning Films: *Half Spirit* (feature), *Meat* (short), *Rainbow Man/John 3:16* (Documentary), *Premenstrual Spotting* (Experimental)

Last Winning Directors: Henri Barges (Feature), Jason Hernandez-Rosenblatt (Short), Sam Green (Documentary), Machiko Saito (Experimental).

Past Judges: Tom Palazzolo, Bryan Wendorf, Jay Bliznick, Donna Jagela, Wendy Solomon, Mike Miller, Jonathan Lavan.

Application Tips: Read the mission statement. Think about whether our festival is the right place to showcase your film. Read the guidelines and follow them!

Application Fee: $25 (60 minutes or less) $35 (over 60 minutes)

Insider Advice: Can't stress enough that you must feel sure that this is the festival where your film belongs. Each year we screen a lot of good entries that are just not right for us. Do your research—don't enter festivals just because you get an application in the mail. If you're not sure, call the festival and talk to a human. That will save you much money and aggravation!

Odds of Acceptance: 1 in 8

Filmmaker Perks: Opening and closing night filmmakers are flown in and lodged at our expense. We always have a special hotel rate for filmmakers at a sponsor hotel. A list of press contacts is available prior to the festival to anyone who asks for one. We always have hosted parties where filmmakers drink for free or way cheap. And of course, we host the annual VPL (Visible Panty League) (you figure it out) Bowling Night, during which visiting filmmakers and local CUFFers descend upon an all-night bowling alley and roll them balls 'til the sun comes up! Charles Pinion of San Francisco has won the trophy two years running. . . can anyone beat him?

CINE ACCIÓN ¡CINE LATINO!

346 Ninth St.

San Francisco, CA 94103

Tel: 415-553-8140

Fax: 415-553-8137

Email: cineaccion@aol.com

Web Site: www.cineaccion.com

Festival Date: September 13-16; September 20-23, 2001

Entry Deadline: Spring 2001, TBD

Year Festival Began: 1992

Director: Rosalia Valencia

Category: Ethnic Latin

Profile: Cine Acción's mission is to foster Latino self representation in the media arts. We are a non-profit membership organization committed to the production and exhibition of film and video which gives voice to the complexity and diversity of the Latino experience.

Cine Acción's Festival ¡Cine Latino! showcases short and feature films by, for and about the Latino community. Our 8th annual festival takes place in the Bay Area in September during Hispanic Heritage Month. The festival screens works by first time filmmakers and established artists from the United States and Latin America. Our festival also includes special free youth screenings offered to Bay Area high schools.

Application Fee: $25.00 (includes one-year membership to Cine Acción)

Common Mistakes: The filmmakers do not send adequate press material, bios, stills or synopses for press work.

Insider Advice: Help promote your screening.

Average Films Entered: All genres are accepted in both short and feature length. The festival is most interested in works created within the last four years.

Films Screened: Usually 8-12 features and approximately 50 shorts are screened.

Odds of Acceptance: 1 in 2

Filmmaker Perks: Travel and accomodations are offered by Cine Acción for some of the visiting filmmakers.

Attendance: 3,000-4,000

Random Tidbits: Famous Guests: Rita Moreno and Cheech Marin. Festival ¡Cine Latino! is the largest gathering of Latino filmmakers in the Bay Area.

CINEMA OUT— ORANGE COUNTY, SOUTH BAY BEACHES & LONG BEACH

3592 North Lewis

Long Beach, CA 90807

Tel: 562-492-9239

Fax: 310-787-1965

Email: mattemerritt@ hotmail.com

Web Site: www.cinemaout.com

Festival Date: February & August

Entry Deadline: December & May

Contact: Matt Merritt

Director: Matt Merritt, Claudia Piras, Ella Matthes

Application Fee: None

CINEMATEXAS INTERNATIONAL SHORT FILM & VIDEO FESTIVAL

Dept. of Radio-TV-Film

University of Texas CMA 6.118

Austin, TX 78712-1091

Tel: 512-471-6497

Fax: 512-471-4077

Email: cinematexas@ cinematexas.org

Web Site: http://uts.cc.utexas.edu/ ~cinematx/home.html

Festival Date: October

Entry Deadline: June

Year Festival Began: 1995

Contact: Micah Magee

Director: Athina Raschel Tsangari (Founding Director), Micah Magee (Managing Director)

Programmer: Spencer Parsons

Category: American Films, Animation, Digital, Digital Animation, Documentary, DVD, Ethnic African, Ethnic Asian, Ethnic Black, Ethnic Jewish, Ethnic Latin, Ethnic Spanish, Experimental, First-Time Independent Filmmakers, Gay Lesbian, Independent, International, Microcinema, Multimedia, PXL, Short, Student, Super 8/8mm, Underground, Video, Weird, Woman

Seminars: Yes

Panels: Yes

Famous Speakers: Yes

Market: No

Competitions: Yes

Value of Awards: $15,000 total awarded

Application Fee: $25 early $30 late

Common Mistakes: Spending too much money dressing the VHS cassette.

Insider Advice: Don't forget your stills.

Average Films Entered: 800 (international competition), 100 (UT competition)

Films Screened: 90 (International competition) 40 (UT competition)

Odds of Acceptance: 1 in 10 (International competition) 1 in 3 (UT competition)

Filmmaker Perks: Lodging

CINEQUEST FILM FESTIVAL

See "The Top Ten Film Festivals" beginning on page 214.

CINEVEGAS FILM FESTIVAL

2501 N. Green Valley Parkway, #118 D

Henderson, NV 89014

Tel: 702-477-7530

Fax: 702-477-7533

Email: cinevegas@aol.com

Web Site: www.cine.vegas.com

Festival Date: November-December

Entry Deadline: October

Year Festival Began: 1998

Contact: Joshua Abbey

Director: Paul Bodner

Category: Independent

Profile: CineVegas is about more than bringing culture to the desert; it's about redefining Las Vegas for the next century as the most progressive and compelling tourist destination in the world.

The goal of CineVegas is to engage the imagination and participation of the entertainment industry and filmgoing public by producing a festival that captures and emulates the inventiveness that has made Las Vegas the focal point of popular American culture.

Gore Score · · · · · · · · · · · · · ·

Combining the phony glitz of gambling in Vegas with the phony Hollywood film community could be a stroke of genius. The festival began its first year with the premiere of a stripper documentary. Not your typical indie fest.

Films Screened: Featured the premiere of the feature-length documentary, *Stripped and Teased: Tales of Las Vegas Women*, directed by award-winning documentary filmmaker Amie Williams.

CLEVELAND iNTERNATiONAL FiLM FESTiVAL

2510 Market Avenue
Cleveland, OH 44113-3434
Tel: 216-623-3456
Fax: 216-623-0103
Email: cfs@clevelandfilm.org
Web Site: www.clevelandfilm.org
Festival Date: March
Entry Deadline: November
Year Festival Began: 1976
Contact: Marcie Goodman
Director: David Wittkowsky, Artistic Director; Marcie Goodman, Managing Director
Programmer: David Wittkowsky, William Guentzler
Other Staff: Tonya Page, Membership Director; Mara Stifter, Cleveland Filmmakers Director; Jeffery Mannies, Development Director
Category: American Films, Documentary, Ethnic Asian, Ethnic Black, Ethnic Latin, Ethnic Spanish, Experimental, First-Time Independent Filmmakers, Gay Lesbian, Independent, International, Short
Profile: Founded in 1976, the Cleveland International Film Festival is the premier film event in the region. For eleven days every March, the Festival presents a full survey of contemporary filmmaking from around the world. Approximately 80 features from more than 30 countries and over 100 short subjects are shown to an audience that now exceeds 36,000.

Gore Score · · · · · · · · · · · · · · · ·

More than a festival, Cleveland is extremely supportive of filmmaking in the Midwest.

Seminars: The Midwest Independent Filmmakers Conference is held during the last weekend of the Festival each year
Panels: FilmForums with visiting filmmakers and local experts as panelists
Application Tips: submit on time—don't miss the deadline.
Application Fee: $35 (short) and $60 (feature)
Common Mistakes: Sometimes the form is incomplete or payment is not included.
Average Films Entered: More shorts are accepted than features.
Films Screened: 80
Odds of Acceptance: 1 in 5
Filmmaker Perks: We provide travel and accommodations for certain visiting filmmakers.
Attendance: 36,400
Journalist Attendance: 50 local
Tourist Information: Rock and Roll Hall of Fame and Museum; Cleveland Museum of Art; Cleveland Orchestra at Severance Hall
Best Cheap Hotels: Holiday Inn Lakeside
Best Luxury Hotels: Ritz-Carlton Cleveland
Best Restaurants: Century at the Ritz-Carlton Cleveland
Best Bars: Lava Lounge
Best Hangout for Filmmakers: The Film Festival, of course!
Best Place for Breakfast: Century at the Ritz-Carlton Cleveland

CMJ FiLMFEST

810 7th Ave., 21st Floor
New York, NY 10019
Tel: 646-485-6596; 1-877-633-4878
Fax: 646-557-0010
Email: filmfest@cmj.com
Web Site: www.cmj.com/ Marathon
Festival Date: October
Entry Deadline: September

Year Festival Began: 1999
Contact: Dana Varon, Festival Coordinator
Director: Donita Dooley
Programmer: Donita Dooley
Other Staff: Chad Feinstein, Promotions Director, Michelle Thomas, Producer
Profile: CMJ FilmFest is a film festival that focuses on the best use of music in film. The four-day event explores the landscape of music and film with a slate of distinctive independent production and major studio premieres. The mission of the CMJ FilmFest is to create a community where filmmakers can network with emerging musicians as well as music industry professionals. Whether the film is an effort from a first time filmmaker or a recognized, established talent—if it has great music, it has a place at CMJ.
Seminars: Yes
Panels: Yes
Famous Speakers: Todd Haynes, Christine Vachon, Kevin Smith, and many music supervisors.
Market: No
Competitions: Yes
Major Awards: The CMJ Signature Award for Best Use of Music in Film
Value of Awards: 1999 marked our first competition; awards were valued at $1,000 each in goods and services.
Application Fee: $20 for shorts, $30 for features and documentaries
Common Mistakes: Not providing enough information via press kits or filling out forms incorrectly.
Insider Advice: If accepted into the festival, bring your music supervisor.
Average Films Entered: Features, documentaries and shorts with interesting or unique use of music; we also look for narrative films and documentaries that use music as part of the plot.
Films Screened: 25
Odds of Acceptance: 1 in 10
Attendance: Last year over 9,000 attended CMJ. The film festival attracted another 2500.

Journalist Attendance: The CMJ Music Marathon, MusicFest & FilmFest is covered annually by major newspapers and magazines such as the *New York Times, Rolling Stone, Los Angeles Times,* etc.

Travel Tips: Travel light, check into airport shuttles.

Best Hangout for Filmmakers: Check out the Anthology Film Archives on 2nd Avenue, and see what's playing at the Angelika.

Festival Tale: In 1999 we hosted a sneak preview of Fox's *Fight Club* because it had an awesome soundtrack. The night of the screening, Hurricane Floyd hit NYC out of nowhere—the mayor was calling for the entire city to close down, it was pissing down torrential rain. But we held firm and went on with the screening. About 500 people showed up at the DGA Theater—400 got in. We screened an unmarried cut and half an hour into it, the film broke. No one could leave because of the rain. We had Samuel Jackson and John Singleton in the house and it was tense. After twenty minutes, we repaired it and the show went on.

COLUMBUS INTERNATIONAL FILM AND VIDEO FESTIVAL "Chris Awards"

Film Council of Greater Columbus
5701 North High St., Suite 200
Worthington, OH 43085
Tel: 614-841-1666
Fax: 614-841-1666
Email: info@chrisawards.org
Web Site: www.chrisawards.org
Festival Date: October
Entry Deadline: July
Year Festival Began: 1952
Contact: Joyce Long
Director: Richard Long
Programmer: Linda Thornburg
Category: Animation, Experimental, Independent, International
Application Fee: $75–$125

CONNECTICUT GAY & LESBIAN FILM FESTIVAL

P.O. Box 231191
Hartford, CT 06123
Festival Location:
Cinestudio
300 Summit Street
Hartford, CT 06106-3100
Tel: 860-586-1136;
Cinestudio: 860-297-2463
Fax: 860-232-3402
Email: glff@yahoo.com
Web Site: www.CTGLFF.org
Festival Date: June 1-9, 2001
Entry Deadline: March 31, 2001
Year Festival Began: 1988
Director: Dan Millett
Programmer: Dan Millett
Category: Gay Lesbian
Profile: A showcase for lesbian, gay, bisexual and transgender films.
Application Fee: $10
Filmmaker Perks: We do pay for some travel expenses and we do put up guests of the festival.
Attendance: 2,000
Tourist Information: Wadsworth Atheneum, Mark Twain House, Trinity College, Hartford Stage
Best Cheap Hotels: Ramada Inn
Best Luxury Hotels: Goodwin Hotel
Best Restaurants: Max Downtown
Best Bars: Polo Club
Best Hangout for Filmmakers: Cinestudio
Best Place for Breakfast: Mo's Midtown

CONTEMPORARY AFRICAN DIASPORA FILM FESTIVAL

535 Cathedral Parkway, Suite 14-B
New York, NY 10025
Tel: 212-749-6020
Fax: 212-316-6020
Web Site: www.Africanfilm.com
Festival Date: November—December
Entry Deadline: August
Director: Reynaldo Spech

CRIPPLE CREEK FILM FESTIVAL

P.O. Box 219 (General Mail)
400 West Midland Ave., Suite 232 (UPS & Fedex)
Woodland Park, CO 80866
Tel: 719-686-9249 ; 1-877-499-FILM (Outside of Colorado)
Fax: 719-686-9249
Email: michaelherst@cripple creekfilmfest.com
Web Site: www.cripplecreekfilm fest.com
Festival Date: September—October
Entry Deadline: August
Director: Michael Herst
Programmer: Michael Herst
Category: Animation, Documentary, Short
Competitions: Yes
Major Awards: Adelphia/Bravo, Excellence in Independent Filmmaking Award and $500.00 cash prize.
Average Films Entered: Completed Feature, Documentary, Short Subject, or Animated Film.

CUCALORUS FILM FESTIVAL

Mailing Address: P.O. Box 2763
Street Address: 420 Orange St.
Wilmington, NC 28401
Tel: 910-343-5995
Fax: 910-343-5227
Email: info@cucalorus.org
Web Site: www.cucalorus.org
Festival Date: March 22-25, 2001
Entry Deadline: Early: November; Late: December
Year Festival Began: 1994
Contact: Dan Brawley
Director: Kristy Byrd, Brent Watkins, Dan Brawley
Category: American Films, Animation, Documentary, Experimental, First-Time Independent Filmmakers, Independent, International, Short, Super 8/8mm, Underground, Video, Weird
Profile: The goal of the festival is to bring independent film culture and awareness to Wilmington. We strive to display deserving

work, creating a noncompetitive showcase of films spawned from all budgets, by filmakers of all backgrounds.

Cucalorus supports the independent artist, providing a beneficial environment for projection, discussion and promotion of the work before a general audience and other filmmakers.

Gore Score · · · · · · · · · · · · · · ·
A great regional indie fest.

Seminars: Filmmaker Discussion Groups ("Coffee Chats"), the Annual Filmmaker's Brunch, Sponsors' Receptions, Live Music at various clubs

Market: No

Competitions: No

Application Fee: $20

Common Mistakes: Horrible dubs that are missing sound or information, several entries with one fee, late submissions.

Insider Advice: Editing, editing, editing. We get a lot of entries that are an hour long that could have been ten minutes long. Lousy acting usually puts us off as well.

Average Films Entered: Genre and format don't matter. Well-made, enthusiastic, different, competent, entertaining, thought-provoking

Films Screened: 40

Odds of Acceptance: 1 in 6

Filmmaker Perks: Discounted or free lodging (the Adopt-a-Filmmaker program), lots of free food and drink, live music and late-nights, lots of discussion among filmmakers, coupons at local stores, relaxed atmosphere, the beach, lovely weather...

Journalist Attendance: 10

Tourist Information: Wrightsville Beach (lovely swimming, surfing), USS NC Battleship, Screen Gems Studios

Travel Tips: I-40 if you're driving. If you're flying, sometimes it's cheaper to fly to Raleigh-Durham and drive to Wilmington.

Best Cheap Hotels: French House B&B

Best Luxury Hotels: Inn at St. Thomas

Best Restaurants: Deluxe

Best Bars: Blue Post Bar & Billiards

Best Hangout for Filmmakers: Blue Post, Barbary Coast, Cucalorus Hospitality Lounge

Best Place for Breakfast: Front Street Diner

Random Tidbits: Wilmington is the third largest film production town in the country, so there are always celebs here working on movies.

D.FiLM
DiGiTAL FiLM FESTiVAL

"One of the 25 players bringing Hollywood into the 21st century"
—*WIRED Magazine*

"(D.FILM's) films push the boundaries of what can be created on computers"
—*Roger Ebert*

564 Mission St., Suite 429
San Francisco, CA 94105

Email: bart@dfilm.com

Web Site: www.dfilm.com

Festival Date: Touring. DFilm travels to Los Angeles, San Francisco, New York, Boston; London and Manchester; Rio.

Entry Deadline: None. Since the festival is continually being shown in different cities throughout the year, deadlines are ongoing.

Year Festival Began: 1997

Director: Bart Cheever

Other Staff: Nikos Constant, Claire McNulty, Publicity

Category: Animation, Digital, Documentary, Independent, International, Short, Student, Touring, Video, Weird

Profile: Our goal is to showcase the very best work being created within the digital medium. We prefer pieces which are approximately five minutes in length or less, or excerpts from longer films. We're looking for work that demonstrates some innovative new use of technology. Although we show abstract work, we especially value pieces which are able to strongly convey ideas or tell stories; pieces which will entertain and inspire

our audiences to create films themselves.

Our goal at D.FILM is to not only showcase the best in digital filmmaking through our screenings and website but to also actively inspire our audiences to make film themselves. Do it.

Gore Score · · · · · · · · · · · · · · ·
Offers amazing opportunities for filmmakers to expose their innovative digital works to audiences as well as providing an impressive number of press opportunities. In addition, screenings and parties provide opportunities to discuss the future of the digital medium.

Application Fee: None. Entry fees suck.

DA ViNCi FiLM
AND ViDEO FESTiVAL

P.O. Box 1536 (Mailing)
760 S.W. Madison Ave., Suite #200 (UPS & FEDEX)
Corvallis, OR 97339 (Mailing)
97333 (UPS & FEDEX)

Tel: 541-757-6363

Fax: 541-754-7590

Email: davinci@davinci-days.org

Web Site: www.davinci-days.org

Festival Date: July

Entry Deadline: Early

Contact: Tina Hutchens

Category: Animation, Documentary, Short, Video

Attendance: Approximately 10,000—15,000

DALLAS ViDEO FESTiVAL

1405 Woodlawn Ave.
Dallas, TX 75208

Tel: 214-999-8999

Fax: 214-999-8998

Email: info@videofest.org or bart@videofest.org

Web Site: www.videofest.org or vvvv.dallasvideo.org

Festival Date: March

Entry Deadline: November

Contact: Bart Weiss

Category: Animation, Documentary, Experimental, Independent, Short, Video

Profile: Requires to enter via website. Additional charge for using paper entry form.

Application Fee: $40 ($30 if member of Video Association of Dallas)

DANCES WiTH FiLMS

"The defiant festival of raw talent."
—*The Hollywood Reporter*

The Lot
1041 N. Formosa Ave.
Formosa Bldg., Rm 217
West Hollywood, CA 90046
Tel: 323-850-2929
Fax: 323-850-2928
Email: info@danceswithfilms.com
Web Site: www.danceswithfilms.com
Festival Date: June
Entry Deadline: March; Late Deadline: April
Year Festival Began: 1998
Contact: Michael Trent
Director: Michael Trent
Programmer: Leslee Scallon

Other Staff: Maura Barry—Volunteer Coordinator
Nancy Fassett—Producing Coordinator
Erich Klain—Transportation Coordinator
Category: American Films, Digital Animation, Documentary, Ethnic African, Ethnic Asian, Ethnic Black, Ethnic Jewish, Ethnic Latin, Ethnic Spanish, Experimental, Fantasy/Science Fiction, First-Time Independent Filmmakers, Gay Lesbian, Independent, International, Short, Video, Woman
Profile: DancesWithFilms is the only film festival in the United States geared solely to the true independents mandating that all competition films have no "known" directors, actors or producers.

Gore Score · · · · · · · · · · · · · · ·
As much a schmooze fest as a festival.

Seminars: Sometimes
Panels: Sometimes

Famous Speakers: Sometimes
Market: No
Competitions: Yes
Major Awards: Best of DancesWithFilms—Feature & Short Categories
Value of Awards: Varies year to year
Application Tips: We place everyone on a level playing field—no politics—no tips
Application Fee: Features $50, Shorts $35. All Late submissions $75
Common Mistakes: Submitting at the last minute and not printing their information clearly. Nothing is worse than finding a terrific film and not be able to get a hold of the filmmaker!
Insider Advice: Submit early—it will only help you. And when you've thought you've edited it as much as you possibly can . . . edit some more.
Films Screened: 50
Odds of Acceptance: 1 in 20
Attendance: 7,000

Journalist Attendance: Approx. 50 and growing

Travel Tips: Get here!

Best Cheap Hotels: The Standard

Best Luxury Hotels: The Standard

Best Restaurants: Hey, we got it all—from Spago to Baja Fresh.

Best Place for Breakfast: Norm's Restaurant on La Cienega

Festival Tale: Celebrity sightings: Drew Barrymore and Tom Greene perusing the DancesWithFilms selections during the 2000 fest.

Random Tidbits: Check your egos at the door. If you have attitude, we have no interest.

> Check your egos at the door. If you have attitude, we have no interest (Dances With Films).

DEEP ELLUM FiLM FESTiVAL

2622 Commerce St.

Dallas, TX 75226

Tel: 214-752-6741

Fax: 214-752-6863

Email: deffest2000@aol.com

Web Site: www.def2.org

Festival Date: November

Entry Deadline: September

Year Festival Began: 1999

Contact: Melina McKinnon

Director: Executive Director: Michael Cain; Managing Director: Melina McKinnon

Programmer: Michael Cain, King Hollis, Karl Kimbrough, Joaquin Lira

Category: American Films, Animation, Digital, Documentary, Ethnic Latin, Experimental, First-Time Independent Filmmakers, Microcinema, Online Festival, Unfinished works in progress, Short, Student, Super 8/8mm, Underground, Video, Weird

Profile: The Deep Ellum Film Festival was founded by lovers of cinema and the arts, who saw an opportunity to create an atmosphere where American and Latin American filmmakers could find their new ideas nurtured, their creativity rewarded and their original voices heard. We wanted to create a place where pushing the art form would be recognized as well as a festival that

would be very filmmaker and film buff friendly.

Gore Score · · · · · · · · · · · · · ·
Texas' best kept secret—a worthwhile underground fest.

Market: Yes

Competitions: Yes

Major Awards: DEFMAN Grand Jury Prize

Value of Awards: $5,000, 25,000 feet of film processing

Past Judges: Denise DiNovi, David Dobkin, Rich Goldberg, LM Kit Carson

Application Fee: $40 feature $30 Short $40 Unfinished with script $30 Script competition $NA PSAs $35 Website

Common Mistakes: They wait to hear from Sundance, don't get in and try to submit after our deadline. Send in your film, if you get into Sundance we'll understand.

Insider Advice: Make it personal. We love movies with feeling, whatever they may be. Don't be afraid of asking questions. Attach the submission form to tape, we hate getting a tape with no info. Last year we received over 400 submissions and screened over 50 films; 100 arrived after the deadline—don't wait for the last moment.

Films Screened: 55

Odds of Acceptance: 1 in 8

Attendance: 3,500

Journalist Attendance: 5-7

Tourist Information: Dallas Stars Game, Lone Star Race Track, Texas Motor Speedway, Kennedy Museum

Travel Tips: Check out our website for deals. Southwest is cheap. Legend is very cool.

Best Cheap Hotels: The Paramount or The Aristocrat (We've got a deal here)

Best Luxury Hotels: The Magnolia (Amazing)

Best Restaurants: Sol's Taco Lounge (open until 3 am); Great Queso or The Green Room to impress the girls.

Best Bars: Club Clearview, Art Bar, Blind Lemon, The Rooftop and Red. All housed in one bad space.

Best Place for Breakfast: Café Brazil

DENVER iNTERNATiONAL FiLM FESTiVAL

1430 Larimer Square, Suite 320

Denver, CO 80202

Tel: 303-595-3456

Fax: 303-595-0956

Email: dfs@denverfilm.org

Web Site: www.denverfilm.org

Festival Date: October

Entry Deadline: July

Director: Ron Henderson

DENVER JEWiSH FiLM FESTiVAL

1430 Larimer Square, Suite 320

Denver, CO 80202

Tel: 303-595-3456; 303-595-0956

Email: dfs@denverfilm.org

Web Site: www.denverfilm.org

Festival Date: August

Director: Ron Henderson

DENVER PAN AFRiCAN FiLM FESTiVAL

1430 Larimer Square, Suite 320

Denver, CO 80202

Tel: 303-595-3456

Fax: 303-595-0956

Email: dfs@denverfilm.org

Web Site: www.denverfilm.org

Festival Date: April

Director: Ron Henderson

DOCFEST— NEW YORK iNTERNATiONAL DOCUMENTARY FESTiVAL

159 Maiden Lane

New York, NY 10038

Tel: 212-668-1100; 212-943-6333

Fax: 212-943-6396

Email: docfest@aol.com

Web Site: www.docfest.org

Festival Date: April–May

Entry Deadline: By invitation only.

Year Festival Began: 1998

Contact: Gary Pollard

Director: Gary Pollard

Programmer: David Leitner

Other Staff: Alla Verlotsky, Managing Director

David Leitner, Program Director

Susan Norget, Public Relations & Marketing

Category: Documentary, Independent

Profile: An annual international non-competitive event to celebrate and promote the documentary form. Programs are selected from among the best new and classic documentaries worldwide in every format. Of the hundreds of film festivals worldwide, only a handful are dedicated exclusively to documentaries. Docfest—uniquely—is the one festival in the U.S. that embraces the entirety of the documentary spectrum: TV, cable, video and film; from low-budget Hi8 videos to network reportage, from Super 8mm to IMAX.

Awards: Independent Film Channel (IFC) $2000 "Documentary Vision Award" and the Zuma Digital DVD Award ($15,000 worth of services to create a complete DVD of a film)

Competitions: No

Application Tips: Filmmakers are welcome to send tapes of their works but the selection is by invitation only.

Application Fee: None

Average Films Entered: Documentaries of all lengths, formats, themes etc.

Filmmaker Perks: Travel and lodging (the famed Algonquin Hotel). Lots of opportunities to network with other documentarians.

DOCUMENTAL

2427 1/2 Glyndon Ave.
Venice, CA 90291
Tel: 310-306-7330
Year Festival Began: 1995
Contact: Gerry Fialka
Director: Gerry Fialka
Category: Documentary, Experimental

DOUBLETAKE DOCUMENTARY FILM FESTIVAL

c/o The Center for Documentary Studies
1317 W. Pettigrew St.
Durham, NC 27705

Tel: 919-660-3699
Fax: 919-681-7600
Email: ddff@duke.edu
Web Site: www.ddff.org
Festival Date: May
Entry Deadline: December (Late Deadline: January)
Director: Nancy Buirski
Programmer: Karen Cirillo
Category: Documentary, International

DURANGO FILM FESTIVAL

1022 1/2 Main Ave.
Durango, CO 81301
Tel: 970-385-8686
Email: info@durangofilmfestival.com
Web Site: www.durangofilmfestival.com
Festival Date: Mid-March
Entry Deadline: December
Year Festival Began: 2000
Director: Erik Burke
Category: Documentary, Independent, Short

Profile: Escape to Durango, a small town in the mountains of Southwestern Colorado. Enjoy and explore the regional winter playground, and see innovative independent features, animation, documentaries, new media works, and short films at the Durango Film Festival. Here you can meet filmmakers and film enthusiasts in a unique and friendly environment. Learn about the art of filmmaking at educational salons and panel discussions.

EAT MY SHORTS

c/o Just For Laughs
2101 S. Laurent
Montreal, PQ H2X 2TS Canada
Tel: 514-845-3155
Fax: 514-845-4140
Email: brentmonster@hotmail.com
Web Site: http://hahaha.com
Festival Date: July
Contact: Brent Schiess

EDMONDS INTERNATIONAL FILM FESTIVAL

EasySpeak Productions
P.O. Box 1885
Edmonds, WA 98020-1885
Tel: 425-787-1021
Fax: 425-787-0821
Email: MichelynG@aol.com
Web Site: www.edmondsfilm.com
Festival Date: August
Entry Deadline: June 30
Year Festival Began: 2000
Contact: Michelyn Gjurasic
Director: Michelyn Gjurasic
Programmer: Michelyn Gjurasic, Paul Sinor, Jacob Young
Category: American Films, Animation, Digital, Digital Animation, DVD, Ethnic African, Ethnic Asian, Ethnic Black, Ethnic Jewish, Ethnic Latin, Ethnic Other, Ethnic Spanish, Experimental, Fantasy/Science Fiction, First-Time Independent Filmmakers, Independent, Markets, Multimedia, Short, Super 8/8mm, Video, Weird, Woman

Profile: Launched in 2000, The Edmonds International Film Festival is dedicated to encouraging, promoting, and enhancing the independent film industry. The festival features approximately 21 juried feature films. A screenplay contest also is included, as well as pre-festival seminars on such topics as writing, acting, producing and marketing. Festival celebrations include an Opening Night Party and an Awards Night Celebration, and celebrity judges decide the top honors.

Gore Score · · · · · · · · · · · · · · · ·

The debut festival featured five little-known indie features along with an impressive line-up of shorts. The immensely positive response means Edmonds will be entertaining audiences in Washington for years to come.

Seminars: Two days of seminars preceding the festival will offer such topics as writing, acting, producing and marketing.
Competitions: Yes
Application Fee: $25-$45

Average Films Entered: Feature length films, all genres. We plan to accept shorts in 2001.

Films Screened: 21

Filmmaker Perks: Contacts in Hollywood: four scheduled-for-you meetings in Hollywood with a reputable, recognized manager, an agent and two production companies, plus cash.

Tourist Information: Beaches, restaurants, antique malls, retail shops, Boeing (largest building in the world), downtown Seattle, Olympic Peninsula, ferries, etc.

Travel Tips: Take Shuttle Express from SeaTac airport to Edmonds ($17) or just rent a car so you can take the ferry and travel around.

God won't help you, but ingenuity will (Fantasia Film Festival)

Best Cheap Hotels: Edmonds Harbor Inn, 4 blocks from the theatre.

Best Luxury Hotels: Embassy Suites, Lynnwood

Best Restaurants: Chanterelle, across the street from the theatre.

Best Bars: Edmonds West Tavern, across the street from the theatre. Or Rory's Pub, 1st and Main, across from the ferry dock and Puget Sound.

Best Hangout for Filmmakers: Edmonds West Tavern or Rory's Pub

Best Place for Breakfast: Claire's Pantry, 3rd and Main.

EURO UNDERGROUND

1658 N. Milwaukee Ave.
Suite 142
Chicago, IL 60647
Tel: 888-864-9644 (U.S. Only); 312-401-7178 (Outside of U.S.)
Fax: 773-292-9205
Email: info@eurounderground.org
Web Site: www.eurounderground.org
Festival Date: November
Entry Deadline: July
Year Festival Began: 1996
Contact: Mark Siska
Director: Mark Siska
Programmer: Amy Beste
Other Staff: Justyna Mielnikiewicz, Ilko Davidov, Eugene Barksdale, Paul Rimple,

Franck Ravel, David Pyle, Victor Radev.

Category: Independent, Underground, Video, Weird

Profile: Euro Underground is a cross-cultural film organization produced by The International Film and Performance Society a not-for-profit film organization exhibiting new and emerging work of international filmmakers. Euro Underground has just completed a three city festival tour that included Sofia, Bulgaria; Krakow, Poland and Berlin, Germany. Euro Underground's mission is to exhibit Europeans and Americans as well as filmmakers throughout the world by producing a yearly festivals in selected European cities and then tour films presented in Europe in American by presenting a series of screening in selected American Cities.

Awards: Yes

Competitions: Yes

Application Tips: Send entries in early

Application Fee: $25 for short. $35 for feature.

Insider Advice: Try to put together and present your film the best way you can. with limited budgets try your best and be resourcefull there is a lot of ways to get things for free. It is highly competitive out there.

Films Screened: 100. But since we are a different festival that presents work throughout the year we screen a lot more. We continually take films and are currently exhibiting somewhere in the world every month.

Odds of Acceptance: 1 in 10

FANTASiA FiLM FESTIVAL

"The ultimate fantasy/horror film festival in the world today. Simply awesome"
—*Harvey Fenton, Flesh & Blood Magazine*

640 St. Paul West, Suite 502
Montreal, Quebec H3C 1L9
Canada
Tel: 514-393-8919; 514-488-5620
Fax: 514-393-8750; 514-488-4653
Email: festival1@videotron.ca or mdavis@total.net

Web Site: www.fantasiafest.com
Festival Date: July 13-31, 2001
Entry Deadline: early June, 2001
Year Festival Began: 1996
Contact: Julien Fonfrede, director of Asian Programming, 514-393-8919
fantasiafest@hotmail.com
Mitch Davis, director of International Programming, 514-488-5620
mdavis@total.net
Director: Pierre Corbeil
Programmer: Mitch Davis, Andre Dubois, Julien Fonfrede, Karim Hussain, Anna Mi-Jeong Lee, Anthony Timpone
Category: American Films, Animation, Digital Animation, Ethnic African, Ethnic Asian, Ethnic Black, Ethnic Jewish, Ethnic Latin, Ethnic Other, Ethnic Spanish, Experimental, Fantasy/Science Fiction, First-Time Independent Filmmakers, Independent, International, Multimedia, Short, Underground, Weird, Woman

Profile: FanTasia exists principally as a showcase for innovative fantasy, action and horror cinema from all edges of the world. At least 40 percent of each year's program consists of films from Asia, and we've also been known to get excited over strange comedies, subversive dramas and chaotic experimental films. In other words, our typical programming hooks are as easy to classify as the words "alternative," "vegetarian," "indie" or "cool."

Market: Not officially, but a number of films have been sold at our event.

Competitions: Yes

Major Awards: Public's Prize

Past Judges: The audience, via ballots.

Application Fee: None

Common Mistakes: Make horrible, uninspired films that have absolutely no voice behind them, then make us watch them!

Insider Advice: God won't help you, but ingenuity will.

Films Screened: Approximately 70

Odds of Acceptance: Approximately 1 in 3

Filmmaker Perks: Lodging, contacts, hardcore press attention, hardcore sex, the odd free meal, free popcorn, drinks and movies!

Attendance: Roughly 80,000 per festival!

Journalist Attendance: 40-60

Tourist Information: The Montreal Insectarium—Like it sounds. More freaky insects than you can shake an insectarium at. Fun and horror for everyone. Dario Argento has said that this is the place that inspired *Phenomena*.

Travel Tips: Our bus and metro system can't be beat. Everything's accessible, and there's no shortage of mutants to keep you entertained throughout your ride!

Best Cheap Hotels: Le Zebre. Actually, it's a bed & breakfast. Close to the cinema and ultra affordable at about $24 USD per night. It's run by an enthusiastic film journalist so you know that you're in safe hands (or do you?). 3767 Avenue Laval; 514-844-9868

Best Luxury Hotels: The Delta—huge, posh, and less than four minutes from our cinema. 475 President Kennedy Avenue; toll free 877-286-1986

Best Bars: Foufounes Electriques—Montreal's legendary punk/alternative venue. Whether there's a band or not, the taps are always flowing and the atmosphere's fantastic. There's a terrace, a dance floor, pool tables etc, with great tunes being blared. Very laid back. Hell, they let GG Allin play here once! Luba Lounge—right down the road from our cinema, and decked with a freakish psychedelic lounge atmosphere right out of an AIP dope film—there are even couches next to the toilets in the johns!

Festival Tale: A scheduled retro screening of Dario Argento's *Deep Red* was somewhat thwarted by the revelation that the print had been shipped minus the all-important reel 3. Undaunted, organizer Karim Hussain took the stage and proceeded to act out the entire missing reel for the completely stunned masses.

FiLM FEST NEW HAVEN

P.O. Box 9644,
New Haven, CT 06536
For delivery of films:
c/o Citizens Television,
873 State St.
New Haven, CT 06511-3923
Tel: 203-776-6789
Fax: 203-481-6789
Email: info@filmfest.org
Web Site: www.filmfest.org

Festival Date: Check website for all updated 2001 information

Entry Deadline: Check website for all updated 2001 information

Year Festival Began: 1995

Contact: Nicola Mantzaris, Katherine Cole

Director: Nina Adams

Category: Independent, International

Profile: The vision of FFNH is to produce an internationally recognized, independent film festival celebrating films and videos from around the world, nurturing filmmakers, and entertaining and enlightening audiences. We screen over 60 independent film or video features, shorts, and documentaries in three venues and over the course of three days.

Seminars: No, but we have an annual Screenplay Reading co-produced with New Century Writer Awards

Panels: Film Makers Forum co-sponsored by Media Arts Center

Market: No

Competitions: Yes

Major Awards: Jury awards Audience awards (by balloting) Kodak cinematography award

Value of Awards: Recognition and award certificate

Application Tips: Check the website for forms, etc. be clear about genre category, stay faithful and hopeful—we're very open and very filmmaker-friendly

Application Fee: Check website for all updated 2001 information

Common Mistakes: Forget to enclose the check for entry fee; (for international entries: make sure screening tape is in NTSC)

Average Films Entered: Innovative, original films by independent filmmakers.

Films Screened: 60

Odds of Acceptance: Approximately 1 in 6

Filmmaker Perks: Our budget doesn't allow for free travel or lodging, but we have discounted arrangements with most New Haven hotels, and can offer some lodging in private homes to filmmakers with limited budgets.

Attendance: 4,000-6,000

Journalist Attendance: *New Haven Advocate, Register, Yale Daily* and *Hartford Courant* have been regulars; *New York Times* (Pat Granjean), Channel 8, 3, 30, and radio stations WSHU, WPLR, WELI

Tourist Information: Yale University campus and galleries, British Art Center, Amistad Memorial, Long Island Sound waterfront, Wooster Square, Long Wharf Theatre district

Travel Tips: New Haven is easily accessible from New York City via Metro-North railroad, from further afield by Amtrak or plane to Tweed/New Haven airport or Bradley Int'l Airport (Hartford/Springfield)

Best Cheap Hotels: The Duncan

Best Luxury Hotels: The Omni

Best Restaurants: New Haven is, of course, most famous for its pizza (hotly debated: did it begin here???), but lots of other goodies are available, ranging from hip New York-style Nuevo Latino (Roomba) to Thai (Bangkok Gardens) to Ethiopian (two of them!) to Italian (Hot Tomato)

Best Bars: "Bar"

Best Hangout for Filmmakers: The bars and restaurants along Chapel St. and Broadway.

Best Place for Breakfast: The Pantry.

Festival Tale: The popcorn machine caught on fire, cancelling a screening in midstream, but the film got a repeat screening the next day and it was the best-attended of the festival (fame through fire!).

FiLM NiTE

2029 Eastwood Rd., #131
Wilmington, NC 28403
Tel: 910-509-2890
Email: dhardin@wilmington.net
Web Site: localsonly.wilmington.net/dhardin
Festival Date: The last Friday of every month
Entry Deadline: submissions accepted year 'round
Year Festival Began: July 1998
Contact: David or Cable Hardin
Director: David Hardin
Programmer: David Hardin, Cable Hardin
Category: American Films, Animation, Documentary, Ethnic African, Experimental, First-Time Independent Filmmakers, Independent, International, Short, Super 8/8mm, Underground, Weird
Profile: Film Nite seeks out the coolest short films around and shows them for free to promote short films and independent filmmakers.
Market: No
Competitions: No
Application Fee: None
Common Mistakes: Bad sound and video. Trying to be Quentin Tarantino or Kevin Smith.
Insider Advice: Keep it short and shoot on film.
Films Screened: 6-8 per month
Filmmaker Perks: The sheer satisfaction of getting in.
Attendance: 50-60 per screening
Journalist Attendance: 2-3
Tourist Information: Wrightsville Beach & downtown Wilmington has many shops, bars, clubs and restaurants right along the Cape Fear River.
Travel Tips: Carpool
Best Cheap Hotels: Super 8
Best Restaurants: Circa 1922 is good if you've got some $$$, LaCosta is a good, inexpensive Mexican place, great seafood is everywhere.
Best Bars: Otters
Best Hangout for Filmmakers: Otters, Bessie's, Barbary Coast, Mollye's Market.
Best Place for Breakfast: Goody Goody Omelet House

Festival Tale: Wilmington has a few celebrities now and then. The *Dawson's Creek* folks are around a lot. Frank Capra Jr. runs Screen Gems Studios in town and has attended screenings in the past.

FiRSTGLANCE: PHiLADELPHiA iNDEPENDENT FiLM AND ViDEO FESTiVAL

PO Box 571105
Tarzana, CA 91356
Email: WROPRO1@email.msn.com
Web Site: www.newimaging.com
Festival Date: March
Entry Deadline: December 15
Year Festival Began: 1996
Contact: Bill Ostroff
Category: Animation, Documentary
Profile: FirstGlance is proud to be taking place in Philadelphia again. We are excited to be back and look forward to the biggest and best festival yet. We encourage student and professional film and videomakers with any budget. We are an underground, alternative festival whose mission is to exhibit all genres of work (film, video and digital productions) from mainstream to controversial in a competitive casual atmosphere.
Awards: Free Airline Ticket, Festival Tickets, Festival T-shirt, and/or "Best of Philly" prize package and Prize money for Student category.
Application Fee: $30, students $25.

FLiCKAPALOOZA FiLM FESTiVAL

7775 Sunset Blvd. PMB 200
Hollywood, CA 90046
Tel: 323-654-5809
Email: Flickapalooza@aol.com
Web Site: www.flickapalooza.com
Festival Date: June
Entry Deadline: February (early); April (late)
Year Festival Began: 2000
Director: Mark Andrushko

Category: Independent
Profile: Flickapalooza is a boutique film festival catering to both filmmakers and industry executives by creating an arena to view, buy or sell films of all genres in an entertaining atmosphere that is conducive to promoting careers in filmmaking.

FLO FiLM FEST

502 Kanuga Drive
West Palm Beach, FL 33401
Tel: 561-804-9393
Email: bicycledays@yahoo.com or flofilmfest@yahoo.com
Web Site: www.flofilmfest.com
Festival Date: March
Entry Deadline: February
Contact: Kris Kemp
Director: Kris Kemp
Programmer: Kris Kemp
Category: Short
Application Fee: $15

FLORiDA FiLM FESTiVAL

See "The Top Ten Film Festivals" beginning on page 214.

FORT LAUDERDALE iNT'L FiLM FESTiVAL

"The Fort Lauderdale Int'l Film Festival, 14 years young, has rightly earned high praise as one of the most important regional film festivals in the U.S. One of the reasons Fort Lauderdale is so respected is because of its commitment to first-time filmmakers, particularly U.S. independents."
—Barbara & Scott Siegel,
Film Journal International

1314 E. Las Olas #007
Ft. Lauderdale, FL 33301
Tel: 954-760-9898
Fax: 954-760-9099
Email: brofilm@aol.com
Web Site: www.fliff.com
Festival Date: October 15–November 11, 2001
Entry Deadline: Early: August 1, 2001; Late: September 1, 2001
Year Festival Began: 1985
Contact: Lily Majjul-Pardo, Public Relations Director

Director: Gregory von Hausch

Programmer: Bonnie Leigh Adams

Category: American Films, Documentary, Ethnic African, Ethnic Asian, Ethnic Black, Ethnic Jewish, Ethnic Latin, Ethnic Spanish, Experimental, First-Time Independent Filmmakers, Gay Lesbian, Independent, International, Short, Student, Underground, Woman

Seminars: Yes

Panels: Yes

Market: No

Awards: Yes

Competitions: Yes

Major Awards: Best Film, Best Actress, Best Actor, Robert Wise Director of Distinction Award, Lifetime Achievement Award, Special Jury Prize and Audience Award

Application Fee: $40 for professional full length feature

$30 for shorts

$25 for student films

Insider Advice: 1) Start with a good script.

2) Keep the film small

3) Cast well

4) Limit camera movement

5) Keep the film tigh; don't make a 75 min film into a 115 min epic

Average Films Entered: We accept all kinds of films however, we look for films with great stories. Stories that involve the human condition with universal appeal.

Films Screened: 135

Odds of Acceptance: Approximately 1 in 11

Filmmaker Perks: We fly in all our directors (sometimes up to four filmmakers per film). We provide lodging and basically food (thru parties and a hospitality suite). We also provide numerous networking opportunities for filmmakers with press and distributors.

Attendance: 66,000

Journalist Attendance: 80-100

Tourist Information: Locally, a filmmaker might want to visit: The Beach, Las Olas Boulevard, Museum of Art, Museum of Discovery, Riverwalk, Graves Muesum of Natural History, the malls (we've got a million of them!), The Water Taxi (to bars and clubs), South Beach, Beach Place, Las Olas Riverfront, Bonnet House, Stranahan House, Birch Taylor State Park

Travel Tips: Bring your swim suit, sunscreen, camera, comfy shoes, windbreaker for sailing, dancing shoes, business cards, boat shoes.

Best Cheap Hotels: Three Suns Inn, Holiday Inn Express

Best Luxury Hotels: Marriott Harbor Beach, Pier 66, Doubletree Galleria

Best Restaurants: Primaverra, Jacksons, Burt & Jack's II Tartufo, Samba Room, Evangeline's, Black Orchid

Best Bars: Elbo Room, Shooters, Mangos

16th Annual

The Fort Lauderdale International Film Festival

10.15.01 - 11.11.01

www.fliff.com

954.760.9898

a vacation from ordinary film

Best Hangout for Filmmakers: Bar at Doubletree

Best Place for Breakfast: Indigo at Riverside Hotel

Festival Tale: Wildest story(ies): Kevin Spacey was set to come to the Festival on a Monday. He was expected the following Saturday. We didn't know where he was coming from or with whom. Kevin told us to leave two airline tickets. Twenty hours before he was to appear, Miramax finally said he was coming alone from L.A. After he got here and screened his film, *Albino Alligator*, our Closing Night Film, he went to the wrap party. I left him there at midnight letting him know his driver was ready to take him back to the hotel whenever he was ready. He said he was fine and went out to party with my staff (until 4 a.m.). During the wee hours of the morning, a journalist from N.Y., who had family in Lauderdale, took the party to her parents' home where she played a cassette recording and sang opera for ten minutes.

Robert Evans, here to speak on producing, had his date flown in from New York for the Black Tie Gala. If this girl was 18, it would have been a miracle.

Victor Nunez, here to promote *Ruby In Paradise* with his whole cast and crew, had arrived but Ashley Judd seemed to be a no-show. Before the flick starts, Victor tells the crowd that he is apologizing for Ashley who wanted to come but her house in L.A. burned down last night and she is just too upset. Movie screens and at the end of the film, the cast and crew go up to take Q&A. As they do, Ashley enters from the back smiling (a shit eating grin) and waltzing down the aisle, stating she had missed her flight and had to fly in to Miami.

FORT WORTH—
Q CiNEMA—
FORT WORTH'S GAY & LESBiAN FiLM FESTiVAL

215 W. Eighth Ave.
Fort Worth, TX 76102
Tel: 817-462-3368
Fax: 817-390-7257
Email: tcamp@star-telegram.com
Web Site: www.qcinema.org
Festival Date: June
Entry Deadline: April
Contact: Todd Camp—Artistic Director
Director: Shawn Moore—Event Director
Programmer: Todd Camp
Category: Gay Lesbian

FOUR*BY*FOUR
SUPER 8 FiLMFEST

"There's beer!"
　　　　　—Collective Anonymous

Austin Cinemaker Co-op
Austin, TX
Tel: 512-236-8877
Email: cinemkr@Texas.net
Web Site: www.cinemaker.org
Festival Date: Late August
Entry Deadline: Early August
Year Festival Began: 1998
Director: Jeff Britt
Other Staff: Gonzo Gonzalez, Richard McIntosh, Danny Chavez, Barna Kantor
Category: Independent, Underground
Profile: "Shut up and shoot something!!"

4X4 Film Festivals are "indie" festivals, in that many of our entrants often spend their "rent paycheck" to make their films. The Cinemaker Co-op has hosted 7 festivals of locally produced short films since 1996.

Application Tips: 1) Shot and submitted on super 8 film, four minutes maximum in length.

2) Edited in camera, utilizing a maximum of 4 splices.

3) Accompanied by an original soundtrack.

4) Submitted with a five second countdown at the beginning of the film (either animate it at the beginning of your film, or take your white leader, and write 18 5's, 18 4's, and so on, with a black Sharpie pen, carefully on each frame).

Application Fee: $5

Insider Advice: Films must be clean. Run your film through a projector a couple of times (and clean it afterwards) to make sure we will not have any projection problems during the screening.

Films Screened: 20-30

Odds of Acceptance: Usually all films are accepted.

Travel Tips: Avoid IH35, it's always a huge mess.

Best Restaurants: Tamale House on Airport Blvd. (this place has great tacos for super cheap!) and Red River Cafe (right off of Red River between 26th and 32nd streets).

Best Bars: Lovejoy's ($2 house pints all the time, great jukebox).

FREAKY
FiLM FESTiVAL (FFF)

Tel: 217-344-3296
Fax: 217-398-5850
Email: info@freakyfilms
Web Site: www.freakyfilms.com
Festival Date: October 26-31, 2001
Entry Deadline: August 1, 2001
Year Festival Began: 1997
Contact: Grace Giorgio
Director: Eric Fisher and Grace Giorgio
Programmer: Eric Fisher, Grace Giorgio, Steve Bailey, Anita Michel, Jason Pankoke
Other Staff: Brian Robertson, Michael J. Correll, Jennifer Auler
Category: American Films, Animation, Documentary, Ethnic African, Ethnic Asian, Ethnic Black, Ethnic Jewish, Ethnic Latin, Ethnic Other, Ethnic Spanish, Experimental, First-Time Independent Filmmakers, Gay Lesbian, International, Short, Student, Super 8/8mm, Underground, Video, Weird, Woman
Profile: What Freaky is.

Freaky (freek-ee)—adj. quirky; exciting; other-than-mainstream; non-conforming.

Bring your swim suit, sunscreen, camera, comfy shoes, windbreaker for sailing, dancing shoes, business cards, boat shoes (Fort Lauderdale International Film Festival).

As you can see, the very definition of freaky describes independent film (and filmmakers, for that matter) quite nicely and by no means is meant to represent a category or genre of film to which we are partial. Rather, we encourage all shapes, sizes, colors, flavors, genders, sexuality, alignments, makes, models and methods of independent filmmaking, thereby fulfilling our annual mission to provide our audience with diverse and unpredictable programs.

Market: No

Competitions: Yes

Major Awards: Best of Fest Jury Award

Value of Awards: Approximately $600

Application Fee: $20

Common Mistakes: The most frequent submittal error is simply not carefully reading the submission guidelines.

Insider Advice: Keep in mind an audience that is not familiar with you or your work and ask yourself if you can realistically expect your film to hold the attention of that audience. If the answer is yes, then submit that damn film! If no, edit until answer is yes.

Films Screened: 75

Odds of Acceptance: 3 in 4

Filmmaker Perks: Lots of free beer!

Attendance: 2,500

Journalist Attendance: Unknown

Tourist Information: Campus of the University of Illinois

Travel Tips: Taxis are very inexpensive in the area but you must call for pick-up well in advance of your intended departure time.

Best Cheap Hotels: The Hodge Podge Lodge

Best Luxury Hotels: Jumer's Castle Lodge

Best Restaurants: Radio Maria, a sponsor!

Best Bars: The Highdive

Best Hangout for Filmmakers: Mike & Molly's

Best Place for Breakfast: Sam's Cafe

FREE FiLM FESTiVAL FiTCHBURG (THE F 4)

22 Beacon Street
Fitchburg, MA 01420
Tel: 978-353-6881
Fax: 419-844-6463
Email: oneifby@revolutionary images.com
Web Site: www.revolutionary images.com
Festival Date: September 2001
Entry Deadline: July 2001
Year Festival Began: 2000
Contact: J.C. Bouvier
Director: Jean-Claude (J.C.) Bouvier
Programmer: J.C. Bouvier Director—Feature/Short film programs
Tim Doyle—Minister of Submissions
Category: American Films, Documentary, Experimental, First-Time Independent Filmmakers, Independent, Underground, Weird
Profile: The Free Film Festival Fitchburg was created as a dynamic venue available primarily to students of the moving image. Its goal is to create new paths or directions for filmmakers, videographers, or anyone working with electronic visual media.
Seminars: Story 101
Lighting 101
Audio 101
Camera 101
Editing 101
Distribution 101

Market: Not yet.
Competitions: Yes
Major Awards: The Fitchy.
Application Fee: Students w/ documentation $ 20
Starving artists with documentation $25
Distributors, studio folk and agents. $1,500.
Common Mistakes: Play politics, not submit because they think they don't have a chance and second guess themselves.
Insider Advice: If you can truly say that you're happy with what you see on the display and you want to share that feeling with others, find a way to do that.

Tourist Information: Fitchburg Art Musuem
Travel Tips: Don't make eye contact with anyone you don't know. Stay off Main Street after sundown and lock your car.
Best Cheap Hotels: The Super 8 by Marshalls.
Best Luxury Hotels: Sheraton Tara
Best Restaurants: Il Forno on Crawford St.
Best Bars: The Wine Cellar
Best Hangout for Filmmakers: Mocha Alley
Best Place for Breakfast: Cozy Corner

FREEDOM FiLM FESTiVAL

9911 W. Pico Boulevard, #510
Los Angeles, CA 90035
Tel: 310-286-9420
Fax: 310-286-7914
Email: acinema@cinema foundation.com
Web Site: www.cinema foundation.com
Festival Date: Feb. 22-25, 2001
Entry Deadline: The Freedom Film Festival does not accept submissions. Films are by invitation only, and are primarily chosen from Eastern Europe.
Year Festival Began: 1997
Contact: Carla Sanders, Project Manager
Director: Gary McVey
Programmer: Gary McVey
Other Staff: Nancy Oppenheim, Artistic Director, Special Projects
Category: Ethnic Other, International
Profile: The American Cinema Foundation presents an annual non-competitive showcase program of films from Eastern and Central Europe and the ex-CIS countries. The films relate to the theme of freedom and specifically to the impact of Stalinism in the region, from the beginning to today. The festival was founded and is curated by Gary McVey, executive director of the American Cinema Foundation. It is in the interest of the Freedom Film Festival to support the important voices of quality filmmaking in the East by giving the

films greater exposure in Hollywood and in the opinion-making media internationally.

Market: No

Competitions: No

Application Fee: None

GAY AND LESBIAN ARTS FESTIVAL OF OKLAHOMA, INC. dba OUTART

Post Office Box 16461
Oklahoma City, OK 73113

Tel: 405-752-2762

Email: outartok@usa.net

Web Site: www.outartok.com

Festival Date: October 12-15, 2001

Entry Deadline: August 10, 2001

Year Festival Began: 1999

Contact: Mark D. Maxey

Director: Tony Francis

Programmer: Michael Yellope, Jr.

Other Staff: Robert Matson / Theatre, Donald Clothier / Music, Mark Maxey / Art

Category: American Films, Animation, Documentary, Ethnic African, Ethnic Asian, Ethnic Black, Ethnic Jewish, Ethnic Spanish, First-Time Independent Filmmakers, Gay Lesbian, Independent, International

Profile: Outart will educate and inform through the media of gay and lesbian films, music, theatre and art. We will provide an environment for gay and lesbian artists to express their talents and provide funding through grants and other means to promote gay and lesbian art and artists in Oklahoma. Each year we highlight the best of current theatrical release movies to the public allowing gay and lesbian film makers to be seen. Each year we grow with new artists, new areas of interest and an overal artistic expression of diversity.

Market: No

Competitions: No

Application Fee: None

Films Screened: 11

Odds of Acceptance: 1 in 3

Filmmaker Perks: Please contact the OUTART board at their

email for more information regarding perks.

Attendance: 2,000

Journalist Attendance: 5-10

Tourist Information: The Oklahoma City Bombing Memorial, OKC Zoo, Omnidome, OmniPlex, Octoberfest, Bricktown.

Best Cheap Hotels: Habana Inn (only gay and lesbian resort in the south)

Best Luxury Hotels: Waterford

Best Bars: Angles, Copa, Finishline

Best Hangout for Filmmakers: Diversity Coffee Shoppe

Best Place for Breakfast: Classen Grille

GEN ART FILM FESTIVAL

"New York's premiere hipster event"

—*New York Magazine*

145 W. 28th St. 11th fl.
New York, NY 10001

Tel: 212-290-0312

Fax: 212-290-0254

Email: info@genart.org

Web Site: www.genart.org

Festival Date: May 2-8, 2001

Entry Deadline: February 15, 2001

Year Festival Began: 1996

Contact: Dominick Balletta

Director: Dominick Balletta

Category: American Films, Animation, Documentary, Experimental, First-Time Independent Filmmakers, Gay Lesbian, Independent, Short, Video, Weird, Woman

Profile: The Gen Art Film Festival is a curated festival that champions independent film and its audiences. The Gen Art Film Festival connects emerging, independent filmmakers with the industry and their non-industry peers interested in exploring the independent film scene. The festival offers a gala New York premiere attended by enthusiastic filmgoers, critics and industry professionals, followed by a spectacular party at one of Manhattan's hippest nightspots. This unique format of screening one feature and one short film per night for seven nights allows Gen Art to truly highlight the work of the filmmakers.

Gore Score · · · · · · · · · · · · · ·

The Gen Art crowd is sometimes more concerned about the parties than the films.

Seminars: None

Panels: None

Market: No

Awards: Yes

Competitions: Yes

BEST FILM FESTIVAL PRIZES AWARDED

$100,000 American Indie Award (Seattle International Film Festival)

$50,000 Grand Prize, six filmmakers divide $100,000 (Heartland Film Festival)

$25,000 in Post Production Services (GEN ART Film Festival)

$20,000 worth of Editing Equipment (Slamdance International Film Festival)

$10,000 Grand Jury Prize (AFI Los Angeles International Film Festival)

$10,000 Tiger Award (Rotterdam International Film Festival)

$10,000 and $1,000 SKYY Prize and Golden Gate Award Grand Prizes (San Francisco International Film Festival)

$5,000 (Chicago Latino Film Festival)

$5,000 and 25,000 feet of film processing (Deep Ellum Film Festival)

Five Acres of Land (Taos Talking Pictures Festival)

Major Awards: Cataland Films/Cyclops Pictures & Sound Audience Award

Value of Awards: $25,000 in post production services.

Past Judges: audience

Application Tips: Don't freak out—the selection process takes time.

Application Fee: Early Deadline: $15 short/$20 feature. Late Deadline $20 short/$25 feature

Common Mistakes: They try to send work that isn't finished—to have us look at work before it's really festival ready—both in our minds and their minds. Relax and submit when you're happy with the product

Average Films Entered: All types, we're looking primarily at first and second time American feature film directors

Films Screened: 14

Odds of Acceptance: 1 in 16

Filmmaker Perks: Great opening night premiere screening and post screening party. Great gifts depending on presenting sponsor.

Attendance: 5,000

Journalist Attendance: 100-200

Travel Tips: Cooler to stay either downtown—Soho Grand, Mercer, Tribeca Grand or at Ian Shrager Hotels: Royalton, Morgan's or Paramount

Best Cheap Hotels: Gerswin Hotel

Best Luxury Hotels: Tribeca Grand

Best Restaurants: Nobu

Best Bars: Veruka

Best Hangout for Filmmakers: Screening Room

Best Place for Breakfast: B&B Grill—Outside

Festival Tale: Everyone from actor Leonardo DiCaprio to supermodels Helena Christenson and Bridget Hall have attended.

GLOBAL AFRICA INTERNATIONAL FILM AND VIDEO FESTIVAL

900 Fallon St., 9th Floor
Oakland, CA 94607

Tel: 510-464-3253

Fax: 510-464-3418

Festival Date: June

Entry Deadline: March

Contact: Frankie A. Sanders

Category: Video

GOLDEN SHOWER VIDEO FESTIVAL

Adam Rocha
8039 Callaghan Rd. PMB 611
San Antonio, TX 78230

Tel: 512-457-8780

Email: info@safilm.com

Web Site: www.safilm.com

Festival Date: June 15 & 16, 2001

Entry Deadline: April 12, 2001

Year Festival Began: 1994

Director: Adam Rocha

Category: American Films, Animation, Digital, Digital Animation, Documentary, Ethnic African, Ethnic Asian, Ethnic Black, Ethnic Jewish, Ethnic Latin, Ethnic Other, Ethnic Spanish, Experimental, Fantasy/Science Fiction, Independent, International, Microcinema, Multimedia, PXL, Short, Student, Super 8/8mm, Underground, Video, Weird, Woman

Profile: No watersports here, the GSVF has a light-hearted approach to a serious business. The title refers to our independent Do-It-Yourself punk rock attitude as in "piss off, Hollywood." The GSVF is a "mom & pop" fest with no eye-gouging box office attendance prices and tons of fun. If selected for the fest, you receive a fest poster & t-shirt. First place receives a lowrider bicycle, 2nd a miniature accordion, 3rd lucha libre (Spanish for Mexican Wrestling) gear.

Market: No

Competitions: Yes

Major Awards: 2001 Lowrider Bicycle

Value of Awards: $400

Application Fee: $10 bucks, Cash Only!

Common Mistakes: Cash Only! Do not send checks. Do not send money orders. Cash Only!

Insider Advice: Send pictures (not a xerox copy) of your production. We get press coverage. (Imagine the picture that you sent on the front of The Hollywood Reporter.)

Average Films Entered: Shorts & Features. The shorter the piece, the more of a chance that it will be included in the festival. All formats are okay but must be transferred onto VHS Only!

Films Screened: 65

Odds of Acceptance: Approximately 63%

Filmmaker Perks: Free tacos and beer.

Attendance: 100-300

Journalist Attendance: 5

Tourist Information: The Alamo, Earl Able's Diner, Tacoland, the Riverwalk.

Best Cheap Hotels: Alamo Travel Lodge

Best Luxury Hotels: Hilton Paso del Rio

Best Restaurants: Mi Tierra

Best Bars: Bar America

Best Hangout for Filmmakers: Rosario's

Best Place for Breakfast: Tacos Martinez

Festival Tale: During the third year, there were over six hundred people in attendance when a festival attendee streaked the audience.

Random Tidbits: San Antonio is a big city with a small town flavor. El Santo (the Mexican wrestler) made an appearance this year.

GREAT PLAINS FILM FESTIVAL

Mary Riempa Ross Film Theater
P.O. Box 880302
Lincoln, NE 68588-0302
(Shipping)
211 N. 12th St., Suite 405
Lincoln, NE 68508

Tel: 402-472-9100

Fax: 402-472-2576

Email: d.ladely1@unl.edu

Web Site: www.rossfilm
theather.org
Festival Date: July
Entry Deadline: April
Director: Danny Lee Ladely
Application Fee: $15—$25

GREEN BADGE
FILM EVENT

50 East Palisade Avenue
Suite #426
Englewood, NJ 07631
Tel: 201-567-0560
Fax: 201-567-1053
Email: Michael Champlin,
redb522@IDT.net
Web Site: www.greenbadge.com
Festival Date: Fall
Entry Deadline: Fall
Year Festival Began: 1998
Contact: Michael Champlin
Director: Alex Svezia
Programmer: Michael Champlin,
William Pennell
Profile: The Green Badge Film
Event, devoted to returning indie
film to its roots, offers new cine-
ma, panel discussions, receptions
and an after party for all ticket
holders.
Seminars: No
Panels: Yes
Application Fee: free to all film-
makers
Attendance: 400

HAMPTONS
INTERNATIONAL
FILM FESTIVAL

3 Newtown Mews
East Hampton, NY 11937
Tel: 516-324-4600; 516-324-2870
Fax: 516-324-5116
Email: filmfest@peconic.net
Web Site: www.thehamptons.
com/film/main.html
Festival Date: October
Entry Deadline: August
Contact: Denise Kasell
Director: Denise Kasell
Programmer: David Schwartz
Other Staff: Linda Blackaby,
Lynda Hansen, Shawn Caila Folz
Category: Independent
Profile: The Hamptons
International Film Festival was

created to provide a forum for
filmmakers around the world
who express an independent
vision at an annual five day event
each October.

A distinctive component of
the Festival is its cash grants to
students and a generous in-kind
award to outstanding filmmakers.

This festival focuses on sup-
porting student and independent
filmmaking. Approximately
20,000 attend.
Seminars: yes
Awards: Yes
Competitions: No
Major Awards: Most Popular
Film, Best Director, Best
Documentary Feature and Best
Short Film.

The Golden Arrow Award—
Based on audience balloting, this
award is presented to the Most
Popular Film, Best Director, Best
Documentary Feature and Best
Short film in the Festival.

Distinguished Achievement
Award to be announced for the
opening of the Festival.

Golden Starfish Award—A
currated selection of American
Independent films will introduce
the work of newly emerging
filmmakers. A jury of film industry professionals, filmmakers and
film critics select the winning
director of the Festival's Golden
Starfish Award from among them
and present the recipient with a
package of goods and services
totaling over $100,000.

Student Scholarship Awards—
The Student Scholarhsip Awards,
totaling $25,000 in cash prizes,
are presented to 10 outstanding
film students whose works will
be presented at the Festival. A
special prize, sponsored by RKO
Pictures, is awarded to the grad-
uate student film selected as
being the best example of cinematic storytelling.

Documentary Award—A spe-
cial jury prize, sponsored by the
Eastman Kodak Company, will be
awarded to the Best
Documentary.

Short Film Award—A special
jury prize will be awarded to the
best Short Subject in this year's
Festival.

Application Fee: $25 (up to 30
minutes) / $50 (over 30 minutes)
Films Screened: 40

HARDSHARE
INDEPENDENT
FILM FESTIVAL

P.O. Box 123
Winslow, AR 72959
Tel: 501-634-5901
Web Site: www.hardshare
filmefest.com
Contact: Susan Hutchcroft
Category: Short
Application Fee: $30

HAWAII INTERNATIONAL
FILM FESTIVAL

1001 Bishop St, Pacific Tower,
Suite 745
Honolulu, HI 96813
Tel: 808-528-3456
Fax: 808-528-1410
Email: info@hiff.org
Web Site: www.hiff.org
Festival Date: November
Entry Deadline: July-August
Contact: Anderson Le
Director: Chuck Boller
Programmer: Bruce Fletcher
Other Staff: Didi Chang.
Director of Development
Chuck Boller, Director of
Adminstration
Lani Miyahara, Hawaii Film Fans
Coordinator (Film Society)
Donne Dawson, Media Director
Category: Ethnic Asian,
Independent, International, Pacific
Rim
Profile: Founded in 1981, HIFF is
dedicated to promoting cross-
cultural understanding among
peoples of Asia, North America
and the Pacific region. We pres-
ent film screenings, discussions,
workshops, panels, special
awards and media events. HIFF
remains committed to presenting
artistic, political, and commercial
works from around the world
with an emphasis on Pacific Rim
filmmakers.
Seminars: Yes
Famous Speakers: Most Figures
in Asian Industry....Hou Hsiao

Hsien, Chen Kaige, Zhang Yimou, Juzo Itami, etc.

Competitions: Yes

Major Awards: Golden Maile Award

Past Judges: Toni Collette, Peter Rainer, Paul Theroux, Malti Sahai, Kim Dong-Ho

Application Fee: $35.00 (waived for Hawaii filmmakers)

Insider Advice: Complete the entire call for entries...make sure all technical information is complete

Average Films Entered: Films that relate in some way to a Pacific Rim theme (which includes the U.S., of course).

Odds of Acceptance: 1 in 10

Filmmaker Perks: We can always provide accommodation for filmmakers, and we are able to fly in quite a few. And, well, it's Hawaii. Also, if your film is playing on the neighbor islands, you can follow it along to some more fun, out of the way places in Maui, on the Big Island, Kauai etc. The big she-bang is in Honolulu (cool parties, big crowds and media etc), and the community, mellow part is on the neighbor islands.

Travel Tips: The nicer you are, the better you're treated!

Best Restaurants: Japanese: Tokkuru-tei; Chinese: Chans; Pacific Rim: A Pacific Cafe, Sam Choys Etc; Local Grinds: Zippy's

Best Bars: Havana Cabana, Anna Bananas

Best Hangout for Filmmakers: Havana Cabana and Centaur Zone Coffee Shop

Best Place for Breakfast: Eggs 'N' Things and Liliha Bakery.

HEARTLAND FILM FESTIVAL

613 North East Street
Indianapolis, IN 46202
Tel: 317-464-9405; 317-635-4201
Email: hff@pop.iquest.net
Web Site: www.heartlandfilmfest.org
Festival Date: October
Entry Deadline: June
Contact: Claire C. Wishard, Festival Coordinator

Director: Jeffrey L. Sparks, Artistic Director

Programmer: Claire C. Wishard, Festival Coordinator

Other Staff: Victor H. Ruthig, Executive Director, Cindy Williams, Office Manager

Category: Animation, Documentary, Short

Profile: To recognize and honor filmmakers whose work explores the human journey by artistically expressing hope and respect for the positive values of life.

Seminars: Yes

Panels: Yes

Awards: Yes

Competitions: Yes

Major Awards: Crystal Heart Award

Value of Awards: $50,000 Grand Prize, $100,000 cash split between six filmmakers.

Application Tips: Follow our statement of purpose

Application Fee: $35 to $55, depending on film type

Average Films Entered: 225

Odds of Acceptance: 1 in 20.

Filmmaker Perks: Free travel and Lodging, as well as Crystal Heart Awards and $100,000 in cash

Travel Tips: Weather could be 60 or 20. Welcome to Indianapolis!

Best Restaurants: Palomino, Mikado, Ruth's Chris, St. Elmo's

Best Bars: Canterbury Bar

Hi MOM! FILM FESTIVAL

401 Pritchard Ave.
Chapel Hill, NC 27514
Tel: 919-967-8969
Fax: N/A
Email: himomfilmfest@yahoo.com
Web Site: http://metalab.unc.edu/cpg
Festival Date: March
Entry Deadline: Early: December; Late: January
Contact: Michael Connor
Category: Short, Video, Weird
Profile: The Hi Mom! Film Festival packs rowdiness, food, drink, free stuff, music and (oh yeah) movies into three glorious

days and two swingin' nights. Hi Mom! is a festival for filmmakers with big ideas and little bank accounts, deep thinkers with shallow pockets, short on gimmicks but long on talent.

Hi/LO FILM FESTIVAL

P.O. Box 170309
San Francisco, CA 94117
Tel: 415-267-0642
Email: hilo@killingmylobster.com
Web Site: www.killingmylobster.com/hilo/

HILTON HEAD FILM FESTIVAL

c/o Hilton Oceanfront Resort
23 Ocean Lane
Hilton Head Island, SC 29928
Tel: 843-341-8063
Email: psivco@hargray.com
Contact: Peter Sivco

HOLLYWOOD BLACK FILM FESTIVAL

1620 Centinela Ave., Suite 204
Inglewood, CA 90302
Tel: 310-348-2942
Fax: 310-348-3949
Email: Info@hbff.org
Web Site: www.hbff.org
Festival Date: February 14-18, 2001
Entry Deadline: August (Early Bird); September (Final)
Year Festival Began: 1999
Contact: Tanya Kersey-Henley, Festival Director
Director: Tanya Kersey-Henley
Programmer: Tanya Kersey-Henley. Jacqueline Blaylock, Gerald Haynes
Category: American Films, Animation, Digital, Documentary, Ethnic Black, First-Time Independent Filmmakers, Gay Lesbian, Independent, International, Student, Super 8/8mm, Video, Woman
Profile: The Hollywood Black Film Festival (HBFF) is an annual film festival which showcases the work of emerging and established black filmmakers (direc-

tors and/or writers) from North America.

The Festival's presenting and founding sponsor is *Black Talent News*, the leading trade publication for blacks in the entertainment industry.

The Hollywood Black Film Festival, Inc. is a non-profit organization whose mission is to enhance the careers of emerging and established black North American filmmakers and screenwriters through a public exhibition and competition program; and to bring independent works by black filmmakers to Southern California area audiences, thereby fostering a greater appreciation for black filmmaking.

Gore Score · · · · · · · · · · · · · · ·

For black filmmakers there is no better place for exposure and to network.

Seminars: Infotainment, a 4-day educational and networking conference, takes place concurrently with the Hollywood Black Film Festival.

Market: No

Competitions: Yes

Major Awards: Jury Award for Feature-Length Film

Jury Award for Short Film

Jury Award for Documentary Film

Jury Award for Student Film

Audience Choice Award

Value of Awards: $25,000 in cash and prizes

Application Fee: $25 (Early Bird before August); $35 (after August)

Common Mistakes: They submit films with very poor production value—lighting, sound, etc. Many first-time filmmakers are in a rush to get their films in and don't take the time to make sure their films are ready for viewing. We advise filmmakers to have their film screened by people other than family and friends to get their honest opinion. If the film isn't ready, wait until it is finished before submitting.

Insider Advice: Get your films in as early as possible—it gives the screening committee more time to review your film. Include as

Matthew McConaughey takes the stage and turns on the charm at a festival seminar.
PHOTO BY ANDREA TURNER/ JACK PLUNKETT

much background information as possible—production notes, bios of key talent, etc.

Films Screened: 60

Odds of Acceptance: 1 in 4

Attendance: 5,000

Journalist Attendance: 40-50

Random Tidbits: It's a networking frenzy, an opportunity for black filmmakers to meet and greet colleagues from all across the U.S. and abroad. It's an annual gathering for the black entertainment community.

HOLLYWOOD FILM FESTIVAL

433 N. Camden Dr., Suite 600
Beverly Hills, CA 90210

Tel: 310-288-1882

Fax: 310-475-0193

Email: awards@hollywood awards.com

Web Site: www.hollywoodfilm festival.com

Festival Date: August

Entry Deadline: March

Contact: Carlos de Abreu

Director: Carlos de Abreu

Programmer: Janice de Abreu

Category: Independent, International

Profile: The Hollywood Film Festival was created to bridge the gap between established

Hollywood and emerging independent filmmakers.

Seminars: We have four days of intensive seminars. From concept to post-production and distribution.

Panels: Over 100 established industry professional participate in our panels.

Famous Speakers: Almost all our speakers are famous.

Awards: Yes

Competitions: Yes

Major Awards: Hollywood Discovery Awards

Hollywood Young Filmmakers Award

Hollywood Cyberaward

Moviemaker Breakthrough Award

Value of Awards: Packages valued at more than $100,000

Application Tips: The artistic quality of the film will be the final factor that will determine if said film will be selected or not.

Application Fee: $50

Insider Advice: The submission package should be packaged professionally—Clean and making sure that it includes all necessary items as per application form.

Average Films Entered: 400

Odds of Acceptance: 1 in 10

Filmmaker Perks: VIP Passes for two. Major industry contacts and press exposure.

Travel Tips: Make your reservations early so you can get bargain prices.

Best Restaurants: Spago in Beverly Hills.

Best Bars: Sky Bar at the Mondrian Hotel.

Best Place for Breakfast: Four Seasons and the Peninsula Hotels in Beverly Hills.

HOMETOWN CiNEMA iNC

"Come to Hometown Cinema. I guarentee you won't go back the same filmmaker."
— *Indiana Daily Student Newspaper*

22425 Ventura Blvd. PMB 296
Woodland Hills, CA 91364
Tel: 818-932-9509
Fax: 818-595-1131
Email: hometownc@ hotmail.com
Web Site: www.hometown.z. com
Festival Date: April 27-29, 2001- Online festival is ongoing
Entry Deadline: April 2001
Year Festival Began: 1996
Contact: Shannah Compton
Director: Shannah Compton
Programmer: Shannah Compton, Ward Roberts, Chris Sutton
Category: Digital Animation, Multimedia, Online Festival, Short, Student, Video, Weird
Profile: Hometown Cinema is a Midwestern student film festival and a national online student film festival. The festival was created to provide a stepping stone between a student's film education and film career. Hometown Cinema aims to bridge the gap between the two in a festival weekend comprised of student film showings, panels, and innovative seminars. We have brought over thirty-five entertainment industry professionals to the festival, and over twenty students have received top internships and job opportunities as a result.
Seminars: Traditionally there are many seminars held—acting, pitching, producing, writing and directing.

Panels: Opening night there will be a panel discussion with all the entertainment industry participating guests.
Famous Speakers: Frank Capra Jr, Tommy O'Haver, Shane Black, Alex Rose.
Market: No
Competitions: Yes there is a contest. The awards will be updated frequently.
Major Awards: Best of Show
Value of Awards: Usually a laboratory sponsors the award with a credit good at their facility.
Application Fee: $15 for event, $0 for online
Insider Advice: Getting your film out there is the only way you are going to grow as a filmmaker and get the exposure you need to make your next film. Festivals are great because they allow you to network amongst other filmmakers.
Odds of Acceptance: 1 in 25
Filmmaker Perks: Filmmakers who are accepted receive free lodging and transportation during the festival. They also have unique opportunities to network with entertainment industry professionals.
Attendance: 500-800
Journalist Attendance: Approx 5-10
Tourist Information: Indianapolis, Indiana is loaded with artsy streets, great bars and good food.
Best Cheap Hotels: Motel 6
Best Luxury Hotels: Century Suites
Best Restaurants: Irish Lion
Best Bars: Bluebird
Best Place for Breakfast: Village Deli
Random Tidbits: The online festival, or as we call it, an "experience," will feature unique, innovative and interactive programming. We host pitch contests where filmmakers can win a chance for us to help produce their film; there are interviews, online chat sessions and interactive ways to learn about filmmaking. What they don't teach you at school.

If you want to have a good time, without Hollywood atti-

tudes, learn about filmmaking, network, see a great town, and make more solid contacts in one weekend, Hometown is where you want to be!

HOMETOWN ViDEO FESTiVAL

666 11th St., Suite 740
Washington, DC 20001
Tel: 202-393-2650
Fax: 202-393-2653
Email: acm@alliancecm.org
Web Site: www.alliancecm.org
Festival Date: July
Entry Deadline: January
Contact: Bunnie Ridell— Executive Director

HONOLULU GAY & LESBiAN FiLM FESTiVAL

1877 Kalakaua Ave.
Honolulu, HI 96815
Tel: 808-941-0424
Fax: 808-943-1724
Email: info@hglcf.org
Web Site: www.hglcf.org
Festival Date: May–June
Entry Deadline: March
Contact: Jon Bryant or Connie Florez
Director: Jon Bryant
Programmer: Connie Florez
Category: Gay Lesbian

HOT DOCS CANADiAN iNTERNATiONAL DOCUMENTARY FESTiVAL

517 College St., Suite 420
Toronto, Ontario M6G 4A2
Canada
Tel: 416-203-2155
Fax: 416-203-0446
Email: pgrove@hotdocs.ca
Web Site: www.hotdocs.ca
Festival Date: April–May
Entry Deadline: December
Director: Chris McDonald— Executive Director
Category: Documentary, International
Profile: Hot Docs, Canada's premier international documentary festival, with over 70 of the

year's most exciting, provocative and audacious non-fiction films from Canada and around the world. An annual celebration of excellence in documentary film and television, Hot Docs has built a reputation for showcasing the best of documentary cinema.

Seminars: Yes

Panels: Yes

Awards: Yes

HOT SPRiNGS DOCUMENTARY FiLM FESTiVAL

819 Central Ave.

P.O. Box 6450

Hot Springs, AR 71902-6450

Tel: 501-321-4747

Fax: 501-321-0211

Email: hsdff@docufilminst.org

Web Site: www.docufilminst.org

Festival Date: October

Entry Deadline: May

Year Festival Began: 1992

Contact: Linda Blackburn— Executive Director

Director: Linda Blackburn— Executive Director

Programmer: Gretchen Miller

Other Staff: Michael Bracy

Category: Documentary, Independent

Seminars: Humanities forums accompanying films

Panels: Lecture series

Awards: No

Competitions: No

Application Tips: Enter early.

Application Fee: $25.00 U.S., $35.00 international

Insider Advice: Send as much information on your film as possible.

Films Screened: Each member of our Screening Committee screens each film submitted; a total of 60 films are shown at the festival.

Odds of Acceptance: 1 in 10

Filmmaker Perks: We offer lodging and contacts.

Tourist Information: Gorgeous mountain town with art galleries, museums, hiking trails, natural spring bathhouses, excellent restaurants and friendly people

Best Restaurants: Belle Arti, Three Monkeys, Brauhaus

Best Bars: Bronze Gorilla

Best Hangout for Filmmakers: Arlington Resort Hotel & Spa.

Best Place for Breakfast: Pancake House

HOUSTON GAY AND LESBiAN FiLM FESTiVAL

Southwest Alternate Media Project (SWAMP)

1519 West Main

Houston, TX 77006

Tel: 713-522-8592

Fax: 713-522-0953

Email: Hglff@swamp.org

Web Site: www.hglff.org

Festival Date: May/June

Entry Deadline: N/A—Non Competitive

Contact: Mary Lampe

Category: Gay Lesbian

HOUSTON iNTERNATiONAL FiLM AND ViDEO FESTiVAL— ANNUAL WORLDFEST "WORLDFEST HOUSTON"

P. O. Box 56566

Houston, TX 77256-6566

Tel: 713-965-9955

Fax: 713-965-9960

Email: Worldfest@aol.com

Web Site: www.worldfest.org

Festival Date: April

Entry Deadline: December

Contact: Kathleen Haney

Director: J. Hunter Todd

Programmer: Kathleen Haney

HUDSON VALLEY FiLM FESTiVAL

40 Garden St.

Poughkeepsie, NY 12601

Tel: 914-473-0318

Fax: 914-473-0082

Email: hvfo@vh.net

Web Site: www.sandbook. com/hvfo

Festival Date: May

Entry Deadline: March

Year Festival Began: 1995

Contact: Shawn Caila Folz

Director: Denise Kasell

Programmer: Shawn Caila Folz

Other Staff: Nancy Cozean, Media Director

Category: Independent

Profile: Focus on and celebrate the screenwriter. We showcase new work from established and emerging writers and filmmakers. Over 7,000 attend.

Panels: Writers Panel Discussion

Awards: Yes

Competitions: No cash prizes

Major Awards: We give a Distinguished Screenwriters Award to one established person each year

Application Tips: Submit new work/scripts in proper format

Application Fee: $15-screenplays, $20-shorts, $25-features/documentaries

Films Screened: All films and scripts entered are read

Odds of Acceptance: Films: 1 in 10. Scripts: 1 in 16.

Filmmaker Perks: Travel and lodging for event they are participating in, as well as additional passes to festival events. We offer exposure via direct mail, other press, including press conference, and there are many contacts to be made at the festival itself.

Tourist Information: Mohonk Mountain House and the Shawangunk Range (hiking, biking and world famous rock climbing), many historic mansions on the Hudson River, quaint historic towns

Travel Tips: If you can, get a rental car. We have discount rates with Enterprise Rent-A-Car.

Best Restaurants: Calico Restaurant/Patisserie, Le Petit Bistro

Best Bars: Stoney Creek

Best Hangout for Filmmakers: Cafe Pongo, Stoney Creek, La Parmigiana

Best Place for Breakfast: Blondie's, Schemmy's, Another Roadside Attraction Diner

HUMAN RiGHTS WATCH iNTERNATiONAL FiLM FESTiVAL

"Superb World Cinema"
—*Geoff Gilmore,*
Sundance Film Festival

350 Fifth Ave., 34th floor
New York, NY 10118
Tel: 212-216-1264
Fax: 212-736-1300
Email: burresb@hrw.org
Web Site: www.hrw.org/iff
Festival Date: June (New York),
October (London).
Entry Deadline: January
Year Festival Began: 1988
Contact: Heather Harding
Director: Bruni Burres
Programmer: Bruni Burres
Other Staff: John Anderson,
Festival Coordinator
Category: Independent
Profile: The Human Rights
Watch International Film Festival
was created to advance public
education on human rights issues
and concerns using the unique
medium of film. Each year, the
Human Rights Watch
International Film Festival
exhibits the finest human rights
films and videos in commercial
and archival theaters and on
public and cable television
throughout the United States.
Highlights of the Festival are
now presented in a growing
number of cities around the
world, a reflection of both the
international scope of the
Festival and the increasingly
global appeal that the project has
generated.
Seminars: Vary with location and
festival schedule
Panels: Vary with location and
festival schedule
Famous Speakers: The Festival
has been chaired by a host of
committed members of the film
industry. Hosts and Co-Chairs
and Opening Night Filmmakers
have included: (alphabetical) Sam
Cohn, Jonathan Demme,
Harrison Ford, Costa Gavras,
Anita Hill, Dustin Hoffman,
Arthur Miller, Michael Moore,
Julia Ormond, Alan Pakula, Rosie
Perez, Robert Redford, Tim
Robbins, Isabella Rosselini, John
Turturro, Susan Sarandon, John
Sayles, John Singleton, Trudie
Styler and Uma Thurman.
Awards: Yes
Major Awards: The Nestor
Almendros Prize is a $5,000
award given annually to a coura-
geous newer filmmaker and the
Irene Diamond Lifetime
Achievement Award is presented
annually to a filmmaker for his
or her lifetime contribution to
human rights and film.
Value of Awards: Nestor
Almendros Prize: $5,000
Irene Diamond Lifetime
Achievement Award: Title only
Past Judges: Festival Planning
Committee
Application Tips: In selecting
films for the Festival, Human
Rights Watch concentrates
equally on artistic merit and
human rights content. The
Festival encourages filmmakers
around the world to address
human rights subject matter in
their work and presents films
and videos from both new and
established international human
rights filmmakers. Each year, the
Festival's programming committee screens more than 800 films
and videos to create a program
that represents a wide number
of countries and issues. Once a
film is nominated for a place in
the program, staff of the relevant
division of Human Rights Watch
also view it to confirm its accu-
racy in the portrayal of human
rights concerns.
Application Fee: None—In lieu
of fee, VHS screening tapes are
not returned
Insider Advice: Submit early and
fully complete all forms
Average Films Entered: Human
Rights related features, documentaries, animated and experimental films and videos.
Films Screened: 5-30 in the
New York Festival, 10 in the
London Festival and approximately 12 in the traveling festival
in the US. On average 5-8 for
language tailored overseas "global showcases."
Odds of Acceptance: 1 in 30
Filmmaker Perks: We try to fly
in and put up as many filmmakers as possible depending on
grants we receive annually.

HUMBOLDT iNTERNATiONAL FiLM AND ViDEO FESTiVAL

Humboldt State University
Theatre Arts Dept.
Arcata, CA 95521
Tel: 707-826-4113
Fax: 707-826-5494
Email: alter@axe.humboldt.edu
Festival Date: March
Entry Deadline: February
Contact: Ann Alter
Application Fee: $30

iMAGEOUT— THE ROCHESTER LESBiAN & GAY FiLM & ViDEO FESTiVAL

274 N. Goodman Street
Rochester, NY 14607
Tel: 716/271-2640
Fax: 716/271-3798
Web Site: www.imageout.com
Application Fee: $5

THE iMAGES FESTiVAL OF iNDEPENDENT FiLM AND ViDEO

". . . the hottest ticket in
Canada for independent film
and video . . . Brimming
with fresh, idiosyncratic film
and videos from around the
world, this festival is unri-
valled."
—*Independent Weekly*

401 Richmond St. W. #448
Suite 228
Toronto, Ontario M5V 3A8
Canada
Tel: 416-971-8405
Fax: 416-971-7412
Email: images@interlog.com
Festival Date: April
Entry Deadline: November
Year Festival Began: 1988
Contact: Larissa Fan
Director: Kelly Langgard
Programmer: Chris Gehman
Category: Animation,
Documentary, Experimental,
First-Time Independent
Filmmakers, Independent,
International, Multimedia, Short,
Super 8/8mm, Video

Profile: The largest event of its kind in Canada, Images is dedicated to showcasing and supporting independent and experimental works in video, film, new media and installation from across Canada and around the world. We aim to provide an alternative to the mainstream, a place where engaging, challenging, thoughtful, brave and beautiful works in all genres and from diverse communities can find a home.

Panels: The festival regularly features panels, workshops and discussions.

Market: No

Competitions: Yes

Major Awards: The Telefilm Canada Prize

Value of Awards: $4,000

Application Fee: $15

Common Mistakes: Filling out forms illegibly, not following instructions, sending no promo material, sending too much promo material, submitting work that is not suitable to the festival.

Insider Advice: Make sure you have a still from your film.

Odds of Acceptance: 1 in 4

Filmmaker Perks: Images invites a number of filmmakers to the festival each year who are provided with travel expenses and lodging. We are also able to help filmmakers interested in attending find inexpensive or free accomodation (depending on availability). There are parties and events throughout the festival which provide good opportunities to schmooze and meet other filmmakers.

Attendance: 5,000

Journalist Attendance: 30

INDEPENDENT EXPOSURE

"Joel Bachar's monthly venue of short films and videos has been getting stronger and stronger over the years, and is recommended not only for those who enjoy making short narrative and experimental works, but even for anyone who even thinks they might like to watch them."

—*Andy Spletzer, The Stranger,*

c/o Microcinema, Inc.
2318 Second Ave., #313-A
Seattle, WA 98121
Tel: 206-568-6051
Email: Info@microcinema.com
Web Site: www.microcinema.com

Festival Date: The fourth Thursday of every month—January through October

Entry Deadline: Ongoing

Year Festival Began: 1996

Contact: Joel S. Bachar

Director: Joel S. Bachar

Other Staff: Roderick Hatfield

Category: Animation, Digital, Digital Animation, Documentary, Experimental, First-Time Independent Filmmakers, Independent, International, Microcinema, Online Festival, PXL, Short, Super 8/8mm, Touring (has been played in 25 countries), Underground, Video, Weird, Woman

Profile: Seattle video and film artist, Joel S. Bachar founded Blackchair Productions in 1992. Due to the overwhelming lack of independent-oriented screening venues, Blackchair Productions began the Independent Exposure Microcinema screening program in 1996. This program, held every month at the Speakeasy Café's Backroom in Seattle, has presented the short film, video and digital works of over 400 artists from 95 cities in 40 states and 15 countries. The program has also gained an enviable reputation in the international

Stephen Bachar of Seattle's Independent Exposure.

microcinema network maintained in 60 cities, 20 states and 25 countries from Tacoma to Albuquerque and Barcelona to Belgrade and Bangkok.

Gore Score · · · · · · · · · · · · · · ·
Seattle's best showcase for new underground work.

Market: No
Awards: No
Competitions: No
Application Tips: Clearly labeled VHS entries and support materials.
Application Fee: $5. Returned if work not accepted and SASE provided.
Common Mistakes: They don't label their tapes. They don't include contact information on all of their materials (tapes, bio, letter, etc) They don't follow entry instructions.
Insider Advice: Never use fiber-filled envelopes—the fibers get all over our VCRs. Follow the entry instructions 100 percent!
Films Screened: 10-12 per month
Odds of Acceptance: 1 in 4
Filmmaker Perks: We have lots of contacts internationally. You can crash on my floor if you come to Seattle and we know bartenders all over town.
Attendance: 70-100/month
Journalist Attendance: Both of the local weeklies give a preview of each show.
Tourist Information: The area where the Kingdome once stood. Belltown—the 'hip' part of Seattle. Jimi Hendrix's grave.
Travel Tips: Don't rent a car if you are only staying in Seattle. Everything is in walking distance. Leave your umbrella at home.
Best Cheap Hotels: Ace Hotel
Best Luxury Hotels: The Sorrento
Best Restaurants: Marco's Supper Club, Cyclops
Best Bars: Cyclops
Best Hangout for Filmmakers: Speakeasy Café, Alibi Room
Place for Breakfast: Pike Place Market
Festival Tale: Independent Exposure played in Belgrade,

during a torrential rainstorm but over 300 people still showed up. One week later, NATO started dropping bombs on the city.

INDEPENDENT FEATURE FILM MARKET

104 W. 29th St.
12th Floor
New York, NY 10001-5310
Tel: 212-465-8200
Fax: 212-465-8525
Email: ifpny@ifp.org
Web Site: www.ifp.org
Festival Date: September
Entry Deadline: May/June
Contact: Milton Talbot
Director: Catherine Tait, Executive Director
Category: Markets
Average Films Entered: 200+
Attendance: 2,000+

INDIANA FILM AND VIDEO FESTIVAL

c/o Indiana Film Society
820 E. 67th St.
Indianapolis, IN 46220
Tel: 317-923-4484
Fax: 317-923-4495
Web Site: www.indiefilm society.org
Festival Date: July
Entry Deadline: June
Contact: Terry Black
Director: Terry Black
Profile: Regional competition open to Indiana and five surronding states. Be in school, live or have made film in Indiana or one of surrounding states.
Value of Awards: Give $5000—$7000 in awards yearly.

INDIURBAN INDEPENDENT FILM FESTIVAL

P.O. Box 532299
Indianapolis, IN 46253
Tel: 317-767-2795
Fax: 317-924-8043
Email: imediamakers@aol.com
Web Site: www.envision pictures.com/indiurban
Festival Date: April

Entry Deadline: November
Year Festival Began: 2001
Contact: Nicole Kearney-Cooper
Director: Nicole Kearney-Cooper
Category: Documentary, Independent, Features, Music Video, Short
Profile: The goal of The IndiUrban Independent Film Festival is to provide an annual showcase and educational forums while exposing independent urban enterainment to the wides audience possible.

INSIDE OUT LESBIAN AND GAY FILM FESTIVAL OF TORONTO

401 Richmond St W, Ste 219
Toronto, Ontario M5V 3A8
Canada
Tel: 416-977-6847
Fax: 416-977-8025
Email: inside@insideout.on.ca
Web Site: www.insideout.on.ca
Festival Date: Late May
Entry Deadline: February
Contact: Shane Smith
Director: Ellen Flanders
Programmer: Shane Smith
Category: Gay Lesbian, Independent
Profile: We're eight years old and growing up fast... The third largest queer festival in the world, we present over 200 works over ten days to 15,000 attendees. The festival is run by filmmakers these days and we try hard to be the friendly festival, friendly to the audience and friendly to filmmakers.
Seminars: We usually have a few, likewise with panels.
Panels: See above.
Famous Speakers: We have our share of galas, visiting dignitaries, glitzy parties and media hype, but we concentrate on showing extremely high quality work to the always appreciative audience and treating the filmmakers well with all-access passes and fun parties. We're in it for the films, honest.
Awards: Yes
Competitions: Yes
Major Awards: Bulloch Award is for the Best New Canadian

You can crash on my floor if you come to Seattle and we know bartenders all over town (Independent Exposure).

Work, and the Akau Framing Award is for Best Canadian Lesbian Short

Value of Awards: Bulloch $2,500, plus a beautiful plaque Akau Framing award = $500.

Application Tips: Send the tape earlier than the deadline

Application Fee: None

Insider Advice: Make sure you include a publicity still and a one-sheet with a quick description of your work, including time, year, exhibition format, and so on.

Odds of Acceptance: 1 in 3

Filmmaker Perks: We give you an all access pass, parties, billets if you want them and sometimes, if it's a feature film, we make travel and accomodation arrangements.

Travel Tips: Trains are pretty cool and they apparently derail a lot less frequently than Amtrak.

Best Restaurants: The Hacienda, down and dirty Mexican food, cool music and a great patio. The waiters are sometimes snarky, but that's just because they're all such sensitive artists, poke a bit harder and you'll find a friend for life.

Best Bars: College Street has an array of trendy wine-bar conversation type hang-outs.

Best Hangout for Filmmakers: Pleasuredome is the coolest indie film exhibitor collective and they put on screenings about once a month. That's where the real indie action is.

Best Place for Breakfast: KOS on College St or the Lakeview on Dundas West.

INTERNATIONAL FESTIVAL OF FILMS ON ART "FIFART FESTIVAL"

640 St. Paul St. West, Suite 406
Montreal, Quebec H3C 1L9
Canada
Tel: 514-874-1637
Fax: 514-874-9929
Festival Date: March
Entry Deadline: October for registration and pre-selection
Contact: Rene Rozon

INTERNATIONAL WILDLIFE FILM FESTIVAL

27 Fort Missoula Road, Suite 2
Missoula, MT 59804
Tel: 406-728-9380
Fax: 406-728-2881
Email: iwff@wildlifefilms.org
Web Site: www.wildlifefilme.org
Festival Date: April
Entry Deadline: December
Year Festival Began: 1978
Contact: Lisa Kersher
Other Staff: Randy Ammon—Executive Director
Category: Independent
Profile: The mission of the International Wildlife Film Festival is to foster knowledge and understanding about wildlife and habitat through excellent and honest wildlife films and other media. Any films or videotapes produced with a central focus on non-domesticated wildlife species either singly or in combination with other species qualifies for the International Wildlife Film Festival. Films involving habitat, conservation, ecology, research management, plants, special art forms or other people's interaction with wildlife are also eligible, but must relate specifically relate to wildlife.
Awards: Best of Festival, 1st, 2nd, 3rd
Best of Craft including Photography, Soundmix, Narration, Script, Editing
Best Special Award including: Educational Value, Scientific Content
Best of (each) Category
Competitions: Yes
Major Awards: Best of Festival (First, Second, Third)
Value of Awards: Monetary value is minimal, Status Value is immeasurable

Application Tips: Follow the directions on the entry form
Application Fee: $25–$200 (depends on category)
Insider Advice: Call us!
Average Films Entered: Wildlife, Environmental, Conservation, Human Interaction with Wildlife
Films Screened: 50
Odds of Acceptance: 1 in 3
Filmmaker Perks: Discounted registration
Tourist Information: High points: Rocky Mountain Elk Foundaiton, Carousel downtown, art galleries galore, wilderness areas surrounding.
Travel Tips: Car not necessary! Missoula is very walkable.
Best Restaurants: The Bridge Bistro
Best Bars: Union Club
Best Hangout for Filmmakers: Union Club
Best Place for Breakfast: The Shack

ISRAEL FILM FESTIVAL

IsraFest Foundation
6404 Wilshire Blvd.
Suite 1151
Los Angeles, CA 90048
Tel: 213-966-4166
Fax: 213-658-6346
Web Site: www.bway.net/israel
Festival Date: October
Contact: Meir Fenigstein
Category: Ethnic Other

JACKSON HOLE WILDLIFE FILM FESTIVAL

125 E. Pearl St.
P. O. Box AD
P.O. Box 3940 (Mailing address)
Jackson, WY 83001
Tel: 307-733-7016
Fax: 307-733-7376
Email: info@jhfestival.org or sdreizle@wyoming.com
Web Site: www.jhfestival.org
Festival Date: September (Every other year on odd years)
Entry Deadline: June
Contact: Mary Ford
Director: Mary Ford
Competitions: Yes

Car not necessary! Missoula is very walkable (International Wildlife Film Festival).

JOHNS HOPKINS FILM FESTIVAL

3015 St. Paul Street, Apt. 2
Baltimore, MD 21218
Tel: 410-889-9596
Email: jhff2001@jhu.edu
Web Site: www.jhu.edu/
~jhufilm/fest
Festival Date: Mid-March
Entry Deadline: January
Year Festival Began: 1998
Contact: Wil Ryan
Director: Wil Ryan
Programmer: Andy O'Bannon,
Jason Shahinfar, Virginia Lee
Category: American Films,
Animation, Documentary,
Experimental, First-Time
Independent Filmmakers,
Independent, International,
Microcinema, Short, Student,
Super 8/8mm, Underground,
Weird
Profile: Originality, creativity,
wackiness, uniqueness. A real
alternative to Hollywood sludge,
not a cheap imitation. We know
there are those out there that
have something to say in a totally
new, exciting, hilarious way. And
we wanna see it, so we can show
it to the world!
Market: No
Competitions: No
Application Fee: $15.00 before
1/5/01; $25.00 after 1/5/01
Insider Advice: Just be honest
with yourself. Are you satisfied
with what you've done? Does
anyone other than your mother
enjoy watching it?
Films Screened: 80
Odds of Acceptance: 1 in 3
Filmmaker Perks: We do what
we can, but no promises.
Attendance: 2,500
Tourist Information: The
Charles Theatre, The Visionary
Art Museum is a must, and The
Red Room if it's open.
Travel Tips: The Light Rail leaves
from BWI to Penn Station every
20 minutes and costs only $1.35.
Best Luxury Hotels: DoubleTree
Inn at the Colonnade
Best Restaurants: The best and
closest would be the Silk Road
Café.

Best Bars: Club Charles, you
might meet John Waters.
Best Place for Breakfast: Pete's
Grill

KANSAS CITY FILMMAKERS JUBILEE

4826 W. 77th Terrace
Prairie Village, KS 66208-4321
Tel: 913/383-8551
Email: KCJub@kcjubilee.org
Web Site: www.kcjubilee.org
Festival Date: April
Entry Deadline: Early:
December; Final: January
Category: Animation,
Documentary, Experimental,
Short
Profile: The Jubilee is a celebra-
tion of the creativity and hard
work of filmmakers in the
Kansas City metro area and
from around the world. It is a
juried showcase of the short and
feature length films. Films and
videos must have been complet-
ed within the last two years.
Awards: Yes
Competitions: Yes
Value of Awards: $1000 of cash,
film stock, lab & post production
services, animation software or
equipment rental.
Application Fee: $20 for early
entry. $25 late entry

KANSAS CITY GAY & LESBIAN FILM FESTIVAL

4330 Holly St.
Kansas City, MO 64111
Tel: 816-960-4636
Fax: 425-6969-9484
Email: jamierich@swbell.net
Web Site: www.kcgayfilmfest.org
Festival Date: June 15-28, 2001
Entry Deadline: April
Contact: Jamie Rich
Director: Jamie Rich
Category: Gay Lesbian, Short,
Video
Profile: Competition is primarily
regional Minnesota to Texas.

KUDZU FILM FESTIVAL (aka ATHENS FILM FESTIVAL)

P.O. Box 1461
Athens, GA 30603
Tel: 706.227.6090
Fax: 706.227.1083
Email: kudzufest@aol.com
Web Site: www.prometheus-
x.com
Festival Date: Early to mid
October
Entry Deadline: August
Year Festival Began: 1997 as the
Athens Film Festival
Other Staff: Paul Marchant—
Festival Co-Director
Category: Independent, Open
and diverse
Profile: The Kudzu Film Festival
is hoping to turn a music town
with a film festival into a film
town with a music scene. The
overall idea behind the festival is
to provide film based events in a
culturally rich city which has
lacked an organized film contin-
gent. Athens is a proud community with much to offer, and by
providing Athens with a film outlet we hope to inspire artists and
business people alike to take a
more active role in filmmaking in
the Southeastern United States.
Plus it's just a really great place
to be.

Gore Score · · · · · · · · · · · · · · ·
*It's no surprise that producer
Michael Stipe's hometown is also
home to one of the hottest up and
coming new fests.*

Seminars: Independent
Filmmaking 101, The Role of the
Cinematographer, The Art and
Craft of Handmade Cinema,
Getting Started in The Film
Business in The South,
Genealogies & Hieroglyphs with
David Gatten
Panels: Exhibition and the
Independent Filmmaker
Awards: Yes
Competitions: Yes
Major Awards: The Kudzu
Application Tips: Make a good
looking film or at least make an
interesting film; crappy camera
work, lighting and sound can kill
a films chances.

Application Fee: $40 ($35 students) early deadline; $50 ($40 students) late deadline

Insider Advice: A nice presentation helps, but many slick packages don't deliver. If your film is really good, it won't matter how much you spend for press kits.

Average Films Entered: Deep and twisted plots, animation, and films with "music or southern" themes play well here.

Films Screened: About 25-35 films are screened.

Odds of Acceptance: 1 in 8

Filmmaker Perks: Well, we throw some kick ass parties, you might catch a glimpse of some local celebrities and you might even get to sleep on the Program Director's couch.

Tourist Information: For old Athens historic value "The Double-Barrel Cannon" and "The Tree that owns itself" are oddities. University of Georgia campus is beautiful and within a minute or two from anywhere downtown.

Travel Tips: For those people flying, if you don't mind connecting in Charlotte, NC. USAir flies direct from Charlotte to Athens, otherwise you have to fly into Atlanta and take an hour plus shuttle ride or rent a car to get to Athens.

Best Restaurants: Depends on who's sponsoring us any given year! The Grit is touted by many as the best but I'd just as soon chill out at The Taco Stand with a cheap burrito and a cold beer.

Best Bars: The Manhattan if you want to see Athens hipsters or The Globe if you want an upscale environment with an academic appeal. Bars are a dime a dozen here, there's one on every corner.

Best Hangout for Filmmakers: Jittery Joe's, for some reason film people love sitting around getting wired on coffee and chatting about movies at all hours of the day or night.

Best Place for Breakfast: The Grill, a 1950s style diner located right in the heart of downtown Athens.

L.A. ASIAN PACIFIC FILM VIDEO FESTIVAL

Visual Communications
263 S. Los Angeles St., Suite 307
Los Angeles, CA 90012
Tel: 213-680-4462
Fax: 213-687-4848
Email: viscom@apanet.org
Web Site: www.vconline.org
Festival Date: May
Entry Deadline: January
Contact: Abraham Ferrer/David Magdael
Other Staff: Programming Committee, Abraham Ferrer/David Magdael

LA LESBIAN FILM FESTIVAL

320 45th St
Oakland, CA 94609
Tel: 510-654-6346
Fax: 510-654-0346
Email: Hesternet@jps.net
Web Site: www.lapena.org
Festival Date: November
Entry Deadline: August
Year Festival Began: 1998
Contact: Karen Hester
Director: Karen Hester and Lisa Rudman
Category: American Films, Documentary, Ethnic African, Ethnic Asian, Ethnic Black, Ethnic Jewish, Ethnic Latin, Ethnic Spanish, Experimental, First-Time Independent Filmmakers, Gay Lesbian, International, Short, Student, Super 8/8mm, Underground, Video, Woman
Profile: La Lesbian Film Festival is a grass roots festival dedicated to building multicultural lesbian identity and community. Our goal is to bring lesbian film makers and film goers together to work for social change. We support work by, for and/or about lesbians, highlighting the works of San Francisco Bay Area lesbians of color. The festival features a provocative mix of full-length documentary, short and experimental video, and 16mm and 35mm film.
Panels: Discussions with local filmmakers.
Market: No

Competitions: No
Application Fee: None
Insider Advice: Send it if it has lesbian content or is a quality work by a lesbian filmmaker with minimal lesbian content. Please include a self-addressed stamped return envelope with enough postage.
Average Films Entered: shorts, but always looking for quality lesbian features.
Films Screened: 30
Odds of Acceptance: 1 in 3
Filmmaker Perks: An enthusiastic, receptive audience and community lodging.
Attendance: 1,200
Journalist Attendance: 3-5
Tourist Information: San Francisco Bay Area, a tourist mecca, especially for lesbians
Travel Tips: Ask film coordinators directly for tips.
Best Cheap Hotels: Shattuck Hotel, Berkeley
Best Luxury Hotels: Claremont Spa and Resort, Oakland
Best Restaurants: Nan Yang, Oakland
Best Bars: La Peña Cultural Center, Berkeley
Best Hangout for Filmmakers: La Peña Cultural Center, Berkeley
Best Place for Breakfast: Lois the Pie Queen, Oakland
Random Tidbits: Our festival is produced in cooperation with La Peña Cultural Center, celebrating its 25th anniversary of bringing artists and art together to work for social change.

LAKE PLACID FILM FORUM

PO Box 489
Lake Placid, NY 12946
Tel: 518-523-3456; 518-576-2063
Fax: 518-523-4746
Email: adkfim@gisco.net
Web Site: www.lakeplacid-filmforum.org
Festival Date: June 7-10, 2001
Entry Deadline: Feb 1, 2001
Year Festival Began: 2000
Contact: Naj Wikoff

Director: Naj Wikoff, Executive Director

Programmer: Kathleen Carroll, Artistic Director

Category: American Films, Animation, Digital, Digital Animation, Documentary, DVD, Experimental, First-Time Independent Filmmakers, Independent, International, Multimedia, Europe, Asia, South America, Canada and the U.S., Short, Student, Video, Woman

Profile: The Lake Placid Film Forum is held in the famed Olympic resort in northern New York State. We call it a Forum rather than a Festival because we see it as a site for filmmakers and film lovers to come together to see films and discuss in formal and informal venues issues of content and the medium.

Seminars: Two seminars each day that addressed major topics/themes.

Panels: Simultaneous "how to" workshops held during the day (i.e self distribution, pitching your screenplay).

Famous Speakers: Milos Forman, Paul Schrader, Russell Banks, Michael Ondaatje, Donald Westlake, Chris Noth, Cliff Robertson, Eugene Hernandez, Michale Barker

Market: No

Competitions: Yes

Major Awards: Best feature, Best documentary, Best short

Value of Awards: Silver Deer Award: an engraved statuette

Past Judges: The audience fill out ballots after each screening rating the films, the ballots are tabulated and awards given.

Common Mistakes: Once accepted, fail to get in photos and bios in a timely manner.

Insider Advice: Send a self addressed return envelope if they want their tapes back. Include bios and info on filmmakers.

Films Screened: Approximately 85

Filmmaker Perks: Lodging, 50 percent discounts for their friends, in some cases free travel, lots of hospitality, workshops, lots of opportunities to make contacts and gain information.

Attendance: 3,000

Journalist Attendance: 32

Tourist Information: Filmmakers enjoyed going down the bobsled and luge runs, the opening party on top of the 120 meter ski jump, fly fishing, golf and skating in the Olympic arena.

Travel Tips: Take the the train, fly in/out of either Montreal or Albany, N.Y. or drive from NYC.

Best Cheap Hotels: Art Devlin's Olympic Motor Inn

Best Luxury Hotels: Lake Placid Lodge, Mirror Lake Inn

Best Restaurants: Nicolas Over Main was the popular eatery, the Lake Placid Lodge was the favorite for fine dining, and the Brown Bog was the favorite for a light snack and glass of wine.

Best Bars: The Cottage

Best Hangout for Filmmakers: Nicola's Over Main, Russell Bank's kitchen

Best Place for Breakfast: Northwood Inn

LOCAL HEROES INTERNATIONAL SCREEN FESTIVAL

"I'm sure it must be the only festival in the entire world where they send a driver to pick up the maker of a short film at the airport. That sort of sets the tone for the festival. The amount of attention they give short filmmakers is rare and appreciated. The other great thing about the festival is that the screenings of the films are sequential—no two films are screening at the same time so that over the course of the festival a kind of collective experience is built up between all the filmmakers."

—Guy Bennett, Vancouver

10159 108th. ST.
Edmonton, Alberta T5J 1L1
Canada
Tel: 403-421-4084;
In Canada: 1-800-480-4084
Fax: 403-425-8098
Email: filmhero@nsi-canada.ca
Web Site: www.nsi-canada.ca

Festival Date: March

Entry Deadline: November

Year Festival Began: 1986

Contact: Any staff member

Director: Bill Evans

Programmer: Bill Evans

Category: Independent, International

Profile: Local Heroes brings the finest independent films and their creators to Edmonton, to share the spotlight with Canada's most exciting new dramatic filmmakers. For five days filmmakers, industry professionals, and the general public mingle together in the open, friendly atmosphere that has made Local Heroes famous. Launched in 1984, it has become one of Canada's most talked about film events.

Awards: No

Competitions: No. We are proudly non-competitive.

Application Fee: Early bird fee—$20; Regular fee—$25.

Average Films Entered: We only accept Canadian short films, but we do accept international features. We do not accept documentaries, experimental films or student films.

Films Screened: 21. We screen the films sequentially so no two films are screened at the same time. This way all the filmmakers get individual attention.

Odds of Acceptance: Shorts—1 in 8; Features—1 in 10

Filmmaker Perks: We cover half of the travel and accomodation costs for Canadian filmmakers featured in the short film section. We also provide one screening pass to them per film. We cover the entire cost of travel and lodging for our international guests and they also receive a festival pass.

Tourist Information: West Edmonton Mall

Travel Tips: The Local Heroes festival tries to make travel to Edmonton as convenient as possible so please contact our travel coordinator for help. Transportation to and from the airport is also available free of charge.

Filmmakers enjoyed going down the bobsled and luge runs, the opening party on top of the 120 meter ski jump, fly fishing, golf and skating in the Olympic arena (Lake Placid Film Forum).

Best Restaurants: There are lots of great restaurants in town. In fact we provide a restaurant guide and the hospitality suite is always a great place to get recommendations from locals.

Best Bars: The best bars in town are the ones where the Local Heroes parties are held. Each night all of the festival guests are invited to attend the receptions along with the movie-goers.

Best Place for Breakfast: The best place for breakfast during the festival is at the morning seminars where we serve a continental breakfast to the festival goers and filmmakers.

LONG iSLAND FiLM FESTiVAL

P.O. Box 13243
Hauppauge, NY 11788
Tel: 800-762-4769; 516-853-4800
Fax: 516-853-4888
Email: festival@lifilm.org
Web Site: www.lifilm.org/festival
Festival Date: July-August
Entry Deadline: May
Contact: Christopher Cooke
Director: Christopher Cooke
Other Staff: Staller Center for the Arts—Stony Brook
Category: Independent
Profile: The Long Island Film Festival is devoted to the screening and support to independently produced films.
Seminars: "Script to Screen" Workshop
Panels: "Filmmaker's Panel"
Awards: Yes
Competitions: Yes
Application Fee: Up to 15min $25.00
Up to 30min $40.00
Up to 60min $60.00
Over 60min $75.00
Films Screened: Approximately 40 features and documentaries are screened and about 60 shorts.
Odds of Acceptance: 1 in 3
Filmmaker Perks: Travel and lodging is provided for filmmakers accepted for screenings.
Travel Tips: Long Island Railroad from N.Y.C. to Stony Brook. By

plane into Islip-MacArthur Airport or LaGuardia Airport.
Best Restaurants: The Park Bench, which is near the festival (long walk) and train station. Good festival grub and great bar too.
Best Hangout for Filmmakers: Hospitality Suite

LONG iSLAND GAY & LESBiAN FiLM FESTiVAL

Cinema Arts Centre
423 Park Avenue
Huntington NY 11743
Tel: 631-242-9727
Email: fly81657@aol.com
Web Site: www.choli.org
Contact: Stephen Flynn
Category: Gay Lesbian

LOS ANGELES iNDEPENDENT FiLM FESTiVAL (LAiFF)

1964 Westwood Blvd., Suite 205
Los Angeles, CA 90025
Tel: 323-951-7090
Fax: 323-937-7770
Email: info@laiff.com
Web Site: www.laiff.com
Festival Date: Mid April
Entry Deadline: Early January
Year Festival Began: 1995
Contact: Ian Channing, Festival Coordinator
Director: Richard Raddon
Programmer: Thomas Ethan Harris
Other Staff: RJ Millard, Director of Publicity/Marketing; Linda Rattner, Managing Director
Category: American Films, Animation, Digital, Digital Animation, Documentary, DVD, Ethnic African, Ethnic Asian, Ethnic Black, Ethnic Jewish, Ethnic Latin, Ethnic Spanish, Experimental, First-Time Independent Filmmakers, Gay Lesbian, Independent, Multimedia, Short, Student, Underground, Video, Weird, Woman
Profile: Now in its eighth year, the Festival has become an essential stop on the festival circuit premiering North American features and shorts. The festival also showcases music videos,

seminars and the annual Craft Series for an audience of over 25,000 each year.
Seminars: Rotating list of topics. Past seminars have focused on Marketing and Distribution, using the internet, post-production tips, and music supervision.
Famous Speakers: Such notable actors and directors have participated in the festival such as Holly Hunter, Curtis Hanson, Agnieszka Holland, Steven Soderbergh, Neil LaBute, Sydney Pollack, Shirley MacLaine and many more.
Market: No
Competitions: Yes
Major Awards: LAIFF Critics Prize
Application Fee: Shorts/Music Videos $35.00; Features $60.00
Common Mistakes: They forget to fill out the application completely.
Insider Advice: Submit your film as early as possible in the programming period.
Average Films Entered: Diverse, original and highly personal independent—documentary and narrative North American films.
Films Screened: 80
Odds of Acceptance: 1 in 25
Filmmaker Perks: The festival is regularly attended by both independent and commercial film executives.
Attendance: 27,000
Journalist Attendance: 175
Best Cheap Hotels: La Reve Hotel, the Standard
Best Luxury Hotels: Mondrian, Bel-Age, Chateau Marmot
Best Bars: Sky Bar
Best Hangout for Filmmakers: Festival VIP Lounge
Best Place for Breakfast: Hugos
Random Tidbits: Celebrity sightings: William Hurt, Sean Penn, Keanu Reeves, Madonna, Holly Hunter, Lenny Kravitz, Shirley MacLaine and many more celebrities attend the LAIFF screenings.

LOS ANGELES INTERNATIONAL SHORT FILM FESTIVAL

1260 N. Alexandria Ave.
Los Angeles, CA 90029
Tel: 323-663-0242
Fax: 323-663-0242
Email: info@lashortsfest.com
Web Site: www.lashortsfest.com
Festival Date: September/
October
Contact: Robert Arentz
Category: Short, Video
Major Awards: Best American
Film, Best Foreign Film
Value of Awards: Certificate of
award in each category.
Application Tips: In order to
qualify, films must be under 45
minutes in length, and shot in
35mm, 16mm or video. Those
shorts selected will compete for
Best Domestic Film and Best
Foreign Film, as well as
Certificate Awards in Animation,
Comedy, Drama, Documentary
and Experimental. All submis-
sions should be on VHS.
Average Films Entered: Films
must be under 60 minutes in
length Formats: 35mm, 16mm,
video
Films Screened: 100
Odds of Acceptance: 1 in 6

LOS ANGELES ITALIAN FILM AWARDS (LAIFA)

P.O. Box 93206
Hollywood, CA 90093
Tel: 213-955-1888
Fax: 213-989-1588;
323-436-2928
Web Site: www.italfilmfest.com
Festival Date: April 24-28, 2001
Entry Deadline: Feb. 28, 2001
Category: Ethnic Other, Short
Profile: LAIFA's primary goal is
bringing to Los Angeles the work
of Italian filmmakers, but the festival wishes to offer a platform
for Italian-American artists to
express their "Italianness," thus
sharing their particular view of a
cultural heritage so strong and
undeniable.
Competitions: Yes
Major Awards: The festival will
present the LAIFA Award for

Best Picture (Italian & Italian-
American), Awards and
Certificates for various place-
ments and the People's Choice
Award for the most popular film
short and feature.
Films Screened: 25

LOS ANGELES LATINO INTERNATIONAL FILM FESTIVAL

6777 Hollywood Blvd., Suite 500
Los Angeles, CA 90028
Tel: 323-469-9066
Fax: 323-469-9067
Email: anvega@latinofilm.org
Web Site: www.latinofilm.org
Festival Date: August
Entry Deadline: June
Year Festival Began: 1996
Contact: Alan Noel Vega
Director: Edward James Olmos
Programmer: Marlene Dermer
Category: Documentary, Ethnic
Latin, Independent, Short
Profile: Covering all aspects of
Latino film, the Latino Film
Festival is entering its fourth
successful year. Films should relate
to Latino culture in some way,
via origin, story, cast or crew. The
program screened is made up of
features, documentaries, shorts
and independent films. The festi-
val offers six panels each year,
free of charge. Seminars are also
offered.
Seminars: Yes
Panels: Yes
Famous Speakers: Rita Moreno,
Mike Medavoy, Andy Garcia,
Jimmy Smits
Awards: Yes

Major Awards: "The Gabby"—
Lifetime Achievement Award
"The Rita"—Best Film
Value of Awards: The awards
total over $35,000
Application Fee: None
Average Films Entered: 150
Films Screened: 70
Odds of Acceptance: 1 in 2
Filmmaker Perks: For feature
filmmakers: airfare, food, lodging
Attendance: 16,000

THE LOST FILM FESTIVAL

4434 Ludlow St.
Philadelphia, PA 19104
Tel: 215-662-0397
Fax: 215-489-1002
Email: Lostff@aol.com
Web Site: www.lostfilmfest.com
Festival Date: The festival is
quarterly.
Entry Deadline: Rolling
Submissions
Year Festival Began: 1998
Contact: Mike Carroll @
lostff@aol.com
Scott Beiben @ 215-662-0397
Skot Beaudoin @ 215-230-0499
Director: Mike Carroll, Skot
Beaudoin, Scott Beibin, Mike Hall,
Giovanni Ciaccio
Category: Animation, Digital,
Digital Animation, Documentary,
Ethnic African, Ethnic Asian,
Ethnic Black, Ethnic Jewish,
Ethnic Latin, Ethnic Spanish,
Experimental, First-Time
Independent Filmmakers, Gay
Lesbian, Independent,
International, Microcinema,
Online Festival, Short, Student,
Touring (Every city/Every town),

BEST PARTY FESTIVALS

Chicago Underground Film Festival
Florida Film Festival
GEN ART Film Festival
Hamptons International Film Festival
Los Angeles International Film Festival
Slamdance International Film Festival
Sundance Film Festival
South By Southwest (SXSW) Film Festival
Toronto InternationalFilm Festival
USA Film Festival

Underground, Video, Weird, Woman

Profile: We want to de-pants the Indie film world, which we feel is too mired in the uptight and snooty theater paradigm. Indie filmmaking should be about stepping away from Hollywood and destroying the non-inclusive and competitive attitudes that capitalism espouses.

The Lost Film Collective believes that any group of folks can create a great movie with a non-hierarchical crew on a shoestring budget, and will support most projects of that ideology. By holding this festival in the locations we are using, we believe we are opening up alternate routes for guerilla film screenings. Our traveling festival tours encourage widespread DIY distribution. We screen feature length and short films that we feel deserve to be seen. We could care less if the film was done on a $3 million dollar budget, or on a $3 budget.

Film is about communication and community! Revolution through Celluloid!

Market: No

Competitions: No

Application Fee: None

Common Mistakes: Omit addresses and crucial info. Mislabel tapes or not label at all.

Insider Advice: Go beyond! Think non-linear always (even if you cut your film on a Steenbeck). Go for the unexpected. Share Information with others. Money is not always the Golden Carrot.

Films Screened: 27

Odds of Acceptance: 1 in 4

Filmmaker Perks: Sometimes we offer travel accommodations. On occasion we offer lodging. Contacts abound.

Attendance: 500

Journalist Attendance: 5-10

Tourist Information: West Philadelphia/ University City, South Street, The Galleries in old City, Space 1026, 4040 Space.

The RITZ theater, Amazing Vegan Restaurants, The Rocky Steps at the Art Museum, Art Museum (Free on Sundays), Italian Market, Mummers

Museum, Delaware River Waterfront, Chinatown

Best Cheap Hotels: Scott Beibin's floor

Best Luxury Hotels: Embassy Suites

Best Restaurants: Abyssinia (Ethiopian)

Best Bars: The Astral Plane, Tattooed Moms

Best Hangout for Filmmakers: Comet Café. International House. The Last Drop. The Bean.

Festival Tale: After advertising for our first film festival, the venue which was holding it was afraid it would be "the next Woodstock" so they backed out on us a week before the fest. Our alternates were two warehouses in the ghetto of West Philadelphia.

Random Tidbits: We show stuff most film festivals won't or can't. We welcome openness and people who care about the art and social significance of filmmaking. Leave snobbery at home.

MADCAT WOMEN'S INTERNATIONAL FILM FESTIVAL

"Both the festival's content and concept are radical in a manicured film landscape where only those marginal makers working in standard formats and digestible genres can get past the groundskeepers."
—*Susan Gerhard, SF Guardian*

639 Steiner St., Apartment C
San Francisco, CA 94117
Tel: 415-436-9523
Email: alionbear@earthlink.net
Web Site: www.somaglow.com/madcat

Festival Date: Approx dates September 4, 11, 18, 25, 2001. More dates and cities to be added.

Entry Deadline: July 20, 2001 (confirm with office)

Year Festival Began: 1996

Contact: Ariella Ben-Dov

Director: Ariella Ben-Dov

Other Staff: Rebecca McBride, Associate Director

Category: Animation, Digital, Digital Animation, Documentary, DVD, Ethnic African, Ethnic Asian, Ethnic Black, Ethnic Jewish, Ethnic Latin, Ethnic Spanish, Experimental, First-Time Independent Filmmakers, Gay Lesbian, Independent, International, Avant Garde, PXL, Short, Student, Super 8/8mm, Touring, Underground, Video, Weird, Woman

Profile: The MadCat Women's International Film Festival is committed to showcasing women film and videomakers who challenge the use of sound and image and explore notions of visual story telling. MadCat has established a strong reputation for programming series of acute and insightful films you'd be hard pressed to see anywhere else.

MadCat's unique programming incorporates experimental and avant-garde films with more accessible independent works and links them thematically to draw in a diverse audience and allow viewers to understand the films set before them.

MadCat sets itself apart from other women's festivals by curating its programs thematically as opposed to looking for films about women's issues. Thus, with each year comes a completely new set of films and themes. MadCat allows viewers to look into the vast array of topics women film and videomakers are wrestling with.

Panels: Yes

Market: No

Competitions: No

Application Fee: Sliding scale $10-30. Give what you can afford!

Insider Advice: Include a SASE

Films Screened: 30-55

Odds of Acceptance: Approximately 1 in 10

Filmmaker Perks: Lodging, Contacts

Attendance: 2,000

Best Restaurants: Burrito's at Cancun on 19th and Mission or fancy food at Firefly on 24th and Douglass.

Best Place for Breakfast: Spagetti Western on Haight and

Steiner, Kate's Kitchen on Haight and Fillmore, Chloe's on Church and Clipper.

MAiNE STUDENT FiLM AND ViDEO FESTiVAL

P.O. Box 4320
Portland, ME 04101
Tel: 207-773-1130
Email: hueyfilm@nlis.net
Web Site: www.agate.net/ ~ile/mama
Festival Date: July
Entry Deadline: June
Director: Huey
Category: Student
Profile: The Maine Student Film and Video Festival is open to Maine residents, 19 years of age and younger only.
Application Fee: None

MAKiNG SCENES

Arts Court, 2 Daly Avenue
Ottawa, Ontario K1N 6E2
Canada
Tel: 819-775-5423
Fax: 819-775-5422
Email: scenes@fox.nstn.ca
Web Site: fox.nstn.ca/~scenes
Festival Date: September
Entry Deadline: May
Contact: Donna Quince
Director: Donna Quince
Category: Gay Lesbian
Seminars: We offer production workshops every year. In 1998 we presented an animation workshop aimed at queers.
Awards: Yes
Competitions: Yes
Major Awards: VIACOM Canada Best Canadian Feature Film Award
2. The Independent Filmmaker's Coop of Ottawa's Best locally-produced Film Award 3. SAW Video Coop's Best locally-produced Video Award
Value of Awards: 1. $1,500 CAN
2. $ 500 CAN
3. $ 500 CAN
Application Tips: Plain & simple, the story or concept must be good, but not necessarily the production value. I have seen a lot of well-produced works but

the story is dreadful. On the other hand I have seen some really weak productions with fabulous concepts.
Application Fee: We don't charge one, preferring to present as many works as possible without that kind of hindrance.
Insider Advice: Hang in there, do not quit.
Films Screened: 75
Odds of Acceptance: 1 in 2
Filmmaker Perks: Free travel—not usually, but it depends
Best Restaurants: Corriander Thai on Kent Street

MALiBU FiLM FESTiVAL

c/o Malibu Film Foundation
30765 PCH, #122
Malibu, CA 90265
Tel: 310-589-2149
Fax: 310-589-2169
Email: mff@malibufilm festival.org
Web Site: www.malibufilm festival.org
Festival Date: February
Entry Deadline: December
Contact: Sheree Chapman or Geanann Gilliland or Dan Cannon
Director: David Katz
Programmer: TBA
Competitions: Yes
Application Fee: $50
Average Films Entered: 30-50

MARCO iSLAND FiLM FESTiVAL

601 Elkcam Circle, B6
Marco Island, FL 34145
Tel: 941-642-3378
Fax: 941-394-1736
Email: info@marcoisland filmfest.com
Web Site: www.marcoisland filmfest.com
Festival Date: October 17-21, 2001
Entry Deadline: July 15, 2001
Year Festival Began: 1998
Contact: Vickie Kelber
Director: Pat Berry
Programmer: Vickie Kelber

Category: American Films, Animation, Documentary, First-Time Independent Filmmakers, Gay Lesbian, Independent, International, Short, Super 8/8mm, Video
Seminars: Yes
Panels: Yes
Market: No
Competitions: Yes
Application Fee: $40 feature; $25 short
Films Screened: 80
Odds of Acceptance: 1 in 5
Attendance: 10,000
Journalist Attendance: 5
Tourist Information: The beach, golfing
Best Cheap Hotels: Paramount
Best Luxury Hotels: Marriott
Best Restaurants: Marek's
Best Place for Breakfast: SW Diner
Random Tidbits: Opening night is called "Sandals and Cinema"—the opening night feature is presented on the beach.

Opening night is called "Sandals and Cinema" the opening night feature is presented on the beach (Marco Island Film Festival).

MARGARET MEAD FiLM FESTIVAL

American Museum of Natural History
Central Park West at 79th St.
New York, NY 10024-5192
Tel: 212-769-5305
Fax: 212-769-5329
Email: meadfest@amnh.org
Web Site: www.amnh.org
Festival Date: November
Entry Deadline: May
Contact: Kate Hurowitz
Director: Elaine Charnov

MARiN COUNTY NATiONAL FiLM AND ViDEO FESTiVAL

Marin County Fairgrounds
Ave. of the Flags
San Rafael, CA 94903
Tel: 415-499-6400
Fax: 415-433-3700
Web Site: www.marinfair.org
Festival Date: June-July
Entry Deadline: May
Other Staff: Jim Farley, Fair Manager
Category: Independent

MARYLAND FILM FESTIVAL

107 East Read Street
Baltimore, MD 21202
Tel: 410-752-8083
Fax: 410-752-8273
Email: info@mdfilmfest.com
Web Site: www.mdfilmfest.com
Festival Date: April
Entry Deadline: N/A—By invitation only
Year Festival Began: 1999
Contact: Chris Cable
Director: Jed Dietz
Programmer: TBA
Profile: The Maryland Film Festival, funded by an unusual public/private partnership in Maryland, has two practical economic development goals: 1) to create a world class film festival centered in Baltimore, and 2) to bring filmmakers to Maryland as a way to encourage future production in the state.

We want a festival experience that is fun—celebrating the whole film culture, with no distinction between types of films. To us, a great movie is a great movie. We realize this is a privilege the marketplace does not have. We strive to make Maryland Film Festival screenings distinct.

MAUI FILM FESTIVAL

P.O. Box 669
Paia, HI 96779
Tel: 808-579-9996
Fax: 808-579-9552
Email: insol@mauifilm festival.com
Web Site: www.mauifilm festival.com
Festival Date: June
Entry Deadline: Early: March
Late: May
Year Festival Began: 1997
Contact: Barry Rivers
Director: Barry Rivers
Category: Animation, Documentary, Independent, International

MEDIA ALLIANCE FILM FESTIVAL

814 Mission St #205
San Francisco, CA 94103
Tel: 415-546-6334 x315
Fax: 415-546-6218
Email: filmfest@media-alliance.org
Web Site: www.media-alliance.org/filmfest
Festival Date: August
Entry Deadline: July
Year Festival Began: 2000
Contact: Lisa Sousa
Director: Lisa Sousa, Rebeka Rodriguez
Category: Documentary, Experimental, First-Time Independent Filmmakers, Independent, Short
Profile: The Media Alliance Film Festival brings activists and filmmakers together. We are seeking daring films that inspire people to act, films that defy the warped messages perpetrated by the corporate media, and films that boldly question the concept of identity in our media-overstimulated culture.
Panels: The Media Alliance Film Festival kicks off with a panel discussion featuring video and filmmakers who use the medium as a tool for activism and organizing in their communities. Members of Whispered Media, TILT media, and other video collectives and independent filmmakers will teach you how to use film and video to increase the impact of your activism.
Market: No
Competitions: No
Application Fee: $15

METHOD FEST

"The Method Festival, designed to celebrate notable performances in independent films, accomplishes exactly what it sets out to do. Every one of the films selected for preview ... is marked by outstanding performances.
—*Kevin Thomas, "Screening Room," Los Angeles Times*

880 Apollo St., Suite 337
El Segundo, CA 90245
Tel: 310-535-9230
Fax: 310-535-9128
Email: Don@methodfest.com
Methodfest@aol.com
Festival Date: June 15-22, 2001
Entry Deadline: Entries open on October 1st. Early Deadline, February 20th, late deadline, April 16th.
Year Festival Began: 1999
Director: Don Franken
Programmer: Elaine Wood
Category: Gay Lesbian, Independent, Short
Profile: Caring, close-knit staff. Passion for Independent Film. Public relations, marketing push behind the films screening and the festival itself. Also, festival is unafraid to take chances with its programming. Tremendous sense of community around the festival. All venues within walking distances. Parties every night, Indie Music Night, VIP Indie Filmmaker lounge, great participation by actors, filmmakers in festival. Acting and Indie Filmmaking workshops help at Pasadena Playhouse Balcony Theatre. Skyy Vodka & Firestone supplies plenty of refreshments for parties/ Indie Film lounge. Limited program, 31 films shown total, 17 features, 14 shorts, will keep similar program in 2001. Focus on quality, not quantity. Solid, very active Advisory Board for festival that meet's year around.
Seminars: Yes
Panels: Yes
Market: No
Competitions: Yes
Major Awards: John Garfield Award for Best Actor, Geraldine Page Award for Best Actress, Best Picture Best Director, Best Screenplay, Maverick Film Award, Best Supporting Actor Award, Best Supporting Actress, Breakout Acting Award, New Maverick Actor Award National Audience Award, various awards for shorts.
Application Fee: short, $25, late fee, $35. Features, $35, late fee, $50.
Common Mistakes: Sending incomplete information, or send-

ing it in increments rather than a comprehensive package. Because so many films come in, bits and pieces of your film package could get lost in the shuffle. Again, we also stress the inclusion of complete production notes and at least three good stills that can readily be published by a paper or easily be reproduced.

Insider Advice: Get press kits with pix to festival organizers and festival screeners as media is very important.

Odds of Acceptance: 1 in 10

Attendance: 3,000-5,000

Journalist Attendance: 36

Tourist Information: Pasadena is famous for its thriving cultural scene that includes live theater, museums, music performance clubs and fine restaurants.

Best Luxury Hotels: The Ritz Carlton Hotel, Pasadena

Best Restaurants: Twin Palms and Cayo are superb

Best Bars: The Muse nightclub

Best Hangout for Filmmakers: Zona Rosa is a perfect coffee bar outlet, especially since it is so close to the theaters where our panel discussions are hosted. But we really love The Wine Merchant, which is an elegant and tasteful place to host a reception.

MiAMi FiLM FESTiVAL

444 Brickell Ave #229
Miami, FL 33131

Tel: 305-377-3456; 305-662-6960

Fax: 305-577-9768

Email: mff@gate.net

Web Site: www.miamifilm festival.com

Festival Date: February

Entry Deadline: November

Year Festival Began: 1984

Contact: Eddie Lytton

Director: Nat Chediak

Programmer: Nat Chediak

Category: American Films, Animation, Digital, Documentary, Ethnic African, Ethnic Asian,

Ethnic Black, Ethnic Jewish, Ethnic Latin, Ethnic Spanish, Experimental, First-Time Independent Filmmakers, Independent, International, Short, Student, Woman

Profile: The Miami Film Festival strives to be among the leading showcases of international cinema. The festival promotes the understanding and appreciation of the art of film and encourages communication among the multiethnic citizens of our community. The motto of the Miami Film Festival is "For the love of film."

Seminars: Every year the Miami Film Festival presents a series of informative and educational seminars that highlight the latest trends in film today and important topics in film history, featuring well-known critics and filmmakers from around the world.

Market: No

Awards: Yes

Competitions: Yes

Major Awards: Miami Film Festival Audience Award

HBO Latin America Group Golden Reel Award for Outstanding Achievement

Application Fee: $30

Common Mistakes: Incomplete forms, non-working fax phone numbers...

Insider Advice: Be professional.

Films Screened: 25-30

Odds of Acceptance: 1 in16

Filmmaker Perks: The Miami Film Festival tries to encourage filmmakers, and stars to accompany their films. Travel and accommodations are provided to festival guests.

Attendance: 45,000

Journalist Attendance: MFF has over 500 local, national, international media partners

Tourist Information: South Beach, Downtown Miami, Vizcaya, Key Biscayne, Sawgrass Mills (shopping)

Travel Tips: Bring shorts, wear sunscreen

Best Cheap Hotels: Anything on Ocean Drive

Best Luxury Hotels: The Mandarin Oriental, Miami

Best Restaurants: Joe's Stone Crabs

Best Bars: The Delano, Miami Beach

Best Hangout for Filmmakers: Baileys Festival Club

Best Place for Breakfast: News Cafe

MIAMI GAY AND LESBIAN FILM FESTIVAL

1521 Alton Road, #147
Miami Beach, CA 33139
Tel: 305-534-9924
Fax: 305-535-2377
Email: festivalinfo@
the-beach.net
Web Site: www.MiamiGay
LesbianFilm.com
Festival Date: April
Contact: Robert Rosenberg
Director: Robert Rosenberg
Category: Gay Lesbian

MIAMI UNDERGROUND FILM & VIDEO FESTIVAL (ONLINE)

3701 N.E. 2nd AVE
Miami, FL 33137
Tel: 305-576-1336
Fax: 305-571-5003
Email: indieparla@
worldnet.att.net
Web Site: www.powerstudios.
com and www.miami
underground.org/
Festival Date: May 17-20, 2001
Entry Deadline: April 1, 2001
Year Festival Began: 2000
Contact: David Wallack, Ross Power, Rey Parla
Director: David Wallack, Ross Power, Rey Parla
Programmer: David Wallack, Ross Power, Rey Parla
Category: American Films, Animation, Digital, Digital Animation, Documentary, DVD, Ethnic African, Ethnic Asian, Ethnic Black, Ethnic Jewish, Ethnic Latin, Ethnic Spanish, Experimental, First-Time Independent Filmmakers, Gay Lesbian, Independent, International, Markets, Microcinema, Multimedia, Online Festival, Scratch Films, Music Videos, Short, Student, Super 8/8mm, Underground, Video, Woman
Profile: Miamiunderground.org is an organization dedicated to the support of cultural arts development and exhibition of independent filmmakers, video artists, screenwriters and artists in general.
Seminars: Film Florida
Panels: On filmmaking, music, video technology
Market: Yes
Competitions: Yes
Value of Awards: Film or video stock for next project depending on length of work.
Past Judges: The voting is achieved by committee and audience participation.
Application Fee: $30 for all entries.
Common Mistakes: Do not include junk and extra miscellaneous stuff.

Insider Advice: Know your specific film genre and submit your entry as early as possible, follow instructions, label correctly, inquire about a festival's pre-screening process, write a competent synopsis that truly describes the project, do not inlude promotional junk and most important of all: Have a great story!

Odds of Acceptance: We are a new fest, but we're really picky!

Filmmaker Perks: Contacts

Attendance: 1,000

Tourist Information: Hey, there's always time to go to South Beach, hang out at Power Studios in the Miami Design District, visit the new basketball arena, and fall in love with some of the most beautiful women on the planet!

Travel Tips: Be ready for the beach!

Best Cheap Hotels: Clevelander

Best Luxury Hotels: Fontainebleau Hotel

Best Restaurants: Mango's Tropical Cafe on Ocean Drive!

Best Bars: Power Studios

Best Hangout for Filmmakers: Power Studios

Best Place for Breakfast: Denny's

Random Tidbits: Celebrity sightings: Gloria Estefan on Lincoln Road, Cameron Diaz, Al Pacino, Oliver Stone, Sylvester Stallone, Madonna, Steven Bauer, Andy Garcia.

MICROCINEFEST

3700 Beech Ave.
Baltimore, MD 21211
Tel: 410-243-5307
Email: bfink@bcpl.net
Web Site: www.bcpl.net/~bfink/
microcinefest/
Festival Date: early November
Entry Deadline: end of July
Year Festival Began: 1997
Contact: Skizz Cyzyk
Director: Skizz Cyzyk
Category: Independent, Microcinema, Short, Touring (Atlanta, GA; Liverpool, England; Washington DC), Underground, Video, Weird

Profile: MicroCineFest's mission is to expose audiences to ambitious, low-budget, psychotronic, substream, off-beat, creative, original, do-it-yourself, daring underground films and videos from all over the world; big ambition on little budget.

Held every fall in Baltimore, Maryland, MicroCineFest is an extension of The H.O.M.E. Group's Independent Open Film & Video Screenings—Baltimore's longest running consistent underground film screening outlet. MicroCineFest is set up and operated in similar spirit to the guerilla film producitons that we screen; both are created out of strong passion regardless of minimal resources and obstacles.

Market: No

Competitions: Yes

Major Awards: Grand Jury Award

Value of Awards: Prizes are donated by sponsors, therefore value changes according to what is donated to us.

Application Fee: $15 for 30 minutes and under; $25 for over 30 minutes.

Special entry fees are as follows: For very short projects: For works under 7 minutes, round the length up to the nearest minute and multiply by 2. That figure is the entry fee. Example: If your work is 3+ minutes long, round it up to 4, multiply that by 2, which gives you 8—your entry fee is $8.

For multiple entries: If you have several short works but can't decide which one(s) to enter and can't afford to enter more than one, enter up to 30 minutes worth for the price of one "over 30 minutes" project ($25). Just be sure to include the appropriate entry information for each work and label the tape with the correct order of the works.

Common Mistakes: Most entry forms ask for a synopsis. There is a big difference between a synopsis and a critique. When asked for a synopsis, you're being asked to briefly explain what the film is about, not how good it is. Also, many filmmakers tend not to know the difference between

their shooting format and their screening format. The shooting format is the format (film or video type) in which you shot your film, and the screening format is the format you provide the festival to screen your finished film.

Insider Advice: Before submitting to a film festival, a filmmaker should take a moment to find out what sort of material that particular festival is interested in. For instance, a glance at the description for MicroCineFest should make it obvious that MicroCineFest is not looking for any serious dramas, mainstream romantic comedies or PBS-ish documentaries. Second, carefully follow the instructions on entry forms. Third, always expect to have your film rejected—never expect an acceptance letter. That way you won't be disappointed if your film is rejected, but it will be a nice surprise if it's accepted.

Films Screened: 100

Odds of Acceptance: 1 in 2

Filmmaker Perks: Since our primary source of funding comes from the entry fees, we cannot afford too many luxuries. However, any visiting filmmaker is offered a ride from the airport/train station/bus depot and a place to crash (usually a floor, couch, or spare bed provided by a staff member or local filmmaker). We know that low-budget filmmakers are usually poor, as are we, so we try to do what we can for them to make their trip to Baltimore as cheap and easy as possible.

Attendance: 2,000

Journalist Attendance: 10

Tourist Information: Duckpin bowling, The Dime Museum, The American Visionary Art Museum in the Inner Harbor, Atomic Books, Normal's Used Books & Music in Waverly, Reptilian Records in Fells Point

Travel Tips: Baltimore is a nice city, but be careful. Lock all valuables in your trunk and think twice before walking around the city alone after dark.

Best Cheap Hotels: We recommend the Quality Inn at The Carlyle (500 W. University Pkwy., 410-889-4500), on the northern

border of Charles Village, Hopkins University, and Wyman Park.

Best Restaurants: The MCF staff favorite is Holy Frijoles (cheap but good Mexican food) in the heart of Hampden.

Best Bars: The Club Charles (it's next door to a good restaurant—Zodiac—and across the street from the best movie theater—The Charles—and it's where John Waters hangs out).

Best Hangout for Filmmakers: In lower Charles Village, just north of Penn Station, on N. Charles Street, is a block that houses The Charles Theater, The Club Charles (see best bar), and the Zodiac Restaurant. Around the corner is Atomic Books and The American Dime Museum.

Best Place for Breakfast: Hampden's Avenue (36th Street) has both Café Hon and Golden West Café.

Festival Tale: A few weeks before our 1999 festival, I went to Liverpool, England, to show a "Best Of MicroCineFest" program at the North By Northwest Independent Film & Art Festival. While I was away, our festival program book was supposed to be laid out so that when I got back I could approve the layout and quickly send it off to the printer and get the books back in time to distribute around town to promote the festival. When I got back, the person laying out the program informed me he had not finished yet. "How far have you gotten?" I asked. "I've haven't started yet," he said, "I've been waiting for you." So on top of all the other last minute things I had to do, I now had to work on the program book and get it shipped to the printer as quickly as possible in order to have it in time for the festival. The printer finally called on opening day to say the programs were ready. With no other car-owning staff members available, I drove from Baltimore to New Jersey to pick them up. On the way back I realized I needed to pick up some filmmakers and a judge at the airport and that I would not have enough time to drop off the pro-

Mweze Ngangura and Robin Williams at the Mill Valley Film Festival

grams and put the seats back in my van. I got pulled over and was given a $180 speeding ticket. When I finally made it to the airport, all the flights I was waiting for had been delayed due to bad weather. By the time I left the airport, I had just enough time to get to the theater and introduce the opening night film. Not having the program books in time for opening night, or personally missing opening all together would have felt like a disaster. Luckily, things worked out, no other disasters surfaced that week, and the festival was a great success.

Random Tidbits: We take our visiting filmmakers duckpin bowling, to cool museums (The Dime Museum, The American Visionary Art Museum), and to parties.

MILL VALLEY FILM FESTIVAL

38 Miller Ave., Suite 6
Mill Valley, CA 94941
Tel: 415-383-5256
Fax: 415-383-8606
Email: finc@well.com
Web Site: www.finc.org
Festival Date: October
Entry Deadline: May (Early deadline)—June (Final Deadline)
Contact: Zoë Elton
Director: Mark Fishkin

Programmer: Zoë Elton
Category: American Films, Independent, International
Profile: MVFF was founded in 1978; it celebrates and promotes film, video and new media as art and education. It's an annual, non-competitive, eleven-day festival with more than a hundred programs of independent features, world cinema, documentaries, shorts, family films, video and new media.

The festival is run under the auspices of the Film Institute of Northern California. Over 40,000 attend annually.

Seminars: Two weekends of seminars and panels, which cover issues related to independent filmmakers and filmmaking, cutting-edge technology, innovations in video and new media, kids' films.

Panels: Panelists have included Waldo Salt, John Sayles, Barry Levinson, Saul Zaentz, Maggie Renzi, Allison Anders, Marianne Sägebrecht, James L. Brooks and Sam Shepard, among others.

Competitions: No. The festival will remain non-competitive.

Application Tips: Sappy as it may sound, make the film you want to make as best you can. Acceptance to a festival is like auditioning—you may be a great actor, but you may not be right for some particular part. You want the right festival for your film—it's not always a match, so don't be disheartened if your film doesn't get in.

Application Fee: Check Call for Entry form for current fees.

Insider Advice: If you have questions about the process, call us.

Odds of Acceptance: 1 in 8

Filmmaker Perks: For feature filmmakers, or for makers whose work is the main hook of a program:
1. Free travel
2. Free Lodging
3. Contacts
4. Publicity
5. Festival Accreditation
6. A relaxed and friendly place to meet people, make contacts, schmooze and hang out
For others, 3—6 apply if they attend the festival, plus we usual-

ly have deals with hotels and car rentals which are available to them.

Travel Tips: We're near San Francisco. Fly in through SFO, bring your hiking gear if the mountains call you, bring your party gear if the clubs call you, bring a driver if you're going to hit the wineries. People are often unsure where Mill Valley is: it's fifteen minutes north of San Francisco over the Golden Gate Bridge.

Best Restaurants: Piatti

Best Bars: The Sweetwater (and during the festival, there have been shows there with the likes of The Bacon Brothers, Rickie Lee Jones and Elvis Costello, as well as locals like Huey Lewis, members of the Grateful Dead, Hot Tuna).

Best Hangout for Filmmakers: The OAC (Outdoor Art Club)

Best Place for Breakfast: Sunnyside Café

MINICINE VISITING FILMMAKER SERIES

824 Texas Ave.
Shreveport, LA 71101
Tel: 318-424-6399
Fax: 318-424-7799
Email: minicine@swampland.org
Web Site: www.swampland.org
Festival Date: September to May (The minicine Visiting Filmmaker Series is actually an eight month long series of monthly screenings that coincide with semester schedules of area colleges and universities.)
Entry Deadline: February 1st for screening in following fall or spring, this proceeds deadlines of state granting organizations we apply to for funding assistance.
Year Festival Began: 1997
Contact: David
Director: Twister
Programmer: Tevin
Category: Ethnic Other, Experimental, First-Time Independent Filmmakers, Microcinema, Multimedia, PXL, Short, Super 8/8mm, Underground, Video
Profile: minicine is a tiny little microcinema dedicated to pulling

off urban film screenings in random and often precarious locations including galleries, coffee shops, alleys and deserted buildings. We do not have a specific festival per se, but program live film events that are intended to create an artist/audience interaction.

Market: Yes

Competitions: No

Application Fee: None

Insider Advice: We concentrate on booking touring filmmakers who will be present to screen work and discuss with audience.

Films Screened: 24

Odds of Acceptance: 1 in 2

Filmmaker Perks: Free accommodations in program director's studio residence and Swamp Tour. Access to crawfish etouffe' & Po'Boys. Can help network and organize tour with other microcinemas.

Attendance: 50-100 per screening

Journalist Attendance: 2-3

Best Cheap Hotels: David's Motel, Bossier City

Best Restaurants: Herby K's

Best Bars: Lee Wright's Lee's Lounge

Best Hangout for Filmmakers: The Burning Spear Caribe Cafe

Best Place for Breakfast: Murrell's

MONTREAL INTERNATIONAL FESTIVAL OF NEW CINEMA AND NEW MEDIA

3530, Boul. Saint-Laurent
Montréal, Québec H2X 2V1
Canada

Tel: 514-847-9272

Fax: 514-847-0732

Email: montrealfest@fcmm.com

Web Site: www.fcmm.com

Festival Date: October

Entry Deadline: September

Year Festival Began: 1972

Contact: Paule Vaillancourt

Director: Luc Bourdan and Claude Chamberlan

Programmer: Claude Chamberlan and Marie-Christine Picard (Feature Length Film) Keril Samodai and Philipe Gendreau (Short and medium length film) Philippe Gajan (Digital Cinema) Alain Mongeau and Frédéric Gauthier (New Media)

Category: Digital, Short

Profile: The event banks on new approaches and technologies while working as a springboard for artists eager to explore the confines of their art.

Awards: Yes

Competitions: Yes

MONTREAL WORLD FILM FESTIVAL

1432 de Bleury Street
Montreal, Quebec H3A 2J1
Canada

Tel: 514-848-3883

Fax: 514-848-3886

Email: ffm@gc.aira.com

Web Site: www.ffm-montreal.org/

Festival Date: August 23–September 3, 2001

Entry Deadline: June

Contact: Serge Losique

Director: Serge Losique

Category: International

Profile: Approximately 350,000 attend.

Awards: Yes

Competitions: Yes

Major Awards: Grand Prix of Americas

Application Fee: None

Odds of Acceptance: over 200 films entered

MONTREAL'S INTERNATIONAL LESBIAN & GAY FILM AND VIDEO FESTIVAL

4067 boul. St. Laurent #404
Montréal, Quebec H2W 1Y7
Canada

Tel: 514-285-4467

Fax: 514-285-1562

Email: info@image-nation.org

Web Site: www: image-nation.org

Entry Deadline: July 1, 2001

Year Festival Began: 1987

Contact: Charline Boudreau, Katharine Setzer

Director: Charline Boudreau

Programmer: Katharine Setzer

Category: Documentary, Experimental, Gay Lesbian, Independent, International, Multimedia, Short, Video

Profile: Image&nation is an international film/video festival which encourages, promotes and showcases media productions done by and for queers. Over the past thirteen years the festival has stood as the queer cultural event in Montreal and Canada.

Competitions: Yes

Major Awards: Bell Mobility Audience Choice Award for Best Feature Film

Value of Awards: $1000 CDN

Application Fee: $10

Common Mistakes: Filmmakers don't send the preview tape.

Insider Advice: When sending a submission, be sure to include a bio and fill out the submission form in full.

Average Films Entered: Narrative, documentary, experimental.

Films Screened: 200

Odds of Acceptance: 1 in 2

Filmmaker Perks: Free travel (usually only for feature works) lodging (same) and contacts (of course!).

Attendance: 16,000

Journalist Attendance: 50

Tourist Information: See the gay village (Ste Catherine between Wolfe and Papineau)

Best Cheap Hotels: Bourbon Hotel

Best Luxury Hotels: Wynman

Best Restaurants: Continental (St. Denis & Rachel)

Best Bars: Unity

Best Place for Breakfast: Beauty's (corner of Mont Royal and Clark)

We're near San Francisco. Fly in through SFO, bring your hiking gear if the mountains call you, bring your party gear if the clubs call you, bring a driver if you're going to hit the wineries (Mill Valley Film Festival).

MOONDANCE iNTERNATiONAL FiLM FESTiVAL

Moondance Film Festival
P.O. Box 3348
Boulder, CO 80307
Office:
970 Ninth Street
Boulder, CO 80302
Tel: 303-545-0202
Fax: 303-494-0879 (fax cover page must include festival office phone number: 303-545-0202)
Email: Moondanceff@aol.com
Web Site: www.moondancefilmfestival.com
Festival Date: January
Entry Deadline: October
Year Festival Began: 1999
Contact: Elizabeth English
Director: Elizabeth English
Category: American Films, Animation, Documentary, Experimental, First-Time Independent Filmmakers, Independent, International, Markets, Short, Video, Woman
Profile: The Moondance International Film Festival is by and for women. Our objective is to promote and encourage women screenwriters, playwrights, short-story writers and women who make independent films, and the best work by women, in any genre of feature films, animation, documentaries, short films, stage plays and short stories. Moondance provides a forum in which those women can have the opportunity for their work to be viewed and accepted by the powers that be, within the international film community.
Seminars: Up to thirty workshops and seminars on screenwriting, film production, TV writing, adaptations, pitching, selling/marketing/promotion, how to get an agent/write a query letter/give a pitch, documentaries, animation, short film production, short-stories to film, stageplays to film, editing film, editing screenplays, characterization in screenplays, directing film and TV, comedy writing, drama writing, improv for writers, making a good script great, out of Hollywood: writing for the rest

of the world, video production, independent low-budget film production...and many others!
Panels: Agents and producers pitch sessions for screenwriters, playwrights and short-story writers
Market: Yes
Competitions: Yes
Major Awards: The Spirit of Moondance awards (for films, screenplays, stageplays, short stories); The Columbine Awards for non-violent conflict resolution in the arts & film.
Value of Awards: Spirit of Moondance: $1000 each winner
Columbine Awards: non-cash prizes
Application Fee: $50 for entries postmarked April 1-June 1
$60 for entries postmarked June 2-August 1
$75 for entries postmarked August 2-October 1
Common Mistakes: Not labeling preview videos/tape cassettes with contact info and running time of film, not enclosing publicity stills and credits/awards of film-maker(s), not enclosing the script.
Insider Advice: Moondance judges look for A-list, top quality in all elements of films: story, direction, producing, cinematography, editing, acting, dialog, sound, lighting, set design, costumes, and production design.
Average Films Entered: All genres of: features, shorts, documentaries, animation, experimental, noir, avant-garde.
Films Screened: 13
Odds of Acceptance: 1 in 2
Filmmaker Perks: The Moondance director promotes the winning and finalist films, screenplays, stageplays and short stories to producers and agents.
Attendance: 1000
Journalist Attendance: 10
Tourist Information: Nearby ski areas (Aspen, Vail, Telluride, Breckenridge, Steamboat, A-basin, Copper), dude ranches, mountain hikes, world-famous Pearl Street mall, famed Red Rocks Ampitheatre, the Denver mint, Boulder creek path, Dushanbe tea house, Boulder

Museum of Contemporary Arts, Boulder Falls, Broadmoor hotel where *The Shining* was filmed, Mork & Mindy's house in Boulder.
Travel Tips: Arrive at Denver International Airport (DIA), catch Super Shuttle ($25) the 50 miles to Boulder, rent a car in Boulder, if needed.

If going on to Sundance from Moondance, it's a one-hour flight to Salt Lake City from DIA.
Best Cheap Hotels: Broker Inn (reasonable, not "cheap"), Foot of the Mountain Motel is inexpensive & charming: individual log cabins with fireplaces & by the creek, Briar Rose bed & breakfast is reasonable & is a lovely Victorian home.
Best Luxury Hotels: Historic Boulderado hotel & Regal Harvest House
Best Restaurants: Latest Zagats Survey & others list these as tops: Zolo's, Sushi Zanmai, John's, Flagstaff House, Rhumba, Red Fish, Q's, Greenbriar Inn, Mataam Fez, Siamese Plate, Ras Kassa, Boulder Cork.
Best Bars: Rhumba, Connor O'Brien's Irish Pub, West-End Tavern, Rio Grande, Boulderado Corner Bar, The Dark Horse.
Best Hangout for Filmmakers: The Med, Full Moon Grill, Tom's Tavern, Trident Coffee House, Dushanbe Tea House
Best Place for Breakfast: Turley's, Mom's Diner, Plaza Coffee Shop, Chautauqua Dining Hall, Lucille's.

MOUNTAiNFiLM

Box 1088
300 South Pine St.
Telluride, CO 81435
Tel: 970-728-4123
Fax: 970-728-6458
Email: info@mountainfilm.org
Web Site: www.mountainfilm.org
Festival Date: Memorial Day Weekend
Entry Deadline: April
Year Festival Began: 1979
Contact: Rick Silverman
Director: Rick Silverman
Category: Documentary. Mountainfilm is America's pre-

mier festival of mountain, adventure, cultural and environmental film and video since 1979.

Profile: Mountainfilm is an extraordinary celebration of film, wild places, and the people that inhabit, explore and protect them. Set against the backdrop of the high San Juan Mountains, the Festival is a mix of film and filmmaker, gallery exhibits, speakers, authors, symposiums, picnics, climbing, backcountry skiing and rich conversation. With an emphasis on cutting-edge programming and personal interaction, the Festival has become a gathering place for directors, producers, buyers, activists, photographers, writers, and those who savor this uniquely informal gathering.

Awards: Yes

Competitions: Yes

Major Awards: Best Of Mountainfilm

Films Screened: About 50

Odds of Acceptance: 1 in 5

Tourist Information: Former mining town turned ski resort, surrounded by 13,000 foot peaks, hot springs nearby, biking, hiking, backcountry skiing, wildflowers and wild animals: bring your camera—it's spectacular.

Travel Tips: Difficult to get to, but always worth the trip.

Best Hangout for Filmmakers: The Hospitality and Main Street

MOXiE! / SANTA MONiCA FiLM FESTiVAL

3000 Olympic Blvd., Bldg. #4
Santa Monica, CA 90404
Tel: 310-264-4274
Fax: 310-388-1538;
310-289-2399
Email: moxy@smff.com
Web Site: www.smff.com

Festival Date: February 14-19
Entry Deadline: December
Year Festival Began: 1997
Contact: Albert de Quay or Robert Boyd
Director: Albert de Quay
Programmer: Robert Boyd
Category: Digital Animation, Ethnic Latin, Ethnic Spanish, Experimental, Independent, International, Multimedia, Online Festival, Touring
Profile: The Santa Monica Film Festival was created in 1997 as a way to recognize local and international Independent filmmakers. We've created a year-round film festival that leads to an annual accolade called Moxie! Awards. This unique format allows us to showcase a greater number of Independent films to a much larger and diversified audience.
Competitions: Yes
Application Fee: $15 (Short); $22 (Feature); $35 (Screenplay), Students Free.
Average Films Entered: 1200
Films Screened: 180
Odds of Acceptance: 1 in 12
Filmmaker Perks: Gala/festival passes. Free food/drinks. Gift package. Introductions to agents, producers and press. Free travel to five filmmakers. Lodging to five filmmakers
Attendance: 7,500+

MUSKEGON FiLM FESTiVAL

1922 Peck Street
Muskegon, MI 49441
Tel: 231-722-3012
Fax: 231-722-3124
Email: joeedick@pelican productions.com
Web Site: www.muskegonfilm festival.com
Festival Date: May
Entry Deadline: February
Contact: Jim Hanley
Director: Joe Edick
Programmer: Roberta King
Application Fee: $40 Features; $30 Short, Documentary, Experimental; $25 Animation; $15 Student Film

NANTUCKET FiLM FESTiVAL

P.O. Box 688 Prince Street Station
New York, NY 10012
Email: ackfest@aol.com
Web Site: www.nantucketfilm festival.org/
Festival Date: June
Entry Deadline: April
Contact: Jonathan Burkhart
Profile: This festival focuses on the art of screenwriting. It remains mostly non-competitive except for the screenplay competition. All film types are accepted. However, VHS and NTSC formats are preferred. All screenplays must be written in English.
Panels: Yes
Awards: Yes
Competitions: Yes
Major Awards: Best Screenplay
Past Judges: A jury awards prizes.
Application Fee: $20 (shorts) $35 (features) ($5 added for video return)

NASHViLLE iNDEPENDENT FiLM FESTiVAL

P.O. Box 24330
Nashville, TN 37202-4330
Tel: 615-742-2500
Fax: 615-742-1004
Email: niffilm@bellsouth.net
Web Site: www.nashvillefilm festival.org
Festival Date: June
Entry Deadline: April
Year Festival Began: 1969
Contact: Kelly Brownlee
Director: Kelly Brownlee
Category: Digital Animation, Documentary, Experimental, Independent, Markets, Episodic Television/Television Pilots, Young film/video maker & family & childrens films, Short, Student
Profile: We are the longest running film festival in the South. This is our thirtieth year of being dedicated to the development and expansion of independent film and video. We screen experimental, documen-

tary, student, feature, animated and high school films. These films cover all subject matter are received from all over the world.

Seminars: Yes

Panels: Yes

Famous Speakers: C.J. Cox, Cynthia Carl, Keith Crawford, Linda Seminski, Michael York, Les Blanc, Margeret Drain, Lilly Thomlin and Joan Tweeksbury.

Awards: Yes

Competitions: Yes

Major Awards: Best of Festival

Value of Awards: $1,500

Last Winning Directors: Barry J. Hershey

Application Tips: We judge on all around quality; story, production values and originality. Tell as strong story with good actors and clean prodution

Application Fee: yes. $10—Young Filmmaker; $35—Under 60 minutes; $50—over 60 minutes; $40—Television Entries

Insider Advice: Follow the instructions and submit all materials on time.

Average Films Entered: Approximately 600

Films Screened: 175

Odds of Acceptance: 1 in 4

Best Restaurants: Sunset Grill

Best Bars: Bluebird Cafe

Best Hangout for Filmmakers: Bongo Java Coffeehouse

Best Place for Breakfast: Fido

NEW DiRECTORS NEW FiLMS FESTiVAL

70 Lincoln Center Plaza
New York, NY 10023
Tel: 212-875-5610
Fax: 212-875-5636
Email: sbensman@filmlinc.com
Web Site: www.filmlinc.com
Festival Date: Spring
Entry Deadline: December
Contact: Sarah Bensman
Director: Marion Masone
Programmer: Richard Peña

NEW ENGLAND FiLM AND ViDEO FESTiVAL

Boston Film/Video Foundation
1126 Boylston Street, Suite 201
Boston, MA 02215
Tel: 617-536-1540
Fax: 617-536-3576
Email: info@bfvf.org
Web Site: www.bfvf.org
Festival Date: March–April
Entry Deadline: December
Contact: Devon Damonte
Director: Devon Damonte
Category: Independent
Profile: We offer audiences access to a diverse body of work by independent and student video and filmmakers and build the audience base for independent film.
Awards: Yes
Competitions: Yes
Major Awards: 14 awards given
Value of Awards: The awards total over $7,000
Application Fee: $35 (Independents) and $25 (Students)
Films Screened: 14 films screened

NEW ORLEANS FiLM AND ViDEO FESTiVAL

225 Baronne St., Suite 1712
New Orleans, LA 70112
Tel: 504-523-3818
Fax: 504-529-2430
Email: neworleansfilmfest@worldnet.att.net
Web Site: www.neworleans filmfest.com
Festival Date: October
Entry Deadline: April/May
Contact: Lindsay Ross
Director: Lindsay Ross
Category: Video

NEW YORK EXPO OF SHORT FiLM AND ViDEO

163 Amsterdam Avenue, PMB 107
New York, NY 10013-5001
Tel: 212-505-7742
Fax: 212-586-6391
Email: nyexpo@aol.com
Web Site: www.yrd.com/nyexpo

Festival Date: November
Entry Deadline: July
Contact: Robert Withers
Director: Anne Borin
Category: Short
Profile: One of the first festivals to recognize the talents of Spike Lee, George Lucas and Martha Coolidge. Approximately 1,500 attend.
Awards: Yes
Competitions: Yes
Major Awards: Jury Award; Gold, Silver, and Bronze Prizes
Value of Awards: Cash and film-stock awards given.
Application Fee: $35
Films Screened: 45
Odds of Acceptance: 1 in 17

NEW YORK FiLM FESTiVAL

Film Society of Lincoln Center
70 Lincoln Center Plaza
New York, NY 10023-6595
Tel: 212-875-5610
Fax: 212-875-5636
Email: sbensman@filmlinc.com
Web Site: www.filmlinc.com
Festival Date: September—October
Entry Deadline: July
Contact: Sarah Bensman
Director: Richard Peña
Category: International
Profile: The New York Film Festival ushers Autumn in with the newest and most significant works by directors—established icons and new discoveries alike—from all over the world. An enormously popular event, the festival stirs the hearts and minds of audiences and stimulates critical debate on the season's best movie-making.

Over the years, the New York Film Festival has proudly premiered films by Martin Scorsese, Jean-Luc Godard, François Truffaut, Akira Kurosawa, Jane Campion, Louis Malle, Jonathan Demme, James Ivory, Robert Altman, Barbara Kopple and Quentin Tarantino, among others.

The New York Film Festival prefers to screen a small number

of films despite its large nature. It has previously showcased a number of popular films such as *Pulp Fiction* (1994), *Secrets & Lies* (1996) and *The People vs. Larry Flynt* (1996).

Co-sponsored with the Museum of Modern Art, New Directors/New Films has earned an international reputation as the foremost forum for film art that breaks or re-makes the cinematic mold. As a festival dedicated to discovering emerging and overlooked artists, newcomers on the verge of mainstream success and distinguished veterans whose work deserves wider public attention, New Directors nurtures directorial talent by creating an invaluable opportunity for that talent to win public support and acceptance.

Awards: Yes
Competitions: No
Application Fee: None
Films Screened: Approximately 30
Odds of Acceptance: 1 in 40
Attendance: 75,000

NEW YORK GAY AND LESBIAN FILM FESTIVAL (THE NEW FESTIVAL)

47 Great Jones St., 6th floor
New York, NY 10012
Tel: 212-254-7228
Fax: 212-254-8655
Email: newfest@idt.net
Web Site: www.newfestival.org
Festival Date: June
Entry Deadline: Early: December Late: February
Contact: Basil Tsiokos
Director: Basil Tsiokos
Category: Gay Lesbian, Independent
Awards: Yes
Competitions: Yes
Major Awards: Best Feature, Best Documentary, Short Film
Application Fee: $15
Films Screened: 150
Odds of Acceptance: 1 in 3

NEW YORK INTERNATIONAL LATINO FILM FESTIVAL

(Mailing)
P. O. Box 1041
New York, NY 10023
(UPS & FEDEX)
170 East 116th St., Suite 1W
New York, NY 10029
Tel: 212-828-2433
Fax: 212-828-2450
Email: info@nylatinofilm.com
Web Site: www.NYLatinoFilm.com
Festival Date: May–June
Entry Deadline: March
Contact: Charles Rice-Gonzales
Director: Calixto Chinchilla
Programmer: Monica Wagenberg, International Programmer
Category: Documentary, Experimental, Short, Student
Profile: The New York International Latino Film Festival's (NYILFF) mission is to showcase films and the artists behind them that offer expansive images of the Latino experience during a weeklong event held in the world's media capital.

NEW YORK INTERNATIONAL VIDEO FESTIVAL

70 Lincoln Center Plaza
New York, NY 10023
Tel: 212-875-5610
Fax: 212-875-5636
Email: sbensman@filmlinc.com
Web Site: www.filmlinc.com
Festival Date: July
Entry Deadline: March
Contact: Sarah Bensman
Director: Marion Masone
Programmer: Richard Peña
Category: Video
Application Fee: None

NEW YORK LESBIAN AND GAY EXPERIMENTAL FILM AND VIDEO FESTIVAL (MIX FESTIVAL)

29 John St., PMB 132
New York, NY 10038
Tel: 212-571-4242
Fax: 212-571-5155
Email: info@mixnyc.org
Web Site: www.mixnyc.org
Festival Date: November
Entry Deadline: Early: June Late: July
Contact: Jonathan Aubrey
Director: Jonathan Aubrey
Category: Gay Lesbian, Experimental
Profile: It focuses mainly on experimental filmmaking. Approximately 3,000 attend.
Awards: No
Competitions: No
Application Fee: $10
Films Screened: 100-150
Odds of Acceptance: 1 in 4

NEW YORK LOWER EAST SIDE FILM FESTIVAL

360 E. 55th St., Suite 20
New York, NY 10022
Tel: 212-358-3557
Email: lisa@nylesff.com
Web Site: www.nylesff.com
Festival Date: April
Entry Deadline: March
Contact: Lisa Woo
Director: Lisa Woo
Programmer: Tom Dunkley
Category: Animation, Documentary, Short

NEW YORK NATIONAL HIGH SCHOOL FILM AND VIDEO FESTIVAL

Trinity School
101 W. 91st St.
New York, NY 10024
Tel: 212-873-1650
Fax: 212-799-3417
Entry Deadline: February
Contact: John Dooley
Category: Student

NEW YORK UNDERGROUND FiLM FESTIVAL

453 W. 16th St., Office Six
New York, NY 10011
Tel: 212-675-1137
Fax: 212-675-1152
Email: festival@nyuff.com
Web Site: www.nyuff.com/
Festival Date: March
Entry Deadline: Early: December; Late: January
Contact: Ed Halter
Director: Ed Halter
Category: Independent
Profile: This annual festival showcases independent and unique films. It focuses on innovative projects that go beyond mainstream filmmaking. Approximately 10,000 attend annually.

Gore Score · · · · · · · · · · · · · · ·
NYUFF is the "must-attend" event in New York. If you have a weird film in need of exposure or if you just want to experience the best of the strangest films ever made, NYUFF is the place to see exciting, vibrant work.

Seminars: Yes
Awards: Yes
Competitions: Yes
Major Awards: Best Feature, Short, Documentary, Animation, Experimental and Festival Choice Award.
Application Fee: $30-35 U.S.
Films Screened: 75 screened
Odds of Acceptance: 1 in 8

NEWPORT BEACH FiLM FESTIVAL

4540 Campus Dr., Suite 100
Newport Beach, CA 92660
Tel: 949-253-2880
Fax: 949-253-2881
Web Site: www.newportbeach
filmfest.com
Festival Date: March—April
Entry Deadline: January
Contact: Todd Quartararo
Director: Gregg Schwenk
Category: Animation, Documentary, Short
Awards: Yes

Major Awards: Jury Award, Audience Award, Director's Award

NEWPORT INTERNATIONAL FiLM FESTIVAL

P.O. Box 146
Newport, RI 02840
Tel: 212-755-2743
Fax: 212-755-2717
Email: newportff@aol.com
Web Site: www.newportfilm
festival.com
Festival Date: June
Entry Deadline: February
Contact: Nancy Donahoe
Director: Nancy Donahoe
Programmer: Maude Chilton
Category: Animation, Independent, Short

NEXT FRAME: UFVA'S TOURiNG FESTiVAL OF iNTERNATiONAL STUDENT FiLM AND ViDEO

Dept. of Film & Media Arts
9 Annenberg Hall
13th & Diamond St.
Temple University 011-00
Philadelphia, PA 19122
Tel: 215-923-3532; 800-499-UFVA (Within USA)
Fax: 215-204-6740
Email: ufva@zm.temple.edu
Web Site: www.temple.edu/
nextframe
Festival Date: October
Entry Deadline: May
Year Festival Began: 1993
Contact: Vanessa Briceño & Brian Johns
Director: Vanessa Briceño & Brian Johns
Other Staff: Zoe Haley, Tour Coordinator
Category: Animation, Documentary, Experimental, Narrative, Student, Touring (Australia, Canada, Columbia, Mexico, New Zealand, Philippines, Portugal and Uruguay)
Awards: Yes
Competitions: Yes

Application Fee: USA—$20, $25 if late. International and UFVA Members $15, $20 if late.

NO DANCE FiLM FESTIVAL

(Entries/deliveries)
703 Pier Avenue #675
Hermosa Beach, CA 90254
(Nodance HQ during January)
Main Street Mall
333 Main Street
Park City, Utah
Tel: 310-939-6269
Fax: 310-374-0134
Email: info@nodance.com
Web Site: www.nodance.com
Festival Date: January
Entry Deadline: November/December
Year Festival Began: 1998
Contact: James Boyd
Director: James Boyd
Programmer: Mike Kernan, Will Hartman, Ali Hileman, Echo Gaffney
Other Staff: Drew Pinson, Bob Ray
Category: American Films, Digital, Documentary, DVD, First-Time Independent Filmmakers, Gay Lesbian, Markets, Microcinema, Multimedia, Online Festival, Short, Touring (Austin, TX; Cannes, France; Toronto, Canada; Los Angeles, CA), Underground
Profile: Held annually in Park City, Utah, The Nodance.com Film & Multimedia Festival is the world's first DVD-projected film festival, running alongside the Sundance and Slamdance Film Festivals.

Gore Score · · · · · · · · · · · · · · ·
Nodance is doing important work by giving digital shorts and features a much-needed voice. For exposure of shorts and new digital work, there is no better place in Park City. Sundance take note: Nodance is here to stay.

Competitions: Yes
Major Awards: Grand Jury Award, Audience Award, Golden Orbs (best marketing)
Value of Awards: Nominal

Application Fee: $25 (early); $50 (late)

Common Mistakes: Don't follow application guidelines. Late entry.

Insider Advice: Don't get into Sundance or Slamdance. Concentrate on story structure. Enter early.

Films Screened: 30

Odds of Acceptance: 1 in 10

Attendance: 500 per day

Journalist Attendance: 50-100 estimated

Tourist Information: Egyptian Theater on Main Street

Travel Tips: Plan to attend Park City early enough to get lodging: www.parkcitylodging.com

Best Restaurants: Texas Reds

Best Bars: Harry-O's

Best Parties: Nodance after-hours parties (nightly)

Best Hangout for Filmmakers: Nodance HQ, Slamdance HQ, Front of Egyptian Theater, Front of Harry-O's Bar

Best Place for Breakfast: Sleep through it. Get your rest.

NORTH CAROLiNA GAY AND LESBiAN FiLM FESTiVAL

309 West Morgan St.

Durham, NC 27701

Tel: 919-560-3040 ext. 232

Fax: 919-560-3065

Email: jim@carolinatheatre.org

Web Site: www.carolinatheatre. org

Festival Date: August

Entry Deadline: May

Year Festival Began: 1995

Contact: Jim Carl

Programmer: Jim Carl, Director of Programming

Category: Gay Lesbian

Market: No

Competitions: Yes

Major Awards: Emerging Film Award

Value of Awards: Certificate

Past Judges: Programming Committee of 20-25 community volunteers selects winner.

Common Mistakes: Submit videos in PAL format; do not supply contact info; no marketing materials.

Gus Van Sant makes the rounds at the Northwest Film & Video Festival.

Insider Advice: Transfer videos to 16mm or 35mm; do not contact festival programmers too early!

Average Films Entered: 16mm, 35mm only

Films Screened: 27

Odds of Acceptance: 1 in 3

Filmmaker Perks: Dependent on budget, we offer free travel, lodging and festival passes, as well as opportunity to "present" their films to the audience.

Attendance: Over 4,000 and growing.

Journalist Attendance: Varies

Best Luxury Hotels: Durham Marriott, located adjacent to the theatre. 919-683-6664

Best Restaurants: Pop's, Brightleaf 905, Anotherthyme

NORTHAMPTON FiLM FESTiVAL

351 Pleasant St. No. 213

Northampton, MA 01060

Tel: 413-586-3471

Fax: 413-584-4432

Email: filmfest@nohofilm.org

Web Site: www.nohofilm.org

Festival Date: November

Entry Deadline: June

Contact: Howard Polansky or Dee De Geiso

Director: Howard Polansky

Programmer: Dee De Geiso

Category: Animation, Documentary, Experimental, Short

NORTHWEST FiLM & ViDEO FESTiVAL

"Some of the origins of my filmmaking come from this Festival. I have always considered this regional ritual to be one of the most exciting and beautiful things about filmmaking."

—Gus Van Sant, Director, 21st Festival Judge.

1219 SW Park Ave.

Portland, OR 97205

Tel: 503-221-1156

Fax: 503-294-0874

Email: info@nwfilm.org

Web Site: www.nwfilm.org

Festival Date: November 2-11, 2001

Entry Deadline: August 1, 2001

Year Festival Began: 1972

Contact: Jenny Jones

Director: Bill Foster

Programmer: Meagan Atiyeh

Category: American Films, Animation, Digital, Documentary, Experimental, First-Time Independent Filmmakers, Independent, Multimedia, Performance, Short, Super 8/8mm, Touring (Seattle, WA; Vancouver, BC; Anchorage, AK; Olympia, WA; Boise, ID; Helena, WA; Eugene OR), Video, Weird

Profile: The NWF&VF is an annual juried survey of new moving image art produced by artists residing in Oregon, Washington, Idaho, Montana, Alaska and British Colombia. Following the screenings in Portland, a touring program of Festival Winners travels throughout the Northwest and to select national venues.

Seminars: Yes

Panels: Yes

Famous Speakers: Yes

Market: No

Awards: Yes

Competitions: Yes

Major Awards: Judges Awards

Value of Awards: $12-15,000

Application Fee: No entry fee, but $15 for return shipping costs per entry (U.S. $20 for Canadian residents). For return of tape, enclose check for U.S. $15 for domestic shipping, U.S. $20 for international.

Insider Advice: Good video copy for the jurying—strong photos for program and press

Average Films Entered: Personal ones

Films Screened: 30-60

Odds of Acceptance: 10%—15%

Filmmaker Perks: Free travel, lodging

Attendance: 6,000

Journalist Attendance: 12

Tourist Information: Powell's Books

Travel Tips: Suntan lotion, of course.

Best Cheap Hotels: Mallory

Best Luxury Hotels: Heathman

Best Bars: Saucebox

Best Hangout for Filmmakers: Montage

Best Place for Breakfast: Bijou

ODYSSEYFEST SCiENCE FiCTION AND FANTASY FiLM FESTiVAL

978 South Main

Lindon, UT 84042

Tel: 801-418-8123

Fax: 801-225-5135

Email: Submissions@OdysseyFest.com

Web Site: www.OdysseyFest.com

Festival Date: January

Entry Deadline: October

Category: Fantasy/Science Fiction

Profile: A festival to showcase the work of independent science fiction and fantasy film makers.

We'd like to help establish the field of science fiction and fantasy as legitimate film/art.

Competitions: Yes

Major Awards: Best Independent Film, Best Worldbuilding, Most Original Idea.

Application Fee: $15 for shorts, $40 for full-length

Insider Advice: No horror. No properties for which you don't have the license. If you send us Star Wars material, you'd better be George Lucas. Strong story and originality given precedence.

OHiO iNDEPENDENT FiLM FESTiVAL

1121 Clark Ave.

Cleveland, OH 44109

Tel: 216-781-1755

Fax: 216-696-6610

Email: OhioIndieFilmFest@juno.com

Web Site: www.ohiofilms.com

Festival Date: November 2001

Entry Deadline: Early: August 1, 2001; Late: September 1, 2001

Year Festival Began: 1994

Contact: Bernadette Gillota, Annetta Marion

Director: Bernadette Gillota, Annetta Marion

Category: American Films, Animation, Digital, Digital Animation, Documentary, Ethnic African, Ethnic Asian, Ethnic Black, Ethnic Jewish, Ethnic Latin, Ethnic Other, Ethnic Spanish, Experimental, First-Time Independent Filmmakers, Gay Lesbian, Independent, International, Markets, Multimedia, Online Festival, Short, Student, Super 8/8mm, Underground, Video, Weird, Woman

Profile: The mission of the OIFF is to be the leading organization in Ohio dedicated to freedom of expression through the art of independent media, by encouraging emerging artists, and by providing a consistent, reputable venue for work the public may not otherwise see. The OIFF accomplishes our mission by facilitating grassroots networking for independent media makers, by acting as the accessible step

between local filmmakers and the larger world of independent film, and through educational programs and workshops.

Gore Score ···············

OIFF deserves a lot of credit for not only bringing indie film to the midwest, but for providing helpful guidance to filmmakers.

Seminars: Yes

Panels: Yes

Market: Yes, usually a couple of shorts buyers in attendance.

Competitions: Yes, audience awards

Major Awards: Best of the Fest

Value of Awards: varies (usually film stock or processing certificates).

Application Tips: Even though we accept work from around the world, it would be beneficial to play up any Ohio connections you (or anyone involved with the project) might have.

Application Fee: $15 for anything under 20 minutes and $20 for 20 minutes and over—August 1st deadline

Fees double for late entries—September 1st

Common Mistakes: Fill out the entry form wrong/give inadequate information.

Insider Advice: Keep it short.

Films Screened: Approximately 100

Odds of Acceptance: Approximately 1 in 3

Filmmaker Perks: Food, drinks.

Attendance: 2,500

Journalist Attendance: Varies—usually 5 or so (TV and print)

Tourist Information: Tremont, Warehouse district, the Lakefront

Best Luxury Hotels: Marriott, Ritz Carlton

Best Restaurants: Grumpy's, Luchita's

Best Bars: The Literary

Best Hangout for Filmmakers: Parkview, Civilization

Best Place for Breakfast: Grumpy's

OJAi FiLM FESTiVAL

P.O. Box 545
Ojai, CA 93024
Tel: 805-640-1947
Email: filmfestival@ojai.net
Web Site: www.filmfestival.
ojai.net
Director: Pauletta Walsh
805-649-4394
pwalsh1998@aol.com
Programmer: Elizabeth
Grumette
805-649-4000
stevo@ix.netcom.com
Category: All genres, Video
Profile: The Ojai Film Festival is
a celebration of cinema, featuring
screenings, workshops, a youth
film festival and celebrity receptions in a village atmosphere.
Outstanding films will be recognized at a gala awards banquet.
Application Fee: $35 for 35mm,
$25 for all other formats, and
$20 for student-produced work
in any category.

OLYMPiA—GENDER QUEER: NORTHWEST TRANSGENDER AND iNTERSEX FiLM

Evergreen Queer Alliance
Cab 314
The Evergreen State College
Olympia, WA 98505
Tel: 360-867-6544
Fax: 360-866-6685
Email: genderqueerfilmfest@
hotmail.com or
evergreen_queer_alliance@
hotmail.com
Web Site:
http://EvergreenQueers.tripod.
com/genderqueer/main.html
Festival Date: May
Entry Deadline: April
Contact: Walker Burch-Lewis
Category: Gay Lesbian

OTTAWA iNTERNATiONAL ANiMATiON FESTiVAL

2 Daly Ave., Suite 120
Ottawa, Ontario K1N 6E2
Canada
Tel: 613-232-8769
Fax: 613-232-6315
Email: oiaf@ottawa.com
Web Site: www.awn.com/ottawa
Festival Date: Fall
Entry Deadline: July
Year Festival Began: 1976
Contact: Chris Robinson
Director: Chris Robinson
Programmer: Chris Robinson.
We also contract a variety of
animation professionals to pro-
gram our retrospectives and
tribute programs.
Category: Animation
Profile: The Ottawa International
Animation Festival is North
America's only competitive ani-
mation festival, and one of the
largest animation events in the
world. The festival attracts a
total audience of more than
25,000.

Like the industry itself, the
OIAF is getting bigger, yet we
remain very much committed to
the art and culture of animation;
independent animators and small
animation studios have always-
and will always-represent the
heart of the OIAF and its activities. New scholarships, networking and recruiting parties, subsi-
dized sponsorships, cash prizes,
and free student workshops are
only a few of the ways in which
we "give back." More than simply
a biennial festival, the OIAF has
become a year round resource
center for independent animators and the animation community alike.
Seminars: Yes
Panels: Yes
Awards: Yes
Competitions: Yes
Major Awards: Grand Prize
Value of Awards: Priceless. No
actual cash prize at this time, but
the exposure from the
Grand Prize is a great asset.
Application Tips: Make a good
film. Seriously though, the OIAF
is not interested in stagnant television animation. Uniqueness and
a willing to experiment are
important. Innovative stories and
techniques are also encouraged.
Application Fee: None.
Insider Advice: Label tapes correctly and make sure that they
are cued to the beginning of the
film. Don't get down if your film
is not selected. The OIAF

receives over 1000 entries and
features a strict selection
process. In order to ensure that
we screen only the best films,
our competition program features only six screenings.
Films Screened: Including retrospectives, well over 300 films.
Odds of Acceptance: 1 in 10
Filmmaker Perks: We offer lodging, festival pass and a small
per diem (for independent filmmakers only). For other attendees, we do our best to find
them the best rates on lodging
and travel. Ottawa also features
a number of social activities
including our world famous animator's picnic, Chez-Ani (a gathering place for attendees), and a
handful of sponsor hosted parties. It is the place to be for anyone and everyone in animation.
Every major and minor player in
animation comes to the festival.
Tourist Information: Ottawa,
Canada's capital city, features a
number of tourist sites: National
Art Gallery, Museum of
Civilization, Parliament Buildings,
Byward Market, Rideau Canal
(longest skating rink in the world
come winter), a number of parks
and bike paths for those interested in the natural side.
Travel Tips: In October, you
never know what the weather
will be like. Prepare for warm
and cold winter. Ottawa is walkable. Don't bother renting a car.
Best Restaurants: There are a
number of restaurants in the
Byward Market and along Elgin
Street (2-3 minute walk from the
festival).
Best Bars: Depends on the person. If you want to drink and
chat, the Black Tomato is easily
the best bar. They feature a number of local beers and have a
menu for whiskies. They also feature great food and sell CDs!
Best Hangout for Filmmakers:
Our own Chez-Ani is where
everyone goes
Best Place for Breakfast: Boko
Bakery in the Byward Market.

OUT AT THE MOViES: SAN ANTONiO'S ANNUAL FESTiVAL OF LESBiAN & GAY FiLM

922 San Pedro
San Antonio, TX 78212
Tel: 210-228-0201
Fax: Fax: 210-228-0000
Email: outfilmtx@aol.com
Web Site: www.esperanza center.org
Festival Date: September
Contact: Phillip Avilla
Director: Phillip Avilla
Category: Gay Lesbian
Profile: It is the aim of Out At The Movies to exhibit contemporary Lesbian & Gay film/video, to demonstrate the strength and diversity of Lesbian & Gay culture, to increase discussion of current social issues within Queer communities, and to promote media education.
Panels: Yes
Awards: No
Competitions: No
Application Fee: No
Odds of Acceptance: 1 in 4
Filmmaker Perks: We offer free travel and lodging.

OUT iN AKRON QUEER SHORTS FiLM FESTiVAL

1663 Main St.
Peninsula, OH 44264
Email: grant348@juno.com
Web Site: outinakron.org

Year Festival Began: 1997
Contact: Lori Grant
Director: Chris Hixon (Chair)
Sandra Kurt (Co-Chair)
Programmer: Lori Grant
Category: American Films, Experimental, Gay Lesbian, Independent, Multimedia, Short, Weird
Profile: "Out in Akron, Inc." was created in 1997 to foster awareness of gay, lesbian, bisexual and transgender culture through the presentation of the annual "Out in Akron Cultural Festival," an annual weekend of film, performance and forums. "Out in Akron" aims to celebrate diversity, educate the community, and provide an experience that is an accurate reflection of the contributions of GLBT people to our culture.
Market: No
Competitions: Yes
Application Fee: None
Films Screened: 10-20
Odds of Acceptance: 1 in 5
Journalist Attendance: 1-5
Tourist Information: Akron Art Museum, Inventor's Hall of Fame, Stan Hywett Hall, Cuyahoga Valley Parks and Recreation Area
Best Restaurants: Ken Stewart's
Best Bars: Babylon
Best Hangout for Filmmakers: Angel Falls Coffehouse
Best Place for Breakfast: Dodie's (not smoke-free)

OUT TAKES DALLAS THE ANNUAL LESBiAN AND GAY FiLM FESTiVAL

3818 Cedar Springs Rd., 101-405
Dallas, TX 75219
Tel: 214-350-1540
Email: outtakes@iname.com
Web Site: www.outtakesdallas. org
Festival Date: November
Entry Deadline: August
Contact: Tim McMullen or David Sullivan
Director: Tim McMullen or David Sullivan
Category: Gay Lesbian

OUTFAR!— ANNUAL PHOENiX iNTERNATiONAL LESBiAN AND GAY FiLM FESTiVAL

819 W. Solano Dr.
Phoenix, AZ 85013
Tel: 602-249-1074
Email: outfarfest@excite.com
Web Site: www.outfar.org
Festival Date: February 15-18, 2001
Entry Deadline: December
Year Festival Began: 1997
Contact: Amy Ettinger
Director: Amy Ettinger
Category: American Films, Animation, Documentary, First-Time Independent Filmmakers, Gay Lesbian, Independent, International, Markets, Short, Video
Profile: OutFar! seeks to program the most current, compelling, entertaining and educational films for the lesbian, gay, bi and trans community. And, to raise funds for other community related causes. The film festival occurs every February for four days and nights. Films are geared towards the alternative community at large and include a variety of subjects, themes and messages. The programming is meant to foster a sense of belonging, togetherness and to forge alliances.
Market: No
Competitions: Yes
Major Awards: Best Film, Best Gay Film, Best Lesbian Film,

BEST GAY FILM FESTIVALS

Atlanta Gay and Lesbian Film Festival - Out on Film
Out At The Movies: San Antonio's Annual Festival of Lesbian & Gay Film
Out in Akron Queer Shorts Film Festival
OutFar! - Annual Phoenix International Lesbian and Gay Film Festival
Out Fest: Los Angeles International Gay and Lesbian Film & Video Festival
North Carolina Gay and Lesbian Film Festival
Philadelphia International Gay and Lesbian Film Festival
Sacramento International Gay and Lesbian Film Festival
San Francisco Lesbian and Gay Film Festival
Seattle Lesbian & Gay Film Festival

Vision Award for Best Short Subject

Value of Awards: Vision Award for Best Short Subject—$250

Application Fee: None

Common Mistakes: Please send a final version of your video if at all possible. Watching digitized videos is difficult.

Insider Advice: Submit early! Many filmmakers have a tendency to send on or after the last deadline day. Although the deadline seems distant, much of the programming begins to take shape by September. There is less chance of adding material into the program blocks as the deadline approaches.

Average Films Entered: Produced by and/or about lesbians, gays, bisexual and transgender people. Content must be relevant to gays, lesbians, bisexual and transgender people. Production must exhibit technical proficiency and creative/artistic execution.

Films Screened: 10

Odds of Acceptance: 1 in 4

Filmmaker Perks: Free travel and lodging for a director or actor in lieu of film rental fees.

Attendance: 3,500

Tourist Information: Scottsdale's Old Town to the Grand Canyon

Travel Tips: Book lodging in advance as October through April is tourist season. Most hotels will sell out well before February.

Best Luxury Hotels: The Ritz, The Biltmore, The Phoenician

Best Restaurants: Vincent Gerithault, Tarbells, Christopher's

Best Bars: AZ88, Tarbells, Royal Palms

Best Place for Breakfast: Golden Swan in the Gainey Hyatt—Brunch!!!

OUTFEST: LOS ANGELES INTERNATIONAL GAY AND LESBIAN FILM & VIDEO FESTIVAL

1125 N. McCadden Place
Suite 235
Los Angeles, CA 90038
Tel: 323-960-9200

Fax: 323-960-2397
Email: outfest@outfest.org
Web Site: www.outfest.org
Festival Date: July
Entry Deadline: March
Year Festival Began: 1982
Contact: Stephen Gutwillig
Director: Stephen Gutwillig
Category: Gay Lesbian, Independent
Awards: Yes
Competitions: Yes
Major Awards: Three winners for excellence in filmmaking. Six audience awards
Value of Awards: Cash awards

PALM BEACH INTERNATIONAL FILM FESTIVAL

1555 Palm Beach Lakes Blvd., Suite 804
West Palm Beach, FL 33401
Tel: 561-233-1044; 561-866-6113
Fax: 561-683-6655
Email: PBFilmFest@aol.com
Web Site: www.pbifilmfest.org
Festival Date: April
Entry Deadline: February
Contact: Susan Fraine
Director: Susan Fraine
Programmer: Mark Diamond
Competitions: Yes
Films Screened: 50+

PALM SPRINGS GAY & LESBIAN FILM FESTIVAL

67900 Carroll Drive
Cathedral City, CA 92234
Tel: 760-770-2042
Fax: 760-770-2042
Email: MAndrunas@aol.com
Web Site: N/A
Festival Date: October
Entry Deadline: July
Contact: Michael Andrunas
Director: Michael Andrunas
Category: Gay Lesbian

PALM SPRINGS INTERNATIONAL FILM FESTIVAL

P. O. Box 2230
Palm Springs, CA 92263-2230
Tel: 760-322-2930
Fax: 760-322-4087
Email: info@psfilmfest.org
Web Site: www.psfilmfest.org
Festival Date: January
Entry Deadline: November
Director: Denis Pregnolato
Awards: Yes
Competitions: No
Major Awards: Charles A. Crain Desert Pam Acheivement Award; International Filmmaker Award; Director's Lifetime Achievement; Frederick Loewe Acheivement Award; Outstanding Acheivement in Craft Award
Application Fee: $25 (shorts) $60 (features)
Attendance: 50,000

PAN AFRICAN FILM & ARTS FESTIVAL

P.O. Box 2418
Beverly Hills, CA 90213
Tel: 323-295-1706
Fax: 323-295-1952
Email: LAPAFF@aol.cm
Web Site: www.paff.org
Festival Date: February
Entry Deadline: October
Contact: Asantewa Olatunji
Director: Ayuko Babu
Programmer: Asantewa Olatunji

PHILADELPHIA FESTIVAL OF WORLD CINEMA

TLA Video
234 Market St., 4th Floor
Philadelphia, PA 19106
Tel: 215-733-0608; 800-333-8521
Fax: 215-733-0668
Email: rmurray@tlavideo.com
Web Site: www.tlavideo.com/pfwc
Festival Date: April–May
Entry Deadline: February
Contact: Jennifer Arndt
Director: Jennifer Arndt
Programmer: Ray Murray
Category: International

Competitions: No
Application Fee: Varies
Odds of Acceptance: over 300 films entered.

PHILADELPHIA INTERNATIONAL GAY AND LESBIAN FILM FESTIVAL

234 Market Street, Fifth Floor
Philadelphia, PA 19106
Tel: 215-733-0608
Fax: 215-733-0637
Email: tcardwell@tlavideo.com
Web Site: www.tlavideo.com
Festival Date: July
Entry Deadline: April
Contact: Tom Cardwell x 37—Managing Director
Director: Raymond Murray
Programmer: Features: Raymond Murray; Shorts: Bent Hill and Tiffany Naiman
Category: Gay Lesbian
Profile: The Philadelphia International Gay and Lesbian Film Festival screens over 130 films, making it one of the largest gay and lesbian festivals in the country.
Panels: Yes
Awards: Yes
Competitions: Yes
Major Awards: Audience Award for Best Feature Film and Audience Award for Best Documentary Film.
Value of Awards: None
Past Judges: Audience ballots
Application Fee: None
Average Films Entered: All types of films that either feature gay and lesbian characters prominately in the film, films directed by or starring out gays and lesbians
Odds of Acceptance: Hundreds are submitted for the approximately 80 slots.
Filmmaker Perks: We offer free travel, a food stipend and lodging for the director or star
Best Restaurants: Judy's
Best Bars: Gay: Woody's; Lesbian: Sisters

PHOENIX FILM FESTIVAL

5501 N. 7th Ave., #719
Phoenix, AZ 85013
Tel: 877-358-1574
Fax: 800-293-7936
Email: director@phxfilm.com
Web Site: www.phoenixfilm festival.com
Festival Date: February
Entry Deadline: December
Year Festival Began: 2000
Category: Independent
Profile: The Phoenix Film Festival, held at the AMC Arizona Center Cinema, is an international event celebrating the art of true independent film. All features, aside from those included in the Tributes or the Midnight Independent Classic Series, have a budget of one million dollars or under. The festival is a gathering of film aficionados (both lovers and creators of cinema) who come together from all over the world and from all walks of life to see and discuss and celebrate the art of independent film. The program consists of thirty major film events, including three Tributes to individual artists, two short film competitions, and four Midnight Independent Classics. These events are supplemented by formal and informal conversations and seminars with the filmmakers and artists in attendance, as well as parties and other events.

PITTSBURGH INTERNATIONAL LESBIAN AND GAY FILM FESTIVAL

P.O. Box 81237
Pittsburgh, PA 15217
Tel: 412-232-3277
Email: pilgffest@aol.com
Web Site: www.pilgff.org
Contact: Vanessa Doico and Trina Brown
Category: Gay Lesbian

PORTLAND INTERNATIONAL FILM FESTIVAL

Northwest Film Center
1219 SW Park Ave.
Portland, OR 97205
Tel: 503-221-1156
Fax: 503-294-0874
Email: info@nwfilm.org
Web Site: www.nwfilm.org
Festival Date: Feb. 9-27, 2001
Entry Deadline: November
Year Festival Began: 1977
Contact: Jenny Jones
Director: Bill Foster, Director of the Northwest Film Center
Programmer: Meagan Atiyeh
Category: American Films, Documentary, First-Time Independent Filmmakers, Independent, International, Short, Video
Profile: The Portland International Film festival is an annual invitational survey of new world cinema produced by the Northwest Film Center. The major film event in Oregon, the Festival draws 30,000+ people from throughout the region to see approximately seventy feature and thirty short films from over two dozen countries.
Seminars: Yes
Panels: Yes
Competitions: Yes
Major Awards: Bravo/AT&T Best of the Festival Award
Application Fee: $25 fee for entry. All formats accepted, no entry form required. For return of tape, enclose check for U.S. $15 for domestic shipping, U.S. $20 for international.
Insider Advice: Submit a good video cassette; strong photos and materials for program & press.
Films Screened: 90-100
Odds of Acceptance: 1 in 15
Filmmaker Perks: Free travel, lodging, fame...
Attendance: 30-32,000
Tourist Information: Powell's Books
Best Restaurants: Saucebox
Best Bars: Mallory
Best Hangout for Filmmakers: Montage
Best Place for Breakfast: Bijou

PXL THiS

2427 1/2 Glyndon Ave.
Venice, CA 90291
Tel: 310-306-7330
Festival Date: August
Entry Deadline: August
Contact: Gerry Fialka
Category: Documentary,
Experimental, Underground,
Weird
Profile: PXL This is a video festival featuring videos made with the PXL-2000 toy camera—pixelvision.

REEL AFFiRMATiONS FiLM FESTiVAL

P.O. Box 73528
Washington, DC 20005
(Shipping)
1333 H Street NW, Suite 600 W
Washington, DC 20056
Tel: 202-986-1119
Fax: 202-326-0402
Email: info@reelaffirmations.org
Web Site: www.reelaffirmations.org
Festival Date: October
Entry Deadline: May
Contact: Sarah Kellogg
Director: Sarah Kellogg
Category: Gay Lesbian, Independent
Awards: Yes
Competitions: Yes
Value of Awards: $1000 Work in Progress Grant for Excellence in Filmmaking
Application Fee: $10
Odds of Acceptance: 1 in 5
Filmmaker Perks: We provide feature filmmakers and the director's award winners free travel, lodging, etc. As we grow in size, we hope to have the sponsors to provide travel and lodging for all filmmakers. We have two Hospitality Coordinators who will work out the details of your travel, hotel accomodations and travel to and from venues for you.
Travel Tips: If you're coming from NYC, take Peter Pan or Trailways—it's less used than Amtrak and never has those irritating, excruciating delays out of Penn Station.

Best Restaurants: Best Chinese: City Lights of China
Best New American: Nora's or the Old Tabard Inn
Best Lunch: Luna Grill or Teaism
Best Italian: Goldoni's
Best Hangout for Filmmakers: JRs and Slyde
Best Place for Breakfast: Luna Grill

REEL MUSiC FESTiVAL

Northwest Film Center of Portland Art Museum
1219 SW Park Ave.
Portland, OR 97205
Tel: 503-221-1156
Fax: 503-294-0874
Email: info@nwfilm.org
Web Site: www.nwfilm.org
Festival Date: January
Entry Deadline: November
Contact: Public Relations Coordinator
Director: Bill Foster
Programmer: Bill Foster
Profile: The Northwest Film Center's annual winter celebration of music and film showcases a diversity of musical forms and visions. New documentaries, artist profiles and visiting artists will be presented.
Average Films Entered: All formats accepted, no entry form required.
Random Tidbits: For return of tape, enclose check for U.S. $15 for domestic shipping and handling, U.S. $20 for international.

RESFEST DiGiTAL FiLM FESTiVAL

601 W. 26th St., 11th Floor
New York, NY 10001
Tel: 212-217-1154
Fax: 212-937-7134
Email: resfest@resfest.com
Web Site: www.resfest.com
Entry Deadline: None. Accepts entries year-round.
Year Festival Began: 1997
Contact: Jonathan Wells
Director: Jonathan Wells
Programmer: Jonathan Wells, Johnny Scalisse, John Turk

Category: Digital, Digital Animation, DVD, Independent, Short, Super 8/8mm, Touring
Profile: ResFest is a touring festival dedicated to the exhibition and promotion of digital filmmaking. We showcase innovative short films that have been empowered by new digital production tools. Entries can be shot on any acquisition format (film, analog/digital video, CGI etc.), but must make use of computer editing and/or effects software. ResFest only exhibits videotape, with the exception of 35mm features, CD-ROMs and DVDs.

Gore Score · · · · · · · · · · · · · · ·
Perhaps one of the best touring festivals in the U.S., if not the world. One part rave party and one part film festival, ResFest has established itself as the place to see the most innovative new digital work. Period. ResFest also publishes a magazine about digital filmmaking and releases DVDs of short digital films.

Application Fee: $15—$20
Average Films Entered: 1200
Films Screened: 75
Odds of Acceptance: 1 in 16

RHODE iSLAND iNTERNATiONAL FiLM FESTiVAL

P.O. Box 162
Newport RI 02840-0002
Tel: 401-861-4445
Fax: 401-847-7590;
401-861-4443
Email: flicksart@aol.com
Web Site: www.film-festival.org
Festival Date: August
Entry Deadline: June
Year Festival Began: 1997
Director: George T. Marshall, Executive Director
Elisabeth Newberry Galligan, Managing Director
Programmer: Christian de Rezendes, Programming Director
Category: American Films, Animation, Digital, Digital Animation, Documentary, DVD, Ethnic African, Ethnic Asian, Ethnic Black, Ethnic Jewish, Ethnic Latin, Ethnic Spanish, Experimental, Fantasy/Science

Fiction, First-Time Independent Filmmakers, Gay Lesbian, Independent, International, Markets, Multimedia, Online Festival, Short, Student, Underground, Video, Weird, Woman

Profile: From its debut in 1997, the Rhode Island International Film Festival (RIIFF) has captured the attention of movers and shakers in the world of independent film. Rhode Island native Bobby Farrelly was so impressed with what he saw in the festival's first year that he agreed to premier his next film at the second year's festival, a film titled *There's Something About Mary*.

The Festival is dedicated to the creation of opportunities for artistic interaction and exchange among independent film directors, producers, distributors, backers and the film-going community. Its intent is to help preserve the past and promote the future of filmmaking. The Festival's goal is to bridge the gap between the entertainment industry and the global creative community and promote opportunities for distribution.

Gore Score ················
One of the most exciting new festivals to come along, RIIFF aggressively supports its filmmakers.

Seminars: We offer three educational programs: KidsEye™ a four-day summer camp for kids ages 8-17 years old; ScriptBiz™ an intensive day-long seminar of selling your script; and Take One, Two, Three: Filmmaking with the Pros: a three-day master class on production which includes a shoot and edit component.

Panels: Yes
Market: Yes
Awards: Yes
Competitions: Yes
Major Awards: We offer several awards during the Festival, plus Honorary Awards. These include: The RIIFF Roger Williams Humanitarian Award; the RIIFF Individual Vision Award; the RIIFF Screenwriting Award; the RIIFF Independent Man Award for Best Feature, Best Short, Best Editing, Best Animation, Best Director, Best Documentary, The Tourisme Québec Award for Foreign Film, Best Score, The Brooks Pharmacy Positive Lifestyle Award, Kodak Vision Award, The Final Draft Original Screenplay Award, and the RI Fest Favorites (chosen by the public in four categories).

Value of Awards: The Screenplay Award is worth $2,500. The other awards may include cash, film stock, trophies and prizes.

Application Fee: $30 for shorts under 45 mins.
$50 for films over 45 mins.
$30 for screenplay entries
$5 for KidsEye™ entries

Common Mistakes: They do not always label their tapes. That becomes a problem for judges.

Insider Advice: Submit early to the film festival and with as much complete information about you and your film as possible.

Films Screened: 150 over 5 days
Odds of Acceptance: 1 in 2
Filmmaker Perks: We offer flight discounts, food/restaurant discounts, free access to special festival parties, a filmmaker lounge, internet access, press room for interview, film review location,

Q&A opportunities, and access to distribution contacts.
Attendance: 13,500
Journalist Attendance: 35
Tourist Information: Since our festival takes place during the summer, the beaches on our coast, Waterfire and historic sites/museums in Providence, walking and biking trails, the Newport Mansions or our Discover Rhode Island location tour during the Festival. Our state's close proximity (one hour's drive) to Boston is also a plus.

Travel Tips: Contact Donovan Travel at www.donovantravel. com, RIIFF's official Travel Agency for personalized service and best pricing. Book early since rooms tend to fill up fast in Providence.

Best Cheap Hotels: Days Inn and the Hampton Court
Best Luxury Hotels: The new Marriott Courtard Providence is a class act.

Best Restaurants: Providence is known for world-class restaurants such as Al Forno. We recommend: India, Davios, the Blue Grotto and Rue de L'Espoir. The staff also hangs out at the Gourmet House in Providence.

Best Bars: Union Station Brewery, CAV and The Call
Best Hangout for Filmmakers: The Cable Car Cinema's Cafe, Starbucks on the East Side, and and the Marriott Courtyard lounge (our host hotel).

Best Place for Breakfast: J. Elliotts on Hope Street.

RiVER CiTY FiLM FESTiVAL

c/o Taproot Inc.
N. 1872 670 St.
Bay City, WI 54723
Tel: 715-594-3880
Fax: 715-594-3787
Web Site: www.thematrix model.com
Festival Date: November
Entry Deadline: October
Contact: Linda Flanders
Director: Linda Flanders
Category: Documentary, Student

BEST KEPT SECRET FESTIVALS

Ann Arbor Film Festival
Ohio Independent Film Festival
Peachtree International Film Festival
Portland International Film Festival
Rhode Island International Film Festival
San Diego International Film Festival
San Francisco Independent Film Festival (aka SF IndieFest)
Sedona International Film Festival and Workshop
Temecula Valley International Film Festival

Profile: The River City Film Festival features "Artistic Documentaries" created by high school teens from Minnesota and Wisconsin.

Application Fee: $10

RiVERRUN iNTERNATiONAL FiLM FESTiVAL

Bella Visione Film Society
P.O. Box 927
Brevard, NC 28712
Tel: 828-862-3618
Fax: 828-883-8806
Email: gpd232@citcom.net
Web Site:
www.brevard.edu/riverrun or
www.bellavisione.com
Festival Date: September
Entry Deadline: August
Contact: Gene D'Onofrio
Director: Gene D'Onofrio
Application Fee: Fee waived for North Carolina residents. $20 for Documentaries, Shorts and Animation. $30 for Features

ROCHESTER iNTERNATiONAL iNDEPENDENT FiLM FESTiVAL

Box 17746
Rochester, NY 14617
Tel: 716-288-5607
Festival Date: May
Entry Deadline: March
Contact: Josephine Perini
Category: Independent, International
Profile: The Rochester International Independent Film Festival accepts only short films no longer than 38 minutes.

ROGER EBERT'S OVERLOOKED FiLM FESTiVAL

c/o College of Journalism
University of Georgia
Athens, GA 30602-3018
Tel: 706-542-4972
Fax: 706-542-2183
Email: nkohn@arches.uga.edu
Web Site: www.ebertfest.com
Festival Date: April

Entry Deadline: N/A
Contact: Nate Kohn
Director: Nate Kohn
Programmer: Roger Ebert
Profile: Screenings of a selection of films that, for a variety of reasons, never received their full due or deserved to be re-examined and appreciated.
Competitions: No

SACRAMENTO iNTERNATiONAL GAY AND LESBiAN FiLM FESTiVAL

C/O Deos & McGill
225 30th St., suite 306
Sacramento, CA 95816
Tel: 916-689-3284
Fax: 916-325-1993
Web Site: www.bluedesert
productions/siglff
Festival Date: October 10-21, 2001
Entry Deadline: Submissions accepted year round. Entries for this year's festival must be submitted by July 15th.
Year Festival Began: 1992
Contact: Kerry Sawyer, Vice President
Director: Greg Brooks, President
Programmer: Film Selection Committee Co-Chairs: Tom Swanner & Linda Deos
Committee is comprised of 22 members
Category: Documentary, Gay Lesbian, Independent, International, Short, Video
Profile: The primary objective and purpose of the Sacramento International Gay & Lesbian Film Festival is to produce an annual film festival, and other like programs, to educate and to raise awareness of gay, lesbian, bisexual and transgender issues within the greater Sacramento area. SIGLFF works with local theatre management to bring quality gay and lesbian films to Sacramento with the focus of showing the LGBT community in positive roles. Almost all of the films are independently produced.
Seminars: No
Panels: No
Market: No

Competitions: No
Application Fee: None. A $5.00 fee is charged for returns of VHS screening submissions.
Common Mistakes: They forget to identify themselves and do not discuss the film.
Insider Advice: Be sure to include a synopsis of your film along with a VHS copy. Put your name and address on the tape, the tape box and somewhere in the video taped production.
Films Screened: 16-25
Odds of Acceptance: 1 in 6
Filmmaker Perks: We occasionally fly filmmakers to Sacramento and provide lodging for special appearances.
Attendance: 2,000
Tourist Information: Old Sacramento Tourist Area, Folsom Lake, American and Sacramento Rivers, California State Capitol, Rail Road Museum.
Travel Tips: Drive or rent a car, public transportation is minimal.
Best Cheap Hotels: Hartley House Inn, Clarion, Radisson off 160
Best Luxury Hotels: The Sterling Hotel, Vizcaya, Hyatt Downtown, Holiday Inn Downtown.
Best Restaurants: Moxie's, Andiamo, Aoili, River City Café, and many more.
Best Bars: Faces, The Depot
Best Hangout for Filmmakers: The Open Book, Faces
Best Place for Breakfast: Tres Hermanas, Café Bernardo

SAGUARO FiLM FESTiVAL

P.O. Box 9147
Scottsdale, AZ 85252
Tel: 480-970-8711
Fax: 480-423-0696
Email: filmz@primenet.com
Web Site: www.extracheese.com/afs
Festival Date: June
Entry Deadline: March
Contact: Durrie Parks

Edie Adams and Winona Ryder at the San Francisco International Film Festival.

SAN DiEGO iNTERNATiONAL FiLM FESTiVAL

Dept. 0078, UEO, UCSD
9500 Gilman Dr.
La Jolla, CA 92093-0078
Tel: 858-822-3199; 858-534-0497
Fax: 858-534-7665
Email: rbaily@ucsd.edu
Web Site: http://ueo.ucsd.edu or www.sdiff.com
Festival Date: February
Entry Deadline: November
Year Festival Began: 1984
Contact: Ruth Baily, Elaine Lea-Chou
Director: Ruth Baily
Category: Animation, Independent, International, We present premieres of major foreign films, but we are also very interested in independent and foreign films that have not been optioned for American distribution. We have one night dedicated to Short Films and another to Animation.
Profile: To bring the best of all forms of contemporary filmmaking to San Diego. Successful realization of a distinctive personal vision is important. SDIFF is a relaxed, friendly festival.
Awards: Yes

Competitions: Yes
Major Awards: Patron's Award for Best Film; Festival Award for Best Film
Value of Awards: Crystal Trophies; Best Short film includes a $500 cash prize
Application Tips: No tricks. Just send your best work. A balance of substance and style is always good.
Application Fee: $30
Insider Advice: Slickness, pretention, "attitude" don't carry much weight. Sensitivity, substance, wit, humor, knowing that a movie is more than a bunch of images on film helps. Don't imitate other filmmakers.
Odds of Acceptance: 1 in 6
Filmmaker Perks: Domestic airfare, lodging, meals.
Travel Tips: Suncreen. The Wild Animal Park is better than the Zoo if you have to choose.
Best Restaurants: Kemosabe
Best Bars: Cafe Japengo
Best Hangout for Filmmakers: Pannikin in La Jolla
Best Place for Breakfast: Mission Beach Cafe

SAN FRANCiSCO iNDEPENDENT FiLM FESTiVAL (aka SF iNDiEFEST)

530 Divisadero St., #183
San Francisco, CA 94117
Tel: 415-929-5038
Email: sfindie@sirius.com
Web Site: www.i.am/indie
Festival Date: January
Entry Deadline: October
Year Festival Began: 1999
Director: Jeff Ross
Category: American Films, Animation, Digital, Digital Animation, Documentary, DVD, Ethnic Asian, Ethnic Black, Ethnic Latin, Experimental, Fantasy/Science Fiction, First-Time Independent Filmmakers, Gay Lesbian, Independent, Musicals, involving car chases, Short, Touring (Northern California campus tour), Underground, Video, Weird, Woman
Profile: The mission of the SF IndieFest is to introduce San Francisco audiences to the coolest, wackiest, slickest, roughest, glorious, trashy, original, unique, interesting, amusing, moving, beautiful, deep, high concept, low brow and everything-in-between flicks we can get our

hands on. And camp. Camp is good. And art films with car chases. Nothing beats a good art film full of car chases and explosions.

Gore Score · · · · · · · · · · · · · · ·

San Francisco's best kept secret and a great venue to see new and up and coming indie films.

Seminars: No

Panels: No

Famous Speakers: No

Market: No

Competitions: Yes

Major Awards: Audience Awards for Best Feature, Short and Animation and we offer a prize for Staff Favorite.

Value of Awards: Prestige

Application Fee: $20

Common Mistakes: Always include a reply post card to make sure we got your entry. Don't bug us with updates on what else your film has been up to. Some of these things come daily! Don't insist on showing us your work on film. We watch everything on video and understand the inherent flaws in the format. Do tell us however if you've updated the sound or made any other change that could affect our decision.

Insider Advice: Pay attention to the type of festival you are submitting to. Our audience will probably not be interested in your documentary about your grandmother and her adventures through Tibet.

Average Films Entered: We try to produce an event with a varied program. From slick, high production value, romantic comedies to whacked-out, far out, low low budget stuff. And everything in between. Especially if car chases are involved. We call it "a little bit LA IndieFest, a little bit New York Underground Fest."

Films Screened: 36

Odds of Acceptance: 1 in 4

Attendance: 4,200

Journalist Attendance: We get massive coverage in the Bay Area papers, *Variety* and the online publications like IndieWire, FilmThreat, Sidewalk etc.

Tourist Information: The Castro Theater. SOMA nightclubs, the Haight Ashbury neighborhood, the bars in the Mission. The Barrio not too far from the bars in the Mission. Ton Kiang's dim sum for Sunday brunch. Punk rock karaoke at Annie's Bar down by the Hall of Justice. Bondage a Go Go on Wednesday Nights. And if you're feeling drunk and disorderly, Fishermans Wharf might be fun. Oh, and the Musee Mechanique is really cool.

Travel Tips: Priceline.com seems to be able to get folks here for $200 all the time. Don't rent a car.

Best Cheap Hotels: One of the youth hostels. Nothing else is cheap in this town.

Best Luxury Hotels: Ritz Carleton

Best Restaurants: Toke Sushi is cheap and great, on Noe and 15th. PPQ has the best pho in the avenues, 19th and Irving. Georgios has the best pizza, 3rd and Clement. Port Cafe has great breakfast/lunch: 16th and Noe. Sparky's works for french fries and coffee at 3 a.m., Church and Market.

Best Bars: Zeitgeist at Valencia and Duboce or Cassanova on Valencia and 16th.

Best Hangout for Filmmakers: At IndieFest, it's Bohemia because it's a block from the theater. Otherwise maybe Mars Bar.

Best Place for Breakfast: Port Cafe. Or Kate's Kitchen in Lower Haight.

SAN FRANCISCO INTERNATIONAL ASIAN AMERICAN FILM FESTIVAL

346 Ninth St., 2nd Floor
San Francisco, CA 94103

Tel: 415-863-0814

Fax: 415-863-7428

Email: festival@naatanet.org

Web Site: www.naatanet.org/festival

Festival Date: March 8-15, 2001

Entry Deadline: Early Deadline: September; Final Deadline: October

Year Festival Began: 1982

Director: Chi-Hui Yang, 415-863-0814 x110

Programmer: Linda Blackaby 415-863-0814 x109

Category: Documentary, Ethnic Other, Experimental, First-Time Independent Filmmakers, Gay Lesbian, Independent, International, Short, Video

Profile: Each year, the SFIAAFF creates an eight day program of Asian American films screened to an audience of 15,000, including filmgoers, filmmakers and industry guests around the world. The festival now screens 90-100 documentary, narrative, and experimental works in film, video and new media, this is supplemented with works from Asia and its diaspora. Specially organized filmmaker Q&A's, panel discussions, seminars, receptions and cultural events round out the week and provide more context with which to further appreciate the screenings. The SFIAAFF is also a significant cultural event for Asian American communities throughout the United States. Created to serve filmmakers and audiences by bringing accurate stories and images of Asian Pacific American experiences to the big screen, the SFIAAFF and its sister festivals in Chicago, Las Vegas, Minneapolis, New York, San Diego, Seattle, Washington D.C., and other cities have helped pave the way for a better understanding of Asian Pacific America for all Americans.

Gore Score · · · · · · · · · · · · · · ·

Extremely supportive of new Asian films from the U.S. and around the world. Often this festival is the only place to see films of this type so it is not to be missed.

Application Fee: $20 Early; $25 Final; Free for NAATA members

SAN FRANCISCO INTERNATIONAL FILM FESTIVAL

San Francisco Film Society
39 Mesa St., Suite 110,
The Presidio
San Francisco, CA 94129

Camp is good. And art films with car chases. Nothing beats a good art film full of car chases and explosions (San Francisco Independent Film Festival).

Tel: 415-929-5000
Fax: 415-921-5032
Email: sfiff@sfiff.org
Web Site: www.sfiff.org
Festival Date: April 19–May 3, 2001
Entry Deadline: Narrative— early January; Documentary, short, animation and experimental—early December
Year Festival Began: 1957, making this the oldest film festival in the Americas
Contact: Brian Gordon or Rachel Rosen
Director: Peter Scarlet, Artistic Director; Amy Leissner, Executive Director
Programmer: Rachel Rosen, Brian Gordon, Doug Jones
Category: American Films, Animation, Documentary, Experimental, First-Time Independent Filmmakers, Independent, International, Short, Student, Video
Profile: The San Francisco International Film Festival, is presented each spring by the San Francisco Film Society, a non-profit arts organization whose aim is to lead in expanding the knowledge and appreciation of international film art and its artists. A showcase for nearly 200 new features, documentaries and shorts, the Festival, presents a savvy selection of each year's most striking new fiction and documentary filmmaking and video production, with an emphasis on work which has not yet secured U.S. distribution.

Gore Score · · · · · · · · · · · · · · · ·
The reputation of SFIFF is well earned. Not only that, the festival should be applauded for taking risks. Other festivals should take note.

Seminars: Yes
Panels: Yes
Market: No
Awards: Yes
Competitions: Yes
Major Awards: SKYY Prize and Golden Gate Award Grand Prizes. Kurosawa Award, Mel Novikoff Award, Persistence of Vision Award, Peter J. Owens Award.

Value of Awards: $10,000 and $1,000
Application Fee: Ranges from $15-200 based on division, category and running time.
Common Mistakes: Putting a trailer for the film in front of the film itself.
Insider Advice: Don't worry about providing fancy promotional materials or expensive glossy flyers. It's your film we're interested in.
Average Films Entered: Approximately 2000
Films Screened: 170
Odds of Acceptance: 1 in 11
Filmmaker Perks: Free travel, lodging, contacts, hospitality suite and networking, socializing occasions
Attendance: Approximately 77,000
Journalist Attendance: over 200
Tourist Information: Camera Obscura at Cliff House, Castro Theatre, Hitchcock's Vertigo locations, Alcatraz, The Presidio, Golden Gate Bridge, City Lights Bookstore
Travel Tips: Bring a jacket, remember this is Northern California
Best Cheap Hotels: Beresford Hotel or Queen Anne
Best Luxury Hotels: Hotel Palomar
Best Restaurants: Zuni Cafe
Best Bars: Tosca Cafe
Best Hangout for Filmmakers: Tosca Cafe, Japantown Bowl or any of the karaoke bars near the Festival
Best Place for Breakfast: Jim's-The Friendliest Diner in San Francisco

SAN FRANCISCO JEWISH FILM FESTIVAL

346 Ninth St.
San Francisco, CA 94103
Tel: 415-621-0556
Fax: 415-621-0568
Email: jewishfilm@sfjff.org
Web Site: www.sfjff.org
Festival Date: Late July 2001
Entry Deadline: March 15, 2001
Year Festival Began: 1981

Director: Janis Plotkin and Samuel Ball
Other Staff: Elizabeth Greene, Administrative Director; Peter Jacobson, Operations Director.
Category: Ethnic Jewish
Profile: The San Francisco Jewish Film Festival showcases new independent American and international Jewish cinema. Now in its twentieth year, the festival is the largest, oldest, and most prestigious Jewish Film Festival in the world, with an attendance of over 34,000 over the course of four weeks. The Festival presents dramatic, experimental, and animated features and shorts about Jewish history, culture, and identity.
Application Fee: None
Journalist Attendance: 25-50

SAN FRANCISCO LESBIAN AND GAY FILM FESTIVAL

c/o Frameline
346 9th St.
San Francisco, CA 94103
Tel: 415-703-8650
Fax: 415-861-1404
Email: info@frameline.org
Web Site: www.frameline.org
Festival Date: June
Entry Deadline: February
Contact: Michael Lumkin & Jennifer Morris
Director: Michael Lumkin & Jennifer Morris
Category: Gay Lesbian, Independent
Profile: This diverse festival celebrates lesbian and gay filmmaking. The last day of the festival is always on San Francisco's annual Gay Pride day. Over 53,000 attend.
Awards: No
Competitions: No
Application Fee: $10 ($20-35 late)
Odds of Acceptance: 1 in 3

SAN LUIS OBISPO INTERNATIONAL FILM FESTIVAL

P. O. Box 1449
San Luis Obispo, CA 93406
Tel: 805-546-3456
Fax: 805-781-6799
E-mail: slofilmfest@slofilmfest.org
Profile: This year marks the eighth anniversary of the Festival, and we are excited about another great lineup of films and events. We will be screening an interesting mix of classic films, along with new features, documentaries, foreign films and animation. We will kick off the festival with a presentation of our annual "King Vidor Memorial Award."
Tourist Information: San Luis Obispo is:
106 miles from Santa Barbara;
198 miles from Los Angeles;
226 miles from San Francisco

SANTA BARBARA INTERNATIONAL FILM FESTIVAL (SBiFF)

1216 State St. #710
Santa Barbara, CA 93101-2623
Tel: 805-963-0023
Fax: 805-962-2524
Email: info@sbfilmfestival.org
Web Site: www.sbfilmfestival.org
Festival Date: March
Entry Deadline: December
Year Festival Began: 1986
Contact: Chris Gilmer
Director: Renee Missel
Programmer: Renee Missel
Category: Digital, Documentary, Independent, International, Short, Video
Profile: This festival is an eleven-day event which focuses on independent films, videos, shorts and documentaries. 32,000 attend annually.
Awards: Yes
Competitions: Yes

Major Awards: Best U.S. Feature, Best Foreign Feature, Best Director, Best Documentary Feature and Short, Best Live Action Short, Award for Artistic Excellence, Best Santa Barbara Filmmaker, Audience Choice Award
Application Fee: $40 (U.S.) $45 (International)
Films Screened: 125

SANTA CLARiTA INTERNATIONAL FILM FESTIVAL

P.O. Box 801507
Santa Clarita, CA 91380-1507
Tel: 661-257-3131
Fax: 661-257-8989;
661-250-0167
Email: pattedee@cs.com
Web Site: www.sciff.org
Festival Date: March
Entry Deadline: January
Contact: Patte Dee
Director: Chris Shoemaker
Programmer: Patte Dee
Category: Animation, Documentary, PSA (Public Service Announcement), Short, Student
Application Fee: $100—Feature Film (30 minutes or longer; $50 Short Film (Up to 30 minutes); $60—Screenplays

SARASOTA FILM FESTIVAL

1365 Fruitville Road
Sarasota, FL 34236
Tel: 941-364-9514
Fax: 941-364-8411
Email: festivalmark@aol.com or sarasotafilmfest@msn.com
Web Site: www.sarasotafilmfest.com
Festival Date: January
Entry Deadline: December
Contact: Mark Marvell
Director: Jody Kielbasa
Competitions: No

SAVANNAH FiLM AND ViDEO FESTiVAL

c/o Savannah College of Art and Design
PO Box 3146
Savannah, GA 31402-3146
Tel: 912-525-5051
Fax: 912-525-5052
Email: filmfest@scad.edu
Web Site: www.scad.edu/filmfest
Festival Date: October-November 2001
Entry Deadline: August 2001
Year Festival Began: 1998
Contact: Danny Filson, Len Cripe, Jennifer Culicchia
Director: Danny Filson
Programmer: Len Cripe
Category: American Films, Animation, Documentary, First-Time Independent Filmmakers, Independent, International, Short, Student
Profile: The festival showcases the talents of the latest and greatest filmmakers and offers a chance for movie buffs to experience the art of film. From feature-length films to two-minute shorts, the festival runs the gamut of cinematic creativity.
Competitions: Yes
Major Awards: Best Feature
Application Fee: $40 professional, $20 students
Common Mistakes: They don't provide all the necessary information, things are not labeled, they forget to pay!
Insider Advice: Presentation is key. Don't cram everything into a little envelope, scribble out your entry form or give us a messed up tape.
Films Screened: 45
Odds of Acceptance: 1 in 3
Attendance: 8-10,000
Tourist Information: River Street, City Market
Travel Tips: Book as early as possible because the hotels in the area fill up very quickly.
Best Cheap Hotels: Marriott
Best Luxury Hotels: Marshall House
Best Restaurants: Sapphire Grill
Best Bars: Churchill's
Best Hangout for Filmmakers: Bar Bar, Café M
Best Place for Breakfast: Clary's

SEATTLE INTERNATIONAL FILM FESTIVAL

911 Pine Street
Seattle, WA 98101
Tel: 206-464-5830
Fax: 206-324-9998
Email: mail@seattlefilm.com or kathleen@seattlefilm.com
Web Site: www.seattlefilm.com
Festival Date: May-June
Entry Deadline: March
Contact: Carl Spence
Director: Darryl Macdonald
Category: Documentary, Gay Lesbian, Independent, International
Profile: Recently cited by the *New York Times* as one of the most influential film festivals in the world. SIFF is the largest and most highly attended film festival in the United States, presenting 170 features and 100 shorts from 40 countries around the world to an audience of over 130,000 film-goers.

Special sections include Contemporary World Cinema, the New Director's Showcase, the Secret Festival, the Films 4 Families, a Tribute Section, Archival Presentations, the Short Film Showcase, Best of the Northwest, Midnight Series, an Annual Foreign Film Poster Auction and the Filmmakers Forum, an intensive, three day program of seminars, workshops and panel discussions which includes The Amazing Fly Filmmaking: A challenge to three directors to conceive, shoot and edit a film the last six days of the festival to screen on closing day. The filmmakers are given 400 feet of 16mm film, local producers and crews and limited equipment.

SIFF has been selected by the Independent Feature Project as one of five North American festivals in which a film's presentation qualifies it for the Independent Spirit Awards, the independent film industry's most prestigious awards.
Seminars: The Filmmakers Forum includes master classes, panels, seminars, one on one discussion, etc. Also included is the Screenwriters Salon, a one on one conversation with various screenwriters as well as the Script Read Through, a special presentation of a selected script cast with professional actors and directed by a film director.
Panels: Yes
Awards: Yes
Competitions: Yes
Major Awards: Golden Space Needle Audience Award; New Directors Showcase (juried); American Independent Award (juried); Reel Network Short Award (juried)
Value of Awards: American Indie Award: $100,0000
Application Tips: Complete all supporting material and application. Don't call to say you know someone famous who will vouch for your film. Get as clean and strong a preview tape as possible; if it is a rough cut, say so on the tape (that's fine as long as we know); put your name, the title of the film and your phone number on the cassette.
Application Fee: $25 for 0-30 min.; $35 for 30-60 min.; $50 for 60-whatever minutes.
Insider Advice: Get your films in early if possible; sound is your best friend for film festivals— make sure it's great; get your production values as high as possible. The competition is tough out there so do what you can to make sure your production values help your film; make sure you have really strong writing (stong script can help overcome almost anything) and let your editor do their job! Rarely is it a good idea for first time filmmakers to be producer, director, writer, actor and editor all at once.
Films Screened: 180 features, 70 short films
Odds of Acceptance: 1 in 5
Filmmaker Perks: We invite premiere status directors as our guests, and offer them travel and lodging as well. All filmmakes who come have access to contacts; we help facilitate by parties, functions, a hospitality suite, events, etc.
Travel Tips: Wear layers!
Best Restaurants: For hip indie filmmakers it's the Alibi Room in the Pike Place Market. owned by fellow indie filmmakers with high profile Hollywood money as investors (the Donners, Rob Morrow, Peter Horton, Tom Skerritt, etc.). Closer to the festival theaters is the Capitol Club (great for Middle Eastern influenced food and outstanding bar drinks); the Wild Ginger (Asian and Pacific Rim) for highbrow filmmakers on a studio expense account; Palace Kitchen to be seen; Cafe Septieme for European style cafe and food; New American Broadway Grill for good food and great atmosphere... Also very cool with great food and lots of the "in" crowd to watch: Flying Fish, Queen City Grill, Metropolitan Grill, Sazarac.
Best Bars: See above. Also the Baltic Room, The Pink Door and Linda's
Best Hangout for Filmmakers: The Alibi Room, The Speakeasy Cafe
Best Place for Breakfast: The Green Cat

SEATTLE LESBIAN & GAY FILM FESTIVAL

c/o Three Dollar Bill Cinema
1122 E. Pike St., #1313
Seattle, WA 98122-3934
Tel: 206-323-4247
Fax: 206-323-4275
Email: filmfest@drizzle.com
Web Site: www.seattlequeerfilm.com
Festival Date: October
Entry Deadline: July
Year Festival Began: 1996
Director: Justine Barda
Programmer: Kirsten Shaffer
Category: Gay Lesbian
Profile: A week-long international film and video festival.
Panels: Yes
Application Fee: $10.00
Average Films Entered: 150+
Films Screened: 70
Filmmaker Perks: Airfare, accomodations, meals, gratitude.
Attendance: 5,000

THE SEATTLE UNDERGROUND FiLM FESTiVAL

1412 18th Ave.
Seattle WA 98122
Tel: 206-382-0926; 206-860-8590
Email: bolexman@msn.com
Web Site: www.seattle
undergroundfilm.com
Entry Deadline: May 1
Year Festival Began: 1999
Director: Jon Behrens, Steve
Creson, Marc Burgio
Category: American Films,
Digital, Documentary, Ethnic
Black, Experimental, First-Time
Independent Filmmakers, Gay
Lesbian, Independent,
International, Super 8/8mm,
Underground, Video, Weird
Profile: The Seattle Underground
Film Festival (SUFF) is dedicated
to bringing you the very best in
avant garde, experimental and
offbeat short and feature films
from around the world. This
Festival will be held for seven
days in October and will take
place at two venues on Seattle's
Capitol Hill district.
Seminars: No
Panels: No
Famous Speakers: No
Market: No
Competitions: Yes, we do award
a trophy to the best short, feature and experimental film each
year.
Major Awards: The SUFF Award
Value of Awards: We made 24k
gold plated film reel trophies
that cost about $600 each.
Application Fee: $20
Common Mistakes: Sometimes
they don't fill out an entry form
and sometimes they forget to
include the entry fee. But not all
the time.
Insider Advice: Keep trying. The
more festivals you submit to, the
more festivals you will get into
and also just getting your name
out there is all too important.
Films Screened: 280
Odds of Acceptance: 1 in 2
Attendance: 2,000
Journalist Attendance: 25
Tourist Information: The
Experience music project.

Travel Tips: Bring money.
Best Cheap Hotels: This is
Seattle; there are no cheap
hotels. However, just a little out-
side of town you can find a
Motel 6.
Best Luxury Hotels: The
Olympic Four Seasons
Best Restaurants: The Six Arms
Pub
Best Bars: Linda's; Six Arms Pub
Best Hangout for Filmmakers:
Linda's Tavern.
Best Place for Breakfast: The
Shanty Hut

SEDONA iNTERNATiONAL FiLM FESTiVAL AND WORKSHOP

*"...I would like to congratulate
the Sedona International Film
Festival for recognizing an
issue that is very close to us."*
—William Daniels, President,
Screen Actors Guild

PO Box 2515, Sedona, AZ 86339
(entries by post)
1725 W. Hwy 89A Ste 2, Sedona,
AZ 86336 (entries by FedEx or
UPS)
Tel: 520-282-0747;
800-780-ARTS
Fax: 520-282-5358
Email: scp@sedona.net
Web Site: www.sedonafilm
festival.com
Festival Date: March 2-4, 2001
Entry Deadline: December 1 for
early submission ($10 discount
on fee), January 8 for final sub-
mission
Year Festival Began: 1994
Contact: Liz Warren
Director: Nadia Caillou
Programmer: Dan Schay, Linda
K. Smith (Shorts Programs)
Category: American Films,
Animation, Documentary, Ethnic
African, Ethnic Asian, Ethnic
Black, Ethnic Jewish, Ethnic Latin,
Ethnic Other, Ethnic Spanish,
First-Time Independent
Filmmakers, Gay Lesbian,
Independent, International, Short,
Woman
Profile: The Sedona International
Film Festival and Workshop
spotlights indie films from
around the globe each March for
Arizona audiences, as well as
providing an in-depth look at a
different aspect of filmmaking
each year. Set in the gorgeous
red rocks of Sedona, the three-
day marathon features between
fifty and sixty independent dramatic, documentary, short and
animated films at the state-of-
the-art Harkins Sedona 6 Luxury
Cinemas. Festivities include a
gala/tribute evening at the
award-winning Enchantment
Resort, complete with a celebrity honoree, music and stellar
refreshments. The annual
Workshop is led by a panel of
industry professionals and is
coordinated yearly by Academy
Award®-winning sound designer
Frank Warner.
Seminars: Every year, the festival
features an in-depth one-day
workshop focusing on a specific
aspect of filmmaking.
Famous Speakers: Past work-
shop faculty members include
Elmer Bernstein, Gloria Borders,
John Burnett, Richard Chew,
David Fein, Gary Gerlich, Bonnie
Kohler, Carol Littleton, Mark
Magini, Walter Murch, Richard
Portman and Thelma
Schoonmaker.
Market: No
Competitions: Yes, audience
awards
Major Awards: Best of Festival
Value of Awards: non-monetary
Last Winning Films: *All My Loved
Ones* (Best of Festival), *Genghis
Blues* (Best Documentary)
Last Winning Directors: Matej
Minac (*All My Loved Ones*), Roko
Belic (*Genghis Blues*)
Application Tips: Don't forget to
include fees, forget to complete
submission forms.
Application Fee: $35 for shorts
of 30 minutes or less, $50 for
full-length feature

Common Mistakes: Forget to include fees, forget to complete submission forms.

Insider Advice: Read and follow all instructions carefully. Don't give up if your film doesn't make it; often our decisions have more to do with developing the right programming mix than whether or not a film is good.

Films Screened: 50-60

Odds of Acceptance: 1 in 10

Filmmaker Perks: Passes to the festival and gala event, break on cost of workshop, private party Saturday night, hotel accommodations for feature filmmakers, honorarium.

Attendance: 6,000

Journalist Attendance: 30-40

Tourist Information: Red Rock Canyon, the vortexes, the Grand Canyon, shops, lots of ruins...

Travel Tips: Pack layers—there is no rhyme or reason to the March weather patterns in Sedona.

Best Cheap Hotels: There are plenty of mom-and-pop places here.

Best Luxury Hotels: Enchantment Resort, L'Auberge de Sedona Resort

Best Bars: Oak Creek Brewery, The Rainbow's End

Best Hangout for Filmmakers: The festival!

Best Place for Breakfast: Desert Flour Bakery

Random Tidbits: We do a lot of networking and cooperative work with other film festivals, and we are all about helping filmmakers get their films seen. We don't forget about filmmakers when the festival is over!

SHORT ATTENTiON SPAN FiLM AND ViDEO FESTiVAL (SASFVF)

1615 Montana Avenue
Santa Monica, CA 90403
Tel: LA: 310-260-1551;
Athens, GA: 706-540-0847
New York: 718-609-0144
Fax: 310-260-1533
Email: beth@dreamspan.com or paul@dreamspan.com
Web Site: www.shortspan.com

Festival Date: Tour begins late Spring

Entry Deadline: February

Year Festival Began: 1991

Contact: Paul Marchant, 718-609-0144

Paul@dreamspan.com

Director: Elizabeth Hall (Founder/ Exec. Dir.)

Paul Marchant (Managing Director)

Category: Animation, Digital, Digital Animation, Ethnic Other, Experimental, Fantasy/Science Fiction, First-Time Independent Filmmakers, Independent, International, Microcinema, Online Festival, PXL, Short, Student, Super 8/8mm, Touring (San Francisco, CA; Oakland, CA; Portland, OR; Seattle, WA; Tucson, AZ; Atlanta, GA; Athens, GA; Savannah, GA; New Orleans, LA; Washington D.C.; New York, NY; Cleveland, OH; Boston, MA; Vancouver, BC; Los Angeles, CA), Underground, Video, Weird, Woman

Profile: SASFVF is a two-hour competitive program made up of two minute, or shorter, non-commercial works. Established in 1991, the festival is the oldest international showcase of its kind for short, short works. Our goal is to promote and celebrate creativity at the grassroots level and to provide a network of support for all short film/video makers in the U.S. and around the world. SASFVF has also had a strong presence on the web since way back in '94, paving the way for online short film festivals and short film related sites.

Gore Score · · · · · · · · · · · · · · ·

Short and sweet, there are a lot of films to love at SASFVF and if you see something you don't like, just wait a minute and it'll be over.

Market: No

Awards: Yes

Competitions: Yes

Major Awards: Best of Festival— $2500

Best Animation— $1000

Viewers' Choice Award— $1000

Value of Awards: $4,500

Application Fee: $10 payable to Dreamspan. (This entry fee gets

entrant plus one into the festival free of charge regardless of whether or not entry is accepted.) College students, high school students and International entries, no fee required.

Common Mistakes: Submit late.

Insider Advice: Submit early. Make sure to leave "leader" in the form of color bars and black at the beginning of piece for editing purposes. Be sure that filmmaker has releases/rights for any actors/music/etc. Make a Beta master of your piece. If you need your tapes returned, be sure to include a self-addressed and *prepaid* mailer.

Films Screened: 60 to 70

Odds of Acceptance: 1 in 4

Filmmaker Perks: Contacts— through our new venture, the Dreamspan Network, we will be able to offer SASFVF artists the chance to work on big budget commercials. We will also be able to pitch the artists' work into all media-games, toys, animation! We receive calls daily from online and offline companies searching for content: we can help the filmmakers get their work to the right folks!

Attendance: 4,500

Journalist Attendance: 20-40

Tourist Information: The festival tours to 16 cities this year. Links on our web site point to the local theaters-many of the theater web sites contain local color tips/tidbits at www.shortspan.com

Travel Tips: Follow SASFVF around the country!

SiLVER iMAGES FiLM FESTiVAL

c/o Terra Nova Films
9848 South Winchester
Chicago, IL 60643
Tel: 773-881-6940
Fax: 773-881-3368
Email: siff@terranova.org
Web Site: www.terranova.org
Festival Date: April
Entry Deadline: December
Contact: Sheila Malkind
Director: Sheila Malkind
Programmer: Sheila Malkind

This is Seattle; there are no cheap hotels. However, just a little outside of town you can find a Motel 6 (The Seattle Underground Film Festival).

Category: Documentary, Experimental, Senior Citizen, Short, Video

Profile: The only festival of its kind, SIFF showcases films and videos from around the world that celebrate older adulthood.

SILVER LAKE FILM FESTIVAL

2658 Griffith Park Blvd., #389
Los Angeles, CA 90039
Tel: 323-221-1763
Email: info@silverlakefilm festival.com
Web Site: www.silverlakefilm festival.com
Entry Deadline: June
Year Festival Began: September
Contact: Greg Ptacek or Vangie Griego
Director: P. David Ebersol
Category: Animation, Digital, Documentary, Ethnic Black, Ethnic Chicano, Ethnic Jewish, Experimental, Gay Lesbian, Independent, International, Markets, Retro Classics, Retro Science, Retro Westerns, Short, Student, Underground, Video, Weird
Profile: A California nonprofit, public benefit corporation, the Silver Lake Film Festival was created to celebrate through cinema the cultural diversity and avant-garde creativity that historically has characterized Silver Lake in Los Angeles. The SLFF serves as a conduit for bringing together the film community in this local area with the rest of Hollywood and hopefully the rest of the world, both filmmakers and fans alike.
Competitions: The Silver Lake Film Festival is also sponsoring a screenwriting competition and is interested in showcasing local artists and musicians.
Average Films Entered: We are interested in all films: features, docs, shorts, experimental. Also, all types are welcome. While this is a predominately gay community, we are looking for both gay and straight themed films, chicano, local films, African-American, animations, music works, art documentaries, anything. While we don't want

pornographic materials, we welcome nearly anything else. All formats are accepted, although we will need a VHS screener. We have already received many films, but we are looking for the best of the best to really kick this off right, and I know that you must have something completed in the last year-and-a-half that would be dynamite.

SLAMDANCE INTERNATIONAL FILM FESTIVAL

See "The Top Ten Film Festivals" beginning on page 214.

SLAMDUNK FILM FESTIVAL

202 Main Street, Suite 14
Venice, CA 90291
Tel: 310-399-3358
Web Site: www.slamdunk.cc
Festival Date: January

SMALL PICTURES INTERNATIONAL FILM FESTIVAL (SPIFF)

P.O. Box 18447
Beverly Hills, CA 90209
Tel: 310-558-6691
Email: info@spiffest.com
Web Site: www.spiffest.com
Festival Date: October
Entry Deadline: August
Year Festival Began: 1996
Contact: Joy Kenelly
Director: Joy Kenelly
Category: Digital, Independent, Short, Underground, Video, Weird
Profile: Short Pictures International Film Festival (SPIFF) is an international film festival hosted by a comedic Mistress/Master of Ceremonies featuring shorts, animation, documentaries, spec. commercials (all 15 min. or less) showcasing the short film genre and benefitting disadvantaged children around the world. Each year a different charity is selected. Last year's beneficiaries were Irish children's charities recommended by the American Ireland Fund. This year's benefit will support inner

city children here in the United States.
Awards: Yes
Application Fee: $35, $55 for late entries.

ST. LOUIS INTERNATIONAL FILM FESTIVAL

55 Maryland Plaza, Suite A
St. Louis, MA 63108-1501
Tel: 314-454-0042
Fax: 314-454-0540
Email: info@sliff.org
Web Site: www.sliff.org
Festival Date: November
Entry Deadline: August
Contact: Shirley Marvin
Director: Shirley Marvin
Programmer: Chris Clark
Category: Documentary, Ethnic Black, Independent, Student

ST. LOUIS INTERNATIONAL LESBIAN & GAY (SLILAG) FILM FESTIVAL

6614 Clayton Rd., # 388
St. Louis, MO 63117-1602
Tel: 314-997-9846
Fax: 314-863-6993
Email: slilagff@aol.com
Web Site: www.slilagfilmfestival. org
Festival Date: September 7-16, 2001
Entry Deadline: May 1, 2001
Year Festival Began: 1992
Contact: Linda Serafini
Category: Documentary, First-Time Independent Filmmakers, Gay Lesbian, Independent, International, Short
Profile: To bring the best of l/g/b/t interest feature length and short films to St. Louis audiences.
Seminars: No
Panels: No
Market: No
Competitions: No
Insider Advice: Please check our website for submission instructions.

STONY BROOK FILM FESTIVAL

Staller Center for the Arts
University at Stony Brook
Stony Brook, NY 11794-5425
Tel: 631-632-7235
Fax: 631-632-7354
Email: festival@stallercenter.com
Web Site: stallercenter.com
Festival Date: July 19-29, 2001
Entry Deadline: April 1, 2001
Year Festival Began: 1996
Contact: PR/Marketing—Patricia Cohen
Director: Alan Inkles
Programmer: Alan Inkles
Other Staff: Production Manager—Patrick Kelly
Category: American Films, Animation, Documentary, Experimental, First-Time Independent Filmmakers, Independent, International, Short
Seminars: Yes
Panels: Yes
Market: Yes
Competitions: Yes
Major Awards: Best Feature Film, Best Short Film, Audience Choice
Application Fee: Feature: $50; Short: $25
Common Mistakes: They do not include a complete press kit.
Insider Advice: Be creative, organized and thorough.
Films Screened: 40
Odds of Acceptance: 1 in 5
Filmmaker Perks: Travel and hotel accommodations
Attendance: 15,000
Journalist Attendance: 10-12
Tourist Information: NYC, Historic Stony Brook Village and Museums, Port Jefferson, The Hamptons
Travel Tips: Fly into Islip Airport
Best Cheap Hotels: Holiday Inn
Best Luxury Hotels: Three Village Inn and Wyndham Wind Watch
Best Restaurants: Pasta Pasta
Best Bars: Planet Dublin of Stony Brook
Best Hangout for Filmmakers: Planet Dublin
Best Place for Breakfast: Anywhere in Port Jefferson Village
Random Tidbits: Our theatre seats 1,050 people and the screen is 40 feet wide, the largest on all of Long Island, NY.

SUNDANCE FILM FESTIVAL

See "The Top Ten Film Festivals" beginning on page 214.

SXSW: SOUTH BY SOUTHWEST FILM FESTIVAL

See "The Top Ten Film Festivals" beginning on page 214.

TAOS TALKING PiCTURES FESTiVAL

"One of the country's leading film festivals"
            —MovieMaker Magazine

7217 NDCBU
1337 Gusdorf, Suite B
Taos, NM 87571
Tel: 505-751-0637
Fax: 505-751-7385
Email: ttpix@ttpix.org
Web Site: www.ttpix.org
Festival Date: April
Entry Deadline: Early: November Late: January
Year Festival Began: 1994
Contact: Kelly Clement
Director: Morton Nilssen
Programmer: Kelly Clement
Category: International
Profile: The festival is produced by Taos Talking Pictures, a New Mexico-based non-profit media arts organization founded in 1994 to encourage the thoughtful production and informed consumption of moving images.

In one of the most dramatic landscapes in the world, Taos is a nature-bound community in a high valley at the edge of a great lava plain at the foot of the Sangre de Cristo Mountains. Situated around an ancient Pueblo, it supports three diverse cultures. One can easily glance backwards here at myths and legends of the Indian/Spanish/American West.

The Taos Talking Picture Festival should be seen as more than just another film festival. It aspires to serve as a rendezvous where people meet to trade ideas and inspiration in an atmosphere conducive to clear, uncluttered thought; a unique context in which to view and discuss the art of film and media in general in this rapidly unfolding Age of Information.

Gore Score · · · · · · · · · · · · · · ·
This small festival continues to support lesser known indies and they
award the best prize for any festival—five acres of land.

Panels: Yes. The Taos Talking Picture Festival is also known for its Media Forum, which brings together media makers and scholars to discuss the impact of film and TV on our culture and society.
Awards: Yes
Competitions: Yes
Major Awards:—Innovation Award

The Taos Mountain Award recognizes outstanding achievement by a Native American media professional.

The Maverick Award is presented to an individual who has retained his or her personal vision while working within the film industry.

The Howard Hawks Storyteller Award recognizes a writer/director who tells powerful stories in innovative ways

Cineaste Award: This award is given to a filmmaker whose works help promote cultural understanding.

The famed Land Grant Award—five acres of land given to encourage filmmakers to take a fresh approach to storytelling and/or the cinematic media

The Land Grant Award, which has received worldwide attention from filmmakers and the media, is given each year at the Taos Talking Picture Festival to recognize a talented, passionate and innovative filmmaker who uses his or her talents to tell powerful, socially relevant stories. The ultimate goal of the Land Grant Award is the foundation of a community of talented filmmakers in Taos.
Value of Awards: Five acres of land on beautiful Taos Cerro Montoso.
Application Fee: $15 (up to 30 minutes) / $25 (30 minutes or over)
Films Screened: The Festival features a number of special events and screenings, including:

• Four new family films
• A comprehensive survey of public access TV, one of our greatest democratic forums

• A special program in which movies and poetry meet
• A two-part film program entitled Girl Culture, featuring videos about growing up female in our culture
• Two programs featuring the best new works produced by Native filmmakers
• A program featuring innovative animation from around the world
• The festival's now-famed shorts programs with work from the filmmakers of tomorrow and highlighted by the George Méliès Award presentation
• Parties, filmmaker receptions and more.
Tourist Information: Taos is also an international tourist destination, a world-class ski resort and one of America's oldest art colonies. Simplicity and sophistication coexist here.

Taos remains a last outpost. Almost remote. The town is still adobe, the countryside still rural. For hundreds of years it has attracted adventurers and artists. And, today, its distance from the anxious post-Modern World gives Taos a powerful mind-clearing quietness.

Taos is an ideal place to think through and explore the ethical/technological issues of entertainment and communication in the New Media Age.

See Taos Virtual Vacation Guide, Taos Ski Valley online and La Plaza de Taos Telecommunity, our nonprofit community network, for more about Taos.

TECH TV'S CAM FiLM FESTiVAL

650 Townsend St.
San Francisco, CA 94103
Tel: 415-551-4500
Fax: 415-551-4564
Web Site: www.techtv.com
Festival Date: May
Entry Deadline: March
Contact: Toni Whiteman
Director: Toni Whiteman
Category: Digital, Independent
Profile: The Tech TV Cam Film Festival accepts two minute long digital videos only. The festival is

designed to teach people how to use their new digital cameras and home editing equipment.
Application Fee: None

TELLURiDE FiLM FESTiVAL

See "The Top Ten Film Festivals" beginning on page 214.

TELLURiDE iNDiEFEST

P.O. Box 860 (Mailing)
398 W. Colorado Ave., #223 (FedEx & UPS)
Telluride, CO 81435
Tel: 970-728-3747
Fax: 970-728-8128
Email: festival@ tellurideindiefest.com
Web Site: www. tellurideindiefest.com
Festival Date: December
Entry Deadline: September
Contact: Michael Carr
Director: Michael Carr
Category: Telluride IndieFest is more like "Film Camp" for the artists, a superb viewing festival, and an informative seminar for both festival entrants and attendees.
Profile: A unique festival/seminar dedicated to the spirit and advancement of independent film/videomaking and screenwriting.

Gore Score · · · · · · · · · · · · · · ·
Telluride's "other" film festival focuses more on "making" movies than seeing them. A great place to schmooze if you're an aspiring screenwriter. Also a great vacation.

Seminars: Yes
Panels: Yes
Awards: No
Competitions: No
Application Tips: 1) Try and make "personal" contact with the festival director, 2) mention any festival competitions in which your film, video, and/or screenplay did well, 3) follow the rules (exactly) that each festival announces, 4) present your material in an interesting manner—include press releases, artwork—anything that may distinguish your material from others.

Application Fee: $35 for short films/videos (under 60 minutes), $40 for screenplays (no more than 120 pages), and $45 for feature films/videos.
Insider Advice: Always include a SASE for entry confirmation and an SASE for return of materials.
Average Films Entered: All Genres. Short Films/Videos and Documentaries are encouraged, as well.
Filmmaker Perks: Entrants may receive:
1) roundtrip airfare
2) four nights complimentary luxury accomodations during the festival
3) an evening dinner sleigh ride
4) snowmobile tour or horseback riding
5) free ski passes, and
6) complimentary equipment rentals.
Travel Tips: Plan on landing in Montrose, CO (65 miles away). The shuttle service to Telluride and back is excellent and reliable.
Best Restaurants: The Powderhouse, La Campagna, La Marmotte, Floradora
Best Bars: Last Dollar Saloon, Sheridan Bar
Best Hangout for Filmmakers: Steaming Bean Coffee House
Best Place for Breakfast: Sofio's, Excelsior

TEMECULA VALLEY iNTERNATiONAL FiLM FESTiVAL

27740 Jefferson Ave. Suite 100
Temecula, CA 92590
Tel: 909-699-6267
Fax: 909-506-4193
Email: jmmoulton@earthlink.net
Web Site: www.tviff.com
Festival Date: Sept. 13-17, 2001
Entry Deadline: August 1, 2001
Year Festival Began: 1995
Contact: Jo Moulton
Director: Jo Moulton
Programmer: Kevin Haasarud, Mike Kerrigan
Category: American Films, Animation, Digital, Documentary, Ethnic Asian, Ethnic Black, Ethnic Jewish, Ethnic Spanish, Experimental, First-Time Independent Filmmakers, Independent, International, Short, Student
Profile: The Temecula Valley International Film festival mission is clear—to promote, enhance and showcase the cinematic vision and artistic wizardry of independent filmmakers from all over the world.
Seminars: Yes
Panels: Yes
Famous Speakers: Yes
Market: No
Competitions: Yes
Application Fee: $25 processing fee / $10, if student.
Common Mistakes: Most often, filmmakers leave off key information on the entry form.
Insider Advice: Enter early and provide complete cast/crew and good production notes.
Average Films Entered: We generally accept all genres except films with excessive nudity, violence or language.
Films Screened: 80
Odds of Acceptance: 1 in 6
Filmmaker Perks: Lodging, extra tickets to special events, sometimes free lodging for out of state and foreign participants.
Attendance: 6,000
Journalist Attendance: 50
Tourist Information: Our wineries and vineyards, old town (antique alley)
Best Cheap Hotels: Motel 6
Best Luxury Hotels: Temecula Creek Inn
Best Restaurants: Baily's
Best Bars: TGI Fridays
Best Hangout for Filmmakers: Aloha Joe's
Best Place for Breakfast: Ziggy's

TEXAS FiLM FESTiVAL

MSC Film Society
Memorial Student Center, Box J-1
College Station, TX 77841
Tel: 409-845-1515
Fax: 409-845-5117
Email: noshowing@ msc.tamu.edu

Always include a SASE for entry confirmation and an SASE for return of materials (Telluride Indiefest).

Web Site: http://films.tamu.edu/festival
Festival Date: February
Entry Deadline: November
Year Festival Began: 1992
Contact: Sarah Forbey and Logan Youree
Director: Sarah Forbey and Logan Youree
Category: Independent
Profile: To promote film as an art medium. Our focus is on education rather than securing distribution. The mission of the Texas Film Festival is to celebrate the vision and enterprise of America's finest contemporary independent filmmakers.
Panels: No
Awards: No
Competitions: No
Application Tips: Get your entry in early so a hasty decision is not made at the last minute.
Application Fee: $10 longer than 45 minutes, $5 shorter than 45 minutes, $15 additional charge for films postmarked after deadline.
Insider Advice: Make something you like and are proud of.
Average Films Entered: We generally accept films with content, a uniqness all their own, and independent film that don't follow mainstream models.
Odds of Acceptance: 1 in 5
Filmmaker Perks: We provide travel, food, and lodging for our feature filmmakers.

THAW VIDEO, FILM, AND DIGITAL MEDIA FESTIVAL

Institute for Cinema and Culture
162 BCSB
Iowa City, IA 52242
Tel: 319-335-1348

Fax: 319-335-2930
Email: thaw@uiowa.edu
Web Site: www.uiowa.edu/~thaw
Festival Date: April
Entry Deadline: January
Year Festival Began: 1996
Contact: Alison LaTendresse
Director: Adam Burke, Alison LaTendresse, Jason Livingston
Category: Animation, Digital, Digital Animation, Documentary, DVD, Experimental, Independent, International, Microcinema, Multimedia, Online Festival, Short, Student, Super 8/8mm, Underground, Video, Weird
Profile: Thaw 01 is an international festival of video, film and digital media open to all artists who challenge the conventional language of their media through innovation in both form and content.

Since its beginning in 1996, Thaw has maintained four principles which set it apart from other festivals. First, it is organized by a scrappy group of media makers, artists, students and scholars. Second, there are no restrictions on content. Third, we are committed to a very modest entry fee. Finally, Thaw celebrates the idea that artistic expression is never bound to a single format. Accordingly, Thaw presents film, video, websites, CD-Roms, digital audio and other forward-looking media art forms, all in the context of one festival. Thaw's momentum builds throughout a four-day series of free theatrical screenings, juror shows, multimedia events, musical performances, parties and a digital "lounge." Each year, Thaw chooses a new panel of feisty, quick-witted media makers to award cash prizes at their discre-

tion. Our non-corporate, star-free environment is sure to please.

Our name was chosen for its implications of emergence, movement, transition and change. Appropriately, the festival occurs during Iowa's seasonal thaw. As the ice melts away and the fields are planted, our audience is reminded of Iowa City's dynamic intellectual, social and artistic life.
Market: No
Competitions: Yes
Major Awards: Names and amounts of awards are determined by each year's panel of jurors.
Application Fee: $15 under 30 min; $30 over 30 min
Insider Advice: Cue your tapes. Keep your chin up.
Films Screened: 70+
Odds of Acceptance: 1 in 3
Filmmaker Perks: Parties, couches, spare beds, good company.
Attendance: 1,000
Journalist Attendance: 5
Travel Tips: Let us know you're coming.
Best Cheap Hotels: Haverkamp's
Best Restaurants: Baldy's
Best Bars: Motley Cow
Best Hangout for Filmmakers: The Foxhead
Best Place for Breakfast: Hambrug Inn No. 2
Random Tidbits: All events are free and open to the public.

30 BELOW FILM & VIDEO COMPETITION

Brandon, Manitoba, Canada
Web Site: www.brandonu.ca/bff/30below/
Profile: The 30 Below Film & Video competition requires that either the producer or director must be a Canada citizen and be under 30.

TORONTO INTERNATIONAL FILM FESTIVAL
See "The Top Ten Film Festivals" beginning on page 214.

BEST DIGITAL FILM FESTIVALS
D.FILM Digital Film Festival
Cinequest: The San Jose Film Festival
Independent Exposure
No Dance Film Festival
onedotzero Digital Creativity Festival
ResFest Digital Film Festival
THAW Video, Film, and Digital Media Festival

TORONTO WORLDWIDE SHORT FILM FESTIVAL

60 Atlantic Avenue, Suite 106
Toronto, Ontario M4K IX9
Canada
Tel: 416-535-8506
Fax: 416-535-8342
Email: twsff@direct.com
Web Site: www.torontoshort.com/film/festival
Category: Animation, Digital Animation, Documentary, Experimental, Short

TROMADANCE FiLM FESTiVAL

"TromaDance proved that big things come in small packages. The guerrilla marketing techniques employed by Troma sparked my interest, so I wound up spending the rest of the day at their event."
—Mark Doyle, Publisher of Guerrilla Filmmaker

TromaDance Selection Committee
733 Ninth Ave.
New York, NY 10019
Tel: NY Office: 212-757-4555;
LA Office: 310-827-6360
Fax: NY: 212-399-9885;
LA: 310-827-0412
Email: TromaDance@troma.com
Web Site: www.troma.com/tromadance2001/
Festival Date: January 26, 2001
Entry Deadline: December
Year Festival Began: 2000
Contact: Doug Sakmann, Yaniv Sharon- Troma NYC
Adam Jahnke, Scott McKinlay- Troma LA
Director: Lloyd Kaufman
Other Staff: TromaDance is staffed entirely by volunteers. If you are going to be in Park City, Utah next January, and you wish to volunteer for TromaDance, the organizers will provide you with a floor to sleep on and plenty of work to do. Email

TromaDance@troma.com for more information.
Category: Animation, Digital, Digital Animation, DVD, Ethnic African, Ethnic Asian, Ethnic Black, Ethnic Jewish, Ethnic Latin, Ethnic Other, Ethnic Spanish, Experimental, Fantasy/Science Fiction, First-Time Independent Filmmakers, Gay Lesbian, Independent, International, Short, Student, Super 8/8mm, Underground, Video, Weird, Woman
Profile: Last year with the TromaDance slogan, "Give independent film back to the people," Troma inaugurated TromaDance as the first Film Festival devoted exclusively to filmmakers and fans. There are no V.I.P. reservations, no charge to submit your films, and entrance to the screenings is free to the public. The founders of TromaDance believe films are meant to be seen, especially when it comes to new filmmakers. Art is for the people! After selling a kidney on the black-

market to complete a short film, the organizers believe it is simply too cruel to charge an additional entry fee to have your film judged.

By coincidence, for twenty-six years it has been Troma's corporate policy not to pay for a film to be judged, especially by a corrupt elitist system. Many independent filmmakers believe that Sundance and other film festivals like it are controlled by the major studios and their public relations lackeys. It seems that too often, only those filmmakers who have a creepy fifty-year-old, bald, pigtailed, cell-phone-toting press agent wearing black get their films accepted to Sundance. If you are not connected to one of the major studios, your film will probably not be selected.

Tromadance is an opportunity for everyone who's ever picked up a camera to have their work seen without the compromises required by corporate interference. Help the people take back independent cinema by entering your movies in the Tromadance Film Festival!

Gore Score · · · · · · · · · · · · · · · ·
You won't find pretentious filmmakers at TromaDance, but you may find a woman in a bikini. Troma's support of genre films in Park City during Sundance is a refreshing break from depressing documentaries and earnest indies. Viva La Troma!

Application Fee: Absolutely no entry fees! The filmmakers put their lives into making their films, why should they have to pay to be judged or for the public to see it?

Common Mistakes: The worst thing you can do is submit your film but not put your contact information. Please make sure to include any press the film has received and a synopsis of the film, along with your contact info.

Insider Advice: Do not be afraid. You made your film for people to see it, so submit it! Even if it is not chosen, it is not necessarily because it is bad. We can only choose so many films. You can always try again next year! There

is no entry fee, so what do you have to lose?

Average Films Entered: We accept all kinds of films. Generally we have a tendency to pick the strangest, grossest and scariest of films, basically the films that evoke some kind of reaction. However, it doesn't matter what kind of film it is, as long as it is a good film and you can see that the filmmaker put his heart and soul into it.

Films Screened: 30-40

Odds of Acceptance: 1 in 25

Filmmaker Perks: If a filmmaker is willing to volunteer his or her services to work on Troma-Dance, we will put him or her up in our modest accommodations. All selections will be printed in all programs and advertisements we announce the official schedule in. Publications include *Variety* and many major Utah newspapers and publications around the time of the festival.

Best Parties: After the day-long festival, a huge party is thrown. There are always plenty of surprises and special guests.

Random Tidbits: Unfortunately, due to the mass numbers of videotapes we receive, films cannot be returned. All submissions must be on VHS 1/2" cassette.

TUBE FiLM FESTiVAL

c/o Outland Films
2378 Fairglen Drive
San Jose, CA 95125
Tel: 408-266-0242
Fax: 408-445-1335
Email: tube@expn.com
Web Site: www.expn.com
Festival Date: August
Entry Deadline: May
Year Festival Began: 2000
Contact: Ken Karn
Director: Ken Karn & Gary Meyer
Programmer: Gary Meyer
Category: Documentary, Independent
Awards: Yes
Competitions: Yes
Major Awards: Best Overall Film

TWiN RiVERS MEDiA FESTiVAL

SPVVA Inc.
Twin Rivers Art Center
P. O. Box 277
Minden, WV 25879
Tel: 304-469-4499
Fax: 304-465-1692
Email: outdoor@dnet.net
Web Site: www.spvva.com
Festival Date: October
Entry Deadline: October
Awards: Canoe & Kayak Magazine Outdoor Award: Special awards will be given to outdoor subjects, such as mountain biking, paddling, environmental concerns, outdoor appreciation, etc. All divisions are eligible.
Application Fee: Yes

UNiTED NATiONS ASSOCiATiON FiLM FESTiVAL

"I was delighted to learn about UNAFF and its successful inauguration."
—Ted Turner, Time Warner

P.O. Box 19369
Stanford, CA 94309
For entries only:
UNAFF
Department of Slavic Languages & Literatures
Stanford University
Stanford, CA 94305-2006
Tel: 650/724-5544; 650/725-0012
Fax: 650/725-0011
Email: info@unaff.org
Web Site: www.unaff.org
Festival Date: October
Entry Deadline: June
Contact: Sarah Wolcher
Director: Jasmina Bojic
Programmer: Jasmina Bojic
Other Staff: Brenda Wagner, Tina Ebey, Leah Edwards, Jane Clemmons, Joyce Leonard, Scott Sharpe, Beth Robinowiz
Category: Documentary, International
Profile: UNAFF is a non-competitive festival that screens documentaries by international filmmakers dealing with UN topics—human rights, environmental survival, women's issues, refugees

---

If a filmmaker is willing to volunteer his or her services to work on TromaDance, we will put him or her up in our modest accommodations (TromaDance).

protection, homelessness, racism, disease control, universal education, war and peace. UNAFF offers a unique opportunity to view films that are rarely screened for public audiences, to become familiar with global problems, and to provide a better understanding of the means to address these problems.

Seminars: Yes

Panels: Yes

Famous Speakers: John Savage, Barbara Trent, Peter Coyote

Market: No

Competitions: No

Application Fee: $25

Average Films Entered: 70

Films Screened: 22

Filmmaker Perks: Lodging and contacts.

Attendance: 2000

Journalist Attendance: 10

Best Cheap Hotels: California

Best Luxury Hotels: Sheraton

Best Restaurants: Il Fornaio

Best Bars: Blue Chalk

UNiTED STATES SUPER 8 FiLM/ViDEO FESTiVAL

c/o Rutgers Film Co-op/
NJ Media Arts Center
131 George St.
Rutgers University
New Brunswick, NJ 08901-1414
Tel: 732-932-8482
Fax: 732-932-1935
Email: NJMAC@aol.com
Web Site: www.rci.rutgers.edu/~nigrin
Festival Date: February
Entry Deadline: January
Contact: A. G. Nigrin
Director: A. G. Nigrin
Category: 8mm film/video
Profile: The Festival encourages any genre (animation, documentary, experimental, fiction, personal, etc.), but the work must have predominantly originated on Super 8mm film or 8mm video. All works will be screened by a panel of judges who will award $1200 in cash and prizes. The Festival takes as its mandate the spreading of the 8mm word. Toward that end, the Rutgers Film Co-op/NJMAC has spon-

sored four touring programs culled from Super 8 Festival prize winners for the past four years.

Seminars: Yes

Panels: Yes

Awards: Yes, $1200 in cash and prizes

Competitions: Yes

Major Awards: Six Best of Categories and Audience Choice Prize

Application Fee: $35

Insider Advice: Follow entry procedures.

Films Screened: 19

Filmmaker Perks: Exhibition, reduced rate at beautiful Hyatt Regency Hotel in NB, parties, contacts, etc.

Travel Tips: We are walking distance from train and bus Stations, half hour from Newark airport and 45 minutes from New York City

Best Restaurants: Old Bay (Cajun), Makeeda (Ethiopian), Sapporo (Japanese), Theresa's

Best Place for Breakfast: Bagel Dish cafe, Highland Park, NJ

UNiVERSiTY OF OREGON QUEER FiLM FESTiVAL

Student Activities Resource Office (SARO), Erb Memorial Union, University of Oregon
Eugene, OR 97403
Tel: 541-346-4000
Fax: 541-346-4400
Email: qff@darkwing.uoregon.edu
Web Site: darkwing.uoregon.edu/~qff/
Festival Date: February
Entry Deadline: November
Year Festival Began: 1993
Contact: Debby Martin (staff)
dmartin@oregon.uoregon.edu
541-346-4375
Director: Morgen Smith
Category: American Films, Animation, Documentary, Ethnic Other, Experimental, Gay Lesbian, Independent, International, Short, Student, Underground, Video, Weird
Market: No
Competitions: Yes

Major Awards: Jury's Choice

Value of Awards: Jury's Choice $200

1st place in experimental, documentary and fiction: $100

2nd place in experimental, documentary and fiction: $50

Honorable Mention: screening only

Application Fee: None

Common Mistakes: No return envelope for video.

Insider Advice: Go for it, it's free.

Average Films Entered: Anything queer related.

Films Screened: 8-16

Odds of Acceptance: 1 in 3

Attendance: 1,000

Journalist Attendance: Local press coverage, three publications.

Tourist Information: McKenzie River, Beach, Saturday Market

Best Cheap Hotels: New Oregon

Best Luxury Hotels: Valley River Inn

Best Restaurants: Zenon

Best Bars: Neighbors (gay)

Best Best Place for Breakfast: The Glenwood

URBANWORLD FiLM FESTiVAL

375 Greenwich St.
New York, NY 10013
Tel: 212-501-9668
Fax: 212-941-3849
Web Site: www.urbanworld.com
Festival Date: August
Year Festival Began: 1997
Director: Tony Murphy
Programmer: Joy Huang (Producer)
Other Staff: Stacy Spikes (Executive Director)
Category: Documentary, Ethnic Asian, Ethnic Black, Ethnic Latin, International, Short
Profile: The first internationally competitive film festival solely dedicated to redefining and enhancing the role of minority films in contemporary cinema.
Seminars: Yes
Panels: Yes

Famous Speakers: Debbie Allen, Samuel Jackson, LaTanya Richardson Jackson, Danny Glover, Russell Simmons, Tracey and Kenneth "Babyface" Edmonds and Andre Harrell.

Awards: Yes

Competitions: Yes

Major Awards: Grand Jury Prize

Value of Awards: $1000 in film stock

US INTERNATIONAL FILM & VIDEO FESTIVAL

United States Festivals Assoc.
841 N. Addison Ave.
Elmhurst, IL 60126-1291

Tel: 630-834-773

Fax: 630-834-5565

Festival Date: June

Entry Deadline: March

Director: J.W. Anderson

Category: Video

Application Fee: $100—$200

USA FILM FESTIVAL

6116 N. Central Exressway
Dalla, TX 75206

Tel: 214-821-6300

Fax: 214-821-6364

Email: usafilmfestival@aol.com

Web Site: www.usafilmfestival.com

Festival Date: April

Entry Deadline: March

Contact: Beth Jasper

Director: Ann Alexander

Category: American Films, Animation, Experimental, First-Time Independent Filmmakers, Independent, International, Short, Video

Profile: Eight day festival with over 13,000 attendees.

Gore Score · · · · · · · · · · · · · · ·

A staff that really cares makes the difference for the USA Film Festival. Filmmakers are treated like royalty and the parties, which take place mainly at the mansions of Dallas' elite, are fantastic.

Awards: Yes

Competitions: Yes

Major Awards: National Short Film and Video Competition

Value of Awards: $1,000 (drama, non-fiction, animation, and experimental categories) $500 (given to the family, Texas, and student winners) $250 (best music video)

Application Fee: $40

Odds of Acceptance: Over 700 entered

VALLEYFEST INDEPENDENT FILM FESTIVAL

P. O. Box 9312
Knoxville, TN 37940

Tel: 865-971-1792; 865-546-8885

Fax: 865-673-8264; 423-573-9447

Email: mswolfe@esper.com or euphoric@esper.com or u4icfilms@aol.com

Web Site: www.valleyfest.com

Festival Date: March

Entry Deadline: Early: November; Late: January

Year Festival Began: 1999

Contact: Melinda Wolfe

Director: Donna Maxwell

Programmer: Glen Glover

Category: American Films, Animation, Digital Animation, Documentary, Ethnic Asian, Ethnic Black, Ethnic Jewish, Experimental, Fantasy/Science Fiction, First-Time Independent Filmmakers, Gay Lesbian, Independent, International, Multimedia, Short, Student, Underground, Video, Weird, Woman

Profile: To showcase undistributed film and video works, especially first time efforts. To provide a fair and friendly atmosphere in which films may compete and to entertain and educate the film audience.

Seminars: Yes

Panels: Yes

Market: No

Competitions: Yes

Major Awards: Best Feature, Best Documentary, Best Short, Best Animation, Best of "Film is a Four Letter Word" and an Audience Award.

Value of Awards: Trophies are awarded. Cash as sponsorship allows.

Application Fee: Early entry: $30; Late entry: $50

Common Mistakes: Not filling out an application completely.

Insider Advice: Don't submit a film unless it is finished. When submitting the running time of your film, include the time it takes to run credits. If you are accepted, stay in touch with our website for specific information.

Films Screened: Our festival runs for four days and we do not predetermine a specific number of films to be screened.

Odds of Acceptance: 1 in 2

Filmmaker Perks: Lots of parties go along with Valleyfest and the filmmakers are always the guests of honor. Valleyfest has a very intimate and friendly atmosphere that filmmakers have appreciated and plenty of opportunities to network and make contacts.

Attendance: 500-1,000

Journalist Attendance: 5-10

Tourist Information: Great Smokey Mountains National Park

Travel Tips: You never know what the weather will be like in March.

Best Cheap Hotels: We've had great success in helping to arrange hotels for filmmakers. We've been able to work a few deals with a couple of hotels so that everyone can afford to stay in really nice places.

Best Restaurants: Mango, Tomato Head, Lula's

Best Bars: Try the Cumberland Strip on the UT campus or visit the many bars in the Old City.

VANCOUVER INTERNATIONAL FILM FESTIVAL

Suite 410—1008 Homer St.
Vancouver, BC V6B 2X1 Canada

Tel: Admin: 604-685-0260
Box Office (Open 10 days before the festival begins): 604-685-8297

Fax: 604-688-8221

Email: viff@viff.org

Web Site: viff.org

Festival Date: September-October

Entry Deadline: July

Director, writer, action figure Kevin Smith is lured by the Toxic Avenger into the TromaDance festivities.

Contact: Nick Tattersall

Director: Alan Franey

Programmer: Alan Franey, Festival Director

Category: Documentary, Independent, International

Profile: The purpose of the Vancouver International Film Festival is to encourage understanding of other nations through the art of cinema, to foster the art of cinema, to facilitate the meeting in British Columbia of cinema professionals from around the world, and to stimulate the motion picture industry in British Columbia and Canada.

Seminars: Each year our festival hosts The Film and Television Trade Forum—a four-day event of seminars and guest speakers covering the myriad issues filmmakers face in the community. Subjects covered include: distribution, marketing, documentaries, animation, directing your own script, navigating the financial landscapes, satire for television, TV series, co-productions, development, new media, pitching your ides, tricks of the trade, keynote luncheon speakers, etc.

Awards: No

Competitions: No

Major Awards: Air Canada People's Choice Award for Most Popular Film

Application Tips: Follow the directions on the regulations carefully, don't submit after dead-line, fill out the form legibly...make good films.

Application Fee: None

Films Screened: Approximately 300 films.

Travel Tips: Be prepared for plenty of rain, try and get to the North Shore Mountains, Stanley Park is an urban must-see, American money works almost as well here as the third world.

Best Restaurants: Diva at the Metropolitan Hotel or Lola's

Best Bars: Babalu's at the Dakota

Best Hangout for Filmmakers: Gerrards lounge at the Sutton Place Hotel.

Best Place for Breakfast: The Elbow Room Cafe

VANCOUVER iSLAND MEDiA FEST

P.O. Box 754

Sooke BC, V0S 1N0 Canada

Tel: 250-642-6745; 250-642-6142

Fax: 250-642-7722

Email: filmfest@film.bc.ca

Web Site: film.bc.ca/filmfest

Festival Date: August 18-20, 2001

Entry Deadline: July 1, 2001

Year Festival Began: 2000 (First Annual)

Contact: Linda Gordon, 250-642-6745

Director: Linda Gordon, Mel Dobres, Edward Milne Community School

Programmer: Shannon Valentine, Gary Nicholls

Category: Animation, Digital, Digital Animation, DVD, Experimental, Fantasy/Science Fiction, First-Time Independent Filmmakers, Independent, International, Microcinema, Multimedia, Short, Student, Super 8/8mm, Underground, Video, Weird

Profile: This festival will showcase film, video and new media. It is the first year of a projected anual event, and our emphasis is on student projects. New media productions from Flash, Director, 3D Studio Max and even Power Point presentations are being showcased. The festival promotes the cutting edge of animation, non-linear editing and how today's youth is exploring the new technology.

Seminars: Yes

Market: No

Competitions: Yes

Major Awards: Best Film, Best Video, Best New Media

Value of Awards: Plaque and $50

Application Fee: $20 students or schools (Schools may present one tape with multiple students for $20)

Independent Professional $40

Feature Length $100

Common Mistakes: Not including a return address.

Insider Advice: Don't be your own worst critic. Don't let it out that the "mistake" is not a planned "special effect."

Films Screened: 21+

Odds of Acceptance: 1 in 1

Filmmaker Perks: Lodging and Contacts. Scholarships to cover accommodation during the festival are available.

Attendance: 1,000

Tourist Information: Hiking trails, beaches, fishing charters, hunting.

Travel Tips: We are on an island, allow extra travel time on the ferry. Bring sunscreen!

Best Cheap Hotels: Malahat Farm

Best Luxury Hotels: Parkside Marine

Best Restaurants: Sooke Harbour House

Best Bars: Castle Pub

Best Hangout for Filmmakers: Fox's Grill

Best Place for Breakfast: Mom's Cafe

VANCOUVER—OUT ON SCREEN QUEER FILM & VIDEO FESTIVAL

405-207 West Hastings Street
Vancouver, BC V6B 1H7 Canada
Tel: 604-844-1615
Fax: 604-844-1698
Email: general@outonscreen.com
Web Site: www.outonscreen.com
Festival Date: August
Entry Deadline: April/May
Contact: Drew Dennis
Director: Drew Dennis
Programmer: Michael Barrett
Category: Gay Lesbian

VANCOUVER UNDERGROUND FILM FESTIVAL

Canada
Email: panic@istar.ca
Web Site: www.blindinglight.com
Festival Date: November
Entry Deadline: October
Year Festival Began: 1998
Director: Alex MacKenzie
Programmer: Alex MacKenzie

Category: Short, Underground, Video, Weird

Profile: Recently voted "Vancouver's Best Alternative Cinema." The Blinding Light is proud to be presenting Vancouver's first ever underground film festival. Expect the best in radical film and video works: hand processed, homemade, strange, experimental and challenging.

VERMONT INTERNATIONAL FILM FESTIVAL: IMAGES AND ISSUES FOR SOCIAL CHANGE

One Main St., Suite 307
Burlington, VT 05401
Tel: 802-660-2600
Fax: 802-860-9555
Email: viff@together.net
Web Site: www.vtiff.org
Festival Date: October
Entry Deadline: July
Year Festival Began: 1985
Contact: Robin Paul
Director: Kenneth Peck
Programmer: Barry Snyder
Profile: Our mission is to inform and motivate people, through film and video, to work for peace, justice and respect for the natural world. We except films in three categories for competition: War and Peace, Justice and Human Rights, and The Environment. All films must be made in the year prior to the festival, and by independent filmmakers.

Awards: Yes. Awards are given or the best of each category, as well as Heart of Festival and People's Choice. Awards are a plaque with the filmmakers name and the title of the film.

Competitions: Yes

Major Awards: Best of the Festival

Application Tips: Follow the format given in the all-For-Entry form, include the $65 fee.

Application Fee: $65

Insider Advice: Our judges appreciate time and care taken to make the submitted works of outstanding cinematic quality.

Odds of Acceptance: Over 100 films are submitted into our festival, about 25-30 will be shown.

Best Restaurants: Bourbon Street Grill, Trattoria Delia, Leunig's, Sweet Tomatoes, Parima, Isabel's On the Waterfront, Smokejacks

Best Bars: Red Square, Nectars, Metronome, Higher Ground, Nickanoose.

Best Hangout for Filmmakers: Muddy Waters (Coffee House), Stone Soup (Vegetarian Bistro)

Best Place for Breakfast: Sneakers in Winooski, G's, Oasis Diner, First Waltz Cafe, Leunig's.

VICTORIA INDEPENDENT FILM AND VIDEO FESTIVAL

101-610 Johnson St.
Victoria, BC, V8W 1M4 Canada
Tel: 250-389-0444
Fax: 250-380-1547
Email: vifvf@direct.ca
Web Site: mypage.direct.ca/v/vifvf
Festival Date: February
Entry Deadline: October
Year Festival Began: 1995
Contact: Kathy Kay or Donovan Aikman
Director: Kathy Kay
Programmer: Donovan Aikman
Category: American Films, Animation, Documentary, Experimental, First-Time Independent Filmmakers, Gay Lesbian, Independent, International, Short, Student, Video, Woman
Profile: Bringing filmmakers and the public together in celebration of creativity, comraderie and sharing information.

Seminars: Yes

Panels: Yes

Market: No

Awards: Yes

Competitions: Yes

Major Awards: Best Feature Film

Value of Awards: No value, but you're brought to the festival and get a funky looking award.

Application Tips: Print legibly, read and understand the form you are signing and write a great synopsis.

Application Fee: $10

Common Mistakes: Fill in the form incorrectly.

Films Screened: 120

Odds of Acceptance: 1 in 4

Filmmaker Perks: To selected filmmakers we provide air travel and a suite at the fabulous Laurel Point Inn. In addition, all directors with accepted films receive a VIP pass. Lots of contact with established film types because everyone's got their guard down and thinks they're on vacation.

Attendance: 6,100

Journalist Attendance: It goes up each year, in 2000 we had 18.

Tourist Information: Victoria has a fantastic museum, the Royal British Columbia Museum. Whale watching for the outdoor types.

Travel Tips: Write your name in all your clothing then book your flight all the way to Victoria—getting dropped off in Vancouver leaves you with an additional three-hour journey (gorgeous though). The weather is generally mild with a mix of cloud and sun, don't forget a jacket. Don't drink too much on the plane—you'll feel terrible later.

Best Cheap Hotels: The Laurel Point Inn is a luxury hotel that provides an inexpensive rate to festival-goers

Best Luxury Hotels: The Laurel Point Inn

Best Restaurants: Il Terrazzo for the stuffed squid; Izumi for the best sushi; Med Grill for pizza

Best Bars: Hugo's, or for strange and bizarre—Big Bad John's

Best Parties: We have a great party: The Mad Hatter's Croquet Party. It features wonky mallets, human wickets, white rabbits with liqueur-filled pill bottles and a Queen with an attitude.

Best Hangout for Filmmakers: The Lounge at the Laurel Point Inn

Best Place for Breakfast: Scott's on Yates for a morning cheeseburger and coffee

VIRGINIA FILM FESTIVAL

Department of Drama
109 Culbreth Rd.
Charlottesville, VA 22903-2446
Tel: 804-982-5277
Fax: 804-924-1447
Email: filmfest@virginia.edu
Web Site: www.vafilm.com
Festival Date: October
Entry Deadline: July
Contact: Richard Herskowitz
Director: Richard Herskowitz
Category: A retreat for filmmakers, scholars and film lovers emphasizing education and entertainment. The Festival examines American film in the context of the international films it influences and reflects. A different theme is explored every year through a mix of classics, mainstream and indie premieres. This is a Festival especially for people who like to talk about film; in fact, it's probably the only Festival with more speakers than films.

Profile: The Virginia Film Festival explores American film and the international cinema it influences and reflects in an annual academic forum that brings together authors, critics, directors, actors, artists, and scholars from across the nation.

Awards: None

Competitions: No

Application Tips: Cue your tape to the best scene for panel viewing. It helps if the film relates to the festival's theme that year, but this is not essential.

Application Fee: $30

Insider Advice: Make your film brilliant, innovative and revelatory, so we're sure to accept it.

Average Films Entered: 150

Films Screened: 60

Odds of Acceptance: 1 in 3

Filmmaker Perks: Lodging and free access to Festival events and parties, plus contacts with many film industry guests.

Attendance: 10,000+

Travel Tips: You can get here by plane or train. We're two hours from D.C. and one hour from Richmond. Charlottesville is spectacular in the fall, and we catch the leaves turning at their peak. Jefferson's Monticello and Rotunda are nearby for visits.

Best Restaurants: Metropolitain.

Best Bars: Miller's

Best Hangout for Filmmakers: The Mudhouse.

Best Place for Breakfast: The Tavern.

WASHINGTON, DC INTERNATIONAL FILM FESTIVAL—FILMFEST DC

P. O. Box 21396
Washington, DC 20009
Tel: 202-724-5613
Fax: 202-724-6578
Email: filmfestdc@filmfestdc.org
Web Site: www.filmfestdc.org
Festival Date: April 18-29, 2001
Entry Deadline: January
Contact: Anthony Gittens, Director
Shirin Ghareeb, Assistant Director
Director: Anthony Gittens
Category: American Films, Ethnic African, Ethnic Asian, Ethnic Black, Ethnic Jewish, Ethnic Latin, Ethnic Other, Ethnic Spanish, First-Time Independent Filmmakers, Independent, International, Short

Profile: Our mission is to bring the best in new international cinema to the nation's capital, and to present these works in a spirit of appreciation and cooperation. We are committed to excellence in both the artistic presentation and management of our event.

Filmfest DC, presented annually, offers over seventy feature premieres, as well as an opening night gala, closing night event, receptions, panels and CineCafes. Many guest directors are in attendance. Filmfest DC is non-competitive, however an Audience Award for favorite film is offered. All categories: shorts, animation, documentaries, children, but mostly features.

Seminars: Yes

Panels: Yes

Market: No

Competitions: Yes

Major Awards: Audience Award

> Cue your tape to the best scene for panel viewing (Virginia Film Festival).

Application Fee: Under 30 min./$15.00

30 min. or over/$25.00

Films Screened: 70

Odds of Acceptance: 1 in 4

Filmmaker Perks: Free travel, lodging, contacts.

Attendance: 36,000

Journalist Attendance: 15

Tourist Information: Museums, national monuments, ethnic neighborhoods

Best Luxury Hotels: The Willard, Four Seasons

Best Restaurants: Georgia Brown's, Obelisk

WATERFRONT FILM FESTIVAL

P.O. Box 387

712 Lake St. (UPS and FedEx)

Saugatuck, MI 49453

Tel: 616-857-8351

Fax: 616-393-0964

Email: Info@waterfrontfilm.com

Web Site: www.waterfrontfilm.com

Festival Date: June 7-10, 2001

Entry Deadline: March 16, 2001

Year Festival Began: 1999

Contact: Dori DePree, dori@waterfrontfilm.com

Director: Hopwood DePree, info@waterfrontfilm.com, Kori Eldean, kori@waterfrontfilm.com

Category: American Films, Independent

Profile: A non-competitive festival celebrating and entertaining the American Independent Filmmaker. Said to be "the number one party festival" by filmmakers, the Waterfront Film Festival offers a unique and festive artists' retreat for fostering an exchange of ideas, discovering films, and having a fantastic time in the lively summer resort village of Saugatuck, Michigan. The Waterfront Film Festival is, according to one guest, "quite possibly the most hospitable festival in the United States." The Festival is open to 16 and 35mm films of any genre (Features, Shorts, Documentaries, Animation, etc.)

Seminars: Yes

Panels: Yes

Famous Speakers: Each year, the Festival brings in a person to honor who has made a large contribution to American Independent filmmaking. This person speaks at the opening ceremony.

Market: No

Competitions: No

Application Fee: $25 if less than 60 minutes; $45 if 60 minutes or longer

Insider Advice: Send a complete package of all the materials requested with the application. If you would like your film returned, include a self-addressed, stamped envelope.

Average Films Entered: We accept all kinds of films but, we tend to lean toward comedies.

Films Screened: 30

Odds of Acceptance: 1 in 10

Filmmaker Perks: We offer free hospitality to some feature filmmakers—this includes airfare, ground transportation, lodging and access to the hospitality lanai (as much food and drink as one cares to consume.) Accommodations are located on the water's edge. Hospitality is our specialty. One of the benefits of the Festival is that all guests stay in the same hotel.

Attendance: 6,000

Journalist Attendance: 60-70

Tourist Information: The lively summer resort village of Saugatuck, situated amongst the towering white sand dunes of Lake Michigan, is already a well-known tourist stop with its quaint shops, homey B&B's, crazy night life and fabulous beaches ranked as one of the top five in the U.S. by MTV.

Travel Tips: Bring summer wear, sunscreen, and a good attitude

Best Cheap Hotels: Ship-n-Shore Motel Boatel

Best Luxury Hotels: Wickwood Inn B&B

Best Restaurants: Marro's

Best Bars: Coral Gables

Best Hangout for Filmmakers: Waterfront's Hospitality Lanai with live poolside music, free water sports, and a 24-hour complimentary Margarita Machine.

Best Place for Breakfast: Ida Red's

Festival Tale: Things tend to get out of hand at Waterfront and people tend to drink more than they usually would. This was most evident last year when a well-known male celebrity (to remain nameless) and two female Festival guests went drunkenly skinny-dipping at 4 a.m. When the trio realized they were out of cigarettes, they commandeered a Festival golf cart and sputtered along for ten miles where they came upon a local pie factory. Imagine the shock, or delight, of the third-shift, hair-netted, pie-factory workers who were greeted by a naked woman, a celebrity in his tighty-whities, and a well-endowed female wearing nothing but a torn plastic tablecloth—all looking to bum a smoke. Needless to say, they returned with almost a full carton of cigarettes.

Random Tidbits: Major sponsors include: The William Morris Agency, Kodak, and The Screen Actors Guild.

WAYS IN BEING GAY (BIANNUAL)

2495 Main St., Suite 425

Buffalo, NY 14214

Tel: 716-835-7362

Fax: 716-835-7364

Email: Office@hallwalls.org

Web Site: www.hallwalls.org

Festival Date: November 2002 (festival is biannual)

Entry Deadline: August 15, 2002

Year Festival Began: 1988

Director: Ed Cardoni, Executive Director

Category: Gay Lesbian

Profile: This biannual festival of works by gay, lesbian, and transgendered artists includes visual art, literature, film, video, and performance.

Market: No

Competitions: No

Application Fee: None

Insider Advice: Send VHS sample reel with description, bio and SASE.

Films Screened: 15-20

Filmmaker Perks: Selected artists are invited for in-person presentations, including travel, accomodations, and honorarium.

Attendance: 500

Tourist Information: Niagara Falls

Best Hangout for Filmmakers: Squeaky Wheel media center

WEST ViRGiNiA iNTERNATiONAL FiLM FESTiVAL

P.O. Box 2165
Charleston, WV 25328-2165

Tel: 304-342-7100

Fax: 304-759-2501

Email: haynespam@aol.com

Web Site: www.wviff.org

Festival Date: May 4-8, 2001

Entry Deadline: March 1, 2001

Year Festival Began: 1985

Contact: Pamela Haynes

Director: Pamela Haynes

Programmer: Tim Alderman

Category: Animation, Documentary, Ethnic Other, Independent, International, Multi-Cultural, Student

Profile: The WVIFF is a non-profit organization dedicated to the celebration and cultivation of film as art and is one of the premier cultural arts organizations in the Appalachian region. The WVIFF offers spring and fall cinematic programming and special events to the general public, reaching some 4,000 film-lovers annually. The Spring Festival program consists of limited release foreign and domestic feature and short films as well as locally-produced films unlikely to be exhibited theatrically in West Virginia. The WVIFF serves an important purpose and community service by bringing cultural, ethnic, and special interest communities closer together by promoting and sharing glimpses of diverse cultures around the world through the magic of the movies.

Panels: Yes

Market: No

Competitions: No

Value of Awards: Total award value: $2,400

Films Screened: 16

Odds of Acceptance: 1 in 2

Filmmaker Perks: Travel and lodging are provided to guests of the festival.

Attendance: 1,500

Journalist Attendance: 6

Tourist Information: Blenko Glass, Sunrise Museum & Science Hall, Snowshoe Ski Resort, Canaan Valley Ski Resort, The Mystery Hole, The Greenbrier Hotel & Resort, Blennerhassett Island, Marshall University (home of the Thundering Herd), and plenty of the best whitewater rafting this side of the Mississippi!

Travel Tips: Don't let your travel agent tell you that jets don't fly into Charleston; they do!

Best Cheap Hotels: Fairfield Inn by Marriott

Best Luxury Hotels: Marriott Town Center

Best Restaurants: Tidewater (fresh fish flown in daily!)

Best Bars: Joey's Bar & Grill

Best Hangout for Filmmakers: Taylor Books

Best Place for Breakfast: Marriott Town Center brunch

WHiSTLER iNTERNATiONAL FiLM & TELEViSiON

601 West Broadway, Suite 400
Vancouver, British Columbia V5Z 4C2 Canada

Tel: 604/871-4328

Fax: 604/871-4338

Email: info@whistlerfilmtv festival.com

Web Site: www.whistlerfilmtv festival.com

Festival Date: March

Entry Deadline: January

Year Festival Began: 2001

Contact: Leagh Gabriel

Director: Leagh Gabriel & Susan Cooke Dosot

Programmer: Tom Lightburn and David Forget (features) & Coreen Mayrs (shorts)

Category: Animation, Digital, Digital Animation, DVD, Experimental, First-Time Independent Filmmakers, Independent, International, Markets, Multimedia, Short, Video

Profile: This world-class film and television festival will debut March 28-31, 2001 in Whistler, British Columbia, one of the world's pre-eminent resorts, and will screen 60 feature-length and short films from around the world.

The Festival will host an Industry Conference where the impact of leading edge convergence technologies on the entertainment industry will be explored. The conference will involve some of the biggest names in New Media, film and television. It will attract professional who will want to be brought up-to-date on current creative and marketing trends, and will provide workshops to assist emerging talent in makeing the leap into the international marketplace.

There are a number of social events planned, including a celebrity ski race. Whistler is one of the most beautiful towns on the face of this earth. It is not just a stunning backdrop, it is a center of glamour and excitement that will provide all of

BEST NEW FESTIVALS

Deep Ellum Film Festival
Edmonds International Film Festival
Hollywood Black Film Festival
Method Fest
Moondance International Film Festival
Silver Lake Film Festival
Valleyfest Independent Film Festival
Waterfront Film Festival
Williamstown Film Festival
Wisconsin Film Festival

Robert Redford ponders a question from the audience during a panel discussion.

PHOTO BY
RANDALL MICHELSON

those attending with wonderful memories.

Seminars: Yes

Panels: Yes

Famous Speakers: Yes

Films Screened: 30 Features and 30 shorts

Best Luxury Hotels: Chateau Whistler & The Westin Hotel

Best Restaurants: Umbertos

WILLIAMSTOWN FILM FESTIVAL

"The beauty of location makes the Williamstown Film Festival a draw for visitors to the Berkshires ... Massachusetts is fast becoming Sundance East."

—Boston Globe

P.O. Box 81

Williamstown, MA 01267

Tel: 413-458-9700

Fax: 413-458-9700

Email: filmfest@mailcity.com

Web Site: www.williamstown filmfest.com

Festival Date: September 21-30, 2001

Entry Deadline: August

Year Festival Began: 1999

Director: Steve Lawson

Category: American Films, DVD, Experimental, First-Time Independent Filmmakers, Independent, Short, Student, Weird

Profile: WFF was founded for several reasons: to add the element of film to an otherwise culturally-rich region (art, dance, music, theater galore); to hook up with the proliferating startup companies in the Berkshires with advanced links to new technologies (DVD, et al), and to bring together a provocative blend of film fans, scholars, critics, artists, and industry professionals in order to honor film's past (classics), celebrate a major figure in the film arena today, and try to figure out where the hell film may be heading.

Seminars: Yes

Panels: Yes

Awards: No

Application Fee: $20

Common Mistakes: Send films that look and sound like other films.

Insider Advice: Have something to say and make it your own voice.

Films Screened: 6

Odds of Acceptance: 1 in 3

Filmmaker Perks: Occasional free travel; always lodging.

Attendance: 1,200

Journalist Attendance: 10

Tourist Information: Williamstown Theatre Festival, Tanglewood, Images Cinema, MASS MoCA, Clark Art Institute

Travel Tips: Reserve early!

Best Cheap Hotels: Field Farm

Best Luxury Hotels: The Orchards

Best Restaurants: Main Street Cafe, Wild Amber Grill

Best Bars: Mezze

Best Place for Breakfast: Blue Benn, Bennington, VT

WINE COUNTRY FILM FESTIVAL

P.O. Box 303 (Mailing Address)

12000 Henno Rd. (FedEx and UPS)

Glen Ellen, CA 95442

Tel: 707-996-2536

Fax: 707-996-6964

Email: wcfilmfest@aol.com

Web Site: www.winecountry filmfest.com

Festival Date: July-August

Entry Deadline: April

Contact: Stephen Ashton

Director: Stephen Ashton, Creative Director

Category: Short

Application Fee: $25

WISCONSIN FILM FESTIVAL

UW–Madison Arts Institute

Vilas Hall 6th Floor

821 University Ave.

Madison, WI 53706

Tel: 608-262-9009 ; 877-963-FILM

Fax: 608-262-6589

Email: filmfest@arts.wisc.edu

Web Site: www.arts.wisc.edu

Festival Date: March 29-April 1, 2001

Year Festival Began: 1999

Contact: Mary Carbine, Director

Director: Mary Carbine, UW-Madison Arts Institute

Category: American Films, Animation, Documentary, Ethnic African, Ethnic Asian, Ethnic Black, Ethnic Jewish, Ethnic Latin, Ethnic Spanish, Experimental, First-Time Independent Filmmakers, Gay Lesbian, Independent, International, Multimedia, Short, Underground, Video, Woman

Profile: Now in its third year, the Wisconsin Film Festival is a university-community festival in Madison that brings the best of independent, experimental and world cinema and new media to Wisconsin and showcases Wisconsin filmmakers.

Seminars: Yes
Panels: Yes
Market: No
Competitions: No
Common Mistakes: Don't read the guidelines. Don't have good photos or press kits. Have photos that are grainy, muddy or not of principal characters in key scenes. Don't respond to follow-ups from programmers. Argue with the programmers decision instead of asking for feedback or referrals.

Insider Advice: Create a one-page info sheet with basic information—film name, director, principal credits, year of completion, language, format(s) available, technical information, contact information, and both a one-sentence and three-sentence film summary. Include key press quotes if available.

Also, put together a press kit with the above as well as a longer film summary, brief bios of key players, and some story material or background on the film's production. Include at least one photo from the film-a close-up or medium shot that captures the film content and gives the audience some idea of what kind of experience they will have seeing the film. Or, save money by sending printouts of the photos and providing a disc or way to electronically send 600 x 900 high-resolution JPG files (the kind needed by newspapers, printers).

Average Films Entered: The Wisconsin Film Festival accepts submissions from filmmakers with Wisconsin ties—within those guidelines, we accept features, shorts, documentary, animated films and new media. We do not accept educational, instructional or industrial films.
Films Screened: Approximately 70
Filmmaker Perks: If we choose the film for the festival, we will work to make it a positive experience for the filmmaker and make it possible for them to attend.

Attendance: 12,000
Journalist Attendance: 15
Tourist Information: Madison has been on the *Money Magazine* "Best Places to Live" lists—great restaurants, funky shops, good art museums, coffeeshops, music clubs, lakes, outdoors. But during the festival weekend, visitors will want to visit our venues, Orpheum Theatre, Madison Art Center, UW-Madison Cinematheque and Memorial Union. Check our website before attending—we'll point you towards things to do and see in Madison.

WOODSTOCK FiLM FESTIVAL
P.O. Box 1406
Woodstock, NY 12498
Tel: 845-679-4265
Fax: 509-479-5414
Email: info@woodstockfilm festival.com
Web Site: www.woodstockfilm festival.com or www.radiowoodstock.com
Festival Date: September
Entry Deadline: July
Year Festival Began: 2000
Contact: Meira Blaustein
Director: Meira Blaustein
Category: Digital, Documentary, Independent, Short

YORKTON SHORT FiLM AND ViDEO FESTIVAL
49 Smith St. East
Yorkton, Saskatchewan S3N 0H4
Canada
Tel: 306-782-7077
Fax: 306-782-1550
Email: info@yorktonshort film.org
Web Site: www.yorktonshort film.org
Festival Date: May
Entry Deadline: February
Contact: Fay Kowal
Director: Fay Kowal
Category: Short, Video

BEST INTERNATIONAL FESTIVALS IN THE USA
Cleveland International Film Festival
Denver International Film Festival
Fort Lauderdale International Film Festival
Houston International Film and Video Festival (Worldfest Houston)
Santa Barbara International Film Festival
Santa Clarita International Film Festival
San Francisco International Film Festival
Seattle International Film Festival
St. Louis International Film Festival
West Virginia International Film Festival

Teen projectionist Galen Rosenthal tucked away in the makeshift booth.

PROJECTING AN IMAGE

What can filmmakers do to make a projectionist's job easier when it comes to sending their prints? You have just spent your life savings on your film, and it's about to premiere at a film festival. Bear in mind you are not opening at Grauman's Chinese Theater. Here are some very simple things you can do to ensure the smoothest possible screening:

1. Make sure your film arrives early and that the cans are marked with the title. If the film is in two cans, label them: 1 of 2, 2 of 2.
2. Label the heads and tails of your print clearly. Include details of the gauge and the reel number on every head and tail: "CITIZEN KANE, B&W, sound, R 1 of 6, 1.33:1, Heads."
3. Write any special projection instructions on a separate sheet and attach it to the inside of the film case. Example: "Focus on Academy Leader, as film begins on a soft image." or "There is no sound for the first thirty seconds of movie."
4. Mark all change-overs clearly (or ask the lab to do so.)
5. Deliver your film ready to project. Your entire film should arrive inspected, heads out on reels (not cores), with all leaders double-side spliced.

Remember: Once the film is up on the screen, it is out of your hands. If there are problems with the sound, focus, framing, or change-overs, deal with them gracefully. Speaking ill of the equipment, festival, or projectionist during the obligatory Q&A makes you look petty. And most importantly—don't give the projectionist a hard time. You never know when they may turn out to be a festival judge.

—Gabe Wardell, projectionist, programmer and jury member
for Slamdance and the Atlanta Film & Video Festival

iNTERNATiONAL FiLM FESTiVALS
Alphabetical by Country

ARGENTINA
---

iNTERNATiONAL FESTiVAL OF FiLMS MADE BY WOMEN

Lavalle 1578 9o piso "B"
1048 Buenos Aires, Argentina
Tel: 54-1-374-7318
Fax: 54-1-311-3062
Contact: Beatriz de Villalba Welsh
Category: International, Women

AUSTRALIA

ADELAiDE iNTERNATiONAL CHiLDREN'S FiLM AND ViDEO FESTiVAL

South Australian Film & Video Centre, Lumiere Lane,
Westside Commerce Center
113 Tapleys Hill Rd.
Hendon, South Australia 5014
Australia
Tel: 08-348-9355
Fax: 08-345-4222
Festival Date: Biennial (even years)
Director: Priscilla Thomas, Project Officer; Andrew Zielinski, Director

ANiMANiA: iNTERNATiONAL FESTiVAL OF ANiMATiON AND MULTiMEDiA

Flickerfest
P.O. Box 52
Haymarket NSW 2000, Australia
Tel: 61-2-251-4960
Fax: 61-2-251-4970
Festival Date: April
Entry Deadline: November
Contact: Craig B. Kirkwood
Category: Animation

AUSTRALiAN iNTERNATiONAL OUTDOOR SHORT FiLM FESTiVAL

Flickerfest
1/21 Gould St.
Bondi Beach, NSW 2026
Australia
Tel: 61-2-9365-6877
Fax: 61-2-251-4970;
61-2-9365-6899
Email: flickerfest@bigpond.com
Web Site: www.flickerfest.com.au
Festival Date: January
Entry Deadline: October
Contact: Bronwyn Kidd
Category: International, Short
Competitions: Yes
Major Awards: Kodak Award for Best Film of Festival
Value of Awards: $2000 AUD
Application Fee: $20 AUD

BRiSBANE iNTERNATiONAL FiLM FESTiVAL

Level 3
Hoyts Regents Bldg.
167 Queen St. Mall
Brisbane, Q 4000 Australia
Tel: 61-7-22-00-333
Fax: 61-7-22-00-400
Festival Date: August
Entry Deadline: June
Contact: Gary Ellis

HiGH BEAM iNTERNATiONAL iNDEPENDENT DRiVE-iN FiLM FESTiVAL

Syndey, Australia
Email: highbeam@ihug.com.au
Contact: Lachlan Imrie
Category: Independent, Short
Profile: High Beam is a competitive festival for indepndently made feature films and shorts. The fest is an outdoor Drive-In combined with an indoor competitive film festival with open film forums and discussions.
Competitions: Yes

MELBOURNE iNTERNATiONAL FiLM AND ViDEO FESTiVAL

P.O. Box 43
St. Kilda
3182 Victoria, Australia
Tel: 03-534-3964
Fax: 03-534-3467
Festival Date: June
Entry Deadline: June
Contact: Harvey Hutchinson

MELBOURNE iNTERNATiONAL FiLM FESTiVAL

P.O. Box 2206
Fitzroy Mail Centre, VIC. 3065
Australia
Tel: 61-3-9417-2011
Fax: 61-3-9417-3804
Email: miff@vicnet.net.au
Web Site: www.melbournefilmfestival.com.au
Festival Date: July-August
Entry Deadline: March (Short Films); April (Features)
Year Festival Began: 1952

Contact: Brett Woodward

Category: International

Profile: Established in 1952, the Melbourne International Film Festival is one of the country's oldest running arts events and the oldest and largest established film festival in the Southern Hemisphere. It is a major event on the Australian arts calendar.

Screened in some of Melbourne's most celebrated inner city cinemas and theatres, the Festival comprises an eclectic mix of outstanding filmmaking from around the world. The Melbourne International Film Festival is a showcase for the latest developments in Australian and International filmmaking, offering audiences a wide range of features and shorts, documentaries, animation and experimental films.

The Festival presents a significant showcase of new Australian cinema and its programme of nearly 200 films is viewed by an enthusiastic and dedicated audience of over 67,000 people.

Seminars: Yes

Famous Speakers: Varies from year to year

Awards: Yes

Competitions: Yes, for short films only.

Major Awards: Best Short Film: $5000 Australian

Best Documentary Short Film: $2000 Australian

Best Experimental Short Film: $2000 Australian

Best Animated Short Film: $2000 Australian

Best Fiction Short Film: $2000 Australian

Value of Awards: Prize money value may vary from year to year

Application Tips: Follow guidelines

Application Fee: Only for the Short Film Competition—$25 U.S. or $30 Australian

Films Screened: 116 features were screened in 1998.

Odds of Acceptance: Features entries are generally by invitation only. The festival receives approximately 600 short film entries each year; approximately

> Melbourne is a very easygoing city, with plenty of bars, cafes and restaurants at reasonable prices. People are very friendly (Melbourne International Film Festival).

100 shorts are included in the program.

Filmmaker Perks: Travel and accommodations are only offered to guests invited to the festival.

Tourist Information: Melbourne is a very easygoing city, with plenty of bars, cafes and restaurants at reasonable prices. People are very friendly.

MELBOURNE QUEER FiLM & ViDEO FESTiVAL

1/35 Cato Street
Prahran, VIC 3181 Australia
Tel: 613-9510-5576
Fax: 613-9510-5699
Email: qfa@rucc.net.au
Web Site: mqfvf.also.org.au
Festival Date: March
Entry Deadline: December
Year Festival Began: 1990
Contact: Lisa Daniel
Director: Lisa Daniel
Programmer: Lisa Daniel, Claire Jackson, Gaye Naismith, Kevin d'Souza, Sam Harrison, Ben Zipper, Joseph Alessi, Olivia Khoo, Lachlan McDowell, Guinevere Narraway, Tim Hunter, Chris Osborne, Paul Jeffery.
Category: American Films, Animation, Documentary, Ethnic African, Ethnic Asian, Ethnic Black, Ethnic Jewish, Ethnic Latin, Ethnic Other, Ethnic Spanish, Experimental, First-Time Independent Filmmakers, Gay Lesbian, Independent, International, Online Festival, Short, Student, Super 8/8mm, Underground, Video, Weird, Woman
Profile: The Festival aims to show quality films for by and about queers from Australia and around the world.
Seminars: Yes
Panels: Yes
Market: No
Competitions: Yes
Major Awards: City of Melbourne Emerging Filmmaker Award
Value of Awards: $1000 cash
Last Winning Directors: Andrew Soo

Application Fee: None
Insider Advice: Give as much info about film as possible (i.e., good press kit or info pack), clear contact details, entry form.
Average Films Entered: Queer films of with a good, original idea, hopefully entertaining, informative.
Films Screened: 98
Odds of Acceptance: 1 in 2
Filmmaker Perks: We are non-profit so are unable to afford travel. Although we usually supply lodging where possible.
Attendance: 8,000
Journalist Attendance: 36
Tourist Information: Victoria Market (biggest outdoor market in Southern Hemisphere), Melbourne Aquarium, Galleries, sporting events, local restaurants, bars.
Travel Tips: Have plenty of time.
Best Restaurants: Langtons
Best Bars: Mink Bar
Best Hangout for Filmmakers: St Kilda or Brunswick Street.
Best Place for Breakfast: Babka

MOOMBA iNTERNATiONAL AMATEUR FiLM FESTiVAL

c/o P. O. Box 286
Preston, Victoria 3072 Australia
Tel: 03-470-1816
Festival Date: March
Entry Deadline: February
Contact: Dudley Harris

REVELATiON iNDEPENDENT FiLM FESTiVAL

PO Box 135, Sth Fremantle
WA, 6162 Australia
Tel: 61-8-9336-2482 phone/fax
Email: dakota@omen.net.au
Web Site: www.omen.net.au/~dakota/riff.htm
Festival Date: Touring
Entry Deadline: December
Director: Richard Sowada
Category: Independent
Profile: Australia's major alternative touring international film festival, the 2nd REVelation Independent Film Festival is call-

ing for entries for the forthcoming event from Australia and beyond.

R.I.F.F. is a strongly curated and contextualised film festival designed to showcase the most progressive in new and archival film works to Australian pop/youth/counter-culture audiences.

Now in its second year, R.I.F.F. has featured retrospective works from Beat generation filmmakers, wonderful archival animations as well as new feature, short, documentary and experimental works.

SHORT POPPiES: iNTERNATiONAL FESTiVAL OF STUDENT FiLM AND ViDEO

Flickerfest
P. O. Box 52
Haymarket NSW 2000, Australia
Tel: 61-2-251-4960
Fax: 61-2-251-4970
Festival Date: July
Entry Deadline: April
Contact: Craig B. Kirkwood
Category: Student

SYDNEY FiLM FESTiVAL

PO Box 950
Glebe NSW 2037
Sydney, Australia
Tel: 61-2-9660-3844
Fax: 61-2-9692-8793
Email: info@sydfilm-fest.com.au
Web Site: www.sydfilm-fest.com.au
Festival Date: June
Entry Deadline: February
Year Festival Began: 1954
Contact: Jenny Neighbour
Category: International. We show a wide range of films from all over the world-features, documentaries, shorts, video work, experimental work, retrospectives—primarily for a film-loving audience, but distributors from throughout Australia also attend to see the latest works and assess public reaction before purchasing titles.
Profile: This international festival focuses on new features, shorts,

and documentaries.
Approximately 140,000 attend.
Awards: Yes
Competitions: Yes, but for Australian short films only.
Major Awards: The Dendy Awards for Australian Short Films; The Yoram Gross Animation Award; The EAC Award; and The NSW Film and Television Office Rouben Mamoulian Award.
Value of Awards: $7,500 (Australian dollars) in the first; $2,500 each in the remaining three.
Application Tips: Send your viewing tape early, make sure you enclose a good press kit and contact details.
Application Fee: $15 (AUD) if you would like your viewing tape returned, otherwise it's free.
Average Films Entered: Anything good.
Films Screened: Around 200
Odds of Acceptance: 1 in 8
Tourist Information: Sydney Harbour, Bondi Beach, Blue Mountains...
Best Hangout for Filmmakers: Victoria Street, Darlinghurst
Best Place for Breakfast: Victoria Street, Darlinghurst or Bondi Beach

SYDNEY MARDi GRAS FiLM FESTiVAL/ QUEER SCREEN LTD.

P.O. Box 1081/12A
94 Oxford St.
Darlinghurst, NSW 2010
Australia
Tel: 61-2-9332-4938
Fax: 61-2-9331-2999
Email: info@queerscreen.com.au or ricahrd@queerscreen.com.au
Web Site: www.queerscreen.com.au
Festival Date: February
Entry Deadline: December
Contact: Richard King or Clare Strong
Category: Gay Lesbian
Competitions: No
Films Screened: 150
Attendance: 20,000

AUSTRIA

AMERiCAN FiLM FESTiVAL

Museumstrausse 31
A-6020 Innsbruck, Austria
Tel: 43-512-580723
Fax: 43-512-581762

AUSTRiAN FiLM DAYS "FiLM FEST WELS"

Austrian Film Office
Columbusgasse 2
A-1100 Vienna, Austria
Tel: 604-0126
Fax: 602-0795
Festival Date: June
Contact: Reinhard Pyrker

FESTiVAL DER FESTiVALS

Schaumburgergasse 18
A-1040 Wien, Austria
Tel: 0222-505-53-37
Fax: 0222-505-53-07
Festival Date: February
Entry Deadline: December
Contact: Alexander V. Kammel

FiLM + ARC iNTERNATiONAL FiLM FESTiVAL

International Festival fur Film + Architektur
Armitage
Rechbauerstrasse 38
A-8010 Graz, Austria
Tel: 43-316-84-24-87
Fax: 43-316-82-95-11
Festival Date: Biennial; November
Entry Deadline: July
Director: Charlotte Pochhacker

iNTERNATiONAL JUVENALE FOR YOUNG FiLM AND ViDEO AMATEURS

Bahnhofstrasse 59 III
Kaerten
A-9020 Klagenfurt, Austria
Tel: 0463-319654
Festival Date: Biennial, odd years; August

Entry Deadline: July
Director: OSR Dir. Wilhelm Elsner
Category: International, Student

INTERNATIONALE FILMFESTIVAL DES NICHTPROFESSIONELLEN FILMS

International Festival of Non-Professional Films
Hauptplatz 11
9100 Volkermakt/Kranten
(Buchalm 42 A-P141 Eberndorf),
Austria
Tel: 04236-2645
Festival Date: August-September
Entry Deadline: August
Contact: Paul Kraiger

VIENNALE—VIENNA INTERNATIONAL FILM FESTIVAL

Stiftgasse 6
A-1070 Vienna, Austria
Stiftgasse 6
Tel: 43-1-526-59-47;
43-1-523-41-72
Email: office@viennale.or.at
Web Site: www.viennale.or.at
Festival Date: October
Entry Deadline: Mid-August
Year Festival Began: 1960
Director: Hans Hurch
Programmer: Hans Hurch
Category: International
Profile: The VIENNALE is a "fest of fests," introducing local audiences to major films of annual fest circuit. It is fest "in praise of independent politics & visions," emphasizing films off beaten track.
Awards: No
Competitions: No, But at the Viennale the FIPRESCI-Prize is awarded for the first or second film of a director.
Major Awards: FIPRESCI Award
Application Tips: Just make a good film.
Application Fee: None
Insider Advice: Send synopsis, cast & credits, VHS Tape (PAL/NTSC)
Films Screened: 170 main programme and tributes

Odds of Acceptance: 1 in 6
Filmmaker Perks: If invited hotel accomodation & travel, meetings, Q&As
Tourist Information: There are so many famous sights worth seeing in Vienna, tours and special info are provided
Best Hangout for Filmmakers: Festival tent

BANGLADESH

DHAKA INTERNATIONAL SHORT FILM FESTIVAL

46 New Elephant Rd.
Dhaka 1205, Bangladesh
Tel: 864682, 500382, 864128
Fax: 880-2-863060
Festival Date: January
Entry Deadline: November for entry forms; December for prints
Contact: Festival Office
Category: Short

BELGIUM

ART MOVIE

Kortrijksesteenweg 1104
B-9051 Ghent, Belgium
Tel: 32-9-221-8946
Fax: 32-9-221-9074
Festival Date: April
Director: Jacques Dubrulle, General Secretary

BRUSSELS INTERNATIONAL CINEMA FESTIVAL

Chausee de Louvain, 30
B-1210 Brussels, Belgium
Tel: 32-2-227-3980
Fax: 32-2-218-1860
Email: tiff@bgnett.no
Web Site: www.bgnett.no/tiff
Festival Date: January
Entry Deadline: October
Contact: Christian Thomas
Category: Documentary
Competitions: Yes
Films Screened: 180-200
Attendance: 47,000

FESTIVAL DE FILM SUR L'ART (LIEGE ART FILM FESTIVAL)

University De Liege
Place Du Vingt-Aout, 32
B 4000 Liege, Belgium
Tel: 32-41-42-00-80
Festival Date: March
Entry Deadline: January
Contact: Jean-Michel Sarlet

FESTIVAL DU FILM GAY ET LESBIEN DE BRUXELLES (BRUSSELS GAY AND LESBIAN FILM FESTIVAL)

Tels Quels asbl, rue du Marchè au Charbon 81
Bruxelles, B-1000 Belgium
Tel: 32-2-512-45-87
Fax: 32-2-511-31-48
Email: fglb@hotmail.com
Web Site: www.fglb.org
Festival Date: January
Entry Deadline: September
Year Festival Began: 1979
Contact: Festival du Film Gay et Lesbien, c/o Tels Quels asbl
Category: Documentary, Gay Lesbian, Independent, International, Short
Profile: The Brussels Gay & Lesbian Film Festival takes place every year in January. The festival draws audiences of over 12.000, screening a large selection of films and videos in the "Botanique," the cultural centre of the French-speaking Community of Belgium. It has a large media and press coverage. Many of the works are Belgian, European or World Premieres. The festival is not only a major cultural and social event in Europe, but also an important networking opportunity. Located in the European capital Brussels, the festival is still growing in international importance.

The festival is co-produced by the Botanique and Tels Quels, a non-profit Gay and Lesbian organisation funded by the French-speaking Community of Belgium. The staff members are all volunteers.
Market: No

Competitions: No

Application Fee: None

Average Films Entered: Gay and lesbian related films, not yet shown in Belgium (features, documentary, shorts)

Films Screened: 100

Odds of Acceptance: Almost 100%

Filmmaker Perks: Lodging (by festival team members), sometimes free travel (only if a sponsor can be found).

Attendance: 12,000

Journalist Attendance: 30

Tourist Information: Brussels, capital city of Belgium and Europe-also Brugge, Ghent, nearby ancient cities.

FESTIVAL INTERNATIONAL DU COURT METRAGE DE MONS (MONS SHORT FILM FESTIVAL)

106, Rue dese Arbalestriers
7000 Mons, Belgium

Tel: 65-31-81-75

Fax: 65-31-30-27

Festival Date: March

Entry Deadline: February

Contact: Alain Cardon

FESTIVAL INTERNATIONAL DU FILM FANTASTIQUE, DE SCIENCE FICTION THRILLER DE BRUXELLES

144 Avenue De La Reine Koninginelaan
Brussels 120, Belgium

Tel: 32-2-201-1713

Fax: 32-2-201-1469

Festival Date: March

Entry Deadline: January

Contact: M. G. Delmote

Category: Retro Science

FESTIVAL INTERNATIONAL DU FILM FRANCOPHONE—NAMUR

175 Rue des Brasseurs
B-5000 Namur, Belgium

Tel: 32-81-24-1236

Fax: 32-81-22-4384

Kelly McGillis and Tim Roth on the festival circuit

Web Site: www.ciger.be/namur/evenements/fiff95/index.html

Festival Date: September-October

Entry Deadline: August

Contact: Dany Martin

FLANDERS INTERNATIONAL FILM FESTIVAL—GHENT

Kortrijksesteenweg 1104
B-9051 Ghent Belgium

Tel: 32-9-221-8946

Fax: 32-9-221-9074

Web Site: www.rug.ac.be/filmfestival/Welcome.html

Festival Date: October

Entry Deadline: August

Director: Jacque Dubrulle, General Secretary

INTERNATIONAL ANIMATED FILM AND CARTOON FESTIVAL

Folioscope ABSL
Rue de la Rhetorique, 19
B-1060 Brussels, Belgium

Tel: 32-2-534-41-25

Fax: 32-2-534-22-79

Festival Date: February

Entry Deadline: December

Contact: Phillippe Moins, Doris Cleven

BERMUDA

BERMUDA INTERNATIONAL FILM FESTIVAL

Correspondence:
P.O. Box HM 2963,
Hamilton HMMX

Deliveries: Broadway House,
1 Crow Lane, Pembroke HM19
Bermuda

Tel: 441-293-3456

Fax: 441-293-7769

Email: bdafilm@ibl.bm

Web Site: www.bermuda filmfest.com

Festival Date: April 20-26, 2001

Entry Deadline: December

Year Festival Began: 1997

Contact: Aideen Ratteray Pryse

Director: Aideen Ratteray Pryse

Programmer: David O'Beirne

Category: American Films, Animation, Documentary, Ethnic African, Ethnic Asian, Ethnic Black, Ethnic Jewish, Ethnic Latin, Ethnic Spanish, First-Time Independent Filmmakers, Gay Lesbian, Independent, International, Short, Woman

Profile: The Bermuda International Film Festival (BIFF) is a showcase for the best in independent film, which entertains and educates both local and international audiences.

Filmmakers, filmgoers and industry professionals come together in a signature location and discuss their passion for the art and business of filmmaking.

Gore Score · · · · · · · · · · · · · · ·

As much a vacation as a festival. Combine a vacation and a trip to a festival in one of the most beautiful places in the world.

Panels: Each year BIFF lines up excellent panellists to conduct workshops on topics such as film finance, scriptwriting, digital filmmaking, producing, etc.

Market: No

Competitions: Yes

Major Awards: Jury Award Starting in '01, there are two awards—one for narrative films and the other for documentaries.

Value of Awards: Return trip to Bermuda!

Past Judges: George Segal, Jane Alexander, Larry Auerbach, Arthur Rankin, Tom Shoebridge, Elliot Grove.

Application Fee: So far it's free!

Common Mistakes: Insufficient information can be a problem that requires needless work on our part to overcome. For example, if the entry submission is supposed to include stills, please provide decent ones.

Insider Advice: Go for it! We want to see as many films as possible.

Films Screened: 28

Odds of Acceptance: 1 in 9

Filmmaker Perks: We bring the filmmakers of the feature length and short films to Bermuda for the event and put them up. We don't think perks get any better than that!

Attendance: 5,000

Journalist Attendance: 6

Tourist Information: Tourists would want to play golf and tennis, go scuba diving, enjoy local art galleries and museums.

Travel Tips: Leave your recreational drugs at home—HMS Customs does not approve!

Best Cheap Hotels: Oxford Guest House

Best Luxury Hotels: Waterloo House

Best Restaurants: Seahorse Grill

Best Bars: Casey's

Best Hangout for Filmmakers: BIFF Bar

Best Place for Breakfast: Rudy's

BRAZIL

BANCO NACIONAL INTERNATIONAL FILM FESTIVAL

Rua Voluntarios de Patria 97
Rio de Janeiro, 22270 RJ Brazil
Tel: 55-21-286-8505
Fax: 55-21-286-4029
Web Site: www.ibase.org.br/
~estacao/tabu.htm
Festival Date: September
Contact: Adhemar Oliveira
Category: International

BRASILIA FILM FESTIVAL

Cultural Foundation of Brasilia
Ave. N2 Norte
Anexo Teatro Nacional Claudio Santoro
70040 Brasilia DF, Brazil
Tel: 55-61-226-3016
Fax: 55-61-224-2738
Festival Date: July
Contact: Fernando Adolfo

GRAMADO INTERNATIONAL FILM FESTIVAL

Rua dos Andradas 736
3 Andar Centro
90 020 004 Porto Alegre, Brazil
Tel: 55-54-286-2335
Fax: 55-54-286-2397
Festival Date: August
Contact: Esdras Rubinn

MiX BRASIL FESTIVAL OF SEXUAL DIVERSITY

Rua Agisse 72 05439-010
Sao Paulo, SP, Brazil
Tel: 55-11-2127390;
55-11-2127390
Email: mixbrasil@uol.com.br
Web Site: www.mixbrasil.com.br
Festival Date: September

Entry Deadline: Mid-July

Director: Andre Fischer

Programmer: Andre Fischer, Andre Fonseca

Category: Gay Lesbian, Independent, Experimental

Profile: Present and discuss the different expressions of sexuality. Improve the audio-visual production in Brazil on gay/lesbian issues.

The Festival takes place every year since '93 in Fortaleza (the capital of Ceara state, known in Brazil for its very macho population) in the gardens of the Government Palace (!), on a big screen between mango trees. The audience can watch for free gay, lesbian, SM, etc. films and videos while enjoying the fruit that falls during the screenings

Seminars: Aids, Independent production, gay literature.

Panels: With foreign directors

Awards: Yes

Competitions: Yes

Major Awards: Silver Rabbit

Value of Awards: Air tickets

Application Fee: No

Average Films Entered: All kind of films. Experimental, more commercial, video, 16/35. Specially the good humourous ones.

Odds of Acceptance: 1 in 2

Filmmaker Perks: Free travel (some), lodging, contacts

Best Restaurants: Spot

Best Bars: Ritz and Glitter

Best Hangout for Filmmakers: All major nightclubs, bar and restaurants in São Paulo sponsor MiX Brasil Festival. So, there are Festival Parties every night during MiX Brasil

Random Tidbits: The Festival tours 8-10 cities in Brazil every year. In '97 the 5th MiX Brasil went for the first time to smaller cities, some known for their homophobia, and it did really well. MiX Brasil will have special evenings with Brazilian Gay and Lesbian shorts this year at Mexico, Tokyo, New York Lisbon and (not confirmed yet) Los Angeles.

RIO DE JANEIRO INTERNATIONAL SHORT FILM FESTIVAL

c/o A.R Produções & Promoções
Praia de Botafogo, 210 Sala
1103-Botafogo
Rio de Janeiro-RJ,
CEP-222550-040 Brazil
Tel: 55-21-553-8918
Fax: 55-21-554-9059
Email: arempre@ax.apc.org
Festival Date: November
Director: Ailton Franco, Jr.
Category: Short
Profile: The Rio De Janeiro International Short Film Festival is a non-competitive festival for 16mm and 35mm films which takes place annually in the month of November at the Centro Cultural Banco do Brasil and Cine Estação Botafogo. Curta Cinema is the principal forum in the Rio de Janeiro for the exhibition and discussion of the importance of shorts in the cinematographic context. It began to exhibit international shorts in it's fifth year, with the intention of showing the international production of films in this format to the Rio audience.

SÃO PAULO INTERNATIONAL FILM FESTIVAL

Al. Lorena, 937 #303
São Paulo-SP CEP 01424-001
Brazil
Tel: 55-11-883-5137;
55-11-3064-5819
Fax: 55-11-853-7936
Email: info@mostra.org
Web Site: www.mostra.org
Festival Date: October
Entry Deadline: August
Contact: Christian Poccard
Director: Leon Cakoff
Programmer: Renata de Almeida
Category: International
Profile: The Festival is a cultural, non-profit event, held by the "Associação Brasileira Mostra Internacional de Cinema" and recognized by the International Federation of the Association of Film Producers.

It's a competitive event with features and shorts from around 60 countries emphasizing on independents.
Competitions: Yes
Major Awards: Bandeira Paulista
Best Restaurants: Restaurante Arábia
Best Hangout for Filmmakers: Maksoud Plaza Hotel
Best Place for Breakfast: Maksoud Plaza Hotel

SÃO PAULO INTERNATIONAL SHORT FILM FESTIVAL

Rua Simao Alvares 784/2
05417-020 São Paulo SP, Brazil
Tel: 55-11-852-9601
Fax: 55-11-282-9601
Email: spshort@ibm.net
Web Site: www.puc-rio.br/mis
Festival Date: April
Director: Zita Carvalhosa
Programmer: Francisco Cesar Fihlo
Category: International, Short

BULGARIA

INTERNATIONAL FESTIVAL OF COMEDY FILMS

House of Humor and Satire
P. O. Box 104
5300 Gabrovo, Bulgaria
Tel: 066-27229; 066-29300
Fax: 066-26989
Festival Date: May
Entry Deadline: March for entry forms; April for prints.
Contact: Tatyana Tsankova

PARTNERSHIP FOR PEACE INTERNATIONAL FILM FESTIVAL

Army Audiovisual Centre
23 Stoletov Blvd.
1233 Sofia, Bulgaria
Tel: 359-2-31-71-55
Fax: 359-2-32-00-18
Festival Date: May
Entry Deadline: March
Contact: Antonii Donchev, Rossitta Valkanova

CHILE

FESTIVAL INTERNATIONAL DE CINE DE VINA DEL MAR

Villavicencio 352
Santiago, Chile
Tel: 562-632-6387; 562-632-2892
Fax: 562-632-6389
Festival Date: October
Contact: Sergio Trabucco, Jaun J. Ulriksen

CHINA

BEIJING INTERNATIONAL CHILDREN'S FILM FESTIVAL

Juvenile Dept. BTV
No. 2A Zaojunmiao
Haidian District
Beijing, 100086 China
Tel: 861-202-5815; 861-202-5810
Fax: 861-202-5814
Festival Date: May-June
Contact: Zhang Pengling
Category: Kid

BEIJING INTERNATIONAL SCIENTIFIC FILM FESTIVAL

25 Xin Wai St.
Beijing, China
Tel: 201-5533
Festival Date: November
Entry Deadline: August
Contact: Ju Jian, Organizational Committee of the ISFF

CHINA INTERNATIONAL SCIENTIFIC FILM FESTIVAL

2567 Xietu Road
Shanghai, China
Tel: 389121
Festival Date: October
Entry Deadline: March for application forms; May for entries
Contact: Xu Zhiyi

CHINA INTERNATIONAL SPORTS FILM FESTIVAL
9 Tiyuguan Road
Beijing, China
Festival Date: May-June
Contact: Chinese Olympic Committee

HONG KONG GAY AND LESBIAN FILM FESTIVAL
Hong Kong Arts Centre, Film & Video Dept.
8F 2 Harbour Road
Wanchai, Hong Kong China
Tel: 852-2582-0200
Fax: 852-2802-0798
Email: tkwong@hkac.org.hk or feverray@netvigator.com
Contact: Teresa Kwong or Raymond Yeung
Category: Gay Lesbian

HONG KONG INTERNATIONAL FILM FESTIVAL (HKiFF)
Level 7
Administration Building
Hong Kong
Cultural Centre
10 Salisbury Road
TsimShaTsui
Kowloon, Hong Kong
Tel: 852-734-2903
Fax: 852-366-5206
Web Site: imsp007.netvigator.com/hkiff/
Festival Date: April
Entry Deadline: December
Contact: Angela Tong
Category: International

Profile: This annual festival is a non-competitive showcase of international films. It is 16 days in length and is held in 6 theaters. Over 80,000 attend.
Awards: No
Competitions: No
Application Fee: None

SHANGHAI INTERNATIONAL ANIMATION FILM FESTIVAL
618 Wang Hang Du Road
Shanghai 200042, China
Tel: 8621-2524349
Fax: 8621-2523352
Festival Date: December
Entry Deadline: May
Contact: Li Gian Guo, Film Festival Organizing Committee
Category: Animation

COLOMBIA

CARTAGENA INTERNATIONAL FILM FESTIVAL
Baluarte San Francisco Javier
Calle San Juan de Dios, Apartado Aereo 1834
Cartagena, Colombia
Tel: 575-6642345-6600966
Fax: 575-6600970-6601037
Email: festicinecartagena@axisgate.com
Web Site: www.rednet.net.co/festicinecartagena
Festival Date: March
Entry Deadline: January
Contact: Gerardo Nieto

Director: Victor Nieto
Programmer: Victor Nieto
Category: Independent, International, Children's
Famous Speakers: Luciano Castillo (Cuba), Nelson Carro (Mexico)
Awards: Opera Prima, Photograph, Script, Actor, Actress, Supporting Actor/Actress, Director, Film
Competitions: Yes
Major Awards: India Catalina (Gold)
Value of Awards: None
Application Tips: Spanish subtitles
Application Fee: None
Insider Advice: Make sure copies arrive on time
Odds of Acceptance: 1 in 2
Filmmaker Perks: Some free travel, lodging, and contacts.
Travel Tips: Cartagena is a tropical place. Very safe. Built in 1533.
Best Restaurants: La Vitrola
Best Bars: Pacos
Best Hangout for Filmmakers: Cafe Santo Domingo
Best Place for Breakfast: Cafe De La Plaza

FESTIVAL DE CINE IBEROAMERICANO PARA LARGOMETRAGES DE FICCION
Apartado aereo 46361
Bogota, Colombia
Tel: 672-82-59
Festival Date: March
Contact: Javier Rey

SANTA FE DE BOGOTA INTERNATIONAL FILM FESTIVAL
Calle 26 No. 4-92
Santa Fe de Bogota, Colombia
Tel: 57-1-282-5196
Fax: 57-1-342-2872
Festival Date: September
Director: Henry Laguado
Category: International

BEST WEIRD FILM FESTIVALS
Brainwash Movie Festival
Golden Shower Film and Video Festival
Hi Mom! Film Festival
minicine Visiting Filmmaker Series
MiX Brasil Festival of Sexual Diversity
Reject FilmFest
Short Attention Span Film and Video Festival
Tacoma Tortured Artists Film Festival
TromaDance Film Festival
Tube Film Festival

CROATIA

WORLD FESTIVAL OF ANIMATED FILMS IN ZAGREB
Kneza Mislava 18
Zagreb, 10 000 Croatia
Tel: 385-1-46-11-808;
385-46-11-709; 385-46-11-589
Fax: 385-1-46-11-808;
385-46-11-807
Email: kdz@zg.tel.hr
Web Site: animafest.hr
Year Festival Began: 1972
Contact: Sanja Borcic-Toth,
Festival Secretary
Director: Margit Antauer,
Organising Director
Programmer: Josko Marusic,
Programme Director
Category: Animation,
International
Profile: The Festival is a biennial event held every even year. The primary goal of the festival is the support of innovation in animation.

Films must be at least 50 percent animated, regardless of the category being entered. Films between 30 seconds and 30 minutes are eligible.
Seminars: Roundtables,
Retrospectives, Exhibitions, etc.
Awards: Yes
Competitions: Yes
Major Awards: Grand Prix
Value of Awards: 15 000 HKN
First Prize in Each of 3 categories, 10 000 HKN
Debute, 15 000 HKN
Best Student Film, 10 000 HKN
Application Fee: No
Odds of Acceptance: 1 in 12
Filmmaker Perks: Lodging and meals are provided for the filmmakers.
Tourist Information: Zagreb is a historical, middle European town with one million inhabitants. There are a lot of cultural monuments, museums, etc.

CUBA

INTERNATIONAL FESTIVAL OF NEW LATIN-AMERICAN CINEMA
Calle 23
N. 1155 Plaza de le Revolucion
Vedado, Havana, Cuba
Tel: 34400; 305041
Festival Date: December
Profile: The purpose of the International Festival of the New Latin American Cinema is to promote and award those works whose significance and artistic values contribute to enrich and reaffirm the Latin American and Caribbean cultural identity.

CZECH REPUBLIC

AGROFILM FESTIVAL
c/o Emerging Film
Praha Boleslavská 11
130 00 Prague 3, CZ
Czech Republic
Tel: 00-42-2-298290
Web Site: www.uvtip.sk/english/awc/agrofilm/main.htm
Festival Date: October
Entry Deadline: July
Contact: Prof. Ing. Ján Plesník

BRUNO 16 INTERNATIONAL NONCOMMERCIAL FILM AND VIDEO FESTIVAL
Kulturni a informacni centrum mesta Bruno
B16, Radnicka 4
658 78 Bruno, Czech Republic
Tel: 05-4221-6260
Fax: 05-4221-4625
Festival Date: October
Entry Deadline: August-September
Contact: Sarka Tryhukova

KARLOVY VARY INTERNATIONAL FILM FESTIVAL
c/o Film Festival Karlovy Vary Foundation
Panska 1
11000 Prague 1, Czech Republic
Tel: 420-2-2423-5448
Fax: 420-2-2423-3408
Email: iffkv@tlp.cz
Web Site: www.iffkv.cz
Festival Date: July
Entry Deadline: April
Programmer: Eva Zaoralova
Category: International
Competitions: Yes
Major Awards: Grand Prix
Crystal Globe
Value of Awards: $20,000

DENMARK

COPENHAGEN FILM FESTIVAL
Bulowsvej 50A
DK-1870 Frederiksberg C
Copenhagen, Denmark
Tel: 45-35372507
Fax: 45-31355758
Festival Date: October
Contact: Jonna Jensen

COPENHAGEN GAY AND LESBIAN FILM FESTIVAL
Attn: Lasse Soll Sunde, Oester Farimagsgade
18 A, 4 tv
Copenhagen, DK-2100 Denmark
Tel: 45 28 40 35 45
Fax: 45 33 74 34 03
Email: lss@gayfilm.dk or
ane.skak@post.tele.dk
Web Site: www.gayfilm.dk
Festival Date: October-November
Entry Deadline: July
Contact: Lasse Soll Soude or Ane Skak
Category: Gay Lesbian

Cartagena is a tropical place. Very safe. Built in 1533 (Cartagena International Film Festival).

INTERNATIONAL ODENSE FILM FESTIVAL

Vindegade 18
DK-5000 Odense C, Denmark
Tel: 45-66-131372 ext. 4044
Fax: 45-65-914318
Festival Date: August
Entry Deadline: May for materials; July for films
Director: Jorgen Roos

DOMINICAN REPUBLIC

INTERNATIONAL WOMEN'S FILM FESTIVAL

Equis-Intec
Ap. Postal 342-9, Zona 2
Santo Domingo
Dominican Republic
Tel: 809-567-9271 x287
Festival Date: Biennial, odd years; March
Category: International, Women

EGYPT

CAIRO INTERNATIONAL FILM FESTIVAL

17 Kasr El Nil St.
Cairo 202, Egypt
Tel: 20-2-392-3562
Fax: 20-2-393-8979
Festival Date: November-December
Entry Deadline: September for entry materials; October for films.
Contact: Saad Eldin Wahba
Category: International

CAIRO INTERNATIONAL FILM FESTIVAL FOR CHILDREN

17 Kasr El Nil St.
Cairo 202, Egypt
Tel: 20-2-392-3562
Fax: 20-2-393-8979
Festival Date: September
Entry Deadline: August
Contact: Saad Eldin Wahba
Category: International, Kid

ENGLAND

BIRMINGHAM INTERNATIONAL FILM AND TV FESTIVAL

9 Margaret St.
Birmingham, B3 3SB England
Tel: 44-121-212-0777
Fax: 44-121-212-0666
Festival Date: November
Entry Deadline: By invitation
Contact: Sarah McKenzie

BRIGHTON FESTIVAL

21-22 Old Steine
Brighton, BN1 1EL England
Tel: 44-273-713-875
Fax: 44-273-622-453
Festival Date: May
Contact: Jim Hornsby

BRITISH SHORT FILM FESTIVAL

BBC Centre House
Room A-214
56 Wood Lane
London, W12 7SB England
Tel: 81-7438000
Fax: 81-7408540
Festival Date: September
Contact: Amanda Casson
Category: Short

CAMBRIDGE INTERNATIONAL FILM FESTIVAL

City Screen LTD
86 Dean St.
London, WIV 5AA England
Tel: 171-734-4342
Fax: 171-734-4027
Email: festival@cambarts.co.uk
Festival Date: Mid-July
Entry Deadline: April
Year Festival Began: 1977
Contact: Tony Jones
Director: Tony Jones
Category: Independent, International
Profile: Over the years the Festival has provided Cambridge film-goers with an opportunity to broaden their horizons and enjoy some of the most exciting and innovative work of contemporary cinema. It has charted the British production, new cinema in Eastern Europe and the emergence of U.S. independents. It has also given many filmmakers their first, and sometimes only, opportunity to screen work in Britain.
Panels: Critic's debate.
Famous Speakers: Wim Wenders, Krzysztof Kieslowski
Awards: No
Competitions: No
Films Screened: 40 features and 40 shorts
Tourist Information: University Colleges
Travel Tips: Flight to Stansted. Then rail or bus to Cambridge (50 minutes)
Best Bars: Bar at Cinema

CHILDREN'S LONDON FILM FESTIVAL

South Bank, Waterloo
London, SE1 8XT England
Tel: 071-815-1322/3
Fax: 071-633-0786
Festival Date: January-February
Contact: Sheila Whitaker
Category: Kids

THE FESTIVAL OF FANTASTIC FILMS

95 Meadowgate Road
Salford, Manchester M68EN England
Tel: 44-161-707-3747
Fax: 44-161-792-0991
Email: hnad@globalnet.co.uk
Web Site: savvy.com/~festival
Festival Date: September
Entry Deadline: August
Contact: Tony Edwards
Director: Gil Lane-Young
Programmer: Harry Nadler
Category: Science Fiction, Fantasy, Horror, Retro Science
Profile: A weekend convention celebrating ten decades of Amazing Movies. The Festival of Fantastic Films is a festival of Film and Television which aims to further the art of Fantasy, Science Fiction and Horror Cinema. This event will be the

centre of debate and act as a catalyst for new films and a fond retrospective of past classic motion pictures of the three interconnected genres.

Seminars: Science Fiction, Fantasy and Horror movie fan convention

Panels: Past events have included: Censorship, The Woman's Place in the Horror Film, Distribution of Independent Productions, Script to Screen, Showreels and How to Edit Them.

Awards: The SOFFIA (The Society of Fantastic Films International Award (presented to Guests of Honour), The Delta Award (presented to Best Amateur Film), Best Independent Feature Award and Best Independent Short Film Award.

Competitions: Yes

Application Tips: Film must be in the Science Fiction, Fantasy or Horror genre.

Application Fee: Yes. Under $66,000 production/acquisition value $40

Over $66,000 production/acquisition value $150

Insider Advice: Send us a VHS in first instance with application form.

Films Screened: Over 35 features and up to 30 shorts, depending on length

Odds of Acceptance: We are new—last year 28 films submitted and 22 were accepted.

Filmmaker Perks: Free one-day Festival Membership

Travel Tips: All members given info via newsletters during year. Manchester Airport is only 20 minutes via direct rail to City Centre and our convention hotel.

Best Restaurants: Manchester has a big range of great restaurants—our Chinatown is the biggest in Europe. Big selection of multi-ethnic eateries. Hotel based event—good French restaurant.

Best Bars: Lowest priced is our special bar in the hotel—Beer at £1 per pint!

Best Hangout for Filmmakers: Hotel event-fans and filmmakers get together all weekend.

Best Place for Breakfast: Hotel: Excellent all you can eat included in room rate.

INTERNATIONAL ANIMATION FESTIVAL

79 Wardour St.
London, W1V 3PH England
Tel: 71-580-6202
Fax: 71-287-2112
Festival Date: April-May
Category: Animation, International

INTERNATIONAL ANIMATION FESTIVAL, CARDIFF, WALES

c/o The British Film Institute
21 Stephen St.
London, W1P 1PL England
Tel: 071-255-1444 x142
Fax: 071-255-2315
Festival Date: May
Entry Deadline: June
Director: Irene Kotlarz
Category: Animation, International

INTERNATIONAL DOCUMENTARY FILM FESTIVAL

The Workstation
15 Paternoster Row
Sheffield, S1 2BX England
Tel: 44-742-796511
Fax: 44-742-706522
Festival Date: March
Contact: Midge Mackenzie
Category: Documentary

INTERNATIONAL FILM AND VIDEO COMPETITION (IAC COMPETITION)

24c West Street
Epsom
Surrey, KT18 7RJ England
Tel: 0372-739672
Festival Date: March
Entry Deadline: January
Contact: IAC
Category: Video

JEWISH FILM FESTIVAL—LONDON

South Bank
Waterloo
London, SE1 8XT England
Tel: 071-815-1322/3
Fax: 071-633-0786
Festival Date: October
Entry Deadline: June
Contact: Jane Ivey

KINO AMERICAN UNDERGROUND & STUDENT SHOWCASE FILM FEST

Kinofilm
Kino Screen Ltd
48 Princess Street
Manchester, M1 6HR England
Tel: 44-161-288-2494; 44-161-281-1374
Fax: 44-161-237-3423
Email: john.kino@good.co.uk
Web Site: www.hals.demon.co.uk/kino
Festival Date: November
Entry Deadline: September
Director: John S. Wojowski
Programmer: John S. Wojowski
Other Staff: Terry Ponsillo/IT Coordinator
Vannessa Millward/IT R& D
Miles Prowse/Technical Manager
Abigail Christenson/Festival Coordinator
Emma Crisp/Festival Assistant Administrator
Category: Independent, Student, Underground
Profile: To promote the short film art form in its widest form, to support new and young film makers and to develop new audiences for such work. To compliment other cinematic events in the city and to provide a wider and diverse appreciation of new forms of moving image culture.
Awards: Yes
Application Tips: Though we accept films up to 30 mins long, best shorts are no longer than 15 mins. Keep them short and sweet.
Application Fee: £2.50 (UK) £.00 (International)
Insider Advice: Make it good.

Average Films Entered: Quirky and unusual, different than the norm.

Odds of Acceptance: 60 entered (50 shown)

Filmmaker Perks: We don't have the budget so we can only offer free tickets for screenings and the opportunities to meet others

Tourist Information: Manchester's clubs and bars, music venues and arts attractions throught the year.

Travel Tips: Use the trams or get a taxi, the buses are crap!

Best Hangout for Filmmakers: Kino and Cornerhouse cinemas. Sandbar, Granbys

Best Place for Breakfast: Bloom Street Cafe

KiNOFiLM, MANCHESTER iNTERNATiONAL SHORT FiLM & ViDEO FESTiVAL

42 Edge Street,

Northern Quarter,

Manchester, M4 1HN England

Tel: 44-161-288-2494

Fax: 44-161-281-1374

Email: General-kino.info@good.co.uk

Director-john.kino@good.co.uk

Web Site: www.kinofilm.org.uk

Festival Date: October/November

Entry Deadline: August

Year Festival Began: 1995

Contact: Either John or Michael

Director: John Wojowski

Programmer: Michael Knowles

Category: Ethnic Asian, Ethnic Black, Independent, Short

Profile: To promote the short film art form in its widest form, to support new and young film makers and to develop new audiences for such work. To compliment other cinematic events in the city and to provide a wider and diverse appreciation of new forms of moving image culture.

Awards: Yes

Competitions: Yes (but only the Irish festival) We would like to offer awards for all but we do not have the budget

Major Awards: Innovation for a new Irish Feature (others are all

shorts—categories differ each year)

Value of Awards: no cash award at present—trophies only

Application Tips: Though we accept films upto 30 mins long, best shorts are no longer than 15 mins. Keep them short and sweet

Application Fee: £2.50 (UK) £.00 (International)

Insider Advice: Make it good.

Odds of Acceptance: 1 in 2

Filmmaker Perks: We don't have the budget so we can only offer free tickets for screenings and the opportunities to meet others.

Tourist Information: Manchester's clubs and bars, music venues and arts attractions throught the year.

Travel Tips: Use the trams or get a taxi, the buses are crap!

Best Hangout for Filmmakers: Kino and Cornerhouse cinemas. Sandbar, Granbys

Best Place for Breakfast: Bloom Street Cafe

LEEDS iNTERNATiONAL FiLM FESTiVAL

"What a bloody marvelous Film Festival!"

—Pete Postlethwaite, Oscar® Winner, In The Name Of The Father.

The Town Hall, The Headrow

Leeds LS1 3AD

West Yorkshire, England

Tel: 44 (0)113-247-8389 ; 44 (0)113-247-8308

Fax: 44 (0) 113-247-8397

Email: liz.rymer@leeds.gov.uk

Web Site: www.leeds.gov.uk/liff

Festival Date: October

Entry Deadline: August

Year Festival Began: 1987

Contact: Liz Rymer and Carmel Langstaff

Director: Liz Rymer

Category: L.I.F.F is an umbrella event for all types of cinema

Profile: L.I.F.F is now the third largest event of its kind in the UK. The Festival celebrates the most influential artform of the 20th Century and seeks to promote the moving image as a

major contributor to the cultural life of the city, the region, and the nation as a whole.

Seminars: Educational workshops, lectures and seminars are held each year; some of these will underpin the retrospective season, other examine aspects of film-making and media issues.

Famous Speakers: Speakers range from writers, actors, commissioning editors, legal representatives, European funding experts, sales agents etc.,

Awards: No

Competitions: No

Application Tips: Our forms are quite straightforward and easy to fill in—be sure to include all information asked for, especially the format. Failure to do this can really make selection and programming difficult. Please don't send home videos or films shot on VHS, we can't do anything with them as the screening quality is so poor and they are rarely of any real interest to audiences. If your film is selected and is coming from abroad, make sure it is labelled correctly as a TEMPORARY IMPORT FOR CULTURAL USE ONLY. If not, we get stung for 100s of pounds in Customs payments and we can't claim it back.

Application Fee: £5.00 within the UK, £10.00 outside.

Average Films Entered: We (and the audiences) love quirky films, Indies which are well written and produced, often humorous slants on life, love, relationships, that kind of thing. We are a big student city so grunge/slacker films go down well. Also, there is a huge audience for animation of all types.

Films Screened: 200+ including retrospectives and new UK releases.

Odds of Acceptance: 1 in 5

Filmmaker Perks: Usually free travel from anywhere in the world (budget and sponsorship permitting), failing that, we can assist with the cost. Flights can be arranged to allow guests to travel to other parts of the UK, e.g. if they've got business in London. At least one night's accommodation in a good hotel—if you've come a long way, we usually stretch this to two. Some food is provided and there is usually some kind of reception and/or hospitality daily throughout the Film Festival. We try to be very friendly and helpful.

Do remember though that we operate on a very tight budget, we like to invite as many people as possible and this costs money—so help us out if you can, by offering to buy the odd round of drinks—you will be rewarded with our undying admiration.

Tourist Information: Tourist attractions etc. Lots of beautiful countryside not far away. Leeds has fantastic bars, cafes and night life—the best in the country apparently.

Travel Tips: Fly into Manchester and offer to take the train straight to Leeds from the airport—our drivers would much appreciate it even though we would love to pick you all up in person. Those of you from warmer climes, bring warm clothes—you'll need them.

Best Restaurants: Too many to name but Soho is pretty good, not too expensive. Cheap and cheerful comes in the form of the fastest (and best) Chinese restaurant in the west.

Best Bars: Oporto, Liquid, Soho, in The Exchange Quarter, and Mojo's, a blues/rock 'n' roll kind of joint—all hip and happening.

Best Hangout for Filmmakers: The Coburg and The Barge—pubs right next to the Film School.

Best Place for Breakfast: Other than the free one in the Hotel...The Hellenic Cafe, full fried English breakfast at its best (or worst) just the thing after a long night.

Festival Tale: I remember a story about someone (who shall remain nameless) putting director Terry Gilliam in a Mercedes facing downhill and the chauffeur had forgotten to put the handbrake on. The sight of an award-winning director rolling off, albeit slowly, into oncoming traffic was mortifying, but it probably seemed worse than it was. A brave Festival helper turned hero and snatched the hand-

brake therefore ensuring Gilliam went on to make *The Fisher King*. I think the lovely man has forgiven us.

LONDON FiLM FESTiVAL

National Film Theatre
South Bank, Waterloo
London, SE1 8XT England
Tel: 44-171-813-1323
Fax: 44-171-633-0786
Email: sarah.lutton@bfi.org.uk
carol.coombes@bfi.org.uk
Web Site: www.ibmpcug.co.uk/
IFF.html
Festival Date: November
Entry Deadline: August
Contact: Sarah Lutton
Director: Adrian Wootton
Programmer: Sandra Hebron
Other Staff: Carol Coombes
(Festival Assistant)
Category: International
Profile: The London Film Festival is an established non-competitive international film festival. It does not have a market or competition. There is no application fee for filmmakers or delegates wishing either to submit work or go to the festival. Over 100,000 attend this 18 day festival.
Competitions: No
Application Tips: Film must have been made in last 2 years, must be a UK premiere.
Application Fee: None
Insider Advice: Feature films get rejected simply because the programmers do not think (a) they are not good enough to be screened, blunt but truthful (b) we have to think who our audience is, would we be able to

promote and sell this film to an audience, and (c) it has to fit into our programme of work which we are encouraging and developing for that particular year.

Shorts—we simply get far too many submitted. While acknowledging it is difficult to tell, or get a story across in 10 mins, or even 5 mins, shorts have to fit into a programme of other short films that have been submitted in a particular year. Last year shorts were broken down into the following programmes (a) British animation (b) international animation (c) (broadly) British shorts (d) (broadly) international shorts.

Those that don't make it: Films about trecking in the Grand Canyon, or documentaries on the great bear, etc., will not get selected simply because there have been so many other films made on a similar theme. Believe me, these films come in. Badly made, out of focus, badly edited shorts do not get selected. **Odds of Acceptance:** we had 2000 tapes submitted last year, out of these 170 features and 70 shorts made up the final programme. The odds of being rejected are therefore really high, this might scare off new filmmakers.

Tourist Information: London, is a lively and vibrant city and there is really no "best" hangout as such as there is such a variety of choice. *Time Out Magazine*, a listings guide to London published weekly, probably offers the best guide to restaurants, gigs, breakfast venues, films, exhibitions and so on to the new visitor to the capital.

BEST INTERNATIONAL FESTIVALS

Berlin International Film Festival
Cannes Film Festival
Durban International Film Festival
London Film Festival
Melbourne International Film Festival
The International Film Festival Rotterdam
Sydney Film Festival
Tokyo International Film Festival
Toronto International Film Festival
Venice International Film Festival

LONDON LESBIAN & GAY FILM FESTIVAL

c/o National Film Theatre, South Bank
London, SE1 8XT England
Tel: 44-20-7815-1323
Fax: 44-20-7633-0786
Email: carol.coombes@bfi.org.uk or
stew@dixynixy.demon.co.uk
Web Site: www.bfi.org.uk/showing/festivals/lgff_sub.html
Contact: Carol Coombes
Category: Gay Lesbian

NORTH DEVON FILM FESTIVAL

The Plough, Fore Street
Torrington
North Devon, EX38 8HQ
England
Tel: 0805-22552
Fax: 0805-24624
Festival Date: June

ONEDOTZERO DIGITAL CREATIVITY FESTIVAL

Shane Walter, onedotzero,
14M Abbey Orchard Street
Estate SW1P 2DL
For Submission Material:
Onedotzero, c/o Matt Hanson,
312 Lexington Building
Fairfield Road
E32UE London, England
Tel: 44-468-893-466;
44-181-983-0463
Fax: 44-171-256-1122
Email: shane@onedotzero.com
matt@onedotzero.com
info@onedotzero.com
Web Site: www.onedotzero.com
Festival Date: late April–Early May
Entry Deadline: February
Year Festival Began: 1997
Contact: Shane Walter and Matt Hanson
Director: Shane Walter and Matt Hanson
Other Staff: Team of freelancers
Category: Digital Film + Creativity Festival
Profile: Onedotzero is a festival which presents bleeding edge moving image work from the worlds of digital film, computer gaming, and new media. It features work from critically acclaimed names and rising stars, often through pieces specially made for the festival.
Onedotzero is also a year-round digital creativity initiative which actively explores the digital aesthetic and new creative paradigms through productions which cut through working disciplines to cross-fertilise the area. The festival entertains, educates and showcases to a new digitally literate audience a range of cutting edge moving image work. New forms of working with desktop digital tools and methods are explored.
Seminars: Yes. Examples include: Non-linear narrative creation by AntiRom, Digital Filmmaking case study by Richard Jobson, Building Gaming Experiences with Sony Net Yaroze workshop
Panels: Yes. Future of Filmmaking cross-disciplinary panels.
Awards: No
Competitions: No
Application Tips: Festival premiere or work never before shown in Europe or UK has a better chance of acceptance. Send innovative, digitally manipulated work—well thought out and with a polished concept. The quirkier the better. Additional supporting materials with application (whether work in other media or other films, test reels, etc.) may lend itself to our innovative intranet supporting programme, or spark of further ideas for new work inclusion.
Application Fee: None at present, but postage and packing need to be supplied if material is required to be returned. Details on Website.
Insider Advice: Send quality VHS or pal copies and supporting material. We are looking for unique styles rather than clumsy trend following pieces.
Films Screened: 70 (mainly shorts)
Odds of Acceptance: About 1 in 7, but in addition to submission we have new work included by invitation and commission

Filmmaker Perks: Great contact, exposure for their work to a unique and opinion forming audience, networking opportunities that lead to innovative new projects and collaborations.
Best Restaurants: Italian Kitchen: 43 New Oxford Street, tel: 0171 836 1011—great Italian food, nice service too. well recommended
Moro: 34-36 Exmouth Market EC1: tel: 0171 833 8336—top place, friendly service, full mix of beautiful food with a Spanish/Moroccan type hint.

ONEDOTZERO: DIGITAL MOVING IMAGE FESTIVAL

P.O. Box 25187
London, SW1 2WE England
Email: submit@onedotzero.com
Web Site: www.onedotzero.com
Category: DVD, Independent, International
Profile: The Onedotzero: Digital Moving Image Festival explores new forms and hybrids of moving image and have been a catalyst for a wide range of innovative digital moving imagemaking.

SHEFFIELD INTERNATIONAL DOCUMENTARY FESTIVAL

The Workstation
15 Paternoster Row
Sheffield, S1 2BX England
Tel: 44 (0)114-276-5141
Fax: 44 (0)114-272-1849
Email: info@sidf.co.uk
Web Site: www.sidf.co.uk
Festival Date: October 15-21, 2001 or October 22-28, 2001
Entry Deadline: June 1, 2001
Year Festival Began: 1994
Contact: Karen Barber
Director: Kathy Loizou
Programmer: Alex Cooke
Other Staff: Brent Woods (Festival Coordinator), Alice Perman (Festival Press Officer)
Category: Documentary
Profile: Sheffield International Documentary Festival aims to facilitate the dissemination of information, exhibition and dis-

cussion of documentary in order to promote the development, growth and understanding of the documentary form, craft and ideas.

Established in 1994, the festival is the only festival in the UK exclusively dedicated to documentary film and television. The festival is in the vanguard of the movement to promote theatrical exhibition of documentary film to the public. The festival screens over 60 documentary films from around the world, many seen for the first time in the UK and it is the only time in the UK when members of the public can see a full programme of documentary films at the cinema.

Seminars: Yes

Panels: Yes

Awards: No

Competitions: No

Application Fee: No

Insider Advice: Please read the film submission form and festival regulations and wherever possible provide the material requested. Send good stills, try not to send rough cuts, and please don't leave submissions until the eleventh hour.

Films Screened: 45

Odds of Acceptance: 1 in 6

Filmmaker Perks: Great parties and what we believe is a truly friendly atmosphere! Wherever possible within the parameters of our budget we try to assist filmmakers exhibiting work at the festival with travel and accommodation. The festival is attended by established directors, independent producers, commissioners, TV company executives, academics and up-and-coming film makers from both the UK and abroad.

Attendance: 520 delegates / 1,200 public

Journalist Attendance: 25-30

Tourist Information: Sheffield is the fifth biggest city in the UK, so there are plenty of good art galleries and museums including the new Millennium Gallery (due to open at the end of 2000) and the National Centre for Popular Music, plus theatres The Crucible and The Lyceum to visit. The festival would advise any tourist vis-

iting Sheffield with a little bit of time to spare to visit its surrounding countryside, as the city is on the edge of the Peak District-some of the most beautiful scenery in the UK.

Travel Tips: Sheffield is located 157 miles north of London. Trains from London St. Pancras to Sheffield take two hours, it is cheaper if travel is off-peak and cheaper still if booked in advance. Timetable and fare information are available from national rail enquiries on 44 (0) 345-48-49-50.

By car, Sheffield City Centre is 5 miles from the M1 motorway, Junction 33. The journey from London to Sheffield by car takes a little bit more than the train.

By air, Sheffield City Airport has scheduled links from Belfast, Brussels, Dublin and Jersey. Other airports in the region include Manchester (41 miles), Leeds/Bradford (40 miles), East Midlands (47 miles).

Best Cheap Hotels: The Ibis is the cheapest hotel. There are plenty of cheap and good bed and breakfasts in Sheffield. Sheffield Visitor Information Centre runs a free Accommodation Hotline for the festival, on 44 (0) 114-201-1011—just quote the festival name when making enquiries or bookings.

Best Luxury Hotels: The Hilton is luxurious.

Best Restaurants: We like Nonna's on Ecclesall Road, for great Italian food. Or Thai food from the family-run Bahn Nah in Broomhill.

Best Bars: For those who like to drink where it's lively and loud, The Forum or The Halcyon on Devonshire Street. For those who prefer their drinking establishments quieter and more relaxed, Trippets on Trippets Lane or Casablanca's on Devonshire Street.

Best Hangout for Filmmakers: Showroom Bar or The Rutland pub.

Best Place for Breakfast: Coffee Revolution on Ecclesall Road is a favourite. Nearer the festival, the Site Gallery café does good coffee, croissants and great bacon

sandwiches. Nibbler's greasy spoon offers more traditional breakfast fare (which Errol Morris seemed to like on his last visit to the festival).

Festival Tale: Observing one of the Board of Directors of the festival having to sprint down to the nearest all-night garage to purchase Michael Moore some non-sugar-free chewing gum in the middle of his interview at the 1998 festival was quite entertaining.

TYNESiDE iNTERNATiONAL FiLM FESTiVAL

10 Pilgrim St.
Newcastle-upon-Tyne, NE1 6QG
England

Tel: 44-91-232-8289

Fax: 44-91-221-0535

Festival Date: November-December

Contact: Roy Bristow

Category: International

FiNLAND

ESPOO CiNÉ iNTERNATiONAL FiLM FESTiVAL

PO. Box 95
Espoo, 02101 Finland

Tel: 358-9-466-599

Fax: 358-9-466-458

Email: aromaa@helsinki.fi

Web Site: www.espoo.fi/cine/

Festival Date: August

Entry Deadline: May

Year Festival Began: 1990

Contact: Liisa Suominen

Director: Timo Kuismin

Programmer: Mikko Aromaa

Other Staff: Kaija Suni, Peter Toiviainen, Petteri Paasila, Marko Mastomaki,

Category: Independent

Profile: Espoo Ciné International Film Festival is mainly recognized as the biggest annual showcase of contemporary European cinema in Finland. We focus on fictional features, and occasionally screen some shorts in between as well.

The line is drawn just before the documentary works; that's practically the only genre we do not specialize in. Our target audience is as broad as the Finnish cinema audience overall. Thus, we're not genre-driven in any way either. And even though European cinema is very strongly associated with the festival, we do screen the best offerings from other continents and countries annually, too. Diversity is also our strength, which helps us to attract 20,000+ people to the beautiful garden city of Tapiola, Espoo, for the six hectic festival days every year.

Awards: No

Competitions: No

Application Fee: None. On short film section the production company is suggested to pay the transportation of the print.

Insider Advice: Send the VHS (NTSC or PAL) review copies of the entries well in advance since the festival board (7 members) is occasionally willing to take a look at them thoroughly.

Average Films Entered: As we're not really genre- or budget-driven, this one's difficult to answer. We have several sections (for US indies, for European arthouse stuff, for big productions, for sneak previews, for midnight movies...), so there is potential space for almost everyone.

Films Screened: 60-70

Odds of Acceptance: 1 in 4

Filmmaker Perks: The festival invites annually up to five foreign special guests over, providing them with travel and lodging. Filmmakers that have entries in our programme but do not make it in the "special guests" category get free accommodation from the festival; other arrangements are also possible on a case-to-case basis.

Tourist Information: The Suomenlinna Fortress on an island just outside Helsinki (the garden city of Tapiola, Espoo, is just a 15-minute ride away from the heart of Helsinki), is easily (and cheaply) accessible via local ferries. The Hvittrask Mansion is a place definitely worth a visit during the summertime; beautiful

The Hvittrask Mansion is a place definitely worth a visit during the summertime; beautiful architecture in even more beautiful surroundings (very spooky at nights). (Espoo Ciné International Film Festival)

architecture in even more beautiful surroundings (very spooky at night). That's the place we take our special guests to annually for a bath in the original Finnish sauna.

Travel Tips: There are at least ten bus lines going directly from the Helsinki city center to Tapiola, Espoo, so it's very easy (and cheap) to get around from the earliest morning hours to past midnight.

Best Restaurants: Well, people going to Tapiola, Espoo, to see the films tend to go to Helsinki during the night; that's where the best restaurants and bars are, and it's just 15 minutes away.

Best Hangout for Filmmakers: The Corona Bar in Helsinki

Best Place for Breakfast: Tapiola Garden

HELSINKI INTERNATIONAL FILM FESTIVAL— LOVE AND ANARCHY

Unioninkatu 10
FIN-00130 Helsinki, Finland
Tel: 358-9-629-528; 358-9-177-501
Fax: 358-9-631-450
Web Site: www.kaapeli.fi/~hff/
Festival Date: May
Contact: Pekka Lanerva
Films Screened: 100
Attendance: 30,000

MIDNIGHT SUN FILM FESTIVAL

Malminkatu 36
00100 Helsinki, Finland
Tel: 358-9-685-2242
Fax: 358-9-694-5560
Festival Date: June
Contact: Peter Von Bagh

TAMPERE FILM FESTIVAL

Box 305
33101 Tampere, Finland
Tel: 358-31-213-0034; 358-31-219-6149
Fax: 358-41-20-08-27
Festival Date: March
Entry Deadline: January
Contact: Kirsi Kinnunen

TAMPERE INTERNATIONAL SHORT FILM FESTIVAL

P.O. Box 305
FIN-33101
Tampere, Finland
Tel: 358-3-213-0034; 358-3-3146-6149, 358-3-223-5188
Fax: 358-3-223-0121
Email: film.festival@tt.tampere.fi
Web Site: www.tampere.fi/festival/film
Festival Date: March
Entry Deadline: January
Year Festival Began: 1970
Contact: Kirsi Kinnunen (Int'l relations)
tel. 358-3-213-0034
Director: Pertti Paltila
Programmer: Raimo Silius
Other Staff: Co-director: Juhani Alanen, tel. 358-3-223-5681
Category: International, Short
Profile: Tampere Film Festival wants to improve the position of short film and documentary film in Finland and internationally.

Tampere Film Festival is one of the biggest short film festivals in Europe. The International Competition of Tampere is highly esteemed. The special characteristic of Tampere is the emphasis given to different short film genres: there are category prizes for the best documentary, best fiction and best animation. The International Short Film Market has become a lively forum for distributors and buyers. Particular attention is given to the latest productions from Finland and northern and Eastern Europe.

Seminars: Multimedia Seminar and Production seminar for professionals.

Awards: Yes

Competitions: Yes

Major Awards: Grand Prize: Festival trophy, a kiss and 25,000 FIM for the best film in International Competition

Value of Awards: A kiss and 5,000 FIM for the best animation, documentary and fiction film.

Application Fee: None

Insider Advice: Send a VHS copy of the film with a fully filled entry form and a complete list of

Fest-goers clamor for a moment of Tammy Faye's attention.

dialogue in original language and in one internationally used language and one still photo. Films must be 35 mm or 16 mm prints with optical or magnetic sound and the running time may not exeed 30 minutes.

Films Screened: 80

Odds of Acceptance: 1 in 37

Filmmaker Perks: We offer free accommodation in Tampere during the festival, no travel expenses.

Tourist Information: Beautiful lakes around the city of Tampere. In the beginning of March you can walk on ice and even swim in a frozen lake. Actually the festival is famous for its sauna party for the foreign guests and it's a tradition that every guest swims in a frozen lake, too.

Best Restaurants: Rostisseria La Perla

Best Bars: Europa, Club Telakka

TURKU LESBIAN AND GAY FILM FESTIVAL

P.O. Box 288
Turku, FIN 20101 Finland
Tel: 358-2-2500695
Fax: 358-2-2512905
Email: tuseta@sci.fi
Web Site: www.sci.fi/~tuseta/
Festival Date: October
Entry Deadline: July

Programmer: Erkki Lietzen, email: lietzen@utu.fi

Category: Gay Lesbian

Profile: The film festival is organized for the 8th time by Turun Seudun SETA ry which is a local organization for sexual minorities. It is the only lesbian and gay film festival in Finland. Turun Seudun SETA ry is a member of the National SETA in Finland and also a member of the International Lesbian and Gay Association ILGA. The film festival is arranged on a non-profit making basis. Our main goal is to screen films with lesbian/gay/bisexual/trans-gendered themes that would not reach the Finnish audience through commercial distribution channels.

Awards: None

Application Tips: Offer a preview tape in VHS (NTSC or PAL format), the film should be in English/Swedish or have English/Swedish subtitles.

Application Fee: None

Insider Advice: Offer a preview tape in VHS (NTSC or PAL) format.

Average Films Entered: Long feature films, documentaries and short films

Odds of Acceptance: 1 in 4. Mostly we pick the films from international festivals like London Lesbian and Gay Film Festival.

FRANCE

AFRICAS CINEMA

3 bis quai Gambetta
49100 Angers, France
Tel: 41-20-08-22
Fax: 41-20-08-27
Festival Date: May
Contact: Michele Barrault, Gerard Moreau
Category: Ethnic Black

ALES CINEMA FESTIVAL—ITINERANCES

Mas-Bringer rue, Stendhal
30100 Ales, France
Tel: 66-30-24-26
Fax: 66-56-87-24
Festival Date: March-April
Entry Deadline: February
Contact: Holley Benoit

AMATUER AND NON-PROFESSIONAL FILM AND VIDEO FESTIVAL

Maison des Jeunes et de la Culture rue Rene Binet
89100 Sens, France
Tel: 86-64-44-42
Festival Date: April
Entry Deadline: February
Director: Michelle Moisson
Category: Student

ANiMATED FiLMS ABOUT SCiENCE (ANiMASCiENCE FESTiVAL)

Mediatheque
Cite des Sciences est de l'Industrie
30 Avenue Corentin Cariou 75930
Oaris Cedex 19, France
Tel: 40-05-71-29
Fax: 40-05-71-06
Festival Date: October-November
Contact: Marie-Helene Herr
Category: Animation

ANNECY iNTERNATiONAL ANiMATED FiLM FESTiVAL

6 Avenue des Iles, BP399
74013 Annecy Cedex, France
Tel: 33-50-57-41-72
Fax: 33-50-67-81-95
Festival Date: Bienniel (odd years); May-June
Entry Deadline: January for forms; February for prints/tapes
Contact: M. Jean-Luc Xiberras
Category: Animation

ARGELES-SUR-MER CiNEMA FORUM

Cinemaginaire
Rue de l'Eglise
66720 Rasigueres, France
Tel: 68-29-13-61
Festival Date: May
Director: Francois Boutonnet, President

AROUND THE WORLD FESTiVAL

Autour du Monde
3 Avenue Jean Laigret
41000 Blois, France
Tel: 54-43-64-19
Festival Date: November
Director: Philippe Boulais, President

BASTiA FiLM FESTiVAL OF MEDiTERRANEAN CULTURES

Association du Festival du Film Mediterranean
Rue Favelelli
Theatre Municipal
20200 Bastia, France
Tel: 95-32-08-32; 95-32-08-86
Fax: 95-32-57-65
Festival Date: October
Director: Julia Rioni, General Secretary
Category: Ethnic Other

BiENNALE iNTERNATiONALE DU FiLM D'ARCHiTECTURE, D'URBANiSME ET D'ENViRONMENT DE BORDEAUX (FiFARC FESTiVAL)

17, Quai de la Monnaie
2eme Etage
33800 Bordeaux, France
Tel: 33-56-94-79-05
Fax: 33-56-91-48-04
Festival Date: December
Entry Deadline: June
Contact: Nicole Ducourau
Category: International

BiLAN DU FiLM ETHNOGRAPHiQUE

Musee de l'Homme
Place du Trocadero
75116 Paris, France
Tel: 47-04-38-20
Fax: 45-53-52-82
Festival Date: March
Entry Deadline: Forms: December; Films: January
Contact: Francois Foucault
Category: International

BLOiS CiNEMA FORUM

Association Maison de Begon
Rue Pierre et Marie Curie
41000 Blois, France
Tel: 54-43-35-36
Festival Date: January
Director: Laurence Gondoin
Category: International

BONDY CiNEMA FESTiVAL

Association Bondy Culture
23 bis rue Roger Salengro
93140 Bondy, France
Tel: 1-48-47-18-27
Festival Date: February
Director: Guy Allombert

BREST SHORT FiLM FESTiVAL

Association Cote Quest
40 bis
Rue de la Republique
BP 173
29269 Brest Cedex, France
Tel: 98-44-03-94
Fax: 98-80-25-24
Festival Date: November
Entry Deadline: August
Contact: Gilbert Le Traon
Category: Short

BRiTiSH CiNEMA FESTiVAL

Association Travelling
8 Passage Digard
50100 Cherbourg, France
Tel: 3-93-38-94
Fax: 33-01-20-78
Festival Date: November
Director: Alain Bunel, President

BRiTiSH FiLM FESTiVAL

8 Passage Digard
F-50100 Cherbourg, France
Tel: 33-2-3393-3894
Fax: 33-2-3301-2078
Festival Date: November
Entry Deadline: October
Director: Jean-Charles Saint
Programmer: Jean-Francois Cornu

CABOURG FESTiVAL OF ROMANTiC FiLMS

106 bis Avenue de Villiers
75017 Paris, France
Tel: 33-1-4267-2626
Fax: 33-1-4622-9303
Festival Date: June
Contact: F. Mahout
Category: Romantic

CANNES FiLM FESTiVAL

See "The Top Ten Film Festivals" beginning on page 214.

CARiBBEAN FiLM FESTiVAL

Images Caribes
77 Route de le Folie
97200 Fort-de-France
Martinique, FWI, France
Tel: 60-21-42; 64-22-90
Fax: 64-11-30
Festival Date: Biennial; June
Director: Suzy Landau, President

CARREFOUR iNTERNATiONAL DE L'AUDiOViSUEL SCiENTiFiC

Cite des Sciences et de l'Industrie
30 Avenue Corentin-Cariou
75930 Paris Cedex 19, France
Tel: 1-40-05-72-49
Fax: 1-40-05-73-44
Festival Date: November
Entry Deadline: September
Contact: Dominique Cartier

CERGY-PONTOiSE CiNEMA FESTiVAL

Theatre des Arts de Cergy-Pontoise
Centre d'Action Culturelle
Place des Arts
BP 307
95027 Cergy, France
Tel: 30-30-33-33
Festival Date: January-February
Programmer: Helen Icart

CEVENNES FESTiVAL OF iNTERNATiONAL ViDEO

L'Ecran cevenol
"La Moliere"
48400 Verbron, France
Tel: 66-44-02-59
Fax: 66-44-02-59
Festival Date: July

CHiNESE FiLM FESTiVAL

Association Chinois de Montepellier
Hotel de Ville
1 Place Francis Ponge
34059 Montpellier cedex, France
Tel: 67-34-73-78; 67-34-70-54
Fax: 67-64-15-81
Festival Date: February
Contact: Genevieve Droz

CiNEMA AU FEMiNiN

Marseilles, France
Tel: 331-4068
Fax: 331-4068-0570
Festival Date: September
Contact: Charlotte Monginet
Category: Women

CiNEMA DU REEL

BPI Centre Georges Pompidou
19 Rue Beaubourg
75197 Paris Cedex 04, France
Tel: 44-78-45-26; 44-78-44-21
Fax: 44-78-21-24
Festival Date: March
Entry Deadline: November for foreign entries.
Contact: Suzette Glenadel

CiNEMAS D'AFRiQUE (AFRiCAN CiNEMA FESTiVAL)

Hotel de Ville, 1
Rue Gambetta
86200 Loudon, France
Tel: 49-98-77-79
Fax: 49-98-12-88
Festival Date: February
Contact: Jean-Claude Rullier
Category: Ethnic Black

CiTiES ViDEO FESTiVAL

Mairie de Poitiers
Hotel de Ville
Place du Marechal Leclerc
86021 Poitiers Cedex, France
Tel: 49-88-82-07
Fax: 49-55-13-48
Festival Date: Biennial; June
Contact: Dominique Royoux

CLERMONT-FERRAND SHORT FiLM FESTiVAL

La Jetée, place Michel del l'Hospital
63058 Clermont-Ferrand cedex France
Tel: 33-04-73-91-65-73
Fax: 33-04-73-92-11-93
Email: info@clermont-filmfest.com
Web Site: http://212.208.133.157
Festival Date: January-February
Entry Deadline: October
Contact: Christian Guinot
Category: Short
Competitions: Yes
Average Films Entered: 350
Attendance: 122,000

CLiSSON FiLM FESTiVAL

Cinema "Le Connetable"
Festival "Le Connetable"
Rue des Halles
44190 Clisson, France
Tel: 40-54-01-49
Festival Date: October-November
Director: Dominique Boisselier, President

COGNAC iNTERNATiONAL FiLM FESTiVAL OF THE THRiLLER

36 Rue Pierret
92200 Neuilly-sur-Seine, France
Tel: 33-1-46-40-5500
Fax: 33-1-46-40-5539
Festival Date: April
Contact: M. Lionel Chouchan

DOUARNENEZ FESTiVAL OF ETHNiC MiNORiTY CiNEMA

Festival de Cinema Douarnenez
BP 6
29172 Douarnenez, France
Tel: 98-92-09-21
Fax: 98-92-28-10
Festival Date: August
Director: Patrick Marziale, President
Category: Ethnic Other

DUNKIRK CINEMA FORUM

Studio 43/MJC
43 Rue du Docteur Louis
Lemaire
59140 Dunkerque, France
Tel: 28-66-47-89
Fax: 28-65-06-98
Festival Date: October
Director: Jacques Deniel

ENTREVUES FILM FESTIVAL

Cinemas d'Aujourd'hui
Hotel de Ville
Place d'Armes
90020 Belfort Cedex, France
Tel: 84-54-24-43
Fax: 84-21-71-71
Festival Date: November-
December
Contact: Mairie de Belfort,
Direction des Affaires Culturelles

EUROPEAN FILM FESTIVAL

Cinemauteur
Mairie de Vichy
03200 Vichy, France
Tel: 70-97-75-75
Fax: 70-97-84-44
Festival Date: June
Director: Nario Robert,
President

FESTIVAL DU FILM D'ANIMATION POUR LA JEUNESSE

Maison de Societes
Boulevard Joliot Curie
01000 Bourg-en-Bresse, France
Tel: 74-23-60-39
Fax: 74-21-16-62; 75-45-25-18
Festival Date: October-
November
Entry Deadline: August
Contact: M. Rene Brendel
Category: Animation

FESTIVAL FOR NATURE AND ENVIRONMENT FILMS

FRAPNA-Section Isere
M. N. E.
5 Place Bir-Hakeim
38000 Grenoble, France
Tel: 33-76-42-64-08
Fax: 33-76-44-63-36
Festival Date: Biennial (even
years); February-March
Director: Jean-Michel Blanc

FESTIVAL INTERNATIONAL DU 1ER FILM ET DE LA JEUNESSE

M. J. C. d'Annonay
Avenue Jean Jaures
07100 Annonay, France
Tel: 33-75-33-11-77
Fax: 33-75-67-64-63
Festival Date: February
Entry Deadline: November
Director: Jean-Louis Vey,
Directeur Adjoint de la M. J. C.

FESTIVAL INTERNATIONAL DU FILM MEDICAL DE MAURIAC (MAURIAC FILM FESTIVAL)

14, Place Georges Pompidou
B. P. 53
15200 Mauriac, France
Tel: 33-71-67-37-37
Fax: 33-71-68-10-00
Festival Date: March-April
Entry Deadline: September
Contact: Michel Chassang

FESTIVAL OF ARTS CINEMA FOR CHILDREN

Groupe TSE
Theatre de la Commune
2 Rue Edouard Poisson
BP 157
93304 Aubervilliers Cedex,
France
Tel: 1-48-33-16-16
Fax: 1-48-34-35-55
Festival Date: October
Contact: Christian Richard
Category: Kids

FESTIVAL OF DEAUVILLE FOR AMERICAN CINEMA (LE FESTIVAL DU CINEMA AMERICAIN IN DEAUVILLE)

Deauville is known for offering "the wildest possible showcase for American cinema, always keeping in mind that is is a reflection of what American Film is—studios, independents, documentaries and shorts."
—*Daniel Benzakein*

Promo 2000
36 rue Pierret
92200 Neuilly-sur-Seine, France
Tel: 33-1-46-40-55-00
Fax: 33-1-46-40-55-39
Email: publics@imaginnet.fl
Web Site: www.imaginet.fr/
deauvillefest
Festival Date: September
Contact: M. Lionel Chouchan
Director: Bruno Barde/Ruda
Dauphin (US Director)
Category: Documentary,
Independent, Short
Profile: France is seen as a market offering good opportunities for independent films. Deauville especially attracts of hundreds of European journalists, giving a major boost to the European box office performance of American films. Approximately 45,000 attend.

Unlike other fests, which give off an elitist air, Deauville is very accessible to the average Jean-Pierre. Press accreditation is available on a first-come, first-served basis, with screenings and photo calls open to anyone with with a ticket. Intimacy and a relaxed atmosphere are the keys to Deauville's success.
Competitions: Deauville has been building up a new noncompetitive section called Panorama, focused on 11 independent films.
Past Judges: Jean-Paul Rappeneau, Liam Neeson, Eric Serra
Application Fee: None
Films Screened: 48

FESTIVAL OF INTERNATIONAL FILM FOR YOUTH AND CHILDREN

FIFEJ

35 rue d'Alsace Courcellor II
95231 Levallois-Perret, France
Tel: 1-47-54-11-00
Fax: 1-47-54-13-42
Festival Date: June
Contact: Louise Maurin, General Delegate
Category: Kids

INTERNATIONAL FILM FESTIVAL

99 Boulevard Malesherbes
Paris, 75008 France
Tel: Registration Dept. 33 1-45-61-66-00; Press-Registration Dept. 33 1-45-61-66-08
Fax: Registration Dept. 33 1-45-61-97-60; Press-Registration Dept. 33 1-45-61-97-61
Festival Date: May

PARIS GAY AND LESBIAN FILM FESTIVAL/FESTIVAL DE FILMS GAYS ET LESBIENS DE PARIS

FFGLP

154 rue Oberkampf
Paris, 75011 France
Tel: 33 1 55 28 38 84
Fax: 33 1 55 28 38 84
Web Site: http://assoc.wanadoo.fr/cineffable/
Category: Gay Lesbian

GERMANY

BERLIN INTERNATIONAL FILM FESTIVAL

See "The Top Ten Film Festivals" beginning on page 214.

BERLIN—VERZAUBERT INTERNATIONAL GAY & LESBIAN FILM FESTIVAL

Rosebud Entertainment
Wittelsbacherstr 26
Berlin, D-10707 Germany
Tel: 49 30 861 45 32

Fax: 49 30 861 45 39
Email: rosebud_entertainment@t-online.de or b.scheuch@snafu.de
Web Site: www.queer-view.com/verzaubert
Contact: Marc Mouci or Maddalena Tognola
Category: Gay Lesbian

EXGROUND— DAS FILMFEST

Jahnstr. 17
Wiesbaden, D-65185 Germany
Tel: 49-611-371156
Fax: 49-611-371157
Email: info@exground.com
Web Site: www.exground.com
Festival Date: November 16-25, 2001
Entry Deadline: August 31, 2001
Year Festival Began: 1990
Contact: Katja Faulhaber
Director: Andrea Wink, Thomas Kluth
Programmer: Marion Klomfass, Brigitte Strubel-Mattes
Category: American Films, Animation, Digital Animation, Documentary, Ethnic Asian, Experimental, First-Time Independent Filmmakers, Independent, International, Short, Underground, Weird
Profile: Exground, the filmfest for new, unusual, droll and exciting productions, is presenting everything that usually gets lost in the mainstream. To the open-minded and interested fan of the big screen, exground offers discoveries and emphases like American Independents, films from Asia, Shorts and national Specials.
Seminars: No
Panels: No
Famous Speakers: No
Market: No
Awards: Yes
Competitions: Yes
Major Awards: exground short film award (only German short films)
Value of Awards: 8,000 German Marks
Application Tips: Good quality VHS-tape and a press kit.

Application Fee: No
Common Mistakes: No information about the length and format.
Films Screened: 30 features, 100 shorts
Odds of Acceptance: Approximately 1 in 7
Filmmaker Perks: Free travel for feature filmmakers, and part of the travel fee for short filmmakers. Lodging: Private accomodation and in some cases a hotel.
Contacts: German Distribution Companies and German Press
Attendance: 7,000
Journalist Attendance: 35
Tourist Information: Roman Spa
Travel Tips: The Rhine Valley
Best Cheap Hotels: Das Kleine Hotel
Best Luxury Hotels: Nassauer Hof
Best Restaurants: Palasthotel
Best Bars: Finale
Best Hangout for Filmmakers: exground lounge
Best Place for Breakfast: Palasthotel

FANTASY FILMFEST— INTERNATIONAL FILM FESTIVAL FOR SCIENCE FICTION, FICTION, HORROR AND THRILLER

Rosebud Entertainment
Herzog-Wilhelmstr. 27
80331 Munich, Germany
Tel: 49-89-2601-2838
Fax: 49-89-2602-2839
Email: rosebud-entertainment@t-online.de
Web Site: home.t-online.de/home/rosebud_entertainment
Contact: Schorsch Muller
Director: Rainer Stefan, Schorsch Muller
Category: Independent
Awards: No
Competitions: No
Application Fee: None
Attendance: 52,000-60,000

Unlike other fests, which give off an elitist air, Deauville is very accessible to the average Jean-Pierre . . . Intimacy and a relaxed atmosphere are the keys to Deauville's success (Festival of Deauville for American Cinema).

FILMFEST BRAUNSCHWEIG

Hochstr 21

Braunschweig, 38102 Germany

Tel: 49-531-75597

Fax: 49-531-75523

Email: filmfest@t-online.de

Web Site: forum.gaertner.de/filmfest/

Festival Date: November

Entry Deadline: End of August

Year Festival Began: 1986

Contact: Martina Fuchs

Director: Our chairmen are Stephan Vockrodt, Edgar Merkel and Roland Kirsch

Category: Animation, Independent, International, Short

Profile: Filmfest Braunschweig has established itself as the audience-orientated film festival, with many guests and opportunities for discussions, on the cultural map of the province of Lower Saxony and beyond. Circa 12,000 cinema-loving members of our audience attend screenings in several film theatres.

Seminars: Seldom

Competitions: Yes, for long films

Major Awards: A prize is awarded for the film selected by our audience as their favourite (only for films over 61 min. long).

Value of Awards: DM 20,000 (one prize)

Application Tips: German premieres of international feature films

Application Fee: No

Insider Advice: Send a VHS copy of the film (NTSC is fine) and answer our application form

Films Screened: About 130 films (60 short films)

Filmmaker Perks: We don't have the money to invite all, but if you are invited, we pay for travel and lodging.

Tourist Information: The Braunschweig dome, Burg Dankwarderode, the world famous Bibliotheka Augusta (Lessing Library) in Wolfenbüttel or what about a factory tour at Volkswagen in Wolfsburg?

Travel Tips: There are two nice national mountain resorts close to Braunschweig: the Harz and the elm, Hannover (expocity in 2000) is 60 kilometers and the former border (GDR) is only 30 kilometers.

Best Restaurants: Ritter St. Georg (French) or Al Trullo (Italian)

Best Bars: Fischbach and Latino

Best Hangout for Filmmakers: Our festival center in the LOT-Theatre

Best Place for Breakfast: Our festival center

FILMFEST HAMBURG

Friedensalle 44

22765 Hamburg Germany

Tel: 49-40-399-19000

Email: wutz@filmfesthamburg.de

Web Site: www.filmfest hamburg.de

Festival Date: September

Director: Josef Wutz

FILMFEST MUNCHEN

c/o IMF GmbH

Kaiserstrasse 39

Munich, D-80801 Germany

Tel: 49-89-38-19-040

Fax: 49-89-38-19-04-27

Festival Date: June-July

Entry Deadline: January-April

Contact: Eberhard Hauff

Category: Animation, Documentary, International

Profile: Filmfest Munchen includes international films, documentaries and animation.

Awards: No

Competitions: No

Application Fee: None

FILMFESTIVAL MAX OPHÜLS PREIS

Mainzerstr. 8

Saarbrücken, 66111 Germany

Tel: 49-681-39452

Fax: 49-681-905-1943

Email: Filmhaus@aol.com

Web Site: www.saarbruecken.de/filmhaus.htm

Festival Date: January

Entry Deadline: November

Year Festival Began: 1980

Contact: G. Bandel

Director: Christel Drawer

Programmer: E. Blum, P. Thilges, M. Neumann, C. Drawer, A. Knuchel, Th. Altmeyer

Awards: Yes

Competitions: Yes

Major Awards: Max Ophüls Preis

Value of Awards: 30.000,- DM

Past Judges: Elfi Mikesch, Judith Waldner, Zoran Solomun, Hans König, Rüdiger Vogler

Odds of Acceptance: 1 in 3

Filmmaker Perks: Lodging.

Best Hangout for Filmmakers: Lola's Bistro

FRANKFURT GAY AND LESBIAN FILM FESTIVAL

Werkstattkino mal seh'n

Adlerflychtstr. 6

Frankfurt am Main, D-10707 Germany

Tel: 49-69-55-73-42

Fax: 49-69-55-73-42

Email: HagenGott@aol.com

Contact: Anjte Witte or Hagen Gottschalck

Category: Gay Lesbian

HAMBURG INTERNATIONAL SHORT FILM FESTIVAL

KurzFilmAgentur Hamburg e.V.

Friedensallee 7

Hamburg, D-22765 Germany

Tel: 49-40-399-093-75

Fax: 49-40-39-10-63-20

Email: kfa@shortfilm.com

BEST FESTIVALS FOR GENRE FILMS

Festival of Fantastic Films

Fantasia Film Festival

Fantasy Film Fest – International Film Festival for Science Fiction, Horror and Thriller

OdysseyFest Science Fiction and Fantasy Film Festival

TromaDance Film Festival

Web Site: www.shortfilm.com

Category: Digital, Digital Animation, International, Short, Super 8/8mm

INTERNATIONAL FESTIVAL OF ANIMATED FILM STUTTGART

Festival Büro

Teckstraße 56

Stuttgart, D-70190 Germany

Tel: 49-71-925-46-0

Fax: 49-711-925-46-15

Email: info@itfs.de

Web Site: www.itfs.de

Category: Animation, Student

INTERNATIONAL FILMFESTIVAL

Collini-Center, Galerie

D-68161

Mannheim, Germany

Tel: 49-621-10-29-43 ;
49-621-15-23-16

Fax: 49-621-29-15-64

Email: ifmh@mannheim-filmfestival.com

Web Site: www.mannheim-filmfestival.com

Festival Date: October

Entry Deadline: Mid-July

Contact: Christine Schmieder

Director: Michael Koetz

Programmer: Michael Koetz

Category: Independent

Profile: The time of film festivals that present only good films, and nothing else, is past. The future lies in simultaneously offering a marketplace for people who trade in film.

Seminars: Together with FIPRESCI (Federation of International Film Critics)

Competitions: Yes

Major Awards: International Independent Award of Mannheim Heidelberg

Value of Awards: Best Feature: DM 30.000

Best Documentary: DM 10.000

Best Short: DM 5.000

Special prize in memoriam of Rainer Werner Fassbinder: DM 10.000

Application Tips: Make a good film!

Application Fee: None

Insider Advice: Produce as much promo material you can afford and send it to the festival (e.g. photographs, epks—but remember there is a different TV format in Europe, no NTSC)

Films Screened: 75

Odds of Acceptance: 1 in 10

Filmmaker Perks: Free travel, lodging, contacts and a productive atmosphere

Travel Tips: Heidelberg Castle, the vineyards of Palatine

Best Restaurants: Grissini im Mannheim

Best Bars: Max Bar in Heidelberg

Best Hangout for Filmmakers: The Festival Lounge, Cafe Odeon in Mannheim

Best Place for Breakfast: Cafe Journal in Mannheim and Heidelberg

INTERNATIONAL GAY AND LESBIAN FILM FESTIVAL

Rosebud Entertainment, Wittelsbacher Str. 26, 10707 Berlin, Germany

Tel: 49-30-861-4532

Fax: 49-30-861-4539

Email: rosebud_entertainment@t-online.de

Web Site: home.t-online.de/home/rosebud_entertainment

Festival Date: November-December

Entry Deadline: August

Director: Schorsch Müller, Rainer Stefan, in cooperation with Barbara Wieler and Birgit Scheuch

Category: Documentary, Experimental, First-Time Independent Filmmakers, Gay Lesbian, International, Woman

Profile: Non-competitive; largest European genre festival; touring festival; five major German cities, one week each; focus on features, documentaries and shorts of interest to Lesbian, Gay, Bisexual and Transgendered people. The festival tours Munich, Stuttgart, Frankfurt, Cologne, Berlin.

Competitions: No

Application Fee: $25

INTERNATIONAL LEIPZIG FESTIVAL FOR DOCUMENTARY AND ANIMATED FILM

Box 940

Leipzig, 04009 Germany

Tel: 49-341-980-39-21 (festival office); 49-341-980-61-43 (press office)

Fax: 49-341-980-61-41 (festival office); 49-341-980-61-43 (press office)

Email: dok-leipzig@t-online.de

Web Site: www.mdr.de/dokfestival

Festival Date: October

Entry Deadline: September

Year Festival Began: 1955

Director: Fred Gehler

Programmer: selection commitee: Fred Gehler, Tamara Trampe, Dieter Rieken, Klaus Wischnewski, Otto Alder; programme organisation: Kerstin Mauersberger (tel/fax: 49-341-980-48-28)

Category: Animation, Documentary

Seminars: workshops are included in the festival programme, themes depend on current programming

Panels: Yes

Awards: Yes

Competitions: Yes

Application Fee: None

Films Screened: In general there are about 300 films screened.

Odds of Acceptance: more than 100 accepted: 20 documentaries in competition, 40 animated films in competion, about 100 documentaries and animated films for information programmes

Filmmaker Perks: Free travel: In exceptional cases. Lodging: if the film is accepted for competition, six nights (whole festival); if the film is accepted for another section: three nights.

Attendance: 16,000

Tourist Information: Historical city cebtre of Leipzig (old Leipzig fair buildings) nation's battle monument new Leipzig fair complex.

Best Restaurants:

Best Hangout for Filmmakers: Festival club at the festival centre

INTERNATIONAL SHORT FILM FESTIVAL OBERHAUSEN

Grillostr. 34

Oberhausen, D-46045 Germany

Tel: 49-208-825-2652

Fax: 49-208-825-5413

Email: info@kurzfilmtage.de

Web Site: www.kurzfilmtage.de

Festival Date: Late April/early May

Entry Deadline: January 15th (tbc)

Year Festival Began: 1954

Director: Lars Henrik Gass

Category: International, Markets, All genres, Short, Video

Profile: The festival organizes four competitions: International, German, Children's Short Films (also international), and the MuVi-Award for the best German music video clip. All genres and formats are accepted, both on film and video. Productions in the International Competition must not exceed a length of 35 minutes, 45 minutes in the German Competition.

In addition to the competition, the Festival offers a short film market where all submitted films can be viewed (an average of around 3,000 short films from all over the world per year), all featured in the annual German/English film market catalogue.

All in all, an average of 17 prizes worth about 75.000 DEM are awarded every year.

The International Short Film Festival Oberhausen is the oldest of its kind, founded in 1954 by Hilmar Hoffmann.

Panels: Yes, as part of the Special Programmes

Market: Yes

Awards: Yes

Competitions: Yes

Major Awards: Grand Prize of the City of Oberhausen plus 16 other awards

Value of Awards: Grand Prize: 15.000 DEM

total value all awards: ca. 75.000 DEM

Application Fee: No

Common Mistakes: Not filling in the entry forms properly (illegible, wrong address).

Films Screened: 460

Odds of Acceptance: 1 in 16

Filmmaker Perks: Travel assistance, accommodation, meal tickets

Journalist Attendance: 150-200 international journalists

KASSELER DOKUMENTARFILM— UND VIDEOFEST

c/o Filmladen Kassel e.V., Goethestr. 31

Kassel, 34119 Germany

Tel: 49-561-7076421

Fax: 49-561-7076441

Email: dokfest@filmladen.de

Web Site: www.filmladen.de/dokfest

Festival Date: November 14-18, 2001

Entry Deadline: August 15, 2001

Year Festival Began: 1982

Director: Gerhard Wissner

Programmer: Wieland Hoehne, Alexandra Ventura, Verena Kuni, Irmhild Scheuer

Category: Documentary, DVD, Experimental, Independent, International, Video

Profile: In times of extreme political, economic and cultural changes, documentary films and videos can play a large part in raising highly controversial topics and in examining background information. Next to other documentary film festivals like Duisburg, Munich and Leipzig, the Kassel festival is one of the few that devotes itself completely to documentaries and its variations. In Germany, this genre is still far away from public awareness since it can't be shown very often.

Market: No

Competitions: No

Application Fee: None

Films Screened: 150

Odds of Acceptance: 1 in 6

Filmmaker Perks: Lodging, Contacts

MAGDEBURG INTERNATIONAL FILM FESTIVAL

Magdeburg Filmburo

Coquistrasse 18a

D-39104 Magdeburg, Germany

Tel: 49-391-48668

Fax: 49-391-48668

Festival Date: September

Entry Deadline: August

Contact: Michael Blume

Category: International

OKOMEDIA INTERNATIONAL ECOLOGICAL FILM FESTIVAL

Okomedia Institute

Habsburgerstr. 9

D-79104 Freiburg, Germany

Tel: 0761-52024

Fax: 0761-555724

Festival Date: November

Entry Deadline: July for forms; August for films

Contact: Heidi Knott

Category: International

OLDENBURG INTERNATIONAL FILM FESTIVAL

Bahnhofstr. 15

Oldenburg, 26122 Germany

Tel: 49-441-25659

Fax: 49-441-26155

Email: Presse@filmfest-oldenburg.de

Web Site: www.filmfest-oldenburg.de

Festival Date: September

Entry Deadline: June

Contact: Thorsten Ritter

Director: Torsten Neumann, Thorsten Ritter

Programmer: Torsten Neumann, Thorsten Ritter

Other Staff: Jan Wittkopp, Tina Tietjen

Category: Independent

Profile: The Oldenburg International Film Festival is dedicated to showcasing a wide range of versatile and individual filmmaking from all over the world. In a personal atmosphere of communication and exchange, films and guests find themselves presented to a responsive and openminded audience.

Aside from the International Section, the Portrait is dedicated to a female director with a distinctive voice and vision, and the Retrospective is dedicated to a unique and outstanding body of work, the festival focuses on U.S. American independent filmmaking with the Independent Section at the heart of the festival.

Awards: No

Competitions: No

Application Tips: Please include photos!

Application Fee: No

Average Films Entered: feature, short, documentary

Films Screened: 50 feature films, 20 short films

Odds of Acceptance: 1 in 10

Filmmaker Perks: For main sections we offer free travel and free lodging for the director and one/two actors/actresses. Free lodging for the short film section. Contacts for all participants.

Best Restaurants: Restaurant Tafelfreuden, Restaurant Leon.

Best Bars: Der Schwan, Schmitz café

Best Hangout for Filmmakers: Kulturetage

Best Place for Breakfast: Restaurant Leon, Schmitz café

POTSDAM FILM FESTIVAL

Friedrich-Ebert-Str. 90
14467 Potsdam, Germany
Tel: 49-331-2801271
Fax: 49-331-2801273
Festival Date: June
Director: Irina Knochenauer

PRIX JEUNESSE INTERNATIONAL

Bayerischer Rundfunk
München, D 80300 Germany
Tel: 49-89-5900-2058
Fax: 49-89-5900-3053
Email: info@prixjeunesse.de
uvz@prixjeunese.de
Web Site: www.prixjeunesse.de
Festival Date: June

Steve Buscemi at the Q&A for his film "Animal Factory."

Year Festival Began: 1964

Contact: U.S. contact David Kleeman, Director of the American Children's Television Center in Chicago, dkleeman@mcs.com

Director: Ursula von Zallinger

Programmer: Kirsten Schneid

Category: The world's premier festival for children's and youth television programmes

Seminars: during the off-years, mainly in Third World countries

Awards: Yes

Competitions: Yes

Major Awards: Prix Jeunesse

Value of Awards: No prize money

Past Judges: All participants vote in the contest: over 300 producers, executives and researchers from more than 50 nations come to Prix Jeunesse. They spend days screening and discussing the nominated programs.

Application Tips: Enter a high-quality program (innovative in content or technique) which is geared to children or young people (age categories: up to 7, 7- 12, 12-17 split in fiction and non-fiction)

Application Fee: No

Average Films Entered: Innovative kids programs

Films Screened: 84

Odds of Acceptance: 1 in 3

Filmmaker Perks: No registration fee for programs nor participants. Contacts with specialists

from around the world-more than 50 countries represented.

Tourist Information: Munich is a great city to go. Opera, concerts, museums but also the famous "beergardens," good restaurants, etc.etc.

Best Restaurants: 3-star restaurant "Tantris" Johann Fichte Str. 7 Tel 36-19-59-0) and the newcomer in the city center "Marstall," Maximilianstr. 16 Tel 29-16-55-11

Best Hangout for Filmmakers: Park Café, Lenbach, Sausalito, Cafe Puck, etc.

SCHWULE FILMWOCHE FREIBURG (GAY FILM FESTIVAL OF FREIBURG)

c/o Kommunales Kino Freiburg
Urachstr.40
Freiburg, 79102 Germany
Tel: 49-761-709033
Fax: 49-761-407592
Email: MFIsele@aol.com
or scivos@sun6.mathematik.
uni-freiburg.de
Web Site: www.geocities.com/
WestHollywood/4623/index.html
Festival Date: April, 2001
Entry Deadline: February
Year Festival Began: 1985
Contact: Michael Isele, Merzhauser Str. 32, D-79110 Freiburg, Germany.
Director: Michael Isele

Programmer: Jürgen Preuss, Jürgen Recknagel, Alexander Scivos, Christoph Heisig.

Category: Documentary, Gay Lesbian, Independent, International, Short

Profile: The annual Gay Film Festival of Freiburg is Germany's second oldest gay film festival and presents selected movies with gay topics. The focus is on the most recent productions which reflect contemporary gay life in all its diversity. We also present historically valuable classics with gay subtext and silent movies with live piano accompaniment. Out of more than 30 long and short films that are presented within one week, the audience elects their favorite movie.

Seminars: No

Panels: No

Famous Speakers: Regionally famous gay authors read parts of their books

Market: No

Competitions: Yes

Major Awards: Audience Award

Value of Awards: Varies from year to year

Application Fee: None

Common Mistakes: All mail from countries which are not members of the European Community *has* to be declared: "No commercial value—for cultural purposes only." Screening copies from countries which are not members of European Community have to include a "pro forma invoice" with a declaration of value less than $50 U.S. This was sometimes forgotten. We will not accept any mail with a different customs declaration.

Filmmaker Perks: Usually we can provide free lodging, a travel by train (within Europe), and contacts.

Tourist Information: Freiburg is a very nice old, medivial town. The gothic cathedral is one of Germany's highest ones. There are ruins of an old castle.

Freiburg is the gate to the beautiful and world-famous Black Forest, a large forest area, ideal for hiking, mountainbiking and skiing, but also for relaxing at

one of its lakes. It is easily accessible by train and car. From all surrounding peaks, of altitudes of 300 m or 1500 m, you have a fantastic view over the valley of the river Rhein and the Kaiserstuhl, an old volcano, nowadays inactive but still famous for its delicious wine.

Travel Tips: The Black Forest is worth a trip. Visit Furtwangen with a large waterfall and the world's largest cockoo clock, or the top of the "Feldberg," the area's highest mountain. Hike through the Wutach gorge where it is cool and shadowy, even in summer. Not far are the cities of Strasbourg in France, Zurich and Basel in Switzerland; or simply have a glass of wine somewhere in the surrounding vineyard villages in the areas Markgräfler Land, Kaiserstuhl or (in France) Alsace.

For skinny-dipping, sunbathing and gay cruising, the lake of Niederrimsingen (20 km from Freiburg) is very popular.

Best Restaurants: No proper restaurant in town is gay. But there are gay bars (see below). Most exquisite, but expensive, are Freiburg's oldest restaurant, Bären and the Colombi Hotel, also Schwär's Hotel and Schloßrestaurant (the latter with a nice view over the town). There are many reasonably priced restaurants around the cathedral. A very nice location with a little lake and the Black Forest right beside you is Waldsee which regularly is also the place of a gay disco/party. Another place with good music is Blue Monday.

Best Bars: Again, it depends on what you like. Popular gay bars are Sonderbar and Rouge. Le Garecons (inside the main station, usually mixed) is in gay ownership and sometimes the location of a gay party.

Best Hangout for Filmmakers: The cafe of the Kommunales Kino, right at the festival's location. It is a good place to get in contact with the audience of the festival, too.

STUTTGART FiLMWiNTER

Friedrichstrabe 23/a
Stuttgart, D-70174 Germany
Tel: 49-711-226-91-60
Fax: 49-711-226-91-61
Email: wanda@wand5.de
Web Site: www.wand5.de
Festival Date: January
Entry Deadline: October
Contact: Barbel Neumann
Category: Short, Video
Competitions: yes
Average Films Entered: 800
Attendance: 9,000

WURZBURG iNTERNATiONAL FiLM FESTiVAL

Filminitiative Wurzburg
Gosbertsteige 2
D-8700 Wurzburg, Germany
Tel: 49-931-414-098
Fax: 49-931-416-279
Festival Date: January
Contact: Berthold Kremmler
Category: International

GREECE

ATHENS iNTERNATiONAL FiLM FESTiVAL

Eleftherotypia/Daily Paper
8 Kolokotroni St.
10561 Athens, Greece
Tel: 32-42-071; 32-44-048
Fax: 32-42-418
Director: Ninos Feneck Mikelides
Category: International

iNTERNATiONAL THESSALONiKi FiLM FESTiVAL

Paparigopoulou 40
11473 Athens, Greece
Tel: 30-1-645-3668
Fax: 30-1-644-8143
Email: info@filmfestival.gr
Festival Date: November
Entry Deadline: October
Director: Michel Demopoulos

INDIA

BOMBAY INTERNATIONAL FILM FESTIVAL FOR DOCUMENTARY, SHORT AND ANIMATION FILMS

Films Division, Ministry of Information & Broadcasting
Film Bhavan,
24 Dr. Golparao Deshmukh Marg.
Bombay, 400 026 India
Tel: 91-22-3864633, 3861421, 3861461
Fax: 91-22-3860308
Festival Date: Biennial; February
Entry Deadline: October for entry forms; November for cassettes; December for film prints
Director: R. Krishna Mohan
Category: Animation, Documentary, International, Short

CALCUTTA FILM FESTIVAL ON MOUNTAINS

81/2/3 Biren Roy Rd. West
Calcutta, 700 061 India
Tel: 77-64-52
Fax: 91-33-26-49-22
Festival Date: January
Entry Deadline: December
Contact: K. K. Ray

FILMOTSAV DOCUMENTARY FILM FESTIVAL

Federation of Film Societies of India
No. 3, Northend Complex
R K Ashram Marg
New Delhi, 110 001 India
Tel: 32-04-30
Festival Date: January
Entry Deadline: December
Contact: Pankaj Butalia

INTERNATIONAL FILM FESTIVAL OF INDIA

Directorate of Film Festivals
Ministry of Information & Broadcasting
4th Floor
Lok Nayak Bhavan
Khan Market
New Delhi, 110 003 India
Tel: 91-11-461-59-53
Fax: 91-11-462-34-30
Festival Date: January
Entry Deadline: November
Contact: Malti Sahai

IRAN

FAJR INTERNATIONAL FILM FESTIVAL

Farhang Cinema
Dr. Shariati Ave.
Gholhak
Tehran 19139, Iran
Tel: 98-21-200-2088
Fax: 98-21-267-082
Festival Date: January
Entry Deadline: January
Contact: Jamal Omid

IRELAND

CORK FILM FESTIVAL— LESBIAN & GAY SECTION

10 Washington Street
Cork City, Ireland
Tel: 353-21-427-1711
Fax: 353-21-427-5945
Email: info@corkfilmfest.org
Web Site: www.corkfilmfest.org
Contact: Sue Wainwright or Jim Lowther
Director: Michael Hannigan
Category: Gay Lesbian

CORK INTERNATIONAL FILM FESTIVAL

10 Washington St.
Cork City, Ireland
Tel: 353-21-4271711
Fax: 353-21-4275945
Email: info@corkfilmfest.org
Web Site: www.corkfilmfest.org
Festival Date: October
Entry Deadline: July
Year Festival Began: 1956
Contact: Angela Jones
Director: Michael Hannigan
Programmer: Rory Concannon
Category: American Films, Digital Animation, Documentary, Ethnic African, Ethnic Asian, Ethnic Black, Ethnic Jewish, Ethnic Latin, Ethnic Other, Ethnic Spanish, Experimental, First-Time Independent Filmmakers, Gay Lesbian, Independent, International, Short, Video, Woman
Seminars: Seminars and workshops of interest to filmmakers
Market: No, but possibly this year.
Competitions: Yes
Major Awards: Best International Short Film
Value of Awards: £3,000
Application Fee: None
Average Films Entered: 1200 (shorts)
Films Screened: over 200
Odds of Acceptance: 1 in 6
Filmmaker Perks: Three nights accommodation for overseas filmmakers of accepted films.
Attendance: 30,000
Journalist Attendance: 50
Tourist Information: Jameson Distillery, Blarney Castle
Best Restaurants: Office has a list of festival friendly restaurants, bars and reasonable accommodation

CORK YOUTH INTERNATIONAL FILM, VIDEO AND ARTS FESTIVAL

Festival Office
94 Arderin Way
The Glen, Cork, Ireland
Tel: 021-306019
Fax: 021-272839
Festival Date: May
Entry Deadline: April
Contact: Helen Prout

DUBLiN FiLM FESTiVAL

1 Suffolk St.
Dublin 2, Ireland
Tel: 353-1-679-2937
Fax: 353-1-679-2939
Festival Date: March
Entry Deadline: December
Contact: Martin Mahon, David McLoughlin

DUBLiN LESBiAN AND GAY FiLM FESTiVAL

Attn: OUThouse Center
6 South William Street
Dublin 2, Ireland
Tel: 353-1-672-7211 (office);
353-1-284-2910 (programmers)
Fax: 353-1-679-1306
Contact: Patricia Carey or Brian Finnegan or Mick Quinlan or Ailbhe Smyth
Category: Gay Lesbian

iNTERNATiONAL CELTiC FiLM AND TELEViSiON FESTiVAL

Celtic Film & TV Office
BBC Northern Ireland
Ormeau Ave.
Belfast, County Antrim BT2 8HQ
Northern Ireland Ireland
Tel: 44-232-338569
Fax: 44-232-338572
Festival Date: March-April
Contact: Suzy O'Hara

JUNiOR DUBLiN FiLM FESTiVAL

Irish Film Center
Eustache St.
Dublin 2, Ireland
Tel: 3531-671-4095
Fax: 3531-677-8755
Festival Date: November
Contact: Alan Robinson=

---

iSRAEL

HAiFA iNTERNATiONAL FiLM FESTiVAL

142 Hanassi Ave.
Haifa, Israel
Tel: 04-386246
Fax: 04-384327
Festival Date: October
Entry Deadline: July
Director: Pnina Blyer

JERUSALEM iNTERNATiONAL FiLM FESTiVAL

Derech Hebron 11 POB 8561
Jerusalem, 91083 Israel
Tel: 972-2-672-4131 ;
972-2-671-5117
Fax: 972-2-673-3076 ;
972-2-671-3044
Email: jer_cine@inter.net.il
Web Site: www.qrd.tau.ac.il/
israel_update.html#jerusalem
Festival Date: July
Entry Deadline: April
Year Festival Began: 1983
Director: Lia van Leer
Programmer: Avinoam Harpak, Lia van Leer, Gilli Mendel
Category: Independent
Profile: Over 160 films are screened in ten days representing the finest in recent cinema; documentaries, short films, avant garde, gay, animation, retrospectives, classics, Israeli Cinema, Mediterranean Cinema and Jewish Themes. Prizes are given for films that focus on human rights, peace and tolerance. Approximately 50,000 attend.
Seminars: Yes
Panels: Yes
Famous Speakers: Yes
Awards: Yes
Competitions: Yes
Major Awards: Two categories for international competition: Wim van Leer "In Spirit of Freedom" Award; Mediterranean Cinema "In Pursuit of Peace & Tolerance" Award
Past Judges: Guglielmo Biraghi, Clyde Jeavons, etc.
Application Fee: None
Odds of Acceptance: 1 in 3

---

iTALY

ALPE ADRiA FEST

Via della Pesscheria 4
34121 Trieste, Italy
Tel: 3940-311-153
Fax: 3940-311-993
Festival Date: January
Director: Anamaria Percavassi

AMBiENTE—iNCONTRi FiLM FESTiVAL iNTERNAZiONALE SU NATURA E AMBiENTE

Segretaria ODESSA-Steps
Cassella Postale 186
33170 Pordenone, Italy
Tel: 39-434-520-404
Fax: 39-434-520-584
Festival Date: July
Entry Deadline: June
Director: Andrea Crozzoli

ANTENNA CiNEMA FESTiVAL (ANTENNACiNEMA)

Palazzo Sarcinelli
Via XX Septembre 132
31015 Conegliano, Italy
Tel: 39-438-411007
Fax: 39-438-32777
Contact: Gianfranco Zoppas

ARCiPELAGO SHORT FiLM FESTiVAL

c/o Associazione Culturale
3E-medi@
Circonvallazione Clodia 88
(apt. #20)
Rome, 00195 Italy
Tel: 39-6-3751-6571
Fax: 39-6-3751-8672
Email: arcipelago@webcom.com
Web Site: www.webcom.com/
3e_media/arcipelago or
www.mondocorto.org
Festival Date: June
Entry Deadline: April
Director: Fabio Bo, Stefano Martina, and Massimo Forleo
Category: International, Short
Profile: Explores new artistic and productive horizons. This festival welcomes works from all countries.

ARMED FORCES AND PEOPLE FiLM FESTiVAL

Rassegna Cinematografica
Internazionale
Eserciti E Popoli
Via A. Catalani, 31
00199 Rome, Italy
Tel: 06-86-20-02-75
Fax: 06-86-20-71-77
Festival Date: November
Entry Deadline: September
Contact: Giorgio Zucchetti

ASOLO iNTERNAtiONAL ANiMAtiON FESTiVAL

Amministrazione Provinciale
31100 Treviso, Italy
Tel: 0422-548327
Fax: 0422-50086
Festival Date: May
Contact: Alfio Bastiancich, Vanna Visentin
Category: Animation, International

BELLARiA iNDEPENDENT CiNEMA FESTiVAL

Segretaria Organizzativa
Biblioteca Communale
Via Paolo Guide 108
47041 Bellaria (FO), Italy
Tel: 541-347186
Fax: 541-347186
Festival Date: June
Contact: Anteprima per il Cinema Indipendente Italiano

BERGAMO iNTERNATiONAL WEEK OF AUTEUR FiLM

Mostra Internationale del Film
d'Autore
Rotonda Dei Mille, I
24100 Bergamo, Italy
Tel: 035-243-566; 035-243-162
Fax: 035-240-816
Festival Date: March
Entry Deadline: January
Contact: Nino Zuchelli

Filmmaker Ben Affleck out and about on the festival circuit.

COM & COM COMEDY AND COMEDiC FiLM FESTiVAL

Piazza Einaudi 2
25041 Boario Terme BS, Italy
Tel: 39-364-53-16-09
Fax: 39-364-53-22-80
Festival Date: September-October
Contact: Aldo Minelli

DYLAN DOG HORROR FESTiVAL

Sergio Bonelli Editore
Via M. Buonarroti 38
20145 Milan, Italy
Tel: 39-2-4800-2877
Fax: 39-2-4819-5682
Festival Date: June
Entry Deadline: April
Contact: Stefano Marzorati

EUROPACiNEMA FESTiVAL

Via 20 Settembre 3
00187 Rome, Italy
Tel: 39-6-4201-1184;
39-6-4200-0211
Fax: 39-6-4201-0599
Festival Date: November 20-December 4
Entry Deadline: September
Director: Monique Veaute

FESTiVAL DEi POPOLi

Borgo Pinti 82R
50121 Firenze, Italy
Tel: 39-55-244-778
Fax: 39-55-241-364
Email: fespopol@dada.it
Festival Date: November
Entry Deadline: September
Director: Mario Simondi

FLORENCE FiLM FESTiVAL

via S. Zonobi 54r
50129 Firenze, Italy
Tel: 055-298249
Fax: 055-298249
Festival Date: December
Director: Fabrizio Fiumi

GiFFONi FiLM FESTiVAL

Piazzi Umberto I
84095 Giffoni Valle Piana
Salerno, Italy
Tel: 39-89-868-544
Fax: 39-89-866-111
Festival Date: July
Entry Deadline: June
Contact: Claudio Gubitosi

GiORNATE PROFESSiONALi Di CiNEMA

Taormina
Sicily, Italy
Tel: 39-6-884-731
Fax: 39-6-440-4255
Festival Date: June

iNTERNATiONAL CiNEMA AND TELEViSiON MULTiMEDiA MARKET (MiFED)

Largo Domodossola 1
1-20145 Milano MI, Italy
Tel: 02-4997-7267; 02-4801-2912
Fax: 02-4997-7020
Festival Date: October
Entry Deadline: June; October for registration information
Contact: Elena Lloyd, MIFED/Fiera Milano
Category: Markets

iNTERNATiONAL FESTiVAL OF DOCUMENTARiES OF THE SEA

Piazza E. Llussu, 4
80820 San Teodoro (Sardegna), Italy
Tel: 0784-866010
Fax: 0784-866010
Festival Date: May
Entry Deadline: April
Contact: Instituto delle Civita del Mare
Category: Documentary

iNTERNATiONAL LESBiAN FiLM FESTiVAL iMMAGiNARiA

c/o Marina Genovese,
Via Calori 13
Bologna, 40122 Italy
Tel: 39-051-556259
Fax: 39-051-556259
Email: assclv@iperbole.bologna.it
Web Site: www2.comune.bologna.it/assclv
Festival Date: February 22-25, 2001
Entry Deadline: October
Year Festival Began: 1993

Contact: Marina Genovese
Director: Marina Genovese
Programmer: Debora Guma, Claudia Stella. Cristina Zanetti
Category: Documentary, Gay Lesbian, Independent, International
Profile: Immaginaria pursues three main objectives: making lesbian cinema known in Italy, where it is still lacks suitable distribution channels; overcoming prejudice and making institutions understand and realise the cultural importance and value of lesbian and feminist cinema production; presenting the best examples of independent lesbian and feminist cinema production to large cinema and TV distribution companies.
Market: No
Competitions: Yes
Application Fee: None
Average Films Entered: The Festival presents documentaries, fiction, experimental and animation films and videos, directed by women, with lesbian and/or feminist contents.
Films Screened: 56
Odds of Acceptance: 1 in 4
Filmmaker Perks: Free travel and lodging.
Attendance: 4,500
Journalist Attendance: 20

iNTERNATiONAL MYSTERY FiLM FESTiVAL (MYSTFEST)

Centro Culturale Polivalente
Piazza Della Repubblica, 34
47033 Cattolica (FO), Italy
Tel: 39-541-967802
Fax: 39-541-967803
Festival Date: June-July
Entry Deadline: May
Contact: Gian Pietro Brunetta
Category: International, Weird

MYSTERY AND NOiR FiLM FESTiVAL

44 Via Dei Coronai
00186 Rome, Italy
Tel: 39-6-6833844; 39-6-6872890
Fax: 39-6-6867902
Festival Date: December

Director: Giorgio Gosetti
Category: Mystery

PORDENONE SiLENT FiLM FESTiVAL

Le Giornate del Cinema Muto
c/o La Cineteca del Friuli
Via Osoppo 26
I-33013 Gemona (UD), Italy
Tel: 0432-980458
Fax: 0432-970542
Festival Date: October
Director: Livio Jacob, Chair
Category: Silent

RiMiNiCiNEMA iNTERNATiONAL FiLM FESTiVAL

Riminicinema Mostra Internazionale
Via Gambalunga 2 7
47037 Rimini, Italy
Tel: 0541-26399; 0541-22627
Fax: 0561-26167; 0561-24227
Festival Date: September
Entry Deadline: June
Contact: Gianfranco Miro Gori
Category: International

TORiNO FiLM FESTiVAL

Via Monte di Pieta 1
Torino, 10121 Italy
Tel: 39-011-5623309
Fax: 39-011-5629796
Email: info@torinofilmfest.org
Web Site: www.torinofilmfest.org
Festival Date: November
Entry Deadline: August (Shorts). September (Features)
Year Festival Began: 1982
Contact: Alberto Barbera
Director: Alberto Barbera
Programmer: Alberto Barbera, Stefano Della Casa, Alexander Horwath, Roberto Turigliatto, Fabrizio Grosoli
Category: International
Profile: This well organized event (formerly know as Festival Internazionale Cinema Giovani) takes place each autumn and focuses on films made by new directors. There is a competitive section for shorts, features and

Italian independents, as well as a section for retrospective and spotlights. The festival has been recognized as a top-drawer showcase for hot new international talent and dubbed second only to Venice on the crowded Italian festival circuit.

Seminars: No

Panels: No

Awards: Yes

Competitions: Yes

Major Awards: International Feature-Film Competition

Best Film: $16,600 lire

Two Special Jury Prizes: $5,500 lire each

Holden Prize for the best screenplay: $1,600 lire

Nestl... Award for Film Distribution

For the winning film's distributor: $55,500 lire

For the winning film's director: $11,100 lire

International short-Film Competition

Best Film: $2,800 lire

Two Special Jury Prizes: $1,100 lire each

Italian-space Competition

Fiction section

First Prize: $5,500 lire in Kodak film and technical services

Second Prize: $1,100 lire

Non-Fiction section:

First Prize: $5,500 lire in Kodak film and technical services

Second Prize: $1,100 lire

Turin-Space Competition

First Prize: $2,800 lire in technical services offered by the cooperative, ZaBum Uno

Second Prize: $550 lire

Cipputi Prize

Best Film on the World of Work: $2,800 lire

in collaboration with the CGIL-CISL-UIL labor unions

Average Films Entered: 300

Attendance: 56,000

TURiN iNTERNATiONAL GAY & LESBiAN FiLM FESTiVAL "FROM SODOM TO HOLLYWOOD"

Piazza San Carlo 161

Torino, 10123 Italy

Tel: 39-011-534888

Fax: 39-011-535796

Email: info@turinglfilmfestival.com or glfilmfest@assioma.com

Web Site: www.turinglfilmfestival.com

Festival Date: April 19-25, 2001

Entry Deadline: January

Year Festival Began: 1986

Contact: Luca Andreotti

Director: Stefano Della Casa

Programmer: Angelo Acerbi

Other Staff: Adriano Virone

Category: American Films, Documentary, Experimental, Gay Lesbian, Independent, International, Short, Video

Profile: Three competitive sections (features, shorts and documentaries), panorama section, special events.

Market: No

Competitions: Yes

Major Awards: Best Feature Film

Value of Awards: $2500

Application Fee: None

Common Mistakes: Little problems in compiling the entry form.

Insider Advice: If you have a film with gay or lesbian issues, try to submit it, don't be shy.

Average Films Entered: We like all the kinds of movies; drama, comedy, experimental, sexy, documentary, etc.

Films Screened: 150

Odds of Acceptance: 1 in 4

Filmmaker Perks: We can offer lodging for filmmakers and free travel only for the directors that have their film in the main competition.

Journalist Attendance: 80

VENiCE iNTERNATiONAL FiLM FESTiVAL

Ca Giustinian

San Marco 1364-A

30124 Venice, Italy

Tel: 39-41-52-18-711

Fax: 39-41-52-27-539

Email: das@labiennale.com

Web Site: http://194.185.28.38/gb/cinema.html

Festival Date: August-September

Entry Deadline: July

Director: Alberto Barbera

Category: International

Profile: The oldest film festival celebrating over 100 years of awarding filmmakers. It is considered one of the best festivals in the world. Approximately 100,000 attend.

Competitions: Yes

Major Awards: Golden Lion (Best Picture); Silver Lion; Grand Special Jury Prize; Golden Lion (Lifetime Achievement); Best actor/actress/supporting actor/supporting actress.

Application Fee: None

Films Screened: 157

JAMAICA

JAMERiCAN FiLM AND MUSiC FESTiVAL

9000 Sunset Blvd., Suite 709

Los Angeles, CA 90069 USA

Tel: 323-936-8951

Email: info@jamericanfilmfest.com

Web Site: www.jamericanfilmfest.com

Festival Date: November 14-19, 2001

Entry Deadline: Early October

Director: Sheryl Lee Ralph

Profile: Voted "One of the Top Ten Film Festivals in the world" by E! Entertainment TV in its inaugural year, The Jamerican Film and Music Festival is a four-day event held each year in November in Montego. The festival is the brainchild of Jamerican actress/filmmaker Sheryl Lee Ralph, whose company, Island Girl Productions, produces the event.

The festival actively supports diverse, positive and innovative examples of cinematic work. "At a time when the global community recognizes the importance of the arts, it is critical that we provide hope, exposure and opportunity to those who want to pursue filmmaking, acting, directing or producing but don't know how," says Ms. Ralph.

The Jamaica Film Commission, the Jamaica Tourist Board and Ms. Ralph have joined to ensure that the Jamerican Film and Music Festival gets off to a great start each year. Film Commissioner Del Crooks commented; "The Film Commission and Jamaica Tourist Board are working to make sure this festival is a successful annual event just like Cannes."

As CEO of Island Girl Productions, Sheryl Lee Ralph has high expectations for the festival. "You'll rub shoulders with producers, directors, and stars on some of the worlds finest beaches, drinking the world's best coffee (Blue Mountain), rum, beer, and eating jerk chicken! Who could ask for anything more?"

JAPAN

FiLM FESTiVAL OF iNTERNATiONAL CiNEMA STUDENTS (FFiCS)

Secretariat of the FFICS Organizing Committee
c/o Tokyu Agency, Inc.
4-8-18 Akasaka
Minato-ku
Tokyo 107, Japan
Tel: 03-3475-3855
Fax: 03-5411-0382
Director: Haruki Iwasaki, Secretary General

FUKUOKA ASiAN FiLM FESTiVAL

1-8-1 Tenjin, Chuo-ku
Fukuoka 810, Japan
Tel: 81-92-733-5170
Fax: 81-92-733-5595
Festival Date: September 11-20
Contact: Shu Maeda
Director: Tadao Sato

HiROSHiMA iNTERNATiONAL AMATEUR FiLM AND ViDEO FESTiVAL

c/o Chugoku Broadcasting Co.
21-3 Motomachi
Naka-ku
Hiroshima 730, Japan
Tel: 082-222-1133
Fax: 082-222-1319
Festival Date: February
Contact: Shozo Murata

INTERNATIONAL ANIMATION FESTIVAL—APAN, HIROSHIMA

Hiroshima Festival Office
4-17 Kako-machi Naka-ku
Hiroshima 730, Japan
Tel: 81-82-245-0245
Fax: 81-82-245-0246
Web Site: www.urban.ne.jp/home/hiroanim/
Festival Date: August
Entry Deadline: March for entry materials; April for prints and tapes
Director: Sayoko Kinoshita
Category: Animation, International

JAPAN INTERNATIONAL FILM & VIDEO FESTIVAL OF ADVENTURE AND SPORTS

Jifas Organizing Committee
Hakuba City office
7025 Hokujo
Hakuba-mura
Kitaazumi-gun
Nagano-ken, Japan
Tel: 81-261-72-5000
Fax: 81-261-72-6311
Festival Date: June
Entry Deadline: February
Contact: Takayuki Ogida
Category: International, Video

TOKYO INTERNATIONAL FANTASTIC FILM FESTIVAL

5H Asano Bldg.
No 3 2-4-19
Ginza, Chou-ku
Tokyo 104, Japan
Tel: 81-33563-6359
Fax: 81-33563-6235
Festival Date: September-October
Entry Deadline: June
Contact: Y. Komatsuzawa
Category: Retro Science

TOKYO INTERNATIONAL FILM FESTIVAL

4F Landic Ginza Bldg. II
1-6-5 Ginza
Chuo-ku
Tokyo 104, Japan
Tel: 81-3-3563-6305
Fax: 81-3-3563-6310
Web Site: www.tokyo-filmfest.or.jp
Festival Date: September-October
Entry Deadline: June
Contact: Yasuyoshi Tokuma / Toshiyuki Hone
Category: International
Profile: There are two competitions in this nternational film festival. The Young Cinema Competition and the International Competition.
Awards: Yes
Competitions: Yes
Major Awards: Tokyo Grand Prix
Special Jury Prize
Best Director/Actor/Actress
Best Artistic Contribution
Best Screenplay
also: Tokyo Gold, Silver and Bronze awards.
Value of Awards: 5-20 million Yen
Application Fee: None
Average Films Entered: 200+
Attendance: 150,000+

TOKYO INTERNATIONAL LESBIAN & GAY FILM AND VIDEO FESTIVAL

5-24-16 #601 Nakano
Nakano-ku
Tokyo, 164-0001 Japan
Tel: 8- 3-5380-5760
Fax: 81-3-5380-5767
Email: lgff@tokyo.office.ne.jp or chimono@hotmail.com
Web Site: http://l-gff.gender.ne.jp/
Contact: Eri Chimoto
Category: Gay Lesbian

TOKYO VIDEO FESTIVAL

Victor Company of Japan, Ltd.
Victor Bldg.
1-7-1 Shinbashi
Minato-ku
Tokyo 105, Japan
Tel: 03-3289-2815
Fax: 03-3289-2819
Festival Date: January
Entry Deadline: September
Contact: Minoru Sato
Category: Video

YAMAGATA INTERNATIONAL DOCUMENTARY FILM FESTIVAL

Kitagawa Bldg. 4fl.,
6-42 Kagurazaka,
Shinjuku-ku
Tokyo, 162-0825 Japan
Tel: 81-3-3266-9704
Fax: 81-3-3266-9700
Email: yidff@bekkoame.or.jp
Web Site: www.city.yamagata/yamagata.jp/yidff/en/home.html
Festival Date: October
Entry Deadline: March
Year Festival Began: 1989
Contact: Seiko Ono
Director: Kazuyuki Yano
Programmer: Seiko Ono, Asako Fujioka, Hisao Saito
Other Staff: Hiraku Miyazawa, Aaron Gerow, Jennifer Swanton
Category: Documentary
Profile: Located in a verdant, rolling valley far north of Tokyo, Yamagata City is the site for Asia's first international documentary film festival. The first festival (in 1989) was held to commemorate the 100th anniversary of Yamagata City, the sponsor of the festival, and has been presented biennially ever since in Yamagata's best season, October. The atmosphere of the festival is intimate and affords Asian filmmakers a prime opportunity to meet with their Western counterparts in relaxed surroundings. The first and foremost documentary festival in Asia, the week-long YIDFF is a central force in promoting documentary both in Japan and the region, showcasing recent,

ground-breaking work in the International Competition and supporting new Asian filmmakers in New Asian Currents.

Eligiblility for the International Competition:

-Films that have been produced in 16mm or 35mm. Documentaries shot on video have been tranferred to 16mm or 35mm.

-Films that have not been released publicly in Japan prior to their showing at Yamagata (Japanese films are exempt).

-Shorts will not be accepted. (Less than 45 min might be considered as a short.)

New Asian Currents:

Content: Centers on the works of up-and coming Asian documentarists.

Eligiblility: Open to all styles of documentary on all formats of film and video.

Seminars: None

Awards: Yes

Competitions: Yes

Major Awards: Prizes for the International Competition

The Grand Prize (The Robert and Frances Flaherty Prize) 3,000,000 yen

The Mayor's Prize 1,000,000 yen

Two Runner-Up Prizes 300,000 yen each

One Special Prize 300,000 yen

Prizes for New Asian Currents

Ogawa Shinsuke Prize 500,000 yen

Two "Awards of Excellence" 300,000 yen each

Value of Awards: See Above

Application Tips: Applications should be legible and easy to

read (typewritten, if possible). Information about the film, such as synopses, should also be informative, but succinct (i.e., neither too short nor too long).

Application Fee: None

Insider Advice: The YIDFF tends to favor independent, groundbreaking documenaries that, while tackling important topics, are valuable not just for the information they convey, but also for their contribution to cinematic art. Given that only 15 works are accepted out of over 400 entries for the International Competition, films, to be accepted, simply have to stand out above the crowd through innovation, technical mastery, and skill in presenting their subject.

Odds of Acceptance: 1 in 26

Filmmaker Perks: The festival covers all travel fees and lodging for the official guests.

Tourist Information: During the festival, special day trips are organized for filmmakers and guests. Numbers are limited and spaces always fill quickly. There are usually two trips. One group visits Mt. Zao, renowned for its hot springs and great skiing. It must be said those who choose this trip are the more adventurous type as the visit entails a dip in an outdoor communal hot spring with very little regard to modesty. Meanwhile the other group is taking in the beauty of Yamadera, a site made famous by the haiku poet Basho who wrote one of his most famous haikus there. Yamadera is a made up of several temples nestled into a craggy mountainside. To reach the top, one must scale the

1,000 plus stone steps, but the hike, in amongst huge, shady cedars, is well worth it.

Afterwards, the two groups meet up by the Mamigasaki riverside for a traditional and seasonal lunch, followed by local entertainment (taiko drums, traditional dance, etc.) in which guests can participate. There are many other places to see in and around the city, which are within walking distance. Temples, museums, castle ruins.

Travel Tips: Maps and pamphlets in English are available from the many information outlets during the festival and all guests receive a festival guide which includes application forms for the day trips. October in Yamagata can be a little cool, so a jacket of some sort is a must.

Best Restaurants: By far the best value for money is Capriciosa, an Italian restaurant which is more often than not packed of hungry diners. Good prices and massive portions. Oh, and the food's pretty darn good too.

If you're after Japanese food, there are some good soba and ramen places. The ramen restaurant Sakaya is pretty good and as such, there is usually a bit of a wait to be seated. There is also an abundance of izakayas, which are a cross between a bar/restaurant. They offer a mix of Japanese and Western food

Best Bars: Most of Yamagata's bars seem to be concentrated around the train station area. Best one? Jiggers Shot Bar is classy without being pretentious. Billy's is closer to the festival sites and is cosy and wellstocked.

Best Hangout for Filmmakers: Komian Club is the official hangout for festival-goers. A pickle shop by day, this charmingly restored traditional warehouse has become a favorite amongst not only the filmmakers and guests but the locals as well. Yamagata also has some great bakeries

BEST DOCUMENTARY FILM FESTIVALS

DocFest - New York International Documentary Festival

Doubletake Documentary Film Festival

Fort Lauderdale International Film Festival

Hot Docs Canadian International Documentary Festival

Hot Springs Documentary Film Festival

Nashville Independent Film Festival

San Francisco International Film Festival

Seattle International Film Festival

Sheffield International Documentary Festival

Yamagata International Documentary Film Festival

KOREA

SEOUL QUEER FiLM & ViDEO FESTiVAL

Nakwon-dong 195-1,
Midong Bd #301, Chongno-ku
Seoul Korea
Tel: 82-2-766-5626
Fax: 82-2-766-0598
Email: queer21@interpia.net
Festival Date: September
Category: Gay Lesbian

LATVIA

ARSENAL FiLM FORUM

ICNC "Arsenal"
Marstalu Iela 14
P. O. Box 626
Riga, LV 1047 Latvia
Tel: 013-2-221620
Fax: 013-2-8820445
Festival Date: September
Contact: Augustus Sukuts

MEXICO

ACAPULCO BLACK FiLM FESTiVAL

c/o UniWorld Group, Inc.
100 Avenue of the Americas
New York, NY 10013 Mexico
Tel: 212-219-7267; 800-559-3898
(To register)
Web Site: www.abff.com
Year Festival Began: 1996
Contact: Jeff Friday
Director: Byron E. Lewis
Programmer: Jeff Friday
Other Staff: Warrington Hudlin,
Curator
Category: American Films, Ethnic
Black, International, Work in
progress, Short
Profile: The Acapulco Black Film
Festival is a celebration of the
cinematic work of black filmmak-
ers and artists. The ABFF offers a
competitive showcase of inde-
pendent black cinema from
around the world. The festival's
retreatlike atmoshpere provides

an intellectually charged environ-
ment for filmmakers, artists,
industry executives, journalists
and film enthusiasts to network
and share information and ideas.
The exciting backdrop of
Acapulco makes this a week you
do not want to miss. Only 1000
people will be accepted.
Awards: Yes
Competitions: Yes
Major Awards: Lincoln
Filmmakers Trophy
Attendance: 1000

FESTiVAL iNTERNACiONAL CiNEMATOGRAFiCO DE CANCUN

Calzada de Tlalpan 1838
Col. Country club
CP 04220 DF Mexico
Tel: 6-89-08-12
Fax: 6-89-09-88
Festival Date: November-
December
Entry Deadline: October
Contact: Jean-Pierre Leleu
Garcia

MOROCCO

iNTERNATiONAL FESTiVAL OF CASABLANCA

Commune Urbaine Moulay
Youssef
Poste 228
Casablanca, Morocco
Tel: 212-2-22-12-16
Fax: 212-2-29-94-74
Festival Date: September
Entry Deadline: Fifteen days
prior to start of festival.
Contact: A. Masbahi

NETHERLANDS

DUTCH FiLM FESTiVAL

Nederlands Film Festival
Hoogt 4-10
3512 GW Utrecht, Netherlands
Tel: 30-322684

Fax: 30-313200
Festival Date: September
Entry Deadline: July
Director: Jacques E. Van
Heyningen

HOLLAND ANiMATiON FiLM FESTiVAL

Hoogt 4
3512 GW Utrecht, Netherlands
Tel: 30-312216
Fax: 30-312940
Contact: Gerben Schermer
Category: Animation

iNTERNATiONAL DOCUMENTARY FiLM FESTiVAL AMSTERDAM (iDFA)

Kleine-Garmanplantsoen, 10
1017 RR Amsterdam,
Netherlands
Tel: 20-627-33-29
Fax: 20-638-53-88
Festival Date: December
Entry Deadline: September
Director: Ally Derks, General
Director
Category: Documentary

THE iNTERNATiONAL FiLM FESTiVAL ROTTERDAM

PO Box 21696
Rotterdam, 3001 AR
Netherlands
Tel: 31-10-890-90-90
Fax: 31-10-890-90-91
Email: tiger@filmfestival
rotterdam.com or iffr@luna.nl
Web Site: www.filmfestival
rotterdam.com or
www.iffrotterdam.nl
Festival Date: January 24-
February 4, 2001
Entry Deadline: shorts and doc-
umentaries: October 1
features: November 1
CineMart projects: October 15
Contact: CineMart and
International PR: Ido Abram
Director: Simon Field, Sandra
den Hamer
Programmer: Rene van der
Giessen

Maps and
pamphlets in
English are
available
from the
many
information
outlets during
the festival
and all guests
receive a
festival guide
which
includes
application
forms for the
day trips
(Yamagata
International
Documentary
Film Festival).

Category: Documentary, International, Innovative and new talent, Short

Profile: The International Film Festival Rotterdam combines adventurous cinema with more conventional films of quality, and a focus on innovative and new talent in the Tiger Awards Competition. Rotterdam enjoys one of the largest film festival audiences in the world.

Market: CineMart 28 January—1 February 2001

A co-production market. Around 40 film projects are presented by their directors/producers to 450 representatives of film financing corporations and organisations (like funds, banks, tv, film distributors, producers etc.). the CineMart staff mediates more than 4000 meetings between participants and almost all the projects receive financing and/or offers on the spot. the participating projects are invited by the Festival/CineMart.

Awards: Yes

Competitions: Yes

Major Awards: Tiger Awards Competition

Other Awards: Fipresci Award; KNF Prizes (awarded by film journalists)

Value of Awards: $10,000.00 (U.S.)

Application Fee: None

Films Screened: 210 screened

Attendance: 300,000+

NEW ZEALAND

AUCKLAND INTERNATIONAL FILM FESTIVAL

P.O. Box 9544, Te Aro
Wellington 6035 New Zealand
Tel: 64-4-385-0162
Fax: 64-4-801-7304
Email: enzedff@actrix.gen.nz
Web Site: www.enzedff.co.nz/
Festival Date: July
Entry Deadline: April
Year Festival Began: 1969
Contact: Bill Gosden
Category: International

Profile: Over 80,000 attend

Awards: No

Competitions: No

Application Fee: None

Films Screened: 120 features and shorts

Odds of Acceptance: 1 in 7

INCREDIBLY STRANGE FILM FESTIVAL

Box 5653
Wellesley St.
Auckland, New Zealand
Email: at@iconz.co.nz

THE NEW ZEALAND FILM FESTIVAL

PO Box 9544
Te Aro
Wellington, 6035 New Zealand
Tel: 64 -4-385-0162
Fax: 64-4-801-7304
Email: enzedff@actrix.gen.nz
Web Site: www.enzedff.co.nz
Festival Date: July
Entry Deadline: April
Contact: Bill Gosden
Director: Bill Gosden
Profile: Screening an invited program of around 100 features and 50 shorts, the Auckland and Wellington Film Festivals provide a non-competitive New Zealand premiere showcase for a striking diversity of film and video styles. An archival component also enjoys considerable prominence. Now into the second decade of programming under the direction of the apparently tireless Bill Gosden, latest editions played to audiences of 80,000 in Auckland and 50,000 in Wellington.

Application Tips: Application forms can be requested (please provide a mailing address) or found at the Festival's website: www.enzedff.co.nz

Application Fee: No

Insider Advice: There are no restrictions

Films Screened: The Festival screens up to 120 films ranging from features to shorts.

OUT TAKES

REEL QUEER
P O Box 12 201
Wellington, New Zealand
Tel: 64-4-388-5211 (Note: this is a private number; please check the time difference before calling!)
Fax: 64-4-474-3127
Email: rking@globe.net.nz
Web Site: nz.com/NZ/Queer/ReelQueer/
Festival Date: mid-May to early June
Entry Deadline: end of February
Director: There is no director. All staff are voluntary and work as a team.
Category: Gay Lesbian
Profile: Annual New Zealand film festival for the lesbian/gay/bisexual/transgender communities, organised and showing in Wellington, but also touring (in part) to Auckland and Christchurch. Organised by Reel Queer, a non-profit community organization.
Seminars: No
Panels: No
Famous Speakers: If we get funding to bring someone out here
Awards: No
Competitions: No
Application Tips: Provide a film that we like!
Application Fee: None
Insider Advice: Provide us with a VHS of reasonable quality, an application form (requested or downloaded from our website) and preferably a synopsis, as far in advance of the close-off date as possible.
Odds of Acceptance: 1 in 2
Filmmaker Perks: We are rarely able to offer free airfares unless we get a grant for this. Ditto with accommodation, though we are usually able to find somewhere they can stay privately.
Best Restaurants: Logan Brown's, Cuba Street
Best Bars: Ruby Ruby, Edward Street (gay bar)
Best Place for Breakfast: Lido cafe, corner of Victoria and Wakefield Streets

WELLINGTON FILM FESTIVAL AND AUKLAND INTERNATIONAL FILM FESTIVAL

Box 9544 Te Aro
Wellington 6035, New Zealand
Tel: 64-4-385-0162
Fax: 64-4-801-7304
Email: enzedff@actrix.gen.nz
Web Site: www.enzedff.co.nz
Festival Date: July
Entry Deadline: May
Contact: Bill Gosden

NORWAY

NORWEGIAN INTERNATIONAL FILM FESTIVAL

P. O. Box 145
N-5501 Haugesund, Norway
Tel: 47-52-73-44-30
Fax: 47-52-73-44-20
Festival Date: August
Contact: Gunnar Lovvik
Category: International

NORWEGIAN SHORT FILM FESTIVAL

Sorengvn.8B
1342 Jar, Norway
Tel: 47-12-20-13
Fax: 47-12-48-65
Festival Date: June
Entry Deadline: March
Contact: Toril Simonsen
Category: Short

TROMSØ INTERNATIONAL FILM FESTIVAL

Post: Box 285, 9253
Delivery: Grønnegata 94,
Tromsø Norway
Tel: 47-77-75-30-90;
47-77-75-30-92
Fax: 47-77-75-30-99
Email: filmfestival@
tromsokino.no
Web Site: www.tromsokino.no/
filmfestival
Festival Date: January
Entry Deadline: October

Year Festival Began: 1991
Contact: Martha Otte
Director: Hans Henrik Berg
Programmer: Ola Lund Renolen
Category: First-Time Independent Filmmakers, Independent, International
Profile: TIFF is Norway's largest film festival for regular cinemagoers, with more than 32,000 admissions in 2000. It is the world's northernmost film festival, presenting an international cutting-edge program of feature films plus the latest regional productions. Complete with a program of critic's favorites, visiting filmmakers and two international juries, the festival's main emphasis is on quality films that reflect the cultural, visual and narrative diversity of international independent filmmaking, and that would not otherwise be seen in Norwegian cinemas. The festival takes place just after the sun has returned to the horizon after a two-month absence, but while it is still possible to experience the Northern Lights in Tromsø.
Seminars: The festival organizes a seminar for youth between 16 -19 years on a film-related theme. In 2000: Funny Games (on the difference between violence in film and computer games)
Panels: The Norwegian Critics Association organises a panel of experts to discuss a relevant theme. (2000: Dogme 95: What now?)
Market: No, but all the Norwegian distributors are present at the festival, and since 95 percent of the films screened don't have Norwegian distribution, some films do get picked up.
Competitions: Yes
Major Awards: Aurora
Also an audience award (not a cash prize)
Value of Awards: Theatrical release in Norway (= cash grant to the distributor) + 25,000 Norwegian crowns (= approx. 3,500 Euro) to the director.
Application Fee: No, but video cassettes and other material will not be returned unless requested, and at applicant's expense.

Common Mistakes: Too late.
Insider Advice: Provide high-quality video and good press kit.
Average Films Entered: Most of our program is selected from other festivals or through personal contacts. By invitation.
Films Screened: 40
Odds of Acceptance: 1 in 20
Filmmaker Perks: Hospitality and contacts. Travel is the exception.
Attendance: 4,500 participants that account for 32,000 admissions.
Journalist Attendance: 100 Norwegian (local, regional, national/TV, radio, print, Internet) and ten international (mostly from Nordic countries) [PS: we have a great press party!]
Tourist Information: During the film festival, all the bars. Though not exactly a tourist attraction, taking a sauna is also an option. Outdoor activities: Dog sledding, skiiing, ice bathing.
Travel Tips: Two airlines serve Tromsø (SAS and Braathens) with 16 flights daily between Oslo and Tromsø. Flying time is approx 1hr 45 min.
Best Cheap Hotels: Amalie Hotel. Pension Skipperhuset.
Best Luxury Hotels: No luxury, just high standard. Rica Ishavshotel (festival hotel), Grand Nordic, Radisson SAS (most expensive)
Best Bars: Solid, Le Mirage
Best Hangout for filmmakers: Solid, Le Mirage
Best Place for Breakfast: Solid, Kaffebønna
Random Tidbits: The nightlife in this little town is indescribable all year-round (it's a university town), but it goes completely berserk during the film festival. All the bars and cafés are filled to the brim until closing time (3:30 am, followed by after hours parties), and there is live music of all kinds at most venues, with festival discounts at several of them.

The spirit and lifestyle of the people in Northern Norway is often compared what you might find in warmer climates: essentially laid back, don't-worry-be-happy attitude.

PHILIPPINES

AMATEUR/ PROFESSIONAL INTERNATIONAL FILM FESTIVAL

Dream Star Pictures Intl.
Blk 20 Lot 18 Golden City Subd.
Santa Rosa, Laguna 4026
Philippines
Tel: 63917-4553093
Fax: 632-6992139
Email: dreastar25@hotmail.com
Web Site: www.filmfestival.pyar.com
Festival Date: March
Profile: Dream Star Pictures International, a Philippines based international film outfit, wants to give recognition to filmmakers both amateur and professional in the field of filmmaking.

POLAND

FESTIVAL OF SHORT FILMS—KRAKOW

c/o Apollo Film
ul. Pychowicka 7
30 364 Krakow, Poland
Tel: 48-12-67-23-40;
48-12-67-13-55
Fax: 48-12-67-15-52
Festival Date: May-June
Entry Deadline: February
Contact: Wit Dudek
Category: Short

INTERNATIONAL FILM FESTIVAL OF THE ART OF CINEMATOGRAPHY (CAMERAIMAGE FESTIVAL)

Foundation Tumult
Rynek Nowomiejeski 28
87-100 Torun, Poland
Tel: 48-56-248-79,
100-19-194-03
Fax: 48-56-275-95
Festival Date: November-December
Entry Deadline: September
Contact: Kazimierz Parucki, Marek Zydowicz

POLISH FILM FESTIVAL

Box 192
22-23 Piwna St.
80831 Gdansk, Poland
Tel: 48-58-315244
Fax: 48-58-313744
Festival Date: November
Contact: Jerzy Martys

WARSAW FILM FESTIVAL

P. O. Box 816
00-950 Warsaw 1, Poland
Tel: 48-2-635-7591
Festival Date: October
Entry Deadline: June
Contact: Stefan Laudyn

PORTUGAL

FANTASPORTO / OPORTO INTERNATIONAL FILM FESTIVAL

Rua da Constituição 311-4200
Porto, Portugal
Tel: 351-2-507-38-80
Fax: 351-2-550-82-10
Email: fantas@caleida.pt
Web Site: www.caleida.pt/fantasporto
Festival Date: February-March
Entry Deadline: December
Year Festival Began: 1981
Contact: António Reis
Director: Mário Dorminsky
Programmer: Beatriz Pacheco-Pereira
Other Staff: Áurea Soares Ribeiro
Profile: The Oporto International Film Festival is held annually in February and is now in its nineteenth year. The 1st edition of Fantasporto, as the festival is usually known, was held in 1981 and was non-competitive. All the following editions included competitive sections.

The festival receives entry forms from all over the world, mostly from European countries and the United States. It runs in 12 theatres (4,000 seats altogether) and shows over 200 feature films each year. The press coverage of the Festival is made by all the important newspaper,

radio stations and television networks. this allows press dossiers of nearly 2,500 clippings each year which represents an unique media coverage in Portugal for similar cultural events
Awards: Yes
Competitions: Yes
Major Awards: Fantasporto Best Film Award
Value of Awards: No commercial value. It's a trophy
Application Fee: None

FESTIVAL INTERNACIONAL DE CINEMA DO ALGARVE

P. O. Box 8091
1801 Lisboa Codex, Portugal
Tel: 351-1-8513615
Fax: 351-1-8521150
Festival Date: May
Entry Deadline: March
Director: Carlos Manuel, General Director

INTERNATIONAL ANIMATED FILM FESTIVAL—CINANIMA

Rua 62, No. 251
4501 Espinho Codex, Portugal
Tel: 2-721-611
Fax: 2-726-015
Festival Date: November
Category: Animation, International

INTERNATIONAL FESTIVAL OF CINEMA FOR CHILDREN AND YOUTH

R. D. Aurora de Macedo, 72
P-2300 Tomar, Portugal
Tel: 049-31-32-47
Contact: Manuel Faria
Category: Kids

INTERNATIONAL VIDEO FESTIVAL OF ALGARVE

Racal Clube
8300 Silves
Algrave, Portugal
Tel: 082-44-25-87
Fax: 082-44-25-30
Contact: FIVA
Category: Video

VIDEOEIRAS FESTIVAL

Gabinete de Relacoes Publicas
Largo de Marques de Pombal
2780 Oeiras, Portugal
Tel: 4411500
Festival Date: April
Entry Deadline: March
Contact: City Council of Oeiras

PUERTO RICO

PUERTO RICO INTERNATIONAL FILM FESTIVAL

70 Mayaguez St.
Suite B-1
Hato Rey, 00918 Puerto Rico
Tel: 809-763-4997
Fax: 809-753-5367
Festival Date: November
Contact: Juan Gerard Gonzalez
Category: International

RUSSIA

INTERFEST MOSCOW INTERNATIONAL FILM FESTIVAL

10, Khokovsky Pereulok
109028 Moscow, Russia
Tel: 7-095-297-7645
Fax: 7-095-227-4600
Festival Date: July
Entry Deadline: March
Contact: Yuri Khodjaev

INTERNATIONAL DOCUMENTARY, SHORT AND ANIMATED FILMS FESTIVAL

"Your festival is unique. It is the only festival where not only documentaries, but also short feature and animation films from many countries are shown. This event is an opportunity for the young generation of filmmakers-the future of cinema-to show their debut works."

—Boris Yeltsin

Kravannaya str., 12
St. Petersburg, 191011 Russia
Tel: 7-812-235-2660 (Festival Coordinator, Alexandra Leibovitch); 7-812-230-2200 (General Director, Mikhail Litviakov)
Fax: 7-812-235-3995
Email: centaur@mail.wplus.net
Festival Date: Late June-Early July
Entry Deadline: May
Year Festival Began: 1989
Contact: Alexandra (Sasha) Leibovitch
Director: Mikhail S. Litviakov, documentary filmmaker
Category: Animation, Documentary, International, Artistic and Intellectual, Short
Profile: The Festival is a good opportunity for communication and exchanging experience and ideas between filmmakers from different countries, who develop themes of good will, spirituality, justice, morality and peace in their work realizing them by the means of cinema. The Festival aims to encourage the creative search and innovations by young filmmakers.
Awards: Yes
Competitions: Yes
Major Awards: Grand Prize Golden Centauri for the best Festival film
Value of Awards:-Golden Centaur-$5,000
Centaur-$2,000 for the best full length documentary film
Centaur-$2,000 for the best short documentary film
Centaur-$2,000 for the best short feature film
Centaur-$2,000 for the best animated film
Five prizes for the best debut films (in Debut Films International Competition)-$1,000
Application Fee: None
Odds of Acceptance: 1 in 7
Tourist Information: No need to describe all the opportunities for tourist in St. Petersburg, Russia. This town, I believe, is one of the most beautiful European cities, matching Paris, Prague, Bruxelles...

Travel Tips: Don't use a taxi on the way from airport, as well as in the city, unless you speak Russian as a native speaker. Never take a lot of money with you, and don't keep your passport in the outer pocket. Don't expect any help from cops, they don't speak English.
Best Restaurants: Perhaps, Brasserie in Europe Hotel.
Best Bars: Idiot (for Dostoyevsky's romance)—come and see the world's best place for intellectuals, artists or journalists hanging out
Best Hangout for Filmmakers: Manhattan (Kotyol simply), founded by several city filmmakers, particularly, Meskhiev.
Best Place for Breakfast: If you're bored of McDonalds and other fast-food events, you can use Idiot as well. It opens at 11:00 a.m. If it's too late, use different cafes dispersed all over the town.

INTERNATIONAL FESTIVAL OF DOCUMENTARY AND SCIENCE FILMS

Sovinterfest
10 Khokhlovsky Pereulok
109028 Moscow, Russia
Tel: 227-8924
Festival Date: January
Contact: Yuri Khodjaev
Category: Documentary

INTERNATIONAL FILM FESTIVAL OF FESTIVALS

10 Kamennoostrovsky Ave.
197101 St. Petersburg Russia
Tel: 812-238581
Fax: 812-2332174
Festival Date: June
Entry Deadline: May
Contact: Alexander Mamontov

ST. PETERSBURG DOCUMENTARY FESTIVAL—MESSAGE TO MAN NONFICTION FILM FESTIVAL

12 Karavannaya St.
St. Petersburg 191011, Russia

Tel: 7-812-235-2660
Fax: 7-812-235-5318
Festival Date: Biennial, even years; February-March
Entry Deadline: December
Contact: Mikhail Litviakov
Category: Documentary

SCOTLAND

DRAMBUIE EDINBURGH INTERNATIONAL FILM FESTIVAL

Eliff Filmhouse
88 Lothian Rd.
Edinburgh, EH3 9BZ Scotland
Tel: 44-31-228-4051
Fax: 44-31-229-5501
Festival Date: August
Entry Deadline: May
Contact: Penny Thompson
Competitions: Yes
Average Films Entered: 250
Attendance: 30,000

DUNDEE MOUNTAIN FILM FESTIVAL

Tayview
15 Ardestie Place, Monifieth
Dundee, DD5 4PS Scotland
Tel: 0382-533146
Fax: 0382-201767
Festival Date: November
Entry Deadline: August
Director: J.W. Burdin, Programme Director

SERBIA

BELGRADE INTERNATIONAL FILM FESTIVAL

Sava Center
Milentija Popovica 9
11070 Belgrad, Serbia
Tel: 39-11-222-4961
Fax: 38-11-222-1156
Festival Date: January-February
Entry Deadline: January
Contact: Nevena Djonlic

It's hot here so leave your woolies at home! (Durban International Film Festival)

SINGAPORE

SINGAPORE INTERNATIONAL FILM FESTIVAL

29A Keong Saik Rd.
Singapore 089136, Singapore
Tel: 65-738-7567
Fax: 65-738-7579
Email: filmfest@pacific.net.sg
Festival Date: April
Entry Deadline: January
Contact: Phillip Cheah
Director: Philip Cheah & Teo Swee
Category: International

SLOVAK REPUBLIC

PRIX DANUBE FESTIVAL

Slovenska Televizia
Mlynska dolina
845 45 Bratislava, Slovak Republic
Tel: 42-7-727-448
Fax: 42-7-729-440
Festival Date: May-June
Entry Deadline: February
Contact: Mikulas Gavala

ART FILM FESTIVAL TRENCIANSKE TEPLICE

attn. Mr. Vladimir Stric
Art Film, n.f.
Konventna 8
Bratislava, 81103 Slovak Republic (Slovakia)
Tel: 421-7-5441-9481;
421-7-5441-9480
Fax: 421-7-5441-9372;
421-7-5441-1679
Email: festival@artfilm.sk
Web Site: www.artfilm.sk
Festival Date: June 22-29, 2001
Entry Deadline: April 6, 2001
Competitions: Competition categories: Artefacts—competition category for films on art, artists and experimentals; On the Road—students film category for films on art and visual experiments; Art Fiction—full-length feature competition for films using new artistic techniques.

Application Tips: Pre-selection requirements: VHS copy, synopsis, dialogue list, director's biography/filmography and 3 stills, entry form by April 6, 2001.
Application Fee: None
Random Tidbits: Will accept 35mm, 16mm and Beta

SOUTH AFRICA

COCA-COLA JOHANNESBURG INTERNATIONAL STUDENT FILM FESTIVAL— "WASHING THE SPEAR"

P.O. Box 277, Melville 2109
Johannesburg, South Africa
Tel: 27-11-482-8345;
27-82-455-0512
Fax: 27-11-482-8347
Email: info@filmdrama school.co.za or
dazzagordi@hotmail.com
Web Site: www.filmdrama school.co.za
Festival Date: Mid November
Entry Deadline: August 2001
Year Festival Began: 2000
Contact: Darren Gordon
Director: Darren Gordon
Programmer: Ziyanda Ngcaba
Category: Ethnic African, Experimental, First-Time Independent Filmmakers, Independent, Student
Profile: "Washing the Spear" is Africa's initiation ceremony for the new filmwarriors of tomorrow. We would like to invite all student filmmakers and film schools to submit a showcase of films produced during the period Jan 1998-2000. The program should not exceed 120 minutes and not be less than 60 minutes. The program is compiled at the discretion of the film institution. The main program consists of multiple screenings of the selected 15 filmschools, 12 International, 3 domestic.
Market: No
Competitions: Yes
Major Awards: The Coca-Cola Spear

Common Mistakes: Not meeting deadlines

Insider Advice: The films need to be completed only by student filmmakers. A first time film maker category will be run from the microcine sidebar.

Tourist Information: Johannesburg, the city of gold. One of the cheapest countries in the world for partying. Game reserves, Soweto, Alexandra township, Cape Town, beautiful beaches and safaris.

Travel Tips: Fly South African Airways.

Best Cheap Hotels: Various bed & breakfasts in the area.

Best Luxury Hotels: Michelangelo

Best Restaurants: The Grillhouse (best steaks in the world)

Best Bars: The Mess

Best Hangout for Filmmakers: Melville

Best Place for Breakfast: Cigarre Exchange

DURBAN INTERNATIONAL FILM FESTIVAL

Centre for Creative Arts
University of Natal
4041 Durban
Kwazulu-Natal, South Africa

Tel: 27-31-260-2594

Fax: 27-31-260-3074

Email: ivanidea@iafrica.com

Festival Date: August

Entry Deadline: June

Year Festival Began: 1978

Contact: Gulam Mather

Director: Gulam Mather

Category: Independent

Profile: South Africa's largest and longest running non-profit film festival out to challenge, provoke, and stimulate.

Seminars: Yes

Panels: A small committee is formed each year to discuss the films and give notice to those which stood out by rewarding the director with a really cool trophy.

Awards: No

Competitions: No

Famke Janssen receives praise for her film, "Love and Sex," at its festival premiere.

Application Tips: We're not into technical training videos, but really anything else will stand a chance. Try to make the deadline or send something now for the following year. We only select films not sourced by ourselves if budget allows for it. Remember—It's normally the packaging that helps sell the product, so before you drop your video cassette in the post make sure that you have included information on the film, your contact details, photos and anything else that represents both you and your film. Good luck!

Application Fee: None—Don't believe in them.

Insider Advice: We've seen a lot of movies, so we will carefully look at yours and if there is something that we like then we will do our best to make sure that the players in Southern Africa know it.

Average Films Entered: You name it, we show it.

Films Screened: 50 to 100—Depends on a number of factors like budget.

Odds of Acceptance: 1 in 2

Filmmaker Perks: The only perk we can offer is if you do want to come out with your film, then we will do our best to accomodate you. We'll also show you around, help you make contacts and make you feel really important. In return we ask only for your valuable insight into filmmaking and ask that you share it with others through workshops.

Tourist Information: Some of the world's best game parks (it is Africa after all), stunning beaches and resorts, winefarms (best wines in the world), beautiful cities and people. South Africa is a unique country with a booming film and television industry.

Travel Tips: It's hot here so leave your woolies at home!

Best Restaurants: In Durban there is something for everyone. Indian cuisine is popular.

Best Bars: The Windsor, just because we hang out there.

Best Hangout for Filmmakers: Try the Windsor. Unfortunately all the filmmakers hang out in Cape Town at Longkloof Studios.

Best Place for Breakfast: Beachfront—Any hotel with a view of the sea.

Festival Tale: If you can imagine having to handcrank a projector whose reel motors blow five minutes before the screening to a 450+ packed house on one of the hottest days of the year when the air conditioning packed up that afternoon and you only have one shot at getting the speed of the film just right or burn—and to make things worse, it's a three-hour Finnish film!!! Then you know what we mean.

JOHANNESBURG FILM FESTIVAL

Festival Films Pty. Ltd.
8th Floor, Hallmark Towers
54 Siemert Road
P. O. Box 16427
Doornfontein 2028
Johannesburg, South Africa

Tel: 27-11-402-5477/8/9
Fax: 27-11-402-6646
Contact: Len Davis

SPAIN

BARCELONA ASiAN FiLM FESTiVAL (MUESTRA DE CiNE ASiÁTiCO DE BARCELONA)

Ramón y Cajal, 138
Barcelona, 08024 Spain
Tel: 34-93-4159009
Fax: 34-93-4159009
Email: retinas@mail.ono.es
Web Site: www.retinas.org
Festival Date: May 2001
Entry Deadline: End of March
Year Festival Began: 1999
Contact: Carlos R Rios
(rioscar@retinas.org)
Amaia Torrecilla
(retinas@mail.ono.es)
Director: Carlos R. Rios
Programmer: Amaia Torrecilla
Category: Ethnic Asian
Profile: Our main goal is to become the door of entrance for the Asian Cinema to other countries, new audiences, distributors and critical interest. We try to show to audience a different cinem., Because Asian Cinema is usually out of the regular distribution and despite its success in international festivals, it doesn't go beyond their borders or local markets.
Market: No
Competitions: Non-competitive, but we have a Public's Choice Award.
Major Awards: Public's Choice Award
Application Fee: None
Common Mistakes: Deadlines!!! They never think about submitting late or that sending a video takes more time than they thought.
Insider Advice: 1) The most important thing is the movie, not the extras a festival can offer (travel, lodging...).
2) Get over the idea that your movie just goes to a big festival.

The most important thing is that you made it in order that somebody could see it. Movies have to move around and people have to see them!! Even in a small festival.
3) Think where are you sending your movie. Try to know what kind of festival you are submitting. That will save time for filmmakers and festivals.
Films Screened: 21
Odds of Acceptance: 1 in 3
Filmmaker Perks: At the moment, we can offer lodging and contacts, specially with press and local distributors. A nice audience and a couple of great parties.
Attendance: 6,000
Journalist Attendance: 50
Tourist Information: Gaudí architecture, gothic quatier, modern architecture (Calatrava, Foster, Isozaki, Moneo), las Ramblas, beach and terrazas, night life.
Travel Tips: Be prepared for our great food!
Best Cheap Hotels: Jardí
Best Luxury Hotels: Ars Hotel
Best Restaurants: Sushi & News (address: 2 Santa Monica)
Best Bars: Zoo (address: 33 Escudillers)
Best Hangout for Filmmakers: Abaixadors 10 (a: 10 Abaixadors)
Best Place for Breakfast: Bar Ra (Mercat Sq)
Random Tidbits: The official section takes place in Apolo, a former dance club, so it's not a usual movie theatre. People sit at tables with candles before the screening and they can have a beer while waiting for the movie listening to cool music. Our audience has become huge fans of this formula!

BARCELONA iNTERNATiONAL EXHiBiTiON OF GAY AND LESBiAN FiLMS

Casal Lambda, c/o Ample 5, baixos
Barcelona, 08002 Spain
Tel: 34 (93) 412-72-72
Fax: 34 (93) 412-74-76
Email: cinema@lambdaweb.org

Web Site: www.lambdaweb.org
Festival Date: October-November
Entry Deadline: July
Contact: Sergi Mesonero (Technical Coordinator)
Director: Xavier-Daniel
Category: Gay Lesbian

BiENAL DE CiNE Y ViDEO CiENTiFiCO ESPANOL

Independencia No. 10
50004 Zaragova, Spain
Tel: 976-71-81-51
Fax: 976-71-81-53
Festival Date: November
Contact: Eugenio Tutor Larrosa

BiENAL NACiON CAJALiCANTE DE CiNE AMATEUR DE LiBRE CREACiON

No. 41, 3a Planta
Alicante, Spain
Tel: 5206544; 5219556
Festival Date: March
Contact: Rafael Sanchez Olmos, Jefe Dpto. Actividades
Category: International

CADiZ iNTERNATiONAL ViDEO FESTiVAL

Pl. Espana Edf. Roma
11071 Cadiz, Spain
Tel: 56-24-01-03
Fax: 56-22-98-13
Festival Date: November
Entry Deadline: September
Category: International

CERTAMEN DE CiNE AMATEUR

Area de Cine
Delegacion Municipal de Cultura
Juan R. Jimenez, 11
29600 Marbella, Spain
Tel: 5-282-34-85
Fax: 5-282-52-87
Festival Date: March
Entry Deadline: February
Contact: Juan Caracuel

CERTAMEN DE CiNE Y VIDEO ETNOLOGICO DE LAS COMMUNIDADES AUTONMAS

Apartado do Correso, 159
Huesca 22080, Spain
Tel: 947-227058
Festival Date: April
Entry Deadline: February
Contact: Eugenio Monesma Molines

CERTAMEN DE VIDEO ELIES ROGENT REHABILITACIO i RESTAURACIO

Colegio de Aparejadores Y Arquitectos Tecnicos de Barcelona
Carrer Del Bon Pastor #5
08021 Barcelona, Spain
Tel: 34-3-414-33-11
Fax: 34-3-414-34-34;
34-3-414-33-68
Festival Date: May
Entry Deadline: September-October for registration; January for entries
Contact: Secretaria de la Muestra-concurso
Elies Rogetn de Video de Rehabilitacion y Restauracion

CERTAMEN INTERNACIONAL BADALONA

Cineistes Independents de Badalona
Apartat de Correus 286
08911 Badalona BCN, Spain
Tel: 3-464-01-91
Fax: 3-464-04-50
Festival Date: October
Entry Deadline: September
Contact: Jordi Pinana, Agusti Argelich

CERTAMEN INTERNACIONAL DE CiNE AMATEUR— CiUTAT D'iGUALADA

Apartado 378
08700 Igualada
Barcelona, Spain
Tel: 34-3-804-69-07
Fax: 34-3-804-43-62

Festival Date: Biennial; October
Entry Deadline: July
Contact: Joana Morera

CERTAMEN INTERNACIONAL DE CiNE CORTOMETRAJE

c/Salzillo No 7
Murcia 30001, Spain
Tel: 968-217751
Festival Date: March
Category: International

CERTAMEN INTERNACIONAL DE CiNE TURiSTiCO DE MADRiD

Avda. Portugal, s/n
28011 Madrid, Spain
Tel: 4701014
Contact: IFMA FITUR "Madrid, Capitol Mundial del Turismo"
Category: International

CERTAMEN INTERNACIONAL DE CiNE Y VIDEO AGRARIO

Carretera Nacional II
Km. 311
P. O. Box 108
50012 Zaragoza, Spain
Tel: 76-70-11-00
Fax: 76-33-06-49
Festival Date: April
Entry Deadline: February
Contact: Mr. Cativiela, Mr. Llera

CERTAMEN INTERNACIONAL DE CiNY Y VIDEO TURiSTiCO—ORiENTE DE ASTURiAS DE LLANES

c/Nemesio Sobrino
1 Llanes (Principado de Asturias)
33500 Spain
Tel: 98-5400164
Festival Date: July
Contact: Jose Luis Salomon Calvo

CERTAMEN INTERNACIONAL DE VIDEO

c/El Pozo 3
44001 Teruel, Spain
Tel: 974-60-00-12
Festival Date: December
Entry Deadline: October
Contact: Cineocho-Optica Tena

CERTAMEN NACIONAL DE CiNE SiLENCiOSO

Instituto Nacional de Seguridad e Higiene en el Trabajo
c/Torrelaguna, 73
28077 Madrid, Spain
Tel: 91-2465776, 2465674, 2465832
Festival Date: October
Contact: Jesus Pinedo Peydro

DONOSTiA— SAN SEBASTiAN INTERNATIONAL FiLM FESTIVAL

Plaza Oquendo S/N
San Sebastian, 20004 Spain
Tel: 34-943-481212
Fax: 34-943-481218
Email: ssiff@sansebastian festival.com
Web Site: www.sansebastian festival.com
Contact: Diego Galan
Director: Mikel Olaciregui
Category: General subject matter, full length features and retrospectives
Competitions: Yes
Application Fee: None

EUROPEAN FESTIVAL OF RURAL AND FiSHING CiNEMA

Apartado De Correos 74
Candas 33430, Spain
Tel: 34-85-871021
Fax: 34-85-884711
Festival Date: July-August
Entry Deadline: A month prior to festival
Director: Isaac Del Rivero

FESTIVAL DE CiNE L'ALFAS DEL Pi

Festival de Cine
Casa De Cultura
03580 Alfaz Del Pi
Alicante, Spain
Tel: 96-5889423/4
Fax: 96-5889453
Festival Date: July
Entry Deadline: June
Director: Juan Luis Iborra

FESTIVAL iNTERNACiONAL DE BARCELONA DE CiNE Y ViDEO NO PROFESSiONALES

Spain
Tel: 93-246400 ext. 318
Festival Date: November
Entry Deadline: September
Contact: Enrique Lopez Manzano

FESTIVAL iNTERNACiONAL DE CiNE DE COMEDiA

Plaza Picasso s/n
Torremolinos, Spain
Tel: 952-380038
Festival Date: December
Contact: Miguel Excalona Quesada (Alcalde)

FESTIVAL iNTERNACiONAL DE CiNE ECOLOGiCO Y DE LA NATURALEZA

c/Gran Via, 43 9oF
28013 Madrid, Spain
Tel: 5424253; 5421005
Fax: 5420701
Festival Date: November
Contact: Alfonso Eduardo Perez Orozco

FESTIVAL iNTERNACiONAL DE CiNE ESPELEOLOGiCO DE BARCELONA

Espeleo Club de Gracia
Apartado de Correos 9.126
08080 Barcelona, Spain
Tel: 34-3-4571581

Fax: 34-3-4571581
Festival Date: November
Entry Deadline: October
Director: Manel Canameras, President

FESTIVAL iNTERNACiONAL DE CiNE FANTASTiCO

c/Diputacion 279 Bajos.
09007 Barcelona, Spain
Tel: 93-317-35-85
Fax: 93-301-22-47
Festival Date: October

FESTIVAL iNTERNACiONAL DE CiNE REALiZADO POR MUJERES

International Festival of Film
Directed by Women
Ateneo Feminista de Madrid
c/Barquillo 44-2o 1
28004 Madrid, Spain
Tel: 34-1-308-69-35
Fax: 34-1-319-69-02
Festival Date: November
Entry Deadline: June
Contact: Paloma Gonzalez

GiJON iNTERNATiONAL FiLM FESTiVAL FOR YOUNG PEOPLE

Paseo de Begona 24-Ent.
33205 Gijon Asturias, Spain
Tel: 34-98-534-37-39 ;
34-98-535-91-55
Fax: 34-98-535-41-52
Email: festcine@las.es
Web Site: www.las.es/gijon filmfestival/
Festival Date: Last week of November 2001
Entry Deadline: September 20, 2001
Year Festival Began: 1963
Contact: Maria Jose Alvarez
Director: Jose Luis Cienfuegos
Programmer: Fran Gayo
Category: Independent, International, Short, Underground
Profile: Being one of the oldest film festivals in Spain and traditionally considered a festival for young people, Gijón has assumed this condition in all terms, with a programme formed by innovative and independent films made by and for young people, with retrospectives, cycles, exhibitions, musical events and the different film sections with a choice for all tastes, from the fresh Official Section to the vindication of directors which have opened new ways in filmmaking.
Market: No
Competitions: Yes
Major Awards: "Principado de Asturias" (Best Film and Best Short Film)
Value of Awards: 12.000 Euro (Feature) and 3.000 Euro (Short)
Application Tips: We open our selection in April although the deadline is September, we think that the sooner they submit the films, the better it will be considered (we often receive half of the films in the last week before the deadline which makes it very difficult for the selectors).
Common Mistakes: We insist that they should not wait until the last minute to send the tape and, if the film is not in Spanish, subtitles and/or dialogue lists are necessary.
Films Screened: 184 titles including several videos and documentaries.
Odds of Acceptance: Features: 1 in 3; Shorts: 1 in 12
Filmmaker Perks: We invite filmmakers and other crew from Features in competition. The Festival covers travel, accomodation and meals. Also they receive an accreditation which allows entrance to all Festival screenings and the rest of activities are free.
Attendance: 31,000 spectators
Journalist Attendance: 230
Tourist Information: The Roman ruins (baths and wall), the palaces and buildings of the XVII and XVIII centuries. The beaches and the landscapes around town. We provide guests with tourist information about Gijon and surroundings and the tourist office provides also good assistance with this matter.
Travel Tips: Gijon is quite warm in November but is also often

rainy and cloudy; this is not that sunny Spain everybody has heard of, so no need to take your beach costume. Average temperature is 9-12°C.

Best Cheap Hotels: The accomodation is also well-known here for its quality and low prices. Most of the festival guests stay at the Begona Hotel but good and also cheaper are hotels San Miguel and Castilla, among others.

Best Luxury Hotels: The best ones are the National Parador and the Begoña Park, but they are situated a little far from downtown, better situated is Principe de Asturias Hotel, facing the beach, and Hernan Cortes, very close to the Festival venues.

Best Restaurants: Local gastronomy is well-known around the world, being the "fabada," one of the most typical Spanish dishes, served in most of the restaurants in town. Try El Puerto, Ataulfo or Casa Justo.

Best Bars: The Festival organizes parties and meetings in some of the best bars and pubs in town. The best known for visitors are: Bulevar, Baba Wild or Varsovia but much cosier and full of design is Blue Sky Café.

Best Hangout for Filmmakers: Many of the guests and festivalgoers meet at the centenarian Dindurra Café, which is situated next to the main festival venue, Teatro Jovellanos. Also a popular place for filmmakers and other guests is the Hotel Begona bar.

Best Place for Breakfast: Hotels usually offer breakfast with the official fares but there are many good cafes and patisseries where you can taste the typical Spanish breakfast 'chocolate with churros'.

GRAN PREMIO DE CINE ESPANOL

c/Seminario, 4-3o
07001 Palma de Mallorca, Spain
Tel: 722444; 702242
Festival Date: November
Entry Deadline: September
Contact: Manuel Fernandez Penero

HUESCA FILM FESTIVAL

Avda Parque, I piso
Huesca, 22002 Spain
Tel: 34 (9) 74-21-25-82
Fax: 34 (9) 74-21-00-65
Email: huescafest@tsai.es
Web Site: www.huesca-filmfestival.com
Festival Date: June
Entry Deadline: April
Year Festival Began: 1973
Contact: José María Escriche Otal
Director: José María Escriche Otal
Profile: International Short-Film Contest, and Sample of European and Latinamerican Cinema (Feature Films).
Awards: Yes
Competitions: Yes
Major Awards: Danzante de Oro
Value of Awards: 1.000.000 pesetas / $ 6500 approx. / 6000 ecus.
Films Screened: 64 short films are screened
Odds of Acceptance: I in 15
Filmmaker Perks: Lodging
Tourist Information: Apart from the Pyrennes nearby, in the city of Huesca the main attractions include : the 13th Century Cathedral, The Church of San Pedro el Viejo from the 12th Century, The Church of San Lorenzo from the 17th Century, The Provincial Museum, the University, The Park, The Palace of the Kings of Aragón.
Travel Tips: Closest airport: Zaragoza. Other airports: Madrid and Barcelona.
Best Restaurants: El Sotón, Las 3 Torres, Lilla Pastia
Best Bars: In Huesca there are 370 bars
Best Hangout for Filmmakers: Meeting point : The Festival itself
Best Place for Breakfast: Luces de Bohemia in Las Cuatro Esquinas

INTERNATIONAL FESTIVAL OF DOCUMENTARY AND SHORT FILM OF BILBAO

Colon de Larreategui
37-4th D.
Apdo. 579
48009 Bilbao, Spain
Tel: 34-4-424-8696
Fax: 34-4-424-5624
Festival Date: November
Entry Deadline: September
Contact: Luis Iturri
Category: Documentary, Short

INTERNATIONAL MADRID FESTIVAL FOR THE FANTASTIC AND SCIENCE FICTION FILM

Gran Via 62-8o izda.
Madrid 28013, Spain
Tel: 541-55-45; 541-37-21
Fax: 542-54-95
Contact: Rita Sonvella

INTERNATIONAL VIDEO CONTEST

c. El Pozo No. 3
Teruel 44001, Spain
Tel: 974-600012
Festival Date: December
Entry Deadline: November
Contact: Fermin Perez
Category: International

MADRID INTERNATIONAL GAY & LESBIAN FILM FESTIVAL

Apartado de Correos 1269
Madrid, 28080 Spain
Tel: 341-5930540
Fax: 341-5930540
Email: potos@lander.es
Web Site: www.redestb.es/triangulo
Category: Gay Lesbian

SAN SEBASTIAN INTERNATIONAL FILM FESTIVAL

P. O. Box 397
20080 San Sebastian, Spain
Tel: 34-943-481212
Fax: 34-943-481218

Gijon is quite warm in November but is also often rainy and cloudy; this is not that sunny Spain everybody heard of, so no need to take your beach costume (Gijon International Film Festival for Young People).

Email: ssiff@sansebastian
festival.com
Web Site: www.ddnet.es/
san_sebastian_film_festival/
Festival Date: September
Entry Deadline: July
Director: Mikel Olaciregui
Profile: The second fortnight in
September sees San Sebastian
turn into the European capital of
cinema. Eminent directors,
famous actors and actresses,
critics, buffs and the general public flock from all over the world
to this yearly rendezvous.
Awards: Yes
Competitions: Yes
Application Fee: None
Random Tidbits: Since 1986, the
Festival has been using the
Anoeta Velodrome, described by
Oliver Stone as "the best film
theatre in the world," to present
a series of films on an enormous
400m screen together with
state-of-the-art lighting and
sound. A wide range of interesting and attractive cycles have
been admired on this screen,
from 3D works and the first
Spanish screening of a spectacular Magnapax film, to European
and even world premieres.

More than 3,500 seats await
the influx of children and adults
who come along to discover the
magic of cinema in this gigantic
theatre, where the morning sessions for primary and secondary
pupils from the different schools
in San Sebastian and its surrounding areas are one of the
most exciting film-related events
experienced by the Velodrome.

The Festival also puts special
emphasis on Basque cinema, to
which it dedicates an entire day.

Another aspect well worth
the mention is the Festival
Market. This business platform
for potential film buyers takes
the shape of the Sales Office,
which offers distributors the
unique opportunity to view a
collection of more than 500
unreleased productions made
over the 12 last months. This
system makes it possible for producers to ensure that their
products can be viewed by market professionals, and in so doing
gives them the chance to meet

buyers in a relaxed and informal
atmosphere where they can successfully conclude their transactions.

SITGES INTERNATIONAL FILM FESTIVAL OF CATALONIA

Avenida Josep Tarradellas, 135,
escalera A, 3° 2ª
Barcelona, 08029 Spain
Tel: 34-93-419-36-35
Fax: 34-93-439-73-80
Email: cinsit@sitgestur.com
Web Site: www.sitges.com/
cinema
Festival Date: October 4-13,
2001
Entry Deadline: July 31, 2001
Year Festival Began: 1968
Contact: Roc Villas
Director: Roc Villas
Programmer: Roc Villas, Carolina
López, Angel Sala, Jordi Batlle,
Alex Gorina, Joana Raja, Ramon
Font
Category: Animation,
Documentary, Fantasy/Science
Fiction, International
Profile: SITGES International
Film Festival of Catalonia is a 33
year old festival with two official
sections:

"Fantàstic" is a specialised
competitive section for fantasy
films which grants us the recognition of F.I.A.P.F. as a specialised
festival. The films in this section
compete for awards to Best
Film, Director, Actor, Actress,
Screenplay, Cinematography,
Original Soundtrack, Visual
Effects, and Best Fantasy Short
Film.

"Gran Angular" includes films
from all other genres. The winner gets the Audience Award, by
popular vote.

There are seven more sec-
tions: "Anima't" (with the most
recent animation productions,
which compete for the jury
award to the Best Animation
Short, and the audience award to
the Best Animation Short)

"Seven Chances" (seven rare
films discovered by the critics)

"Retrospectiva" (a review of
the best classic cinema)

"Audiovisual Català" (Catalan
audiovisual productions)

"Brigadoon" (an alternative
video space with free admission)

"Segundo de Chomon" (a
recovery of this important pioneer's work)

"Images of a Century" (a
selection of exquisite documentaries on the facts of the 20th
century).
Seminars: Exhibitions, confer-
ences
Competitions: Yes
Major Awards: Best Film
Application Fee: None
Common Mistakes: They don't
enclose enough information
about the film: contact name,
synopsis, technical data,...etc.
Insider Advice: An entry form is
not necessary to submit the
work.
Average Films Entered: All
kinds.
Films Screened: 180
Odds of Acceptance: 1 in 2
Filmmaker Perks: Free travel
and free lodging
Attendance: 105,000 audience
members
Journalist Attendance: 523
accredited journalists from 16
countries
Tourist Information: The town,
with its modernist buildings, and
Barcelona city, at 20 miles north.
Best Luxury Hotels: Hotel Melià
Gran Sitges (Port d'Aiguadolç,
s/n, 08870, Sitges)
Festival Tale: Blair Witch Project
star Heather Donahue flew to
Barcelona airport invited by the
Festival, when Spanish distributor
decided that, in spite of the universal knowledge there was on
the film in October 1999, it
should be released in Spain on
the basis that it was a real story.
Assuming that Heather was actually lost and in the woods, he
stopped her from any promotional activites at the Festival.
With a nice big laugh, she
enjoyed a few days of tourism in
the city of Barcelona, and went
back to Los Angeles.

SWEDEN

GÖTEBORG FILM FESTIVAL

Box 7079
Göteborg, S-40232 Sweden
Tel: 46-31-41-05-46
Fax: 46-31-41-00-63
Email: goteborg@filmfestival.org
Web Site: www.goteborg.filmfestival.org
Festival Date: Late January-Early February
Entry Deadline: November
Year Festival Began: 1979
Contact: Agneta Green, programme coordinator
Ulf Bjurström, managing director
Magnus Telander, festival producer
Director: Gunnar Bergdahl
Profile: International festival for new movies from all over the world. Scandinavian meeting point for film industry
Seminars: Cinemix is the name of the festival's seminar programme. Every year more than 30 seminars are arranged.
Awards: Yes
Competitions: Yes
Major Awards: The Nordic Film Prize for the best new nordic feature.
Value of Awards: 50.000 SEK
Application Fee: All films are screened by invitation only
Films Screened: 300+
Attendance: 15,500

GOTHENBURG FILM FESTIVAL

P. O. Box 7079
S-402 32 Gotenborg, Sweden
Tel: 31-41-05-46
Fax: 31-41-00-63
Festival Date: February
Entry Deadline: December for entry forms, stills, posters
Contact: Kristina Borjesson

NORRKÖPING FILM FESTIVAL FLIMMER

G:a Radstugugatan 30
Norrkoping, S-602 24 Sweden
Tel: 46-11-152650
Fax: 46-11-161840
Email: filmfestival@norrkoping.se
Web Site: www.flimmer.nu
Festival Date: March 7-11, 2001
Entry Deadline: January
Year Festival Began: 1998
Contact: Johan Karlsson
Director: Johan Karlsson
Programmer: Malin Bjorkman-Widell
Category: American Films, Animation, Digital, Documentary, Gay Lesbian, Independent, International, Microcinema, Student, Video
Profile: Welcome to FLIMMER—Östergötlands big film party. Norrköpings film festival is southeast Sweden's biggest film festival. The festival is aiming at film lovers of all ages irrespective of taste. Experiences beyond the ordinary repetoire are offered, but also reruns of earlier premiéres. A total film celebration for all the family.
Panels: About regional political film policy.
Market: No
Competitions: Yes
Major Awards: Flimmer statue
Value of Awards: USD 1000
Application Fee: None
Common Mistakes: They have the wrong type of film for the festival or the competition.
Insider Advice: First send an e-mail before sending in the film.

Average Films Entered: Short films in 35 mm, or feature/documentary in a DV/BETA format.
Films Screened: 5
Odds of Acceptance: 1 in 5
Filmmaker Perks: National: free travel, lodging and food
International: lodging and food
Attendance: 6,100
Journalist Attendance: 15
Tourist Information: The bars, the clubs, the archipelago of Norrkoping, wild life park with dolphin show, the museum of art.
Best Cheap Hotels: Hornans Vandrarhem (city)
Best Luxury Hotels: Grand Hotell
Best Restaurants: Guskelov (in English: Thank God!), crossover cuisine, or the Pappa Grappa with Italian dishes.
Best Bars: The Pappa Grappa

STOCKHOLM INTERNATIONAL FILM FESTIVAL

P.O Box: 3136
Stockholm, S-103 62 Sweden
Tel: 46-8-677-50-00
Fax: 46-8-20-05-90
Email: info@cinema.se
Web Site: www.filmfestivalen.se
Festival Date: November
Entry Deadline: September
Contact: Jakob Abrahamsson
Director: Git Scheynius
Programmer: Jakob Abrahamsson
Other Staff: Astrid Hallenstvedt
Profile: Since its start in 1990, the festival has established itself

BEST UNDERGROUND FESTIVALS

Antimatter Festival of Underground Short Film & Video
B-Movie Film Festival
Chicago Underground Film Festival
Independent Exposure
Miami Underground Film & Video Festival
MicroCineFest
New York Underground Film Festival
Seattle Underground Film Festival
Short Attention Span Film and Video Festival
Vancouver Underground Film Festival

as one of the leading festival and media events in Northern Europe. Stockholm X, a competitive section for directors who have made their first, second or third features; Open Zone, an outlook on where world cinema stands today; U.S. independents; Twilight Zone, films exploring the subculture of cinema; Northern Lights, a Critic's Week for films from the Nordic and Baltic Countries; and Made in Sweden 1999, a summary of the Swedish films released this year.

Renowned for its focus in new directors and cutting edge cinema the festival is also a major Scandinavian media event covered by more than 400 journalists. Quentin Tarantino, Steve Buscemi, Joel & Ethan Coen, Dennis Hopper and Elia Kazan are among the many personalities who have enjoyed the only festival in the world that operates 24 hours per day.

Awards: Yes
Competitions: Yes
Major Awards: Bronze Horse
Value of Awards: Honours/$ 10.000
Application Fee: None
Insider Advice: Send viewing cassette with something on your self and your film.
Films Screened: 150
Odds of Acceptance: 1 in 30
Filmmaker Perks: Limited funds—some do get travel/lodgings, all get guides/dinner treats.
Best Restaurants: Mooncake
Best Bars: Restaurant W.C, Hotel lobby Anglais
Best Hangout for Filmmakers: Café Schpkowski
Best Place for Breakfast: Hannas Deli

UPPSALA iNTERNATiONAL SHORT FiLM FESTiVAL

P.O. Box 1746
Uppsala, S-751 47 Sweden
Tel: 46-18-12-00-25
Fax: 46-18-12-13-50
Email: uppsala@shortfilm festival.com
Web Site: www.shortfilm festival.com

Festival Date: October
Entry Deadline: June 30, 2001
Year Festival Began: 1982
Contact: Asa Garnert
Director: Asa Garnert
Programmer: Christoffer Olofsson
Other Staff:
Category: Animation, Documentary, Experimental, International, Short
Profile: The Uppsala International Short Film Festival is Sweden's premier festival for short films, being the only one exclusively devoted to this genre. Screening more than 200 short films every year, the festival programme includes an International Competition, a Nordic Video Section, Children's Film Festival, Film School Day as well as special programmes and retrospectives. The festival offers the audience a unique chance of seeing short films otherwise not shown in Sweden. The festival also aims to create a meeting place for film professionals, audience and media.
Awards: Yes
Competitions: Yes
Major Awards: Uppsala Grand Prix
Value of Awards: 25 000 SEK (funded by Atom Films) + statuette Uppsala Film Jackdaw
Application Tips: Send us the films early. We get lots of submissions the last week before deadline, this means that the Selection committee gets an enormous workload during a very short period of time. A film submitted in June might get more attention then a film submitted late July.
Application Fee: No
Average Films Entered: Original, imaginative films. Strong subjects, and well written stories. Films that our made with the short film genre in mind. Films that are just made for "my portfolio" are seldom good or interesting.
Films Screened: 150-170
Odds of Acceptance: 1 in 5
Tourist Information: Uppsala is an old university town. The largest cathedral in Northern Europe. The biggest library

(Carolina Rediviva). Uppsala was the capital of "Sweden" during the Viking era, and in Old Uppsala you can visit the burial sites of the ancient kings.
Best Restaurants: Italian: Pinos
Vegetarian: Max & Marie
Fish: Hambergs fisk
Indian: Gandhi
Traditional: Domtrappkällaren
Chinese: China River
Greek: Akropolis
Mexican: Los Mexicanos
Modern: Elaka Måns
Post-modern: Grisen
Best Bars: Katalin
Best Hangout for Filmmakers: The Festival Pub.
Best Place for Breakfast: Tea & Sympathy

SWITZERLAND

CiNEMA TOUT ECRAN / iNTERNATiONAL FiLM & TELEViSiON CONVENTiON

16 rue General Dufour
CP 5305
CH-1211 Geneva 11, Switzerland
Tel: 41 22/328 85 54
Fax: 41 22/329 68 02
Email: info@cinema-tout-ecran.ch
Web Site: www.cinema-tout-ecran.ch
Festival Date: September
Entry Deadline: July
Year Festival Began: 1995
Contact: Leo Kaneman and Stephanie Billeter
Director: Leo Kaneman
Category: Artistic, public and professional
Profile: This festival presents quality films produced by/for television networks. The aim is to prove that "auteurs" may take advantages of television and that television is capable to produce films with originality
Seminars: Yes
Panels: Yes
Awards: Yes
Competitions: Yes

Major Awards: Grand Prix Cinema Tout Ecran

Value of Awards: 10'000 Swiss Francs

Application Tips: Originality and personality (and of course to be produced or co-produced by TV)

Application Fee: None

Average Films Entered: Quality films from 60 min. to 120 min.

Films Screened: 50 shorts, 25 new features, 10 old ones, 8 TV series

Odds of Acceptance: 1 in 13

Filmmaker Perks: Offer free travel, lodging and contacts

Best Restaurants: Opera Bouffe, Echalotte, Cafe Des Bains, Patio

Best Bars: A lot in the Old Town

FESTIVAL DE GENEVE DES EXPOIRS DU CINEMA EUROPEEN

2 Rue Bovy-Lysberg
Case Postale 418
1211 Geneva, Switzerland
Tel: 41-22-321-5466
Fax: 41-22-321-9862
Festival Date: October
Entry Deadline: June
Director: Roland Ray, President

GENEVA FILM FESTIVAL

P. O. Box 5615
1211 Geneva 11, Switzerland
Tel: 41-22-809-9450
Fax: 41-22-809-9444
Festival Date: October
Entry Deadline: October
Contact: Roland Ray

INTERNATIONAL ELECTRONIC CINEMA FESTIVAL

P. O. Box 1451
CH-820 Montreux, Switzerland
Tel: 21-963-32-20
Fax: 21-963-88-51
Festival Date: April-May
Contact: Renee Crawford

INTERNATIONAL FESTIVAL OF COMEDY FILMS OF VEVEY

La Grenette
Grand Place 29
CH-1800 Vevey, Switzerland
Tel: 41-21-92-22-027
Fax: 41-21-92-22-024
Festival Date: July
Entry Deadline: End of June previous year
Contact: Yves Moser, Patrick Henry, Bureau du Festival de Film de Comedie

INTERNATIONAL FESTIVAL OF FILMS ON ART (FIFART FESTIVAL)

P. O. Box 2783
CH-1002 Lausanne, Switzerland
Tel: 021-803-4053
Fax: 021-803-4053
Festival Date: Biennial, even years, October
Entry Deadline: May
Director: Anca Visdei
Category: International

LOCARNO INTERNATIONAL FILM FESTIVAL

Via Della Posta 6
CH-6600 Locarno, Switzerland
Tel: 41-91-751-0232
Fax: 41-91-751-7465
Festival Date: August
Entry Deadline: June
Category: International

NYON INTERNATIONAL DOCUMENTARY FILM FESTIVAL

P. O. Box 98
CH-1260 Nyon, Switzerland
Tel: 41-22-361-70-71
Fax: 41-22-361-70-71
Festival Date: September
Director: Gaston Nicole, President
Category: Documentary, International

PINK APPLE-SCHWULLESBISCHES FILMFESTIVAL

Postfach 28, CH-8501
Frauenfeld, Switzerland
Email: pinkapple@gay.ch
Web Site: www.pinkapple.ch or www.gay.ch/pinkapple
Festival Date: April/May
Entry Deadline: January
Year Festival Began: 1998
Category: Gay Lesbian, Touring (Zurich, Frauenfeld, Lucerne, Basel)
Profile: Gay and lesbian film festival.
Market: No
Competitions: Yes
Major Awards: Pink Apple Publikumspreis
Past Judges: Audience
Insider Advice: Submit VHS European PAL-format.
Average Films Entered: Gay and lesbian films
Films Screened: 20
Odds of Acceptance: 1 in 3

QUEERSICHT-SCHWUL-LESBISCHES FILMFESTIVAL BERN

Postfach 367/Bollwerk 21
CH-3011 Bern, Switzerland
Tel: 41-31-311-41-48
Fax: 41-31-311-41-48
Email: queersicht@hotmail.com
Web Site: mypage.bluewin.ch/queersicht/index.html
Festival Date: 2nd weekend of November
Entry Deadline: July 1, 2001
Year Festival Began: 1997
Director: Maddalena Tognola and Marc Mouci
Programmer: Nathalie Keusen, Patrick Martinez and Stefanie Arnold
Category: Gay Lesbian, Independent, International, Short
Profile: Queersicht is the largest Swiss gay and lesbian film festival. It's a small but nice event with an international short film competition every second year. We try to show features, documentaries and shorts that usually don't find their ways to the local theaters to a larger audience.

Seminars: No
Panels: No
Famous Speakers: No
Market: No
Competitions: Every second year
Major Awards: Rosa Brille
Value of Awards: 1000 sFr
Application Fee: None
Insider Advice: Watch out our application form (homepage) and fill in. Send information on the film first before sending a previous tape (if possible PAL).
Average Films Entered: Quality comes first.
Films Screened: 16
Odds of Acceptance: 1 in 6
Filmmaker Perks: Fame (!!) and a very nice audience.
Attendance: 1600
Tourist Information: Alpes, Old Town (on the UNESCO World Culture list), River Aare, House of Parliament.
Travel Tips: "Berner Oberland" and the Jungfrau mountain. Bern is also in the very center of Switzerland and you can travel to most of the other swiss towns within less than two hours (Zurich, Basel, Geneva, Luzern).
Best Cheap Hotels: Goldener Schlüssel
Best Luxury Hotels: Schweizerhof, Bellevue
Best Restaurants: Du Nord
Best Bars: Kreissaal
Best Place for Breakfast: Brasserie Lorraine on Sundays.
Festival Tale: It's in the Water, our opening film on the second edition got lost between Madrid and Barcelona. It finally arrived at the airport on Saturday morning, but the customs was closed until Monday. So we couldn't show our "best film" at the end.

VIPER INTERNATIONAL FILM AND VIDEO FESTIVAL

VIPER Lucerne
P. O. Box 4929
CH-6002 Lucerne, Switzerland
Tel: 4141-51-74-07
Fax: 4141-52-80-20

Web Site: October
Festival Date: August
Contact: Cristoph Settele
Category: International

TAIWAN

ASIA-PACIFIC FILM FESTIVAL

8F No. 116 Hang Chung St.
Taipei, Taiwan
Tel: 02-371-5191
Fax: 02-311-0681
Festival Date: December
Director: Hsu Li-Kung, VP
Category: Ethnic Other

THAILAND

BANGKOK FILM FESTIVAL

4 Sukhumvit Soi 43
Bangkok, 10110 Thailand
Tel: 66-2-259-3112
Fax: 66-2-259-2987
Email: film@nationgroup.com
Web Site: www.bkkfilmfest.com
Festival Date: end of September
Entry Deadline: June 15, 2001
Year Festival Began: 1998
Contact: Brian Bennett
Director: Brian Bennett
Category: American Films, Documentary, Ethnic Asian, First-Time Independent Filmmakers, Independent, International, Online Festival, Touring
Profile: The festival wants to promote independent film and provides a competition (The Golden Elephant Awards) for Best Feature and Documentary Films. All films are eligible for the Audience Awards.
Seminars: Yes
Panels: Yes
Awards: Yes
Competitions: Yes
Major Awards: Golden Elephant
Value of Awards: Prestige
Application Tips: Note that a value of zero (0) should be declared on all customs documentation.

Application Fee: None
Insider Advice: Send in early
Average Films Entered: 280
Films Screened: 50
Odds of Acceptance: 1 in 5
Filmmaker Perks: Travel, lodging are provided to select films.
Attendance: 22,000
Journalist Attendance: 15

TUNISIA

FESTIVAL INTERNATIONAL DU FILM AMATEUR DE KELIBIA

P. O. Box 116
1015 Tunis, Tunisia
Tel: 216-1-280-207
Fax: 216-1-336-207
Festival Date: July-August
Entry Deadline: May for registration; June for films
Contact: Taoufik Abid

TURKEY

ANKARA INTERNATIONAL FILM FESTIVAL

World Mass Media Research Foundation
Bulten Sokak No.64/2
06700 Kavakladere
Ankara, Turkey
Tel: 90-312-468-7745
Fax: 90-312-467-7830
Festival Date: March
Entry Deadline: December for entry forms; February for prints
Director: Sevna Aygun, General Secretary
Category: International

ISTANBUL SHORT FILM AND VIDEO FESTIVAL

Consulat General de France
80090 Istikst Caddem
No. 8 Tukeim, Turkey
Tel: 144-44-95
Fax: 144-48-95
Festival Date: March
Contact: Consulat General de France

UKRAINE

KYiV INTERNATiONAL FiLM FESTiVAL, MOLODiST

(Molodist means "youth" in Ukrainian)
Molodist, Dom Kino, Suite 115, Saksagansky St, Number 6
Kyiv, 252033 Ukraine
Tel: 280-44-246-67-98
Fax: 380-44-227-4557
Email: molodist@gu.kiev.ua
Web Site: www.compxpress.com/~dkmedia/molodist or www.uis.Kiev.ua/~molodist
Festival Date: October
Entry Deadline: July
Year Festival Began: 1970
Contact: Lyudmila Novikova
Director: Andrei Khalpakhtchi
Programmer: Alexander Shpyliuk
Category: Independent
Competitions: Yes, 4 categories
Major Awards: The Scynthian Deer statuette
Value of Awards: Grand Prix: USD 10,000
Best debut full length feature: USD 2,500
Best debut short film: USD 2,500
Best debut documentary or animation film: USD 2,500
Best actor/actress: FRF 5,000
Application Tips: Send video for pre-selection on time, dialogues list for translation, filmography and contacts for good info in the catalogue. Stills (for the catalogue) and some publicity material such as posters and flyers.
Application Fee: None
Insider Advice: when their film is selected, they should come to the Festival.
Films Screened: for pre-selection and selection: all of them, the selection commitee goes to other film festivals too and brings back videotapes, contacts or strong desire to show the film
Odds of Acceptance: 1 in 6
Filmmaker Perks: Everybody gets free housing on a cruise boat moored on the Dniepr river, free breakfast on the boat and free lunch in the main

House of Cinematographers where good Ukrainian specialties are served. Then, for dinner, every night there is a party and everybody is invited to cocktail parties. The main perk of Molodist festival is certainly the intimate atmosphere where you can meet anybody you want.
Tourist Information: Kyiv is located in Ukraine and therefore is the oldest Rus, the first slavonci state is Ukraine. There are lots of things to visit such as: incredible monasteries, the Laura monasteries (one of the oldest in the ex-USSR) St. Sophia Church (in 1037) the 1900's architecture (the center is beautifully kept and you cannot miss hundreds of cariatydes and atlantes statues everywhere.
Travel Tips: When flying to Kyiv, you need a visa to get in. Make sure you make plans in advance, it's much cheaper. When coming by train, it is a real experience as trains are really slow but full of nice people ready to share a glass of vodka with you.
Best Bars: Eric's (founded by a German dude)
Best Hangout for Filmmakers: The House of Cinematographers/Dom Kino

URUGUAY

INTERNATiONAL FiLM FESTiVAL FOR CHiLDREN AND YOUNG PEOPLE

Lorenzo Carnelli 1311
11200 Montevideo, Uruguay
Tel: 598-2-408-2460; 598-2-409-5795
Fax: 598-2-409-4572
Email: cinemuy@chasque.apc.org
Festival Date: July 5-16
Entry Deadline: May 10
Director: Ricardo Casas
Category: Kids

INTERNATiONAL FiLM FESTiVAL OF MONTEViDEO AND PUNTA DEL ESTE

Lorenzo Carnelli 1311

Casilla de correos 1170
Montevideo, Uruguay
Tel: 598-2-48-24-60
Fax: 598-2-49-45-72
Festival Date: April
Entry Deadline: February
Director: Manuel Martinez Carril, Director Cinematica Uruguaya

WALES

WELSH INTERNATiONAL FiLM FESTiVAL

Ty Meandros, 54A Bute Street
Cardiff, CF1 6AF Wales
Tel: 44 1970 617995
Fax: 44 1970 617942
Email: wiff@pcw-aber.co.uk
Web Site: www.aber.ac.uk/~wff995/ or www.pcw-aber.co.uk/WIFF/
Festival Date: November
Entry Deadline: September
Year Festival Began: 1989
Contact: General enquiries: Grant Vidgen
Press enquiries: Sion Jobbins
Director: Grant Vidgen
Category: General, non-competitive
Profile: The Welsh International Film Festival seeks to bring the best of world cinema to as wide an audience in Wales as possible and to promote the best of Welsh film to as wide an international audience as possible.
Awards: Yes
Competitions: Yes (Only for short films by a Welsh film maker)
Major Awards: D. M. Davies Award
Value of Awards: £30 000 sterling
Application Tips: Get your submission in early, and relate it to one or more of the programme themes.
Insider Advice: Do complete your film as indicated in your application form. If you're not sure of the final format when you send in the application tell us—don't guess! Bribery of the selection panel doesn't work, but

When coming by train, it is a real experience, as trains are really slow but full of nice people ready to share a glass of vodka with you (Kyiv International Film Festival Molodist).

please include as much useful information as possible with your application—any interesting angles for promoting the film, your availability to attend the festival etc. Follow our advice with regard to shipping—it'll often be more expensive and less secure if you don't!

Films Screened: 170

Odds of Acceptance: 1 in 3

Filmmaker Perks: Limited assistance with travel and lodging is available.

Tourist Information: National Museum of Wales, Museum of Welsh Life, Cardiff Castle, Castell Coch

Travel Tips: Our weather in November can be changeable—come prepared!

Best Restaurants: Scott's Brasserie

ZIMBABWE

KINE INTERNATIONAL FILM FESTIVAL

Kine Centre

Box 580

Harare, Zimbabwe

Tel: 73-69-66

Fax: 72-45-15

Festival Date: June

Entry Deadline: March

Contact: Bruce Waters

Category: International

THE TRUTH ABOUT ONLiNE FiLM FESTiVALS

The most important thing you need to know about online film festivals is that they are not really festivals. In fact, I'm getting really annoyed at the way the words "film festival" are being abused. A real film festival takes place where people can interact in the real world. It's the difference between watching a movie at home on television or seeing a film on opening night with a packed audience. There is no comparison. Having said that, online festivals and websites that showcase downloadable short films and features are fantastic ways to expose your movie to a worldwide audience. You want to definitely explore online opportunities for your movie, but only *after* you have made your real film festival debut. Your debut, press that your film receives and any other awards you may collect playing at real film festivals will only make your movie more desirable to online ventures and put you in a better position to negotiate your deal. Keep this in mind.

Many reputable film festivals are adding online elements as part of their programs. Slamdance has been showing shorts online for years now. Not to be outdone, the Sundance Film Festival recently added an online element to its website. Directors of festivals with an aggressive online presence are now able to include more films in their programs in the form of films online. This is good news for filmmakers and film fans everywhere. It gives the filmmaker the benefit of being associated with a well-known festival, and gives fans an opportunity to see quality work online.

The web is an amazing new medium, but I must warn you that some online festivals are merely scams used to gather free content. Be very wary; do your homework and study any online fest you're considering becoming a part of. Ask other filmmakers what kind of deals they got and how they feel they are being treated. Do yourself a favor and pay a lawyer $50 to look over any contract you are offered. One important piece of advice I can't scream loudly enough to every filmmaker reading this book, because this is a book, and it's text printed on the page, but if I were sitting next to you right now I would scream the word "Non-exclusive!" Do not, under any circumstance, allow an online venture to tie up all the rights to your film. (Unless they are willing to pay you what the film is worth, plus a healthy profit for yourself.) You never know what may happen with your film in the future. You might get lucky and one of the actors in your film will become a big celebrity or get involved in a scandal, then you'll have a film that's really worth something! You need to build in non-exclusivity so you can pursue other opportunities that you may not even be thinking about now. There are so many ways to exploit your film—such as adding it to a collection of short films on DVD, releasing your film on video, foreign rights on television, domestic cable and other TV rights, etc.—you can carve out any area of rights you wish, you need only ask. And, there are actually many benefits to being associated with a strong website, like access to press that may not have taken notice of your movie and the fact that anyone with a computer can see your work.

> .....
> You need to build in non-exclusivity so that you can pursue other opportunities that you may not even be thinking about now.
> .....

The web is still a volatile marketplace, so be sure to thoroughly explore any online destination you are seriously considering. Even reputable names like Steven Spielberg have learned hard lessons about the web (when he saw tens of millions go down the toilet with the collapse of the overhyped Pop.com). The listings that follow are some of the most well-known sites for downloadable video. And there are many more being built every week, so do your own searches on the web. Based on the unpredictability of the Internet, some of these sites may not even exist by the time you read this book, so be careful. The web is an incredible marketing tool and can help you enormously, but make sure *you're* using *it*, and *it's* not using *you*.

ONLiNE FiLM FESTiVALS

ALWAYSi

Web Site: www.Alwaysi.com
234 Front Street, 4th Floor
San Francisco, CA 94111
Tel: 415-776-7758
Fax: 415-398-3750
Email: info@alwaysi.com
Director: Howard Rosenberg,
CEO, howard@alwaysi.com
Gary Zeidenstein, Vice President
of Content Acquisition,
gary@alwaysi.com
Profile: Alwaysi is the web's premiere destination for unique,
independent entertainment for
consumers and an indispensable
industry resource for working
professionals. The company's
consumer mission is to deliver
motion picture and television-
type entertainment to a potential audience of millions worldwide. The company's business
mission is serve the creators of
independent entertainment by
developing new revenue and distribution opportunities; to provide an exhibition platform for
independent entertainment creators to showcase their material
to entertainment talent representatives, acquisitions executives
and other industry professionals
and to create a community for
working professionals to keep
current on industry news.
Alwaysi's library of over 1000
feature-length films, short films,
animation and TV-like series is
available to view in streaming
formats.
Application Fee: Alwaysi.com
offers the filmmaker a free combination of services to help promote the filmmaker and his/her
work.

AMERICAN SHORT SHORTS

This festival has an online
component. See "North
American Film Festivals" beginning on page 251 for the festival's complete listing.

ATOMFiLMS

Web Site: www.atomfilms.com
(Seattle Office)
Attn: Acquisitions
815 Western Avenue, Suite 300
Seattle, WA 98104
Email: submit@atomfilms.com

BANGKOK FiLM FESTiVAL

This festival has an online
component. See "International
Film Festivals" beginning on page
345 for the festival's complete
listing.

BiG FiLM SHORTS

Web Site:
www.bigfilmshorts.com
3727 W. Magnolia Blvd., #189
Burbank, CA 91505
Tel: 818-563-2633
Fax: 818-955-7650
Email: info@bigfilmshorts.com
Profile: Big Film Shorts is a distributor and sales agent for
short films and is based in
Burbank, California. The company's mission is to offer top quality, sophisticated entertainment in
the form of short films, primarily
via the Internet, to as wide an
audience as possible.

Founded in 1996, Big Film
Shorts launched this website
soon after, creating the Internet's
first online catalog of short films.

In the ensuing years, Big Film
Shorts has gained the respect
and trust of film buyers, filmmakers and, of course, fans of short
films.

BiJOU CAFE

Web Site: www.bijoucafe.com
5632 Van Nuys Blvd. #186
Van Nuys, CA 91401
Profile: Each week, a new series
of short films by independent
filmmakers from around the
world will be shown here in
their entirety. Once you're multi-
media-ready, get set for: cutting
edge, alternative films, videos,
shorts, documentaries, classics
and features, many exclusive to
the Cafe; an "artist first" view-
point which means no censorship; and on-demand selectability
per title for whenever you want
to view it.

BiNARY THEATER

Web Site:
www.binarytheater.com
Email: chaz@binarytheater.com
Profile: Using our association
with college and university Film
Studies departments, sponsorship of film festivals, and a strong
relationship with skilled student
and professional artists,
Binary Theater is dedicated to
discovering talented film makers
and providing them a free, unlim-
ited distribution channel for
their work. Binary Theater
selects high-quality, compelling
work, digitizes it and puts it on
our website for all the world to
see—fans, reviewers, industry
watchers, talent scouts, employ-
ers, etc. The public is invited to
view and comment on the

videos and even send e-mail messages to the film's creator(s). BinaryTheater has created a win-win situation for both the artist and the viewer—artists now have a method of distribution that takes advantage of cutting-edge technology, and viewers now have a single, definitive source for artistic entertainment.

Imagine having instant access to the best work from the best film schools in the country—all from a few key strokes on your computer. This is what BinaryTheater is all about.

THE BiT SCREEN

Web Site:
www.thebitscreen.com
PO Box 343
Narberth, PA 19072
Email: info@druidmedia.com
Profile: The Internet's a new medium, and it demands new content - which is exactly what you'll find on The Bit Screen. The Bit Screen delivers first-run Internet films and web series directly to your desktop.

We add new programs every week on this site and on The Best of The Bit Screen on Broadcast.com (www.broadcast.com/video). Sign up to receive a copy of our weekly newsletter to find out what's coming up next on the screen.

DDPTV WEEKLY FiLM FESTiVAL

Web Site: www.ddptv.com
Email: info@ddptv.com
Director: Simon Slater
Profile: DDPTV's Weekly Film Festival is an online showcase of videos and films developed with the Internet in mind. Filmmakers can submit their videos by uploading them into DDPTV's online community, which is powered by Hotline Connect technology. Each week, three videos submitted will be broadcast on the DDPTV website. DDPTV viewers then vote on which of the three choices they like the best. Each weekly winner is then

entered into the Film Festival Finals. The Finals are held twice a year in New York City. A panel of entertainment and content producing professionals, including a representative from Hotline Communications, will judge finalists. The winner will win $2000 towards his or her next production, as well as having their next production featured on DDPTV.

DEEP ELLUM FiLM FESTiVAL

This festival has an online component. See "North American Film Festivals" beginning on page 251 for the festival's complete listing.

DFiLM

Web Site: www.dfilm.com
564 Mission St., Suite 429
San Francisco, CA 94105
Email: bart@dfilm.com
Festival Date: Touring.
Entry Deadline: None. Since the festival is continually being shown in different cities throughout the year, deadlines are ongoing.
Director: Bart Cheever
Nikos Constant
Claire McNulty, Publicity
Profile: Our goal is to showcase the very best work being created within the digital medium. We prefer pieces which are approximately 5 minutes in length or less, or excerpts from longer films. We're looking for work that demonstrates some innovative new use of technology. Although we show abstract work, we especially value pieces which are able to strongly convey ideas or tell stories, pieces which will entertain and inspire our audiences to create films themselves.

Our goal at D.film is to not only showcase the best in digital filmmaking through our screenings and website but to also actively inspire our audiences to make film themselves. Do it.

D.film is a touring festival. This year we'll be bringing the festival to nineteen cities around the world. The core traveling festival

will expand from four cities to nine, and we're setting up a special tour of college campuses which will be organized by Brett Russell, formerly of Spike and Mike's Festival of Animation/Sick and Twisted and Warren Miller Films, which will bring the festival to an additional ten cities. Last year, every show in every city was sold out.

Gore Score · · · · · · · · · · · · · · · ·
D.film offers amazing opportunities for filmmakers to expose their innovative digital works to audiences as well as providing an impressive number of press opportunities. In addition, screenings and parties provide opportunities to discuss the future of the digital medium.

Application Fee: None.

DiGiDANCE DiGiTAL CiNEMA FESTiVAL

Web Site:
www.digidanceonline.com
1346 Stanley Ave., Suite 3
Los Angeles, CA 90046
Tel: 323-878-0633
Fax: 323-692-1020
Festival Date: January
Director: Shiron Bell
Profile: "Digidance was formed to promote digital production and digital distribution as a way of giving unique moviemaking a way to find an audience outside of the typical Hollywood system," says festival director and founder Shiron Bell. "In our view the only truly independent moviemaking in today's entertainment industry is digital. If you have a unique voice and vision and don't have access to significant funding you shoot digital, it's that simple."

GETOUTTHERE

Web Site:
www.getoutthere.bt.com
Profile: It is BT's goal to support all forms of communication and Getoutthere.bt.com is part of this program.

Getoutthere.bt.com has been created to empower musicians and filmakers by providing the opportunity for their creative

work to be seen and heard. The site is designed to give a platform for new talent and we hope that all users will respect the work of others.

We want you to think of this as your site. At the same time, we have to have some basic rules. We will not carry work that has obscene, defamatory or racist content. We will patrol the site for this sort of content and we reserve the right to withdraw it immediately without informing the person who uploaded it.

Awards: 1. Tickets to getoutthere Live including one of the daytime events, the awards and a celebrity bash.

2. Uploaders enter the chance to win a dream prize that money can't buy to help further your career, such as a day in a London recording studio with a top record producer. A chance have your track distributed on a white label, with feedback from top DJs or a day in the studio cutting a cinema trailer for a new movie.

3. The ultimate prize for the overall newcomer in both music and film is a marketing and promotions campaign delivered by six of the top agencies in the UK.

4. MP3 players, WAP phones, cinema season tickets are up for grabs for both voters and uploaders.

GOT FiLM FEST

Web Site: www.gotfilmfest.com
Tel: 407-291-8361
Email: iwonderpro@aol.com
Festival Date: December/January
Profile: Got Film Fest is an online based free short film festival geared at student, independent and underground filmmakers. Cash awards and Prizes are given out in all major categories; Jury, Judges, Animation, Tech Awards. Sponsored by iWonderFilm.com.

HOLLYWOOD SHORTS

Web Site: www.lalive.com/hollywoodshorts/
765 N. Ridgewood Place, Suite 4
Los Angeles, CA 90038
Tel: 323-960-3385
Email: hollywoodshorts@yahoo.com
Festival Date: Ongoing
Entry Deadline: Ongoing
Director: Kimberley Browning
Profile: Hollywood Shorts is a monthly series that provides emerging directors, writers, and producers an opportunity to present their short subject films and videos to the world online here at L.A. Live, and at live screenings on the second Sunday of every month at The Gig, 11637 West Pico Blvd. in West Los Angeles. These films are chosen out of hundreds of entries from around the world. To enjoy this month's selections just scroll down and take your pick.
Application Fee: $5.00

HOMETOWN CiNEMA iNC

This festival has an online component. See "North American Film Festivals" beginning on page 251 for the festival's complete listing.

iFiLM

Web Site: www.ifilm.com
1024 N. Orange Drive
Hollywood, CA 90038
Tel: 323-308-3400
Email: info@ifilm.com
Profile: Launched in October 1998, IFILM is the leading authority and directory for the emerging world of Internet film, and the most popular online resource for film fans, filmmakers, and entertainment industry professionals.
Awards: The most popular IFILM filmmakers (as determined by our audience) are also now eligible to earn cash and prizes based on their success. In addition, through its strategic industry partnerships, IFILM will soon be offering offline distribution to the most popular filmmakers, including opportunities to show-

case their work on television, on TiVo and in movie theaters. In some cases, IFILM also partners with filmmakers to promote their work via specially tailored promotional and publicity programs. Recent IFILMmakers in the news received placements in ABC Network News, CNN, *Entertainment Weekly, Los Angeles Times, New York Times, Time Magazine* and *USA Today*.

iNDEPENDENT EXPOSURE

This festival has an online component. See "North American Film Festivals" beginning on page 251 for the festival's complete listing.

iNDiEKiNO iNTERNATiONAL FiLM FESTiVAL

Web Site: ww.indiekino.com
Tel: 82-2-593/6391
Fax: 82-2-593/6291
Email: boonsoo@indiekino.com
Profile: The Indiekino International Film Festival, where digital technology and independent films meet. Contrary to kind of movies up until now, we, at Indiekino, will transform the way of movie thinking and help to raise the standard of independent films.

LEOFEST

Web Site: www.leofest.com
LeoFest Submissions Department
PO Box 4351
PMB 1000
Hollywood, CA 90078
Entry Deadline: Ongoing
Director: Leonardo DiCaprio
Profile: Is film an obsession? Has your desire to make films become a serious need? Already have one in the can? If it's 15 minutes or less, and you'd like to see it in competition with the works of other accomplished, novice or first-time filmmakers just like yourself, Leonardo DiCaprio invites you to participate in the very first film festival of its kind: LeoFest. Message from Leo: I've been around

artists my entire life. Breaking through—when you're just starting out—can seem impossible. This festival seeks to change that; to offer a place for your work can be seen and for you to see the work of others. Even exchange tips, ideas and war stories with other filmmakers. Basically, this festival strives to offer a level playing field on which anyone who wishes may play.

Awards: Yes

Application Fee: $35

THE LOST FiLM FESTiVAL

This festival has an online component. See "North American Film Festivals" beginning on page 251 for the festival's complete listing.

MANiFESTiVAL

Web Site: www.manifestival.com.

P.O. Box 224,

New York, NY 10012

Email: kiley@manifestival.com.

Director: Kiley Bates

Profile: This online festival is maintained by a network of affiliates with an interest in the future of online cinema. Each affiliate supports the festival in specific areas: consultation, design, facility donations, film digitization, public relations and other areas.

MELBOURNE QUEER FiLM & ViDEO FESTIVAL

This festival has an online component. See "North American Film Festivals" beginning on page 251 for the festival's complete listing.

MiAMi UNDERGROUND FiLM & ViDEO FESTIVAL (ONLiNE)

This festival has an online component. See "North American Film Festivals" beginning on page 251 for the festival's complete listing.

MOXiE! / SANTA MONiCA FiLM FESTIVAL

This festival has an online component. See "North American Film Festivals" beginning on page 251 for the festival's complete listing.

NEW VENUE

Web Site: www.newvenue.com

58 Ave C Suite #2B

New York, NY 10009-8526

Tel: 212-606-3488

Email: info@newvenue.com

Director: Creator & Founder Jason Wishnow

Profile: The New Venue is an arbiter of quality, catering to a global media-savvy community, presenting only those movies which push the envelope of cinema on the web.

Every week the New Venue features new independent short films which overcome the aesthetic and technical limitations of the Internet and which offer content you just couldn't see anywhere else.

NO DANCE FiLM FESTIVAL

This festival has an online component. See "North American Film Festivals" beginning on page 251 for the festival's complete listing.

OHiO iNDEPENDENT FiLM FESTIVAL

This festival has an online component. See "North American Film Festivals" beginning on page 251 for the festival's complete listing.

PiTCH TV

Web Site: www.pitchtv.com

304 Hudson St., 6th floor

New York, NY 10013

Tel: 212-584-5840

Email: info@pitchtv.com

Profile: Pitch is a NYC based studio and Pitch TV is our way of showing our own work and the work of the many artists we admire.

REELSHORT

Web Site: www.reelshort.com

80 South Street

New York, NY 10038

Tel: 212-809-3202

Fax: 212-809-3209

Email: info@reelshort.com

Director: Filmmaker contact: Geri Cosenza geri@reelshort.com

Business Development contact: Daniel Gossels daniel@reelshort.com

Advertising and Sponsorship contact: Andy Marks andy@reelshort.com

Marketing and Film Festvial contact: Shawn Folz shawn@reelshort.com

Media contact: Lisa Lori, Lisa Lori Communications 212.925.2300 LisaLoriCom@aol.com

Profile: To enable talented, emerging filmmakers to gain wider and faster access to global audiences and industry leaders by providing online and traditional entertainment platforms for their creative work.

BEST TOURING FILM FESTIVALS

ResFest Digital Film Festival

D.FILM Digital Film Festival

Northwest Film & Video Festival

REVelation Independent Film Festival

RHODE ISLAND INTERNATIONAL FILM FESTIVAL

This festival has an online component. See "North American Film Festivals" beginning on page 251 for the festival's complete listing.

SHORT ATTENTION SPAN FILM AND VIDEO FESTIVAL (SASFVF)

This festival has an online component. See "North American Film Festivals" beginning on page 251 for the festival's complete listing.

SHORTBUZZ.COM

Web Site: www.shortbuzz.com
41 East 11th Street, Floor 11
New York, NY 10003
Tel: 212-699-3624
Fax: 212-331-1109
Email: info@shortbuzz.com
Profile: The key difference between Shortbuzz and its competition is that Shortbuzz is run by filmmakers. We understand the challenges that short filmmakers experience when trying to get exposure for their work. Thus, we provide a free venue for filmmakers to screen their work, we don't ask for the exclusive rights to their film (like other websites do) and we offer filmmakers 50 percent of the profits from any sale or license of their film that Shortbuzz orchestrates!
Application Fee: Free

SHORTTV

Web Site: www.shorttv.com
580 Broadway, Suite 1111
New York, NY 10012
Tel: 212-226-6258
Email: Info@shorttv.com
Profile: Shorttv.com is a truly independent short film channel and Internet company dedicated to supporting independent filmmakers by providing them with the opportunity to show their work before a wide audience. Shorttv is established to bridge the gap between industry professionals; from actors and crew members to directors, producers and distributors.

SPUTNIK7

Web Site: www.sputnik7.com
Fax: 212-645-5971
Email: info@sputnik7.com
Profile: Credited as the world's first real-time audio/video Internet entertainment experience, Sputnik7 is a broadcast network offering a sophisticated mix of independent music, film, and anime programming via interactive Video Stations, Audio Stations, Videos on Demand, and Digital Downloads.

Sputnik7's award winning design allows people to chat, purchase music, make requests, rate videos, and find information on artists, all without interrupting their audio/visual entertainment experience.

Application Fee: Sputnik7 is free. You can enter Sputnik7 as member or a guest, though membership does have its privileges.

STUDENTFILMS.COM THE ONLINE STUDENT FILM FESTIVAL

Web Site: www.studentfilms.com
Studentfilms.com
PO Box 446
Allston, MA 02134
Email: chrisw@studentfilms.com
Festival Date: Ongoing
Entry Deadline: Ongoing
Director: Chris Wright
Webmaster and Founder of Studentfilms.com
Profile: Studentfilms.com was created to provide an almost infinite audience for budding filmmakers and their films. Using QuickTime technology (which is getting better every day), Studentfilms.com gives everyone the means to have their storytelling voice heard around the world.

More importantly, the site is starting to become a place where filmmakers can go to get advice on making their film—a kind of meeting place for film students, either those who are veterans or those who are new to the medium. This I think will begin to be an ever more valuable resource. .

Awards: Films that receive the most votes by viewers become the most popular films. Kind of like high school.

Application Fee: There is no application fee, however, you are encouraged to support the site by buying a t-shirt for $13.

THE SYNC ONLINE FILM FESTIVAL

"The promise that 'this festival never ends' could be taken as either a threat or a hopeful sign."
—*Details*

Web Site: www.thesync.com/festival/
The Sync
312 Laurel Avenue
Laurel, MD 20707
Tel: 301-438-7281
Fax: 301-598-0769
Email: info@thesync.com
Festival Date: Ongoing and always accepting entries.
Entry Deadline: New films are added monthly when voting begins.
Director: Thomas Edwards
thomas@thesync.com
Profile: The purpose of The Sync is to create compelling, interactive content that is specifically tailored for the "Net Generation." This is not television recycled, but the beginning of a totally new medium, aimed at the needs and expectations of the Net Generation audience.

The Sync's shows have won acclaim from publications such as *Entertainment Weekly, Rolling Stone,* and *USA Today.* And The Sync was the first webcaster to have its work displayed at the New York Museum of Modern Art.

Besides all-original productions, The Sync also works with content partners (such as

Slashdot and the JenniCam) as well as independent filmmakers to bring a wide mix of entertainment and tech-entertainment shows to its viewers.

To bring our content to our viewers, The Sync works with streaming technology partners RealNetworks and Microsoft Windows Media, and distribution partners iCast and College Broadcast.

The site also highlights shows like *Snack Boy*, *CyberLove*, *Geeks in Space* among others.

Awards: Every day viewers vote for their favorite shorts in seven categories. New films are added each month, and there are new winners every minute—this festival never ends! Your vote determines which films remain on the site, while less popular films will be periodically replaced with new entries.

Application Fee: None.

THAW VIDEO, FILM, AND DIGITAL MEDIA FESTIVAL

This festival has an online component. See "North American Film Festivals" beginning on page 251 for the festival's complete listing.

UNDERGROUNDFILM.COM

Web Site: www.underground film.com
137 West 14th Street, Suite 202
All submissions should be sent to:
Box 461 70A Greenwich Avenue
New York, NY 10011
Tel: 212-206-1995
Fax: 212-206-1997
Email: info@undergroundfilm. com
Director: Mike Kelly
Steven Bogart
Profile: Undergroundfilm.com's mission is to create an online film community. We are committed to showing and selling the work of independent filmmakers, a sector of the creative community that has little or no access to the traditional tools of distribution.

Undergroundfilm.com is the next wave of the independent film industry, streamlining distribution and exhibition in a single web space that allows filmmakers to take their work to the industry and the audience at once.

By merging film and new media, Undergroundfilm.com hopes to usher in a new era of artistic expression and entertainment on the Internet. We want you to be a part of it.

Application Fee: Free

URBANCHILLERS.COM

Web Site: www.urbanchillers.com
Awards: For those filmmakers who truly shine, we will commission you to make future movies for urbanchillers.com

VIRTUETV.COM

Web Site: www.virtuetv.com
31-32 Eastcastle Street
London, WIN 7PD
Tel: 44-020-7323-6850
Fax: 44-020-7323-6847
Email: info@virtuetv.com
Profile: Virtue Broadcasting is Europe's leading Internet Broadcaster and streaming content creator.

We provide turnkey solutions capable of meeting and exceeding your highest expectations.

Set up in early 1998 to meet the growing demand for technical expertise in the application of digital visual technology, we operate, manage and provide content for Europe's leading Internet video network (virtuetv.com) and provide similar facilities for corporate clients.

By bringing audio and video to the web, both live and on-demand, streaming is unleashing a host of powerful new business and consumer applications, empowering enterprises large and small to take advantage of the opportunities presented by the Internet's global reach and ease of access.

WEBDANCE FILM FESTIVAL

Web Site: www.webdance filmfestival.com
8424A Santa Monica Blvd. #775
West Hollywood, CA 90069
Email: contact@webdance filmfestival.com
Festival Date: Ongoing
Entry Deadline: Ongoing
Awards: Most popular films receive nothing but the recognition of their peers.
Application Fee: None

YAHOO INTERNET LIFE! MAGAZINE ONLINE FILM FESTIVAL

Web Site: www.onlinefilm festival.com
Send Shorts and Animations to:
10850 Wilshire Blvd., Suite 1200
Los Angeles, CA 90024
Features and full-length documentaries:
Ben Greenman
Yahoo! Internet Life Magazine
28 East 28th Street, 12th Floor
New York, NY 10016
Tel: 323-692-8350
Email: yilsubmitfilms@aol.com
Festival Date: March 2001
Entry Deadline: February
Profile: As we move into the next century, we are faced with a transformation of the film industry through the Internet. More people can make films than ever before, and they can distribute their films to a larger audience than ever before more cheaply than ever before.

This festival will elevate the online film space, explore the various ways that content providers are using the Internet to exhibit compelling entertainment, and, most importantly, will provide a viable outlet for independent, shorts, and animation filmmakers.

Application Fee: $25

ZOiE FiLMS iNTERNET FiLM FESTiVAL

Web Site: www.zoiefilms.com
539 Salem Woods Drive
Marietta, GA 30067
Tel: 404-816-0602
Fax: 678-560-6777
Email: filmfest@zoiefilms.com
Festival Date: February 20, 2001
Entry Deadline: March 20, 2001
Director: Kathryn Elliott
Artistic Director
Profile: Zoie Films is about independent filmmaking. and quality programs. We encourage the work of independent filmmakers and employ the Internet as a medium for the exhibition of those films.
Awards: The Zoie Crystal Star Award and Certificates of Merit
Application Fee: All lengths: $25
Screenplays: $25

APPENDiCES

- Index of Film Festivals by Name
- index of Film Festivals by Month
- Index of Film Festivals by Genre
- iFiLMfinders Power Invitation List for Festival Screenings and Parties
- Filmmaker Resources

iNDEX OF FiLM FESTiVALS BY NAME

INDEX OF FiLM FESTiVALS BY MONTH

JANUARY

Alpe Adria Fest
Annual Kidfilm Festival
Australian International Outdoor Short Film
    Festival "Flickerfest"
Black Maria Film and Video Festival
Blois Cinema Forum
Brussels International Cinema Festival
Calcutta Film Festival On Mountains
Charlotte Gay & Lesbian Film Series
    Presented by Outcharlotte
Dhaka International Short Film Festival
Fajr International Film Festival
Festival du Film Gay et Lesbien de Bruxelles
    (Brussels Gay and Lesbian Film Festival)
Filmfestival Max Ophüls Preis
Filmotsav Documentary Film Festival
International Festival of Documentary and
    Science Films
International Film Festival of India
Moondance International Film Festival
No Dance Film Festival
Odysseyfest Science Fiction and Fantasy
    Film Festival
Palm Springs International Film Festival
Reel Music Festival
San Francisco Independent Film Festival
    (aka SF Indiefest)
Sarasota Film Festival
Slamdance International Film Festival
Slamdunk Film Festival
Stuttgart Filmwinter
Sundance Film Festival
Tokyo Video Festival
Tromadance Film Festival
Tromsø International Film Festival
Wurzburg International Film Festival

JANUARY–FEBRUARY

Belgrade International Film Festival
Cergy-Pontoise Cinema Festival
Children's London Film Festival
Clermont-Ferrand Short Film Festival
Göteborg Film Festival
International Film Festival Rotterdam
Rotterdam International Film Festival

FEBRUARY

Angelciti Los Angeles Film Festival & Market
Berlin International Film Festival
Bombay International Film Festival for
    Documentary, Short and Animation Films
Bondy Cinema Festival
Chinese Film Festival
Cinema Out - Orange County, South Bay
    Beaches & Long Beach
Cinemas D'afrique "African Cinema Festival"
Festival der Festivals
Festival International du ler Film et de la
    Jeunesse
Freedom Film Festival
Gothenburg Film Festival
Hiroshima International Amateur Film and
    Video Festival
Hollywood Black Film Festival
International Animated Film and Cartoon
    Festival
International Lesbian Film Festival
    Immaginaria
Malibu Film Festival
Miami Film Festival
Moxie! / Santa Monica Film Festival
Outfar! - Annual Phoenix International
    Lesbian and Gay Film Festival
Pan African Film & Arts Festival
Phoenix Film Festival
Portland International Film Festival
San Diego International Film Festival
Sydney Mardi Gras Film Festival/Queer
    Screen Ltd.

Texas Film Festival
United States Super 8 Film/Video Festival
University of Oregon Queer Film Festival
Victoria Independent Film and Video Festival

FEBRUARY-MARCH

Big Muddy Film Festival
Cinequest Film Festival
Fantasporto / Oporto International Film
Festival
Festival for Nature and Environment Films
St. Petersburg Documentary Festival "Message
to Man Nonfiction Film Festival"

MARCH

Amateur/Professional International Film
Festival
Ankara International Film Festival
Ann Arbor Film Festival
Baca Film and Video Festival
Bare Bones International Film Festival
Bergamo International Week of Auteur Film
Bienal Nacion Cajalicante de Cine Amateur
de Libre Creacion
Bilan du Film Ethnographique
Carolina Film and Video Festival
Cartagena International Film Festival
Certamen de Cine Amateur
Certamen Internacional de Cine
Cortometraje
Cinema du Reel
Cleveland International Film Festival
Cucalorus Film Festival
Dallas Video Festival
Dublin Film Festival
Durango Film Festival
Festival de Cine Iberoamericano para
Largometrages de Ficcion
Festival de Film Sur L'art "Liege Art Film
Festival"
Festival International du Court Metrage de
Mons "Mons Short Film Festival"
Festival International du Film Fantastique, de
Science Fiction Thriller de Bruxelles
Firstglance: Philadelphia Independent Film
and Video Festival
Flo Film Fest
Hi Mom! Film Festival
Humboldt International Film and Video
Festival
International Documentary Film Festival
International Festival of Films On Art "Fifart
Festival"

International Film and Video Competition
"IAC Competition"
International Women's Film Festival
Istanbul Short Film and Video Festival
Johns Hopkins Film Festival
Local Heroes International Screen Festival
Melbourne Queer Film & Video Festival
Moomba International Amateur Film Festival
New York Underground Film Festival
Norrkoping Film Festival Flimmer
San Francisco International Asian American
Film Festival
Santa Barbara International Film Festival
(SBIFF)
Santa Clarita International Film Festival
Sedona International Film Festival and
Workshop
SXSW: South by Southwest Film Festival
Tampere Film Festival
Tampere International Short Film Festival
Valleyfest Independent Film Festival
Whistler International Film & Television

MARCH-APRIL

Ales Cinema Festival - Itinerances
Festival International du Film Medical de
Mauriac "Mauriac Film Festival"
International Celtic Film and Television
Festival
New England Film and Video Festival
Newport Beach Film Festival
Wisconsin Film Festival

APRIL

AFI DVCam Fest Sponsored by Sony
Amateur and Non-Professional Film and
Video Festival
Animania: International Festival of
Animation and Multimedia
Arizona International Film Festival
Arizona State University Short Film and
Video Festival
Art Movie
Aspen Shortsfest
Bermuda International Film Festival
Beverly Hills Film Festival
Certamen de Cine y Video Etnologico de las
Communidades Autonmas
Certamen Internacional de Cine y Video
Agrario
Charlotte Film and Video Festival
Cognac International Film Festival of the
Thriller

Denver Pan African Film Festival
Hometown Cinema Inc
Hong Kong International Film Festival
    (HKIFF)
Houston International Film and Video
    Festival—Annual Worldfest "Worldfest
    Houston"
Images Festival of Independent Film and
    Video
Indiurban Independent Film Festival
International Film Festival of Montevideo
    and Punta del Este
International Wildlife Film Festival
Kansas City Filmmakers Jubilee
Los Angeles Independent Film Festival
    (LAIFF)
Los Angeles Italian Film Awards (LAIFA)
Maryland Film Festival
Miami Gay and Lesbian Film Festival
New York Lower East Side Film Festival
Palm Beach International Film Festival
Roger Ebert's Overlooked Film Festival
São Paulo International Short Film Festival
Schwule Filmwoche Freiburg—Gay Film
    Festival of Freiburg
Silver Images Film Festival
Singapore International Film Festival
Taos Talking Pictures Festival
Turin International Gay & Lesbian Film
    Festival "From Sodom To Hollywood"
USA Film Festival
Videoeiras Festival
Washington, DC International Film Festival—
    Filmfest DC
Thaw Video, Film, and Digital Media Festival

APRIL-MAY

African Film Festival
Athens International Film and Video Festival
Chicago Latino Film Festival
Docfest - New York International
    Documentary Festival
Hot Docs Canadian International
    Documentary Festival
International Animation Festival
International Electronic Cinema Festival
International Short Film Festival Oberhausen
Onedotzero Digital Creativity Festival
Philadelphia Festival of World Cinema
Pink Apple - Schwullesbisches Filmfestival
San Francisco International Film Festival

MAY

Africas Cinema
Argeles-Sur-Mer Cinema Forum
Asolo International Animation Festival
Barcelona Asian Film Festival (Muestra de
    Cine Asiático de Barcelona)
Birmingham International Educational Film
    Festival
Boston Gay & Lesbian Film & Video Festival
Brighton Festival
BWAC Film & Video Festival
Cannes Film Festival
Certamen de Video Elies Rogent
    Rehabilitacio i Restauracio
Charlotte Gay & Lesbian Film Series
    Presented by Outcharlotte
Cork Youth International Film, Video and
    Arts Festival
Doubletake Documentary Film Festival
Festival Internacional de Cinema Do Algarve
Gen Art Film Festival
Helsinki International Film Festival—Love
    and Anarchy
Hudson Valley Film Festival
Inside Out Lesbian and Gay Film Festival of
    Toronto
International Animation Festival, Cardiff,
    Wales
International Festival of Comedy Films
International Festival of Documentaries of
    the Sea
L. A. Asian Pacific Film Video Festival
Miami Underground Film & Video Festival
    (Online)
Mountainfilm
Muskegon Film Festival
Olympia — Gender Queer: Northwest
    Transgender and Intersex Film
Partnership for Peace International Film
    Festival
Rochester International Independent Film
    Festival
Tech TV's Cam Film Festival
West Virginia International Film Festival
Yorkton Short Film and Video Festival

MAY-JUNE

Annecy International Animated Film Festival
Beijing International Children's Film Festival
China International Sports Film Festival
Festival of Short Films—Krakow
Honolulu Gay & Lesbian Film Festival
Houston Gay and Lesbian Film Festival

New York International Latino Film Festival
Out Takes
Prix Danube Festival
Seattle International Film Festival

JUNE

American Short Shorts
Annual American Indian Film and Video
    Competition
Arcipelago Short Film Festival
Art Film Festival Trencianske Teplice
Atlanta Film and Video Festival
Aurora Asian Film Festival
Austrian Film Days "Film Fest Wels"
Bellaria Independent Cinema Festival
Cabourg Festival of Romantic Films
Caribbean Film Festival
Chicago Alt.Film Fest
Cities Video Festival
Connecticut Gay & Lesbian Film Festival
Dances With Films
Dylan Dog Horror Festival
European Film Festival
Festival of International Film for Youth and
    Children
Flickapalooza Film Festival
Florida Film Festival
Fort Worth — Q Cinema - Fort Worth's Gay
    & Lesbian Film Festival
Giornate Professionali di Cinema
Global Africa International Film and Video
    Festival
Golden Shower Video Festival
Huesca Film Festival
Human Rights Watch International Film
    Festival
International Film Festival of Festivals
Japan International Film & Video Festival of
    Adventure and Sports
Kansas City Gay & Lesbian Film Festival
Kine International Film Festival
Lake Placid Film Forum
Maui Film Festival
Melbourne International Film and Video
    Festival
Method Fest
Midnight Sun Film Festival
Nantucket Film Festival
Nashville Independent Film Festival
New York Gay and Lesbian Film Festival (The
    New Festival)
Newport International Film Festival
North Devon Film Festival
Norwegian Short Film Festival

Potsdam Film Festival
Prix Jeunesse International
Saguaro Film Festival
San Francisco Lesbian and Gay Film Festival
Sydney Film Festival
US International Film & Video Festival
Waterfront Film Festival

JUNE-JULY

Filmfest Munchen
International Documentary, Short and
    Animated Films Festival
International Mystery Film Festival "Mystfest"
Marin County National Film and Video
    Festival

JULY

Ambiente-Incontri Film Festival
    Internazionale su Natura e Ambiente
Asian American International Film Festival
Auckland International Film Festival
Brasilia Film Festival
Cambridge International Film Festival
Certamen Internacional de Ciny y Video
    Turistico—Oriente de Asturias de Llanes
Cevennes Festival of International Video
Da Vinci Film and Video Festival
Eat My Shorts
Fantasia Film Festival
Festival de Cine L'alfas del Pi
Giffoni Film Festival
Great Plains Film Festival
Hometown Video Festival
Indiana Film and Video Festival
Interfest Moscow International Film Festival
International Festival of Comedy Films of
    Vevey
International Film Festival for Children and
    Young People
Jerusalem International Film Festival
Karlovy Vary International Film Festival
Maine Student Film and Video Festival
New York International Video Festival
Outfest: Los Angeles International Gay and
    Lesbian Film & Video Festival
Philadelphia International Gay and Lesbian
    Film Festival
San Francisco Jewish Film Festival
Short Poppies: International Festival of
    Student Film and Video
Stony Brook Film Festival
The New Zealand Film Festival
Wellington Film Festival and Aukland
    International Film Festival

The Festival of Fantastic Films
Toronto International Film Festival
Woodstock Film Festival

SEPTEMBER-OCTOBER

Aspen Filmfest
Black Filmworks Festival of Film and Video
Com & Com Comedy and Comedic Film
    Festival
Cripple Creek Film Festival
Festival International du Film Francophone—
    Namur
Los Angeles International Short Film Festival
New York Film Festival
Tokyo International Fantastic Film Festival
Tokyo International Film Festival
Vancouver International Film Festival

OCTOBER

Agrofilm Festival
American Film Institute (AFI) - Los Angeles
    International Film Festival
Austin Film Festival & Heart of Film
    Screenwriters Conference
Bastia Film Festival of Mediterranean
    Cultures
Bruno 16 International Noncommercial Film
    and Video Festival
Burbank International Childrens Film Festival
Certamen Internacional Badalona
Certamen Internacional de Cine Amateur—
    Ciutat D'igualada
Certamen Nacional de Cine Silencioso
Chicago International Children's Film Festival
    (Cicff)
Chicago International Film Festival
China International Scientific Film Festival
Cinematexas International Short Film &
    Video Festival
CMJ Filmfest
Columbus International Film and Video
    Festival "Chris Awards"
Copenhagen Film Festival
Cork International Film Festival
Denver International Film Festival
Dunkirk Cinema Forum
Festival de Geneve des Expoirs du Cinema
    Europeen
Festival Internacional de Cine Fantastico
Festival International de Cine de Vina del Mar
Festival of Arts Cinema for Children
Flanders International Film Festival—Ghent
Freaky Film Festival (FFF)

Gay and Lesbian Arts Festival of Oklahoma,
    Inc. dba Outart
Geneva Film Festival
Haifa International Film Festival
Hamptons International Film Festival
Heartland Film Festival
Hot Springs Documentary Film Festival
International Cinema and Television
    Multimedia Market—MIFED
International Festival of Films on Art "Fifart
    Festival"
International Filmfestival
International Leipzig Festival for
    Documentary and Animated Film
Israel Film Festival
Jewish Film Festival—London
Kudzu Film Festival (aka Athens Film
    Festival)
Kyiv International Film Festival, Molodist
Leeds International Film Festival
Marco Island Film Festival
Mill Valley Film Festival
Montreal International Festival of New
    Cinema and New Media
New Orleans Film and Video Festival
Next Frame: UFVA's Touring Festival of
    International Student Film and Video
Palm Springs Gay & Lesbian Film Festival
Pordenone Silent Film Festival
Reel Affirmations Film Festival
Sacramento International Gay and Lesbian
    Film Festival
São Paulo International Film Festival
Seattle Lesbian & Gay Film Festival
Sheffield International Documentary Festival
Sitges International Film Festival of Catalonia
Small Pictures International Film Festival
    (SPIFF)
Turku Lesbian and Gay Film Festival
Twin Rivers Media Festival
United Nations Association Film Festival
Uppsala International Short Film Festival
Vermont International Film Festival: Images
    and Issues for Social Change
Viennale—Vienna International Film Festival
Virginia Film Festival
Warsaw Film Festival
Yamagata International Documentary Film
    Festival

OCTOBER-NOVEMBER

Animated Films About Science "Animascience Festival"
Barcelona International Exhibition of Gay and Lesbian Films
Clisson Film Festival
Copenhagen Gay and Lesbian Film Festival
Festival du Film D'animation Pour la Jeunesse
Fort Lauderdale Int'l Film Festival
Kinofilm, Manchester International Short Film & Video Festival
Savannah Film and Video Festival

NOVEMBER

Angelus Awards Student Film Festival
Armed Forces and People Film Festival
Around the World Festival
Banff Festival of Mountain Films
Beijing International Scientific Film Festival
Berkeley Video and Film Festival
Bienal de Cine Y Video Cientifico Espanol
Birmingham International Film and TV Festival
Brest Short Film Festival
British Cinema Festival
British Film Festival
Cadiz International Video Festival
Canyonlands Film & Video Festival
Carrefour International de L'audiovisuel Scientific
Coca-Cola Johannesburg International Student Film Festival
Deep Ellum Film Festival
Dundee Mountain Film Festival
Euro Underground
Exground—Das Filmfest
Festival Dei Popoli
Festival Internacional de Barcelona de Cine y Video No Professionales
Festival Internacional de Cine Ecologico y de La Naturaleza
Festival Internacional de Cine Espeleologico de Barcelona
Festival Internacional de Cine Realizado Por Mujeres
Film + Arc International Film Festival
Filmfest Braunschweig
Gijon International Film Festival for Young People
Gran Premio de Cine Espanol
Hawaii International Film Festival
International Animated Film Festival—Cinanima

International Festival of Documentary and Short Film of Bilbao
International Thessaloniki Film Festival
Jamerican Film and Music Festival
Junior Dublin Film Festival
Kasseler Dokumentarfilm—Und Videofest
Kino American Underground & Student Showcase Film Fest
La Lesbian Film Festival
London Film Festival
Margaret Mead Film Festival
Microcinefest
New York Expo of Short Film and Video
New York Lesbian and Gay Experimental Film and Video Festival (Mix Festival)
Northampton Film Festival
Northwest Film & Video Festival
Ohio Independent Film Festival
Okomedia International Ecological Film Festival
Out Takes Dallas—The Annual Lesbian and Gay Film Festival
Polish Film Festival
Puerto Rico International Film Festival
Queersicht - Schwul-Lesbisches Filmfestival Bern
Rio de Janeiro International Short Film Festival
River City Film Festival
St. Louis International Film Festival
Stockholm International Film Festival
Torino Film Festival
Vancouver Underground Film Festival
Ways in Being Gay (Biannual)
Welsh International Film Festival

NOVEMBER-DECEMBER

Cairo International Film Festival
Cinevegas Film Festival
Contemporary African Diaspora Film Festival
Entrevues Film Festival
Europacinema Festival
Festival Internacional Cinematografico de Cancun
International Film Festival of the Art of Cinematography "Cameraimage Festival"
International Gay and Lesbian Film Festival
Tyneside International Film Festival

DECEMBER

Asia-Pacific Film Festival
Biennale Internationale du Film
    D'architecture, D'urbanisme et
    D'environment de Bordeaux "Fifarc
    Festival"
Certamen Internacional de Video
Festival Internacional de Cine de Comedia
Florence Film Festival
International Documentary Film Festival
    Amsterdam (IDFA)
International Festival of New Latin-American
    Cinema
International Video Contest
Mystery and Noir Film Festival
Shanghai International Animation Film
    Festival
Telluride Indiefest

iNDEX OF FiLM FESTiVALS BY GENRE

AMERiCAN FiLMS
Acapulco Black Film Festival
American Film Institute (AFI)—Los Angeles
  International Film Festival
American Short Shorts
Arizona State University Short Film and
  Video Festival
Bangkok Film Festival
Bermuda International Film Festival
Brainwash Movie Festival
Charlotte Gay & Lesbian Film Series
  Presented by Outcharlotte
Chicago International Film Festival
Cinematexas International Short Film &
  Video Festival
Cleveland International Film Festival
Cork International Film Festival
Cucalorus Film Festival
Dances With Films
Deep Ellum Film Festival
Edmonds International Film Festival
Exground—Das Filmfest
Fantasia Film Festival
Film Nite
Fort Lauderdale Int'l Film Festival
Freaky Film Festival (FFF)
Free Film Festival Fitchburg (The F4)
Gay and Lesbian Arts Festival of Oklahoma,
  Inc. dba Outart
Gen Art Film Festival
Golden Shower Video Festival
Hollywood Black Film Festival
Johns Hopkins Film Festival
La Lesbian Film Festival
Lake Placid Film Forum
Los Angeles Independent Film Festival
  (LAIFF)
Marco Island Film Festival
Melbourne Queer Film & Video Festival
Miami Film Festival
Miami Underground Film & Video Festival
  (Online)
Mill Valley Film Festival
Moondance International Film Festival
No Dance Film Festival

Norrkoping Film Festival Flimmer
Northwest Film & Video Festival
Ohio Independent Film Festival
Out in Akron Queer Shorts Film Festival
Outfar!—Annual Phoenix International
  Lesbian and Gay Film Festival
Portland International Film Festival
Rhode Island International Film Festival
San Francisco Independent Film Festival (aka
  SF Indiefest)
San Francisco International Film Festival
Savannah Film and Video Festival
Seattle Underground Film Festival
Sedona International Film Festival and
  Workshop
Stony Brook Film Festival
Temecula Valley International Film Festival
Turin International Gay & Lesbian Film
  Festival "From Sodom To Hollywood"
University of Oregon Queer Film Festival
USA Film Festival
Valleyfest Independent Film Festival
Victoria Independent Film and Video Festival
Washington, DC International Film Festival—
  Filmfest DC
Waterfront Film Festival
Williamstown Film Festival
Wisconsin Film Festival
Zoiefest!

ANiMATiON
American Short Shorts
Angelciti Los Angeles Film Festival & Market
Angelus Awards Student Film Festival
Animania: International Festival of
  Animation and Multimedia
Animated Films About Science "Animascience
  Festival"
Annecy International Animated Film Festival
Antimatter Festival of Underground Short
  Film & Video
Arizona State University Short Film and
  Video Festival
Asolo International Animation Festival

Atlanta Film and Video Festival
Bermuda International Film Festival
Beverly Hills Film Festival
Blue Sky International Film Festival
Bombay International Film Festival for
   Documentary, Short and Animation Films
Brainwash Movie Festival
Charged 60-Second Film Festival
Chicago International Children's Film Festival
   (CICFF)
Chicago International Film Festival
Chicago Latino Film Festival
Cinematexas International Short Film &
   Video Festival
Columbus International Film and Video
   Festival "Chris Awards"
Cripple Creek Film Festival
Cucalorus Film Festival
D.Film Digital Film Festival
Da Vinci Film and Video Festival
Dallas Video Festival
Deep Ellum Film Festival
Edmonds International Film Festival
Exground—Das Filmfest
Fantasia Film Festival
Festival du Film D'animation Pour la Jeunesse
Film Nite
Filmfest Braunschweig
Filmfest Munchen
Firstglance: Philadelphia Independent Film
   and Video Festival
Freaky Film Festival (FFF)
Gay and Lesbian Arts Festival of Oklahoma,
   Inc. dba Outart
Gen Art Film Festival
Golden Shower Video Festival
Heartland Film Festival
Holland Animation Film Festival
Hollywood Black Film Festival
Images Festival of Independent Film and
   Video
Independent Exposure
International Animated Film Festival—
   Cinanima
International Animation Festival
International Animation Festival, Cardiff,
   Wales
International Animation Festival—Japan,
   Hiroshima
International Documentary, Short and
   Animated Films Festival
International Festival of Animated Film
   Stuttgart
International Leipzig Festival for
   Documentary and Animated Film
Johns Hopkins Film Festival
Kansas City Filmmakers Jubilee

Lake Placid Film Forum
Los Angeles Independent Film Festival
   (LAIFF)
The Lost Film Festival
Madcat Women's International Film Festival
Marco Island Film Festival
Maui Film Festival
Melbourne Queer Film & Video Festival
Miami Film Festival
Miami Underground Film & Video Festival
   (Online)
Moondance International Film Festival
New York Lower East Side Film Festival
Newport Beach Film Festival
Newport International Film Festival
Next Frame: UFVA's Touring Festival of
   International Student Film and Video
Norrkoping Film Festival Flimmer
Northampton Film Festival
Northwest Film & Video Festival
Ohio Independent Film Festival
Ottawa International Animation Festival
Outfar!—Annual Phoenix International
   Lesbian and Gay Film Festival
Rhode Island International Film Festival
San Diego International Film Festival
San Francisco Independent Film Festival (aka
   SF Indiefest)
San Francisco International Film Festival
Santa Clarita International Film Festival
Savannah Film and Video Festival
Sedona International Film Festival and
   Workshop
Shanghai International Animation Film
   Festival
Short Attention Span Film and Video Festival
   (SASFVF)
Silver Lake Film Festival
Sitges International Film Festival of Catalonia
Stony Brook Film Festival
Temecula Valley International Film Festival
Thaw Video, Film, and Digital Media Festival
Toronto Worldwide Short Film Festival
Tromadance Film Festival
University of Oregon Queer Film Festival
Uppsala International Short Film Festival
USAFilm Festival
Valleyfest Independent Film Festival
Vancouver Island Media Fest
Victoria Independent Film and Video Festival
West Virginia International Film Festival
Whistler International Film & Television
Wisconsin Film Festival
World Festival of Animated Films in Zagreb
Zoiefest!

DiGiTAL

AFI DVCam Fest Sponsored by Sony
American Film Institute (AFI)—Los Angeles
    International Film Festival
American Short Shorts
Antimatter Festival of Underground Short
    Film & Video
Chicago Latino Film Festival
Cinematexas International Short Film &
    Video Festival
D.Film Digital Film Festival
Deep Ellum Film Festival
Edmonds International Film Festival
Golden Shower Video Festival
Hamburg International Short Film Festival
Hollywood Black Film Festival
Independent Exposure
Lake Placid Film Forum
Los Angeles Independent Film Festival
    (LAIFF)
Lost Film Festival
Madcat Women's International Film Festival
Miami Film Festival
Miami Underground Film & Video Festival
    (Online)
Montreal International Festival of New
    Cinema and New Media
No Dance Film Festival
Norrkoping Film Festival Flimmer
Northwest Film & Video Festival
Ohio Independent Film Festival
Resfest Digital Film Festival
Rhode Island International Film Festival
San Francisco Independent Film Festival (aka
    SF Indiefest)
Santa Barbara International Film Festival
    (SBIFF)
Seattle Underground Film Festival
Short Attention Span Film and Video Festival
    (SASFVF)
Silver Lake Film Festival
Small Pictures International Film Festival
    (SPIFF)
Tech TV's Cam Film Festival
Temecula Valley International Film Festival
Thaw Video, Film, and Digital Media Festival
Tromadance Film Festival
Vancouver Island Media Fest
Whistler International Film & Television
Woodstock Film Festival
Zoiefest!

DiGiTAL ANiMATiON

American Short Shorts
Antimatter Festival of Underground Short
    Film & Video
Arizona State University Short Film and
    Video Festival
Chicago Latino Film Festival
Cinematexas International Short Film &
    Video Festival
Cork International Film Festival
Dances With Films
Edmonds International Film Festival
Exground—Das Filmfest
Fantasia Film Festival
Golden Shower Video Festival
Hamburg International Short Film Festival
Hometown Cinema Inc
Independent Exposure
Lake Placid Film Forum
Los Angeles Independent Film Festival
    (LAIFF)
Lost Film Festival
Madcat Women's International Film Festival
Miami Underground Film & Video Festival
    (Online)
Moxie! / Santa Monica Film Festival
Nashville Independent Film Festival
Ohio Independent Film Festival
Resfest Digital Film Festival
Rhode Island International Film Festival
San Francisco Independent Film Festival (aka
    SF Indiefest)
Short Attention Span Film and Video Festival
    (SASFVF)
Thaw Video, Film, and Digital Media Festival
Toronto Worldwide Short Film Festival
Tromadance Film Festival
Valleyfest Independent Film Festival
Vancouver Island Media Fest
Whistler International Film & Television
Zoiefest!

DOCUMENTARY

AFI DVCam Fest Sponsored by Sony
American Film Institute (AFI)—Los Angeles
    International Film Festival
American Short Shorts
Angelciti Los Angeles Film Festival & Market
Angelus Awards Student Film Festival
Antimatter Festival of Underground Short
    Film & Video
Arizona State University Short Film and
    Video Festival
Aspen Filmfest
Aspen Shortsfest
Atlanta Film and Video Festival

B-Movie Film Festival
Bangkok Film Festival
Bermuda International Film Festival
Blue Sky International Film Festival
Bombay International Film Festival for
Documentary, Short and Animation Films
Brussels Gay and Lesbian Film Festival
Festival du Film Gay et Lesbien de
Bruxelles
Brussels International Cinema Festival
Charlotte Gay & Lesbian Film Series
Presented by Outcharlotte
Chicago International Film Festival
Chicago Latino Film Festival
Cinematexas International Short Film &
Video Festival
Cleveland International Film Festival
Cork International Film Festival
Cripple Creek Film Festival
Cucalorus Film Festival
D.Film Digital Film Festival
Da Vinci Film and Video Festival
Dallas Video Festival
Dances With Films
Deep Ellum Film Festival
Docfest—New York International
Documentary Festival
Documental
Doubletake Documentary Film Festival
Durango Film Festival
Exground—Das Filmfest
Festival du Film Gay et Lesbien de Bruxelles
(Brussels Gay and Lesbian Film Festival)
Festival of Deauville for American Cinema
"Le Festival du Cinema Americain in
Deauville"
Film Nite
Filmfest Munchen
Firstglance: Philadelphia Independent Film
and Video Festival
Fort Lauderdale Int'l Film Festival
Freaky Film Festival (FFF)
Free Film Festival Fitchburg (The F4)
Gay and Lesbian Arts Festival of Oklahoma,
Inc. dba Outart
Gen Art Film Festival
Golden Shower Video Festival
Heartland Film Festival
Hollywood Black Film Festival
Hot Docs Canadian International
Documentary Festival
Hot Springs Documentary Film Festival
Images Festival of Independent Film and
Video
Independent Exposure
Indiurban Independent Film Festival
International Documentary Film Festival

International Documentary Film Festival
Amsterdam (IDFA)
International Documentary, Short and
Animated Films Festival
International Festival of Documentaries of
the Sea
International Festival of Documentary and
Science Films
International Festival of Documentary and
Short Film of Bilbao
International Film Festival Rotterdam
International Gay and Lesbian Film Festival
International Leipzig Festival for
Documentary and Animated Film
International Lesbian Film Festival
Immaginaria
Johns Hopkins Film Festival
Kansas City Filmmakers Jubilee
Kasseler Dokumentarfilm—Und Videofest
La Lesbian Film Festival
Lake Placid Film Forum
Los Angeles Independent Film Festival
(LAIFF)
Los Angeles Latino International Film Festival
Lost Film Festival
Madcat Women's International Film Festival
Marco Island Film Festival
Maui Film Festival
Media Alliance Film Festival
Melbourne Queer Film & Video Festival
Miami Film Festival
Miami Underground Film & Video Festival
(Online)
Montreal's International Lesbian & Gay Film
and Video Festival
Moondance International Film Festival
Mountainfilm
Nashville Independent Film Festival
New York International Latino Film Festival
New York Lower East Side Film Festival
Newport Beach Film Festival
Next Frame: UFVA's Touring Festival of
International Student Film and Video
No Dance Film Festival
Norrkoping Film Festival Flimmer
Northampton Film Festival
Northwest Film & Video Festival
Nyon International Documentary Film
Festival
Ohio Independent Film Festival
Outfar!—Annual Phoenix International
Lesbian and Gay Film Festival
Portland International Film Festival
PXL This
Rhode Island International Film Festival
River City Film Festival
Rotterdam International Film Festival

Sacramento International Gay and Lesbian Film Festival

San Francisco Independent Film Festival (aka SF Indiefest)

San Francisco International Asian American Film Festival

San Francisco International Film Festival

Santa Barbara International Film Festival (SBIFF)

Santa Clarita International Film Festival

Savannah Film and Video Festival

Schwule Filmwoche Freiburg Gay Film Festival of Freiburg

Seattle International Film Festival

Seattle Underground Film Festival

Sedona International Film Festival and Workshop

Sheffield International Documentary Festival

Silver Images Film Festival

Silver Lake Film Festival

Sitges International Film Festival of Catalonia

St. Louis International Film Festival

St. Louis International Lesbian & Gay (SLILAG) Film Festival

St. Petersburg Documentary Festival "Message To Man Nonfiction Film Festival"

Stony Brook Film Festival

Temecula Valley International Film Festival

Thaw Video, Film, and Digital Media Festival

Toronto Worldwide Short Film Festival

Tube Film Festival

Turin International Gay & Lesbian Film Festival "From Sodom To Hollywood"

United Nations Association Film Festival

University of Oregon Queer Film Festival

Uppsala International Short Film Festival

Urbanworld Film Festival

Valleyfest Independent Film Festival

Vancouver International Film Festival

Victoria Independent Film and Video Festival

West Virginia International Film Festival

Wisconsin Film Festival

Woodstock Film Festival

Yamagata International Documentary Film Festival

Zoiefest!

DVD

American Short Shorts

Antimatter Festival of Underground Short Film & Video

Cinematexas International Short Film & Video Festival

Edmonds International Film Festival

Kasseler Dokumentarfilm—Und Videofest

Lake Placid Film Forum

Los Angeles Independent Film Festival (LAIFF)

Madcat Women's International Film Festival

Miami Underground Film & Video Festival (Online)

No Dance Film Festival

Onedotzero: Digital Moving Image Festival

Resfest Digital Film Festival

Rhode Island International Film Festival

San Francisco Independent Film Festival (aka SF Indiefest)

Thaw Video, Film, and Digital Media Festival

Tromadance Film Festival

Vancouver Island Media Fest

Whistler International Film & Television

Williamstown Film Festival

Zoiefest!

ETHNIC AFRICAN

Angelciti Los Angeles Film Festival & Market

Antimatter Festival of Underground Short Film & Video

Arizona State University Short Film and Video Festival

Bermuda International Film Festival

Beverly Hills Film Festival

Charlotte Gay & Lesbian Film Series Presented by Outcharlotte

Chicago International Film Festival

Cinematexas International Short Film & Video Festival

Coca-Cola Johannesburg International Student Film Festival

Cork International Film Festival

Dances With Films

Edmonds International Film Festival

Fantasia Film Festival

Film Nite

Fort Lauderdale Int'l Film Festival

Freaky Film Festival (FFF)

Gay and Lesbian Arts Festival of Oklahoma, Inc. dba Outart

Golden Shower Video Festival

La Lesbian Film Festival

Los Angeles Independent Film Festival (LAIFF)

Lost Film Festival

Madcat Women's International Film Festival

Melbourne Queer Film & Video Festival

Miami Film Festival

Miami Underground Film & Video Festival (Online)

Ohio Independent Film Festival

Rhode Island International Film Festival

Sedona International Film Festival and Workshop

Tromadance Film Festival
Washington, DC International Film Festival—
Filmfest DC
Wisconsin Film Festival
Zoiefest!

Urbanworld Film Festival
Valleyfest Independent Film Festival
Washington, DC International Film Festival—
Filmfest DC
Wisconsin Film Festival

ETHNiC ASiAN

American Film Institute (AFI)—Los Angeles
International Film Festival
Angelciti Los Angeles Film Festival & Market
Antimatter Festival of Underground Short
Film & Video
Arizona State University Short Film and
Video Festival
Bangkok Film Festival
Barcelona Asian Film Festival (Muestra de
Cine Asiático de Barcelona)
Bermuda International Film Festival
Beverly Hills Film Festival
Charlotte Gay & Lesbian Film Series
Presented by Outcharlotte
Chicago International Film Festival
Chicago Latino Film Festival
Cinematexas International Short Film &
Video Festival
Cleveland International Film Festival
Cork International Film Festival
Dances With Films
Edmonds International Film Festival
Exground—Das Filmfest
Fantasia Film Festival
Fort Lauderdale Int'l Film Festival
Freaky Film Festival (FFF)
Gay and Lesbian Arts Festival of Oklahoma,
Inc. dba Outart
Golden Shower Video Festival
Hawaii International Film Festival
Kinofilm, Manchester International Short
Film & Video Festival
La Lesbian Film Festival
Los Angeles Independent Film Festival
(LAIFF)
Lost Film Festival
Madcat Women's International Film Festival
Melbourne Queer Film & Video Festival
Miami Film Festival
Miami Underground Film & Video Festival
(Online)
Ohio Independent Film Festival
Rhode Island International Film Festival
San Francisco Independent Film Festival (aka
SF Indiefest)
Sedona International Film Festival and
Workshop
Temecula Valley International Film Festival
Tromadance Film Festival

ETHNiC BLACK

Acapulco Black Film Festival
Africas Cinema
Angelciti Los Angeles Film Festival & Market
Antimatter Festival of Underground Short
Film & Video
Arizona State University Short Film and
Video Festival
Bermuda International Film Festival
Beverly Hills Film Festival
Black Filmworks Festival of Film and Video
Black Talkies On Parade Film Festival
Charlotte Gay & Lesbian Film Series
Presented by Outcharlotte
Chicago International Film Festival
Chicago Latino Film Festival
Cinemas D'afrique "African Cinema Festival"
Cinematexas International Short Film &
Video Festival
Cleveland International Film Festival
Cork International Film Festival
Dances With Films
Edmonds International Film Festival
Fantasia Film Festival
Fort Lauderdale Int'l Film Festival
Freaky Film Festival (FFF)
Gay and Lesbian Arts Festival of Oklahoma,
Inc. dba Outart
Golden Shower Video Festival
Hollywood Black Film Festival
Kinofilm, Manchester International Short
Film & Video Festival
La Lesbian Film Festival
Los Angeles Independent Film Festival
(LAIFF)
Lost Film Festival
Madcat Women's International Film Festival
Melbourne Queer Film & Video Festival
Miami Film Festival
Miami Underground Film & Video Festival
(Online)
Ohio Independent Film Festival
Rhode Island International Film Festival
San Francisco Independent Film Festival (aka
SF Indiefest)
Seattle Underground Film Festival
Sedona International Film Festival and
Workshop
Silver Lake Film Festival
St. Louis International Film Festival

Temecula Valley International Film Festival
Tromadance Film Festival
Urbanworld Film Festival
Valleyfest Independent Film Festival
Washington, DC International Film Festival—
   Filmfest DC
Wisconsin Film Festival
Zoiefest!

ETHNiC JEWiSH

Angelciti Los Angeles Film Festival & Market
Antimatter Festival of Underground Short
   Film & Video
Arizona State University Short Film and
   Video Festival
Bermuda International Film Festival
Beverly Hills Film Festival
Charlotte Gay & Lesbian Film Series
   Presented by Outcharlotte
Chicago International Film Festival
Chicago Latino Film Festival
Cinematexas International Short Film &
   Video Festival
Cork International Film Festival
Dances With Films
Edmonds International Film Festival
Fantasia Film Festival
Fort Lauderdale Int'l Film Festival
Freaky Film Festival (FFF)
Gay and Lesbian Arts Festival of Oklahoma,
   Inc. dba Outart
Golden Shower Video Festival
La Lesbian Film Festival
Los Angeles Independent Film Festival
   (LAIFF)
Lost Film Festival
Madcat Women's International Film Festival
Melbourne Queer Film & Video Festival
Miami Film Festival
Miami Underground Film & Video Festival
   (Online)
Ohio Independent Film Festival
Rhode Island International Film Festival
San Francisco Jewish Film Festival
Sedona International Film Festival and
   Workshop
Silver Lake Film Festival
Temecula Valley International Film Festival
Tromadance Film Festival
Valleyfest Independent Film Festival
Washington, DC International Film Festival—
   Filmfest DC
Wisconsin Film Festival
Zoiefest!

ETHNiC LATiN

American Film Institute (AFI)—Los Angeles
   International Film Festival
Angelciti Los Angeles Film Festival & Market
Antimatter Festival of Underground Short
   Film & Video
Arizona State University Short Film and
   Video Festival
Bermuda International Film Festival
Beverly Hills Film Festival
Charlotte Gay & Lesbian Film Series
   Presented by Outcharlotte
Chicago International Film Festival
Chicago Latino Film Festival
Cine Acción ¡Cine Latino!
Cinematexas International Short Film &
   Video Festival
Cleveland International Film Festival
Cork International Film Festival
Dances With Films
Deep Ellum Film Festival
Edmonds International Film Festival
Fantasia Film Festival
Fort Lauderdale Int'l Film Festival
Freaky Film Festival (FFF)
Golden Shower Video Festival
La Lesbian Film Festival
Los Angeles Independent Film Festival
   (LAIFF)
Los Angeles Latino International Film Festival
Lost Film Festival
Madcat Women's International Film Festival
Melbourne Queer Film & Video Festival
Miami Film Festival
Miami Underground Film & Video Festival
   (Online)
Moxie! / Santa Monica Film Festival
Ohio Independent Film Festival
Rhode Island International Film Festival
San Francisco Independent Film Festival (aka
   SF Indiefest)
Sedona International Film Festival and
   Workshop
Tromadance Film Festival
Urbanworld Film Festival
Washington, DC International Film Festival—
   Filmfest DC
Wisconsin Film Festival
Zoiefest!

ETHNiC SPANiSH

Angelciti Los Angeles Film Festival & Market
Antimatter Festival of Underground Short
   Film & Video
Arizona State University Short Film and
   Video Festival

Bermuda International Film Festival
Beverly Hills Film Festival
Charlotte Gay & Lesbian Film Series
  Presented by Outcharlotte
Chicago International Film Festival
Chicago Latino Film Festival
Cinematexas International Short Film &
  Video Festival
Cleveland International Film Festival
Cork International Film Festival
Dances With Films
Edmonds International Film Festival
Fantasia Film Festival
Fort Lauderdale Int'l Film Festival
Freaky Film Festival (FFF)
Gay and Lesbian Arts Festival of Oklahoma,
  Inc. dba Outart
Golden Shower Video Festival
La Lesbian Film Festival
Los Angeles Independent Film Festival
  (LAIFF)
Lost Film Festival
Madcat Women's International Film Festival
Melbourne Queer Film & Video Festival
Miami Film Festival
Miami Underground Film & Video Festival
  (Online)
Moxie! / Santa Monica Film Festival
Ohio Independent Film Festival
Rhode Island International Film Festival
Sedona International Film Festival and
  Workshop
Temecula Valley International Film Festival
Tromadance Film Festival
Washington, DC International Film Festival—
  Filmfest DC
Wisconsin Film Festival
Zoiefest!

EXPERIMENTAL

AFI DVCam Fest Sponsored by Sony
American Short Shorts
Angelciti Los Angeles Film Festival & Market
Antimatter Festival of Underground Short
  Film & Video
Arizona State University Short Film and
  Video Festival
Aspen Shortsfest
Atlanta Film and Video Festival
Brainwash Movie Festival
Charlotte Gay & Lesbian Film Series
  Presented by Outcharlotte
Chicago International Film Festival
Chicago Latino Film Festival
Cinematexas International Short Film &
  Video Festival

Cleveland International Film Festival
Coca-Cola Johannesburg International
  Student Film Festival
Columbus International Film and Video
  Festival "Chris Awards"
Cork International Film Festival
Cucalorus Film Festival
Dallas Video Festival
Dances With Films
Deep Ellum Film Festival
Documental
Edmonds International Film Festival
Exground—Das Filmfest
Fantasia Film Festival
Film Nite
Fort Lauderdale Int'l Film Festival
Freaky Film Festival (FFF)
Free Film Festival Fitchburg (The F4)
Gen Art Film Festival
Golden Shower Video Festival
Images Festival of Independent Film and
  Video
Independent Exposure
International Gay and Lesbian Film Festival
Johns Hopkins Film Festival
Kansas City Filmmakers Jubilee
Kasseler Dokumentarfilm—Und Videofest
La Lesbian Film Festival
Lake Placid Film Forum
Los Angeles Independent Film Festival
  (LAIFF)
Lost Film Festival
Madcat Women's International Film Festival
Media Alliance Film Festival
Melbourne Queer Film & Video Festival
Miami Film Festival
Miami Underground Film & Video Festival
  (Online)
Minicine Visiting Filmmaker Series
Montreal's International Lesbian & Gay Film
  and Video Festival
Moondance International Film Festival
Moxie! / Santa Monica Film Festival
Nashville Independent Film Festival
New York International Latino Film Festival
Next Frame: UFVA's Touring Festival of
  International Student Film and Video
Northampton Film Festival
Northwest Film & Video Festival
Ohio Independent Film Festival
Out in Akron Queer Shorts Film Festival
PXL This
Rhode Island International Film Festival
San Francisco Independent Film Festival (aka
  SF Indiefest)
San Francisco International Asian American
  Film Festival

San Francisco International Film Festival
Seattle Underground Film Festival
Short Attention Span Film and Video Festival
  (SASFVF)
Silver Images Film Festival
Silver Lake Film Festival
Stony Brook Film Festival
Temecula Valley International Film Festival
Thaw Video, Film, and Digital Media Festival
Toronto Worldwide Short Film Festival
Tromadance Film Festival
Turin International Gay & Lesbian Film
  Festival "From Sodom To Hollywood"
University of Oregon Queer Film Festival
Uppsala International Short Film Festival
USAFilm Festival
Valleyfest Independent Film Festival
Vancouver Island Media Fest
Victoria Independent Film and Video Festival
Whistler International Film & Television
Williamstown Film Festival
Wisconsin Film Festival
Zoiefest!

FIRST-TIME INDEPENDENT FILMMAKERS

American Film Institute (AFI)—Los Angeles
  International Film Festival
American Short Shorts
Angelciti Los Angeles Film Festival & Market
Arizona State University Short Film and
  Video Festival
Bangkok Film Festival
Bermuda International Film Festival
Beverly Hills Film Festival
Brainwash Movie Festival
Charlotte Gay & Lesbian Film Series
  Presented by Outcharlotte
Chicago International Film Festival
Chicago Latino Film Festival
Cinematexas International Short Film &
  Video Festival
Cleveland International Film Festival
Coca-Cola Johannesburg International
  Student Film Festival
Cork International Film Festival
Cucalorus Film Festival
Dances With Films
Deep Ellum Film Festival
Edmonds International Film Festival
Exground—Das Filmfest
Fantasia Film Festival
Film Nite
Fort Lauderdale Int'l Film Festival
Freaky Film Festival (FFF)
Free Film Festival Fitchburg (The F4)

Gay and Lesbian Arts Festival of Oklahoma,
  Inc. dba Outart
Gen Art Film Festival
Hollywood Black Film Festival
Images Festival of Independent Film and
  Video
Independent Exposure
International Gay and Lesbian Film Festival
Johns Hopkins Film Festival
La Lesbian Film Festival
Lake Placid Film Forum
Los Angeles Independent Film Festival
  (LAIFF)
Lost Film Festival
Madcat Women's International Film Festival
Marco Island Film Festival
Media Alliance Film Festival
Melbourne Queer Film & Video Festival
Miami Film Festival
Miami Underground Film & Video Festival
  (Online)
Minicine Visiting Filmmaker Series
Moondance International Film Festival
No Dance Film Festival
Northwest Film & Video Festival
Ohio Independent Film Festival
Outfar!—Annual Phoenix International
  Lesbian and Gay Film Festival
Portland International Film Festival
Rhode Island International Film Festival
San Francisco Independent Film Festival (aka
  SF Indiefest)
San Francisco International Asian American
  Film Festival
San Francisco International Film Festival
Savannah Film and Video Festival
Seattle Underground Film Festival
Sedona International Film Festival and
  Workshop
Short Attention Span Film and Video Festival
  (SASFVF)
St. Louis International Lesbian & Gay
  (SLILAG) Film Festival
Stony Brook Film Festival
Temecula Valley International Film Festival
Tromadance Film Festival
Tromsø International Film Festival
USA Film Festival
Valleyfest Independent Film Festival
Vancouver Island Media Fest
Victoria Independent Film and Video Festival
Washington, DC International Film Festival—
  Filmfest DC
Whistler International Film & Television
Williamstown Film Festival
Wisconsin Film Festival
Zoiefest!

GAY LESBiAN

Angelciti Los Angeles Film Festival & Market
Antimatter Festival of Underground Short
Film & Video
Arizona State University Short Film and
Video Festival
Aspen Shortsfest
Atlanta Gay and Lesbian Film Festival—Out
on Film
Austin's Gay and Lesbian Film Festival
Barcelona International Exhibition of Gay
and Lesbian Films
Berlin—Verzaubert International Gay &
Lesbian Film Festival
Bermuda International Film Festival
Beverly Hills Film Festival
Brussels Gay and Lesbian Film Festival
Festival du Film Gay et Lesbien de
Bruxelles
Charlotte Gay & Lesbian Film Series
Presented by Outcharlotte
Chicago International Film Festival
Chicago Latino Film Festival
Chicago Lesbian and Gay International Film
Festival
Cinematexas International Short Film &
Video Festival
Cleveland International Film Festival
Connecticut Gay & Lesbian Film Festival
Copenhagen Gay and Lesbian Film Festival
Cork Film Festival—Lesbian & Gay Section
Cork International Film Festival
Dances With Films
Dublin Lesbian and Gay Film Festival
Festival du Film Gay et Lesbien de Bruxelles
(Brussels Gay and Lesbian Film Festival)
Fort Lauderdale Int'l Film Festival
Fort Worth—Cinema—Fort Worth's Gay &
Lesbian Film Festival
Frankfurt Gay and Lesbian Film Festival
Freaky Film Festival (FFF)
Gay and Lesbian Arts Festival of Oklahoma,
Inc. dba Outart
Gen Art Film Festival
Hollywood Black Film Festival
Hong Kong Gay and Lesbian Film Festival
Honolulu Gay & Lesbian Film Festival
Houston Gay and Lesbian Film Festival
Inside Out Lesbian and Gay Film Festival of
Toronto
International Gay and Lesbian Film Festival
International Lesbian Film Festival
Immaginaria
Kansas City Gay & Lesbian Film Festival
La Lesbian Film Festival
London Lesbian & Gay Film Festival
Long Island Gay & Lesbian Film Festival

Los Angeles Independent Film Festival
(LAIFF)
Lost Film Festival
Madcat Women's International Film Festival
Madrid International Gay & Lesbian Film
Festival
Making Scenes
Marco Island Film Festival
Melbourne Queer Film & Video Festival
Method Fest
Miami Gay and Lesbian Film Festival
Miami Underground Film & Video Festival
(Online)
Mix Brasil Festival of Sexual Diversity
Montreal's International Lesbian & Gay Film
and Video Festival
New York Gay and Lesbian Film Festival (The
New Festival)
New York Lesbian and Gay Experimental Film
and Video Festival (Mix Festival)
No Dance Film Festival
Norrkoping Film Festival Flimmer
North Carolina Gay and Lesbian Film Festival
Ohio Independent Film Festival
Olympia—Gender Queer: Northwest
Transgender and Intersex Film
Out At the Movies: San Antonio's Annual
Festival of Lesbian & Gay Film
Out in Akron Queer Shorts Film Festival
Out Takes
Out Takes Dallas the Annual Lesbian and Gay
Film Festival
Outfar!—Annual Phoenix International
Lesbian and Gay Film Festival
Outfest: Los Angeles International Gay and
Lesbian Film & Video Festival
Palm Springs Gay & Lesbian Film Festival
Paris Gay and Lesbian Film Festival/Festival
de Films Gays et Lesbiens de Paris
Philadelphia International Gay and Lesbian
Film Festival
Pink Apple—Schwullesbisches Filmfestival
Pittsburgh International Lesbian and Gay
Film Festival
Queersicht—Schwul-Lesbisches Filmfestival
Bern
Reel Affirmations Film Festival
Rhode Island International Film Festival
Sacramento International Gay and Lesbian
Film Festival
San Francisco Independent Film Festival (aka
SF Indiefest)
San Francisco International Asian American
Film Festival
San Francisco Lesbian and Gay Film Festival
Schwule Filmwoche Freiburg Gay Film
Festival of Freiburg

Seattle International Film Festival
Seattle Lesbian & Gay Film Festival
Seattle Underground Film Festival
Sedona International Film Festival and
    Workshop
Seoul Queer Film & Video Festival
Silver Lake Film Festival
St. Louis International Lesbian & Gay
    (SLILAG) Film Festival
Sydney Mardi Gras Film Festival/Queer
    Screen Ltd.
Tokyo International Lesbian & Gay Film and
    Video Festival
Tromadance Film Festival
Turin International Gay & Lesbian Film
    Festival "From Sodom To Hollywood"
Turku Lesbian and Gay Film Festival
University of Oregon Queer Film Festival
Valleyfest Independent Film Festival
Vancouver—Out On Screen Queer Film &
    Video Festival
Victoria Independent Film and Video Festival
Ways in Being Gay (Biannual)
Wisconsin Film Festival

INDEPENDENT

AFI DVCam Fest Sponsored by Sony
American Film Institute (AFI)—Los Angeles
    International Film Festival
American Short Shorts
Angelciti Los Angeles Film Festival & Market
Angelus Awards Student Film Festival
Ann Arbor Film Festival
Antimatter Festival of Underground Short
    Film & Video
Arizona State University Short Film and
    Video Festival
Aspen Filmfest
Aspen Shortsfest
Atlanta Film and Video Festival
Atlantic Film Festival
Austin Film Festival & Heart of Film
    Screenwriters Conference
Banff Festival of Mountain Films
Bangkok Film Festival
Bargain Basement Independent
    Film/Videofestival
Berlin International Film Festival
Bermuda International Film Festival
Beverly Hills Film Festival
Big Muddy Film Festival
Blue Sky International Film Festival
Brainwash Movie Festival
Breckenridge Festival of Film

Brussels Gay and Lesbian Film Festival
    Festival du Film Gay et Lesbien de
    Bruxelles
Cambridge International Film Festival
Cannes Film Festival
Carolina Film and Video Festival
Cartagena International Film Festival
Charlotte Film and Video Festival
Charlotte Gay & Lesbian Film Series
    Presented by Outcharlotte
Chicago Alt.Film Fest
Chicago International Film Festival
Chicago Latino Film Festival
Chicago Underground Film Festival
Cinematexas International Short Film &
    Video Festival
Cinevegas Film Festival
Cleveland International Film Festival
Coca-Cola Johannesburg International
    Student Film Festival
Columbus International Film and Video
    Festival "Chris Awards"
Cork International Film Festival
Cucalorus Film Festival
D.Film Digital Film Festival
Dallas Video Festival
Dances With Films
Docfest—New York International
    Documentary Festival
Durango Film Festival
Durban International Film Festival
Edmonds International Film Festival
Espoo Ciné International Film Festival
Euro Underground
Exground—Das Filmfest
Fantasia Film Festival
Fantasy Filmfest—International Film Festival
    for Science Fiction, Fiction, Horror and
    Thriller
Festival du Film Gay et Lesbien de Bruxelles
    (Brussels Gay and Lesbian Film Festival)
Festival of Deauville for American Cinema
    "Le Festival du Cinema Americain in
    Deauville"
Film Fest New Haven
Film Nite
Filmfest Braunschweig
Flickapalooza Film Festival
Florida Film Festival
Fort Lauderdale Int'l Film Festival
Four*By*Four Super 8 Filmfest
Free Film Festival Fitchburg (The F4)
Gay and Lesbian Arts Festival of Oklahoma,
    Inc. dba Outart
Gen Art Film Festival
Gijon International Film Festival for Young
    People

Golden Shower Video Festival
Hamptons International Film Festival
Hawaii International Film Festival
High Beam International Independent
  Drive-In Film Festival
Hollywood Black Film Festival
Hollywood Film Festival
Hot Springs Documentary Film Festival
Hudson Valley Film Festival
Human Rights Watch International Film
  Festival
Images Festival of Independent Film and
  Video
Independent Exposure
Indiurban Independent Film Festival
Inside Out Lesbian and Gay Film Festival of
  Toronto
International Filmfestival
International Lesbian Film Festival
  Immaginaria
International Wildlife Film Festival
Jerusalem International Film Festival
Johns Hopkins Film Festival
Kasseler Dokumentarfilm- Und Videofest
Kino American Underground & Student
  Showcase Film Fest
Kinofilm, Manchester International Short
  Film & Video Festival
Kudzu Film Festival (aka Athens Film
  Festival)
Kyiv International Film Festival, Molodist
  (Molodist Means "Youth" in Ukrainian "
Lake Placid Film Forum
Local Heroes International Screen Festival
Long Island Film Festival
Los Angeles Independent Film Festival
  (LAIFF)
Los Angeles Latino International Film Festival
Lost Film Festival
Madcat Women's International Film Festival
Marco Island Film Festival
Marin County National Film and Video
  Festival
Maui Film Festival
Media Alliance Film Festival
Melbourne Queer Film & Video Festival
Method Fest
Miami Film Festival
Miami Underground Film & Video Festival
  (Online)
Microcinefest
Mill Valley Film Festival
Mix Brasil Festival of Sexual Diversity
Montreal's International Lesbian & Gay Film
  and Video Festival
Moondance International Film Festival
Moxie! / Santa Monica Film Festival

Nashville Independent Film Festival
New England Film and Video Festival
New York Gay and Lesbian Film Festival (The
  New Festival)
New York Underground Film Festival
Newport International Film Festival
Norrkoping Film Festival Flimmer
Northwest Film & Video Festival
Ohio Independent Film Festival
Oldenburg International Film Festival
Onedotzero: Digital Moving Image Festival
Out in Akron Queer Shorts Film Festival
Outfar!—Annual Phoenix International
  Lesbian and Gay Film Festival
Outfest: Los Angeles International Gay and
  Lesbian Film & Video Festival
Phoenix Film Festival
Portland International Film Festival
Queersicht—Schwul-Lesbisches Filmfestival
  Bern
Reel Affirmations Film Festival
Resfest Digital Film Festival
Revelation Independent Film Festival
Rhode Island International Film Festival
Rochester International Independent Film
  Festival
Sacramento International Gay and Lesbian
  Film Festival
San Diego International Film Festival
San Francisco Independent Film Festival (aka
  SF Indiefest)
San Francisco International Asian American
  Film Festival
San Francisco International Film Festival
San Francisco Lesbian and Gay Film Festival
Santa Barbara International Film Festival
  (SBIFF)
Savannah Film and Video Festival
Schwule Filmwoche Freiburg Gay Film
  Festival of Freiburg
Seattle International Film Festival
Seattle Underground Film Festival
Sedona International Film Festival and
  Workshop
Short Attention Span Film and Video Festival
  (SASFVF)
Silver Lake Film Festival
Slamdance International Film Festival
Small Pictures International Film Festival
  (SPIFF)
St. Louis International Film Festival
St. Louis International Lesbian & Gay (Slilag)
  Film Festival
Stony Brook Film Festival
Sundance Film Festival
SXSW: South by Southwest Film Festival
Tech Tv's Cam Film Festival

Telluride Film Festival
Temecula Valley International Film Festival
Texas Film Festival
Thaw Video, Film, and Digital Media Festival
Tromadance Film Festival
Tromsø International Film Festival
Tube Film Festival
Turin International Gay & Lesbian Film
  Festival "From Sodom To Hollywood"
University of Oregon Queer Film Festival
USA Film Festival
Valleyfest Independent Film Festival
Vancouver International Film Festival
Vancouver Island Media Fest
Victoria Independent Film and Video Festival
Washington, DC International Film Festival—
  Filmfest DC
Waterfront Film Festival
West Virginia International Film Festival
Whistler International Film & Television
Williamstown Film Festival
Wisconsin Film Festival
Woodstock Film Festival
Zoiefest!

INTERNATIONAL

Acapulco Black Film Festival
American Film Institute (AFI)—Los Angeles
  International Film Festival
American Short Shorts
Angelciti Los Angeles Film Festival & Market
Angelus Awards Student Film Festival
Ankara International Film Festival
Antimatter Festival of Underground Short
  Film & Video
Arcipelago Short Film Festival
Arizona State University Short Film and
  Video Festival
Asolo International Animation Festival
Aspen Filmfest
Athens International Film and Video Festival
Athens International Film Festival
Auckland International Film Festival
Australian International Outdoor Short Film
  Festival "Flickerfest"
Banco Nacional International Film Festival
Bangkok Film Festival
Berlin International Film Festival
Bermuda International Film Festival
Beverly Hills Film Festival
Bienal Nacion Cajalicante de Cine Amateur
  de Libre Creacion
Biennale Internationale du Film
  D'architecture, D'urbanisme et
  D'environment de Bordeaux "Fifarc
  Festival"

Bilan du Film Ethnographique
Blois Cinema Forum
Blue Sky International Film Festival
Bombay International Film Festival for
  Documentary, Short and Animation Films
Brussels Gay and Lesbian Film Festival
  Festival du Film Gay et Lesbien de
  Bruxelles
Cadiz International Video Festival
Cairo International Film Festival
Cairo International Film Festival for Children
Cambridge International Film Festival
Cannes Film Festival
Cartagena International Film Festival
Certamen Internacional de Cine
  Cortometraje
Certamen Internacional de Cine Turistico de
  Madrid
Charlotte Gay & Lesbian Film Series
  Presented by Outcharlotte
Chicago International Film Festival
Chicago Latino Film Festival
Cinematexas International Short Film &
  Video Festival
Cleveland International Film Festival
Columbus International Film and Video
  Festival "Chris Awards"
Cork International Film Festival
Cucalorus Film Festival
D.Film Digital Film Festival
Dances With Films
Doubletake Documentary Film Festival
Exground—Das Filmfest
Fantasia Film Festival
Festival du Film Gay et Lesbien de Bruxelles
  (Brussels Gay and Lesbian Film Festival)
Film Fest New Haven
Film Nite
Filmfest Braunschweig
Filmfest Munchen
Fort Lauderdale Int'l Film Festival
Freaky Film Festival (FFF)
Freedom Film Festival
Gay and Lesbian Arts Festival of Oklahoma,
  Inc. dba Outart
Gijon International Film Festival for Young
  People
Golden Shower Video Festival
Hamburg International Short Film Festival
Hawaii International Film Festival
Hollywood Black Film Festival
Hollywood Film Festival
Hong Kong International Film Festival
  (HKIFF)
Hot Docs Canadian International
  Documentary Festival

Images Festival of Independent Film and Video

Independent Exposure

International Animated Film Festival—Cinanima

International Animation Festival

International Animation Festival, Cardiff, Wales

International Animation Festival—Japan, Hiroshima

International Documentary, Short and Animated Films Festival

International Festival of Films Made by Women

International Festival of Films On Art "Fifart Festival"

International Film Festival Rotterdam

International Gay and Lesbian Film Festival

International Juvenale for Young Film and Video Amateurs

International Lesbian Film Festival Immaginaria

International Mystery Film Festival "Mystfest"

International Short Film Festival Oberhausen

International Video Contest

International Women's Film Festival

Japan International Film & Video Festival of Adventure and Sports

Johns Hopkins Film Festival

Karlovy Vary International Film Festival

Kasseler Dokumentarfilm- Und Videofest

Kine International Film Festival

La Lesbian Film Festival

Lake Placid Film Forum

Local Heroes International Screen Festival

Locarno International Film Festival

London Film Festival

Lost Film Festival

Madcat Women's International Film Festival

Magdeburg International Film Festival

Marco Island Film Festival

Maui Film Festival

Melbourne International Film Festival

Melbourne Queer Film & Video Festival

Miami Film Festival

Miami Underground Film & Video Festival (Online)

Mill Valley Film Festival

Montreal World Film Festival

Montreal's International Lesbian & Gay Film and Video Festival

Moondance International Film Festival

Moxie! / Santa Monica Film Festival

New York Film Festival

Norrkoping Film Festival Flimmer

Norwegian International Film Festival

Nyon International Documentary Film Festival

Ohio Independent Film Festival

Okomedia International Ecological Film Festival

Onedotzero: Digital Moving Image Festival

Outfar!—Annual Phoenix International Lesbian and Gay Film Festival

Philadelphia Festival of World Cinema

Portland International Film Festival

Puerto Rico International Film Festival

Queersicht—Schwul-Lesbisches Filmfestival Bern

Rhode Island International Film Festival

Riminicinema International Film Festival

Rochester International Independent Film Festival

Rotterdam International Film Festival

Sacramento International Gay and Lesbian Film Festival

San Diego International Film Festival

San Francisco International Asian American Film Festival

San Francisco International Film Festival

San Luis Obispo International Film Festival

Santa Barbara International Film Festival (SBIFF)

Santa Fe de Bogota International Film Festival

São Paulo International Film Festival

São Paulo International Short Film Festival

Savannah Film and Video Festival

Schwule Filmwoche Freiburg Gay Film Festival of Freiburg

Seattle International Film Festival

Seattle Underground Film Festival

Sedona International Film Festival and Workshop

Short Attention Span Film and Video Festival (SASFVF)

Silver Lake Film Festival

Singapore International Film Festival

Sitges International Film Festival of Catalonia

Slamdance International Film Festival

St. Louis International Lesbian & Gay (Slilag) Film Festival

Stony Brook Film Festival

Sundance Film Festival

Sydney Film Festival

Tampere International Short Film Festival

Taos Talking Pictures Festival

Temecula Valley International Film Festival

Thaw Video, Film, and Digital Media Festival

Tokyo International Film Festival

Torino Film Festival

Toronto International Film Festival

Tromadance Film Festival

Tromsø International Film Festival

Turin International Gay & Lesbian Film Festival "From Sodom To Hollywood"

Filmfest Braunschweig
Flo Film Fest
Fort Lauderdale Int'l Film Festival
Freaky Film Festival (FFF)
Gen Art Film Festival
Gijon International Film Festival for Young
    People
Golden Shower Video Festival
Hamburg International Short Film Festival
Hardshare Independent Film Festival
Heartland Film Festival
Hi Mom! Film Festival
High Beam International Independent
    Drive-In Film Festival
Hometown Cinema Inc
Images Festival of Independent Film and
    Video
Independent Exposure
Indiurban Independent Film Festival
International Documentary, Short and
    Animated Films Festival
International Festival of Documentary and
    Short Film of Bilbao
International Film Festival Rotterdam
International Short Film Festival Oberhausen
Johns Hopkins Film Festival
Kansas City Filmmakers Jubilee
Kansas City Gay & Lesbian Film Festival
Kinofilm, Manchester International Short
    Film & Video Festival
La Lesbian Film Festival
Lake Placid Film Forum
Los Angeles Independent Film Festival
    (LAIFF)
Los Angeles International Short Film Festival
Los Angeles Italian Film Awards (LAIFA)
Los Angeles Latino International Film Festival
Lost Film Festival
Madcat Women's International Film Festival
Marco Island Film Festival
Media Alliance Film Festival
Melbourne Queer Film & Video Festival
Method Fest
Miami Film Festival
Miami Underground Film & Video Festival
    (Online)
Microcinefest
Minicine Visiting Filmmaker Series
Montreal International Festival of New
    Cinema and New Media
Montreal's International Lesbian & Gay Film
    and Video Festival
Moondance International Film Festival
Nashville Independent Film Festival
New York Expo of Short Film and Video
New York International Latino Film Festival
New York Lower East Side Film Festival

Newport Beach Film Festival
Newport International Film Festival
No Dance Film Festival
Northampton Film Festival
Northwest Film & Video Festival
Norwegian Short Film Festival
Ohio Independent Film Festival
Out in Akron Queer Shorts Film Festival
Outfar!—Annual Phoenix International
    Lesbian and Gay Film Festival
Portland International Film Festival
Queersicht—Schwul-Lesbisches Filmfestival
    Bern
Resfest Digital Film Festival
Rhode Island International Film Festival
Rio de Janeiro International Short Film
    Festival
Rotterdam International Film Festival
Sacramento International Gay and Lesbian
    Film Festival
San Francisco Independent Film Festival (aka
    SF Indiefest)
San Francisco International Asian American
    Film Festival
San Francisco International Film Festival
Santa Barbara International Film Festival
    (SBIFF)
Santa Clarita International Film Festival
São Paulo International Short Film Festival
Savannah Film and Video Festival
Schwule Filmwoche Freiburg Gay Film
    Festival of Freiburg
Sedona International Film Festival and
    Workshop
Short Attention Span Film and Video Festival
    (SASFVF)
Silver Images Film Festival
Silver Lake Film Festival
Slamdance International Film Festival
Small Pictures International Film Festival
    (SPIFF)
St. Louis International Lesbian & Gay
    (SLILAG) Film Festival
Stony Brook Film Festival
Stuttgart Filmwinter
Tampere International Short Film Festival
Temecula Valley International Film Festival
Thaw Video, Film, and Digital Media Festival
Toronto Worldwide Short Film Festival
Tromadance Film Festival
Turin International Gay & Lesbian Film
    Festival "From Sodom To Hollywood"
University of Oregon Queer Film Festival
Uppsala International Short Film Festival
Urbanworld Film Festival
USA Film Festival
Valleyfest Independent Film Festival

Vancouver Island Media Fest
Vancouver Underground Film Festival
Victoria Independent Film and Video Festival
Washington, DC International Film Festival—
    Filmfest DC
Whistler International Film & Television
Williamstown Film Festival
Wine Country Film Festival
Wisconsin Film Festival
Woodstock Film Festival
Yorkton Short Film and Video Festival
Zoiefest!

STUDENT
AFI DVCam Fest Sponsored by Sony
Amatuer and Non-Professional Film and
    Video Festival
American Short Shorts
Arizona State University Short Film and
    Video Festival
Aspen Shortsfest
Atlanta Film and Video Festival
Austin Film Festival & Heart of Film
    Screenwriters Conference
Bargain Basement Independent
    Film/Videofestival
Black Harvest International Film Festival
Burbank International Childrens Film Festival
Carolina Film and Video Festival
Chicago International Film Festival
Cinematexas International Short Film &
    Video Festival
Coca-Cola Johannesburg International
    Student Film Festival
D.Film Digital Film Festival
Deep Ellum Film Festival
Fort Lauderdale Int'l Film Festival
Freaky Film Festival (FFF)
Golden Shower Video Festival
Hollywood Black Film Festival
Hometown Cinema Inc
International Festival of Animated Film
    Stuttgart
International Juvenale for Young Film and
    Video Amateurs
Johns Hopkins Film Festival
Kino American Underground & Student
    Showcase Film Fest
La Lesbian Film Festival
Lake Placid Film Forum
Los Angeles Independent Film Festival
    (LAIFF)
Lost Film Festival
Madcat Women's International Film Festival
Maine Student Film and Video Festival
Melbourne Queer Film & Video Festival

Miami Film Festival
Miami Underground Film & Video Festival
    (Online)
Nashville Independent Film Festival
New York International Latino Film Festival
New York National High School Film and
    Video Festival
Next Frame: UFVA's Touring Festival of
    International Student Film and Video
Norrkoping Film Festival Flimmer
Ohio Independent Film Festival
Rhode Island International Film Festival
River City Film Festival
San Francisco International Film Festival
Santa Clarita International Film Festival
Savannah Film and Video Festival
Short Attention Span Film and Video Festival
    (SASFVF)
Short Poppies: International Festival of
    Student Film and Video
Silver Lake Film Festival
St. Louis International Film Festival
Telluride Film Festival
Temecula Valley International Film Festival
Thaw Video, Film, and Digital Media Festival
Tromadance Film Festival
University of Oregon Queer Film Festival
Valleyfest Independent Film Festival
Vancouver Island Media Fest
Victoria Independent Film and Video Festival
West Virginia International Film Festival
Williamstown Film Festival
Zoiefest!

SUPER 8/8MM
American Short Shorts
Antimatter Festival of Underground Short
    Film & Video
Arizona State University Short Film and
    Video Festival
Cinematexas International Short Film &
    Video Festival
Cucalorus Film Festival
Deep Ellum Film Festival
Edmonds International Film Festival
Film Nite
Freaky Film Festival (FFF)
Golden Shower Video Festival
Hamburg International Short Film Festival
Hollywood Black Film Festival
Images Festival of Independent Film and
    Video
Independent Exposure
Johns Hopkins Film Festival
La Lesbian Film Festival
Madcat Women's International Film Festival

Marco Island Film Festival
Melbourne Queer Film & Video Festival
Miami Underground Film & Video Festival
  (Online)
Minicine Visiting Filmmaker Series
Northwest Film & Video Festival
Ohio Independent Film Festival
Resfest Digital Film Festival
Seattle Underground Film Festival
Short Attention Span Film and Video Festival
  (SASFVF)
Thaw Video, Film, and Digital Media Festival
Tromadance Film Festival
Vancouver Island Media Fest
Zoiefest!

UNDERGROUND

American Short Shorts
Angelciti Los Angeles Film Festival & Market
Antimatter Festival of Underground Short
  Film & Video
Arizona State University Short Film and
  Video Festival
Brainwash Movie Festival
Chicago Underground Film Festival
Cinematexas International Short Film &
  Video Festival
Cucalorus Film Festival
Deep Ellum Film Festival
Euro Underground
Exground—Das Filmfest
Fantasia Film Festival
Film Nite
Fort Lauderdale Int'l Film Festival
Four*By*Four Super 8 Filmfest
Freaky Film Festival (FFF)
Free Film Festival Fitchburg (The F4)
Gijon International Film Festival for Young
  People
Golden Shower Video Festival
Independent Exposure
Johns Hopkins Film Festival
Kino American Underground & Student
  Showcase Film Fest
La Lesbian Film Festival
Los Angeles Independent Film Festival
  (LAIFF)
Lost Film Festival
Madcat Women's International Film Festival
Melbourne Queer Film & Video Festival
Miami Underground Film & Video Festival
  (Online)
Microcinefest
Minicine Visiting Filmmaker Series
No Dance Film Festival
Ohio Independent Film Festival

PXL This
Rhode Island International Film Festival
San Francisco Independent Film Festival (aka
  SF Indiefest)
Seattle Underground Film Festival
Short Attention Span Film and Video Festival
  (SASFVF)
Silver Lake Film Festival
Small Pictures International Film Festival
  (SPIFF)
Thaw Video, Film, and Digital Media Festival
Tromadance Film Festival
University of Oregon Queer Film Festival
Valleyfest Independent Film Festival
Vancouver Island Media Fest
Vancouver Underground Film Festival
Wisconsin Film Festival
Zoiefest!

VIDEO

AFI DVCam Fest Sponsored by Sony
American Short Shorts
Angelciti Los Angeles Film Festival & Market
Angelus Awards Student Film Festival
Antimatter Festival of Underground Short
  Film & Video
Arizona State University Short Film and
  Video Festival
B-Movie Film Festival
Baca Film and Video Festival
Berkeley Video and Film Festival
Brainwash Movie Festival
Charlotte Film and Video Festival
Charlotte Gay & Lesbian Film Series
  Presented by Outcharlotte
Chicago International Children's Film Festival
  (CICFF)
Chicago Latino Film Festival
Cinematexas International Short Film &
  Video Festival
Cork International Film Festival
Cucalorus Film Festival
D.Film Digital Film Festival
Da Vinci Film and Video Festival
Dallas Video Festival
Dances With Films
Deep Ellum Film Festival
Edmonds International Film Festival
Euro Underground
Freaky Film Festival (FFF)
Gen Art Film Festival
Global Africa International Film and Video
  Festival
Golden Shower Video Festival
Hi Mom! Film Festival
Hollywood Black Film Festival

Hometown Cinema Inc
Images Festival of Independent Film and
Video
Independent Exposure
International Film and Video Competition
"IAC Competition"
International Short Film Festival Oberhausen
International Video Festival of Algarve
Japan International Film & Video Festival of
Adventure and Sports
Kansas City Gay & Lesbian Film Festival
Kasseler Dokumentarfilm—Und Videofest
La Lesbian Film Festival
Lake Placid Film Forum
Los Angeles Independent Film Festival
(LAIFF)
Los Angeles International Short Film Festival
Lost Film Festival
Madcat Women's International Film Festival
Marco Island Film Festival
Melbourne Queer Film & Video Festival
Miami Underground Film & Video Festival
(Online)
Microcinefest
Minicine Visiting Filmmaker Series
Montreal's International Lesbian & Gay Film
and Video Festival
Moondance International Film Festival
New Orleans Film and Video Festival
New York International Video Festival
Norrkoping Film Festival Flimmer
Northwest Film & Video Festival
Ohio Independent Film Festival
Ojai Film Festival
Outfar!—Annual Phoenix International
Lesbian and Gay Film Festival
Portland International Film Festival
Rhode Island International Film Festival
Sacramento International Gay and Lesbian
Film Festival
San Francisco Independent Film Festival (aka
SF Indiefest)
San Francisco International Asian American
Film Festival
San Francisco International Film Festival
Santa Barbara International Film Festival
(SBIFF)
Seattle Underground Film Festival
Short Attention Span Film and Video Festival
(SASFVF)
Silver Images Film Festival
Silver Lake Film Festival
Small Pictures International Film Festival
(SPIFF)
Stuttgart Filmwinter
Thaw Video, Film, and Digital Media Festival
Tokyo Video Festival

Tromadance Film Festival
Turin International Gay & Lesbian Film
Festival "From Sodom To Hollywood"
University of Oregon Queer Film Festival
US International Film & Video Festival
USA Film Festival
Valleyfest Independent Film Festival
Vancouver Island Media Fest
Vancouver Underground Film Festival
Victoria Independent Film and Video Festival
Whistler International Film & Television
Wisconsin Film Festival
Yorkton Short Film and Video Festival
Zoiefest!

WEIRD
American Short Shorts
Antimatter Festival of Underground Short
Film & Video
Arizona State University Short Film and
Video Festival
Brainwash Movie Festival
Charged 60-Second Film Festival
Chicago Latino Film Festival
Chicago Underground Film Festival
Cinematexas International Short Film &
Video Festival
Cucalorus Film Festival
D.Film Digital Film Festival
Deep Ellum Film Festival
Edmonds International Film Festival
Euro Underground
Exground—Das Filmfest
Fantasia Film Festival
Film Nite
Freaky Film Festival (FFF)
Free Film Festival Fitchburg (The F4)
Gen Art Film Festival
Golden Shower Video Festival
Hi Mom! Film Festival
Hometown Cinema Inc
Independent Exposure
International Mystery Film Festival "Mystfest"
Johns Hopkins Film Festival
Los Angeles Independent Film Festival
(LAIFF)
Lost Film Festival
Madcat Women's International Film Festival
Melbourne Queer Film & Video Festival
Microcinefest
Northwest Film & Video Festival
Ohio Independent Film Festival
Out in Akron Queer Shorts Film Festival
PXL This
Rhode Island International Film Festival

San Francisco Independent Film Festival (aka
SF Indiefest)
Seattle Underground Film Festival
Short Attention Span Film and Video Festival
(SASFVF)
Silver Lake Film Festival
Small Pictures International Film Festival
(SPIFF)
Thaw Video, Film, and Digital Media Festival
Tromadance Film Festival
University of Oregon Queer Film Festival
Valleyfest Independent Film Festival
Vancouver Island Media Fest
Vancouver Underground Film Festival
Williamstown Film Festival
Zoiefest!

Rhode Island International Film Festival
San Francisco Independent Film Festival (aka
SF Indiefest)
Sedona International Film Festival and
Workshop
Short Attention Span Film and Video Festival
(SASFVF)
Tromadance Film Festival
Valleyfest Independent Film Festival
Victoria Independent Film and Video Festival
Wisconsin Film Festival
Zoiefest!

WOMAN

American Short Shorts
Angelciti Los Angeles Film Festival & Market
Angelus Awards Student Film Festival
Antimatter Festival of Underground Short
Film & Video
Arizona State University Short Film and
Video Festival
Bermuda International Film Festival
Beverly Hills Film Festival
Charlotte Gay & Lesbian Film Series
Presented by Outcharlotte
Chicago International Film Festival
Chicago Latino Film Festival
Cinematexas International Short Film &
Video Festival
Cork International Film Festival
Dances With Films
Edmonds International Film Festival
Fantasia Film Festival
Fort Lauderdale Int'l Film Festival
Freaky Film Festival (FFF)
Gen Art Film Festival
Golden Shower Video Festival
Hollywood Black Film Festival
Independent Exposure
International Gay and Lesbian Film Festival
La Lesbian Film Festival
Lake Placid Film Forum
Los Angeles Independent Film Festival
(LAIFF)
Lost Film Festival
Madcat Women's International Film Festival
Melbourne Queer Film & Video Festival
Miami Film Festival
Miami Underground Film & Video Festival
(Online)
Moondance International Film Festival
Ohio Independent Film Festival

iFiLMFiNDERS POWER iNViTATiON LiST
FOR FESTiVAL SCREENiNGS AND PARTiES

Alliance Atlantis
808 Wilshire Blvd., 3rd Floor
Santa Monica, CA 90403
310-899-8000
Mark Horowitz

Artisan Entertainment
2700 Colorado Ave.
Santa Monica, CA 90404
310-449-9200
Bill Block, Leilani Forby

Attitude Films
300 Mercer Street, #26L
New York, NY 10003
212-995-9008
Andrew Chang

Blockbuster, Inc.
1201 Elm Street, Renaissance Tower
Dallas, TX 75270
214-854-3430
Dean Wilson

Buzz Media
1110 Yonge St.# 201
Toronto, Ont. M4W2L6
416-920-3800
Natalie Vinet

Castle Hill Productions
1414 Ave, of the Americas
New York, NY 10019
212-888-0080
Mel Maron

Cinevista, Inc.
2044 Praire Ave.
Miami, FL 33139
305-532-3400
Rene Fuentes Chao

Code Red Films
200 Varick Street
New York, NY 10014
646-486-4344
Jeff Levy-Hinte

Dimension Films
375 Greenwich St.
New York, NY 10013
212-941-3800
Andrew Rona

Film Forum
209 West Houston Street
New York, NY 10014
212-627-2035
Karen Cooper

Filmopolis Pictures
11300 W. Olympic Blvd. #840
Los Angeles, CA 90064
310-914-1776
Zachary Lovas

Fine Line Features
116 N. Robertson Blvd., #200
Los Angeles, CA 90048
310-854-5811
Mark Ordesky

First Look Pictures
8800 Sunset Blvd. 3rd Floor
Los Angeles, CA 90069
310-855-1199
MJ Peckos

First Run Features
153 Waverly Place, 6th Floor
New York, NY 10014
212-243-0600
Anne Riser

Fox Searchlight
10201 Pico Blvd.
Los Angeles, CA 90035
310-369-1000
Rosanne Korenberg

Good Machine Intl.
417 Canal St., 4th Fl.
New York, NY 10013
212-343-9230
Ted Hope

HBO Films
2049 Century Park East, #3600
Los Angeles, CA 90067
310-201-9200
Colin Callendar, Doris Casup (NY),
Maud Nadler

Icarus Films
123 West 93rd Street
New York, NY 10025
212-864-7603
Jonathan Miller

IFC Films
1111 Stewart Ave.
Bethpage, NY 11714
516-803-4511
Bob Berney

Independent Film Channel
150 Crossways Park
Woodbury, NY 11797
516-364-2222
Jonathan Sehring

International Media Services
599 Broadway, 8th Floor
New York, NY 10012
212-941-1464
Sandy Mandelberger

Jeff Dowd & Associates
2309 25th Street
Santa Monica, CA 90405
310-581-5555
Jeff Dowd

Jet Media
32040 Canterhill Place
Westlake Village, CA 91316
818-707-1080
Eric Taub

Keystone Entertainment
23410 Civic Center Way
Malibu, CA 90265
310-317-4883
Mark Borde

Kino International
333 West 39th Street, #503
New York, NY 10018
212-629-6880
Donald Krim

Kushner-Locke
11601 Wilshire Blvd., 21st Fl.
Los Angeles, CA 90025
310-481-2000
Phil Mittleman

Lynda A. Hansen and Associates
115 E. 92nd Street
New York, NY 10128
212-534-6497
Lynda A. Hansen

Lions Gate Films
561 Broadway, Suite 12 B
New York , NY 10012
212-966-4670
Michael Paseornek

Manga Entertainment
727 North Hudson
Chicago, IL 60610
312-751-0020
Marvin Gleicher

Menemsha Entertainment
1157 S. Beverly Drive. 2nd Floor
Los Angeles, CA 90035
310-712-3720
Neil Friedman

Mirimax Films
375 Greenwich St.
New York, NY 10013
212-941-3800
Harvey Weinstein

Palm Pictures
4 Columbus Circle, 5th Floor
New York, NY 10019
212 506-5800
Chris Blackwell

Prestige Entertainment
335 N Maple Drive, #222
Beverly Hills, CA 90210
310-247-6060
Etchie Stroh

Reeltime Distributing Corp.
353 W. 48th Street, 6th Floor
New York, NY 10036
212-582-5380
Roberta Findlay

Roxie Releasing
3125 16th Street
San Francisco, CA 94103
415-431-3611
Bill Banning

Rudolph & Beer
432 Park Ave. South
New York, NY 10016
212-684-1001
Steven C. Beer

Seventh Art Releasing
7551 Sunset Blvd. #104
Los Angeles, CA 90046
323-845-1455
Udy Epstein

Shooting Gallery
10877 Wilshire Blvd., Suite #1800
Los Angeles, CA 90024
310-443-1926
Andy Given

Showtime Networks
10880 Wilshire Blvd., Suite 1600
Los Angeles, CA 90024
310-234-5200
Sharon Byrens

Sloss Law Office
170 5th Ave.
New York, NY 10010
212-627-9898
John Sloss

Sony Pictures Classics
550 Madison Ave., 8th Floor
Nw York, NY 10022
212-833-8833
Michael Barker, Dylan Leiner

Starz Encore Group
5445 DTC Parkway, #600
Englewood, CO 80111
303-267-4004
Robert Leighton

Strand Releasing
1460 Fourth St., #302
Santa Monica, CA 90401
310-395-5002
Marcus Hu

Stratosphere Entertainment
767 Fifth Ave., #4700
New York, NY 10153
212-605-1010
Ronna Wallace

Sundance Channel
1633 Broadway, 16th Floor
New York, NY 10019
212-708-1434
Barbara Raab

Sunshine Amalgamedia
740 Broadway, 2nd Floor
New York, NY 10003
212-995-2222
Jed Albert

Troma
733 Ninth Avenue
New York, NY 10019
212-757-4555
Lloyd Kaufman

Tulchin Entertainment
11377 W. Olympic Blvd., 2nd Fl.
Los Angeles, CA 90064
310-914-7979
Harris Tulchin

Unicorn Films
37 Cranberry Street
Brooklyn, NY 11201
718-522-5870
Paul Tobias

USA Films
65 Bleeker Street, 2nd Floor
New York, NY 10012
212-539-4030
Scott Greenstein

Zeitgeist Films Limited
247 Centre Street, 2nd Floor
New York, NY 10013
212-274-1989
Emily Russo

Literary Agents for Writers and Directors

Above the Line Agency
9200 Sunset Blvd., #804
Los Angeles, CA 90069
310-859-6115

The Agency
1800 Ave. of the Stars, #1114
Los Angeles, CA 90067
310-551-3000

APA/Agency for the Performing Arts
9200 Sunset Blvd., #900
Los Angeles, CA 90069
310-273-0744

The Artists Agency
10000 Santa Monica Blvd., #305
Los Angeles, CA 90067
310-277-7779

Becsey-Wisdom-Kalajian
9200 Sunset Blvd., #820
Los Angeles, CA 90069
310-550-0535

Broder-Kurland-Webb-Uffner
9242 Beverly Blvd., #200
Beverly Hills, CA 90210
310-281-3400

Don Buchwald & Associates
10 E 44th St.
New York, NY 10017
212-867-1200

Creative Artists Agency
9830 Wilshire Blvd.
Beverly Hills, CA 90212-1825
310-288-4545

Duva-Flack Associates, Inc.
200 W. 57th St., #1008
New York, NY 10019
212-957-9600

Endeavor
9701 Wilshire Blvd., 10th Fl.
Beverly Hills, CA 90212
310-248-2000

The Gage Group
9255 Sunset Blvd., #515
Los Angeles, CA 90069
310-859-8777

The Gersh Agency
232 N. Canon Dr.
Beverly Hills, CA 90210
310-274-6611

Innovative Artists
1999 Ave. of the Stars, #2850
Los Angeles, CA 90067
310-553-5200

International Creative Mgmt.
8942 Wilshire Blvd.
Beverly Hills, CA 90211
310-550-4000

Major Clients Agency
345 Maple Dr., #395
Beverly Hills, CA 90210
310-205-5000

Metropolitan Talent Agency
4526 Wilshire Blvd.
Los Angeles, CA 90010
323-857-4500

William Morris Agency
151 El Camino Dr.
Beverly Hills, CA 90212
310-859-4000

The Daniel Ostroff Agency
9200 Sunset Blvd., #402
Los Angeles, CA 90069
310-278-2020

Paradigm
10100 Santa Monica Blvd.,
25th Floor
Los Angeles, CA 90067
310-277-4400

Preferred Artists
16633 Ventura Blvd., #1421
Encino, CA 91436
818-990-0305

Jim Preminger Agency
450 N. Roxbury Dr., PH 1050
Beverly Hills, CA 90210
310-860-1116

Shapiro-Lichtman, Inc.
8827 Beverly Blvd., #C
Los Angeles, CA 90048
310-859-8877

United Talent Agency
9560 Wilshire Blvd., #500
Beverly Hills, CA 90212
213-273-6700

Writers & Artists
8383 WIlshire Blvd., Suite 550
Bevery Hills, CA 90211
323-866-0900

FiLMMAKER RESOURCES

Screening Rooms— Los Angeles

Charles Aidikoff Screening Room
150 S. Rodeo Dr., #140
Beverly Hills, CA 90212
310-274-0866

The Culver Studios Screening Rooms
9336 W. Washington Blvd
Culver City, CA 90232
310-202-3253

Raleigh Studios
650 N. Bronson
Los Angeles, CA 90038
323-871-5649

Ocean Ave. Screening Room
1401 Ocean Ave., #301
Santa Monica, CA 90401
310-576-1831

Sunset Screening Rooms
2212 W. Magnolia Blvd.
Burbank, CA 91506
818-556-5190
www.screeningrooms.com

Sunset Screening Rooms
8730 Sunset Blvd.
W. Hollywood, CA 90069
310-652-1933

Screening Rooms— New York

The Screening Room
54 Varick St
New York, NY 10013
212-334-2100

The Broadway Screening Room
1619 Broadway
New York, NY
212-307-0990

Magno Sound & Video
729 Broadway
New York, NY
212-302-2505

Millenium
66 East 4th Street
New York, NY 10003
212-673-0090

Tribeca Film Center
375 Greenwich St.
New York, NY 10013
212-941-3930

Lab Services/Transfers (Film and Tape)

Ringer Video Services
2408 W. Olive Ave.
Burbank, CA 91506
818-954-8621

Big Time Dailies
6464 Sunset Blvd., Suite 1090
Hollywood, CA 90028
323-464-0616

Forde Motion Picture Labs
306 Fairview Ave. North
Seattle, WA 98109
206-682-2510

Metropolis Film Labs
300 Phillips Park Road
Mamaroneck, NY 10543
914-381-0893

DuArt Film and Video
245 West 55th Street
Nerw York, NY 10019
212-757-4580

Film Score/ Soundtrack Advice

ASCAP
7920 Sunset Blvd., Suite 300
Los Angeles, CA 90046
323-883-1000
Nancy Knutsen

BMI
8730 Sunset Blvd., 3rd Floor
Los Angeles, CA 90069
310-659-9109
Doreen Ringer-Ross

Production Software

The Writers' Store
2040 Westwood Blvd.
Los Angeles, CA 90025
800-272-8927
310-441-5151

Film Bookstores

Larry Edmund's Bookstore
6644 Hollywood Blvd.
Hollywood, CA 90028
323-463-3273

Samuel French Bookstores
7623 Sunset Blvd,
Los Angeles, CA 90046
323-876-0570

Samuel French Bookstores
11963 Ventura Bl.
Studio City, CA
818-762-0535

Book Soup
8818 Sunset Blvd.
Los Angeles, CA 90069
310-659-3110

Drama Book Shop
723 Seventh Ave.
New York, NY 10019
212-944-0595

Cinema Books
4753 Roosevelt Way N.E.
Seattle, WA 98105
206-547-7667

Theatre Books
11 St. Thomas Street
Toronto, Ontario, Canada   MSS 287
416-922-7175

Biz Books
136 E. Cordova St.
Vancouver, BC V6A 1K9
604-669-6431

Looking for Mr. or Ms. Rights?

ifilmfinders.

The most comprehensive film rights tracking service in the world.

Contact Peter Belsito
ifilmfinders@ifilm.com   323.308.3489 ☎

ABOUT THE AUTHOR

Chris Gore has built a solid reputation as the hilariously honest, down-to-earth creator and editor of Film Threat (www.filmthreat.com). Chris has traveled to over 100 film festivals, having attended his first festival at the age of 12, and has been a judge at Athens, Austin, Edmonds, Florida, Slamdance, and the USA Film Festival. He is also busy as the editor-at-large for *Total Movie Magazine*, a reviewer for "The X Show" and the host of "The New Movie Show" for FOX television. Chris has been called everything from "an easier to relate to Roger Ebert, free of the celebrity status and preachiness . . . " to ". . . the Gen-X Leonard Maltin" to the "pit bull of journalism." He is also the author of *The 50 Greatest Movies Never Made.*

SUBMiT YOUR FiLM FESTiVAL LiSTiNG

Send us your data or update your entry for the next edition of *The Ultimate Film Festival Survival Guide*

To be included in the next edition of *The Ultimate Film Festival Survival Guide*, please contact us via e-mail and we will send you instructions for submitting information for a new festival as well as how to correct, update or add any information to an existing entry. If you are a new festival, please send as much information as possible. In the meantime, send us any additional promotional materials, including press kits, and especially photos—promo items like T-shirts, hats, posters and invites to festivals are also appreciated!

And for your own files, here is our contact info:

Chris Gore
c/o Lone Eagle Film Festival Book Listing
1024 N. Orange Dr.
Hollywood, CA 90038
E-mail: info@loneeagle.com
Fax: 323-308-3595